HERITAGE
Auction Galleries

 W9-DEV-884

Dear Friends,

It is with the greatest of pleasure that I introduce what is without a doubt the most exciting auction catalog I have ever had the privilege to assemble. After over thirty years in the Americana field, it is all too easy to become jaded. Then a project like this comes along to inspire and to remind that we have not "seen it all" after all!

The Henry Luhrs Collection has proven to be more than just a breath of fresh air but more like a whirlwind. As I poured through the hundreds of folders housing its treasures, I hopped up countless times to run to a colleague or call someone on the phone to enthuse over my latest "discovery." Here was a mix of material not seen in years; a literally untouched collection built with expert discernment during the period from the 1930's through the 1950's, when the manuscript field was far more of a "buyer's market," and it was still possible to purchase a wide range of truly special items.

Clearly Mr. Luhrs focus was on American historical figures - with a particular fascination for items relating to Abraham Lincoln. But his eclectic taste also led him to acquire significant autographs from many other fields as well, not to mention a broad array of rare books and even two original Gutenberg Bible leaves!

The collection includes nearly 10,000 items, and it was clearly not possible to present all or even most in a single auction. Accordingly, we have selected what we deem the more significant and interesting for inclusion in this catalog. The balance will be offered in future Heritage auctions. But I feel confident that this present selection will give even the most discriminating collectors and dealers plenty to choose from! One of the nicest aspects of this presentation is the profusion of genuinely interesting and unusual items which are valued monetarily at surprisingly affordable levels. The phrase is oft abused, but this auction truly does include "something for everyone."

In introducing a catalog I usually try to list a few highlights of the sale, but in this case it would require pages. I will cite just two personal favorites. One is the highly important "confidential" letter which President-elect Lincoln wrote to Governor-elect Andrew Curtin of Pennsylvania in December, 1860, offering advice to the new leader of this important swing state regarding "this secession and disunion movement." Lincoln beseeches Curtin to use his office and influence to line up Pennsylvania's support to "maintain the Union at all hazzards," and suggests that he endeavor to get the state legislature to "pass resolutions to that effect." The eloquence of Lincoln's language in this letter, as well as the window it presents into his thinking regarding the gathering storm of secession and the need to create a bulwark against it in Pennsylvania, makes this one of the most important Lincoln letters to come on the market in years.

But for sheer charm, it is hard to top the lovely watch bought by Lincoln as an intended engagement gift for Mary Todd in 1841. It is easy to imagine the love struck, gangly young lawyer spending his last dollar on this gift, only to believe he had ruined his chances with Mary before he ever had the chance to present it, and then giving it as almost an after-thought to another young beauty named Mary whom he barely knew! Scholars have written in great detail about this tortured period in the emotionally troubled Lincoln's life, but the tale of this watch and its physical allure are infinitely more evocative.

I sometimes close these catalog introductions by hoping that the reader will find as much enjoyment in studying and participating in the auction as I myself had in assembling it. In this case, it would be a hard task to accomplish; but you are encouraged to try! I promise it will be an effort well rewarded.

Many interesting, but more modestly valued, items from the Luhrs Collection will also be offered in a series of internet-only auctions to begin later this year. Please watch our web site for news of these important bidding opportunities.

Cordially,

Thomas D. Slater
Director, Heritage-Slater Americana
800-872-6467 ext 441

Terms and Conditions of Auction

AUCTIONEER AND AUCTION:

1. This Auction is presented by Heritage Numismatic Auctions. Inc.; or its subsidiary Currency Auctions of America, Inc.; or their affiliate, Heritage Auctions, Inc. d/b/a Heritage Auction Galleries, Heritage Art Auctions, Heritage Fine & Decorative Arts Auctions, Heritage Comics Auctions, Heritage-Slater Americana, Heritage Vintage Movie Posters, or Heritage Sports Collectibles Auctions, as identified with the applicable licensing information on the title page of the catalog or on the Internet site (the "Auctioneer"). The Auction is conducted under these Terms and Conditions of Auction and applicable state and local law.

BUYER'S PREMIUM:

2. On bids placed through Heritage, a Buyer's Premium of fifteen percent (15%) for Heritage Numismatic Auctions Inc, Heritage-CAA, Heritage Comics Auctions and Heritage Movie Posters or nineteen and one-half percent (19.5%) for Heritage Sports Collectibles, Heritage Music & Entertainment Memorabilia, Heritage Art Auctions and Heritage Americana of the hammer price will be added to the successful bid. If the bid is placed through eBay Live a Buyer's Premium equal to the normal Buyer's Premium plus an additional five percent (5%) of the hammer price will be added to the successful bid up to a maximum Buyer's Premium of Twenty Two and one-half percent (22.5%). There is a minimum Buyer's Premium of $9.00 per lot.

AUCTION VENUES:

3. Exclusively Internet, Continuous Internet, Internet Currency, Amazing Comics Auctions, Amazing Sports Auctions, and Online Session are Auctions conducted on the Internet. Signature Auctions accept bids on the Internet first, followed by a floor bidding session; bids may be placed prior to the floor bidding session by Internet, telephone, fax, or mail.

BIDDERS:

4. Any person participating or registering for the Auction agrees to be bound by and accepts these Terms and Conditions of Auction ("Bidder(s)").
5. All Bidders must meet Auctioneer's qualifications to bid. Any Bidder who is not a customer in good standing of the Auctioneer may be disqualified at Auctioneer's sole option and will not be awarded lots. Such a determination may be made by Auctioneer in its sole and unlimited discretion, at any time prior to, during, or even after the close of the Auction.
6. If an entity places a bid, then the person executing the bid on behalf of the entity agrees to personally guarantee payment for any successful bid.
7. Auctioneer reserves the right to exclude any person it deems in its sole opinion is disruptive to the Auction or is otherwise commercially unsuitable.
8. CREDIT REFERENCES: Bidders who do not have established credit with the Auctioneer must either furnish satisfactory credit information (including two collectibles-related business references) well in advance of the Auction or supply valid credit card information. Bids placed through our Interactive Internet program will only be accepted from pre-registered Bidders; Bidders who are not members of HeritageAuctions.com or affiliates should pre-register at least two business days before the first session to allow adequate time to contact references.

BIDDING OPTIONS:

9. Bids may be placed for a Signature Auction as set forth in the printed catalog section entitled "Choose your bidding method." For Exclusively Internet, Continuous Internet, Internet Currency, Amazing Comics Auctions, Amazing Sports Auctions, and Online Session auctions, see the alternatives shown on each website. Review at HeritageCoins.com/Common/howtobid.php.
10. Presentment of Bids: Non-Internet bids (including but not limited to podium, fax, phone and mail bids) are treated similar to floor bids in that they must be on-increment or at a half increment (called a cut bid). Any podium, fax, phone, or mail bids that do not conform to a full or half increment will be rounded up or down to the nearest full or half increment and will be considered your high bid.
11. Auctioneer's Execution of Certain Bids. Auctioneer cannot be responsible for your errors in bidding, so carefully check that each bid is entered correctly. When identical mail or FAX bids are submitted, preference is given to the first received. To ensure the greatest accuracy, your written bids should be entered on the standard printed bid sheet and be received at Auctioneer's place of business at least two business days before the Auction start. Auctioneer is not responsible for executing mail bids or FAX bids received on or after the day the first lot is sold, nor Internet bids submitted after the published closing time; nor is Auctioneer responsible for proper execution of bids submitted by telephone, mail, FAX, e-mail, Internet, or in person once the Auction begins. Internet bids may not be withdrawn until your written request is received and acknowledged by Auctioneer (FAX: 214-443-8425); such requests must state the reason, and may constitute grounds for withdrawal of bidding privileges. Lots won by mail Bidders will not be delivered at the Auction unless prearranged in advance. The decision of the Auctioneer and declaration of the winning Bidder is final.
12. Caveat as to Bids. Bid increments (over the current bid level) determine the lowest amount you may bid on a particular lot. Bids greater than one increment over the current bid can be any whole dollar amount. It is possible under several circumstances for winning bids to be between increments, sometimes only $1 above the previous increment. Please see: *"How can I lose by less than an increment?"* on our website.
13. Bidding Increments: The following chart governs current bidding increments.

Current Bid	Bid Increment	Current Bid	Bid Increment
< $10	$1	$3,000 - $4,999	$250
$10 - $29	$2	$5,000 - $9,999	$500
$30 - $59	$3	$10,000 - $19,999	$1,000
$60 - $99	$5	$20,000 - $29,999	$2,000
$100 - $199	$10	$30,000 - $49,999	$2,500
$200 - $299	$20	$50,000 - $99,999	$5,000
$300 - $499	$25	$100,000 - $249,999	$10,000
$500 - $999	$50	$250,000 - $499,999	$25,000
$1,000 - $1,999	$100	$500,000 - $1,499,999	$50,000
$2,000 - $2,999	$200	> $1,500,000	$100,000

CONDUCTING THE AUCTION:

14. Notice of the consignor's liberty to place reserve bids on his lots in the Auction is hereby made in accordance with Article 2 of the Texas Uniform Commercial Code. A reserve is an amount below which the lot will not sell. THE CONSIGNOR OF PROPERTY MAY PLACE WRITTEN RESERVE BIDS ON HIS LOTS IN ADVANCE OF THE AUCTION; ON SUCH LOTS, IF THE HAMMER PRICE DOES NOT MEET THE RESERVE, THE CONSIGNOR MAY PAY A REDUCED COMMISSION ON THOSE LOTS. Reserves are generally posted online about 3 days prior to the Auction closing on Internet-Only Auctions, and 7 days prior to the Auction on Signature Auctions. Any successful bid placed by a consignor on his consigned lot on the Auction floor or by telephone during the live session, or after the reserves for an Auction have been posted, will be considered an unqualified bid, and in such instances the consignor agrees to pay full Buyer's Premium and Seller's Commissions on any lot so repurchased.
15. The highest qualified Bidder shall be the buyer. In the event of any dispute between floor Bidders at a Signature Auction, Auctioneer may at his sole discretion reoffer the lot. Auctioneer's decision shall be final and binding upon all Bidders.
16. Auctioneer reserves the right to refuse to honor any bid or to limit the amount of any bid which, in his sole discretion, is not submitted in "Good Faith," or is not supported by satisfactory credit, numismatic references, or otherwise. A bid is considered not made in "Good Faith" when an insolvent or irresponsible person, or a person under the age of eighteen makes it. Regardless of the disclosure of his identity, any bid by a consignor or his agent on a lot consigned by him is deemed to be made in "Good Faith".
17. All items are to be purchased per lot as numerically indicated and no lots will be broken. Auctioneer reserves the right to withdraw, prior to the close, any lots from the Auction.
18. Bids will be accepted in whole dollar amounts only. No "buy" or "unlimited" bids will be accepted. Bidders will be awarded lots at approximately the increment of the next highest bid. No additional commission is charged for executing bids. Off-increment bids may be accepted by the Auctioneer at Signature Auctions.
19. Auctioneer reserves the right to rescind the sale in the event of nonpayment, breach of a warranty, disputed ownership, auctioneer's clerical error or omission in exercising bids and reserves, or otherwise.
20. Outage Policy: Auctioneer occasionally experiences Internet and/or Server outages during which Bidders cannot participate or place bids. If such outage occurs, we may at our discretion extend bidding for the auction up to 24 hours. At our discretion, Auctioneer may consider two outages that occur very closely to one another to be one outage when extending such Auction. This policy applies only to widespread outages and not to isolated problems that occur in various parts of the country from time to time.
21. Scheduled Downtime: Auctioneer periodically schedules system downtime for maintenance and other purposes; this scheduled downtime is not covered by the Outage Policy.
22. The Auctioneer or its affiliates may consign items to be sold in the Auction, and may bid on those lots or any other lots. Auctioneer or affiliates expressly reserve the right to modify any such reserve bids on these items or any others at any time prior to the live auction or the online closing based upon data made known to the Auctioneer or its affiliates. The Auctioneer may extend advances, guarantees, or loans to certain consignors, and may extend financing or other credits at varying rates to certain Bidders in the auction.
23. The Auctioneer has the right to sell certain items after the close of the sale. Items sold by Auctioneer post sale shall be considered sold during the auction and all these Terms and Conditions shall apply to such sales including but not limited to the payment of the buyer's fee, return rights and disclaimers.

PAYMENT:

24. All sales are strictly for cash in United States dollars. Cash includes: U.S. currency, bank wire, cashier checks, travelers checks, and bank money orders, all subject to reporting requirements. Credit Card (Visa or Master Card only) and PayPal payments may be accepted up to $10,000 from non-dealers at the sole discretion of the auctioneer, subject to the following limitations: a) sales are only to the cardholder, b) purchases are shipped to the cardholder's registered and verified address, c) Auctioneer may pre-approve the cardholder's credit line, d) a credit card transaction may not be used in conjunction with any other financing or extended terms offered by the Auctioneer, and must transact immediately upon invoice presentation, e) rights of return are governed by these Terms and Conditions, which supersede those conditions promulgated by the card issuer, f) floor Bidders must present their card. Personal or corporate checks may be subject to clearing before delivery of the purchases.
25. Payment is due upon closing of the Auction session, or upon presentment of an invoice. Auctioneer reserves the right to void an invoice if payment in full of the invoice is not received within 7 days after the close of the Auction.
26. Lots delivered in the States of Texas, California, or other states where the Auction may be held, are subject to all applicable state and local taxes, unless appropriate permits are on file with us. Bidder agrees to pay Auctioneer the actual amount of tax due in the event that sales tax is not properly collected due to: 1) an expired, inaccurate, inappropriate tax certificate or declaration, 2) an incorrect interpretation of the applicable statute, 3) or any other reason.. Lots from different Auctions may not be aggregated for sales tax purposes.
27. In the event that a Bidder's payment is dishonored upon presentment(s), Bidder shall pay the maximum statutory processing fee set by applicable state law.
28. If the Auction invoice(s) submitted by Auctioneer is not paid in full when due, the unpaid balance will bear interest at the highest rate permitted by law from the date of invoice until paid. If the Auctioneer refers the invoice(s) to an attorney for collection, the buyer agrees to pay attorney's fees, court costs, and other collection costs incurred by Auctioneer. If Auctioneer assigns collection to its in-house legal staff, such attorney's time expended on the matter shall be compensated at a rate comparable to the hourly rate of independent attorneys.
29. In the event a successful Bidder fails to pay all amounts due, Auctioneer reserves the right to resell the merchandise, and such Bidder agrees to pay for the reasonable costs of resale, including a 10% seller's commission, and also to pay any difference between the resale price and the price of the previously successful bid.
30. Auctioneer reserves the right to require payment in full in good funds before delivery of the merchandise to the buyer.
31. Auctioneer shall have a lien against the merchandise purchased by the buyer to secure payment of the Auction invoice. Auctioneer is further granted a lien and the right to retain possession of any other property of the buyer then held by the Auctioneer or its affiliates to secure payment of any Auction invoice or any other amounts due the Auctioneer from the buyer. With respect to these lien rights, Auctioneer shall have all the rights of a secured creditor under Article 9 of the Texas Uniform Commercial Code. In addition, with respect to payment of the Auction invoice(s), the buyer waives any and all rights of offset he might otherwise have against the Auctioneer and the consignor of the merchandise included on the invoice.
32. If a Bidder owes Auctioneer or its affiliates on any account, Auctioneer and its affiliates shall have the right to offset such unpaid account by any credit balance due Bidder, and it may secure by possessory lien any unpaid amount by any of the Bidder's property in their possession.
33. Title shall not pass to the successful Bidder until all invoices are paid in full. It is the responsibility of the buyer to provide adequate insurance coverage for the items once they have been delivered.

RETURN POLICIES:

34. A MEMORABILIA lot (Autographs, Sports Collectibles, or Music, Entertainment, Political, Americana and/or Pop Culture memorabilia): The Auction is not on approval. When the lot is accompanied by a Certificate of Authenticity (or its equivalent) from an independent third party authentication provider, buyer has no right of return. Under extremely limited circumstances not including authenticity (e.g. gross cataloging error), a purchaser who did not bid from the floor may request Auctioneer to evaluate voiding a sale; such request must be made in writing detailing the alleged gross error, and submission of the lot to Auctioneer must be pre-approved by Auctioneer. A bidder must notify the appropriate department head (check the inside front cover of the catalog or our website for a listing of department heads) in writing of the purchaser's request and such notice must be mailed within three (3) days of the mail bidder's receipt of the lot. Any lot that is to be evaluated for return must be received in our offices within 30 days after Auction. AFTER THAT 30 DAY PERIOD, NO LOT MAY BE RETURNED FOR ANY REASONS. Lots returned must be in the same condition as when sold and must include the Certificate of Authenticity, if any. No lots purchased by floor bidders may be returned (including those bidders acting as agents for others). Late remittance for purchases may be considered just cause to revoke all return privileges.

MAIL/FAX BID SHEET

Heritage Auction Galleries
Direct Customer Service Line—Toll Free:
1-866-835-3243 (24 hour VM)
HeritageAuctions.com
3500 Maple Avenue, 17th Floor
Dallas, Texas 75219-3941
(All information must be completed.)

NAME _____   CUSTOMER # (if known) _____

ADDRESS _____   E-MAIL ADDRESS _____

CITY/STATE/ZIP _____

DAYTIME PHONE (A/C)_____   EVENING PHONE (A/C) _____

Would you like a FAX or e-mail confirming receipt of your bids? If so, please print your FAX # or e-mail address here: _____
REFERENCES: New bidders who are unknown to us must furnish satisfactory industry references or a valid credit card in advance of the sale date.

Dealer References (City, State) and/or Credit Card Information

_____

_____

_____

_____

You are authorized to release payment history information to other dealers and auctioneers so that I may establish proper credit in the industry. (Line out this statement if you do not authorize release.)

Non-Internet bids (including but not limited to, podium, fax, phone and mail bids) may be submitted at any time and are treated similar to floor bids. These types of bids must be on-increment or at a half increment (called a cut bid). Any podium, fax, phone or mail bids that do not conform to a full or half increment will be rounded up or down to the nearest full or half increment and will be considered your high bid.

Current Bid	Bid Increment	Current Bid	Bid Increment
< $10	$1	$3,000 - $4,999	$250
$10 - $29	$2	$5,000 - $9,999	$500
$30 - $59	$3	$10,000 - $19,999	$1,000
$60 - $99	$5	$20,000 - $29,999	$2,000
$100 - $199	$10	$30,000 - $49,999	$2,500
$200 - $299	$20	$50,000 - $99,999	$5,000
$300 - $499	$25	$100,000 - $249,999	$10,000
$500 - $999	$50	$250,000 - $499,999	$25,000
$1,000 - $1,999	$100	$500,000 - $1,499,999	$50,000
$2,000 - $2,999	$200	> $1,500,000	$100,000

(Bid in whole dollar amounts only.)

LOT NO.	AMOUNT	LOT NO.	AMOUNT	LOT NO.	AMOUNT	LOT NO.	AMOUNT

PLEASE COMPLETE THIS INFORMATION:

1. IF NECESSARY, PLEASE INCREASE MY BIDS BY:
   ❑ 10%   ❑ 20%   ❑ 30%
   Lots will be purchased as much below bids as possible.

2. ❑ I HAVE BOUGHT COINS FROM YOU BEFORE (references are listed above)

I have read and agree to all of the Terms and Conditions of Auction: inclusive of paying interest at the lesser of 1.5% per month (18% per annum) or the maximum contract interest rate under applicable state law from the date of sale (if the account is not timely paid), and the submission of disputes to arbitration.

	SUBTOTAL	
	TOTAL from other side	
	TOTAL BID	

_____
(Signature required) Please make a copy of your bid sheet for your records.

FAX HOTLINE: 214-443-8425

REV. 1_31_06

LOT NO.	AMOUNT	LOT NO.	AMOUNT	LOT NO.	AMOUNT	LOT NO.	AMOUNT

TOTAL this side

Please make a copy of your bid sheet for your records.

The
Henry E. Luhrs Collection

of important American historical manuscripts

HERITAGE GRAND FORMAT AMERICANA AUCTION #626 • FEBRUARY 20-21, 2006 • DALLAS, TEXAS • NEW YORK SIMULCAST

AUCTION LOCATION: Heritage Auction Galleries
1st Floor Auction Room
3500 Maple Avenue • Dallas, Texas 75219

LOT VIEWING
Friday, February 17, 2006
9:00 AM - 5:00 PM CT

Sunday, February 19, 2006
9:00 AM - 5:00 PM CT

Monday, February 20, 2006
9:00 AM - 3:00 PM CT

CUSTOMER SERVICE
Heritage Auction Galleries
3500 Maple Avenue, 17th floor
Dallas, Texas 75219
866.835.3243 • 24 Hour Voice Mail

ABSENTEE BIDS BY FAX
Deadline: Friday, February 17, 2006
12:00 NOON CT • Fax: 214.443.8425

ABSENTEE BIDS BY INTERNET
HeritageAuctions.com/Americana
Bid@HeritageAmericana.com
Internet bidding closes at 10:00 PM CT
the night prior to each session

LIVE TELEPHONE BIDDING
Must be arranged on or before
Friday, February 17, 2006
Customer Service • 1.866.835.3243

SIMULCAST LOCATION: Shreve's Galleries
145 West 57th Street (between 6th & 7th Avenues)
18th Floor • New York, NY 10019 • 212.262.8400

Live bidding and virtual simulcast of this auction will be available for all sessions in New York City.

AUCTION SESSIONS

Session One: The Luhrs Autograph Collection
Lots 25001-25753 • Monday, February 20, 2006 • 5:00 PM CT

Session Two: Books and Manuscripts
Lots 25754-26086 • Tuesday, February 21, 2006 • 1:00 PM CT

Session Three: Autographs and Manuscripts
Lots 26087-26761 • Tuesday, February 21, 2006 • 5:00 PM CT

AUCTIONEER
Sam Foose, TX License #00011727

AUCTION RESULTS
Immediately available at: HeritageAuctions.com/Americana

LOT PICK UP
Tuesday, February 21, 2006 • 10:00 AM - 1:00 PM CT
Wednesday, February 22, 2006 • 9:00 AM - 5:00 PM CT
Also available during and between sessions

CONDITION QUESTIONS OR OTHER INFORMATION REQUESTS
Please submit at least one week before the sale.
Fax to 214.443.8425 or email Tom Slater at
TomS@HeritageAuctions.com, or
Marsha Dixey at MarshaD@HeritageAuctions.com

HERITAGE
Auction Galleries

Direct Customer Service Line: Toll Free 1.866.835.3243 (24-Hour VM)
3500 Maple Avenue, 17th Floor • Dallas, Texas 75219-3941
214.528.3500 • 800.872.6467 • 214.443.8425 (fax)

PRESENTED AND CATALOGUED BY HERITAGE AUCTIONS, INC.
Catalogued by: Tom Slater, Marsha Dixey, Lyndsey Watts, John Hickey and Michael Riley
Guest Experts/Catalogers: Rob Golan, Arby Rolband, John Reznikoff, Sara Willen, Herman Darvick
Edited by: Kim Jones, Jim Steele, Becky Dirting, Marsha Dixey, Andrew Norton, Jennifer Norton, Ka Riley
Photography by: Gerardo Dominguez, Beatriz Faustino, Patric Glenn, Joe Ramirez, Matt Roppolo, Tony Webb, Butch Ziaks, and Shaun Zokaie
Production and Design by: Mandy Bottoms, Cindy Brenner, Janet Brown, Carlos Cardoza, Keith Craker, Cathy Hadd, Mary Hermann,
Matt Pegues, John Petty, Michael Puttonen, Debbie Rexing, Marsha Taylor, Carl Watson
Imaging and Operations: Lucas Garritson, Alexandra Perez, Randy Rice and Colette Warren

View lots online at HeritageAuctions.com/Americana

Steve Ivy
CEO
Co-Chairman
of the Board

Jim Halperin
Co-Chairman
of the Board

Greg Rohan
President

Paul Minshull
C. O. O.

Tom Slater
Director of
Acquisitions

Jared Green
V.P. of Business
Development

Marsha Dixey
Consignment
Director

John Hickey
Consignment
Director

Sam Foose
Consignment
Director

HERITAGE
Auction Galleries

3500 Maple Avenue, 17th Floor
Dallas, Texas 75219-3941
214.528.3500 • 800.872.6467 • 214.443.8425 (fax)

35. COINS, CURRENCY, COMICS AND SPORTSCARDS Signature Auctions: The Auction is not on approval. No certified material may be returned because of possible differences of opinion with respect to the grade offered by any third-party organization, dealer, or service. No guarantee of grade is offered for uncertified Property sold and subsequently submitted to a third-party grading service. There are absolutely no exceptions to this policy. Under extremely limited circumstances, (e.g. gross cataloging error) a purchaser, who did not bid from the floor, may request Auctioneer to evaluate voiding a sale; such request must be made in writing detailing the alleged gross error, and submission of the lot to the Auctioneer must be pre-approved by the Auctioneer; bidder must notify Ron Brackemyre, (ext. 312) in writing of the such request and such notice must be mailed within three (3) days of the mail bidder's receipt of the lot. Any lot that is to be evaluated must be in our offices within 30 days after Auction. Grading or method of manufacture do not qualify for this evaluation process nor do such complaints constitute a basis to challenge the authenticity of a lot. AFTER THAT 30-DAY PERIOD, NO LOTS MAY BE RETURNED FOR REASONS OTHER THAN AUTHENTICITY. Lots returned must be housed intact in the original holder. No lots purchased by floor Bidders may be returned (including those Bidders acting as agents for others). Late remittance for purchases may be considered just cause to revoke all return privileges.

36. Exclusively Internet, Internet Currency, Amazing Comics Auctions, Amazing Sports Auctions, Continuous Internet and Online Session auctions: THREE (3) DAY RETURN POLICY. All lots (Exception: Third party graded notes are not returnable for any reason whatsoever) paid for within seven days of the Auction closing are sold with a three (3) day return privilege. You may return lots under the following conditions: Within three days of receipt of the lot, you must first notify Auctioneer by contacting Customer Service by phone (1-800-872-6467) or e-mail (Bid@HeritageAuctions.com), and immediately mail the lot(s) fully insured to the attention of Returns, Heritage, 3500 Maple Avenue, 17th Floor, Dallas TX 75219-3941. Lots must be housed intact in their original holder and condition. You are responsible for the insured, safe delivery of any lots. A non-negotiable return fee of 5% of the purchase price ($10 per lot minimum) will be deducted from the refund for each returned lot or billed directly. Postage and handling fees are not refunded. After the three-day period (from receipt), no items may be returned for any reason. Late remittance for purchases revokes all Return-Restock privileges.

37. All Bidders who have inspected the lots prior to the auction will not be granted any return privileges, except for reasons of authenticity.

DELIVERY; SHIPPING AND HANDLING CHARGES:

38. Postage, handling and insurance charges will be added to invoices. Please either refer to Auctioneer's website HeritageAuctions.com for the latest charges or call Auctioneer.

39. Auctioneer is unable to combine purchases from other auctions or Heritage Rare Coin Galleries into one package for shipping purposes. Successful overseas Bidders shall provide written shipping instructions, including specified customs declarations, to the Auctioneer for any lots to be delivered outside of the United States. NOTE: Declaration value shall be the item(s) hammer price together with its buyer's premium.

40. All shipping charges will be borne by the successful Bidder. Due to the nature of some items sold, it shall be the responsibility for the successful bidder to arrange pick-up and shipping through third parties, as to such items Auctioneer shall have no liability. Any risk of loss during shipment will be borne by the buyer following Auctioneer's delivery to the designated common carrier, regardless of domestic or foreign shipment. Any request for shipping verification for undelivered packages must be made within 30 days of shipment by Auctioneer.

41. In the event an item is damaged either through handling or in transit, Auctioneer's maximum liability shall be the amount of the successful bid including the Buyer's Premium. On the fall of Auctioneer's hammer, Buyers of Fine Arts and Decorative Arts lots assumes full risk and responsibility for lot, including shipment by common carrier, and must provide their own insurance coverage for shipments.

CATALOGING, WARRANTIES AND DISCLAIMERS:

42. NO WARRANTY, WHETHER EXPRESSED OR IMPLIED, IS MADE WITH RESPECT TO ANY DESCRIPTION CONTAINED IN THIS AUCTION OR ANY SECOND OPINE. Any description of the items or second opine contained in this auction is for the sole purpose of identifying the items for those Bidders who do not have the opportunity to view the lots prior to bidding, and no description of items has been made part of the basis of the bargain or has created any express warranty that the goods would conform to any description made by Auctioneer.

43. Auctioneer is selling only such right or title to the items being sold as Auctioneer may have by virtue of consignment agreements on the date of auction and disclaims any warranty of title to the Property.

44. Translations of foreign language documents are provided as a convenience to interested parties. Heritage makes no representation as to the accuracy of those translations and will not be held responsible for errors in bidding arising from inaccuracies in translation.

45. In the event of an attribution error, Auctioneer may at its sole discretion, correct the error on the Internet, or, if discovered at a later date, to refund the buyer's money without further obligation. Under no circumstances shall the obligation of the Auctioneer to any Bidder be in excess of the purchase price for any lot in dispute.

46. Auctioneer disclaims any warranty of merchantability or fitness for any particular purposes.

47. Auctioneer disclaims all liability for damages, consequential or otherwise, arising out of or in connection with the sale of any property by Auctioneer to Bidder. No third party may rely on any benefit of these Terms and Conditions and any rights, if any, established hereunder are personal to the Bidder and may not be assigned. Any statement made by the Auctioneer is an opinion and does not constitute a warranty or representation. No employee of Auctioneer may alter these Terms and Conditions, and, unless signed by a principal of Auctioneer, any such alteration is null and void.

48E. MEMORABILIA – Auctioneer does not warrant authenticity of a memorabilia lot (Autographs, Sports Collectibles, or Music, Entertainment, Political, Americana and/or Pop Culture memorabilia), when the lot is accompanied by a Certificate of Authenticity, or its equivalent, from an independent third-party authentication provider. Bidder shall solely rely upon warranties of the authentication provider issuing the Certificate or opinion. For information as to such authentication provider's warranties the bidder is directed to: SCD Authentic, 4034 West National Ave., Milwaukee, WI 53215 (800) 345-3168; JO Sports, Inc., P.O. Box 607 Brookhaven, NY 11719 (631) 286-0970; PSA/DNA; 130 Brookshire Lane, Orwigsburg, Pa. 17961; Mike Gutierrez Autographs, 8150 Raintree Drive Suite A, Scottsdale, AZ. 85260; or as otherwise noted on the Certificate. Subject to sections 57 and 58, bidders who intend to challenge authenticity or provenance of a lot must notify Auctioneer in writing within thirty (30) days of the Auction's conclusion. Auctioneer's maximum liability shall not exceed the high bid on that lot, which bid shall be deemed for all purposes the value of the lot. In the event Auctioneer cannot deliver the lot or subsequently it is established that the lot lacks title, provenance, authenticity, or other transfer or condition issue is claimed, Auctioneer's liability shall be limited to recission of sale and refund of purchase price. After one year has elapsed, Auctioneer's maximum liability shall be limited to any commissions and fees Auctioneer earned on that lot.

49. All non-certified coins, currency, and comics are guaranteed genuine, but are not guaranteed as to grade, since grading is a matter of opinion, an art and not a science, and therefore the opinion rendered by the Auctioneer or any third party grading service may not agree with the opinion of others (including trained experts), and the same expert may not grade the same item with the same grade at two different times. Auctioneer has graded the non-certified numismatic items, in the Auctioneer's opinion, to their current interpretation of the American Numismatic Association's standards as of the date the catalog was prepared. There is no guarantee or warranty implied or expressed that the grading standards utilized by the Auctioneer will meet the standards of ANACS, NGC, PCGS, ICG, CGC, CGA or any other grading service at any time in the future.

50. Since we cannot examine encapsulated notes or comics, they are sold "as is" without our grading opinion, and may not be returned for any reason. Auctioneer shall not be liable for any patent or latent defect or controversy pertaining to or arising from any encapsulated collectible. In any such instance, purchaser's remedy, if any, shall be solely against the service certifying the collectible.

51. Due to changing grading standards over time, differing interpretations, and to possible mishandling of items by subsequent owners, Auctioneer reserves the right to grade items differently than shown on certificates from any grading service that accompany the items. Auctioneer also reserves the right to grade items differently than the grades shown in the catalog should such items be reconsigned to any future auction.

52. Although consensus grading is employed by most grading services, it should be noted as aforesaid that grading is not an exact science. In fact, it is entirely possible that if a lot is broken out of a plastic holder and resubmitted to another grading service or even to the same service, the lot could come back with a different grade assigned.

53. Certification does not guarantee protection against the normal risks associated with potentially volatile markets. The degree of liquidity for certified coins and collectibles will vary according to general market conditions and the particular lot involved. For some lots there may be no active market at all at certain points in time.

RELEASE:

54. In consideration of participation in the auction and the placing of a bid, a Bidder expressly releases Auctioneer, its officers, directors and employees, its affiliates, and its outside experts that provide second opines from any and all claims, cause of action, chose of action, whether at law or equity or any arbitration or mediation rights existing under the rules of any professional society or affiliation based upon the assigned grade or a derivative theory, breach of warranty express or implied, representation or other matter set forth within these Terms and Conditions of Auction or otherwise, except as specifically declared herein; e.g., authenticity, typographical error, etc., and as to those matters, the rights and privileges conferred therein are strictly construed and is the exclusive remedy. Purchaser, by non-compliance to its express terms of a granted remedy, shall waive any claim against Auctioneer.

DISPUTE RESOLUTION AND ARBITRATION PROVISION:

55. By placing a bid or otherwise participating in the auction, such person or entity accepts these Terms and Conditions of Auction, and specifically agrees to the alternative dispute resolution provided herein. Arbitration replaces the right to go to court, including the right to a jury trial.

56. Auctioneer in no event shall be responsible for consequential damages, incidental damages, compensatory damages, or other damages arising from the auction of any lot. Auctioneer's maximum liability shall not exceed the high bid on that lot, which bid shall be deemed for all purposes the value of the lot. In the event that Auctioneer cannot deliver the lot or subsequently it is established that the lot lacks title, provenance, authenticity, or other transfer or condition issue is claimed, Auctioneer's liability shall be limited to recission of sale and refund of purchase price. After one year has elapsed, Auctioneer's maximum liability shall be limited to any commissions and fees Auctioneer earned on that lot.

57. Any claim as to provenance or authenticity must be first transmitted to Auctioneer by credible and definitive evidence and there is no assurance after such presentment that Auctioneer will validate the claim. Authentication is not an exact science and contrary opinions may not be recognized by Auctioneer. Even if Auctioneer agrees with the contrary opinion of such authentication, our liability for reimbursement for such service shall not exceed $500.

58. Provenance and authenticity are not guaranteed by the Auctioneer, but rather are guaranteed by the consignor. Any action or claim shall include the consignor with Auctioneer acting as interpleador or nominal party. While every effort is made to determine provenance and authenticity, it is up to the Bidder to arrive at that conclusion prior to bidding.

59. If any dispute arises regarding payment, authenticity, grading, description, provenance, or any other matter pertaining to the Auction, the Bidder or a participant in the Auction and/or the Auctioneer agree that the dispute shall be submitted, if otherwise mutually unresolved, to binding arbitration in accordance with the commercial rules of the American Arbitration Association (A.A.A.). A.A.A. arbitration shall be conducted under the provisions of the Federal Arbitration Act with locale in Dallas, Texas. Any claim made by a Bidder has to be presented within one (1) year or it is barred. The prevailing party may be awarded his reasonable attorney's fees and costs. An award granted in arbitration is enforceable in any court of competent jurisdiction. No claims of any kind (except for reasons of authenticity) can be considered after the settlements have been made with the consignors. Any dispute after the settlement date is strictly between the Bidder and consignor without involvement or responsibility of the Auctioneer. NOTE: Purchasers of rare coins or currency through Heritage have available the option of arbitration by the Professional Numismatists Guild (PNG); if an election is not made within ten (10) days of an unresolved dispute, Auctioneer may elect either PNG or A.A.A. Arbitration.

60. In consideration of his participation in or application for the auction, a person or entity (whether the successful Bidder, a Bidder, a purchaser and/or other Auction participant or registrant) agrees that all disputes in any way relating to, arising under, connected with, or incidental to these Terms and Conditions and purchases or default in payment thereof shall be arbitrated pursuant to the arbitration provision. In the event that any matter including actions to compel arbitration, construe the agreement, actions in aid or arbitration or otherwise needs to be litigated, such litigation shall be exclusively in the Courts of the State of Texas, in Dallas County, Texas, and if necessary the corresponding appellate courts. The successful Bidder, purchaser, or Auction participant also expressly submits himself to the personal jurisdiction of the State of Texas.

MISCELLANEOUS:

61. Agreements between Bidders and consignors to effectuate a non-sale of an item at Auction, inhibit bidding on a consigned item to enter into a private sale agreement for said item, or to utilize the Auctioneer's Auction to obtain sales for non-selling consigned items subsequent to the auction, are strictly prohibited. If a subsequent sale of a previously consigned item occurs in violation of this provision, Auctioneer reserves the right to charge Bidder the applicable Buyer's Premium and consignor a Seller's Commission as determined for each auction venue and by the terms of the seller's agreement.

62. Acceptance of these terms and conditions qualifies Bidder as a Heritage customer who has consented to be contacted by Heritage in the future. In conformity with "do-not-call" regulations promulgated by the Federal or State regulatory agencies, participation by the Bidder is affirmative consent to being contacted at the phone number shown in his application and this consent shall remain in effect until it is revoked in writing. Heritage may from time to time contact Bidder concerning sale, purchase and auction opportunities available through Heritage and its affiliates and subsidiaries.

63. Storage of purchased coins and currency: Purchasers are advised that certain types of plastic may react with a coin's metal or transfer plasticizer to notes and may cause damage. Caution should be used to avoid storage in materials that are not inert.

STATE NOTICES:

64. Notice as to an Auction Sale in California. Auctioneer has in compliance with Title 2.95 of the California Civil Code as amended October 11, 1993 Sec. 1812.600, posted with the California Secretary of State its bonds for it and its employees and the auction is being conducted in compliance with Sec. 2338 of the Commercial Code and Sec. 535 of the Penal Code.

Rev. 1_25_06

Mail Bidding at Auction

Mail bidding at auction is fun and easy and only requires a few simple steps.

1. Look through the catalog, and determine the lots of interest.

2. Research their market value by checking price lists and other price guidelines.

3. Fill out your bid sheet, entering your maximum bid on each lot.

4. Verify your bids!

5. Mail Early. Preference is given to the first bids received in case of a tie. When bidding by mail, you frequently purchase items at less than your maximum bid.

Bidding is opened at the published increment above the second highest mail or Internet bid; we act on your behalf as the highest mail bidder. If bidding proceeds, we act as your agent, bidding in increments over the previous bid. This process is continued until you are awarded the lot or you are outbid.

An example of this procedure: You submit a bid of $100, and the second highest mail bid is at $50. Bidding starts at $51 on your behalf. If no other bids are placed, you purchase the lot for $51. If other bids are placed, we bid for you in the posted increments until we reach your maximum bid of $100. If bidding passes your maximum: if you are bidding through the Internet, we will contact you by e-mail; if you bid by mail, we take no other action. Bidding continues until the final bidder wins.

Telephone Bidding

To participate by telephone, please make arrangements at least one week before the sale date with Customer Service, 1-800-872-6467, Ext. 150.

We strongly recommend that you place preliminary bids by mail, fax, or Internet, even if you intend to participate by telephone. On many occasions this dual approach has helped reduce disappointments due to telephone problems, unexpected travel, late night sessions and time zone differences, etc. We will make sure that you do not bid against yourself.

Mail Bidding Instructions

1. **Name, Address, City, State, Zip**
   Your address is needed to mail your purchases. We need your telephone number to communicate any problems or changes that may affect your bids.

2. **References**
   If you have not established credit with us from previous auctions, you must send a 25% deposit, or list dealers with whom you have credit established.

3. **Lot Numbers and Bids**
   List all lots you desire to purchase. On the reverse are additional columns; you may also use another sheet. Under "Amount" enter the maximum you would pay for that lot (whole dollar amounts only). We will purchase the lot(s) for you as much below your bids as possible.

4. **Total Bid Sheet**
   Add up all bids and list that total in the appropriate box.

5. **Sign Your Bid Sheet**
   By signing the bid sheet, you have agreed to abide by the Terms of Auction listed in the auction catalog.

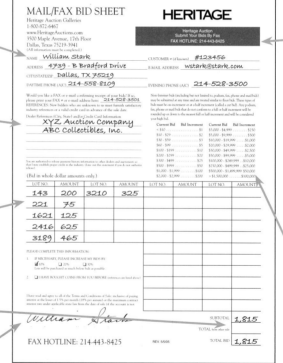

6. **Fax Your Bid Sheet**
   When time is short submit a Mail Bid Sheet on our exclusive Fax Hotline. There's no faster method to get your bids to us *instantly*. Simply use the **Heritage Fax Hotline number: 214-443-8425**.

   When you send us your original after faxing, mark it "Confirmation of Fax" (preferably in red!)

7. **Bidding Increments**
   To facilitate bidding, please consult the following chart. Bids will be accepted on the increments or on the half increments.

The official prices realized list that accompanies our auction catalogs is reserved for bidders and consignors only. We are happy to mail one to others upon receipt of $1.00. Written requests should be directed to Customer Service.

Rev. 1/23/06

Interactive Internet™ Bidding

You can now bid with Heritage's exclusive *Interactive Internet*™ program, available only at our web site: HeritageAuctions.com. It's fun, and it's easy!

1. Register online at: **HeritageAuctions.com**

2. View the full-color photography of every single lot in the online catalog!

3. Construct your own personal catalog for preview.

4. View the current opening bids on lots you want; review the prices realized archive.

5. Bid and receive immediate notification if you are the top bidder; later, if someone else bids higher, you will be notified automatically by e-mail.

6. The *Interactive Internet*™ program opens the lot on the floor at one increment over the second highest bid. As the high bidder, your secret maximum bid will compete for you during the floor auction, and it is possible that you may be outbid on the floor after Internet bidding closes. Bid early, as the earliest bird wins in the event of a tie bid.

7. After the sale, you will be notified of your success. It's that easy!

Interactive Internet™ Bidding Instructions

1. **Log Onto Website**

   Log onto **HeritageAuctions.com** and chose the portal you're interested in (i.e., coins, comics, movie posters, fine arts, etc.).

2. **Search for Lots**

   Search or browse for the lot you are interested in. You can do this from the home page, from the Auctions home page, or from the home page for the particular auction in which you wish to participate.

3. **Select Lots**

   Click on the link or the photo icon for the lot you want to bid on.

4. **Enter Bid**

   At the top of the page, next to a small picture of the item, is a box outlining the current bid. Enter the amount of your secret maximum bid in the textbox next to "Secret Maximum Bid." The secret maximum bid is the maximum amount you are willing to pay for the item you are bidding on (for more information about bidding and bid increments, please see the section labeled "Bidding Increments" elsewhere in this catalog). Click on the button marked "Place Absentee Bid." A new area on the same page will open up for you to enter your username (or e-mail address) and password. Enter these, then click "Place Absentee Bid" again.

5. **Confirm Absentee Bid**

   You are taken to a page labeled, "Please Confirm Your Bid." This page shows you the name of the item you're bidding on, the current bid, and the maximum bid. When you are satisfied that all the information shown is correct, click on the button labeled, "Confirm Bid."

6. **Bidding Status Notification**

   One of two pages is now displayed.

   a. If your bid is the current high bid, you will be notified and given additional information as to what might happen to affect your high bidder status over the course of the remainder of the auction. You will also receive a Bid Confirmation notice via email.

   b. If your bid is not the current high bid, you will be notified of that fact and given the opportunity to increase your bid.

HERE'S A REAL VALENTINE

Let the Prisoner be
released on taking the
oath of Dec. 8. 1863.
A Lincoln

4. 1865.

HEARTED PRESIDENT LINCOLN
T THIS NOTE FEBRUARY 14, 1865.

THIS PARDON GAVE LIBERTY
TO A PRISONER OF THE
NORTH DURING THE
CIVIL WAR.

It has been a real privilege to catalog and present the wonderful collection which Henry Luhrs assembled. While many of the items are in and of themselves beguiling, this experience has transcended the sum of those parts. Henry Luhrs passed away in 1962, before I got my start collecting and dealing in Americana; we never met. But it is impossible to go through the collection he built without developing a real sense and appreciation of the man. Here was someone who truly loved history, and who possessed the intellect and accumulated knowledge to appreciate hundreds of items whose esoteric content would have gone right over the head of the average collector - or dealer for that matter.

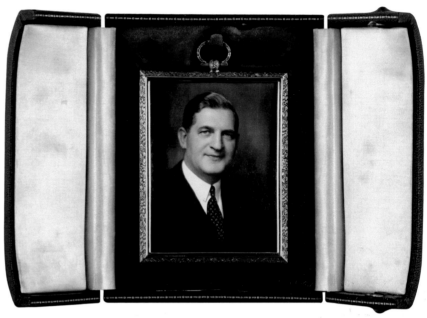

The result of his discerning collecting is perhaps the richest trove of American historical manuscripts to come to market in many, many years. As we "ooh" and "ah" over his treasures, let us not forget the dedicated collector who made it all possible.

One eulogy written upon his death observed that "Henry E. Luhrs was a man who did so many things, and did them so well, that it is difficult to decide which of his interests were most important." Indeed, one cannot help but wonder when he found time to collect!

During the 1920's, Mr. Luhrs resided in New York City, and it was there that he became exposed to some of the pioneer Americana dealers and galleries — and his collecting bug took hold in earnest. In 1927 he married Pearl H. Beistle, and in 1929 he was persuaded to move to Shippensburg, Pennsylvania to help run her family's business. He became the company's chief executive officer in 1935, a responsibility he shouldered until his death. The Beistle Company remains one of the region's major corporate presences, and is today the world's leading manufacturer of party favors and decorations. This would be enough to keep most men more than busy, but Henry Luhrs managed to find the time not only to build this wonderful collection, but, among many other activities, to organize the Shippensburg Public Library and serve as its board chairman for twenty-five years, to serve for fifteen years as executive secretary of the Shippensburg Community Chest, to serve as a longtime member and sometime President of the city's Borough Council, to serve as president of Shippensburg's Rotary Council, to be an active member and "unofficial historian" of the Memorial Lutheran Church, to organize a group of Lincoln scholars into the Lincoln Fellowship of Pennsylvania and serve as its first president, to play an active role in youth groups including the Boy Scouts of America, and to organize the Shippensburg Historical Society!

While he was a sophisticated student of Pennsylvania history and an avid collector of its artifacts, Henry Luhrs reserved his greatest enthusiasm for Abraham Lincoln, whom he considered to be THE greatest American. A student of Lincoln's life since boyhood, he founded his renowned Lincoln Library in 1929 in a single room of his Shippensburg home. It was a repository both of research materials and artifacts of the 16th President, and it grew so rapidly that, when the home next door came up for sale, Mr. Luhrs bought it to house the expanding collection. He planned a much more ambitious facility, but his untimely death at 61 prevented its fulfillment.

Those who knew him said that Henry Luhrs rather enjoyed the irony of such a sophisticated collection coming to reside in this unlikely small town in rural Pennsylvania. But geographical isolation did not hamper his collecting, as he remained in active touch with the country's leading dealers, and continued adding to the collection right up until his death.

It is often said that, once collecting is in one's blood, one may develop an interest in collecting most anything, and Henry Luhrs was walking proof of that observation. We would be remiss in not mentioning that somewhere he also found the time to amass significant collections of coins, postage stamps, clocks and watches, music boxes, commemorative medals, and classical antiquities! He was truly a Renaissance Man, and we are privileged to bring to your attention this remarkable manifestation of his taste and range.

— Tom Slater

TABLE OF CONTENTS

SESSION 1 — THE HENRY E. LUHRS COLLECTION

SESSION ONE
Public-Internet Auction #626
Monday, February 20, 2006, 5:00 PM CST, Lots 25001–25782

Dallas, Texas

A 19.5% Buyer's Premium Will Be Added To All Lots

Visit HeritageAuctions.com/Americana to view scalable images and bid online.

Live bidding and and a Virtual Simulcast of this auction will available for all bidding sessions in New York City at Shreve's Auction Gallery at the following address:

Shreve's Galleries • 145 West 57th Street
(57th St. between 6th & 7th Avenues)
18th Floor • New York, NY 10019
212-262-8400
(Not active until day of auction)

Heritage will broadcast the auction Live (with limited delay) from its showroom in Dallas to the off-site bidding room in New York. At the bidding room, local bidders will be able to register for bidding and bid on lots live through a Heritage phone-bidder dialed into the Dallas auction.

Two projection screens will be viewable, one with the current lot and bid status, the other with a simulcasted video feed of the live auction in Dallas. Snacks will be served at the off-site New York bidding room.

25001 **John Adams on Government:** *"the word Republic as it is used may signify — any thing — everything or nothing"*

John Adams (1734-1726) President, Signer of the Declaration of Independence, extremely fine content Letter Signed *"John Adams"*, two pages, 7.8" x 9.75", Quincy, April 30, 1819, a rich and detailed letter on the nature of republics, his own writings, and mentioning Thomas Jefferson. He writes, to an unknown correspondent:

"Of republicks [sic] the varieties are infinite, or at least as numerous, as the tunes and changes that can be rung upon a complete sett [sic] of Bells. — Of all the Varitety's [sic], a Democracy is the most rational - the most ancient - and the most fundamental - and essential of all others. — In some writing of other of mine I happened — current... to drop the phrase —'the word Republic as it is used may signify - any thing — everything or nothing' — From this escape I have been pelted for twenty or thirty years - with as many stones, as even were throw'n at St Steven - when St Paul held the clothes of the Stoners - but the aphorism is literal, strict, solemn truth - to speak technically, or scientifically, if you will - There are Monarchial Aristocratical and Democratical Republicks - the Government of Britain — and that of Poland - are as strict by republicks - as that of Rhode Island or Connecticut under their old Charter— If mankind have a right to the voice of experience - they ought to furnish that experience with Pen, ink and paper to write it and as amannensis [?] to Copy it- I should have been extremely obliged to you if you had favoured me with Mr Jefferson['] s sentiments upon the Subject — as I see you have an inquiring mind — I sincerely wish you much pleasure Profit, and success in your investigations[.] I have had some pleasure in them - but no Profit - and very little, if any success. —-" Adams then responds to a question about his 1787 pamphlet *A Defence of the Constitutions of Government of the United States of America*: *In some of your Letters you say that my*

defence [sic] - has become rare- this is strange Mr Dilly Published an Edition of it in London... addition of it, was published in Boston — another in New - York - another in Philadelphia — before the Adoption of the present Constitution of the National Government - and before one line of the Federalist was printed - since that Mr Cobbet, Alias Porcupine printed a large Edition of the whole Work in Philadelphia - and Mr Stockdale of Picca-dilly has published another large Edition in London - it has been Translated into the French and German Languages - and what has become of all these Copies "

A truly wonderful letter by one of the most important architects of the American Revolution. Adams' wrote *A Defence of the Constitutions of Government of the United States of America* while serving as United States Minister to the Court of St. James. The wide-ranging work, was in most part, an expansion of his arguments on the needs for checks and balances in government that he expressed in his 1776 pamphlet *Thoughts on Government.* The work, stressing the power of the executive in an effort to thwart aristocracy was, ironically, interpreted by many as monarchial. Abagail Admas wrote to their son, John Quincy about the book: "I tell him they will think in America that he is setting up a king." Adams himself predicted that the work would make him unpopular. But, he conceded to his friend James A. Warren in 1787: "Popularity was never my mistress, nor was I ever, or shall I ever be a popular man." It was at this point too that the political differences between Adams and his old comrade Thomas Jefferson came to the fore. Their relationship deteriorated from that point forward and the two communicated little for many years. At the prompting of Dr. Benjamin Rush, the two began communicating again in 1809 and continued a lively correspondence for the balance of their days. They both died on July 4, 1826. This missive is of tremendous significance; a very special offering. From the Henry E. Luhrs Collection. Accompanied by LOA from PSA/DNA.

Estimate: $20,000-$30,000

25002   John Quincy Adams Orders "*A Set of the Laws of Pennsylvania*" — **for the State Department!** Letter Signed, in full, as Secretary of State, 1 page, 7.5" by 10", Department of State. [Washington], January 31, 1818. To Philadelphia publisher and bookseller Matthew Carey. Mounting traces and a pencilled note at bottom do not detract from the overall pleasing appearance of this letter, which is very good. John Quincy Adams, as perhaps

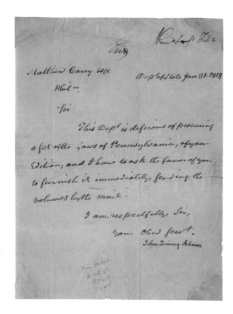

America's greatest Secretary of State, formulated policy, dealt with diplomats, wrote extensively to dozens of U.S. ministers and hundreds of consul, issued passport, arranged for the maintenance, management and even printing of government documents, supervised the Patent Office and the census, established standards for weights and measures and, oh yes, met with the President on a daily basis. Somehow in all this, he also needed some law books — for what we hate to think. "*This Department is desirous of procuring a Set of the Laws of Pennsylvania, of your edition, and I have leave to ask the favor of you to furnish it immediately, sending the volumes by the mail.*" From the Henry E. Luhrs Collection. Accompanied by LOA from PSA/DNA.

Estimate: $400-$600

25004   James Buchanan (1791-1868), President, Letter Signed "*James Buchanan*" as United States Minister to Great Britain, two pages, 7.75" x 12.5", London, November 12, 1855 to General R. B. Campbell, United States Consul in London, and concerning a damaged American ship. He writes in part: "*I regret that in either of these cases an application had been made and refused at the Privy Council before it was possible for me to present the subject at the Foreign Office. If, however, by the action of the British Government and*

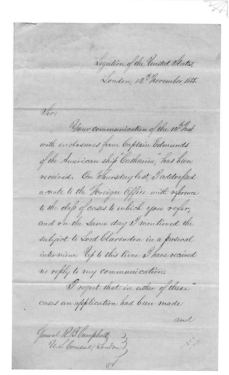

without any fault of theirs, American ships are subjected to detention and damage, their owners will probably take measures through the State Department at Washington, to obtain a fair indemnity for their losses..." Usual folds, very light soiling, else fine condition. From the Henry E. Luhrs Collection. Accompanied by LOA from PSA/DNA.

Estimate: $500-$700

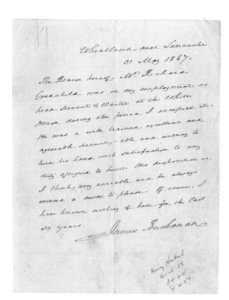

25003   James Buchanan Writes a Letter of Recommendation for a White House Servant Fired By Mary Lincoln! Autograph Letter Signed, 1 page, 6" by 8", Wheatland, May 31, 1867. Some very faint paper clip imprints in upper left, and a soft pencil note, easily erasable, lower right, else fine. Richard Goodchild, an Englishman, was hired by President Buchanan to be "Steward" at the White House, which meant that Goodchild essentially ran the place. Mrs. Lincoln, however, was no sooner through the door than she conducted a purge of Buchanan's staff — the likes of which had never been seen before — and Goodchild was among the first to go. Here the ex-President Buchanan writes him a glowing letter of recommendation. "*The Bearer hereof, Mr. Richard Goodchild was in my employment as head servant and waiter in the White House during the period I occupied it. He was a well trained, excellent and obedient servant, able and willing to turn his hand with satisfaction to any duty assigned him. His disposition is good, very amiable and he has always evinced a desire to please...*" From the Henry E. Luhrs Collection. Accompanied by LOA from PSA/DNA.

Estimate: $600-$800

25005   James Buchanan (1791-1868) President, Autograph Letter Signed "*James Buchanan*" as Congressman, one page with integral address leaf, 8" x 10", Lancaster, June 2, 1830 to a Baltimore merchant informing him that "*The Supreme Court, on yesterday afternoon, decided that they would not grant a re-adjustment of your case. Their decision affirming the judgment of the District Court of York County*

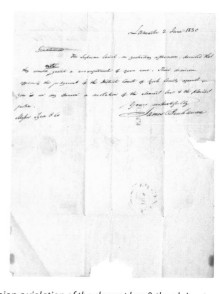

against you is in my opinion a violation of the clearest law & the plainest justice." Buchanan represented his Pennsylvania district in the House of Representatives from 1821 to 1831. The following year he would take the post of U.S. Minister to Russia. He resigned that post in 1834 to take up a vacant seat in the U.S. Senate where he served until 1845 when he became James K. Polk's Secretary of State. Losses form seal tear, small folds split affecting two words of text, otherwise Very Good on bright, clean paper. From the Henry E. Luhrs Collection. Accompanied by LOA from PSA/DNA.

Estimate: $600-$800

25006   James Buchanan (1791-1868) President, Autograph Letter Signed "*James Buchanan*", one page, 8" x 10", "*Senate Chamber*", [Washington], January 8, 1845 to Colonel Reah Frazer requesting political advice. He writes in part: "*Mr. Bair, the postmaster at new Providence has resigned & John Peoples has been recommended as his successor. Is he a suitable person... I know now who will be Mr. Shunk's Attorney General; but consider it most probable that it will be Mr. Kane. He is far from being my first choice; but I do hope that my friends at Lancaster, particularly yourself, will subject to it with a good grace. Whatever complaints you many have, will, however unjustly be attributed to me...*" The future president then turns to speculation on the possible cabinet for the incoming Polk Administration: "*We have literally no news of the least importance form Col: Polk. Different sets are busy in Cabinet making; but all is as yet conjecture...*" Buchanan would be nominated Secretary of State by Polk soon afterwards. A few soiled spots, usual folds, else Very Good condition. Wonderful content from our only bachelor president. From the Henry E. Luhrs Collection. Accompanied by LOA from PSA/DNA.
Estimate: $800-$1,200

25007   Grover Cleveland, (1837-1908), President, partly-printed Document Signed "*Grover Cleveland*" as Governor, two pages, 10.5" x 16", Albany, August 9, 1883 ordering the closing of The Preston Fertilizing Company in Long Island City, Queens because it was a nuisance "*...affecting the security of life and health in Long Island City...*" With embossed foils seal of the State of New York. usual creases, else fine condition. A fun example! From the Henry E. Luhrs Collection. Accompanied by LOA from PSA/DNA.
Estimate: $300-$400

25008   Frances Cleveland, as First Lady, Returns a Not Quite "Worthless" Swimsuit! Autograph Letter Signed (twice: as "Frances E. Cleveland" and "Mrs. Grover Cleveland"), as First Lady, 3 pages, recto and, 4.5" by 7", on her monogrammed stationery, Gray Gables, Buzzards Bay, Massachusetts, August 21, [18]94. To C.F. Hovey & Co., a landmark Boston dry goods establishment. In very fine condition. One of the most popular of First Ladies charmingly returns a defective swimsuit. In full: "*I do not feel like saying that the bathing suit you sent me was a 'worthless article' — it was not that for it could be easily repaired. I only felt it was hardly worth its full price because it frayed in a seam & burst out the second time it was used. I wish to order some ribbon — a piece of cream white satin on one side No 5 plain. Will you kindly send me a bill for it — and what you think a fair price for a slightly damaged $5.50 bathing suit. I wish to thank you for your kindness and courtesy in returning my check. The article did not seem to me sufficiently damaged to accept your generous adjustment.*" From the Henry E. Luhrs Collection. Accompanied by LOA from PSA/DNA.
Estimate: $150-$250

25009   Rose Cleveland: An Uncommon Autograph Letter From the "Executive Mansion." Autograph Letter Signed (in full: "Rose Elizabeth Cleveland"), 2 pages, 4" by 6", on the letterhead of the "Executive Mansion", Washington, November 16, 1888. To Mrs. Horace Goodwin. In excellent condition. Rose Cleveland, the learned spinster sister of the bachelor President Grover Cleveland, served as "First Lady" for little over a year, until her brother married his 21 year-old Ward Frances, in a White House ceremony in 1886. Miss Cleveland was an intellectual and her boredom with social obligations may be inferred from her confession that she occupied herself at state functions by conjugating difficult Greek verbs. This letter, however, is simple: she thanks her correspondent for sending her a photograph of Great-Uncle Charles Cleveland, in which he looks rather like he did when she last saw him. From the Henry E. Luhrs Collection. Accompanied by LOA from PSA/DNA.
Estimate: $300-$400

25010 Calvin Coolidge Letter as President: a Genealogy of Himself - Marked "Personal Not for Publication"! Typed Letter Signed, *as President,* bearing an autograph annotation at top "Personal not for publication", 1 page, on the embossed letterhead of The White House, Washington, March 24, 1927. To Mrs. Florette A. Coolidge in Rochester, New York. In Fine condition, albeit with a faintly pencilled note re provenance at bottom. Silent Cal speaks, but not for the record, about his ancestry. In part: *"I know that there was an Obadiah Coolidge in the census of Plymouth, Vermont, which was taken in 1790, wherein he was reported to have several children. I never knew what became of him. He was not a brother of my great-grandfather, but was probably a brother of his father. My great-grandfather was Calvin and his father was John. John came from Lancaster, Massachusetts, where there is a record of his marriage but we have never found any record of his birth, though we suppose he was the son of Josiah Coolidge who was a son of Obadiah Coolidge. Perhaps you know where Obadiah went from Plymouth and in what part of New York he settled. Of course I would like to see the photograph to which you refer."* From the Henry E. Luhrs Collection. Accompanied by LOA from PSA/DNA.
Estimate: $600-$900

25012 Calvin Coolidge, as President, Comments on the 1926 Congressional Elections. Typed Letter Signed, *as president,* 1 page, 7" by 9", marked "Personal", The White House, Washington, November 9, 1926. To the American Ambassador to France, Myron T. Herrick. Fine, with a faint pencilled note at bottom. The president comments frankly on the congressional elections of the preceding week: *"... Some of the results are of course keenly disappointing, but we have a substantial majority in the House, and as the only election which covered the whole country was for Members of the House, I think we are justified in a feeling of satisfaction on the general result."* From the Henry E. Luhrs Collection. Accompanied by LOA from PSA/DNA.
Estimate: $300-$400

25011 Calvin Coolidge Uncommon Autograph Letter Signed as Vice President Autograph Letter Signed, *as Vice President,* 1 page, on the embossed letterhead of The Vice President's Chamber, Washington, February 3, 1923. To Judge E. A. Armstrong in Princeton. In Fine condition, with a huge signature. Accompanied by the transmittal envelope bearing Coolidge's printed free frank. In full: *"It was very pleasant to get your message by Rep. Patterson. Cordially..."* From the Henry E. Luhrs Collection. Accompanied by LOA from PSA/DNA.
Estimate: $300-$500

RARE BOOKS FROM THE LUHRS COLLECTION

A broad selection of rare and interesting books from this collection are to be found in the afternoon session of our February 21, 2006 catalog. Each is identified as being from the Henry Luhrs Collection. Please do take the opportunity to peruse these significant offerings.

25013 **Coolidge Addresses the Boy Scouts of America**

Calvin Coolidge (1872-1933), President, fine content printed Typescript Signed "*Calvin Coolidge*" as President, one page, 8" x 13", no place given [Washington], July 26, 1924, a press release of his speech delivered before the "*Delegates of the Boy Scouts of America*" prior to their departure to the 1924 Boy Scout Jamboree in Copenhagen,

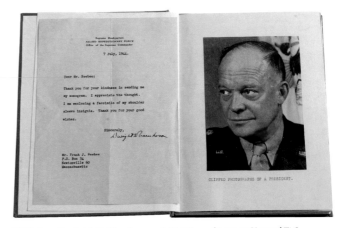

Denmark. Sadly, this is a stirring address delivered less than a month after Coolidge's own son, 16-year-old Calvin Coolidge, Jr. — who had been an active Boy Scout — tragically died of an infection. He spoke to the departing scouts (in small part): "*...As Honorary president of your body, I desire to give you a word of farewell... There was no Boy Scout organization in my boyhood; but every boy who has the privilege of growing up on a farm learns instinctively the three fundamentals of scouthood. The first is a reverence for Nature... There is new life in the soil for every man... The second is a reverence for law. I remember the town meetings of my boyhood... There is something in every such meeting, in every election, that approaches very near to the sublime. I am thrilled at the thought of my audience tonight, for I never address boys without thinking that among them may be a boy who will sit in this White House... Let this nation, under your guidance, be finer nation... The third is a reverence for God. It is hard to see how a great man can be an atheist. Without the sustaining influence of faith in a divine power we could have little faith in ourselves... Doubters do not achieve; skeptics do not contribute; cynics do not create. Faith is the great movie power, and no man realizes his full possibilities unless he has the deep conviction that life is eternally important... These are not only some of the fundamentals of the teachings of the Boy Scouts, they are the fundamentals of our American institutions.... I trust that you can show to your foreign associates in the great Scout movement that you have a deep reverence for the truth, and are determined to live by it; that you wish to protect and cherish your own country and contribute to the well being, right thinking, and true living of the whole world.*" Calvin Coolidge's son's body lay in state in the East Room of the White House and, according to a newspaper account, when the body was carried out to the train station, "Boy Scouts assisted in keeping the lines open for the party to proceed through on their way to Union Station." His son's early death, affected Coolidge deeply. He remarked later "When he [Calvin Jr.] went, the power and glory of the Presidency went with him." Addressing a troop of Boy Scouts so soon after this tragic event must have been a moving experience." Fine condition, and ideal for display. From the Henry E. Luhrs Collection. Accompanied by LOA from PSA/DNA.

Estimate: $750-$1,200

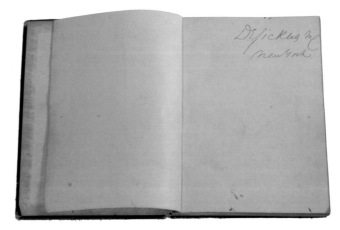

25014 **Dwight D. Eienhower 1944 Typed Letter Signed** TLS: "*Dwight D. Eisenhower*" as Supreme Commander, Allied Expeditionary Force, 1p, 6" x 8". Supreme Headquarters, July 7, 1944. To Frank J. Beebee, Newtonville, Mass. In full: "*Thank you for your kindness in sending me my monogram. I appreciate the thought. I am enclosing a facsimile of my shoulder sleeve insignia. Thank you for your good wishes.*" General Eisenhower had led the invasion of Normandy on D-Day, June 6, 1944, just one month earlier. The letter is affixed to a page of a specially bound, hardcover scrapbook, with "IKE 1953" in gilt lettering imprinted on the spine. The book measures 6.5" x 8.5" and has 68 pages with photographs affixed to one side only. Many are Associated Press black & white photographs, but there are also photographs clipped from magazines and newspapers, all relating to Dwight D. Eisenhower, with most picturing him. A four page typed article from the June 1, 1952 edition of "The New York Times" (about Ike's candidacy for the 1952 presidential nomination) is near the front of the book and a one page typed index is in the back. The 8" x 10.5" color "facsimile of my shoulder sleeve insignia" mentioned by General Eisenhower has been tipped to a page. Letter and insignia facsimile sheet each bear one horizontal and one vertical fold from mailing. Overall, the book is in fine condition. A unique addition to an Eisenhower collection. From the Henry E. Luhrs Collection. Accompanied by LOA from PSA/DNA.

Estimate: $400-$600

25015 **Millard Fillmore & Daniel Sickles Signatures in 1858 Autograph Album.** "*Respectfully Yours Millard Fillmore Albany N.Y. April 15, 1858*" and "*D. E. Sickles MC New York*" along with hundreds of other political signatures. This collection was apparently gathered by Sergeant at Arms Lasher of the New York Assembly of 1858. A veritable "Who's Who" in New York politics of this period, this book's pages are all tight and clean, the front board is loose and the cover has some wear. The signatures are all bold and clear, many with personal sentiments and positions added. Great lot for the researcher. From the Henry E. Luhrs Collection. Accompanied by LOA from PSA/DNA.

Estimate: $400-$600

25016 Dwight D. Eisenhower 1954 Thanksgiving Proclamation Signed in full, as president. A printed, one page, 8" x 14" press release, Washington, D.C., November 6, 1954. In this document Eisenhower officially proclaims November 25, 1954 as Thanksgiving Day and he has signed it beneath his printed name at the bottom. Included is the letter of transmittal from Ann C. Whitman, Eisenhower's personal secretary, and the original "White House" mailing envelope. Very Fine condition, mailing folds barely visible as it has been stored flat. From the Henry E. Luhrs Collection. Accompanied by LOA from PSA/DNA.
Estimate: $800-$1,200

IMMEDIATE RELEASE   NOVEMBER 6, 1954
JAMES C. HAGERTY, PRESS SECRETARY TO THE PRESIDENT
- -

THE WHITE HOUSE
THANKSGIVING DAY, 1954
3077
BY THE PRESIDENT OF THE UNITED STATES OF AMERICA
A PROCLAMATION

Early in our history the Pilgrim fathers inaugurated the custom of dedicating one day at harvest time to rendering thanks to Almighty God for the bounties of the soil and for His mercies throughout the year. At this autumnal season tradition suggests and our hearts require that we follow that hallowed custom and bow in reverent thanks for the blessings bestowed upon us individually and as a Nation.

We are grateful that our beloved country, settled by those forebears in their quest for religious freedom, remains free and strong, and that each of us can worship God in his own way, according to the dictates of his conscience.

We are grateful for the innumerable daily manifestations of Divine goodness in affairs both public and private, for equal opportunities for all to labor and to serve, and for the continuance of those homely joys and satisfactions which enrich our lives.

With gratitude in our hearts for all our blessings, may we be ever mindful of the obligations inherent in our strength, and may we rededicate ourselves to unselfish striving for the common betterment of mankind.

NOW, THEREFORE, I, DWIGHT D. EISENHOWER, President of the United States of America, in consonance with the joint resolution of Congress approved December 26, 1941, designating the fourth Thursday of November of each year as Thanksgiving Day, do hereby proclaim Thursday, November 25, 1954, as a day of national thanksgiving, and I call upon all our citizens to observe the day with prayer. Let us demonstrate in our lives our humble thanks to God for His beneficence in the year which is past, and let us ask His guidance in the year to come.

IN WITNESS WHEREOF, I have hereunto set my hand and caused the Seal of the United States of America to be affixed.

DONE at the City of Washington this sixth day of November in the year of our Lord nineteen hundred and fifty-four, and of the Independence of the United States of America the one hundred and seventy-ninth.

(SEAL)

DWIGHT D. EISENHOWER

By the President:

JOHN FOSTER DULLES
Secretary of State.

#####

25017 Ulysses S. Grant Cabinet Members Autograph Collection. All items are in fine or better condition unless noted. Included in this lot are:

Schuyler Colfax. Vice President. Autograph Letter Signed.

Henry Wilson. Vice President. Autograph Letter Signed.

Zechariah Chandler. Secretary of the Interior. Autograph Endorsement Signed.

James D. Cameron. Secretary of War. Autograph Letter Signed.

Lot M. Morill. Secretary of the Treasury. Autograph Letter Signed (good condition). From the Henry E. Luhrs Collection. Accompanied by LOA from PSA/DNA.
Estimate: $300-$500

25018 Warren G. Harding Manuscript on Lincoln, "The Tenderest and Truest." Typed Manuscript Signed, *as Senator,* entitled *"Lincoln - The Tenderest and Truest"*, 1 page, 5.25" x 6.75", on the letterhead of the United States Senate but dated Marion, Ohio, July 27, 1920. In Fine condition, although the gimlet eye will perceive that the bottom blank half of the leaf has a slight smudge, and two miniscule pinholes. Of special interest is when one President remarks on another: when the other is Lincoln, the remarks are important. In full: *"The English language has been exhausted in extolling Abraham Lincoln, which but proves that he is superior to praise. Perhaps in all the world's history he had no prototype. Unschooled he was learned; untutored he was thoroughly a gentleman. He had the gift of the scholar and the graces of speech of the most polished orator. His 'firmness in the right' absolves him from any charge of weakness. But he will live throughout the ages for his gentleness and humanity."* From the Henry E. Luhrs Collection. Accompanied by LOA from PSA/DNA.
Estimate: $700-$900

United States Senate,
WASHINGTON, D.C.

Marion, Ohio,
July 27, 1920.

LINCOLN - THE TENDEREST AND TRUEST.

The English language has been exhausted in extolling Abraham Lincoln, which but proves that he is superior to praise. Perhaps in all the world's history he had no prototype. Unschooled he was learned; untutored he was thoroughly a gentleman. He had the gift of the scholar and the graces of speech of the most polished orator. His "firmness in the right" absolves him from any charge of weakness. But he will live throughout the ages for his gentleness and humanity.

Warren G Harding

25019 Warren G. Harding Scarce Autograph Letter — Turning Down a Good Time! Autograph Letter Signed, *as Senator,* 1 page, on the letterhead of the United States Senate, Washington, June 6, 1917; to Connecticut Senator Frank Brandegee, a member of Harding's informal drinking and claver club, the "Little Mothers", which met, convivially, after work in the lower rooms of the Hotel Bon Ton. In Very Fine condition. With typical bonhomie, Harding pens this rare letter to his brother "Little Mother." In full: *"I would rejoice to be your luncheon guest speaker next Sunday, June 10th, because it is easy to anticipate a bully good time, but I find myself tied up by the coming of family guests to whom I am committed for that day. You will therefore have to strike my name from the list, for which I am very selfishly sorry."* From the Henry E. Luhrs Collection. Accompanied by LOA from PSA/DNA.
Estimate: $500-$700

25020 Warren G. Harding: Portion of Typed Letter Signed Mentioning Coolidge. Incomplete Typed Letter Signed, *as Senator*, 1 page, 5.25" x 3.5", no place, no date [circa 1919-20]; being the last two paragraphs of a letter. Slightly ragged at top

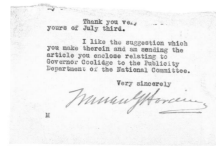

where torn, else Fine. In part: *"I like the suggestion which you make therein and am sending the article you enclose to Governor Coolidge to the Publicity Department of the National Committee..."* Coolidge, Governor of Massachusetts for but a year, was elected Harding's vice-president in 1920. From the Henry E. Luhrs Collection. Accompanied by LOA from PSA/DNA.
Estimate: $200-$300

25021 Rutherford B. Hayes and Other Statesmen Autograph Collection consisting of the following items: R. B. Hayes (Clipped Signature); Levi P. Morton, Benjamin

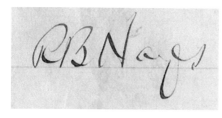

Harrison's vice president (ALS); William E. Chandler, Secretary of the Navy under Arthur (ALS); Samuel J. Kirkwood, Secretary of the Interior under Garfield and Arthur (ALS); Thomas B. Reed, Speaker of the House (ALS); Hilary A. Herbert, Secretary of the Navy under Cleveland (ANS); Charles J. Folger, Secretary of the Treasury under Arthur (Signature); Hoke Smith, Secretary of the Interior under Cleveland (TLS). Items are in generally very good condition. From the Henry E. Luhrs Collection. Accompanied by LOA from PSA/DNA.
Estimate: $300-$400

25022 Herbert Hoover Signed Book: *Addresses Upon the American Road 1933-1938* (New York: Charles Scribner's Sons, 1938), first edition, 390 pages, blue cloth with gilt, 8vo (6" x 8.5"), dust jacket, signed on the front free endpaper *"The Good Wishes of Herbert Hoover"*. A collection, the first in a series, of Hoover's speeches. Very Good condition, corners bumped, original owner's stamp on free front endpaper. The dust jacket has some tattering along the edges, soiling, and a couple of tiny areas of lifting on the back. From the Henry E. Luhrs Collection. Accompanied by LOA from PSA/DNA.
Estimate: $250-$350

25023 Herbert Hoover Printed Speech Signed. Signed, in turquoise ink, on the cover of his speech entitled *"The Protection of Freedom"*, delivered at the reception given by the State of Iowa on the occasion of the 31st President's 80th birthday. 5" x 8", 19 pages, West Branch Iowa, August 10, 1954. In Very Fine condition, albeit there is, in faint pencil, a note in the lower right corner. A beautiful souvenir of a reflective, and cautionary, Cold War address. From the Henry E. Luhrs Collection. Accompanied by LOA from PSA/DNA.
Estimate: $200-$300

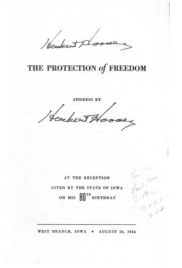

25024 Herbert Hoover (1874-1964), President, his signature *"Herbert Hoover"* on a scarce printed copy of his address, to the 1948 Republican National Convention entitled *"This Crisis in American Life,"* and delivered in Philadelphia on June 22, 1948, thirteen pages, octavo (5.5" x 8.5"), staple bound. He spoke (in small part): *"My fellow Republicans, for the inevitable passing of years, this is indicated as probably the last time I will met with you in convention... Therefore, I repeat, what you say and do here and in this campaign, is for transcendent importance. If you produce nothing but improvised platitudes, you will give no hope. If you produce no leadership here, no virile fighter for the right, you will have done nothing of historic significance.... If you temporize with collectivism in any form, you will stimulate its growth and make certain the defeat of free men..."* A fine example. From the Henry E. Luhrs Collection. Accompanied by LOA from PSA/DNA.
Estimate: $300-$400

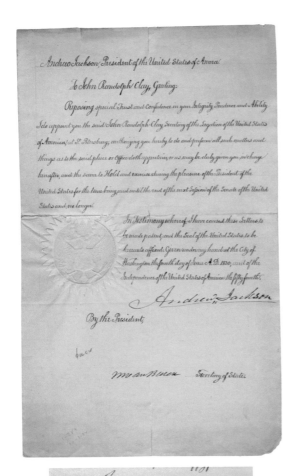

25025   Andrew Jackson & Martin Van Buren Document Signed
"*Andrew Jackson*" as President and "*M Van Buren*" as Secretary of State.
One page, 9" x 14.5", Washington, June 4, 1830. An appointment of John
Randolph Clay to the position of "*...Secretary of the Legation of the United
States of America, at St. Petersburg...*" Interestingly, John Randolph Clay
has been called our country's first career diplomat. This appointment
to Russia was his first post, and he would later serve in Austria and Peru
during his 30-year career. This manuscript document is in very good
condition; general toning, lower left corner chipped some weakness
at folds, minor repairs on verso. From the Henry E. Luhrs Collection.
Accompanied by LOA from PSA/DNA.
Estimate: $1,500-$2,500

25026   Andrew Jackson (1767-1845) President, Letter Signed,
"Andrew Jackson" as President, two pages, 7.5" x 9.75", Washington, June
15, 1835 to John H. Wheeler. Jackson acknowledges "*...your favor of the
6th instant and of the care which accompanied it as a testimonial of the
kind feelings entertained for me by your neighbor Mr. Gordon Gartlin. I
pray you to assure him that I received his present with satisfaction and
pleasure...I cannot doubt from your description of his character, and from
his being a substantial farmer, that he has had the opportunity of examining the measures of my administration and of forming a judgment
upon them without bias. To his class in our society because it is the largest
and the most independent, should the public officer chiefly look for that
measure of approbation which is to outlive the strives of the day and
to connect the memory of his services with the lasting prosperity of his
country...*" Jackson built his political support from independent yeoman
farmers and others outside of the traditional political "class" exemplified
by John Quincy Adams. And, of course, embracing the "common folk"
put Old Hickory in the Executive Mansion. Fold separations repaired, light
toning, else near fine. A wonderful example. From the Henry E. Luhrs
Collection. Accompanied by LOA from PSA/DNA.
Estimate: $1,500-$2,000

25027 **Thomas Jefferson (1743-1826) President and author of the Declaration of Independence,** very fine content Autograph Letter Signed *"Th: Jefferson"* as President, one page, 8" x 9.75" with integral address leaf, Washington, December 31, 1802 to Caesar A. Rodney, the son of the Signer.

Jefferson begins his letter by discussing the matter of an unpaid bill: *"I thank you for the mention you made in yours of the 19th of my subscription to the academy, immediately after subscribing I had set it down on a list of presents... to be made by mr John Barnes of this place, he transacts all my pecuniary affairs. I supposed it paid, and he supposed it was to be called for, and thus it has laid and would have laid but for your letter which recalled my attention to it. mr Barnes will now immediately remit it to mr Latimer according to the printed advertisement."*

Upon concluding the subject of his more than troubled personal finances, he focuses on the coming legislative season: *"Congress is not yet engaged in business of any note. we want men of business among them. I really wish you were here. I am convinced it is in the power of any man who understands business, and who will undertake to keep a file for the business before Congress & to press it as he would his own docket in a court, to shorten the sessions a month one year with another, & to save in that way 30,000 D[ollars] a year. An ill-judged modesty prevents those from undertaking it who are equal to it. You will have seen by the message that there is little interesting proposed to be done. the settlement of the Mississippi territory is among the most important. So also, in my opinion, is the proposition for the preservation of our Navy, which otherwise will either be entirely rotten in 6 or 8 years, or will cost us 3 or 4 millions in repairs. Whether the proposition will surmount the doubts of some, and false economy of others, I know not. Accept assurances of my great esteem & respect. Th: Jefferson"*

While Jefferson served as Vice President under Adams, he opposed the Administration's naval buildup during the quasi-war with France. Once in the White House, however, he was faced with a new crisis. The Barbary state of Tripoli had declared war on the United States after Jefferson refused to pay them what amounted to protection money. In response, he sent a fleet to the Mediterranean and fought a four year naval war. Hence Jefferson saw the need for a strong navy. At the same time, Jefferson was able to cut the federal debt by one third. His focus on settling the Mississippi Territory would be soon overshadowed by his surprise acquisition of the Louisiana Territory. Another offering with wonderful, historic content. Fine condition. Vintage Jefferson engraving included. From the Henry E. Luhrs Collection. Accompanied by LOA from PSA/DNA.
Estimate: $25,000-$35,000

Dear Sir   *Monticello Aug. 27. 08.*

Your favor of the 13.th is recieved. I see no reason against your giving your opinion, in favor of General Allen, to him to be used with the British government. the only doubt I ever entertained on it was that which you mention res--pecting his bail, and I have not yet seen my way out of that. I inclose you the letter of a M. Mouesay, whose case seems to be as hard a one as I have known. I wish you to open a correspondence with the district attorney of Mary--land, get him to do for Mouesay whatever he can, and to state the truth of the case, as it has appeared to him, & transmit it to us while it is fresh in his memory, as I have little doubt it will become a case between government & government. we have not recieved one interesting word from Genl. Armstrong or mr Pinckney since our separation. I salute you with affec--tion & respect.

Th: Jefferson

Mr. Rodney.

25028   **Thomas Jefferson Autograph Letter Signed** *"Th: Jefferson."* One page, 7.25" x 7", Monticello, Virginia, August 27th, 1808. This letter was written to Caesar A. Rodney, the nephew Declaration of Independence Signer, Caesar Rodney. Rodney was currently serving as United States Attorney General under Jefferson. The letter reads in part, *"I see no reason against your giving your opinion, in favor of General Allen, to him to be used with British Government. The only doubt I ever entertained on it was that which you mention respecting his bail, and I have not yet seen my way out of thatWe have not received one interesting word from Genl. Armstrong or Mr. Pickney since our separation. I salute you with affection and respect..."*
The letter is in very fine condition; usual folds are present; signature still bold and dark. From the Henry E. Luhrs Collection.
Accompanied by LOA from PSA/DNA.
Estimate: $10,000-$12,000

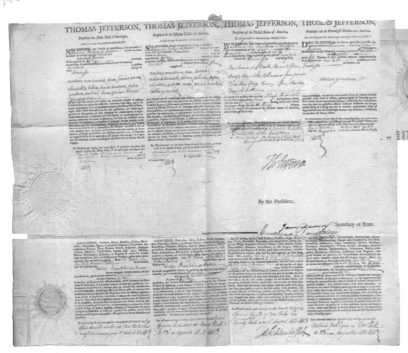

25029   **Thomas Jefferson & James Madison Four Language Ship's Sea Letter** Signed "*Th:Jefferson*" as President and "*James Madison*" as Secretary of State. One page, 19.75" x 15.75", partly printed in four languages-French, Spanish, English, and Dutch, New York, August 23, 1803. In part: "BE IT KNOWN, That leave and permission are hereby given to Alexander Jenkins of Hudson, master or commander of the Sloop called the *Franklin* of the burden of 84 33/95 tons, or thereabouts, lying at present in the port of New York bound for Tenerife and laden with Nankeens, dry Goods, Bread, flour, Soap, Candles, tobacco, gunpowder, Pipes, Tar, Shoes, Rum, Gin, Butter, Boards & Stores to depart and proceed with the said Sloop on his said voyage, such Sloop having been visited, and the said A. Jenkins having made oath before the proper officer, that the said Sloop belongs to one or more of the citizens of the United States of America, and to him or them only..." There is a 2.25" white paper seal of the United States affixed at left with a 1.25" seal of New York beneath it. Also countersigned by David Gelston, as Collector of the Customs, who was a prominent New York politician. Very good condition; several folds, roughness at edges, mounting traces on verso at top, seals are intact and complete. The Jefferson and Madison signatures are bold and dark. Excellent for display. From the Henry E. Luhrs Collection. Accompanied by LOA from PSA/DNA.

Estimate: $4,000-$6,000

25030   **Andrew Johnson: War-Date Letter Regarding the Press in Tennessee.** Letter Signed, *as Senator,* 2 pages albeit signed on recto, 5.75" x 9", laid into a slightly larger sheet, Washington City, March 15, 1861. In Excellent condition. To General W.C. Patterson. Busily campaigning against secession in his home state, here Johnson lists newspapers which he has "*no doubt will republish Col. Williams' Letters.*" He then lists the ten Tennessee papers, and the cities in which they appear. An intriguing communication. From the Henry E. Luhrs Collection. Accompanied by LOA from PSA/DNA.

Estimate: $700-$900

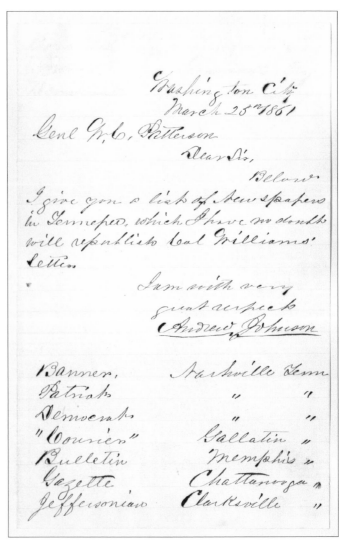

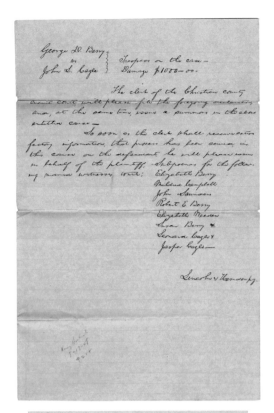

25031 **Abraham Lincoln Requests Witnesses for Case in Which a Man is Accused of Fathering an Illegitimate Child** ADS: *"Lincoln & Herndon p.q.,"* 1p, 8" x 12". Christian County [Illinois], September 12, 1849. Headed by Lincoln: *"George D. Berry/vs./John S. Cagle/Trespass on the case- Damage $1000-00-."* Lincoln continues: *"The clerk of the Christian county circuit court will please file the foregoing declaration, and, at the same time, issue a summons in the above entitled cause— So soon as the clerk shall receive satisfactory information, that process has been served in this cause on the defendant, he will please issue in behalf of the plaintiff, Subpoenas for the following named witnesses to wit: Elizabeth Berry, Mildred Campbell, John Saunders, Robert E. Berry, Elizabeth Weeden, Susan Berry, Leonard Cagle, Jasper Cagle-"* On verso in another hand: "Filed Sept 12/1849/W.S. Moore". George D. Berry, Lincoln & Herndon's client, sued John S. Cagle for trespass. **The declaration Lincoln wrote, which he has asked the clerk to file, alleged that John S. Cagle caused George D. Berry's daughter Elizabeth Berry to bear an illegitimate child and be sick for nine months. Lincoln & Herndon asked for $1000 in damages. Heading their witness list: Elizabeth Berry. It is interesting to note that the baby was already born, that it was not the mother bringing suit against the man who fathered her child, but her father - and the crime allegedly committed was "Trespass".** The law firm of Lincoln & Herndon was formed in 1843. The partnership continued, nominally at least, until Lincoln's death in 1865. Lightly browned at folds. In fine condition. From the Henry E. Luhrs Collection. Accompanied by LOA from PSA/DNA. **Estimate: $8,000-$15,000**

25032 **Abraham Lincoln Massive Bronze-Finish Bust; A Unique Image.** Perhaps the largest Lincoln metal bust we have ever encountered, measuring 53" in height, and 28" in width at the shoulders! Lincoln is shown wearing a Roman-style toga, a common convention among sculptors of the day when depicting statesmen. IT is made of zinc with an applied bronze finish which appears to be original. Minor wear to the finish, particularly around the bottom of the pedestal base, but overall in excellent condition for display. The bust is unsigned and bears no maker's name, so it is impossible to date precisely. But it is of a style popular during the last years of the War. Possibly it may have been made during the mourning period after Lincoln's assassination, but most memorial pieces bear birth and death dates or some sentiment identifying them as memorial in nature. Although it is in typical style, we cannot recall seeing a version of this exact Lincoln sculpture previously. Given the lack of markings and the distinctiveness of the image, it may well be a one-of-a-kind item, possibly made for a specific location or even a manufacturer's trial which was never commercially produced. In any case, one of the most power and arresting Lincoln sculptures we have seen.

For many years this bust was the focal point in the reception area of the Beistle Corporation in Shippensburg, Pennsylvania, Henry Luhr's family company. To many members of the family and others who knew his collection, it became the collection's most familiar symbol. We feel sure it will "rule the room" wherever its new owner chooses to display it. From the Henry E. Luhrs Collection. **Estimate: $8,000-$12,000**

Marked "*Confidential*", Lincoln advises
the governor on how to address the
growing secession crisis. He writes: "*I am
much obliged by your kindness in asking
my views in advance of preparing your
inaugural. I think of nothing proper for me
to suggest except a word about this secession and disunion movement — On that
subject, I think you would do well to express, without passion, threat, or appearance of boasting, but nevertheless, with
firmness, the purpose of yourself and your
state to maintain the Union at all hazards
— Also, if you can, procure the Legislature
to pass resolutions to that effect— A[s] [I]
shall be very glad to see your friend, the
Attorney General [Samuel A. Purviance],
that is to be, but I think he need scarcely
make a trip merely to confer with me on
the subject you mention.*"

This important letter reveals a great deal
of political savvy on the part of the Rail
Splitter. Lincoln recognized the interreg-
num following his election for what it was:
one of the most dangerous periods in
our history. The four full months between
Lincoln's election in 1860 and his inauguration in Washington on March the Fourth
were accompanied by predictions of
assassination. Arguably, the Federal government came close to collapse. Even the
influential New York *Herald* cautioned the
President-elect to consider mollifying his
views... or choose the only sane course:
resignation. "If he persists in his present
position... he will totter into a dishonored
grave, driven there perhaps by the hands
of an assassin." With sincere bravado,
Lincoln responded "I will suffer death
before I will consent or advise my friends
to consent to any concession or compromise which looks like buying the privilege
of taking possession of the Government
to which we have a constitutional right."
(Getting Lincoln safely into Washington
became the concern of Alan Pinkerton and Ward Lamon... a trip fraught with danger.) True, this country had never suffered the heinous, despicable act
of political assassination. (A failed attempt was made on the life of Andrew Jackson in 1835 by a deranged man.) But everyone knew these were extraordinary times creating depths of regional and ideological hatred that had never been seen. We often forget that Abraham Lincoln became a target the
moment he stepped onto the national stage.

Marked "CONFIDENTIAL", this letter reflects Lincoln's use of surrogates to communicate his political intentions. Unwilling to reveal his plans for legislation prior to assuming office — save for his quoting extensively from the Founding Documents in his address at Independence Hall as he traveled to
Washington — he let politicos such as Curtin argue the necessity of no compromise. He did not grant interviews nor reveal to the press his plans for
holding the Union. But... as this letter points out, it would be just fine for Pennsylvania's State Legislature to do so! This missive mirrors what he would reveal in his first Inaugural Address three months later: that he would take whatever steps necessary to "maintain the Union at all hazards." Reports of South
Carolina seceding reached the President-elect the day before writing his letter to Curtin. He is said to have taken the news calmly. But, he likewise made
it clear through private letters — such as this — that he would not govern over a fractured country.

A tremendously important Lincoln letter — one of the finest to remain in private hands. It has every component desired: insight, significant content, revelatory history. It will always remain a cornerstone to any major collection. From the Henry E. Luhrs Collection. Accompanied by LOA from PSA/DNA.
Estimate: $80,000-$120,000

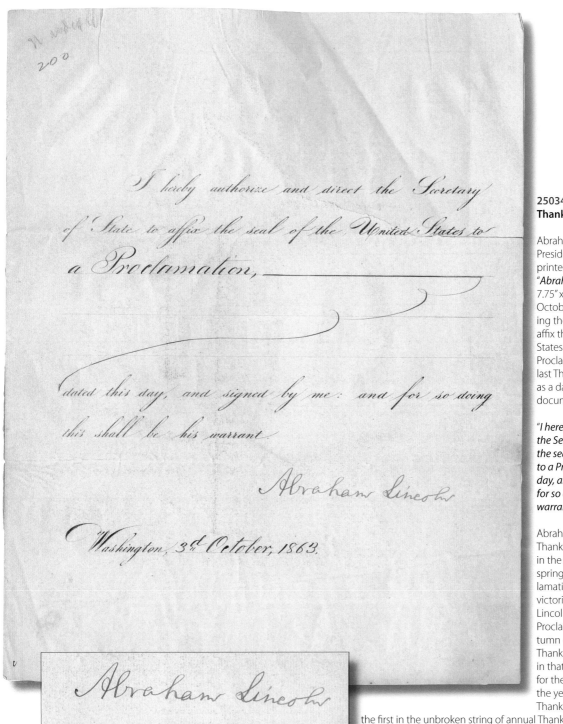

I hereby authorize and direct the Secretary of State to affix the seal of the United States to a Proclamation,

dated this day, and signed by me: and for so doing this shall be his warrant

Abraham Lincoln

Washington, 3d October, 1863.

Abraham Lincoln

25034   For Lincoln's Thanksgiving Proclamation

Abraham Lincoln (1809-1865) President, important partly-printed Document Signed *"Abraham Lincoln"* one page, 7.75" x 10", Washington, October 3, 1863, authorizing the Secretary of State to affix the Seal of the United States to the first Presidential Proclamation designating the last Thursday in November as a day of Thanksgiving. The document reads in full:

"I hereby authorize and direct the Secretary of State to affix the seal of the United States to a Proclamation, dated this day, and signed by me: and for so doing this shall be his warrant."

Abraham Lincoln issued Thanksgiving Proclamations in the spring of 1862 and the spring of 1863; both proclamations gave thanks for victories in battle. Abraham Lincoln's Thanksgiving Proclamation in the autumn of 1863 - the second Thanksgiving Proclamation in that year - gave thanks for the general blessings of the year. This second 1863 Thanksgiving Proclamation, the first in the unbroken string of annual Thanksgiving proclamations, is regarded as the true beginning of the national Thanksgiving holiday.

The original proclamation is housed at the National Archives in Washington. The original manuscript of the proclamation, in the hand of Secretary of State William Seward, was sold to benefit troops at an 1864 Sanitary Fair during the Civil War and its location remains unknown. Mounting traces on integral blank leaf, partial clean fold separation and one small tear into text that lays flat, else Fine. This order to affix the seal to the Thanksgiving Proclamation, boldly signed by the President, set forth a tradition observed every year and remains the favorite holiday of just about every American family. A truly evocative piece of Lincolniana that touches us all. From the Henry E. Luhrs Collection. Accompanied by LOA from PSA/DNA.
Estimate: $50,000-$75,000

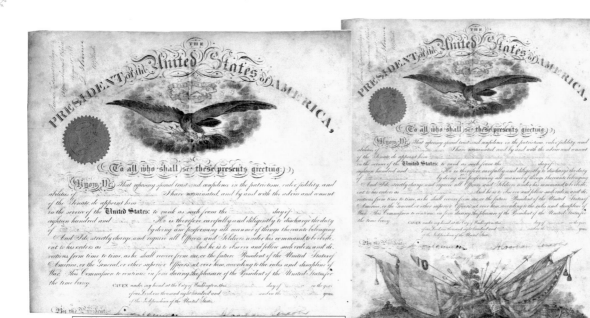

25035   Abraham Lincoln Document Signed
"Abraham Lincoln." 13.8" x 17", one page printed document, signed by both the president and Secretary of War Cameron, dated August 17, 1861 from Washington D.C. This document is a commission for P.H. Durkee to the rank of First Lieutenant in the 14th Regiment of Infantry. It is docketed in the upper left-hand corner. The head and foot of the document feature gorgeous engravings, and the orange seal is still present and intact. The document is in Good condition; the writing is fading slightly, but Lincoln's signature is still bold and crisp; there is adhesive damage and residue on the verso; otherwise amazing! From the Henry E. Luhrs Collection. Accompanied by LOA from PSA/DNA.
Estimate: $4,500-$6,000

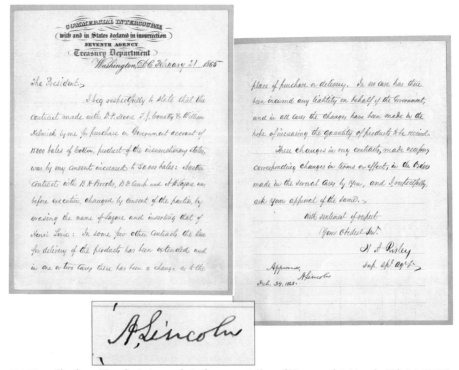

25036   Abraham Lincoln Autograph Endorsement Signed *"Approved, A. Lincoln, Feb. 24. 1865."*
The document Lincoln endorses is on handsome stationery from the Commercial Intercourse Treasury Department. The letter asks him to approve some cases regarding the altering of contracts. The signature is dark and crisp.

The endorsement is in very fine condition; usual folds are present. From the Henry E. Luhrs Collection. Accompanied by LOA from PSA/DNA.
Estimate: $3,500-$4,500

Luzerne County, ss:

Commonwealth of Pennsylvania.

I, *Wm. H. Pier,* Prothonotary
of the Court of Common Pleas of and for said county,
do hereby certify that *Canfield Harrison*
whose name is signed to the forgoing certificate of
acknowledgment, was at the time of taking such
acknowledgment *an associate Judge
of the Court of Common Pleas*
in and for said county, duly commissioned and sworn
and residing in said county, and *was* at the time of taking such acknowledgment, duly authorized to take the same, and authorized by the laws of said State to take the proof and
acknowledgment of deeds and other instruments, and administer oaths generally, and that I am
well acquainted with the handwriting of the said *Canfield Harrison*

and verily believe that the above signature to said certificate of acknowledgment is genuine.
In Testimony Whereof, I have hereunto subscribed my name and affixed my official seal, at
Wilkes-Barre, in said county, this *14th* day of *May,* A. D. 186*4.*

Wm. H. Pier, **Prothonotary.**

25037   Abraham Lincoln Document Signed
"*Abraham Lincoln.*" One page, 15.5" x 19.25", Officer's
Commission, Washington D.C., February 26, 1864. This
document is an officer's commission for the United
States Navy stating that Henry McSherry had been
appointed a Surgeon. Lincoln signs this as does the
Secretary of Navy, Gideon Welles.

The document is in very fine condition; usual folds
are present; seal is still intact and clear; very light soiling on edges. From the Henry E. Luhrs Collection.
Accompanied by LOA from PSA/DNA.
Estimate: $7,000-$9,000

**25038   Abraham Lincoln
Orders Underage Boy Dismissed
From Army - and Bounty Repaid!**
Autograph Endorsement Signed ("A.
Lincoln"), as *president,* 1 page, being
a docket on the verso of a petition
of dismissal, 8" by 12.25", no place
[Washington], May 24, 1864. In fine
condition. Being the official notarized
petition of a father, "*that his son
Charles W. Randall has enlisted in the
United States Service, is now in the
67th Regiment Pa. vols. ... that said
Charles W. Randall enlisted without his knowledge or consent, and further that Charles W.
Randall was born on the fifteenth day February A.D. 1850, and was therefore but fourteen
years of age on the fifteenth day of February A.D. 1844.*" Lincoln has written: "*Let this boy
be discharged upon refunding any bounty received.*" An unusual endorsement. From the
Henry E. Luhrs Collection. Accompanied by LOA from PSA/DNA.
Estimate: $5,500-$6,500

25039 Abraham Lincoln Officer Commission Document Signed in full. This is as nice a document and signature as you're likely to find! One page, 16" x 19.5", Washington, April 7, 1863. An appointment of Pinkney Lugenbeel as "... Major in the Nineteenth Regiment of Infantry..." effective December 31, 1862. Lincoln's signature is dark, bold, and 3.75" long. It is countersigned by Edwin M. Stanton as Secretary of War and by Edward Townsend as Asst. Adjutant General in the docketing information in the upper left on the front. Very fine condition with expected folds, large pink seal present and intact. A most excellent display piece! From the Henry E. Luhrs Collection. Accompanied by LOA from PSA/DNA.

Estimate: $7,000-$9,000

25040 Abraham Lincoln Releases Prisoners Four Days Before His Assassination! An Endorsement Signed "*A Lincoln*" on a lined sheet 3" x 2.625", np, April 10, 1865. In full, "*Let these Prisoners be discharged on taking the oath of Dec. 8, 1863. April 10, 1865*". A very poignant item- Lincoln shows mercy to prisoners of war during the week in which John Wilkes Booth showed no mercy to him. This has to be one of the last times that Abraham Lincoln ever signed his name- an exceptional opportunity! About fine condition; folds light toning on the left edge, hinged at top to larger sheet. From the Henry E. Luhrs Collection. Accompanied by LOA from PSA/DNA.

Estimate: $7,000-$9,000

25041 Abraham Lincoln "Valentine's Day" Prisoner Release Endorsement Signed "*A Lincoln*" on the verso of a lined sheet 3.25" x 2.375", np, February 14, 1865. In full, "Let the Prisoner be released on taking the oath of Dec. 8, 1863...Feb. 14, 1865." written by his secretary, John Hay, and signed above the date by Lincoln himself. Mr. Luhrs purchased this item from John Heise Autographs in 1937. Apparently, he had been seeking a Lincoln item dated on Valentine's Day for some time. He then used this item to produce a souvenir Valentine to be sent to friends of the Lincoln Library. One of these heart-shaped cards is included with the lot. It says, above and below an image of this document, "Here's a Real Valentine. Big Hearted President Lincoln Sent This Note February 14, 1865. This Pardon Gave Liberty to a Prisoner of the North During the Civil War." An interesting association item. Fine condition. From the Henry E. Luhrs Collection. Accompanied by LOA from PSA/DNA.

Estimate: $4,000-$5,000

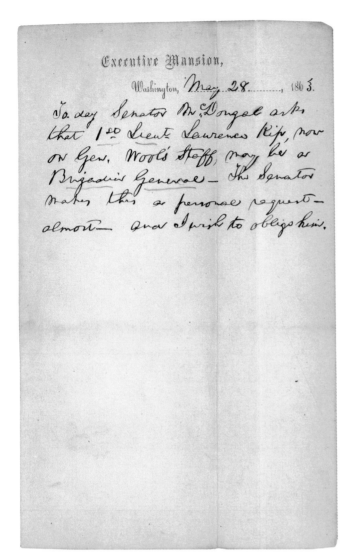

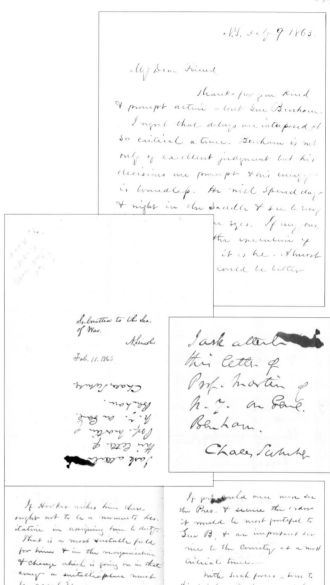

25042　Abraham Lincoln Autograph Letter. One page, 5" x 8", Executive Mansion letterhead, Washington D.C., May 28th, 1863. The letter is written by Lincoln as an approval to a senator's request, it reads, *"To.day* [sic] *Senator McDougal asks that 1st Lieut. Lawrence Kip, now on Gen. Wool's Staff, may be a Brigadier General - The Senator makes this a personal request - almost - and I wish to oblige him."* Lawrence Kip was never awarded this rank, however, he did survive the war and continue to serve in the Army. Accompanying this letter are two photographs of the Lincoln memorial, both in color, and a lovely photogravure of Lincoln. All these items will make lovely display piece for this letter.

The letter is in fine condition; usual folds are present; staining present along fold lines on verso; letter has been silked at some point in the past; slight mounting traces on verso. From the Henry E. Luhrs Collection. Accompanied by LOA from PSA/DNA.

Estimate: $5,000-$6,000

25043　Abraham Lincoln Autograph Endorsement Signed on the verso of a letter to Charles Sumner about General Burham (three pages, 6.5" x 8", New York, February 9, 1863). Lincoln has written *"Submitted to the Sec. of War. A. Lincoln Feb. 11, 1863"*. There is also an Autograph Endorsement Signed above the Lincoln by Charles Sumner: *"I ask attentn to this letter of Prof. Martin of N.Y. on Genl. Burham. Charles Sumner"*. Benjamin N. Martin, a professor at New York University, wrote the original letter. Fine condition; multiple folds, an ink smear at the top of Sumner's note. From the Henry E. Luhrs Collection. Accompanied by LOA from PSA/DNA.

Estimate: $4,500-$5,500

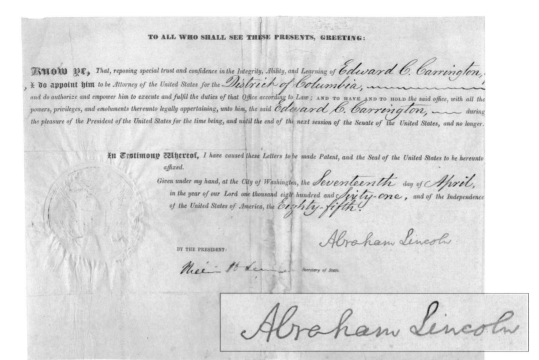

TO ALL WHO SHALL SEE THESE PRESENTS, GREETING:

Know ye, That, reposing special trust and confidence in the Integrity, Ability, and Learning of *Edward C. Carrington,* , **I do appoint him** to be Attorney of the United States for the *District of Columbia,* and do authorize and empower him to execute and fulfil the duties of that Office according to Law ; AND TO HAVE AND TO HOLD the said office, with all the powers, privileges, and emoluments thereunto legally appertaining, unto him, the said *Edward C. Carrington,* during the pleasure of the President of the United States for the time being, and until the end of the next session of the Senate of the United States, and no longer.

In Testimony Whereof, I have caused these Letters to be made Patent, and the Seal of the United States to be hereunto affixed.

Given under my hand, at the City of Washington, the *Seventeenth* day of *April,* in the year of our Lord one thousand eight hundred and *Sixty-one* , and of the Independence of the United States of America, the *Eighty-fifth.*

Abraham Lincoln

BY THE PRESIDENT:

Secretary of State.

25044   Abraham Lincoln Document Signed *"Abraham Lincoln."* One page, 10.75" x 7.75", Washington D.C., April 17th, 1861. This document is an appointment that announces that Edward C. Carrington is appointed as an Attorney for the District of Columbia. The document is signed by President Lincoln as well as Secretary of State William H. Seward. The document is in fine condition; usual folds are present; staining and soiling present along vertical fold; embossed seal still intact; signatures are bold and dark! From the Henry E. Luhrs Collection. Accompanied by LOA from PSA/DNA.
Estimate: $5,000-$6,000

25045   Abraham Lincoln Prisoner Release Autograph Endorsement Signed *"A Lincoln"* on the back of a document 3.125" x 2.375", np, February 6, 1865. In full *"Let these men take the oath of Dec. 8, 1863 & be discharged. Feb. 6, 1865".* Fine condition; writing on the verso can be faintly seen through the paper, laid down to another sheet with vintage hinges present. From the Henry E. Luhrs Collection. Accompanied by LOA from PSA/DNA.
Estimate: $4,000-$5,000

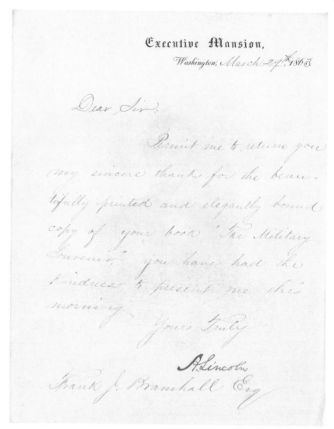

25046 **Abraham Lincoln Document Signed, as president, partially printed and accomplished in manuscript,** *"Abraham Lincoln."* One page, 13.75" x 17.5", Washington D.C., October 25, 1861. Promoting one Richard P.H. Durkee Captain in the Fourteenth Regiment of Infantry in the U.S. Army. Durkee did survive the Civil War, it is documented that he resigned in 1863. The document is boldly signed by Lincoln and Edwin M. Stanton, Secretary of War. The vignettes are in Fine condition, still crisp and detailed; the embossed seal is still intact.

The document is in Very Fine condition; usual folds are present; mounting traces present on verso; docketing information present in upper left corner. From the Henry E. Luhrs Collection. Accompanied by LOA from PSA/DNA.

Estimate: $6,000-$8,000

25047 **Abraham Lincoln (1809-1865), President, Letter Signed** *"A. Lincoln"* as President, one page on Executive Mansion letterhead, 7.75" x 9.75", Washington, March 29, 1863 to Frank J. Bramhall thanking him *"...for the beautifully printed and elegantly bound copy of your book 'the Military Souvenir,' you have had the kindness to present me this morning..."* Written in the hand of Lincoln's personal secretary **John G. Nicholay.** The book to which Lincoln refers is a collection of steel engraved portraits (after photographic images) accomplished by John Chester Buttre entitled *The Military Sounvenir: A Portrait gallery by Frank J. Bramhall* (New York: J. C. Buttre, 1863). It was Buttre's ubiquitous engraving after the Cooper Union portrait that adorned campaign ribbons and biographies and related ephemera that helped propel Lincoln into the White House. Offered together with the font panel of the original transmittal envelope addressed and franked by Nicolay, *"Jno. G. Nicolay".* Besides some extremely light toning, the letter is in very fine condition with a dark, bold signature. A wonderful example with interesting background history. From the Henry E. Luhrs Collection. Accompanied by LOA from PSA/DNA.

Estimate: $6,000-$7,000

Let these men take the oath of Dec. 8. 1863 & be discharged.

A. Lincoln

March 7. 1865

A. Lincoln

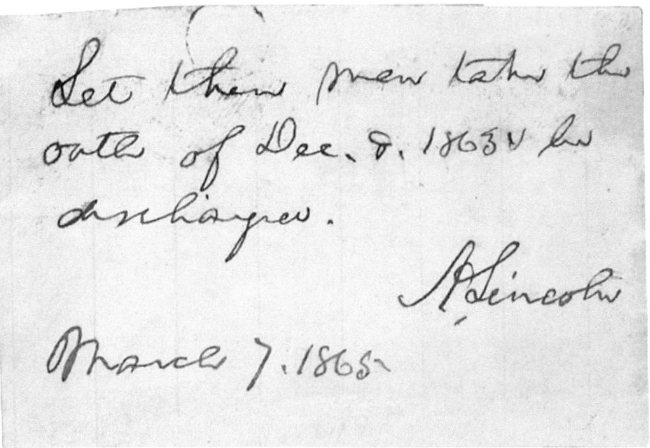

25048 Abraham Lincoln Autograph Endorsement Signed *"A. Lincoln."* The endorsement is on a clipped piece of lined paper from a larger document and laid down on a sturdier backing sheet, it measures 3" x 2" and reads, *"Let the men take the oath of Dec. 8, 1863 & be discharged."* The endorsement is dated March 7, 1865. From the Henry E. Luhrs Collection. Accompanied by LOA from PSA/DNA.

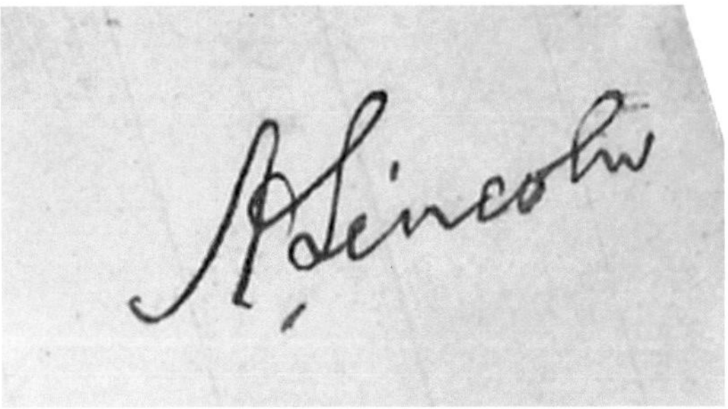

Estimate: $4,000-$5,000

War Department
Washington City,
April 1 1863

Ordered
That John A Brown
under sentence of death by judgment of a Court Martial at Indianapolis Ind and he is hereby pardoned and absolved from the sentence aforesaid; and that he be released from imprisonment and discharged from the service of the United States. By order of the President.

A. Lincoln

Edwin M Stanton
Secretary of War

A. Lincoln

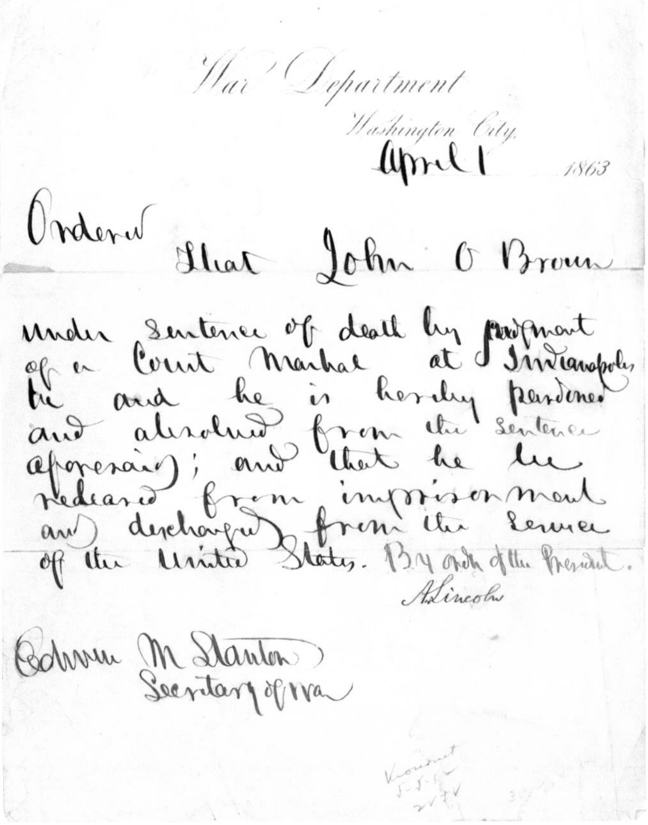

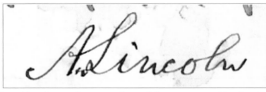

25049 Lincoln pardons a union soldier sentenced to death

Abraham Lincoln (1809-1865) President, unusual manuscript Document Signed, *A. Lincoln"* as President, one page, 7.75" x 9.75", *"War Department"*, Washington, April 1, 1863 with the body of the text in the hand of and countersigned by Secretary of War **Edwin Stanton** (1814-1869). An order to pardon "*...John A Brown under Sentence of death by [illeg.] of a Court Marshal at Indianapolis...*" and directing that he be "*... absolved from Sentence aforesaid; an hat he be released from imprisonment and discharged from the Service of the United States...*" An unusual manuscript accomplished by Stanton in an evidently hurried manner, likely due to the critical nature of avoiding the execution. Very light soiling and light dampstains, folds reinforced with archival tape on verso, else very good condition. Lincoln pardons seldom come to market — this, prepared by Stanton, is an unusual and desirable rarity. From the Henry E. Luhrs Collection. Accompanied by LOA from PSA/DNA.

Estimate: $9,000-$12,000

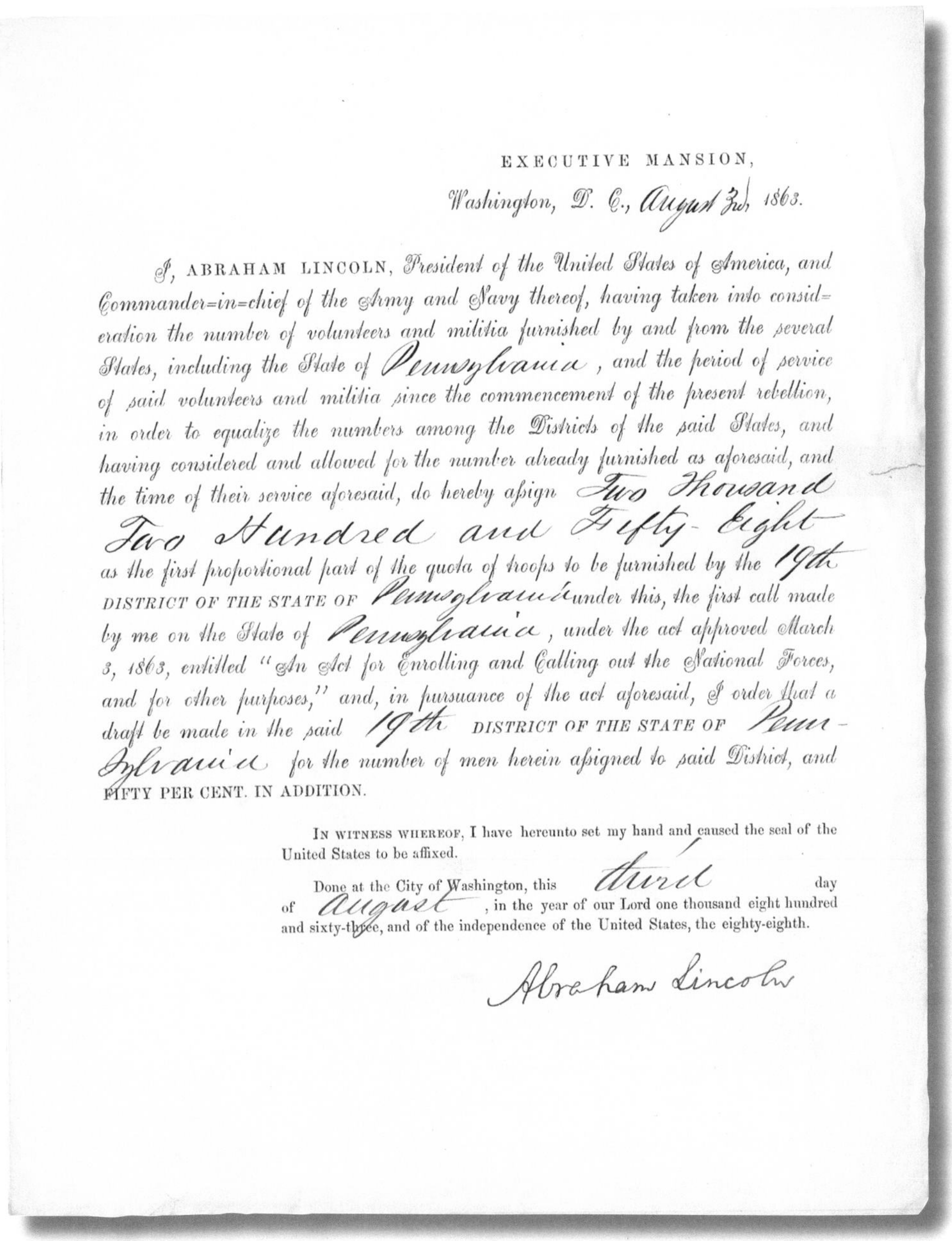

EXECUTIVE MANSION,

Washington, D. C., August 3rd, 1863.

I, ABRAHAM LINCOLN, President of the United States of America, and Commander=in=chief of the Army and Navy thereof, having taken into consideration the number of volunteers and militia furnished by and from the several States, including the State of *Pennsylvania*, and the period of service of said volunteers and militia since the commencement of the present rebellion, in order to equalize the numbers among the Districts of the said States, and having considered and allowed for the number already furnished as aforesaid, and the time of their service aforesaid, do hereby assign *Two Thousand Two Hundred and Fifty-Eight* as the first proportional part of the quota of troops to be furnished by the *19th* DISTRICT OF THE STATE OF *Pennsylvania* under this, the first call made by me on the State of *Pennsylvania*, under the act approved March 3, 1863, entitled "An Act for Enrolling and Calling out the National Forces, and for other purposes," and, in pursuance of the act aforesaid, I order that a draft be made in the said *19th* DISTRICT OF THE STATE OF *Penn-sylvania* for the number of men herein assigned to said District, and FIFTY PER CENT. IN ADDITION.

IN WITNESS WHEREOF, I have hereunto set my hand and caused the seal of the United States to be affixed.

Done at the City of Washington, this *third* day of *August*, in the year of our Lord one thousand eight hundred and sixty-three, and of the independence of the United States, the eighty-eighth.

Abraham Lincoln

25050   Abraham Lincoln issues a draft call to Pennsylvania

 Abraham Lincoln (1808-1865), President, fine content partly printed Document Signed "*Abraham Lincoln*" as President, one page 7.75" x 9.75", Washington, August 3, 1863, a draft call issued to the state of Pennsylvania. The document reads in part: "*I Abraham Lincoln, President of the United States of America, and Commander-in-chief of the Army and navy thereof, having taken into consideration the number of volunteers and militia furnished... and the period of service of said volunteers and militia since the commencement of the present rebellion, in order to equalize the numbers amongst the Districts of the said States,... do hereby assign Two thousand Two Hundred and Fifty-Eight as the first proportional part of the quota of troops to be furnished by the 19th District of the State of Pennsylvania under this, the first call made by me on the State of Pennsylvania, under the act approved March 3, 1863, entitled 'An Act for Enrolling and calling out the National Forces and or other purposes'...*" It was the same act of Congress, that when enforced in the City of New York led to days of rioting and civil unrest involving approximately 50,000 people, and causing untold damage to the city. The unrest stemmed from the practice of "substituting", where someone with $300 could avoid service, thus excluding the wealthy from duty. The draft call brought these class resentments to the surface in a most dramatic fashion. Beside a half-inch marginal tear not affecting the text, this is a clean and bright example, very fine condition. From the Henry E. Luhrs Collection. Accompanied by LOA from PSA/DNA.
Estimate: $12,000-$15,000

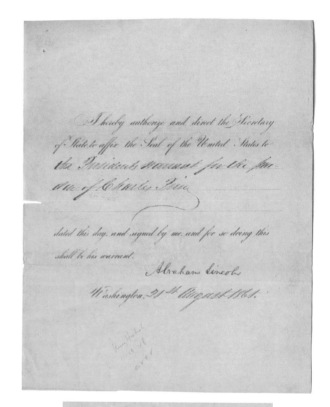

25052   Abraham Lincoln Prisoner Release Autograph
Endorsement Signed "*A Lincoln*" on the verso of a document 3.75" x 2.25", np, February 16, 1865. In full, "*Let these men take the oath of Dec. 8, 1863 & be discharged. Feb. 16, 1865*".Very good condition; some light soiling, ink smeared a bit, laid down to card. From the Henry E. Luhrs Collection. Accompanied by LOA from PSA/DNA.
Estimate: $4,000-$5,000

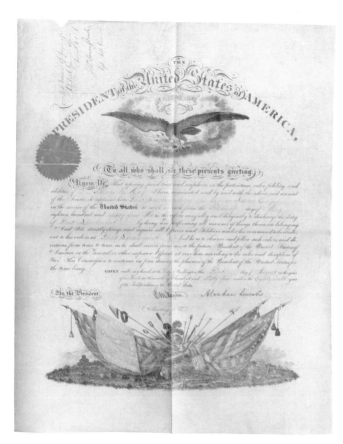

25051   Lincoln commissions a wounded Gettysburg veteran

Abraham Linocln (1809-1865), President, partly-printed Document Signed "*Abraham Lincoln*" as President, one page on vellum, 15.75" x 19.75", Washington, August, 1, 1864, a military commission promoting Thomas H. Hay as "*...First Lieutenant in the Veteran Reserve Corps...*" Countersigned by Secretary of War **Edwin Stanton** ("*E M Stanton*"). Document festooned with an eagle at top and a symbolic display of military accruements at bottom. On July 2, 1865, Hay as a first lieutenant in the 54th New York Infantry, lost 102 men at Cemetery Hill at Gettysburg. Hay was severely wounded in his left leg during the battle, and had it amputated. He then served with the Reserve Corps until he retired in 1870. Unusually bold and clear example of Lincoln's signature with no feathering or skipping. Usual folds, otherwise very good condition. A superior commission for anyone wishing a single example to own. From the Henry E. Luhrs Collection. Accompanied by LOA from PSA/DNA.
Estimate: $6,000-$8,000

25053   Abraham Lincoln (1809-1865) President, important partly-printed Document Signed "*Abraham Lincoln*" one page, 8" x 10", Washington, August 21, 1861, a warrant for the Secretary of State to affix the seal of the United States to a pardon. The document reads in full: "*I hereby authorize and direct the Secretary of State to affix the Seal of the United States to the Presidents warrant for the pardon of Charles Price dated this day and signed by me and for so doing this shall be his warrant.*" Lincoln pardons establish the compassion of our war-time president — he granted them whenever possible. A bold, clean signature. Some soiling at the folds and one tiny tear at left edge away from text, else about Fine. From the Henry E. Luhrs Collection. Accompanied by LOA from PSA/DNA.
Estimate: $6,000-$7,000

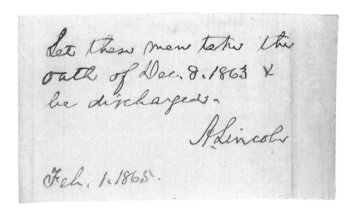

25054   **Abraham Lincoln Prisoner Release Autograph**
Endorsement Signed *"A Lincoln"* on the verso of a lined sheet 3.75" x 2",
np, February 1, 1865. In full *"Let these men take the oath of Dec. 8, 1863*
& be discharged. Feb. 1, 1865." The oath Lincoln mentions was part of his
Proclamation of Amnesty and Reconstruction that allowed persons in
rebellion, with certain exceptions, who take an oath to support and defend the Constitution to be granted full pardon. Fine condition. From the
Henry E. Luhrs Collection. Accompanied by LOA from PSA/DNA.
Estimate: $4,000-$5,000

25056   **Abraham Lincoln Autograph Note Signed** *"A Lincoln"* to
Senator Jacob Collamer (of Vermont). Card, 3.25" x 2", np, January 11,
1863. In full, *"If not going to church please call & see me at once; & if to*
church, please call as soon after, as convenient." with *"Senator Collamer"*
on the verso. Collamer was a conservative anti-slavery Republican who
served in the senate from 1855 until his death in 1865. Fine condition.
From the Henry E. Luhrs Collection. Accompanied by LOA from PSA/DNA.
Estimate: $4,500-$5,500

25055   **Abraham Lincoln Prisoner Release Autograph**
Endorsement Signed *"A Lincoln* on a lined sheet 5" x 1.625", np, February
7, 1865. In full, *"Let these men take the oath of Dec. 8, 1863 & be dis-*
charged. Feb. 7, 1865". The oath that these prisoners would be expected
to take was as follows:

I, _____, do solemnly swear, in presence of Almighty God, that I will
henceforth faithfully support, protect and defend the Constitution of the
United States, and the union of the States thereunder; and that I will, in
like manner, abide by and faithfully support all acts of Congress passed
during the existing rebellion with reference to slaves, so long and so far
as not repealed, modified or held void by Congress, or by decision of
the Supreme Court; and that I will, in like manner, abide by and faithfully
support all proclamations of the President made during the existing
rebellion having reference to slaves, so long and so far as not modified or
declared void by decision of the Supreme Court. So help me God."

Very good condition; one fold, a bit of soiling, laid down to lightweight
card. From the Henry E. Luhrs Collection. Accompanied by LOA from
PSA/DNA.
Estimate: $4,000-$5,000

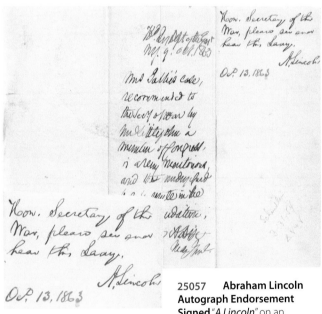

25057   **Abraham Lincoln**
Autograph Endorsement
Signed *"A Lincoln"* on an
Autograph Letter Signed by Maj. Gen. John A. Dix. One page, 9.5" x 7.5",
np, October 13, 1863. The Dix letter from the Department of the East
Headquarters in New York reads, "Mrs. Gallie's case, recommended to the
Secy of War by Mr. Littlejohn a member of Congress, is very meritorious,
and the undersigned begs to write in the recommendation." Lincoln
writes, *"Hon. Secretary of the War, please see and hear this lady."* then
signs and dates it. Researching the Civil War personnel records shows
that there were two soldiers from New York named Gallie: James Gallie
(40 years old) enlisted in June 1863 as a private and was discharged for
disability that September. 22-year old Walter Gallie enlisted in May 1861
as a private, was promoted to corporal, and killed in battle June 1862 in
South Carolina. This letter might possibly refer to the widow or mother
of one of these soldiers. Fine condition; folds with just a small amount of
soiling. From the Henry E. Luhrs Collection. Accompanied by LOA from
PSA/DNA.
Estimate: $4,000-$5,000

Before Abraham Lincoln became enshrined in the American Pantheon as the Great Emancipator, the War President, the Savior of the Union, he was Lincoln the prairie lawyer: a man who spent months of every year traveling, often in heat and dust or rain and mud, to a string of country courthouses. There he tended to legal matters of every conceivable stripe for an array of clients that usually consisted of simple farmers, storekeepers, tradesmen and mechanics, widows, wives and orphans. As routine as his cases often were, it was in that moveable arena of pioneer Illinois courts that he honed his logic, his intellect, and his language. It was there that he was afforded field and scope for his wit, his wisdom, his common sense and his compassion; in brief, for all of the aspects of that human understanding which would so well serve a nation when it came to be tried by civil war. It was there, too, that the common perception of the homespun, folksy, humorous Lincoln blossomed into legend.

The following lots present the largest private holding of legal documents by and about Abraham Lincoln that have ever come to market. They bring life and immediacy to many aspects of Lincoln, the lawyer, that sometimes mythical figure who represented the heavy-burdened without fee, championed the beleaguered despite opprobrium, finessed equity from inflexible law, and won the hearts of skeptical jurymen. But here, too, is the shrewd and successful railroad lawyer who commanded huge fees as well as the anxious attorney who sometimes made mistakes.

The physical dispersal of legal records, the arcana of the law itself, and the overlay of hearsay and story about a handful of Lincoln's most famous cases, have long kept his legal career dim and obscure, even to ardent admirers and those who shared his profession. (Full, scholarly appreciation and meaningful assessment of Lincoln, the lawyer, has now become possible thanks to the twenty-year effort of the Lincoln Legals

Project of the Illinois Historic Preservation Agency. Their mission: to gather and publish the scattered documentation of his legal career.)

The collection offered here includes some remarkable, unknown items and represents an unusual opportunity to acquire manuscripts related to almost every aspect of Lincoln's law practice, both civil and criminal. Aside from many items written and/or signed by Lincoln himself, here are holographs by his three regular law partners: John Todd Stuart (partnered with Lincoln 1837-41), a political as well as legal mentor, and cousin of Mary Todd Lincoln; Stephen T. Logan (1841-44), considered by many of his day as the best lawyer in Illinois; and William H. Herndon (1844-65), whose devotion to Lincoln was such that he spent the last third of his life and much of his fortune in gathering a priceless record of Lincoln's early life. During his career, Lincoln frequently partnered with scores of lawyers of all ranks for either single cases or for particular court terms. The names of many of these will be found on the following documents, among them Ward Hill Lamon, Lincoln's formal partner in Vermilion County who later became his U.S. Marshal in Washington and de-facto bodyguard; and Henry C. Whitney, who wrote the first-hand classic about Life on the Circuit with Lincoln. Here, too, are clerical documents which mention Lincoln or are signed in his name. Whether written by partners or clerks -- or Lincoln himself -- all of the manuscripts offered here are precious relics of one of America's most celebrated lawyers -- and its greatest statesman.

For those who might share the passion for collecting Lincolniana, we highly recommend that you consider joining The Rail Splitters – a national organization that publishes a quarterly journal for collectors and scholars. Information on subscribing and joining can be found at their website: www.railsplitter.com. We are in their debt for assistance in identifying some of the Lincoln material in this catalog.

Abraham Lincoln as a successful Illinois attorney in 1858.
Photo courtesy of Rail Splitter Archives

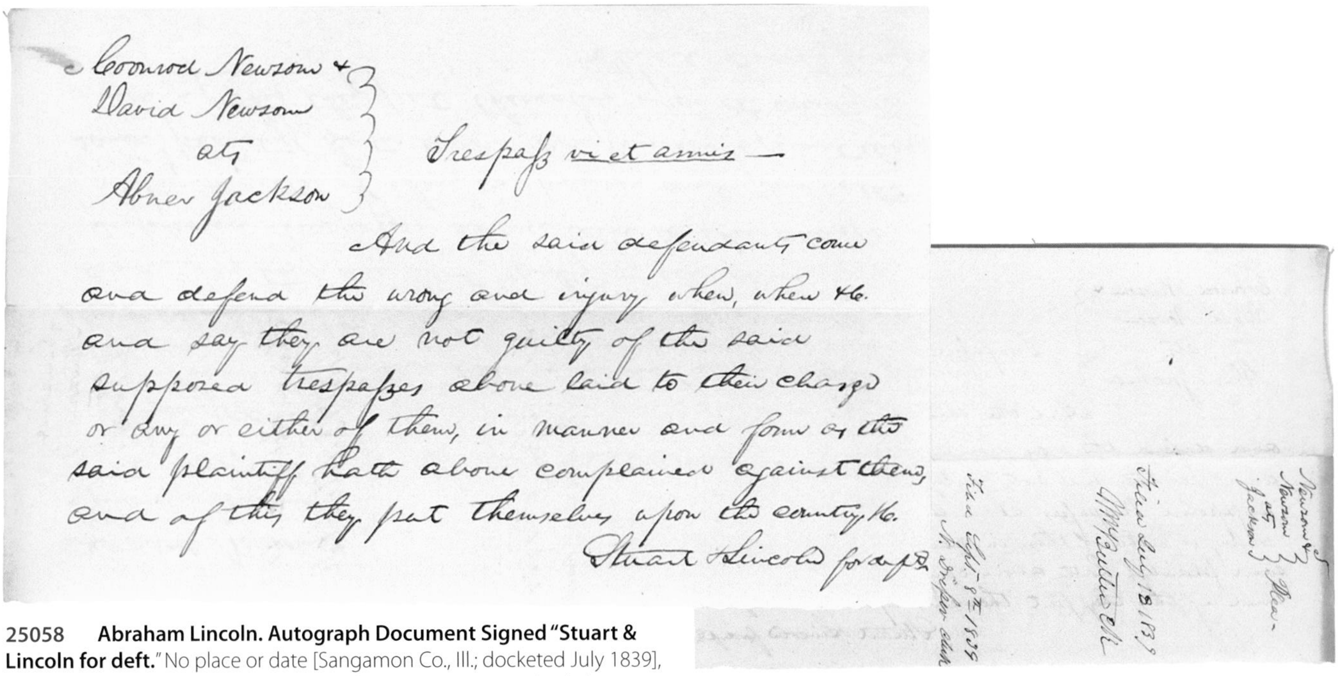

Coonrod Newsom &
David Newsom
ats
Abner Jackson

Trespass vi et armis —

And the said defendants come and defend the wrong and injury, when, where &c. and say they are not guilty of the said supposed trespasses above laid to their charge or any or either of them, in manner and form as the said plaintiff hath above complained against them, and of this they put themselves upon the country &c.

Stuart & Lincoln for deft.

Newsoms
Newsom
ats
Jackson } Plea

Filed July 18 1839

25058 Abraham Lincoln. Autograph Document Signed "Stuart & Lincoln for deft." No place or date [Sangamon Co., Ill.; docketed July 1839], one page, oblong octavo. In an action of trespass ***vi et armis*** (with force and arms) brought by Abner Jackson against Coonrod and David Newsom, the defendants state "***they are not guilty of the…supposed trespasses…laid to their charge…in manner and form as the said plaintiff hath above complained***". A fine, early "Lincoln legal", signed in the name of his first law partnership and dated about two and a half-years after his admission to the bar. A fine example completely in Lincoln's hand. From the Henry E. Luhrs Collection. Accompanied by LOA from PSA/DNA.

Estimate: $7,000-$9,000

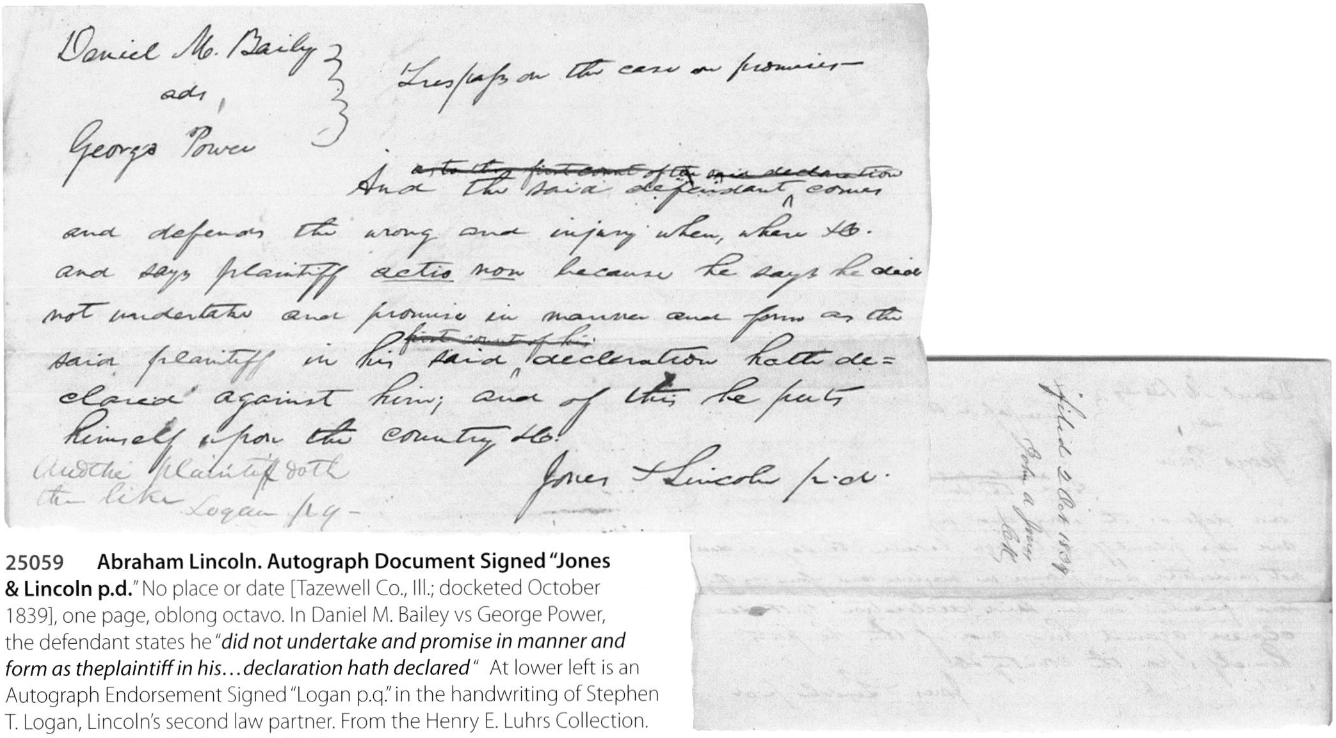

Daniel M. Baily
ads.
George Power

Trespass on the case on promises —

And ~~as to the first count of the said declaration~~ the said defendant comes and defends the wrong and injury when, where &c. and says plaintiff actio non because he says he did not undertake and promise in manner and form as the said plaintiff in his ~~first count of his~~ said declaration hath declared against him; and of this he puts himself upon the country &c.

Jones & Lincoln p.d.

And the plaintiff doth the like Logan p.q.

Filed 2 Oct 1839

25059 Abraham Lincoln. Autograph Document Signed "Jones & Lincoln p.d." No place or date [Tazewell Co., Ill.; docketed October 1839], one page, oblong octavo. In Daniel M. Bailey vs George Power, the defendant states he "***did not undertake and promise in manner and form as theplaintiff in his…declaration hath declared***" At lower left is an Autograph Endorsement Signed "Logan p.q." in the handwriting of Stephen T. Logan, Lincoln's second law partner. From the Henry E. Luhrs Collection. Accompanied by LOA from PSA/DNA.

Estimate: $5,000-$6,000

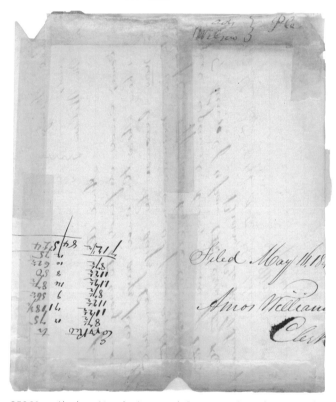

25060   **Abraham Lincoln. Unsigned Autograph Document.** No place or date (Sangamon Co., Ill., ca November 1840), one-half page, folio. A court decree (half in Lincoln's hand, the balance in an unknown hand) granting the petition of Sarah Brown, guardian, to sell some real estate *"at public vendue on the on the twenty-fifth day of December next in the town of Rochester"* She is ordered to advertise the sale in "some newspaper published in Springfield & by posting up noticesinRochester" From the Henry E. Luhrs Collection. Accompanied by LOA from PSA/DNA.
Estimate: $3,000-$3,500

25061   Abraham Lincoln. Autograph Document Signed "Brown, Baker & Lincoln p.d." No place or date (Vermilion Co., Ill.; docketed May 184[1]), one page, oblong octavo. In John M. Wilson vs Samuel Frazier, the defendant states he is *"not [gu]ilty in manner and form as the…plaintiff… hat[h a]lleged"* This suit against Frazier, the county sheriff, was dismissed on Oct. 17, 1842 when Lincoln reported to the court that Wilson was dead; Lincoln was however mistaken, and the case was reinstated the next day because of his error. Trimming at left side and some marginal chips take a letter or two in each line (bracketed in quotation). Verso has reinforced folds and considerable marginal darkening. From the Henry E. Luhrs Collection. Accompanied by LOA from PSA/DNA.
Estimate: $4,000-$5,000

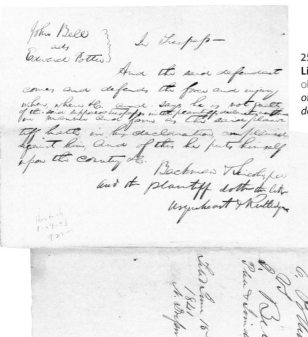

**25062   Abraham Lincoln. Autograph Document Signed "Bachman &
Lincoln, p.d."** No place or date [Menard Co., Ill.; docketed June 1841], one page,
oblong octavo. In Edward Potter vs John Bell, the defendant states he is *"not guilty
of the…supposed trespass…in manner and form as the said plaintiff hath in his
declaration complained"* Records show that this case involved a brown mare which
Bell stole, but Potter recovered. After a jury failed to agree, arbitrators awarded
Potter one cent damages and ordered Bell to pay the costs. This document
also bears an endorsement in the name of attorneys "Urquhart & Rutledge",
the latter being David H. Rutledge, who served in the Black Hawk War under
Lincoln and was a brother of his legendary love, Ann Rutledge. From the
Henry E. Luhrs Collection. Accompanied by LOA from PSA/DNA.
Estimate: $6,000-$7,000

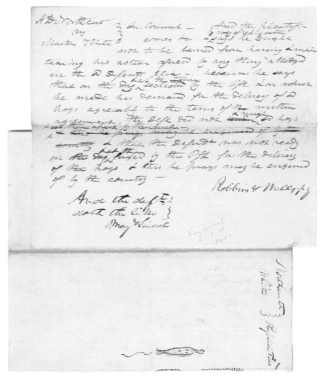

25063   Abraham Lincoln. Document signed by Lincoln for the plaintiff's
attorneys, "Robbins & Wells p.q." with his own Autograph Endorsement Signed
as attorney for the defendant ("And the deft. doth the like / May & Lincoln") at
lower left. No place or date [present Christian Co., Ill.; June 1841], one page,
oblong octavo. The plaintiff in A.D. Northcutt vs Martin White seeks to maintain his suit, alleging that on the date he demanded delivery of some hogs
per written agreement, the defendant did not "weigh sd. hogs and set them
apart by themselves" The verso bears a docket by Lincoln (*"Northcutt vs White
/ Replication"*) and an odd little doodle which, appearing to be in the same
ink, may have been sketched by Lincoln himself. From the Henry E. Luhrs
Collection. Accompanied by LOA from PSA/DNA.
Estimate: $4,000-$5,000

**25064   Abraham Lincoln. Autograph Document
Signed "Logan & Lincoln p.d."** Menard Co. (Ill.), no date
[docketed October 1841], one page, oblong octavo. A
request for issuance of subpoenas in the case of Edward
Potter vs John Bell (see preceding item). Among the parties summoned are Francis Regnier and James Short, old
friends and neighbors of Lincoln from his New Salem days.
Regnier was one of the frontier village's physicians, while
"Uncle Jimmy" Short is remembered for having bought
the impoverished Lincoln's surveying instruments when
they were sold on execution and returning them to him
so that he could continue to earn a living. Short's kindness
was not forgotten, and during his Presidency Lincoln made
him an Indian agent in California. From the Henry E. Luhrs
Collection. Accompanied by LOA from PSA/DNA.
Estimate: $5,000-$6,000

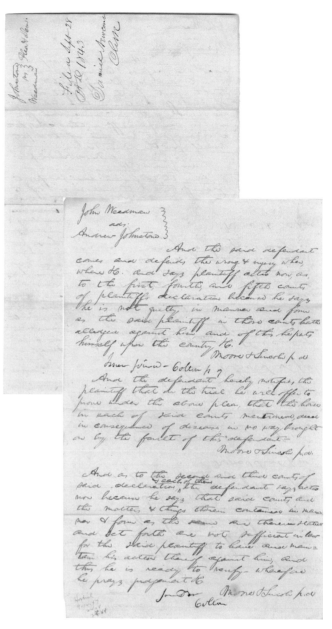

**25065   Abraham Lincoln. Autograph Document Signed twice
"Logan & Lincoln p.q."** Christian Co., Ill., June 1842, about one page in
total, penned on both sides of a folio sheet. A complaint by Jacob Londy,
who alleges that John Cagle and Robert Richardson in November 1841
took from him *"fourteen plaines [sic], one brace and bits…three trying
squares, one dozen firmer chizzels [sic], three saws, and several other
small tools, and the box in which said tools were contained"*, valued at
eighty dollars, and for which he claims damages of $150. On the verso
Lincoln asks the court clerk to *"issue a writ of replevin for the property
described"* Defendant Cagle was apparently a bad seed: seven years later
Lincoln was hired to sue him for fathering an illegitimate child. From the
Henry E. Luhrs Collection. Accompanied by LOA from PSA/DNA.
Estimate: $5,000-$6,000

**25066   Abraham Lincoln. Autograph Document Signed three
times "Moore & Lincoln p.d."** No place or date [DeWitt Co., Ill.; docketed September 1843], one page, folio. In Andrew Johnstone vs John
Weedman, the defendant states that upon trial he will prove that a
certain horse *"died in consequence of disease, in no way brought on by
the fault of this defendant."* Records show that Weedman, hired to feed
and care for Johnstone's horse, rode it a distance of 15 miles just before it
coincidentally died. Johnstone lost both the present case and an appeal
to the state supreme court, partly because he initially brought the wrong
type of suit, an action in trover (i.e., to recover the value of personal
chattels wrongfully converted by another to his own use). His suits did,
however, help lead to the establishment of courts of equity in Illinois.
Lincoln's fellow attorney in this case, Clifton Moore of Clinton, Ill., was one
of his more frequent "circuit partners" and became a millionaire through
land speculation. From the Henry E. Luhrs Collection. Accompanied by
LOA from PSA/DNA.
Estimate: $6,000-$8,000

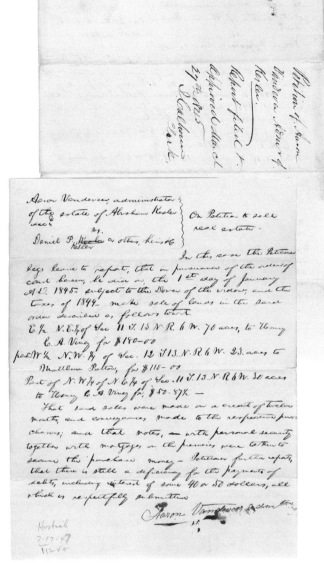

25067   Abraham Lincoln. Autograph Document Signed twice "Wilmot & Lincoln p.d." No place, no date (Tazewell Co., Ill.; docketed April 1844). In Seaborn Moore vs John Davis, the defendant states that on trial he will *"prove and set off against the claim of the plaintiff"* two promissory notes, plus payment of two judgments against Moore on which Davis was security, and *"the value of three hundred trees"* furnished by Davis to Moore, totaling in all about $689. Lincoln writes that the promissory notes are being filed *"and set up in defence in the case. And the defendant claims a judgment over against the plaintiff."* Lincoln's colleague in this suit, William H. Wilmot, died the following year and Lincoln chaired the committee which, on behalf of members of the bar in adjoining counties, drew up sympathy resolutions. From the Henry E. Luhrs Collection. Accompanied by LOA from PSA/DNA.
Estimate: $5,500-$6,500

25068   Abraham Lincoln. Unsigned Autograph Document. No place or date (Sangamon Co., Ill.; docketed March 1845), one page, quarto. A report prepared for and signed by Aaron Vandeveer as administrator of the estate of Abraham Kesler, in his suit against Daniel P. Kesler and others. Vandeveer reports selling, subject to widow's dower and 1844 taxes, three described tracts of land totaling 123 acres *"on a credit of twelve months…with personal security together with mortgages on the premises"*, which sales will nevertheless leave a deficiency against *"payment of debts including interest of some 40 or 50 dollars…"* From the Henry E. Luhrs Collection. Accompanied by LOA from PSA/DNA.
Estimate: $3,200-$3,800

William Mitchell
ads
Daniel Newcomb
In assumpsit

And the said defendant comes and defends the wrong and injury when, where &c. and says plaintiff actio non because he says he did not undertake and promise in manner and form as the said plaintiff in his said declaration hath alleged; and of this he puts himself upon the country &c.

Conkling & Lincoln p.d.

And the plff. doth the like
D. Davis p.q.

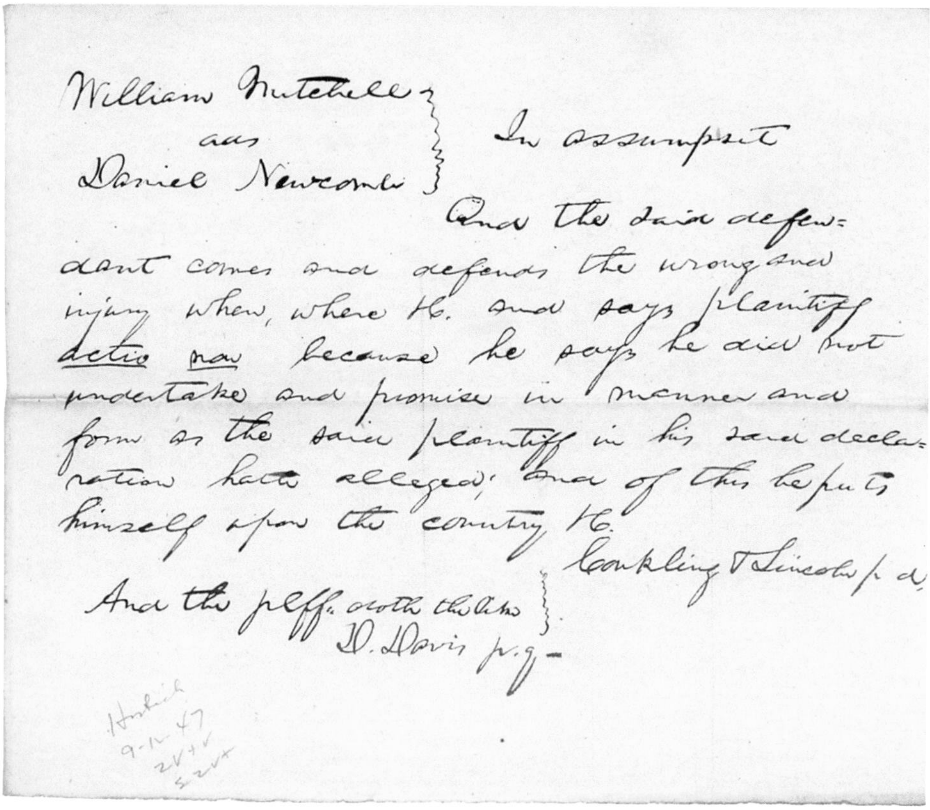

25069 Abraham Lincoln. Autograph Document Signed "Conkling & Lincoln p.d." No place or date [Clinton Co., Ill., April 1846], one page, oblong large octavo. In William Mitchell vs Daniel Newcomb, the defendant declares "***he did not undertake and promise in manner and form as the... plaintiff...hath alleged...*** " Lincoln has also written, at lower left, the response from the plaintiff's attorney, David Davis, and signed for him ("***And the plff. doth the like / D. Davis p.q.***"). Lincoln was very close to Davis, who as a circuit court judge heard hundreds of his cases during the 1850's; on at least a few occasions Lincoln even sat in for Davis on the bench. In 1860 Davis adroitly managed to secure Lincoln the Republican Presidential nomination, and in turn was appointed by Lincoln an Associate Justice of the United States Supreme Court. From the Henry E. Luhrs Collection. Accompanied by LOA from PSA/DNA.
Estimate: $5,000-$6,000

25070 Abraham Lincoln. Autograph Document Signed "Fenn & Lincoln p.d." No place or date [Woodford Co., Ill.; docketed September 1846], one page, folio. In Jesse C. Smith vs John Strawn, the defendant demurs, noting that in Smith's declaration "***no time is alleged as to when the mill...was erected and completed[T]here is no allegation...that the defendant had notice of the fact that the mill was erected...[T]here is no allegation that the defendant was requested to make a conveyance.***" Evidently these objections carried the day, for Lincoln and fellow lawyer Ira Fenn won this case when the plaintiff submitted to a nonsuit (essentially, a dismissal) on 18 September, just eleven days after Lincoln's election to Congress was formally certified. From the Henry E. Luhrs Collection. Accompanied by LOA from PSA/DNA.
Estimate: $4,000-$5,000

John Strawn
ads.
Jesse C. Smith
In covenant

And the said defendant comes and defends the wrong and injury when where &c. and says plaintiff actio non because he says that the said plaintiff's declaration and each & every count thereof separately, and the matters and things therein contained in manner and form as the same are therein stated and set forth are not sufficient in law for the said plaintiff to have or maintain his aforesaid action thereof against him, the said defendant, and this he is ready to verify. Wherefore he prays judgment &c.

Fenn & Lincoln p.d.

And for special causes of demurrer, the defendant sets down the following towit:
1st That no time is alleged as to when the mill in the declaration mentioned, was erected and completed —
2nd That no time is alleged, in the declaration as to when the ten dollars therein mentioned was paid —
3rd That there is no allegation in the declaration, that the defendant had notice of the fact that the mill was erected
4th That there is no allegation that the defendant was requested to make a conveyance —

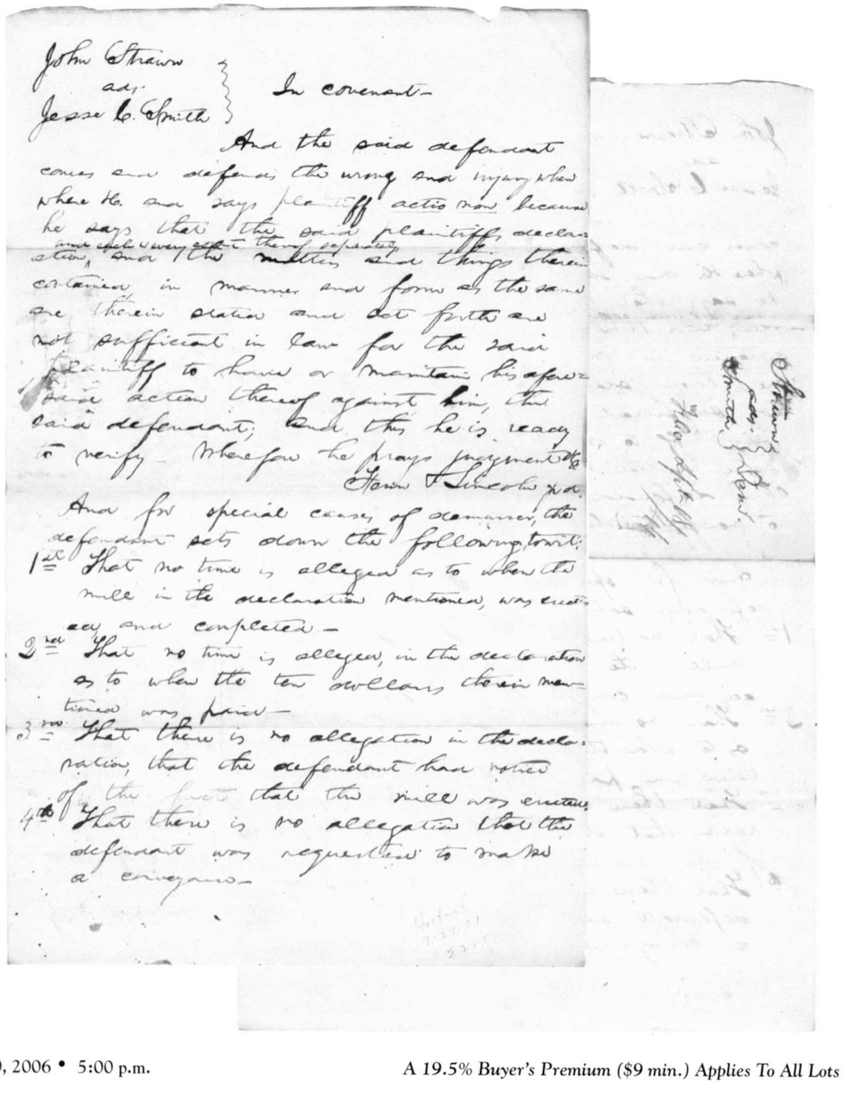

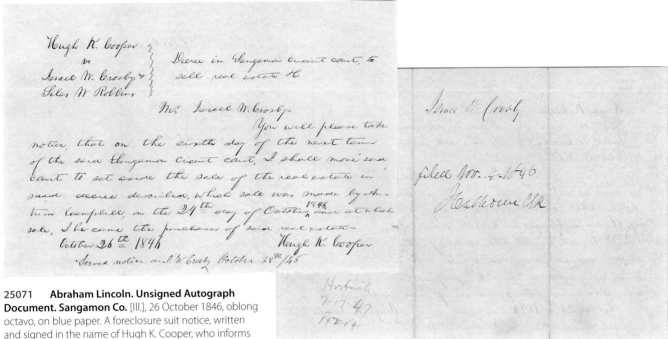

25071   **Abraham Lincoln. Unsigned Autograph Document. Sangamon Co.** [Ill.], 26 October 1846, oblong octavo, on blue paper. A foreclosure suit notice, written and signed in the name of Hugh K. Cooper, who informs Israel W. Crosby that he will move the circuit court to set aside the sale of real estate which it decreed in the case of Cooper vs Crosby and Silas W. Robbins, *"which sale was made by Antrim Campbell, on the 24th day of October 1846, and at which sale, I became the purchaser of said real estate."* Cooper's request for a set-aside and a resale of the property was denied, to which Lincoln and his partner William Herndon excepted; but they lost again in February 1847 on appeal to the state supreme court. From the Henry E. Luhrs Collection. Accompanied by LOA from PSA/DNA.

Estimate: $2,400-$3,200

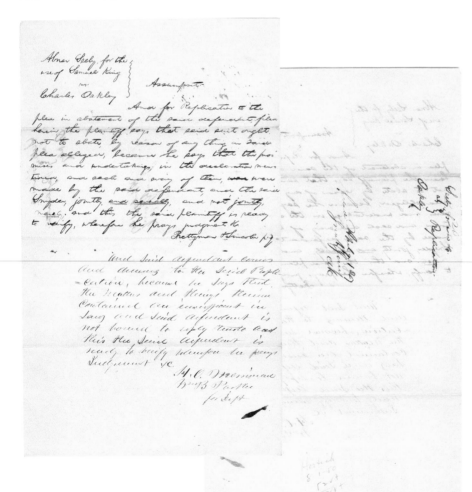

25072   **Abraham Lincoln. Autograph Document Signed "Prettyman & Lincoln p.q."** No place or date (Tazewell Co., Ill.; docketed April 1847), one-half page, folio. In *"Abner Seely for the use of Samuel King vs Charles Oakley",* the plaintiff replies to the defendant's plea in abatement stating that certain *"promises and under…takings…were made by the…defendant, and the said Snyder, jointly, and severally, and not jointly, merely"* From the Henry E. Luhrs Collection. Accompanied by LOA from PSA/DNA.

Estimate: $5,000-$6,000

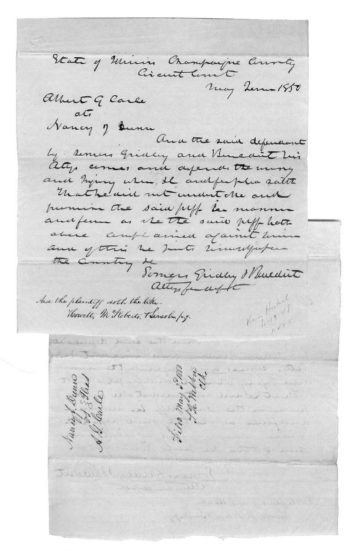

25073 Abraham Lincoln. Autograph Document Signed twice "Holland & Lincoln p.d." Tazewell Co., Ill., June 184(8?), one page, folio. In Nichols and Ewers vs Price Jacobs, the defendant asserts that a *"supposed writing obligatory…is not his deed"* and further that it *"was executed without any good or valuable consideration moving to him"* Jacobs signs a certification at foot. Horizontal fold passes through one signature. From the Henry E. Luhrs Collection. Accompanied by LOA from PSA/DNA.
Estimate: $4,500-$5,200

25074 Abraham Lincoln. Autograph Endorsement Signed "And the plaintiff doth the like / Howett, McRoberts & Lincoln p.q." Penned at the foot of a document by Somers, Gridley & Benedict, attorneys for defendant, Champaign Co., Ill., May 1850, one page, square quarto. In Nancy Dunn vs Albert G. Carle, the defendant demurs and pleads not guilty. This was a bastardy suit, which Lincoln and his colleagues won in May 1852 when a jury declared Carle the father of Dunn's infant and ordered him to pay $50 support annually. At the same time, Lincoln won a trespass suit against Carle brought by Ms. Dunn's father, for seduction; in that case, the jury awarded the father $180.41 in damages! From the Henry E. Luhrs Collection. Accompanied by LOA from PSA/DNA.
Estimate: $3,200-$4,000

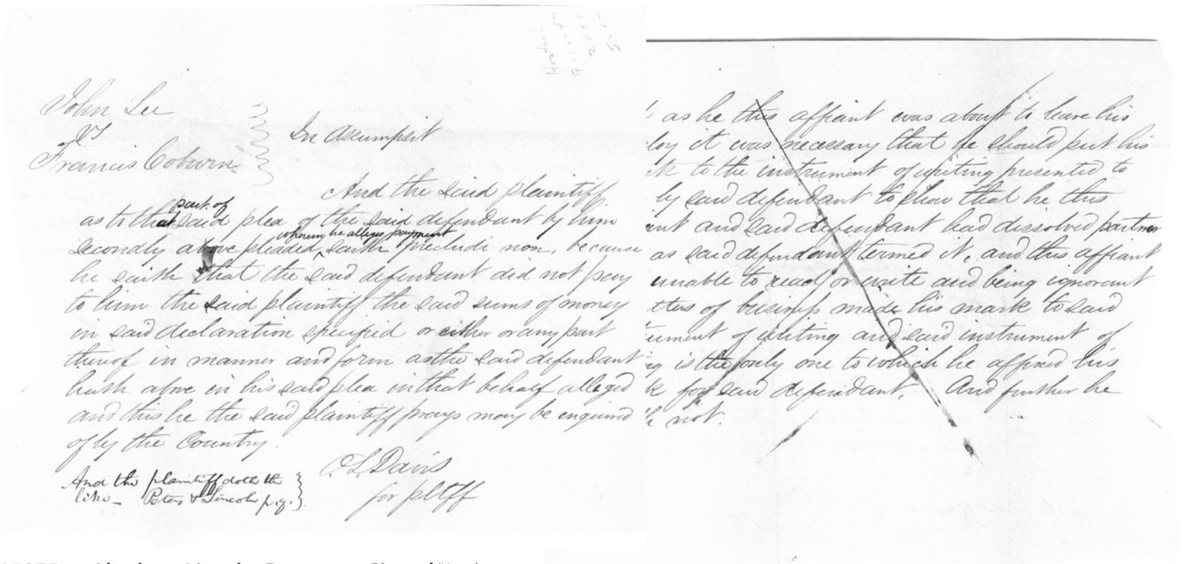
John Lee
vs
Francis Coburn } In Assumpsit

And the said plaintiff as to that part of said plea of the said defendant by him secondly above pleaded wherein he alleges payment saith precludi non, because he saith that the said defendant did not pay to him the said plaintiff the said sums of money in said declaration specified or either or any part thereof in manner and form as the said defendant hath above in his said plea in that behalf alleged and this he the said plaintiff prays may be enquired of by the Country.

O.L. Davis
for plff

And the plaintiff doth the like - Peters & Lincoln p.q.

25075 Abraham Lincoln. Document Signed "And the plaintiff doth the like - Peters & Lincoln p.q." No place or date [Vermilion Co., Ill., May 1850], one page, oblong octavo. Lincoln's endorsement is penned at the lower left of an Autograph Document Signed by O.L. Davis, attorney for the plaintiff in John Lee vs Francis Coburn. The plaintiff demurs to a plea of the defendant, stating the latter did not pay certain sums of money as alleged. Irregular margins, especially at left side; written on a piece of paper torn from another legal document, the text of which has been crossed out overleaf. From the Henry E. Luhrs Collection. Accompanied by LOA from PSA/DNA.
Estimate: $3,200-$4,000

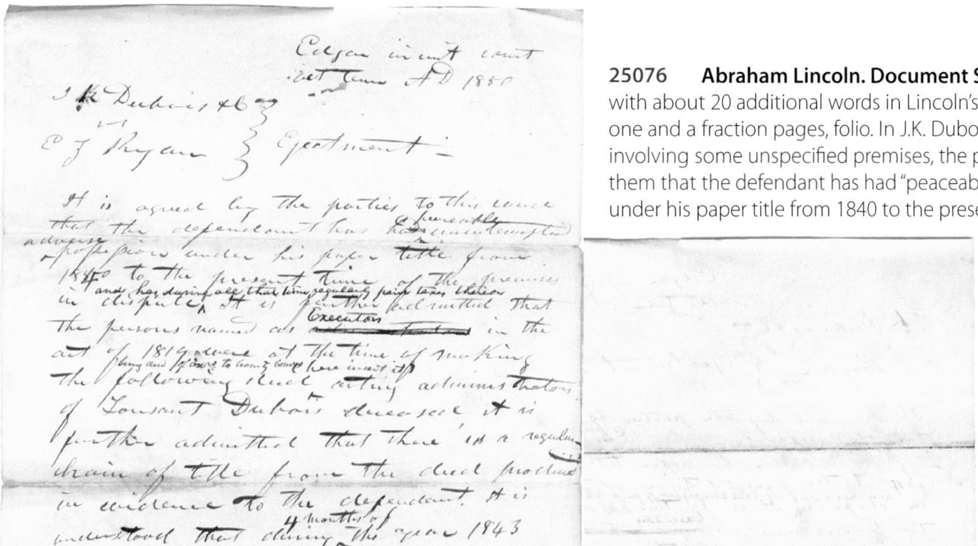
Edgar circuit court
Oct Term AD 1850

J K Dubois & Co
vs
E Z Ryan } Ejectment

It is agreed by the parties to this cause that the defendant has had peaceable uninterrupted adverse possession under his paper title from 1840 to the present time of the premises in dispute and has during all that time regularly paid taxes thereon. It is further admitted that the persons named as Executors in the act of 1819 were at the time of making the following deed acting administrators of Toussaint Dubois deceased. It is further admitted that there is a regular chain of title from the deed produced in evidence to the defendant. It is understood that during 4 months of the year 1843 there was no one actually living on said premises but possession was not abandoned by defendant the houses having been locked and the keys in the possession of defendant. The reason said building was not occupied was that said house was partly a bank or counting house and partly a tavern house. The bank had wound up and the building could only be occupied by renters and during this 4 months no person appeared to rent said property but that as soon as a tenant appeared the Bank by its agent gave possession and said possession has continued to the present time.

25076 Abraham Lincoln. Document Signed "Bowman & Lincoln for plaintiffs", with about 20 additional words in Lincoln's hand. Edgar Co. (Ill.), October 1850, one and a fraction pages, folio. In J.K. Dubois & Co. vs E.Z. Ryan, a suit of ejectment involving some unspecified premises, the parties agree to certain facts, among them that the defendant has had "peaceable uninterrupted adverse possession under his paper title from 1840 to the present time" (Lincoln inserts ***"and has, during all that time, regularly paid taxes thereon"***). It is noted that for four months during 1843 the property was empty, but not abandoned, "the houses having been locked and the keys in the possession of defendant"; the building was temporarily unoccupied because it "was partly a bank or counting house and partly a tavern[T]he bank had wound up and the building could only be occupied by renters, and during this 4 months no person appeared to rent said property butas soon as a tenant appeared the bank by its agent gave possession" On the verso, Lincoln has written ***"The foregoing admissions are made for the purpose of the first trial only"*** and signed. An interesting document showing Lincoln as attorney for his near neighbor and political ally Jesse K. Dubois, who was so ardent a friend that he named one of his three sons for the future President (it was the Dubois sons who pulled the legendary prank of knocking off Lincoln's stovepipe hat by means of a string tied across the sidewalk). From the Henry E. Luhrs Collection. Accompanied by LOA from PSA/DNA.
Estimate: $3,000-$3,500

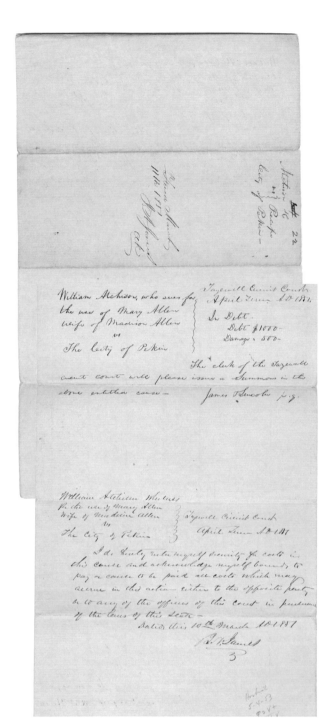

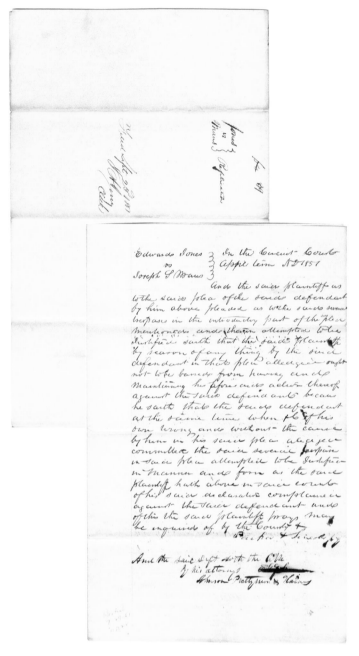

25077 **Abraham Lincoln. Autograph Document Signed** "James & Lincoln p.q." Tazewell Co. (Ill.), April 1851, one-quarter page, folio. The circuit court clerk is requested to *"please issue a summons"* in the case of William Atchison (suing for Mary, wife of Madison Allen) vs the City of Pekin. At foot, attorney B.F. James has written an Autograph Document Signed entering himself as security for costs in the case. Benjamin F. James was one of the few candidates whom Lincoln personally examined for admission to the bar. James entered practice in 1841 and was frequently involved in cases with Lincoln during the following decade. From the Henry E. Luhrs Collection. Accompanied by LOA from PSA/DNA.

Estimate: $3,000-$3,500

25078 **Abraham Lincoln. Document Signed** "& Lincoln p.q.", with a brief docket on verso ("Jones vs Maus / Replication") also in his hand. No place (Tazewell Co., Ill.), April 1851, one page, folio. In Edward Jones vs Joseph S. Maus, the plaintiff declares that he "ought not to be barred from having and maintaining" his suit against the defendant. This suit was an action for trespass *vi et armis* —with force and arms - in which Jones, himself an attorney, sought $5000 damages for loss of an eye in a fight with Dr. Maus (the two men clashed because Jones called Maus a liar for claiming to be a graduate of the prestigious Jefferson Medical College in Pennsylvania). Maus claimed he had fought in self-defense, and each party claimed that the other had used a weapon and not just his fists. By means now unknown, the two men were persuaded to an agreement and in April 1852 Judge David Davis ordered the case dismissed. (For the record, subsequent research suggests that Dr. Maus was a liar and in fact never graduated from Jefferson Medical College). This document was first signed in the name of attorney [William B.] Parker, presumably in his own hand; to this, the future President has added "*& Lincoln p.q.*" Lincoln's signature is a trifle scratchy in appearance, and his "p.q." somewhat blotted, both due to the writing materials and to hasty folding of the document while the ink was wet. From the Henry E. Luhrs Collection. Accompanied by LOA from PSA/DNA.

Estimate: $4,000-$4,500

The following pair of documents relate to one of Abraham Lincoln's most remarkable libel cases, that of Dr. William Fithian vs George W. Casseday. The two men were bitter personal, political and business rivals, each of whom operated a female seminary in the town of Danville, Ill. When Casseday published an article claiming that Fithian had abandoned the corpse of his wife "and left it to be buried at the mercy of others", Fithian sued him for $25,000 damages. In fact, Fithian had left his wife's remains with her family at Paris, Ill., in order to travel to the residence of a sick son. Fithian afterwards returned to Paris by way of Danville, a fact Casseday also seized upon in his article, remarking that there would have been no such delay if "a political election had been on hand in place of a deceased wife…" Fithian was represented by Lincoln, former Illinois Attorney General Usher F. Linder, and Oliver L. Davis. Casseday was defended by four attorneys, including Ward Hill Lamon, a new Danville resident who would within a year become Lincoln's only formally-recognized circuit law partner. After hearing testimony from 95 witnesses, a jury awarded Fithian damages of $547.90, a sum which Casseday for some time thereafter listed on his personal property tax form as "The character of Dr. Fithian…which I bought and paid for."

William Fithian
vs
George W. Casseday

And the said plaintiff comes, and as to the pleas of the said defendant by him firstly, secondly, thirdly, fourthly, and fifthly above pleaded, says, precludi non, because he says that said pleas, and each of them separately, and the matters and things in said pleas, and in each of them separately, contained, in manner and form as the same are therein stated and set forth, are not sufficient in law to bar and preclude the said plaintiff from having and maintaining his said action against him the said defendant, and this the said plaintiff is ready to verify, wherefore, &c.

Davis, Linder & Lincoln p.q.

Fithian vs Casseday Demurrer

Filed October 23rd 1851 James G. Craig Clk

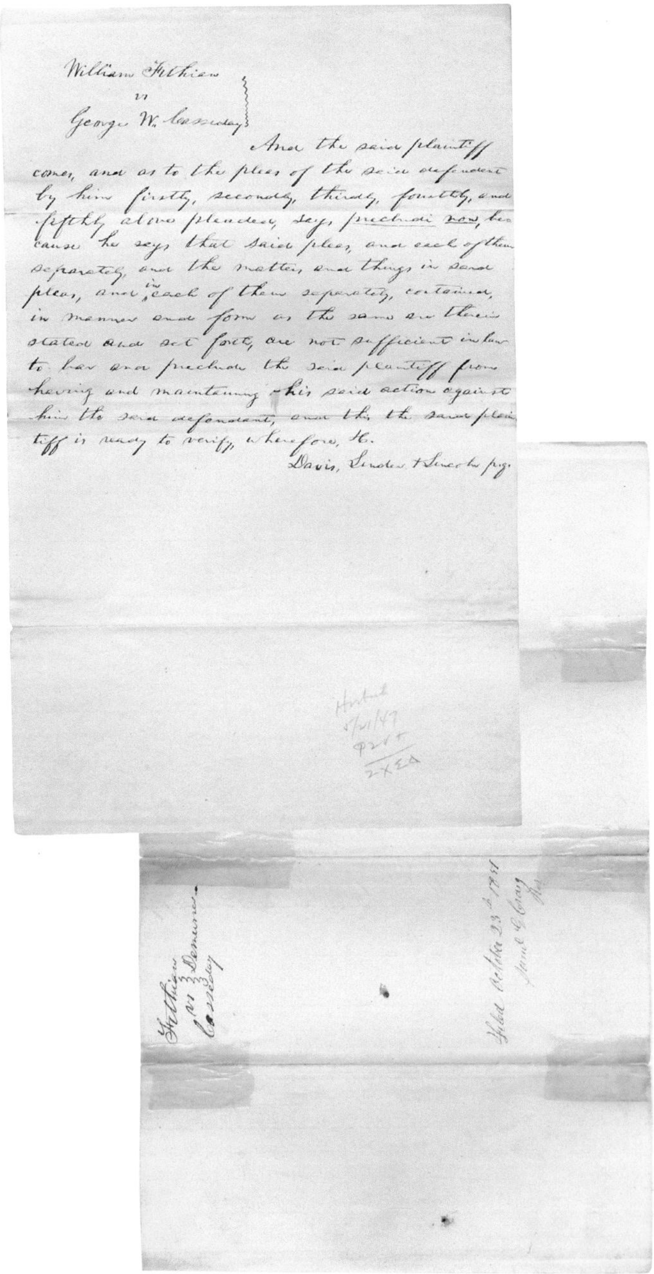

25081 Abraham Lincoln. Autograph Document Signed "Davis, Linder & Lincoln p.q." No place or date (Vermilion Co., Ill.; docketed October 1851), one-half page, folio. A demurrer in the case of William Fithian vs George W. Casseday, claiming that pleas by the defendant ***"are not sufficient in law to bar and preclude the said plaintiff from having and maintaining his said action against...the said defendant..."*** Old glassine repairs on verso to fold breaks at margins. See preceding and following lots. From the Henry E. Luhrs Collection. Accompanied by LOA from PSA/DNA.

Estimate: $4,000-$5,000

State of Illinois }
Vermillion County } ss

Newton Low, being first duly sworn states, on oath, that on or about the day of September A.D. 1851 affiant heard John Ritter speak of Dr. William Fithian in very unfriendly terms, and particularly in relation to the pending law suit between said Fithian and George W. Casseday, in which he expressed the wish that Casseday might gain the suit, that affiant does not recollect the precise language used by said Ritter, but he is sure he is not mistaken in the substance of the statements made by said Ritter.

Newton Low

Subscribed & sworn before me this 24th day of Oct 1851 — D Davis Judge

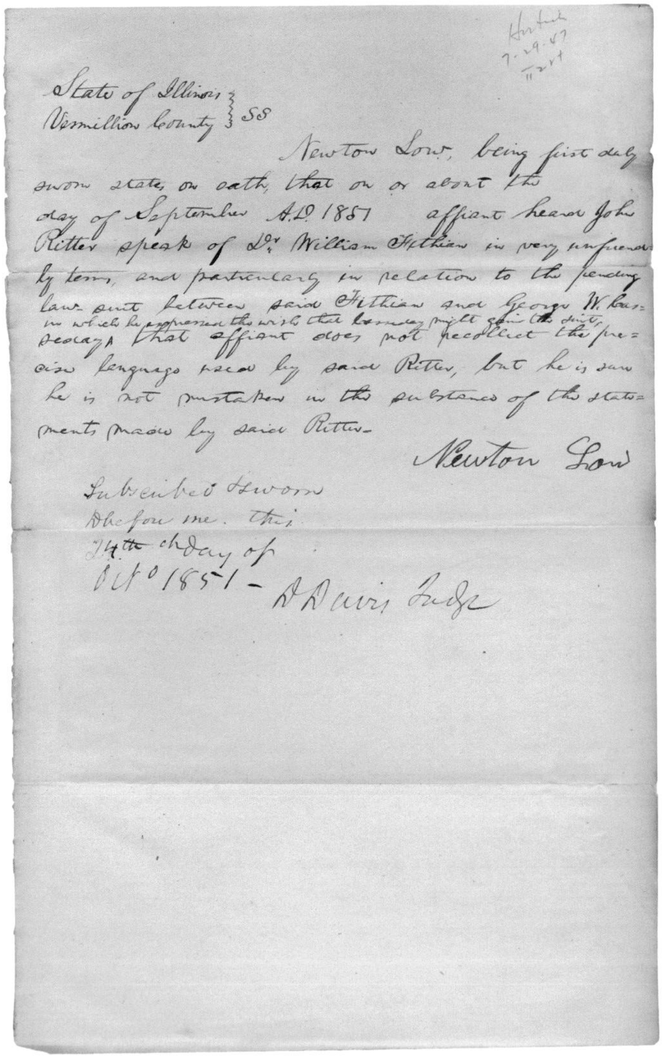

25082 Abraham Lincoln. Unsigned Autograph Document. Vermilion Co. (Ill.), Oct. 24, 1851, one-half page, folio. A deposition prepared for and signed by Newton Low, which has been witnessed by the dated signature of **David Davis** (as "D Davis Judge"). Low swears on oath that sometime in September he ***"heard John Ritter speak of Dr. William Fithian in very unfriendly terms, and particularly in relation to the pending law suit between...Fithian and George W. Casseday in which he expressed the wish that Casseday might gain the suit..."*** Low states that he ***"does not recollect the precise language used by...Ritter, but he is sure he is not mistaken in the substance of the statements..."*** Slightly frayed margins; margins and folds reinforced on verso, which is blank except for a docket. SEE PRECEDING LOTS From the Henry E. Luhrs Collection. Accompanied by LOA from PSA/DNA.

Estimate: $4,000-$5,000

Joseph Wood
vs
James M. Blackburn

And the said plaintiff comes, and as to the plea of the said defendant by him secondly above pleaded, says precludi non because he says the said plaintiff and defendant did not refer "the said several trespasses, and causes of action and all damages sustained by said plaintiff by reason thereof to the final arbitrament and award of one Brown Wilson" in manner and form as is in his said plea alledged; and of this the said plaintiff puts himself upon the country &c.
Benedict & Lincoln p.q.

And for further Replication to said third plea, said says precludi non because he says the said Brown Wilson did not make his final award, in manner and form as is in said plea alledged; and of this the pltff puts himself upon the country &c.
Benedict & Lincoln p.q.

And for further Replication to said third plea said pltff says precludi non because he says the said defendant did not make the tender, in manner and form as is in said plea alledged; and of this the pltff puts himself upon the country &c
Benedict & Lincoln p.q.

Wood vs Blackburn } Replication
Filed Oct 29, 1851
James M. Miller Clerk

Of the September Term of the Tazewell County Circuit Court, A.D. 1852

State of Illinois
Tazewell County } ss

James E. Smith, plaintiff complains of James C. Gaines, defendant, being in custody &c of a plea of trespass on the case:

For that whereas the said defendant, heretofore, towit, on the day of July in the year of our Lord one thousand eight hundred and fiftytwo, at the county aforesaid, in a certain conversation which he then and there had & held, in the presence and hearing of divers good citizens of the state, of and concerning the said plaintiff, and of and concerning the evidence the said plaintiff had theretofore given on the trial of a certain cause before a justice of the Peace, wherein the defendant herein was a party, falsely and maliciously spoke, uttered and published the following false, scandalous, malicious, and defamatory words, towit: "James E. Smith" (the plaintiff meaning) "swore a lie, and I" (deft meaning) "can prove it" "Smith" (the plaintiff meaning) "swore a lie and I" (deft meaning) "can prove it" "He" (the plaintiff meaning) "swore a lie and I" (deft meaning) "can prove it" "James E. Smith (the plaintiff meaning) swore a lie" "Smith" (plaintiff meaning) "swore a lie" "He" (the plaintiff meaning) "swore a lie", he the said defendant thereby then and there meaning and intending to impute to the said plaintiff the crime of perjury—

And whereas also afterwards towit on the day and year aforesaid, at the county aforesaid, he the said defendant, in a certain other ...

... to the damage of the said plaintiff of one thousand dollars, and therefore he brings his suit &c.
Lincoln and Saltonstall, for pltff—

Smith as Gaines } Declaration
Filed August 31st 1852
J. A. Jones Clk

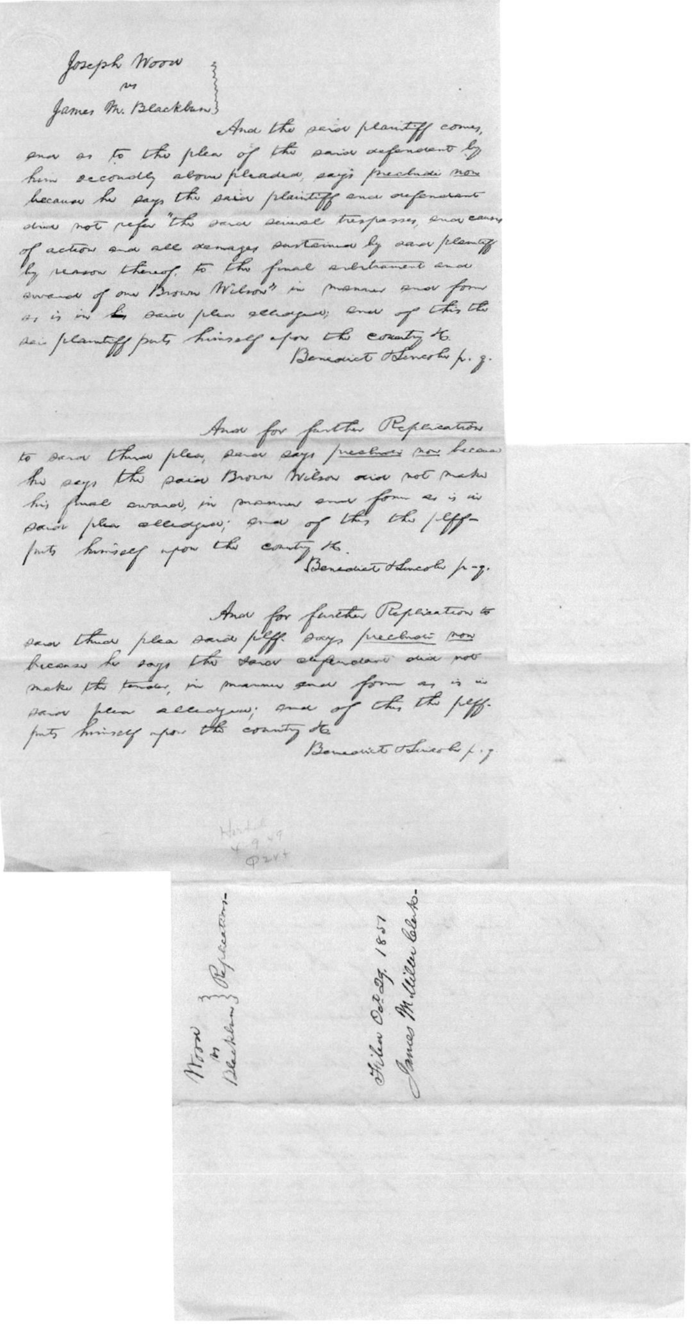

25083 Abraham Lincoln. Autograph Document Signed three times "Benedict & Lincoln p.q." No place [Edgar Co., Ill.], October 1851, one page, folio, on faintly ruled blue paper. On verso Lincoln has written a docket with the parties' names as well as the notation *"Filed Oct. 29, 1851"* underneath which the court clerk has signed. Joseph Wood, in his suit against James M. Blackburn, denies that he and the defendant referred *"'...the said several trespasses, and causes of action and all damages sustained by said plaintiff...to the final arbitrament and award of one Brown Wilson' in manner and form...as is alledged..." or that Wilson made "his final award, in manner and form as is...alledged..."* Excellent. From the Henry E. Luhrs Collection. Accompanied by LOA from PSA/DNA.
Estimate: $4,000-$5,000

25084 Abraham Lincoln. Autograph Document Signed "Saltonstall, for plff". Tazewell Co. (Ill.), September 1852, one and one-half pages, folio, on blue paper. In James E. Smith vs James C. Gaines, the plaintiff declares that the previous July the defendant *"in a...conversation...held in the presence and hearing of divers good citizens...concerning the evidence the said plaintiff had theretofore given on the trial of a certain cause before a justice of the peace, wherein the defendant herein was a party...spoke...the following false, scandalous, malicious and defamatory words, to wit: 'James E. Smith...swore a lie, and I...can prove it'...meaning and intending to impute to the said plaintiff the crime of perjury..."* Records show that on May 5, 1852 a jury decided for Smith, awarding him $100 damages, a tenth of the amount asked for in this document. Lincoln seems to have written this declaration as a favor for his colleague A.H. Saltonstall, and only later joined him in the suit; someone, perhaps county clerk J.A. Jones, has amended the signature by adding "Lincoln and" before what Lincoln himself wrote ("Saltonstall, for plff."). From the Henry E. Luhrs Collection. Accompanied by LOA from PSA/DNA.
Estimate: $4,000-$5,000

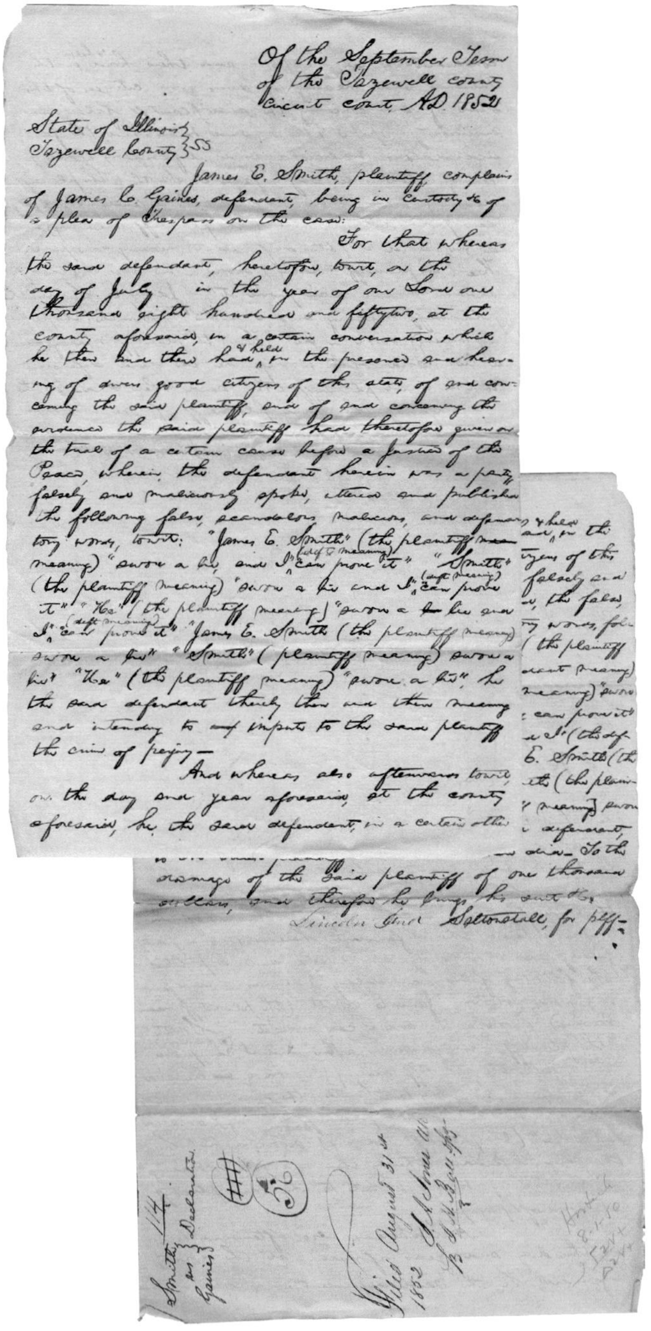

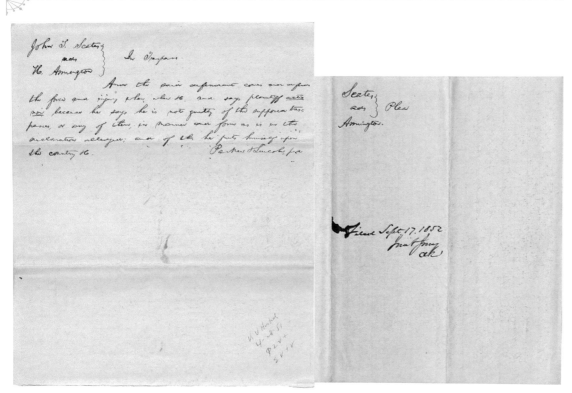

25085   Abraham Lincoln. Autograph Document Signed "Parker & Lincoln, p.d." No place or date [Tazewell Co., Ill.; docketed September 1852], one-third page, quarto, on grayish-blue paper. In H. Armington vs John T. Scates, the defendant states he is *"not guilty of the supposed trespasses, or any of them, in manner and form"* as alleged. From the Henry E. Luhrs Collection. Accompanied by LOA from PSA/DNA. **Estimate: $3,000-$4,000**

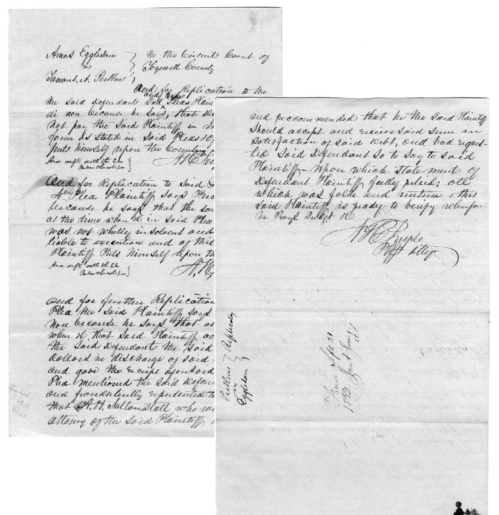

25086   Abraham Lincoln. Two Autograph Endorsements Signed "And deft. doth the like / Parker & Lincoln p.d." Penned on an Autograph Document Signed by N.H. Purple, attorney for the plaintiff in Amos Eggleson vs Tarrant A. Perkins, Tazewell Co. [Ill.], no date [docketed September 1852], one and one-half pages, folio, on blue paper. The plaintiff disputes several pleas of the defendant and specifically accuses him of "falsely and fraudulently" persuading the plaintiff to accept $25 in discharge of a judgment by claiming that such settlement was recommended by the defendant's then attorney, A.H. Saltonstall. Records show that Lincoln lost this case and the plaintiff won a jury award of $110.45. From the Henry E. Luhrs Collection. Accompanied by LOA from PSA/DNA.

Estimate: $4,000-$5,000

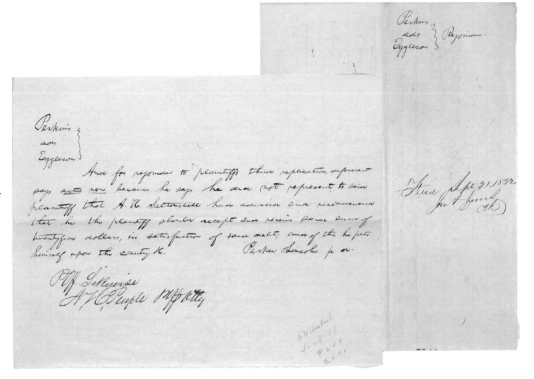

25087 **Abraham Lincoln. Autograph Legal Document Signed "Parker & Lincoln p.d."** No place or date [Tazewell Co., Ill.; docketed September 1852], oblong octavo. In Eggleson vs Perkins, the defendant declares *"he did not represent to…plaintiff that A.H. Saltonstall had advised and recommended that he the plaintiff should accept…said sum of twenty five dollars in satisfaction of said debt…"* From the Henry E. Luhrs Collection. Accompanied by LOA from PSA/DNA.
Estimate: $3,200-$3,800

25088 **Abraham Lincoln. Autograph Document Signed twice "Jones & Lincoln p.d."** No place or date [Tazewell Co., Ill.; docketed May 1853], two-thirds page, folio, on ruled blue paper. In Daniel Crabb and Andrew Watts vs Andrew Wallace, the defendant asserts that he *"did not unjustly detain the cattle of the said plaintiffs, in manner & form as…alledged"* and that the cattle were at the time his own property and *"not then & there the property of the said plaintiffs…"* From the Henry E. Luhrs Collection. Accompanied by LOA from PSA/DNA.
Estimate: $4,000-$5,000

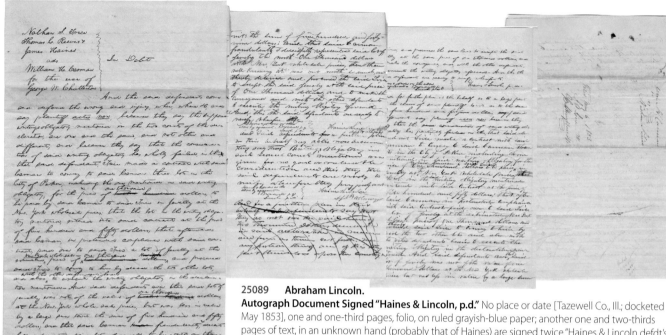

25089   Abraham Lincoln.
Autograph Document Signed "Haines & Lincoln, p.d." No place or date [Tazewell Co., Ill.; docketed May 1853], one and one-third pages, folio, on ruled grayish-blue paper; another one and two-thirds pages of text, in an unknown hand (probably that of Haines) are signed twice "Haines & Lincoln defdt's attorneys"; besides all this, Lincoln has inserted in three places, in a small hand, the endorsement *"Issue & joinder on the above by agreement"* and signed *"Broadwell p.q. / Lincoln p.d."* (thus, in all, Lincoln has written four surname signatures throughout this document). A record from an unusual suit, William H. Carman for the use of George W. Chatterton vs Nathan Trice, Thomas C. Reeves and James Haines, which involved a contract by the defendants to convey three lots in the city of Pekin *"for the price of one thousand dollars, to be paid by said Carman…in jewelry at…New-York wholesale prices…"* The defendants claim that the jewelry was in fact only worth about $450 and that *"Carman fraudulently & deceitfully represented said lot of jewelry to be worth one thousand dollars at the New York wholesale prices, there & then well knowing it was not worth so much…"* Interestingly, the man standing behind this suit, George Chatterton, was Springfield's leading jeweler. In 1842, he had furnished Lincoln with a wedding band for Mary Todd inscribed "Love is eternal". $3,800-4,500
From the Henry E. Luhrs Collection. Accompanied by LOA from PSA/DNA.
Estimate: $4,500-$6,000

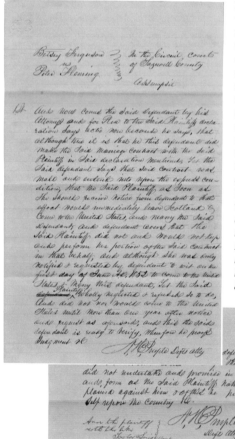

25090   Abraham Lincoln. Unsigned Autograph Document. Vermilion Co., Ill., 3 June 1853, three and one-quarter pages, folio. A long, involved affidavit by Daniel Sturm, principal defendant in a lawsuit brought by John S. Graham, guardian of the minors Mary J., Marena E., and Sarah M. French. Sturm recalls coming to Danville, Ill. from his residence in Indiana to see his attorney, W.H. Lamon, and declares that they could not procure a copy of the bill in Graham's suit at either the offices of the court clerk or the plaintiff's attorney, O.L. Davis. Sturm *"remained in Danville over night, and in the morning again saw said Lamon, who again told him that said bill could not be found, upon which affiant returned to Indiana…[A] week or two afterwards affiant wrote to Mr. Davis, enquiring whether said bill had been found, but got no answer…"* Sturm and the plaintiff subsequently *"agreed upon terms of adjustment, except that complainant reserved to himself to go to Mr. Davis and ascertain whether he would approve of said adjustment; at the same time promising…he would return and inform affiant of the result, and also…of the true time of said term of court, about which there then was some question in the minds of both"* Graham did not however return, and near the end of the court term Sturm *"was astounded by the information that the court had been in session that week…"* A decree by default having been entered against him, Sturm does not object to the allegations in Graham's bill nor the proof taken, but says *"that great injustice will be done him in the final decree, unless he be allowed to alledge and prove some matters, in the nature of set-off…[I]n the account against him he is charged with the rents, issues and profits [of] a certain farm in Indiana belonging to said minors…[W]hen he first bought said farm for said minors…he found it in no condition to be profitably used and enjoyed, and…to make it productive, he did throughout the years of 1845 up to the year 1850 make valuable and lasting improvements…consisting in part of the finishing of a dwelling house, the building of a smoke house & two stables, the planting of an apple orchard of eighteen trees, now bearing, and…clearing in the timber & fencing…fourteen acres and a half of land, and breaking the most of it…"* For this, as well as for real estate taxes, expenses, and for nearly six and a half years of *"custody and care"* of the minors, furnishing their *"necessary food, clothing, lodging, and schooling,"* Sturm seeks a set-off of more than $1600. If *"allowed to make these allegations & proof of them, he will do so upon the terms, that he will dispute none of the proof of the complainant already in; that complainant make any additional proof in his power; that this affidavit stand for his answer in the cause; and that he will now produce his proofs and ask no continuance…He…has been guilty of no bad faith, in not answering sooner…but…has, in all things, intended to do full justice, with reasonable diligence as to time."* Sturm boldly signs at conclusion. Extensive glassine repairs to fold breaks and tenderness; small marginal chip on last page. A long, interesting Lincoln legal, with over 700 words in his hand. $3,800-4,500 From the Henry E. Luhrs Collection. Accompanied by LOA from PSA/DNA.
Estimate: $4,500-$6,000

25091 **Abraham Lincoln. Autograph Endorsement Signed "And the plaintiff doth the like / Taylor & Lincoln p.q."** Written at the end of an Autograph Document Signed by N.H. Purple, attorney for the defendant in Betsey Fergusson vs Peter Fleming, Tazewell Co. (Ill.), no date (docketed May 1854), about two and one-quarter pages, folio, on ruled blue paper. An intriguing record from a breach of promise suit. Fleming here claims that his "*marriage contract with the said plaintiff*" was made on the express condition that she would "*mmediately leave Scotland & come to the United States*" when he notified her, but that she "*wholly neglected & refused so to do, and did not nor would come to the United States until more than one year after notice and request…*" Fleming also claims that Betsey, for a "*good and valuable consideration*," had released him from "*all his promises and understandings*"; further, that he had offered to marry her but she had refused. SEE FOLLOWING LOTs From the Henry E. Luhrs Collection. Accompanied by LOA from PSA/DNA.
Estimate: $4,000-$5,000

25092 **Abraham Lincoln. Document Signed "Taylor & Lincoln p.q."** Tazewell Co. [Ill.], May 1854, three-quarters page, folio. The document states that Peter Fleming "*will admit on the trial of this cause, that some time in…August A.D. 1852 after defendant's arrival in this country he remitted to the plaintiff by cheque on the Commercial Bank of Scotland the sum of twenty pounds to aid her in leaving Scotland and…coming to this country and that the same was received by plaintiff within…two or three months thereafter and that the plaintiff did not leave Scotland to come to the United States until about the last of July A.D. 1853…*" SEE PRECEDING AND FOLLOWING LOTS From the Henry E. Luhrs Collection. Accompanied by LOA from PSA/DNA.
Estimate: $3,000-$4,000

25093 **Abraham Lincoln. Autograph Document Signed three times "Taylor & Lincoln p.q."** No place or date (Tazewell Co., Ill.; docketed May 1854), one and a fraction pages, folio, on ruled blue paper. In Betsey Ferguson vs Peter Fleming, a *"breach of marriage contract,"*, the plaintiff responds to several of the defendant's pleas, calling one *"repugnant, in this, that it admits the contract…and then avers the existence of a condition which would change the contract…into a wholly different contract."* Further, Betsey says she *"did not discharge and release the said defendant"* nor *"neglect and refuse to marry"* him as he claims. SEE PRECEDING AND FOLLOWING LOTS From the Henry E. Luhrs Collection. Accompanied by LOA from PSA/DNA.

Estimate: $4,000-$5,000

25094 **Abraham Lincoln. Autograph Document Signed** "Taylor & Lincoln p.q." Tazewell Co. [Ill.], no date [docketed May 1854], one-half page, folio, on ruled paper. In Betsey Fergusson vs Peter Fleming, the plaintiff objects to a plea by the defendant since it *"amounts to the general issue…is not direct and positive, but argumentative"* and *"pleads evidence and not facts."* The central portion of this document is written in an unknown hand; Lincoln has added the names of the parties, court, and the three specific causes of demurrer, making in all about 40 words in his hand, plus the signature. SEE PRECEDING THREE LOTS $3,000-4,500 From the Henry E. Luhrs Collection. Accompanied by LOA from PSA/DNA.

Estimate: $4,000-$5,000

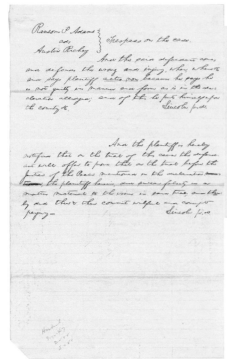

25095 **Abraham Lincoln. Autograph Document** Signed twice "Lincoln p.d." No place or date [DeWitt Co., Ill.; docketed May 1854], two-thirds page, folio, on ruled paper. A plea and notice in Austin Richey vs Ransom P. Adams. The defendant advises the plaintiff that upon trial he *"will offer to prove that on the trial before the Justice of the Peace mentioned in the declaration, the plaintiff herein, did swear falsity in a matter material to the issue in said trial; and thereby did then & there commit willful…perjury."* One blank lower corner clipped, well clear of all writing. From the Henry E. Luhrs Collection. Accompanied by LOA from PSA/DNA.

Estimate: $4,500-$6,000

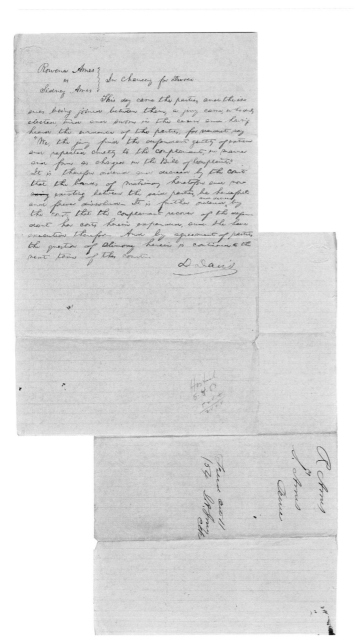

25096 **Abraham Lincoln. Autograph Document, written in Lincoln's hand** but signed by David Davis. No place or date [Tazewell Co., Ill.; docketed October 1854], one-half page, folio, on ruled blue paper. In the divorce suit of Rowena Ames vs Sidney Ames, Lincoln writes out the jury verdict and consequent court decree for the judge to sign: "…*'We, the jury find the defendant guilty of extreme and repeated cruelty to the complainant, in manner and form as charged…….' It is therefore ordered and decreed…that the bands of matrimony…between the said parties be henceforth and forever dissolved. It is further ordered and decreed…that the complainant recover of the defendant her costs herein expended, and she have execution therefor. And by agreement of parties the question of alimony herein is continued to the next term of this court."* Lincoln-related divorce papers are uncommon, and this example is choice for being signed by the circuit court judge and friend who became his 1860 campaign manager and one of his U.S. Supreme Court appointees. From the Henry E. Luhrs Collection. Accompanied by LOA from PSA/DNA.

Estimate: $4,000-$5,000

25097 **Abraham Lincoln. Unsigned Autograph** Document. Champaign Co., Ill., 21 May 1855, one and one-half pages, folio, on faintly ruled paper. An affidavit prepared for and signed by George High, "*defendant in two certain indictments, found against him, by the Grand Jury of Vermilion County, for the supposed stealing of two mareswhich indictments are now pending in…Champaign county…by change of venue…*" High swears that he "*can not safely go to trial at the present term because of the absence of one Jack, alias, John Noland…a material witness*" by whom he expects to prove that on the day the mares were stolen, August 29, 1852, he "*was not within said Vermilion, nor within ten miles of it, at any time during the whole of that day, and the succeeding night, and the larger half of the next day…*" Subpoenas were issued for Noland, but they "*have not been returned, nor has said witness appeared,*" and because he has been "*confined in jail*" High has "*had it not in his power to use any greater diligence…*" He states that he expects to procure Noland's "*attendance at the next term; and that this application is not made for delay but that justice may be done.*" High was in fact found guilty of horse theft and sentenced to three years in prison. In November 1857 Lincoln wrote a petition for High's pardon, which was signed by 27 residents of Vermilion county; after signing it himself, Lincoln personally carried the petition to Gov. William H. Bissell, who granted the appeal and made High a free man. SEE FOLLOWING LOT From the Henry E. Luhrs Collection. Accompanied by LOA from PSA/DNA.

Estimate: $4,500-$6,000

25098   Manuscript Document, signed in an unknown hand "Swett, Lawrence, Lincoln & Lamon D.Q." Champaign Co., Ill., May 1855, three-quarters page, folio, on lined blue paper. In the case of George High, indicted for larceny, the lawyers ask that subpoenas be directed to the sheriffs of Warren, Mason and Iroquois Counties for four named witnesses, including John Noland, "to testify in behalf of the defendant". A brief note by clerk (Thompson R.) Webber states that the subpoenas were issued on 23 April 1855. SEE PRECEDING AND FOLLOWING LOTS. From the Henry E. Luhrs Collection.
Estimate: $1,000-$1,500

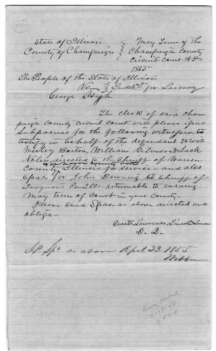

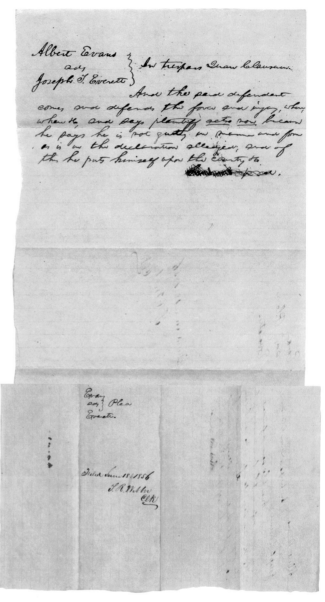

25099   Manuscript letter signed "Swett, Lawrence, Lincoln & Lamon Atty's for deft" in an unknown hand. Danville, Ill., May 1, 1855, to the Champaign County circuit court clerk (T.R. Webber), one page, quarto, on ruled blue paper. In the case of State of Illinois vs George High, the attorneys ask that subpoenas be issued for Wesley Barton, William Gilmore and Jack Noland, directed to Henderson County since it has been learned that the witnesses do not reside in the county first thought, *"but a mile or two over the line in the next county…Great promptness is desired."* At foot Webber has written a note indicating that the subpoenas were issued on 2 May. Crease repaired on verso with old glassine. SEE PRECEDING TWO LOTS $800-1,000 From the Henry E. Luhrs Collection. Accompanied by LOA from PSA/DNA.
Estimate: $1,000-$1,500

25100   Abraham Lincoln. Autograph Document, with crossed-out signature "Lincoln p.d." No place, no date (Champaign Co., Ill.; docketed June 1856), one-third page, folio, on ruled blue paper. A plea in the case of Joseph T. Everett vs Albert Evans, for *"trespass quare clausum"* (literally, "breaking the close"; unlawful entry or trespass upon land). Evans "says he is not guilty in manner and form" as alleged. Lincoln originally signed this document, but then assiduously blotted out his name with cross-hatching; it is still discernible. From the Henry E. Luhrs Collection. Accompanied by LOA from PSA/DNA.
Estimate: $3,500-$4,500

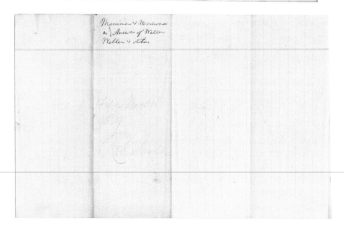

25101   Abraham Lincoln. Unsigned Autograph Document.
Vermilion Co. (Ill.), April 1858, one page, folio, on ruled paper. A plea prepared for and signed by Joseph Peters, defendant in a suit brought by Robbins and Pomeroy. Peters seeks judgment in his favor because a writ was *"served upon him, within the county of Champaign…and because… the county of Vermilion is not the county of the plaintiffs; and because… the causes of action…did not…accrue in the county of Vermilion; and because…said causes of action were not…specifically made payable in said county of Vermilion… [W]herefore he prays judgment of said writ and declaration, and that the same may be quashed &c."* Broken folds reinforced on verso, which is blank except for dockets. From the Henry E. Luhrs Collection. Accompanied by LOA from PSA/DNA.
Estimate: $3,000-$4,000

25102   Abraham Lincoln. Autograph Document Signed "Lincoln & Hill for Respondent". De Witt Co. [Ill.], no date [docketed March 1859], one page, folio, on ruled paper. The separate answer of John F. Wellen *"to a bill in chancery exhibited against him and others…by Harvey H. Merriman and Jesse G. Woodward…"* Having *"read the answer of his co-defendant, DeWitt C. Jones,"* Wellen *"adopts the same so far as applicable to him"* and *"admits the lumber sold by him to said DeWitt C. Jones, was as charged in complainant's bill, purchased by respondent with money obtained from said Snell under the contracts mentioned in complainant's bill. Respondent denies all fraud and combination charged…[and] prays to be…discharged with his reasonable costs."* From the Henry E. Luhrs Collection. Accompanied by LOA from PSA/DNA.
Estimate: $4,500-$6,000

25103   Abraham Lincoln. Autograph Document Signed twice
"Lincoln p.d." No place or date (Vermilion Co., Ill.; docketed May 1859), one and one-half pages, folio. A complex plea and notice in James Dougherty vs *"Matilda Rankin, impleaded with Francis M. Rankin"* involving a life estate Mrs. Rankin had in some land that she had contracted to convey to the plaintiff. Since Dougherty settled with one Milton Davis, who held some interest in the property, and she herself subsequently gave Dougherty *"by deed, her entire interest in said land"* she *"insists that the written contract…was and is entirely superceded, and is of no more effect."* Lincoln's writing is unusually large and distinct. Bottom portion of second leaf trimmed away; broken folds reinforced on versos, which are blank except for dockets. From the Henry E. Luhrs Collection. Accompanied by LOA from PSA/DNA.
Estimate: $6,000-$7,000

25104   Abraham Lincoln. Autograph Document Signed twice
"Beckwith & Lincoln p.d." No place or date [Vermilion Co., Ill.; docketed May 1859], two pages, folio. In Sanford Calvert vs Wm. R. Timmons, Joseph Anderson, Remus McArdle, Barney Day and Albert Heath, the defendants offer to prove upon trial that Timmons was a justice of the peace and that Heath, *"believing that an auger had been stolen, and… was concealed in the dwelling house, out-house, garden, yard or other place or places of…plaintiff"* made a complaint before Timmons, who issued a search warrant that was *"placed…in the hands of…Anderson, who was…an acting constable…Anderson summoned…McArdle (who also was a constable) and Day to assist him in making said search…and found the auger…[I]n doing so, they committed no actual violence or damage…[T]he foregoing is the whole of the supposed trespass in the declaration mentioned."* Glassine repairs/strengthening on verso of each leaf to weak or slightly broken folds. From the Henry E. Luhrs Collection. Accompanied by LOA from PSA/DNA.
Estimate: $5,000-$6,000

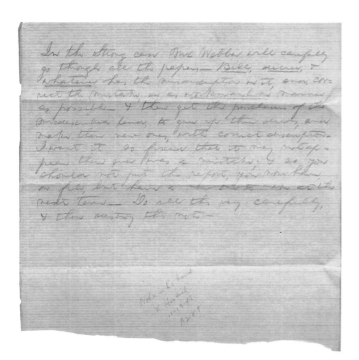

25105 **Abraham Lincoln. Unsigned Autograph Note,** in pencil. No place or date, approximately two-thirds page, quarto, written on a large piece of ruled blue paper torn from a folio sheet. An astonishing missive from "Honest Abe", in which he asks a court clerk to alter legal documents that were already in the clerk's hands, and otherwise "fix" a mistake. This directive was sent to Thompson R. Webber of Champaign County, one of Lincoln's most trusted friends among the court officers of the eighth circuit; in an 1862 recommendation to Secretary of War Edwin Stanton he called Webber "an honest and capable man." The present note evidently refers to Strong vs Thomas, a May 1854 suit in which Lincoln represented the plaintiff and which involved some 47 heirs. A rather anxious Lincoln writes, in full: *"In the Strong case, Mr. Webber will carefully go through all the papers - Bill, decree, & whatever has the misdescription on it, and correct the mistake, in as workmanlike manner as possible — & then get the purchasers of the misdescribed land, to give up their deeds, and make them new ones, with correct description. I want it so fixed that it may not appear there ever was a mistake; & so you should not put the report, you now have, on file, but have a new one to make at the next term. Do all this very carefully, & then destroy this note."* The seeming impropriety (if not illegality) of Lincoln's request makes this an autograph of character-ological and not just historical interest. What he feared most from these legal documents with mistaken land descriptions — aside from potential embarrassment - may have been reflected in a rhetorical question he once wrote down for a law lecture: *"Who can be more nearly a fiend than he who habitually overhauls the register of deeds, in search of defects in titles…to stir up strife, and put money in his pocket?"* Surely one of the most extraordinary documents to survive from Lincoln's law practice - and unpublished! The pencil writing is somewhat light — perhaps intentionally - but it is entirely readable. From the Henry E. Luhrs Collection. Accompanied by LOA from PSA/DNA.
Estimate: $9,000-$11,000

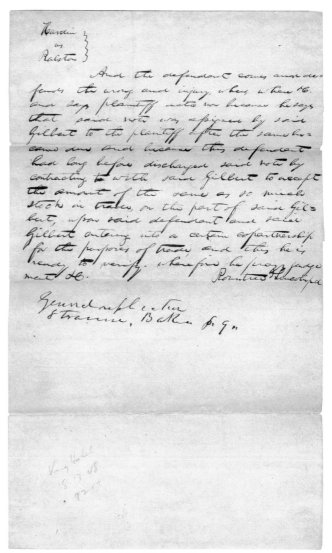

25106 **Abraham Lincoln. Autograph Document Signed "Rountree & Lincoln p.d."** No place or date (probably Christian Co., Ill., ca 1843), one-half page, folio. In the case of *"Hardin vs Ralston"* the defendant avers that a note *"was assigned by…Gilbert to the plaintiff after the same became due and because this defendant had long before discharged said note by contracting with said Gilbert to accept the amount of the same as so much stock in trade…"* A fine specimen. From the Henry E. Luhrs Collection. Accompanied by LOA from PSA/DNA.
Estimate: $4,500-$6,000

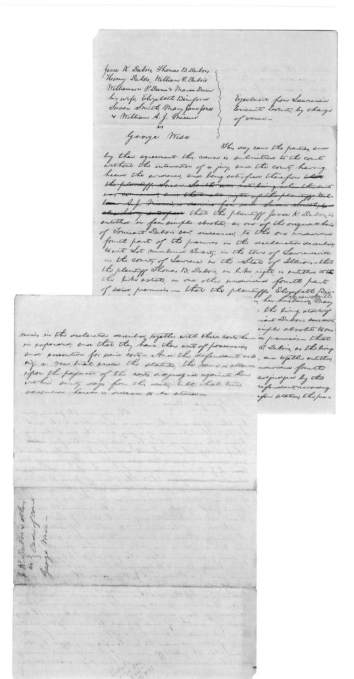

25107   Abraham Lincoln. Lengthy Autograph Endorsement Signed "A. Lincoln for Defts." No place or date (probably Sangamon Co., Ill., ca 1855), two pages, folio, on blue paper. The main text, in an unknown hand, is signed by A. Johnston and comprises the last page of a once-longer deposition in a lawsuit involving cast iron tombs. Johnston, who was a prominent Springfield monument-maker, unsurprisingly declares that "compared with ordinary marble tombstones" the cast-iron kind are "of little or no value" and although he dodges a question as to their difference in cost, he does admit that the best quality of tombstone, Italian marble, would cost $3 "per superficial foot" including "socket and lettering in the best style but not carving." Asked if any cast iron tombs are "in use about Springfield" he replies "none that I know of." At the foot of the document, Lincoln has penned a statement that: *"The parties in this case agree that the above depositions, so far as the questions and answers are proper, may be used in evidence in the cause…and also in the case of William H. Young against Reuben Miller now pending in the Logan county circuit court."* Interestingly it was Johnston who repaired Lincoln's sarcophagus when it was damaged in an 1876 attempt to steal the President's remains. Brownish staining nearly blots out the final word in Lincoln's endorsement ("court") and covers his signature, which nevertheless is quite readable. From the Henry E. Luhrs Collection. Accompanied by LOA from PSA/DNA.
Estimate: $5,000-$6,500

25108   Abraham Lincoln. Unsigned Autograph Document. No place or date, one and one-quarter pages, folio, on faintly ruled blue paper. An "order of court" in the case of Jesse K. Dubois and others vs George Wise, an ejectment suit brought from Lawrence County on change of venue. By mutual agreement the case *"is submitted to the court without the intervention of a jury"* and the court, *"having heard the evidence",* concludes *"that the plaintiff Jesse K. Dubois, is entitled…as one of the original heirs of Touisant Dubois senr., deceased, to…one undivided fourth part of…lot numbered Twenty, in the town of Lawrenceville…"* A similar judgment is entered for numerous other named descendants of Toussaint Dubois. *"It is therefore adjudged by the court that the plaintiffs recover of the defendant…the premises…described, together with their costs…And the defendant asking a new trial under the statute, the same is allowed upon the payment of the costs adjudged against him within sixty days…till which time execution hereon is ordered to be staid."* Missing extreme tips of two corners, well clear of all writing. Lincoln has lined out about three and a half sentences which, although related to the suit, evidently did not belong in this document. From the Henry E. Luhrs Collection. Accompanied by LOA from PSA/DNA.
Estimate: $3,000-$4,000

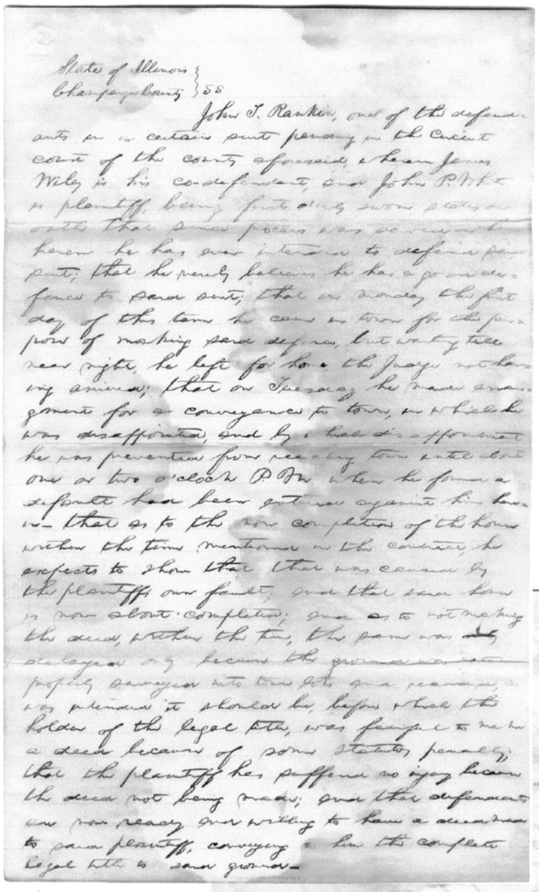
State of Illinois }
Champaign County } SS

John T. Rankin, one of the defendants in a certain suit pending in the Circuit court of the county aforesaid, wherein James Wiley is his co-defendant, and John P. White is plaintiff, being first duly sworn states on oath that since process was served on him he has ever intended to defend said suit; that he verily believes he has a good defence to said suit; that on Monday the first day of this term he came in town for the purpose of making said defence, but waiting till near night, he left for home the Judge not having arrived; that on Tuesday he made arrangement for a conveyance to town, in which he was disappointed, and by which disappointment he was prevented from reaching town until about one or two o'clock P.M. when he found a default had been entered against him — that as to the non completion of the house within the time mentioned in the contract, he expects to show that that was caused by the plaintiff's own fault, and that said house is now about completed; and as to not making the deed, within the time, the same was delayed only because the ground was not properly surveyed into town lots and recorded as it should be, before which the holder of the legal title, was fearful to make a deed because of some statutory penalty; that the plaintiff has suffered no injury because the deed not being made; and that defendants are now ready and willing to have a deed made to said plaintiff, conveying to him the complete legal title to said ground.

25109 Abraham Lincoln. Unsigned Autograph Document. Champaign Co., Ill., no date, one page, folio. John T. Rankin, co-defendant of James Wiley in a suit brought by John P. White, swears that ever since process was served on him *"he has...intended to defend said suit... On Monday the first day of this term he came in town for the purpose of making said defence, but waiting till near night, he left for home, the Judge not having arrived;...on Tuesday he made arrangement for a conveyance to town, in which he was disappointed, and...prevented from reaching town until about one or two o'clock P.M. when he found a default had been entered against him..."* As to *"non-completion of the house within the time mentioned in the contract, he expects to show that that was caused by the plaintiff's own fault, and that said house is now about completed; and as to not making the deed...the same was delayed only because the ground was not properly surveyed into town lots and recorded...before which the holder of the legal title was fearful to make a deed because of some statutory penalty..."* He declares the plaintiff has suffered no injury because of the lack of a deed and that the defendants are *"ready and willing to have a deed made to said plaintiff, conveying...complete legal title to said ground."* An unusual document that highlights the purely logistical difficulties which sometimes plagued attendance at pioneer courts. Large irregular water stain covers most of the document, lightening or faintly blurring a number of words, but all is readable. From the Henry E. Luhrs Collection. Accompanied by LOA from PSA/DNA.
Estimate: $3,000-$4,000

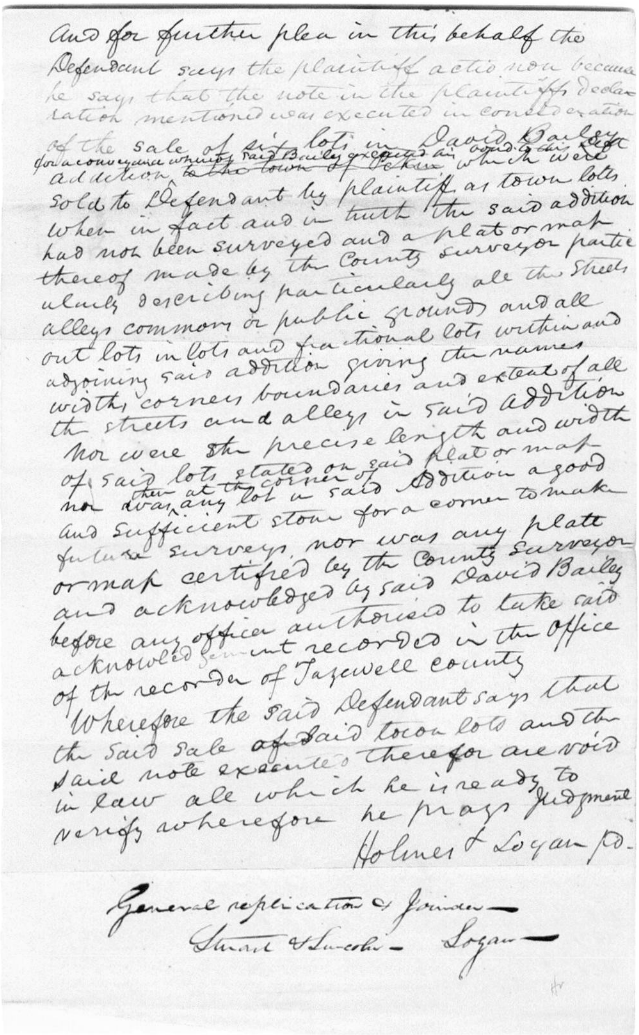
And for further plea in this behalf the Defendant says the plaintiff actio non because he says that the note in the plaintiffs declaration mentioned was executed in consideration of the sale of six lots in David Bailey addition to the town of Pekin which were sold to Defendant by plaintiff as town lots when in fact and in truth the said addition had not been surveyed and a plat or map thereof made by the County surveyor particularly describing all the Streets alleys commons or public grounds and all out lots in lots and fractional lots within and adjoining said addition giving the names width, corners boundaries and extent of all the streets and alleys in said addition nor were the precise length and width of said lots stated on said plat or map nor was there at the corner of any lot in said Addition a good and sufficient stone for a corner to make future surveys, nor was any platt or map certified by the County Surveyor and acknowledged by said David Bailey before any officer authorised to take said acknowledgement recorded in the Office of the recorder of Tazewell county
Wherefore the said Defendant says that the said sale of said town lots and the said note executed therefor are void in law all which he is ready to verify wherefore he prays judgment
Holmes & Logan pd.

General replication & joinder —
Stuart & Lincoln — Logan —

25110 Abraham Lincoln. Document Signed "General replication & joinder - Stuart & Lincoln - Logan". No place [Tazewell Co., Ill.], no date, one page, folio. The main text is an Autograph Document Signed by Stephen T. Logan (as "Holmes & Logan pd") in David Bailey vs Leonard Knox. The defendant pleads that the sale of some lots in a town addition, and his promissory note therefor, should be voided because there is no duly certified and recorded plat of the addition by the county surveyor showing alleys, common grounds, street names, widths, boundaries, etc., "nor was there at the corner of any lot in said addition a good and sufficient stone for a corner to mark future surveys...". From the Henry E. Luhrs Collection. Accompanied by LOA from PSA/DNA.
Estimate: $4,500-$6,000

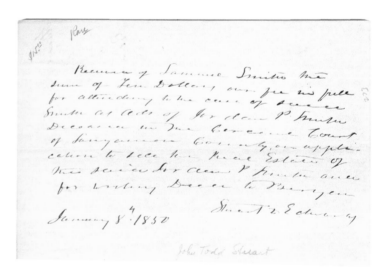

25111   Abraham Lincoln. Unsigned Autograph Document. No place or date, one page, oblong octavo. In Lucetta Stevens vs Phineas Stevens, on her petition for assignment of dower, Lincoln writes out a court order which grants her request since "*John C. Doremus…guardian ad litem to the said Phineas Stevens…knows nothing in bar of said petition*" Lincoln has left a blank space (never filled in) for the description of the lands on which she is to recover dower. It is further ordered that "*Henry Giger and James Bowlin be appointed commissioners to assign and set out her dower…*" Excellent. From the Henry E. Luhrs Collection. Accompanied by LOA from PSA/DNA.
Estimate: $3,800-$4,500

25112   Lincoln Law Partner, John Todd Stuart. Autograph Document Signed "Stuart & Lincoln Solicitors for Compt." Sangamon Co. (Ill.), no date (docketed February 1838). The clerk is directed to issue subpoenas in chancery for Isaac R. and Rachael Braucher in a suit brought by William Hickman, administrator of George Churchill, deceased. Very early: dated less than a year after Lincoln had begun the regular practice of law. Stuart and Lincoln won this suit, securing a $481.69 judgment. From the Henry E. Luhrs Collection. Accompanied by LOA from PSA/DNA.
Estimate: $1,000-$1,500

25113   Lincoln Law Partner, John Todd Stuart. Autograph Document Signed "Stuart & Edwards". No place [Sangamon Co., Ill.], Jan. 8, 1850, one page, oblong octavo. A $10 fee receipt to Samuel Smith, administrator of the estate of Jordan P. Smith, for attending to his court application to sell the latter's real estate. From the Henry E. Luhrs Collection. Accompanied by LOA from PSA/DNA.
Estimate: $500-$800

25114   Lincoln Law Partner, Stephen Trigg Logan. Autograph Document Signed "Logan & Lincoln pq". Sangamon Co. [Ill.], no date (ca July 1844), four pages, quarto. A lengthy complaint by Reuben Thompson, who contracted to sell Edward Stapleford a lot in Iles's addition to the city of Springfield, taking in payment two notes at six and twelve months with 10% annual interest. Stapleford having *"utterly failed & refused to pay said notes"* except for some interest, Thompson asks that he be compelled to fulfill the contract or that a lien be granted and the lot sold to settle the debt and pay legal costs. Records show that Logan and Lincoln won this suit by default of the defendant. From the Henry E. Luhrs Collection. Accompanied by LOA from PSA/DNA.

Estimate: $1,000-$1,500

25115   Lincoln Law Partner, Stephen Trigg Logan. Autograph Document Signed "Logan & Lincoln for Petitioners". Sangamon Co. [Ill.], no date (docketed July 1844), about three pages, folio. Andrew Lanterman and Gunnel McKinney, administrators of John Lanterman, state that he died intestate in March 1842 leaving debts greater than his assets and request an order of court to sell so much of the deceased's real estate as will cover his debts, the costs of their petition, and of sale.
From the Henry E. Luhrs Collection. Accompanied by LOA from PSA/DNA.
Estimate: $800-$1,000

25116   Lincoln Law Partner, William Henry Herndon. Autograph Document Signed "Margarete Porter per / Lincoln & Herndon for Sol." Sangamon Co. [Ill.], Nov. 1851, two pages, folio. The widow of William Porter seeks, from Hoffman et al, her dower right to some property on Fifth Street, although she had duly signed the deed when her husband sold the land long before (the property in question may have formed part of "Hoffman's Row", the block of buildings where Lincoln once had his law office). Lincoln and Herndon won this suit in March 1852, winning Mrs. Porter a dower of $10 a year. From the Henry E. Luhrs Collection. Accompanied by LOA from PSA/DNA.
Estimate: $800-$1,000

25117   Lincoln Law Partner, William Henry Herndon. Autograph Document Signed "Wells Wells & Lake / by Lincoln & Herndon" No place [Sangamon Co., Ill.?], August 1859, one and one-half pages, quarto. Thomas H. and John G. Wells and Jabez W. Lake testify in Morse & Primm, administrators, vs Thompson et al, that they purchased some real estate having been informed that it was free from any encumbrance, and as they *"know nothing further of the facts & allegations and charges made in said complainant's said bill…neither admit nor deny the same"* and ask to be *"dismissed with their reasonable costs…"* From the Henry E. Luhrs Collection. Accompanied by LOA from PSA/DNA.
Estimate: $800-$1,000

To the Honorable the Judge of the Circuit Court of Sangamon County in Chancery Sitting ... Term A.D. 1860

Your Orator — Amasa Booth — would most respectfully show unto your Honor, that on or about the 9th day of Nov A.D. 1858. he married one Matilda now Matilda Booth in Sangamon County and State of Illinois where both Complainant and respondent have lived since said marriage. Your Orator says that at the time of said marriage he believed and hoped that said Matilda was a chaste & virtuous woman; but it so happens that soon after said marriage your Orator started for California to make some money with which to support his said wife & himself — your Orator — and soon after the departure of the Complainant for California as aforesaid for the purposes aforesaid the said Respondent — Matilda Booth did keep a ...

Matilda Booth with having committed in the City of Springfield Sangamon County and State of Illinois adultery & fornication or one or the other since the marriage aforesaid and without the connivance or consent of your Orator —

In tender consideration whereof Your Orator prays that the bonds of matrimony — the contract of marriage — may be wholly set aside and dissolved and a divorce granted to the Complainant and for such further orders — decrees & relief as shall seem meet — just & equitable to your Honor ...

Your Orator further prays that the said Matilda Booth may be made defendant to this Bill and that the writ of subpoena may issue out of this Honorable Court ... and that she be compelled to answer this Bill, though not on oath, as it is hereby waived — and after a final hearing of this cause your Orator will ever pray —

Lincoln & Herndon
Sol for Complt.

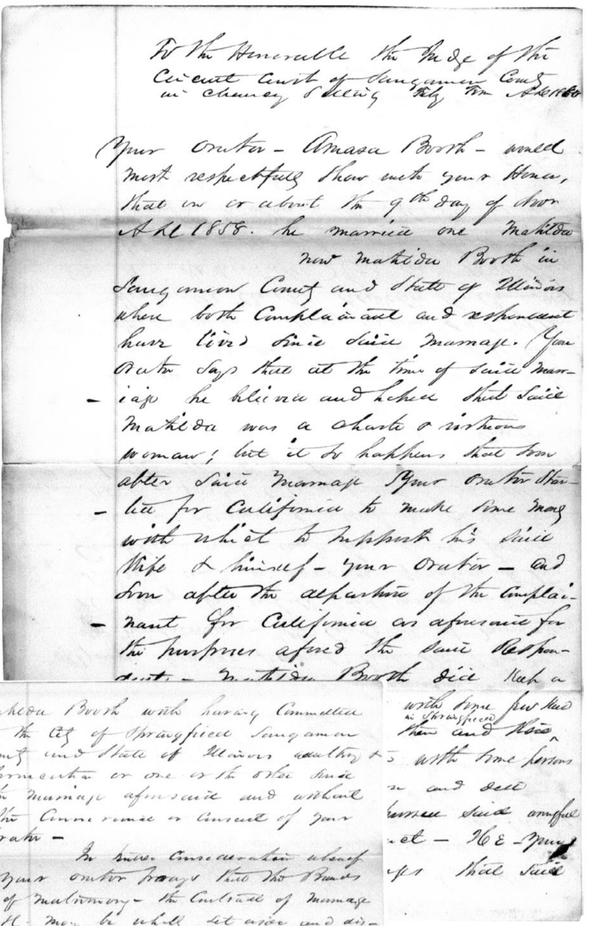

25118 Lincoln Law Partner William Henry Herndon. Autograph Document Signed *"Lincoln & Herndon Sol. For Complt."* Sangamon Co., Ill., Feb. 1860, two pages, folio. A bill for divorce in which Amasa Booth charges his wife Matilda with prostitution. Booth states that he was married in Sangamon County in November 1858, at which time he *"believed and hoped that said Matilda was a chaste & virtuous woman..."* Soon afterward he left for California to make money for their support, whereupon Matilda started keeping *"a bad house"* where she had *"illegal connection with some persons…and has continually pursued said wrongful, illegal & unchaste conduct"* committing *"adultery & fornication or one or the other…without the connivance or consent"* of her husband. $1,500-2,000 From the Henry E. Luhrs Collection. Accompanied by LOA from PSA/DNA.

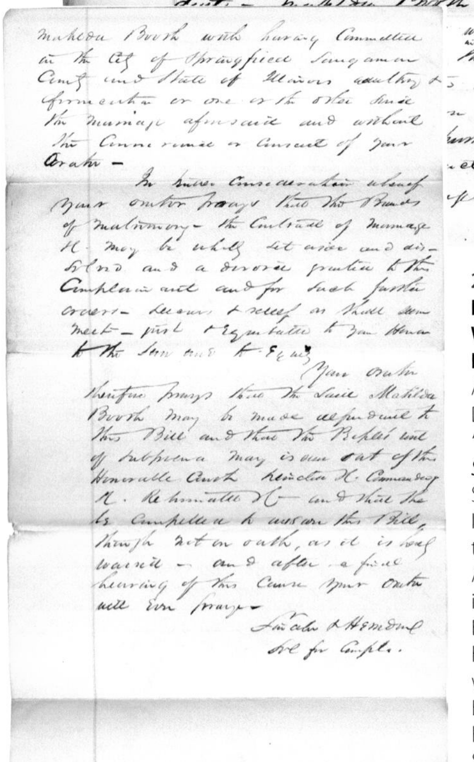

Estimate: $2,000-$2,500

To the Honorable the Judge of the Circuit Court of Sangamon County in Chancery Sitting April Term A.D. 1860

Your Oratrix — Nancy M. Clarkson — would most respectfully show unto your Honor, that on or about the 18th day of May A.D. 1853. she was married to one James J. Clarkson in ... of the State of Texas — and that she your oratrix and said James J. Clarkson, moved to Louisiana where they as husband & wife remained for about one year and from this last State your oratrix and said James as such husband & wife removed to the City of Chicago & State of Illinois and thence to the City of Springfield Sangamon County & State of Illinois where they landed aforesaid about the first day of July A.D. 1856 & have continuously from the first day & year aforesaid lived together as such lawful husband & wife — And your Oratrix would further show unto your Honor that at said City of Chicago said James Clarkson — the Respondent had illicit intercourse with various women of bad character whose names are unknown to your

... commit a rape on her: She is about 10 years of age. and could give no consent; and if she could it is all the same so far as this Bill is concerned. Said Clarkson — the Respondent — in this case was arrested — ... and was bound over to ... and appear before the next term of the Circuit Court of Sangamon County to answer said charges — Your oratrix knew anything of any or all these charges till a few days before

Nancy M. Clarkson
By Lincoln & Herndon
her Sols.

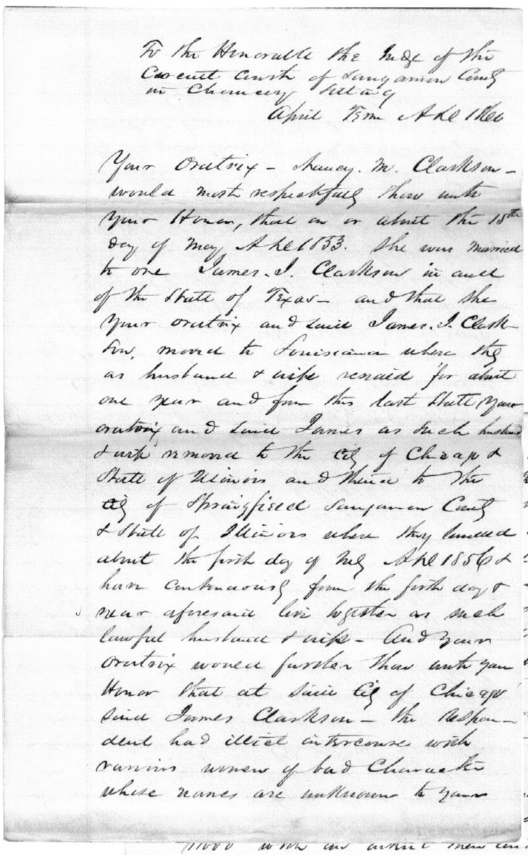

25119 Lincoln Law Partner William Henry Herndon. Autograph Document Signed *"Nancy M. Clarkson by Lincoln & Herndon her Sols".* Sangamon Co. (Ill.), April 1860, three pages, folio. A bill for divorce which, among its grounds, makes a very rare mention of attempted child-rape. Mrs. Clarkson states that she married James J. Clarkson in Texas in 1853 and that they subsequently lived in Louisiana before moving to Illinois, where they settled at Chicago and then, in July 1856, at Springfield. She avers that in Chicago her husband *"had illicit intercourse with various women of bad character"* and that in Springfield he has *"committed adultery with various bad and lewd women...Said Clarkson is a shiftless man, a man of bad habits, drinks & gambles."* Furthermore, on or about Dec. 1, 1860 (sic; presumably 1859) Clarkson *"evilly & wickedly made an assault upon a little girl named Mary Wood with an intent…to commit a rape on her. She is about 10 years of age and could give no consent; and if she could it is all the same so far as this bill is concerned…Clarkson…was arrested…and bound over to…appear before the next term of the circuit court…Clarkson gave bail and has departed to places unknown…"* From the Henry E. Luhrs Collection. Accompanied by LOA from PSA/DNA.

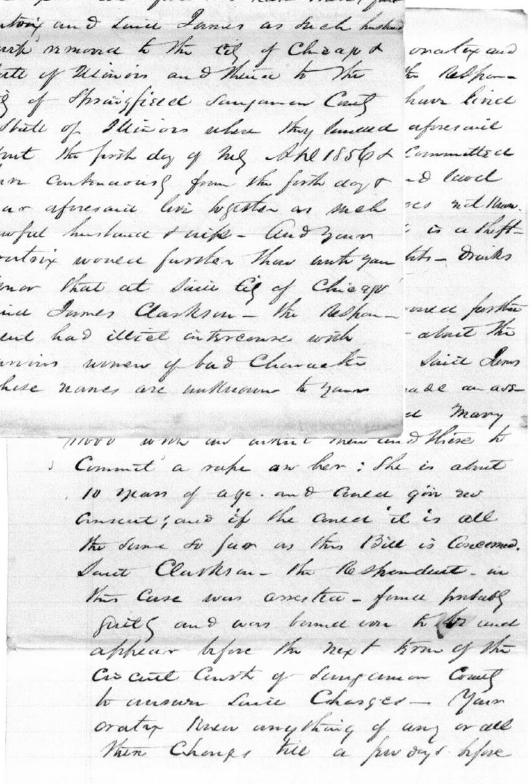

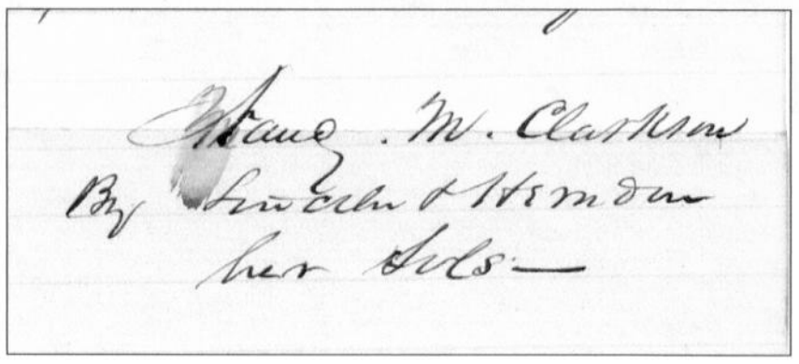

Estimate: $2,200-$2,800

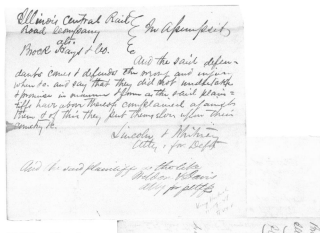

25120   Lincoln Law Partner, William Henry Herndon. Autograph Document Signed "Lincoln & Herndon / Sol for complainant". Sangamon Co. [Ill.], April 1860, three pages, folio. William Rhodes and Isabel Metcalf, executors of John M. Metcalf, seek to foreclose on a tract of land sold to Frederick Bertman, whose note for the same has remained unpaid since April 1859. From the Henry E. Luhrs Collection. Accompanied by LOA from PSA/DNA.

Estimate: $800-$1,000

25122   Lincoln Colleague, Henry Clay Whitney. Autograph Document Signed "Lincoln & Whitney Attys for Deft". No place, no date [Champaign Co., Ill., April 1857], two-thirds page, oblong octavo. In Brock, Hays & Co. vs Illinois Central Rail Road, the defendants state *"they did not undertake & promise in manner & form as the said plaintiffs havecomplained against them…"* Records show that this suit involved a shipment of hogs from Okaw, Ill. to Chicago. Because the journey took three times longer than usual, in extremely cold weather, many of the hogs died and the remainder were seriously underweight upon arrival. A jury awarded the plaintiffs $860.25 damages. On appeal to the state supreme court, Lincoln unsuccessfully contended that the damages assessed against the railroad were excessive. Corner nipped. From the Henry E. Luhrs Collection. Accompanied by LOA from PSA/DNA.

Estimate: $800-$1,000

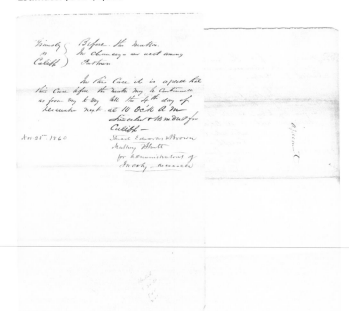

25121   Lincoln Law Partner, William Henry Herndon. Autograph Document Signed "Lincoln & Herndon for Calibb", also signed by John Todd Stuart (as "Stuart Edwards & Brownfor administrators of Jacoby, deceased"). No place (presumably Sangamon Co., Ill.), one-third page, folio,on faintly ruled paper. An agreement that the suit of Grimsley vs Calibb *"may be continued as from day to day till the 4th day of December next…".* Stuart has dated his signature Nov. 23, 1860. An uncommon association of both Lincoln's first and last law partners, and dated in the very month that he was elected President. This was doubtless one of the last cases to be attended in Lincoln's name during his Springfield residency. From the Henry E. Luhrs Collection. Accompanied by LOA from PSA/DNA.

Estimate: $1,200-$1,500

25123   Lincoln Colleague, Henry Clay Whitney. Autograph Document Signed twice "Lincoln & Whitney attys for deft." Champaign Co. [Ill.], April 1858, one and three-quarters pages, quarto, on ruled blue paper. In Cornelius Thompson and Haviland Tompkins vs Illinois Central Rail Road Co., the defendants state that upon trial they will show a release from Thompson which agreed that, in return for reduced freight on some livestock, the railroad would be released *"from any and all claims which might arise from damage or injury to said stock whilst in the cars of defendants or for delay in their carriage or for escape thereof from the cars"* Further, they *"will introduce evidence tending to prove that the stock…was the property of Stevens & Brother merchants in Chicago - alsoreceipts signed by said Stevens & Bro. for the receipt of said stock in good time & in good order at Chicago."* From the Henry E. Luhrs Collection. Accompanied by LOA from PSA/DNA.

Estimate: $600-$700

25124 Lincoln Colleague Henry Clay Whitney Autograph Document Signed.
"Lincoln p.q."
Champaign Co., Ill., October 1859, two pages, folio, on ruled paper. A declaration in Samuel A. Harvey vs Archer Campbell, written and signed by Whitney for Lincoln, his partner in the case. Harvey seeks to recover $20,000 which he claims to have advanced Campbell as of June 1859, plus $2,000 interest. Stained across central horizontal fold and along some margins. From the Henry E. Luhrs Collection. Accompanied by LOA from PSA/DNA.
Estimate: $600-$700

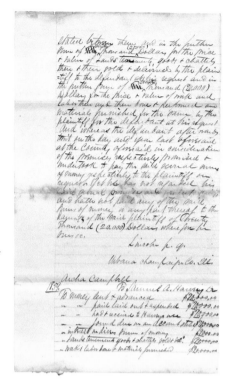

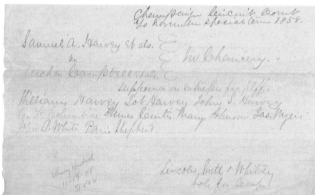

25125 Lincoln Colleague, Henry Clay Whitney.
Autograph Document Signed "Lincoln, Swett & Whitney / Sols for Comp." Champaign Co. [Ill.], November 1858, one page, oblong octavo. A request for the issuance of subpoenas in Samuel A. Harvey et al vs Archer Campbell et al. Ink quite pale in spots, but all readable. From the Henry E. Luhrs Collection. Accompanied by LOA from PSA/DNA.
Estimate: $400-$500

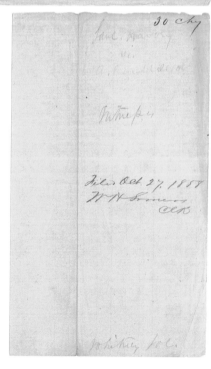

25126 Lincoln Colleague, Henry Clay Whitney. Autograph Legal Document Signed "A. Lincoln & H.C. Whitney Attorneys for Plaintiff". Champaign Co., Ill., October 1859, one-half page, folio, on lightly ruled paper. A praecipe in Samuel A. Harvey vs Archer Campbell, directing issuance of a summons to the defendant, noting that the suit involves a claim *"to the damage of said plaintiff of twenty thousand (20,000) dollars"* Some discoloration. Whitney has signed again (*"Henry C. Whitney p.q."*) at the foot of docketed filing panel on verso. From the Henry E. Luhrs Collection. Accompanied by LOA from PSA/DNA.
Estimate: $400-$500

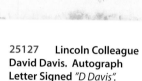

25127 Lincoln Colleague David Davis. Autograph Letter Signed *"D Davis"*.
Bloomington, Ill., July 15, 1854, to "Dear Matheny" (James H. Matheny, court clerk of Sangamon County, Ill.), one page, quarto. *"I find that I had the bill & minutes of evidence in the graveyard case. I have hastily drawn a decree… Please show it to Edwards & Herndon & Judge Logan. If not full enough they can alter it, or if anything is desired to be added by way of getting it up to Supreme Court, let it be done."* A cramped postscript notes that he has sent the Jacksonville suit papers "to Lincoln express." As judge of the 8th Illinois judicial circuit, Davis presided over a vast number of Lincoln's cases, and was directly elevated by him to the U.S. Supreme Court in 1862. A few insignificant ink blots, else excellent. From the Henry E. Luhrs Collection. Accompanied by LOA from PSA/DNA.
Estimate: $500-$600

25128 Lincoln Partly Printed Subpoena,
accomplished and signed by Schuyler County circuit court clerk Robert A. Glenn. Rushville [Ill.], Feb. 18, 1840, one page, oblong octavo. The sheriff of Sangamon County is directed to summon "Abraham Lincoln,

Benjamin Talbott, Charles Arnold, & Peter Van Bergen" to appear and give evidence in the case of Stephen T. Logan vs James Adams. A sheriff's docket on verso indicates all of the parties were served *"by reading the within Mar. 10th 1840"*. During his legal career Lincoln probably directed the issuance of hundreds of subpoenas; it is very unusual to find him on the receiving end! From the Henry E. Luhrs Collection. Accompanied by LOA from PSA/DNA.
Estimate: $400-$500

25129   Lincoln Document Signed

"Conkling & Lincoln & c for J B Moffatt" in an unknown hand. Sangamon Co. [Ill.], March 1849, about two and one-quarter pages, folio. A complicated plea in Willis H. Johnson vs John B. Moffatt and Thomas Lewis, asserting that a cross bill was unnecessary to enable the court "to render complete equity between the parties to the original bill[l]it does not introduce any new party or set up any new defence, nor present the factsin a new light.it contradicts what said Johnson has admitted in his answer to the original bill.it does not seek any affirmative

reliefBecause in the original billMoffatt did not seek any relief against Johnson, but only against Lewis because Lewis had all the assets that were not charged to the partners separately in his hands, and Johnson was a necessary defendant only in consequence of his having been a partnerJohnson was merely a nominal defendant and consequently it was entirely unnecessary for him to file a cross bill and it could not aid him in his defence. That asMoffatt sought no relief against Johnson in the original bill, said Johnson has not shewn in his cross bill that he was entitled to any relief against Moffatt, neither has he shewn that he is entitled to any affirmative relief against Lewis, other than what he could have obtained under the original bill, because he admits in his answer to the original bill that Lewis' answer to the same is true" From the Henry E. Luhrs Collection. Accompanied by LOA from PSA/DNA.

Estimate: $500-$600

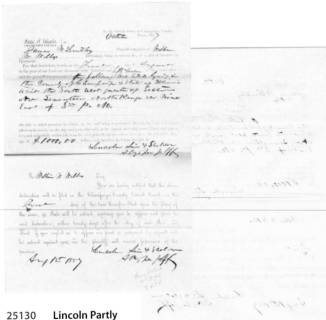

25130   Lincoln Partly Printed Document, signed

twice in an unknown hand "Lincoln, Linn & Sheldon / Attys for plff". Champaign Co., Ill., October 1857, one page, folio. James W. Lindley complains that William W. Wells "unlawfully withholds" possession of a quarter-section of land in Champaign County, to his damage of $1000. A notice at the bottom of the page advises Wells that he must "appear and plead" or suffer judgment by default "and the plaintiff will recover possession" From the Henry E. Luhrs Collection. Accompanied by LOA from PSA/DNA.

Estimate: $400-$500

25131   Lincoln Partly Printed Document, signed

twice in an unknown hand "Lincoln, Linn & Sheldon / Attys for plff". Champaign Co., Ill., October 1857, one page, folio. George Hareslan(?) complains that William Keeble "unlawfully withholds" a quarter-section of land in Champaign County, to his damage of $1000. Keeble is ordered to appear and plead or suffer judgment by default "and the plaintiff will recover possession" From the Henry E. Luhrs Collection. Accompanied by LOA from PSA/DNA.

Estimate: $400-$500

25132   Lincoln Partly Printed Document, signed

twice in an unknown hand "Lincoln, Coles, Linn & Sheldon / Attys for plff". Champaign Co., Ill., October 1857, one page, folio. William C. McReynolds complains that Luther Eades "unlawfully withholds" possession of a quarter-section of land in the county, to his damage of $1000. A notice at bottom advises Eades that he must "appear and plead" or suffer judgment by default "and the plaintiff will recover possession" Marginal separation in upper fold. From the Henry E. Luhrs Collection.

Estimate: $400-$500

25133   Lincoln Partly Printed Document, signed

twice in an unknown hand "Lincoln, Coles & Sheldon / Attys for plff". Champaign Co., Ill., October 1857, one page, folio. Joseph W. Linn Jr. complains that Charles Grubel "unlawfully withholds" possession of a quarter-section of land in the county to his damage of $1000. A notice at bottom warns Grubel to "appear and plead" or suffer judgment by default "and the plaintiff will recover possession" From the Henry E. Luhrs Collection.

Estimate: $400-$500

25134   The 1841 Abraham Lincoln Wedding Gift That Mary Todd Never Saw.

January 1, 1841, by many accounts, was to be not only the start of a new year in Springfield, Illinois, but also the start of a new marriage between a gangly, insecure, self-taught attorney and a young, highly-educated, popular Southern belle. Their names were Abraham Lincoln and Mary Todd and both had been born in Kentucky. Abraham, born to poor, illiterate farmers, had ended up in Springfield in 1837 after a succession of professions and moves; he was there practicing law and serving in the Illinois House of Representatives. Mary, born to wealthy, slave-holding parents, had moved from Lexington, Kentucky to Springfield in 1839 to live with her sister Elizabeth Edwards, quickly taking a leading position in local society. Her arrival apparently caused quite a stir among local bachelors as many courted her, including Lincoln, James Shields, and Stephen Douglas, the "little giant" of Illinois politics. She fell in love with Abraham Lincoln, though, and they were engaged in 1840. The relationship proved to be rocky; their tastes, ambitions, and backgrounds differed, causing frequent arguments. Lincoln grew increasingly despondent, fearing that they were incompatible, and that he would never be able to make her happy in marriage. With the date for the nuptials set, Lincoln set out to buy a wedding present suitable for his sophisticated young fiancÈe- something lovely and enduring.

Lincoln purchased the blue enamel, diamond-studded, 18-karat gold timepiece offered in this lot. He had it engraved "*To Miss Mary Todd from A.L. 1841*" on the inside back cover. As the impending wedding grew nearer, Lincoln grew more moody and depressed, apprehensive of the coming event. According to accounts from W. H. Hearndon, one of Lincoln's law partners, the guests and bride were present at the Edwards home on January 1, 1841, waiting; waiting for a bridegroom that would not show up. Others claim that this was only the day that Lincoln broke the engagement; no wedding was actually planned. Lincoln, in a March 1842 letter to his dear friend Joshua B. Speed, referred to this day, in part: "I am not going beyond the truth, when I tell you, that the short space it took me to read your last letter, gave me more pleasure, than the total sum of all I have enjoyed since that fatal first of Jany.'41. Since then, it seems to me, I should have been entirely happy, but for the never-absent idea, that there is one still unhappy whom I have contributed to make so. That still kills my soul. I can not but reproach myself, for even wishing to be happy while she is otherwise." Whichever is the true story, Lincoln never gave Miss Mary Todd the wedding present watch he had so thoughtfully picked out for her.

Returning to Springfield from a trip on January 14, 1841, Lincoln was at the home of William Butler where he boarded. A celebrated Kentucky beauty named Mary N.

Curtis was visiting there at the time. They had met on several previous occasions and, on this particular day, they sat in the parlor and shared a pleasant conversation. With no warning, Lincoln pulled out the watch and presented it to Miss Curtis, saying something to the effect of "Mary, I've got something for you." He went on up the stairs to his room as she sat there stunned. Mary returned to her home in Louisville the next day, probably thinking she was engaged to an up-and-coming Illinois lawyer and politician. It was some time later, when she took the watch out to wind it, that Mary Curtis noticed the engraving, then realizing that Lincoln possibly just gave her the watch to rid himself of an unpleasant memory. The timepiece was placed away in a trunk for 31 years. In the meantime, Abraham Lincoln and Mary Todd did finally marry, on November 4, 1842. The rest of that story, as they say, is history.

It was only when Mary thought herself to be dying that she passed the Lincoln watch along to a dear friend named Elizabeth DeWitt. In a letter dated June 7, 1872 that is included with this lot, Mary writes, in part: "*Do you remember the beautiful blue watch with the diamond stones our beloved President Lincoln gave me that memorable afternoon of January, 1841, with the inscription inside...Well I want you to accept it from me and keep it as a remembrance of me, when I pass to the great beyond, dear Elizabeth...*" Miss DeWitt then kept the watch for 18 years until financial difficulties forced her part with it. She found a buyer in an acquaintance named Hugh J. Grant, then mayor of New York City and a known Lincoln collector. On May 10, 1890 Miss DeWitt wrote to Mr. Grant in a letter, also included in this lot, in part: "*...It gives me great personal pleasure to feel that the watch of our great President Abraham Lincoln, shall rest in your collection...*" Another letter, also included, dated May 3, 1898, shows that the watch was, at that time, owned by John D. Simmons. The chain of ownership is unclear from that point until December 8, 1931, when an elderly woman walked into a local shop in Washington, D.C. with the watch and a few other Lincoln items. A victim of the depression, she sold it to the dealer with the proviso that her name never be revealed. A few weeks later it was purchased by art collector Mano Swartz of Baltimore, and then passed into the hands of Joseph Kruskal of New York City. In 1936 the watch was placed on display in New York City to great fanfare as part of an exhibit titled "The Life and Times of Abraham Lincoln" held to benefit the Madison Square Boys Club. The watch's interesting history was printed in the local papers including the *Times,* the *Sun,* and the *Herald Tribune* (a file of clippings is included with the lot). Some years later, in their February 16, 1946 issue, *Colliers* featured a two page story with color photos on the romantic and historical background of this fine timepiece (full issue included in lot). It passed into other collections and through a Parke-Bernet Galleries auction before finding a home in Henry Luhrs' Lincoln Library collection in

58   Session One, Auction #626 • Monday, February 20, 2006 • 5:00 p.m.

A 19.5% Buyer's Premium ($9 min.) Applies To All Lots

in 1952. The Mary Todd watch was by far the most expensive item ever purchased by Henry Luhrs for this collection, costing $1800. To put this price in perspective, George Washington Autograph Letters were, at that time, readily available in the $150-200 range.

Heritage Galleries is proud to offer this beautiful and historical example of the horological art to the general public for the first time in 50 or more years. The watch itself is in fine running condition and comes with a winding key and the original wooden box. Its overall diameter is approximately 1.5" and the watchcase is marked "Chrismann Sons & Brown", "Geneva", and "18K". The blue enameling is just a bit worn at the very edges on both sides. All but one of the diamonds are in their mounts (a few were replaced in the 1950s) and that one is present with the watch. The decorative wooden box is 6.5" x 4.5"Àx 3" and features an inlaid floral design on the top and a black velvet interior. It is rare to find a presidential relic of this age and importance with such a chain of provenance. Still, it is true, the chain goes back "only" to 1872. There is no direct, contemporary documentation, but there is no reason to presume that there should or would be. To doubt the veracity of this item, one must presume that Mary Curtis deliberately had the watch fraudulently engraved, and she would certainly seem to lack any motive to do so, inasmuch as she gave the watch away.

An extensive file accompanies the watch, including correspondence indicating that some doubters had temporarily shaken Henry Luhrs' confidence in the authenticity. However, the last letter in the file makes it clear that these doubts stemmed from an absence of proof positive, rather than because of any specific reason to doubt the watch. Indeed, the eminent dealer in Lincolniana Ralph Newman had offered, after conferring with Paul Angle of the Chicago Historical Society, to act as an agent for the sale of the watch.

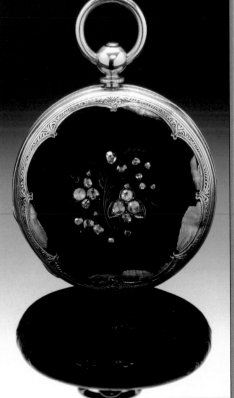

Newman dealt in Lincoln items for over sixty years, beginning when he opened a shop in Chicago on Lincoln's birthday in 1933. Carl Sandberg was an early and regular customer. As a dealer he worked with a range of Civil War material, but was best as the leading Lincoln expert of his day. The fact that, at the conclusion of a flap of controversy over the Mary Todd watch, Ralph Newman was prepared to handle its sale should be, for sophisticated collectors, more or less the final word on the subject.

While it may be impossible to prove the authenticity of this remarkable watch beyond a shadow of a doubt, the documentation is far more extensive and compelling than that accompanying most Lincoln artifacts. We are sure it will be treasured by its new owner, as is has been by several generations of owners who came before. From the Henry E. Luhrs Collection.

Estimate: $50,000 and UP

25135 **Lincoln Document in an unknown hand,** signed "Langley, Lincoln & Jones/ Defts Attys". Champaign Co. [Ill.], April 1859, one-half page, folio. In County of Champaign vs President and Trustees of the Town of West Urbana, the defendants claim they "did not undertake or promise in manner and form" as the plaintiffs allege. From the Henry E. Luhrs Collection.
Estimate: $400-$500

25136 **Abraham Lincoln, Candidate for President, Sends His Autograph.** Letter Signed "*A. Lincoln*", 1 page, 7.5" x 5.25", Springfield, August 14, 1860. To G. W. Wilson. Some mounting traces on verso, and a pencil note at bottom, but the center section containing text and bright signature is fine. Imagine: candidate Lincoln did not make a single speech in 1860. Instead he set up shop in the governor's room in the State House, greeted visitors - saying little of consequence - and, this letter reveals, signed autograpahs. In full: "*Dear Sir. Herewith I send you my autograph, which you request. Yours truly...*" From the Henry E. Luhrs Collection. Accompanied by LOA from PSA/DNA.
Estimate: $7,000-$9,000

25137   Mary Todd Lincoln's Desktop Music Box, Incorporating an Ink Well 15" in length, elaborately carved from walnut in the form of an ear of corn, the hinged lid of which opens to reveal a small music box (with original key, but not working, and two glass ink jars. "Mary Lincoln" is painted on the bottom in what is clearly old gold paint, showing light wear, but easily readable. Good overall display condition, with several minor bits of edge wear and chipping which detract minimally.

Purchased by Henry Luhrs at the legendary Oliver K. Barrett Lincoln Collection sale at Park-Bernet Galleries on Feb. 20, 1952 (lot 179. The original lot I.D sticker is still present). A unique and highly personal artifact from one of America's most famous and yet least understood First Ladies, with the provenance of one to the most famous great Lincoln collections. From the Henry E. Luhrs Collection.
Estimate: $12,000-$18,000

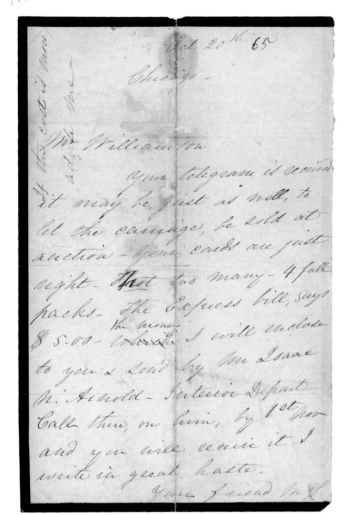

25138 **Mary Todd Lincoln Autograph Letter Signed** "M.L." One page, 4.8" x 7.4", mourning paper, Chicago, October 20, 1865. Written to Alexander Williamson, tutor at the White House. Williamson was hired by Mary Todd to tutor Willie and Tad, her sons. The letter reads in part, *"Your telegram is received. It may be just as well to let the carriage be sold at auction. Your cards are just right, not too many - 4 full packs. The Express bill says $5.00; the money I will enclose to you & send by Mr. Isaac Arnold"*

The letter is in fine condition; usual folds are present; stained along the vertical fold. From the Henry E. Luhrs Collection. Accompanied by LOA from PSA/DNA.
Estimate: $6,000-$8,000

25140 **Abraham Lincoln's Stepmother's Father's Will and Testament Mentioning Sarah Bush Johnston.**

Christopher Bush, extremely rare manuscript Document Signed with his mark, *"x"*, three pages, 7.5" x 12", Elizabethtown, Kentucky, February 24, 1812, being his last will and testament. The will reads in part: "*...calling to mind that all men must die- and being desirous to provide for my loving wife as amply as my little property will admit of and also wishing to do equal justice between my children and concurring I have already given to all my children (except Christopher & John) their full share of my estate both real & personal and being desirous to that my two sons namely Christopher & John shall be secured in my estate equal to what I have given to the rest of my children who has left me namely my son William Samuel Isaac & Elijah and my daughters Hannah Radley Rachael Smallwood and Sally Johnston...*" Sally (or Sarah) Bush Johnston (1788-1869) was then the wife Daniel Johnston, a ne'er-do-well Hardin county farmer, who died two years later in 1816. She would then marry the widower Thomas Lincoln on December 2, 1819. Nancy Hanks Lincoln, Abraham's mother, had died of "milk sickness" the previous autumn in 1818 when Abraham was only 9 years old. Lincoln later described his stepmother as "a good and kind mother" and in correspondence referred to her as "Mother." They enjoyed a superb relationship. Document witnessed and signed by Benjamin Helm who also signs the attestation of probate preformed in February 1813 when the will was executed. A remarkable and quite unique piece of Lincolniana. Provenance, King Hostick to Parke Bernet Galleries, February 6, 1962, Lot 185. We have not seen one example of Christopher Bush appear at any major auction in the past thirty years. Light toning along folds, else Very Good condition. From the Henry E. Luhrs Collection.
Estimate: $3,500-$4,500

25139 **Benjamin Lincoln Signs a Document Running a Woman Out of Town!** Document Signed ("Benjamin Lincoln, Jun."), as Selectman, 1 page, 7.5" by 8.5", Hingham, Massachusetts, July 8, 1766. Also signed by Selectmen Daniel Lincoln, Stephen Cushing and Benjamin Cushing; docketed by Obadiah Lincoln on verso. Stained at margins, worn at folds, but overall good; a pencil note in lower left corner does not effect text. In 1766, not yet the general, and far away from being the new nation's Secretary of War, Lincoln signed on to running a woman out of his home town. *"You are hereby required forthwith to warn Ruth Perrey to Depart this town Within fourteen Days or give Security to the Select Men of Hingham to Indemnify that town from any Charge that May Ever Hereafter arise by her means."* From the Henry E. Luhrs Collection. Accompanied by LOA from PSA/DNA.
Estimate: $300-$500

25141 (Mary Lincoln) Manuscript Letter in an unknown hand on United States Military Telegraph letterhead, one page, 5" x 8", [Washington], 1861 to Robert Todd Lincoln. The telegram reads in full: "*Robert Lincoln Metropolitan Hotel N.Y. I will be there Wednesday evening. Mrs. Lincoln.*" Note below in another hand reads: "*6 / Chg State Dept*" Another notation "*No 205 Rm*" This was likely sent in August 1861 when Mary and Robert, together with John Hay and Elizabeth Todd Grimsley, traveled to Long Branch, New Jersey and then

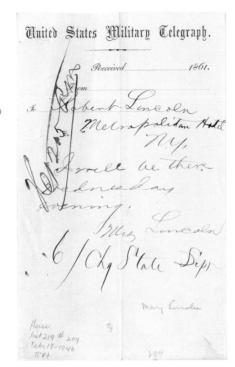

New York — returning in early September. During this trip, Mary visited Haughwont and Company and purchased "One fine Porcelain Dining Service of One Hundred and ninety pieces... decorated Royal Purple, and double gilt, with the Arms of the United States, on each piece, for the Presidential Mansion... $3,195.00." This was one of many extravagant purchases for the White House that elicited tremendous criticism in the press. Usual folds, very light soiling, else fine. A fun piece of collateral Lincolniana! From the Henry E. Luhrs Collection. Accompanied by LOA from PSA/DNA.
Estimate: $800-$1,200

25142 President Lincoln Shot by an Assassin- April 15, 1865 *New York Times.* The full eight-page edition, published between the time Lincoln was shot and his death a few hours later. The column one headlines read, in order: "AWFUL EVENT. President Lincoln Shot by an Assassin. The Deed Done at Ford's Theatre Last Night. The Act of a Desperate Rebel. The President Still Alive at Last Accounts. No Hopes Entertained of His Recovery. Attempted Assassination of Secretary Seward. Details of the Dreadful Tragedy." Four of the six columns on the front page are filled with various reports of the event, and the entire front page is printed with mourning rules (black borders between the columns). In the modern day of up-to-the-second news transmission, it's hard to imagine how hard it was to get accurate and timely reporting in 1865. This historic newspaper is in generally very good condition, unopened at the top and untrimmed at the edge, folds with weakness, one area of foxing near the masthead. Still, a great piece for display and a particularly desirable title. From the Henry E. Luhrs Collection. Accompanied by LOA from PSA/DNA.
Estimate: $600-$800

25143 Abraham Death: Assassination A War-Time Diary Mentioning & Philosophizing on Lincoln's Murder. Manuscript, in an unknown hand, accomplished mostly in pencil, clear and legible throughout, being a leather-bound book comprised of some 71 ruled pages, 4.5" by 7", St. Louis, dating from August 21 1864 to April 16, 1865. The soft cover is worn, but very good, and the manuscript, very fine. With a full typed transcription. Largely

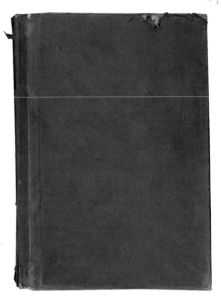

comprised of religious meditations, and catalogued by Charles Hamilton as a book of sermons, the very last entry concerns the murder, the day before, of President Lincoln. In part: "*I... mourn with my fellow mortals for my Country and for the world. Singular it seems and a wonderment to the minds of all how our dear President was taken from us, at the very moment of our rejoicing at the speedy return of Peace. Who can foresee the future. The hearts of many are hung in gloom...*" From the Henry E. Luhrs Collection. Accompanied by LOA from PSA/DNA.
Estimate: $600-$900

25144 **[Abraham Lincoln] Fascinating Collection of Documents & Day Books in the Hands of, and Relating to, the President's American Forebears!** This lot, last sold at Parke Bernet Galleries over a half century ago, is comprised of four 18th century autograph pieces, all of which are either in hands of, and/or relate to, President Lincoln's forebears in America - Mordecai Lincoln, Thomas Lincoln and Abraham Lincoln. Since Lincoln's male line used these names throughout the generations, we leave off presuming to name which Mordecai, Thomas and Abraham Lincoln are involved, and refer interested parties to such valuable works as *American Presidential Families* - an offshoot of *Burke's Peerage & Baronetag* - by Brogan and Mosley (MacMillian, 1993).

The material is, in brief, as follows: 1) Abraham Lincoln, Document Signed ("Abm: Lincoln"), as *Executor,* co-signed by one Lawrence Katekin as the same, 4 pages, recto and verso, 8.25" by 13", Reading, June 3, 1778, being "*Conditions of a Vendue holden this day of the personal Effects, late of Thomas Warren deceased, as follows, Vizt. The highest bidder to be the Buyer (and the subscribers reseive a bid On each Article Sold) ready Money to be paid for all Articles Sold; except the Tobacco and Tobacco Press for which one half thereof Three Months Credit will be given to the purchaser, giving Security if required to Abm: Lincoln* [his signature] and *Lawrence Katekin* [his signature]." There follows an inventory of items offered and prices realized, carrying the information that Abraham Lincoln himself purchased a wheelbarrow for 18 shillings. On the fourth integral leaf are further notes and figures, some dating from June 1793, as concern the aforementioned tobacco. The condition of this document is Good overall, bold and legible, albeit worn, with a piece of the last leaf - not effecting the text - missing. Accompanied by a typed transcription. 2) Document, bearing a pencil note that it is in the hand of Abraham Lincoln, entitled "*An appraisement held the 22th day of December 1791 of John Bechtols Personal Estate*", 3 pages, recto and verso, 8" by 12.5", no place, December 22, 1791. Very Good overall, albeit with a nascent tear at the right margin of the center fold. Inventories here is the late Bechtol's apparel - a fine hat, a new coat, an old coat, britches, buckles, etceteras; his livestock, farming equipment, and guns - the "*Black horse with a bald face*" brought the most, 25 pounds; and his various crops. Accompanied by a typed transcription. 3) 2 Day Books, both measuring 4" by 6", some 76 and 50 pages respectively, each held together by string; dated, ostensibly, 1757 through 1802. Although aged, dog-eared, loosely-bound and looking all the worse for wear, they are written in bold, legible hands. The cover of one reads "*Abraham Lincoln [twice] Beginning to Day at Mordecai Lincolns ye [the] 21st of third month for the year 1757*". The front cover of the companion book is seemingly non-existent, as the book begins mid-sentence, but the back page carries a final entry "*Abraham Lincoln... November 2, 1802*." Both Day Books have numerous entries regarding the business affairs of Mordecai, Thomas and Abraham Lincoln, as well as extensive medical remedies ("*Indian Cure for the Rheumatism*", "*A Cure for the Gonorrhea*" "*To Take Away Freckles*"), metallurgical formulas, and arithmetical rules and calculations. 4) Ledger, leather bound, entitled on cover "*Abraham Lincoln's Day Book January 1st, 1799*", 8" x 12.5", 88 pages, carrying business entries - what sold, and to whom - through 1807. The leather cover is in poor condition but the internal pages are Very Fine. All and all, this remarkable lot is a virtual treasure trove of Lincoln scholarship. From the Henry E. Luhrs Collection. Accompanied by LOA from PSA/DNA.
Estimate: $1,000-$2,000

25145 **[Abraham Lincoln] Joshua Fry Speed: Extremely Scarce Autograph Letter of Lincoln's Most Intimate Friend — Mentioning Lincoln! Autograph Letter** Signed "*J.F. Speed*", 1 page, 7.5" by 10", Washington, December 1, 1861. To Captain — and soon General — Charles Champion Gilbert, who has annotated the letter at bottom: "*Mr. Speed is a gentleman of this city a former law partner of the President and does a considerable private business with him. He has been using a recommendation for my promotion for some time.... It may come to pass...*"; Gilbert's son attests on the verso that the not entirely accurate memoranda is in the hand of his father. In fine condition, with two tiny, and faint, dealer's notes in the top corners; sold by Goodspeed's of Boston in 1956.

Lincoln scholars, and gossip columnists, know all about the letters which Lincoln wrote his most intimate friend, Joshua Speed: there are dozens in Basler's Collected Works. Letters from Speed to Lincoln, however, are considerably less in evidence. Yet much is still known about how Lincoln and Speed met as young men in New Salem; shared a room, and a bed, for four years; fell out, some allege, over love, and all tell, over slavery; and remained friends, despite politics, always. Perhaps an enduring sign of their lifelong intimacy may be gleaned from the fact that Speed saw Lincoln more frequently than was officially recorded - there is, at any rate, no mention in Lincoln Day by Day of the visit this letter memorializes. "*Last night I had an interview with Genl McClellan & the President separately. McClellan promised that on Monday he would make you a brigadier with orders to report to Baltimore. It may be gratifying to you to know that he spoke in high terms of you and was very willing to accede to the request of your friends in recommending your promotion to the President.*"

Gilbert did get his star — temporarily: blamed for botching Perryville, he ended the War a Major, sitting at a desk. From the Henry E. Luhrs Collection. Accompanied by LOA from PSA/DNA.
Estimate: $1,000-$1,500

25146 Senator Ira Harris, A Close Friend of Lincoln's, Sends His Autograph. Autograph Letter Signed, 1 page, 5.5" by 9", Senate Chamber, [Washington], February 18, 1865. In very fine condition, with a few words in pencil at bottom anent provenance. Lincoln collectors who have already put together a set of his Cabinet, may now wish, with this autograph, to compile a definitive set of his friends. New York Senator Ira Harris was among the President's "most frequent evening visitors", making him privy not only to the President's thinking, but his patronage — so much so, Lincoln joked, that he looked underneath his bed each night to check if Senator Harris was there, seeking another favor. One favor, extended by the Lincolns to Harris' daughter Clara and her fiancée, ended tragically: both were theatre guests of the Lincolns the night of April 14th, 1865... Harris' letter, in full: "*I have received your note requesting me to send you my autograph — I take pleasure in complying with your request — You will find the desired signature subscribed to this note...*" From the Henry E. Luhrs Collection. Accompanied by LOA from PSA/DNA.
Estimate: $150-$250

25148 Abraham Lincoln:George Harriman An Uncommon Letter of Lincoln's Acting Secretary of the Treasury Autograph Letter Signed, as *Assistant Secretary of the Treasury*, 1 page, 8" x 10", Treasury Department, [Washington], November 29, 1861. To Andrew Jamieson, Collector of the Town of Alexandria, Virginia. Mounting traces on left margin of verso, else fine. With typed transcription. Your growing collection of Lincoln's Cabinet Secretaries is going to need this uncommon autograph: Harriman served as Treasury Secretary ad interim from July 1, 1864 to July 5, 1864. In full: "*I send for your information and guidance, and as a reply to your letter of 26 Oct. Last, the enclosed Copy of a bill from this Dept. To the Coll. At Philadelphia, dated 27 Inst. As to the charge of permits to Coasting Vessels.*" Carpe Diem. From the Henry E. Luhrs Collection. Accompanied by LOA from PSA/DNA.
Estimate: $300-$400

25147 Lincoln's Secretary of War Simon Cameron Signs as a Sixteen Year old Hospital worker at Fort McHenry; along with the Forts Commanding Officer On April 12,1815 a receipt for payment for 85 days of labor at TEN CENTS PER DAY. The payment is authorized by Lt. Col. James Armistad, who a few months earlier had made the authorship of "The Star Spangled Banner" possible by keeping the flag flying over Ft. McHenry; "... by the dawn's early light..." during the British bombardment. Measures 8.0" x 7.25" and signed twice by Cameron, at the bottom and on verso. Fine appearance, with old amateur repair of fine horizontal separation along original crease line. The Fort's hospital nursed victims of the British attack, and young Cameron signed on as a temporary worker. A unique historical curiosity. From the Henry E. Luhrs Collection. Accompanied by LOA from PSA/DNA.
Estimate: $300-$400

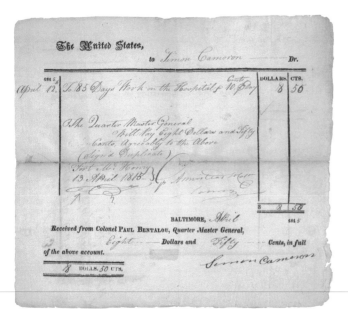

25149 [Abraham Lincoln] Edwin D. Morgan: Letter of the Lincoln Cabinet Appointee Who Wouldn't Serve Autograph Letter Signed as Governor of New York, 1 page, 5" x 8", Albany, February 27, 1861. To New York Comptroller Robert Denniston. In very fine condition, albeit with a couple of pencil dealer's notations, and minor mounting traces on verso of the docketed integral leaf.

Great collectors are nothing if not comprehensive — and so the person who collects this letter will be a great Lincoln collector indeed, for here is the autograph of a man, though appointed by the President to be Secretary of the Treasury, refused to serve. Edward Morgan, then a Senator from New York, first heard the appointment as it was being read on the Senate floor on February 13, 1865. "*I was appointed to the position once during Mr. Lincoln's administration,*" he recalled, "*without being consulted at all. It was to succeed Senator [William P.] Fessenden, and no one was more surprised than myself to hear the appointment read when it was sent to the Senate for approval. I asked them to lay the matter over until I should return, and then drove to the White House and represented to Mr. Lincoln, that for many reasons, I could not accept the position, and the appointment was withdrawn.*" This autograph letter is not about the infamous incident, but does mention Lincoln twice, and "The Treasurer", once. "*I enclose a note to the President of the United States on behalf of the application of our mutual friend, The Treasurer, which you will oblige me by handing to Mr. Lincoln as you may have opportunity upon your arrival in Washington.*" From the Henry E. Luhrs Collection. Accompanied by LOA from PSA/DNA.
Estimate: $200-$300

25150   Francis Spinner, Lincoln's Treasurer of the United States, on War-Date Free Frank. Free Frank,
being an Autograph
Address Leaf franked
as Treasurer of the
United States, 8" x 3.75", on the printed letterhead of Treasury of the
United States, stamped Washington, August 27, 1862. To Luther Haven,
Esq., at the U.S. Depository in Chicago. Some wear to surface, but Fine,
and striking, overall. Francis Spinner's Civil War appointment as Treasurer
marks a milestone in women's history: he hired female clerks, if only
because they weren't subject to military service. But he was the first
government administrator to hire women and moreover, he paid them
well and defended their employment against critics. He also served the
Johnson and Grant administrations. From the Henry E. Luhrs Collection.
Accompanied by LOA from PSA/DNA.

Estimate: $100-$200

25151   Edwin M. Stanton Autograph Letter Signed About Patronage Autograph
Letter Signed, 1 full page, 8" by
10", Washington, December 24,
1859. To the Hon. L.W. Maynard.
In very fine condition. With typed
transcription. "*Lincoln's Mars*" was
hardly the one to go about looking for, and giving away, jobs:
most of his letters are martial
in tone. But before he became
Buchanan's Attorney-General,
or Lincoln's Secretary of War, or
Johnson's, too, he was a lawyer
- and perhaps he hadn't quite per-
fected of his infamous talent for
saying "no" in the most obnoxious way possible, a trait which would, soon
enough, make him hated by virtually everyone. In this letter, he seems
to say "maybe." In part: "*I shall be very glad to see you in Washington.
Nothing new has occurred in relation to the Judgeship and there is not
any immediate prospect that there will be a vacancy 'tho it may happen
any day. When you come here we will confer fully in relation to the matter...*" From the Henry E. Luhrs Collection. Accompanied by LOA from
PSA/DNA.

Estimate: $200-$250

**25152   Executive Order By President Lincoln To The U.S. Army
To Hire Southern Slaves.** Manuscript Executive Order Certified to be
Official Copy by: *R. Williams"* as Assistant Adjutant General, 2p (front
& verso), 4.5" x 7.75". War Department, July 22, 1862. In full *"1. Ordered
that Military Commanders within the States of Virginia, South Carolina,
Georgia, Florida, Alabama, Mississippi, Louisiana, Texas, and Arkansas,
in an orderly manner seize and use any property, real or personal, which
may be necessary or convenient for their several commands, as supplies, or for other military purposes; and that, where property may be
destroyed for proper military objects, none shall be destroyed in wanton-
ess or malice.2. That Military and Naval commanders shall employ
as laborers, within and from said States so many persons of African
descent as can be advantageously used for military or naval purposes, giving them reasonable wages for their labor. 3. That, as to
both property and persons of African descent, accounts shall be kept
sufficiently accurate and in detail to show quantities and amounts,
and from whom both property and such persons shall have come as a
basis upon which compensation can be made in proper cases. And the
several Departments of this Government shall attend to and perform
their appropriate towards the execution of these orders. By order of
the President Edwin M. Stanton Secretary of War."* Born in Virginia,
Robert Williams, who signed this document certifying it to be an official Executive Order, later served as Adjutant General, respectively, of
the Departments of the Missouri and of the Platte, and of the Division
of the Missouri. He was promoted by seniority in his department to the
rank of Lieutenant Colonel in 1869, Colonel in 1881, and by brevet to
the grade of Brigadier General, United States Army "for diligent, faithful,
and meritorious services during the rebellion." In 1866, Robert Williams
married the widow of Stephen A. Douglas. Left edge of first page (right
edge of second page) is tattered from being torn out of a notebook,
affecting the final letters of some words on the second page. The final
letters of a few words at the right edge of the first page are also missing.
**It is interesting to note that while Southerners regarded their slaves
as property, this Executive Order distinguishes between "property
and persons of African descent". A remarkable document of not
only Civil War history, but American history, relating to paying
southern slaves "reasonable wages" to work for the Union Army,
as ordered by President Abraham Lincoln over five months before
his Emancipation Proclamation freed them!** From the Henry E. Luhrs
Collection. Accompanied by LOA from PSA/DNA.

Estimate: $500-$700

25153   Gideon Welles: A War-Date Letter Signed and a Post-War Autograph Letter.
Two for the price of one, but both as Secretary of the Navy, as follows: 1) Letter Signed, as Lincoln's Secretary of the Navy, 8" by 10", on Navy Department letterhead, Washington, June 22, 1864; to Naval Paymaster General George L. David at the strategically positioned Cairo, Illinois Navy Yard. Bearing a stamp on the verso of the integral 4th leaf, *"Respectfully forwarded David D. Porter Rear Admiral"* below which appears a handwritten date, "June 22, 1864." In very fine condition, albeit with a few pencil dealer notations at bottom right corner. With typed transcription. In full: *"Your letter of the 15th instant has been received. Your clerk will be allowed his actual necessary travelling expenses from Brooklyn, N.Y. [home to another Navy Yard] to Cairo."* 2) Autograph Letter Signed, as Johnson's Secretary of the Navy, 1 page, 5" by 8" inches, Hartford, February 26, 1876. To the New York publisher firm of Sheldon & Co. In fine condition, albeit a barely visible internal tear has been repaired on verso, and there are mounting traces on verso as well. With typed transcription. Here the ex-journalist and great diarist orders books: *"...The 'Memoirs of J.Q. Adams' are not yet complete, I believe, but I wish to get the volumes so far as published. If the 1st Vol is out of print I must take such as I can get."* From the Henry E. Luhrs Collection. Accompanied by LOA from PSA/DNA.
Estimate: $250-$350

25154   James Madison 1810 Officer Commission Document Signed.
One page, partly printed on vellum, 14.5" x 17.5", Washington, June 1, 1810. A handsome document with engraved vignettes by I. Draper, appointing William Lavall "A Second Lieutenant in the third Regiment of Infantry" countersigned by W[illiam] Eustis as Secretary of War. Fair condition; minor foxing, weakness and separation at folds with various areas of paper loss, one affecting the *"James Madison"* signature slightly, still an attractive item for display. From the Henry E. Luhrs Collection. Accompanied by LOA from PSA/DNA.
Estimate: $1,000-$1,500

25155   A fine James Madison Autograph Letter Signed. Written at Richmond, VA. Jan. 8, 1830. 7.50" x 9.50", very fine but for old paper tape strip along one edge on verso easily removed. To an unidentified recipient, and signed *"With cordial salutations James Madison."* The first part of the letter addresses a constitutional issue concerning the exercise of Executive Power, while the second discusses specific issues before the Virginia State Convention then in progress to revise the existing state constitution. We reproduce the entire text below. Note the statement *"... the radical caused of our difficulties has the colored population "Dear Sir Yours of Dec. 26 was duly rec.d and I should have yielded less to the causes of your delay, had my recollections furnished any particular information on the subject of it; and my present situation does not permit the measures which might aid them. It would seem that the exercise of Executive power in the cases referred to, without the intervention of the Judiciary was regarded as warranted by the L. of N. as part of the Local Law; and that the State Executives became the federal instruments by virtue of their authority over the Militia. If the term 'instructed' was used in the call on them, it is one that would not be relished now by some of them at least. Will not the debate on Robbins's case particularly the Speech of the present Ch. Justice, disclose the probable grounds on which the Federal Executives proceeded. I have not the means of consulting that source of information; but am under the impression that the cases hinged on analogous principles. Our Convention is now in the pangs of parturition. Whether the result will be an abortion or an offspring worthy of life will shortly be determined. The radical cause of our difficulties has been the coloured population which happens to lie in our geographical half of the States and to have been the great object of taxation. Comprising efforts, required by this peculiarity, have checked the projects and votes, in a very curious, and to strangers unintellible manner. The main object wit many has been to produce modification having the best chance of getting through the Convention and of not being rejected by the people: and at the same time be better than existing constitution which has real as well as unpopular deformation, that would not long be borne without very exciting attempts for a plenipotentiary revision of theirs. With cordial salutations James Madison."* This fine letter is still in the folder in which it was purchased from legendary autograph dealer King Hostick in 1956, and a pencil notation confirms it then fetched the princely sum of $75.00. From the Henry E. Luhrs Collection. Accompanied by LOA from PSA/DNA.
Estimate: $2,500-$3,000

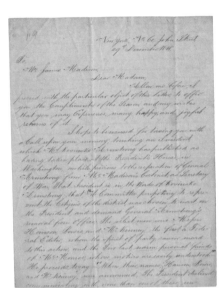

25156   Thomas L. McKenney to Dolley Madison Autograph Letter Signed, *"Tho L McKenney".* Three pages, 7.5" x 10.0", New York City, December 29, 1848. Thomas L. McKenney (1785-1858), a Georgetown merchant, was appointed Superintendent of Indian Affairs in 1816 by President James Madison. He went on to author the 3-volume "History of the Indian Tribes" and maintained a relationship with the Madison Family. This letter partially reads, *"...I hope to be excused for taxing your memory... the only Interview I ever had with Mr. Madison, upon any subject connected with General Armstrong, was on F. Street, (he being on horseback) when I was Commissioned by General Smith, in Company with Major Williams to report to the President, the state of revolt in which the Troops on Windmill Hill, were thrown, on the Appearance of General Armstrong among them, after the Conflagration of the Capitol...It is for History I ask this Information — as well as to shew before it shall have passed to the final record, the falsehood of connecting me with this 'Hanson and Bavie' Committee...".* Light soiling, one small perforation, browning on the center crease. Overall Very Good condition. A few unrelated pencil notations and brief red manuscript biography of McKenney on blank back panel. From the Henry E. Luhrs Collection. Accompanied by LOA from PSA/DNA.
Estimate: $500-$700

25157   James Madison Signature and a Dolley Madison Free Frank — A Beautiful Pair! Two pieces in excellent condition, as follows: 1) James Madison. Signature, on a slip of paper measuring 3" by 1", dark and legible; and 2) Dolley Madison, his wife, a Free Frank signed *"Free — D.P. Madison"* and stamped, in red ink, "FREE" as well, 3.5" by, at it's widest point, 1.75." It is attached to a slighter large slip measuring 4.5" by 2.5". Although Mrs. Madison possessed the franking privilege for 13 years, her franks are quite scarce. From the Henry E. Luhrs Collection. Accompanied by LOA from PSA/DNA.
Estimate: $600-$800

25158   William McKinley Signs An Official Arbor Day Proclamation as Ohio Governor. Original typed 1892 document, signed by McKinley and Ohio Secretary of State Daniel Ryan. Large, showy gold-foil paper official state seal attached. 8.0" x 12.5" and in very fine condition. (2 pp). This is a relic of the earliest days of the environmental conservation movement. McKinley designates April 29, 1892 as Arbor Day: *"Whereas, The forests of the state are rapidly disappearing to an alarming extent;*

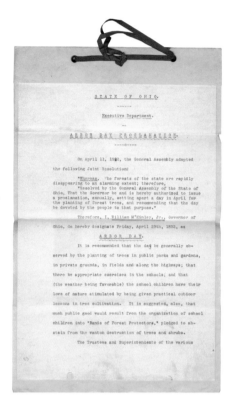

therefore, resolved by the General Assembly of the State of Ohio, That the Governor be and is hereby authorized to issue a proclamation, annually, setting apart a day in April for the planting of forest trees, and recommending that the day be devoted by the people to that purpose." Still in the original folders in which it was purchased, in 1956, from legendary autograph dealer King Hostick. A pencil notation confirms a selling price of $15.00. From the Henry E. Luhrs Collection. Accompanied by LOA from PSA/DNA.
Estimate: $500-$700

25159   William McKinley Autograph Document Signed (twice), as the attorney for the plaintiff, 3 pages, 7.75" x 12.5", Louisville, Ohio, September 3, 1872. Being a legal agreement, regarding services and payment. In Fine condition; docketed on verso. From the Henry E. Luhrs Collection. Accompanied by LOA from PSA/DNA.
Estimate: $300-$400

25160   James Monroe Autograph Letter Signed. Written at *"Richmond June 7th, 1802."* Measures 7.75" x 9.5". Two sides, plus integral exterior sheet with address and frank. Very good, due to scattered foxing. A legal communication, presumable to a fellow attorney, one Vincent Redman, Esq. Monroe represented a plaintiff who had been denied a reward of $100 for the apprehension of a fugitive, or the grounds that the claimant had in fact *"harbored the said offender."* From the Henry E. Luhrs Collection. Accompanied by LOA from PSA/DNA.

Estimate: $600-$900

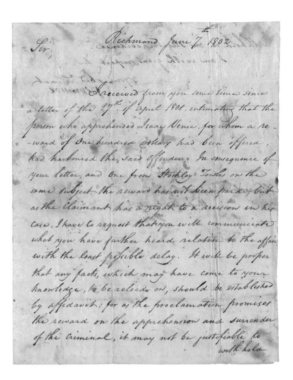

25161   Important 1814 James Monroe Letter Signed Regarding Recovery of "two valuable negro men" who have gone over to the British. Written at the "Department of State, June 21, 1814" to one Col. Wadsworth. 7.5" x 9.5". Very fine but for two old tape repairs to fine horizontal separations along the original fold lines.

Writing as Secretary of State, Monroe instructs the Colonel to assist in the recovery of two runaway slaves. *"Sir, Mr Thomas E. Grantt, in a letter to me under date of the 17th instant, represents that two valuable negro men, belonging to him, have gone off to the enemy, and solicits the favor of a flag for the purpose of endeavoring to reclaim them. If any opportunity of communicating with the British Squadron in the Patuxent should occur, and Mr. Grantt's object can be effected without inconvenience of detriment to the public service, you are requested to afford him such facilities for the recovery of his property as may be in your power. I have the honor to be, Sir, Very respectfully, your mo. ob. sev. Jas. Monroe."* Still in the original folder in which it was purchased from legendary autograph dealer King Hostick in 1956. A pencil notation confirms a selling price of $27.50. From the Henry E. Luhrs Collection. Accompanied by LOA from PSA/DNA.

Estimate: $2,500-$3,500

25162   James Monroe, John Quincy Adams and Associates. This lot contains the following items:

President James Monroe Ship *"Rolla"* Document Signed with Johh Quincy Adams countersigned as Secretary of State. One page, partly printed, 10" x 14", New York, April 3, 1818. Unfortunately this document is in poor condition with paper loss affecting both signatures. A paper conservator could make this a very displayable item though.

William H Crawford, Monroe's Secretary of War. Signed Circular. One page, partly printed, 6.75" x 9", Treasury Department, July 24, 1820. Signed as Secretary of the Treasury. Fine condition.

Richard Rush, Monroe's Attorney General, John Quincy Adams' Secretary of the Treasury. Autograph Letter Signed. Three pages, 5.25" x 8", Paris, February 5, 1848. Fine condition. From the Henry E. Luhrs Collection. Accompanied by LOA from PSA/DNA.
Estimate: $400-$500

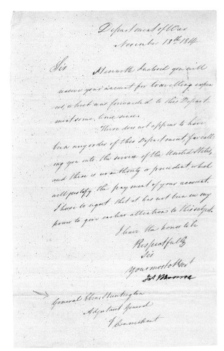

25163   James Monroe Autograph Letter Signed, as Secretary of War, *"Jas. Monroe."* 1 page, 7.5" x 12", Department of War, November 18th, 1814. To a General Ebin. Huntington, the Adjunct General of Connecticut. Explaining the War Department did not summon General Huntington to service, and refunding his traveling expenses.. From the Henry E. Luhrs Collection. Accompanied by LOA from PSA/DNA.
Estimate: $800-$1,000

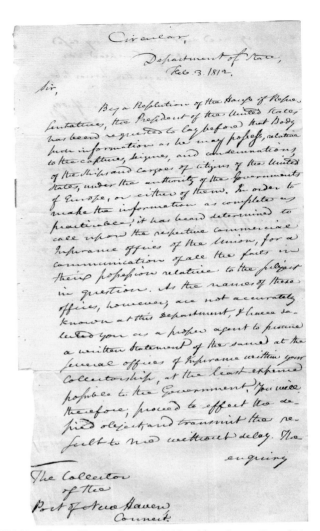

25164   James Monroe (1758-1831) President, Letter Signed *"Jas Monroe"* as Secretary of State, two pages, 7.75" x 13.25", [Washington], February 3, 1812 to The Collector of the Port of New Haven, Connecticut. A fine content letter written only months before the United States declared war on Great Britain (June 4, 1812). The war started after years of abuse by Great Britain and France toward American commercial shipping on the high seas during the Napoleonic Wars. The chief problem was the capture of neutral American ships and their cargoes. Here Madison attempts to gather data on the problem from the customs collectors: *"By a resolution of the House of Representatives, the President of the United States has been requested to lay before that Body such information as he may possess, relative to the capture, seizure, and condemnations, of the ships and cargoes of citizens of the United States, under the authority of the Governments of Europe, or either of them. In order to make the information as complete as practicable, it has been determined to call upon the respective commercial insurance offices of the Union, for a communication of all the facts in their possession relative to the subject in question. As the names of these offices, however, are not accurately known at this Department, I have selected you as a proper agent to procure several offices of Insurance within your collectorship, at the least expense to the Government..."* Although both the French and British seized American ships, it was the British who also impressed sailors into the British Navy. England also made use of forts in the North American interior to incite Indian attacks against American settlements; all of which propelled the United States to declare war on Great Britain. Marginal losses not affecting text, usual folds, else very good condition. A fine specimen with interesting content. From the Henry E. Luhrs Collection. Accompanied by LOA from PSA/DNA.
Estimate: $2,000-$3,000

25165 Historic Archive with Letter by President Franklin Pierce Ordering Arrest of an American Planning His Own Private War.

Franklin Pierce (1804-1869), Letter Signed

"*Franklin Pierce*" as President, two pages, 8" x 13.5", Washington, May 25, 1855 to Captain Charles Boarman, Commander of the Brooklyn Navy Yard ordering the Navy to pursue and capture filibusterer (a private soldier-of-fortune) Henry L. Kinney (1814-1862) then en route to Nicaragua in an attempt mount an insurrection and establish an Anglo-American colony. Kinney's plan to wage this private war would have dire consequences for the balance of power between free and slave states prior to the outbreak of the Civil War. Pierce, already upset the precarious balance between slave and free states with the Kansas-Nebraska Act in 1854, feared a reopening the question of slavery in all the western territories. He further sowed anger among anti-slavery free-soilers by proposing an invasion of Cuba — which would also become open to slavery under the rules set by the Kansas-Nebraska Act. Mercenary filibustering expeditions south of the border would likewise threaten this delicate balance. Here, Pierce orders the arrest of a man bent on establishing an American colony in Central America with an eye toward annexation to the United States. Pierce informs Captain Borman:

"*Sir: Official information has been laid before me to the effect that an indictment has been found in the District Court of the United States for the Southern District of New York, charging that one Henry L. Kinney, and one John W. Fabens, have, in violation of the Act of Congress in this behalf provided, set on foot and have prepared a military expedition against the Republic of Nicaragua, with which the United States are at peace. Further information has been received that an indictment has been found and returned to the District Court of the United States for the Eastern District of Pennsylvania, charging the said Henry L. Kinney with the like offence within that District. Information has also been received that a steamer called the United States has been chartered by the same Henry L. Kinney and John W. Fabens, together with one Fletcher Webster, for the purpose of being employed in such military expedition or enterprise, in violation of law, and is about to sail from the District of New York, to convey the said Kinney and Fabens, their followers, and associates, enlisted or engaged for said enterprise or expedition, to their destination in Nicaragua. You are therefore hereby directed and empowered, in virtue of the eighth section of the Act of Congress, approved the 20th of April, 1818, to take all proper measures, and to employ such part of the Naval force of the United States under your command as may be necessary to prevent the carrying on of such expedition or enterprise, and especially to prevent, the departure of said steamer United States from beyond the limits of the said District of New York...*"

Quite a dramatic appeal indeed! And, as incredible as this forgotten history reads, yet another expedition to Nicaragua was being led at the very same time by career filibusterer William Walker (1824-1860). That expedition originating out of San Francisco. While Walker was consolidating his control of the interior, Kinney, who had managed to board another ship and leave New York, arrived in Greytown, the capital of the British Mosquito Coast protectorate on the Caribbean coast of Nicaragua, in September 1855. Kinney then proclaimed himself Governor of the "City and Territory of Greytown". Faced with opposition from Walker, the Nicaraguans, and the British, Kinney soon lost his financial backing, resigned from office, and was expelled from the country. Interestingly, Franklin Pierce briefly recognized the Nicaraguan government under Walker's leadership. Walker had the support of Cornelius Vanderbilt who wanted to construct a railroad to link the Caribbean and the Pacific. However, once in power, Walker betrayed Vanderbilt and handed the rights to build a railroad to Vanderbilt's rivals, Cornelius K. Garrison and Charles Morgan. Vanderbilt then pressured Pierce to rescinded recognition of the Walker government, and organized an opposition force led by Costa Rica to thwart Walker's attempt to conquer all of Central America. In an attempt to garner Southern support, he legalized black slavery in Nicaragua which had been outlawed in 1824. Walker was defeated in 1857 and surrendered to the U.S. Navy. He was killed in Honduras after mounting a similar expedition there in 1860. Kinney, who also founded the city of Corpus Christi, Texas, outlived Walker but was later shot and killed in Mexico in 1862. The letter bears the usual folds, very light soiling, otherwise in fine condition.

Also included is Capt. Charles Borman's retained response to the Secretary of the Navy, in a secretarial Letter Signed, 8" x 12", "*Navy Yard*", New York, May 28, 1855, informing the secretary that "*I shall in obedience to these orders prepare the U.s. Steamer 'Vixen', the only vessel available at this Yard and place Lieut De Camp in command of her, with a sufficient force of officers, seamen & Marines to secure the arrest and detention of the vessel... the Collector of the Port... has promised to place under my orders the U.S. Revenue Cutter 'Washington' that she may act in concert with the 'Vixen'...*" Light toning, slightly weak at folds, else very good. The *United States* was detained at the 8th Street dock by the *Vixen* while the government attempted to press its claims against Kinney. Kinney managed to leave New York in June with some of his followers aboard the schooner *Emma*. The New York Times questioned Pierce's motives in an article on June 28: "*...why all this persecution of Messrs. Kinney and Fabens. Manifest destiny will march onward, sooner or later... But when the public shall learn the truth, it will be seen that the Nicaragua Transit Company [owned by Vanderbilt] have played a deeper game in preventing the sailing of the Kinney Expedition than any other set of men in the United States...*" According to another letter found in this small archive, an **Autograph Letter Signed from attorney A. Spalding** of New York, three pages, 5" x 8", New York, October 10, 1864, there was some damage to the ship *United States.* The attorney requests the letter from Pierce as evidence in a "*...Suit of John Graham then owner of the Steamship 'United States.'*" He notes that the suit is relative to the navy's "*...detaining in this Post the famous 'Kinney Expedition'.*" Partial fold separation, else very good.

A tremendous group detailing remarkable, albeit somewhat forgotten, military and political history. From the Henry E. Luhrs Collection. Accompanied by LOA from PSA/DNA.

Estimate: $7,000-$9,000

25166   Poignant Franklin Roosevelt Typed Letter Signed Regarding the Conclusion of WW I. Written on Navy Dept. letterhead (FDR was Assistant Secretary) 9 November, 1918. 8.0" x 10.25", extremely fine, but for the two original creases where folded for mailing. Apparently written in response to a letter of congratulations for winning the war. FDR writes, *"What you say is the kind of thing that hearten anybody who is doing the work for the Nation in this crisis."*

"That news of yesterday was premature, to say the least (false report of an Armistice), but by the time you get this we will know one way or the other." From the Henry E. Luhrs Collection. Accompanied by LOA from PSA/DNA.
Estimate: $400-$600

25167   No Lot

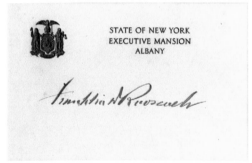

25168   Franklin D. Roosevelt "Executive Mansion - Albany" Signed Card Card Signed, *as governor*, 5" by 3.25", embossed with the gold seal of the State of New York, and reading, "State of New York, Executive Mansion," no date [circa 1931]. Mint. From the Henry E. Luhrs Collection. Accompanied by LOA from PSA/DNA.
Estimate: $150-$250

25169   Franklin D. Roosevelt Cabinet Autograph Collection consisting of the following items: John Nance Garner, Vice President (Signature on VP letterhead); James A. Farley, Postmaster (Signature on Postmaster card); Harold L. Ickes, Secretary of the Interior (Signature on Interior card). All in very fine condition. From the Henry E. Luhrs Collection. Accompanied by LOA from PSA/DNA.

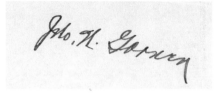

Estimate: $200-$300

25170   Franklin D. Roosevelt "Executive Mansion - Albany" Signed Cards A lot of 3 mint Cards Signed, *as governor*, 5" by 3.25", embossed with the gold seal of the State of New York, and reading, "State of New York, Executive Mansion," no date [circa 1931]. Handsome examples, highly suitable for framing. From the Henry E. Luhrs Collection. Accompanied by LOA from PSA/DNA.

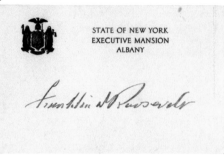

Estimate: $400-$600

25171   Franklin Roosevelt works on restoring Warm Springs

Franklin Delano Roosevelt (1882-1945) President, fine content Typed Letter Signed *"Franklin D. Roosevelt"* one page on Fidelity and Deposit company of Maryland letterhead, 7.25" x 10.5," *at Warm Springs, Georgia"*, April 7, 1927 with additional line in his hand, to R.C. Estes in Atlanta, Georgia concerning blueprints for planned buildings at Warm Springs. He writes noting that *"...I enclose check for $40.56 for the*

blue prints of the whole property. $85. for preview [illeg.] - total $125.56. I spoke to Mr. Cook about our contemplated steam plant to heat the hotel and cottages, and possibly provide power. Would you be good enough to let me know the names of two or three high-class firsts in Atlanta to inspect the lay-out and give me plans and estimates." In 1921 Roosevelt contracted polio which left his legs mostly paralyzed. Refusing to bow to the possibility of spending the balance of his days in a wheelchair, he attempted numerous therapies. In 1924 he visited a spa in Warm Springs, Georgia where he became convinced of the benefits of hydrotherapy toward his rehabilitation. In 1926 he purchased the resort and established the Roosevelt Warm Springs Institute for Rehabilitation and began the process of restoring the nineteenth century buildings into a modern medical facility. Although hydrotherapy never did restore F.D.R.'s ability to walk, he continued visiting the springs regularly for the remainder of his life. He died during his final visit to the spa on April 12, 1945. Very light soiling, else fine condition. From the Henry E. Luhrs Collection. Accompanied by LOA from PSA/DNA.
Estimate: $1,000-$1,500

25172 Franklin D. Roosevelt Typed Letter Signed in full as president. One page, 7" x 8.75", White House letterhead, Washington, January 3, 1933 [sic], to Edward Stern. Interestingly, this letter is mis-dated. Roosevelt was not yet president on the date typed on this letter but based on the included envelope's postmark, it was actually written in 1934. Apparently the typist was still in the habit of typing 1933 early in the new year (I know I do that each

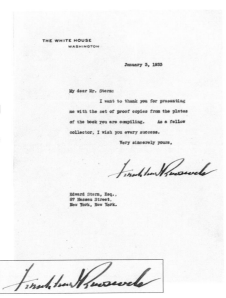

year!). Roosevelt writes, in full: "My dear Mr. Stern: I want to thank you for presenting me with the set of proof copies from the plates of the book you are compiling. As a fellow collector, I wish you every success. Very sincerely yours,". The book referred to is *History of the "Free Franking" of Mail in the United States* which was published in 1936 and this letter was reproduced on page 204 of that work. It is well known that FDR was an avid stamp collector. Very Fine condition; one mailing fold; original envelope included. From the Henry E. Luhrs Collection. Accompanied by LOA from PSA/DNA.
Estimate: $700-$900

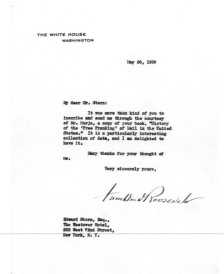

25173 Franklin D. Roosevelt Typed Letter Signed in full as president. One page, 7" x 8.75", White House letterhead, Washington, May 26, 1936, to Edward Stern. FDR thanks Stern for a copy of his newly published book *History of the "Free Franking" of Mail in the United States.* In part, "...It is a particularly interesting collection of data, and I am delighted to have it. Many thanks for your thought of me." Fine condition; one mailing fold; original envelope included. From the Henry E. Luhrs Collection. Accompanied by LOA from PSA/DNA.
Estimate: $700-$900

25174 William Howard Taft Signed Photograph. Here we have a very fine, signed photograph of the 27th president. This black and white photograph measures 9.75" x 13" and is signed on the lower edge in the white border as, *"Sincerely yours, Wm. H. Taft."* The photograph is presently framed for a full size of 11" x 15". The photograph is in very fine condition; slight yellowing has occurred on the white border — will mat out. From the Henry E. Luhrs Collection. Accompanied by LOA from PSA/DNA.
Estimate: $300-$500

25175 William Howard Taft- Two Typed Letters Signed *"Wm H Taft"*. The first, a letter of introduction: one page, 8" x 10.5", Office of the Civil Governor of the Philippine Islands letterhead, Manila, December 22, 1902, to Lord Curzon. In part, "...This will introduce to your Excellency Professor Bernard Moses of the University of California. Professor Moses is a member of a

Commission of eight persons charged with the legislative government of these Islands..." Taft served in this position in the Philippines from 1901 until 1903. Moses was a distinguished educator, a forceful public speaker, and an expert in the field of Spanish-American relations. President McKinley had appointed him to the Philippines Commission in 1900. Lord Curzon was the Viceroy on India from 1899 until 1905. Very Fine condition with mailing folds.

The second letter: one page, 8" x 10.5", Supreme Court of the United States letterhead, Pointe-au-Pic, Canada, August 12, 1926, to a Mr. George E. Thompson, in part, "...in which you offer to me, for $10, a set of 'Officers and Students of Yale College'...I don't care to purchase the set..." Fine condition; mailing folds and some crinkling at the bottom, affecting no text. From the Henry E. Luhrs Collection. Accompanied by LOA from PSA/DNA.
Estimate: $400-$500

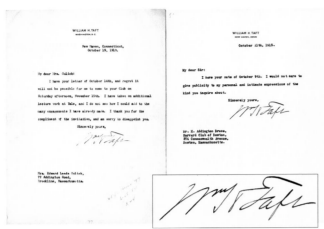

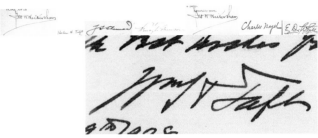

25176   William Howard Taft Document Group. This lot consists of four pieces, two typed letters signed, one autograph letter signed, and one signature on a small card. The handwritten letter measures 5" x 8", and is 3 pages long. The typed letters measure 7" x 9.3", and are both signed in dark, black ink. The typed letters are written from New Haven, Connecticut. The signature card measures 3.3" x 1.5", and is also signed in dark, black ink. The lot features a nice selection of signatures from the 27th president. Taft is still the only man to hold both the office of President and that of Chief Justice of the Supreme Court. All four documents are in Fine condition; all have the usual folds, and the ink still remains dark and crisp. From the Henry E. Luhrs Collection. Accompanied by LOA from PSA/DNA.
Estimate: $450-$650

25178   William Howard Taft and Cabinet Signatures Collection. This lot contains 19 items that are signed individually by Taft and members of his cabinet. The contents of the lot are: William Howard Taft, President (Signature); Helen Taft, First Lady (Free Frank Envelope); James S. Sherman, Vice President (Signature, TLS); Henry L. Stimson, Secretary of War (Signature, TLS); Edward Douglas White, Supreme Court Justice (Signature); George W. Wickersham, Attorney General (4x TLS); Charles Nagel, Secretary of Labor (2x Signature); George von L. Meyer, Secretary of the Navy (2x Signature); Frank H. Hitchcock, Postmaster General (Signature); Walter L. Fisher, Secretary of the Interior (2x Signature); Jacob M. Dickinson, Secretary of War (Signature, TLS).

Other notables in this lot are: Francis B. Harrison, Congressman from New York (TLS); David J. Foster, Congressman from Vermont (TLS); and Joseph G. Cannon, Congressman from Illinois and Speaker of the House (SP, ALS).

The condition of this lot is fine on average; some of the signatures are clipped, while others are cards; the TLSs have the usual folds present. From the Henry E. Luhrs Collection. Accompanied by LOA from PSA/DNA.
Estimate: $600-$800

25177   William and Helen Taft Signature Lot. This lot features three items from the First Family. One typed letter signed by Taft himself, and two signature cards, one signed by William and the other signed by Helen Taft. The typed letter measures 5.5" x 9", and is dated January 13, 1907, he signs it *"Wm. H. Taft."* It was written during Taft's term as Secretary of War. The War Department's letterhead appears at the top. The William H. Taft signature card measures 3.5" x 2.5' and is signed, *"Wm. H. Taft."* The final signature card measures 5" x 3", and reads, *'Sincerely yours-Helen H, Taft. Washington, D.C."* All three pieces are in Good condition; some soiling has occurred on the pieces, staining the white paper. The typed letter has some slight bleeding of the ink it was typed in. In all cases, the signatures are dark and legible. A nice lot! From the Henry E. Luhrs Collection. Accompanied by LOA from PSA/DNA.
Estimate: $400-$500

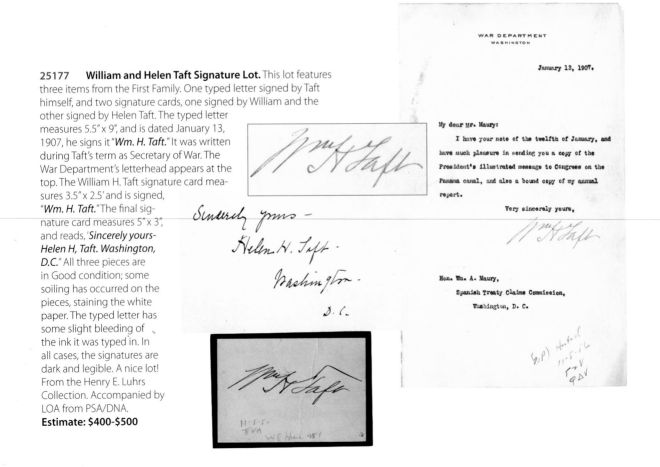

25180 Complete Zachary Taylor Cabinet Autograph Collection.
Included in this awesome grouping are approximately 25 items signed by various officials and associates from this presidency. Included are: President Zachary Taylor (Signature); Vice President (later President) Millard Fillmore (Signature); Secretary of State John M. Clayton (DS, ALS, Signature); Secretary of the Treasury William Meredith (LS); Secretary of War George Crawford (ANS, DS); Attorney General Reverdy Johnson (ALS, ANS, Signature); Postmaster General Jacob Collamer (Signature); Secretary of the Navy William Preston (LS, AES, Signature); Secretary of the Interior Thomas Ewing (ALS, Signature).

Other notables in this lot: Winfield Scott (Signature); Charles Sumner (AMsS); Truman Smith (ALS); Abbott Lawrence (Signature, ALS); R. A. Ballinger (Signature).

Conditions are generally very good to fine. A collection that might take years to assemble can be yours for one simple bid. From the Henry E. Luhrs Collection. Accompanied by LOA from PSA/DNA.
Estimate: $2,000-$3,000

25179 Zachary Taylor Rare Autograph Letter Signed as President - About West Point - to Sam Houston!
Autograph Letter Signed ("Z. Taylor"), as *president,* 2 pages, recto and verso, 8" by 10", Washington, June 30, 1850. To the founder of the Texas Republic, **Sam Houston,** then a U.S. Senator from the State of Texas, but addressed here as "General." In excellent condition. With fine steel engravings of both Taylor and Houston. Here the President discusses an appointment to West Point with Sam Houston - lately the President of a country of his own. "*I have received and duly considered your favor of the 19th inst. setting forth the claims of young Carr to a Cadets appointment, and am sorry to say in reply that it will not be possible to include him among those to be appointed 'at large' for the current year. Those appointments, as you doubtless know, are limited to ten, while the number of applicants is more than one hundred, including many sons of officers who have been killed or died in service and whose claims are certainly very strong, particularly when the intention of the law, giving those appts. to the President, is borne in mind. It would afford me pleasure to meet your wishes in the matter, could I do so consistently with my views of propriety, which I am sure you would be last to expect me to disregard.*" From the Henry E. Luhrs Collection. Accompanied by LOA from PSA/DNA.
Estimate: $4,000-$6,000

25181 Zachary Taylor, Millard Fillmore, Sam Houston, Jefferson Davis.
Signatures included in a fine autograph album. This 4to size autograph album dates from 1850 and includes the autographs of the entire Taylor cabinet, as well as most of the congressman and senators of the 31st Congress. They are neatly arranged by position and state. Included are Secretary of State John M. Clayton, Secretary of the Treasury William Meredith, Secretary of War George Crawford, Attorney General Reverdy Johnson, Postmaster General Jacob Collamer, Secretary of the Navy William Preston, Secretary of the Interior Thomas Ewing, Senators Daniel Webster, William Seward, Stephen A. Douglas, Thomas Hart Benton, David Levy Yulee, and Thomas J. Rusk. An amazing collection. From the Henry E. Luhrs Collection. Accompanied by LOA from PSA/DNA.
Estimate: $2,500-$3,500

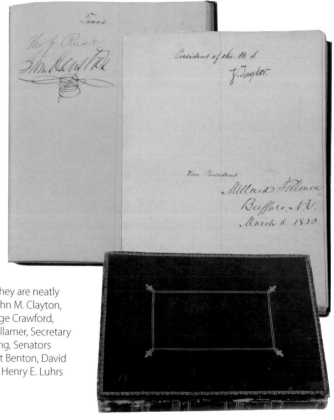

25182 Harry Truman Signed Photo. The photo is a 9" x 7" B&W press photo picturing Truman with his wife Bess and daughter Margaret, signed only by him. Included with this lot are several typed letters from Truman which contain printed and secretarial signatures. One of them is from his last days as Senator.

The photograph is in very fine condition. Accompanied by LOA from PSA/DNA.
Estimate: $200-$300

25185 Scarce Photograph Signed by Harry Truman and his Vice President, Alben Barkley. 8.0" x 9.0" black and white third generation photo, on stiff stock. Boldly signed by Truman in black ink and Barkley in blue. Very fine or better. A tough pairing on a photo. Provenance: Paul Hog, 1956. From the Henry E. Luhrs Collection. Accompanied by LOA from PSA/DNA.
Estimate: $450-$650

25186   No Lot

THE WHITE HOUSE
WASHINGTON

THE WHITE HOUSE
WASHINGTON

25183 Harry and Bess Truman White House Cards Signed individually less than a month after Truman took office upon the death of Franklin D. Roosevelt. These cards are each 4" x 2.5" and beautifully signed in black ink. Included is their original letter of transmittal dated May 7, 1945, and envelope of transmittal postmarked May 8, 1945. From the Henry E. Luhrs Collection. Accompanied by LOA from PSA/DNA.
Estimate: $600-$800

25184 Harry S. Truman Cabinet Autograph Collection. A comprehensive grouping of the various cabinet officers, senators, congressmen, military leaders, Supreme Court justices, and associates that comprised the Truman presidency. There are well over 150 autographs offered in this lot which includes signatures, signed photos, and letters. Truman had approximately 36 different cabinet members and all but two appear to be included! Just a few of the highlights are below:

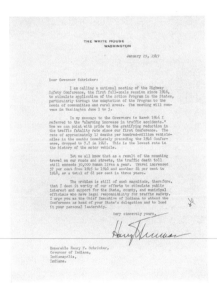

Harry Truman- Typed Letter Signed as President to the Governor of Indiana.

Vice Presidents Garner, Wallace, Barkley, and Nixon — all have signed a 1950 National Capital Sesquicentennial First Day Cover.

General Leslie Groves- Signed photo.

General & Joint Chiefs Chairman Omar Bradley- Signature.

You'll recognize many of the other names also: Bess Truman, Dean Acheson, George C. Marshall, Henry A. Wallace, and W. Averill Harriman. Generally fine or better condition. From the Henry E. Luhrs Collection. Accompanied by LOA from PSA/DNA.
Estimate: $800-$1,200

25187 Harry Truman Photograph Signed "*Harry S. Truman.*" 8" x 10" black and white photograph of the 33rd president. He signs the photograph in dark, black ink. The photograph is in Fine condition; only slight flaking of the emulsion present in the darker areas of the shot. From the Henry E. Luhrs Collection. Accompanied by LOA from PSA/DNA.
Estimate: $400-$600

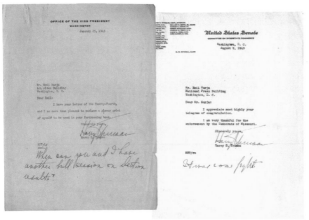

25188   Harry S. Truman (1884-1972), President, scarce Typed Letter Signed *"Harry S Truman"* as Vice President, one page, 8" x 10.5", Washington, January 25, 1945 with autograph postscript, to the earliest professional pollster, Emil Hurja, noting that he was *"...more than pleased to enclose a glossy print of myself to be used in your forthcoming book..."* Truman adds in a short autograph postscript below his signature: *"When can you and I have another bull session on election results?"* Offered together with a second **Harry S. Truman, Typed Letter Signed** *"Harry S Truman"* as Senator, one page, 8" x 10", Washington, August 9, 1940 also to Hurja thanking him for his *"...telegram of congratulation. I am very thankful for the endorsement by the Democrats of Missouri."* He adds a short postscript: *"It was some fight"*. Also together with a 8.5" x 6" telegram from Hurja to Truman, Washington, August 7, 1940 reading: *"If squeezing helps you will win."* Contrary to popular belief, it was not John Kennedy who was the first presidential candidate to extensively use popular opinion polling, nor was Louis Harris the first presidential pollster. Emil Hurja convinced the Democratic National Committee to allow him to conduct polls for Franklin D. Roosevelt's 1932 and 1936 presidential campaigns. Obviously Truman also highly valued Hurja's counsel. A great pair of letters in very good condition. Wonderful history. From the Henry E. Luhrs Collection. Accompanied by LOA from PSA/DNA

Estimate: $700-$900

25189   President Harry Truman's Final Report to the Nation Signed *"Harry Truman."* Six pages, 8" x 14", White House, Washington D.C., delivered at 10:30 Eastern, Thursday, January 15th, 1953. This mimeographed manuscript was a copy of the speech Truman gave in his last week in office. It reads in part, *"Next Tuesday, General Eisenhower will be inaugurated as President of the United States. A short time after the new President takes his oath of office, I will be on the train going back home to Independence, Missouri. I will once again be a plain, private citizen of this RepublicThe greatest part of the President's job is to make decisions-big ones and small ones, dozens of them almost every day. The papers may circulate around the Government for a while but they finally reach his desk. And then, there's no place else for them to go. The President-whoever he is-has to decide. He can't pass the buck to anybody. No one else can do the deciding for him. That's his jobI suppose that history will remember my term in office as the years when the "cold war" began to overshadow our lives. I have had hardly a day in office that has not been dominated by this all-embracing-struggle- this conflict between those who love freedom and those who would lead the world back into slavery and darkness. And always in the background there has been the atomic bomb"* This document is full of historical allusion and memories of the Truman term. A truly handsome Truman document. Accompanied by LOA from PSA/DNA

Estimate: $500-$700

25190   Harry S Truman Signed 1952 State of the Union Address Mimeographed Speech Signed: *"Harry S Truman/Best of luck to the twins!/Feb. 3, 1954"* at conclusion, 9p (front & verso), 8" x 14". The White House, January 9, 1952. Headed, in part: "HOLD FOR RELEASE/CONFIDENTIAL: The following message of the President on the State of the Union is for delivery to the Congress at 12:30 p.m., E.S.T., Wednesday, January 9, 1952, and is for automatic release at that time...." In part: *"In Korea, the forces of the United Nations turned hack the Chinese Communist invasion-and did it without widening the area of conflict. The action of the United Nations in Korea has been a powerful deterrent to a third world war. However, the situation in Korea remains very hazardous. The outcome of the armistice negotiation is still uncertain...At the present session of the United Nations in Paris, we, together with the British and the French, offered a plan to reduce and control all armaments under a foolproof inspection system. This is a concrete, practical proposal for disarmament. But what happened ? Vishinsky laughed at it. Listen to what he said: 'I could hardly sleep at all last night .... I could not sleep because I kept laughing.' The world will be a long time forgetting the spectacle of that fellow laughing at disarmament. Disarmament is not a joke. Vishinsky's laughter met with shock and anger from people all over the world. And, as a result, Mr. Stalin's representative received orders to stop laughing and start talking...The thing that is uppermost in the minds of all of us is the situation in Korea. We must—and we will—keep up the fight there until we get the kind of armistice that will put an end to the aggression and protect the safety of our forces and the security of the Republic of Korea. Beyond that, we shall continue to work for a settlement in Korea that upholds the principles of the United Nations. We went into Korea because we knew that Communist aggression had to be met firmly if freedom was to be preserved in the world. We went into the fight to save the Republic of Korea, a free country, established under the United Nations. These are our aims. We will not give up until we attain them. Meanwhile, we must continue to strengthen the forces of freedom throughout the world. I hope the Senate will take early and favorable action on the Japanese peace treaty, on our security pacts with the Pacific countries, and on the agreement to bring Greece and Turkey into the North Atlantic Treaty. We are also negotiating an agreement with the German Federal Republic under which it can play an honorable and equal part among nations and take its place in the defense of Western Europe...I am glad to hear that home rule for the District of Columbia will be the first item of business before the Senate. I hope that it, as well as statehood for Hawaii and Alaska, will be adopted promptly...In all we do, we should remember who we are and what we stand for. We are Americans. Our forefathers had far greater obstacles than we have, and much poorer chances of success. They did not lose heart, or turn aside from their goals. In that darkest of all winters in American history, at Valley Forge, George Washington said: 'We must not, in so great a contest, expect to meet with nothing but sunshine.' With that spirit they won their fight for freedom. We must have that same faith and vision...."* Stapled at top left corner. Folds, else in fine condition. From the Henry E. Luhrs Collection. Accompanied by LOA from PSA/DNA.

Estimate: $500-$800

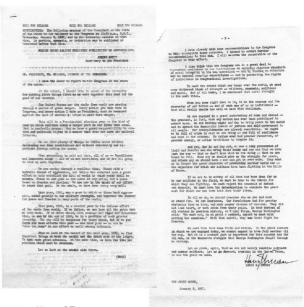

25191   Harry S Truman Signed
1953 State of the Union Address Mimeographed Speech Signed: *"Harry S Truman"* at conclusion, 16p (front & verso), 8" x 14". The White House., January 7, 1953. Headed, in part: "HOLD FOR RELEASE/CONFIDENTIAL: The President's Srate of the Union Message is for automatic release at 12:15 p.m., E.S.T., Wednesday, January 7, 1953...." In part: *"This is the eighth such report that, as President, I have been privileged to present to you and to the country. On previous occasions, it has been my custom to set forth proposals for legislative action in the coming year. But that is not my purpose today. The presentation of a legislative program falls properly to my successor, not to me, and I would not infringe upon his responsibility to chart the forward course. Instead, I wish to speak of the course we have been following the past eight years and the position at which we have arrived. In just two weeks, General Eisenhower will be inaugurated as President of the United States and I will resume—most gladly—my 'place as a private citizen of this Republic. The Presidency last changed hands eight years ago this coming April. That was a tragic time: a time of grieving for President Roosevelt—the great and gallant human being who had been taken from us; a time of unrelieved anxiety to his successor, thrust so suddenly into the complexities and burdens of the Presidential office. Not so this time. This time we see the normal transition under our democratic system. One President, at the conclusion of his term, steps back to private life; his successor, chosen by the people, begins his tenure of the office. And the Presidency of the United States continues to function without a moment's break...I took the oath of office on April 12, 1945. In May of that same year, the Nazis surrendered. Then, in July, that great white flash of light, man-made at Alamogordo, heralded swift and final victory in World War II—and opened the doorway to the atomic age. Consider some of the great questions that were posed for us by sudden, total victory in World War II. Consider also, how well we as a Nation have responded. Would the American economy collapse, after the war? That was one question. Would there be another depression here—a repetition of 1921 or 1929? The free world feared and dreaded it. The communists hoped for it and built their policies upon that hope. We answered that question—answered it with a resounding "no."...For our part, we in this Republic were—and are—free men, heirs of the American Revolution, dedicated to the truths of our Declaration of Independence: '... That all men are created equal, that they are endowed by their Creator with certain unalienable rights...That to secure these rights, governments are instituted among men, deriving their just powers from the consent of the governed.' Our post-war objective has been in keeping with this great idea...The world is divided, not through our fault or failure, but by Soviet design. They, not we, began the cold war. And because the free world saw this happen—because men know we made the effort and the Soviet rulers spurned it—the free nations have accepted leadership from our Republic, in meeting and mastering the Soviet offensive...Now we turn to the inaugural of our new President. And in the great work he is called upon to do he will have need for the support of a united people, a confident people, with firm faith in one another and in our common cause. I pledge him my support as a citizen of our Republic, and I ask you to give him yours. To him, to you, to all my fellow citizens, I say, Godspeed. May God bless our country and our cause."* Stapled at top left corner. Folds, else in fine condition. From the Henry E. Luhrs Collection. Accompanied by LOA from PSA/DNA.
Estimate: $500-$800

25192   Harry S Truman
Signed 1952 State of the Union
Address Mimeographed Speech Signed: *"Harry S Truman"* at conclusion, 9p (front & verso), 8" x 14". The White House, January 9, 1952. Headed, in part: "HOLD FOR RELEASE/CONFIDENTIAL: The following message of the President on the State of the Union is for delivery to the Congress at 12:30 p.m., E.S.T., Wednesday, January 9, 1952, and is for automatic release at that time...." In part: *"In Korea, the forces of the United Nations turned hack the Chinese Communist invasion-and did it without widening the area of conflict. The action of the United Nations in Korea has been a powerful deterrent to a third world war. However, the situation in Korea remains very hazardous. The outcome of the armistice negotiation is still uncertain...At the present session of the United Nations in Paris, we, together with the British and the French, offered a plan to reduce and control all armaments under a foolproof inspection system. This is a concrete, practical proposal for disarmament. But what happened ? Vishinsky laughed at it. Listen to what he said: 'I could hardly sleep at all last night .... I could not sleep because I kept laughing.' The world will be a long time forgetting the spectacle of that fellow laughing at disarmament. Disarmament is not a joke. Vishinsky's laughter met with shock and anger from people all over the world. And, as a result, Mr. Stalin's representative received orders to stop laughing and start talking...The thing that is uppermost in the minds of all of us is the situation in Korea. We must—and we will—keep up the fight there until we get the kind of armistice that will put an end to the aggression and protect the safety of our forces and the security of the Republic of Korea. Beyond that, we shall continue to work for a settlement in Korea that upholds the principles of the United Nations. We went into Korea because we knew that Communist aggression had to be met firmly if freedom was to be preserved in the world. We went into the fight to save the Republic of Korea, a free country, established under the United Nations. These are our aims. We will not give up until we attain them. Meanwhile, we must continue to strengthen the forces of freedom throughout the world. I hope the Senate will take early and favorable action on the Japanese peace treaty, on our security pacts with the Pacific countries, and on the agreement to bring Greece and Turkey into the North Atlantic Treaty. We are also negotiating an agreement with the German Federal Republic under which it can play an honorable and equal part among nations and take its place in the defense of Western Europe...I am glad to hear that home rule for the District of Columbia will be the first item of business before the Senate. I hope that it, as well as statehood for Hawaii and Alaska, will be adopted promptly...In all we do, we should remember who we are and what we stand for. We are Americans. Our forefathers had far greater obstacles than we have, and much poorer chances of success. They did not lose heart, or turn aside from their goals. In that darkest of all winters in American history, at Valley Forge, George Washington said: 'We must not, in so great a contest, expect to meet with nothing but sunshine.' With that spirit they won their fight for freedom. We must have that same faith and vision...."* Stapled at top left corner. Folds, else in fine condition. From the Henry E. Luhrs Collection. Accompanied by LOA from PSA/DNA.
Estimate: $500-$800

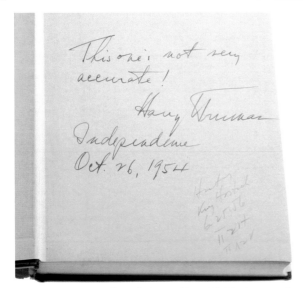

25193 Harry Truman Signed Biographies with His Autograph.
Two books in this lot. *Harry Truman: A Political Biography* by William P. Helm (New York: Duell, Sloan and Pearce, 1947), first edition, vii, 241 pages, black boards with red titles, 8vo (6" x 8.75"), dust jacket, signed on the front free endpaper "*This is not very accurate! Harry Truman Independence Oct. 26, 1954*". Book in very good condition, scuffed at the top edge, corners bumped. The dust jacket has multiple rips and tears.

Harry Truman President A Realistic Appraisal of His Administration by Frank McNaughton and Walter Hehmeyer (New York and Toronto: Whittlesey House, McGraw-Hill Book Company, Inc., 1948), first edition, 294 pages, tan cloth boards, 8vo (5.75" x 8.25"), dust jacket, signed on the front free endpaper "*This one is better than Bill Helm's HST Independence Oct. 26, 1954*" and on the frontispiece photo "*Harry Truman*". Book is in very good condition, spine and back cover soiled where dust jacket is ripped, corners bumped. Dust jacket is in poor condition with a portion missing. From the Henry E. Luhrs Collection. Accompanied by LOA from PSA/DNA.
Estimate: $700-$900

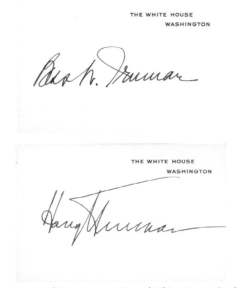

THE WHITE HOUSE
WASHINGTON

THE WHITE HOUSE
WASHINGTON

25194 Harry and Bess Truman Signed White House Cards. An absolutely pristine set of two White House cards, 4" x 2.5", each individually signed in black ink. Both include their original letters and envelopes of transmittal, President Truman's signature dates from 1949 and the First Lady's dates from 1951. From the Henry E. Luhrs Collection. Accompanied by LOA from PSA/DNA.
Estimate: $500-$700

25195 Harry Truman Signed Photo and Typed Letter Signed as President. The first item in this lot is a superb 9.5" x 13.25" B&W Harris & Ewing portrait of Truman signed by him in the lower wide margin "*Kindest Regards Harry Truman*". Fine condition with some creasing and minor tears in the margins, none affecting the signature area.

The second item is a Typed Letter Signed. One page, 7" x 9", White House letterhead, Washington, March 1, 1952, sending an Indiana couple (former Missourians) best wishes on their golden anniversary. Extra fine condition. From the Henry E. Luhrs Collection. Accompanied by LOA from PSA/DNA.
Estimate: $400-$600

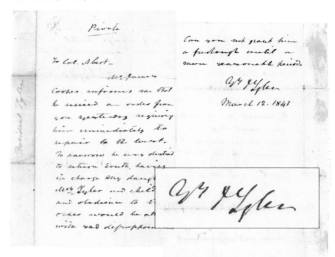

25196 John Tyler (1790-1862) President, Autograph Letter Signed "*John Tyler*" as President, two pages, 4.5" x 7.5", no place given, March 12, 1843, to Colonel J. J. Abert of the Topographical Engineer Corps. marked "*Private*" He writes: "*Mr. James Cooper informs me that he received an order from you yesterday requiring him immediately to repair to the West. To morrow he was destined to return South, having in charge my daughter Mrs. Tyler and children and obedience to the order would be attended with sad disappointment. Can you not grant him a furlough until a more reasonable period.*" Mrs. Tyler was Mrs. Priscilla Cooper Tyler, his son robert's wife who, at the time, had two daughters, and acted as White House hostess in the absence of the First Lady. Overall quite bright and clean save for very light soiling to a portion of the docket page still affixed. From the Henry E. Luhrs Collection. Accompanied by LOA from PSA/DNA.
Estimate: $800-$1,200

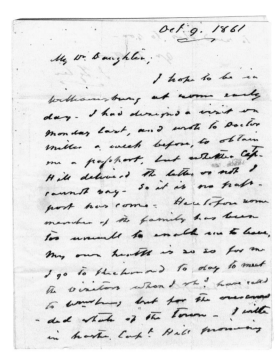

Oct. 9. 1861

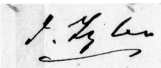

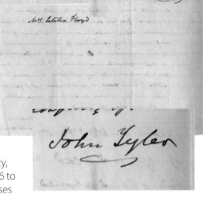

25197   John Tyler (1790-1862) President, Autograph Letter Signed, "*J. Tyler*", two pages with integral address leaf addressed in his hand, 6.5" x 8", [no place given], October 9, 1861 to his daughter Letitia Semple. "*I hope to be in Williamsburg at some early day - I had designed a visit on Monday last, and wrote to Doctor Miller a week before, to obtain me a passport, but whether Capt. Hill delivered the letter or not I cannot say - So it is no passport has come - Heretofore some member of the family has been too unwell to enable me to leave. My own health is so so for me I go to Richmond to day to meet the visitors whom I sh[oul]d have call'd to W[illia]msburg but for the over crowded state of the town - I write in haste. Capt. hill promising to send this to you.*" Tyler presided over the secret peace conference that ran February 4th through the 27th, 1861 in Washington. The recommendations made by the conference were rejected by Congress. Tyler then devoted the short remainder of his life to the development of the Confederate States of America sitting in the provisional Congress in August and elected to the Confederate Congress on November 7, 1861. He died before he could take his seat. Few people appreciate an interesting bit of trivia: John Tyler was the ONLY U.S. President whose death was not officially recognized by the Federal Government. It would not be until the Administration of Woodrow Wilson that an official acknowledgement and directive of mourning was issued... fifty years after the fact! Usual folds, a few minor tones spots, archival tape repair to seal tear on address leaf, else very good condition on bright, white paper. From the Henry E. Luhrs Collection. Accompanied by LOA from PSA/DNA.
Estimate: $1,000-$1,500

25198   John Tyler (1790-1862) President, Autograph Letter Signed "*John Tyler*" two pages with integral address leaf addressed in his hand, and bearing his franking signature "*J. Tyler*", 8" x 10", Sherwood Forrest, Charles City County, [Virginia], October 20, 1846 to Mrs. Letitia Floyd. It discusses a professorial post at the College of William and Mary and gives the news of the birth of his son, David Gardiner Tyler (1846-1894). He writes in part: "*...in the case of Mr. Holmes I should have interposed all the good offices in my power, for his won merit's sake - and I shall without delay, make known to the Rector of Wm and Mary, my conviction of the judiciousness of his appointment to a suitable professorship in that venerable institution- I believed the present arrangements are altogether temporary, and altho I have ceased to be a Visitor, yet I feign hope that my wishes may have some little influence over the board...*" Tyler had been educated at William and Mary, and later, in 1859, served as its chancellor. Tyler continues by mentioning the birth of his son by his second wife, Julia Gardiner Tyler: "*...She has recently presented me a glorious boy, who renews my youth, and constitutes with her a precious link to the chain of existence.*" Loss from seal tear on address leaf not affecting text, usual folds, else very good. Young David would later serve in the Confederate Army as a private in the Rockbridge Artillery, First Virginia Battalion, Army of Northern Virginia. He also served in Congress representing Virginia. A warm, family letter. From the Henry E. Luhrs Collection. Accompanied by LOA from PSA/DNA.
Estimate: $800-$1,000

25199   John Tyler and Key Administration Figures Autograph Collection. This lot contains a fabulous grouping of more than 30 auto-

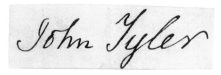

graphs — including signed items from 15 of Tyler's 19 different cabinet members. It could take years to assemble a collection of this size and depth on the Tyler presidency. Here you can own it with just one winning bid. A sampling of the autographs included in the lot (lot in generally fine condition):

John Tyler. President. Bold Signature.

Willie P. Mangum. President Pro Tempore of the U.S. Senate. Since Tyler did not have a vice president, Mangum was next in the line of succession! ALS, Signature.

Abel P. Upshur. Secretary of State, Navy. Signature (2), Free Frank, LS, ALS.

William Wilkins. Secretary of War. LS (2), ALS.

Hugh S. LegarÈ. Attorney General. ADS, Signature.

John C. Calhoun. Secretary of State. Signature.

George M. Bibb. Secretary of the Treasury. LS.

John J. Crittenden. Attorney General. Signature. From the Henry E. Luhrs Collection. Accompanied by LOA from PSA/DNA.
Estimate: $800-$1,000

25200   John Tyler Autograph Letter Signed
"*John Tyler.*" A letter written and signed by John Tyler, one page, 7.6" x 9.9", Gloucester County, Virginia, August 20, 1836. The content is of incredible interest as it has to do with the issue of slavery. It reads, "*My Dear Sir; Will you do me the favor with as little delay as possible to have copied and forward me, the resolutions offered by myself to the Senate last winter, on the subject of abolishing slavery in the District- A loose sheet of journal would be better than a copy. Your compliance will much oblige.*"

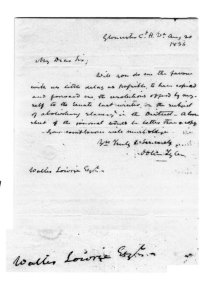

Tyler is writing to Mr. Walter Lowrie Esquire, Secretary of the Senate. This letter was written before Tyler assumed the Vice Presidency and Presidency. Before his role in these two positions Tyler served as a United States Senator for the state of Virginia. Tyler was pro-slavery throughout his political career, and often opposed motions to abolish it in certain districts of the United States.

"His Accidency" as political opponents called him was one of the first presidents to go against his party's ideas and make decisions based on his own logic and merit. For this he earns the distinction of being the only president to leave office "without a party." He even named his home Sherwood Forest, considering himself somewhat of a political outlaw!

The letter is in fine condition, with small areas of ink smudging in the body of the letter, dark smoke stains on the upper edge, and the expected fold lines. The letter comes complete with a typed transcript of the document. Now your collection can be complete with "Tyler too!" From the Henry E. Luhrs Collection. Accompanied by LOA from PSA/DNA.
Estimate: $1,500-$2,000

25201   A Teetotaling Tyler needs more whiskey!

John Tyler (1790-1862), President, Autograph Letter Signed "*John Tyler*" two pages, 7.75" x 9.75", Sherwood Forest, Ch[arle]s City C[our]t House, February 9, 1858, to Colonel Ware. He writes in part: "*I am about to ask a favour of you the granting of which will I trust, give you but slight trouble. I obtained in 1844 through your friendly agency, two barrels of Whiskey of Lt. Richardson. It is due to truth to say that all my visitors from that time to this have drank and sung its praises, and it has been so great a favorite, that it has shared the fate of most other favorites and has been almost all consumed by kindness. The last carton is all that now remains of it. Now my Dr. Sir I wish not only to replenish my stock but to procure a supply for an esteemed friend and neighbour, and should therefore like to get 4 barrels of it. Can you do this for me. It was and is called Richardson's Old whiskey and I should like it to be the same veritable stuff... Perhaps the stock is nearly run out, if so I should be glad to receive two barrels or even one. I am like yourself a de facto temperance man never drinking spirituous liquors myself, but my numerous visitors would scarcely agree to be placed upon the same list...*" Neatly tipped along the left margin to larger sheet bearing a bust engraving of Tyler, else fine. From the Henry E. Luhrs Collection. Accompanied by LOA from PSA/DNA.
Estimate: $800-$1,200

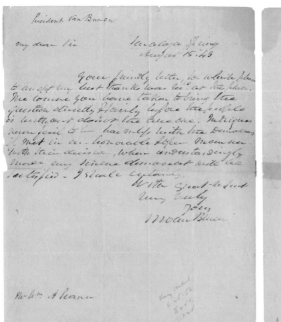

25202 **Martin Van Buren Autograph Letter Signed, with Political Philosophy Content.** Written at *"Saratoga Springs, August 15, '43."* Beige letter paper, measuring 7.5" x 9.75". Very fine save for trivial chips along left edge.

"Saratoga Springs August 15, 1843 My dear Sir Your friendly letter, for which please to accept my best thanks was recd. At this place. The course you have taken to bring the question directly and fairly before the people is without doubt the true one. Intrigues never fail to be harmless with the Democracy if met in an honorable and open manner. With their decision, when understandingly made ever sincere democrat will be satisfied — I shall certainly. With great respect Very truly Yours M. Van Buren." Provenance: King Hostick, 1956. From the Henry E. Luhrs Collection. Accompanied by LOA from PSA/DNA.
Estimate: $800-$1,000

25205 **Martin Van Buren Free Frank and Signature.** Two items. First, a very desirable envelope (cut open with wax seal still intact) signed in the upper right *"Free M Van Buren"*. It is addressed to a Mr. Bancroft in Boston and postmarked January 8, Washington City, D.C. On the verso of the address panel, Van Buren has written *"With the Presidents Kind regards"*. The second item is a clipped signature, 3.5" x 1", signed *"M Van Buren"*, lightly mounted into a presentation folder. Both are in very good condition; the free frank has several very tiny pinholes at the top, two of which affect the signature, noted for accuracy. From the Henry E. Luhrs Collection. Accompanied by LOA from PSA/DNA.
Estimate: $400-$600

25203 **Martin Van Buren and Cabinet Autograph Collection** consisting of a complete group of his cabinet members, short only Benjamin Butler. Most others are represented by multiple items. A few other important statesmen of the day are added in to this lot of at least 20 items. Autographs include: Martin Van Buren (clipped Signature); Richard M. Johnson (ALS); John M. Niles (DS); James K. Paulding (ALS); Levi Woodbury (LS). A great lot for the serious collector or the dealer. Generally fine condition. From the Henry E. Luhrs Collection. Accompanied by LOA from PSA/DNA.
Estimate: $1,000-$1,200

25204 No Lot

25206   **General George Washington Wishes To Settle all Army Accounts With the States Before the Army is Disbanded**

Manuscript LS: *"G. Washington"*, 3p, 8" x 11.75". The third page, 7" x 8.75", has been expertly attached to an 8" x 11.75" sheet, attaching it to the first two pages. [Head Quarters, April 14, 1783]. In full: *"Sir: Previous to the disbanding the Army - an event which it is to be wished, may take place with as much ease & satisfaction as circumstances will admit - Congress have directed that a compleat settlement and liq-uidation of all their Accounts shall be made; To effect this, the Pay*

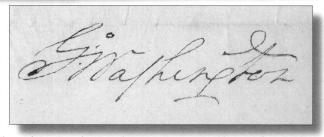

Master Genl. is arrived with full Instructions to enter immediately upon the settlement, and to compleat it as soon as possible; In performing this Duty, he informs me that recourse must be had to the several States, for their Accounts (if they have any) against their respective Lines; - this requisition probably may have been, or will be, made by Mr. Morris; but as I consider it of the utmost importance both for the ease and quiet of the Army, as well as in point of Oeconomy to the Public, that this business should be effected with all the dispatch that it is possible to give it, I have procured from the Pay Master Genl. the enclosed minutes of what he judges necessary to obtain from the States, as part of the ground of his settlement; which I take the liberty to transmit to your Excellency, with my most earnest request, that you will be pleased to give directions that the earliest attention may be given to forward, without the least delay, to Mr. Peirce, the Pay Master Genl., whatever information, accounts or papers, shall on examination of his Minutes, be found necessary; together with any other papers or documents which may be thought proper from your State to effect the settlement proposed. I have taken this liberty the rather, as it is judged, that, on a supposition of the utmost dispatch in the States, the greatest delay in compleating this very important settlement, will most probably arise from the time necessary to obtain their Accounts. I have the honor to be Your excellency's Most Obedient Servant." Copies of this letter, each signed by General Washington, were sent to the states of Connecticut, Massachusetts, New Hampshire, New Jersey, New York, and Rhode Island. Each was accompanied by minutes from the Paymaster General, estimating what was needed from each state, the purpose of which was to enable him to establish a uniform basis for paying off the Army. The minutes sent by the Paymaster General is not present. Accompanied by a 1946 letter from Gordon T. Banks of Goodspeed's Book Shop in Boston in which he states: "It is our impression that this is the copy that was sent to Rhode Island, although we have no tangible evidence." Dark bold signature of Washington. Small hole between lines on third page, slight soiling. Overall, in fine condition. From the Henry E. Luhrs Collection. Accompanied by LOA from PSA/DNA.

Estimate: $60,000-$80,000

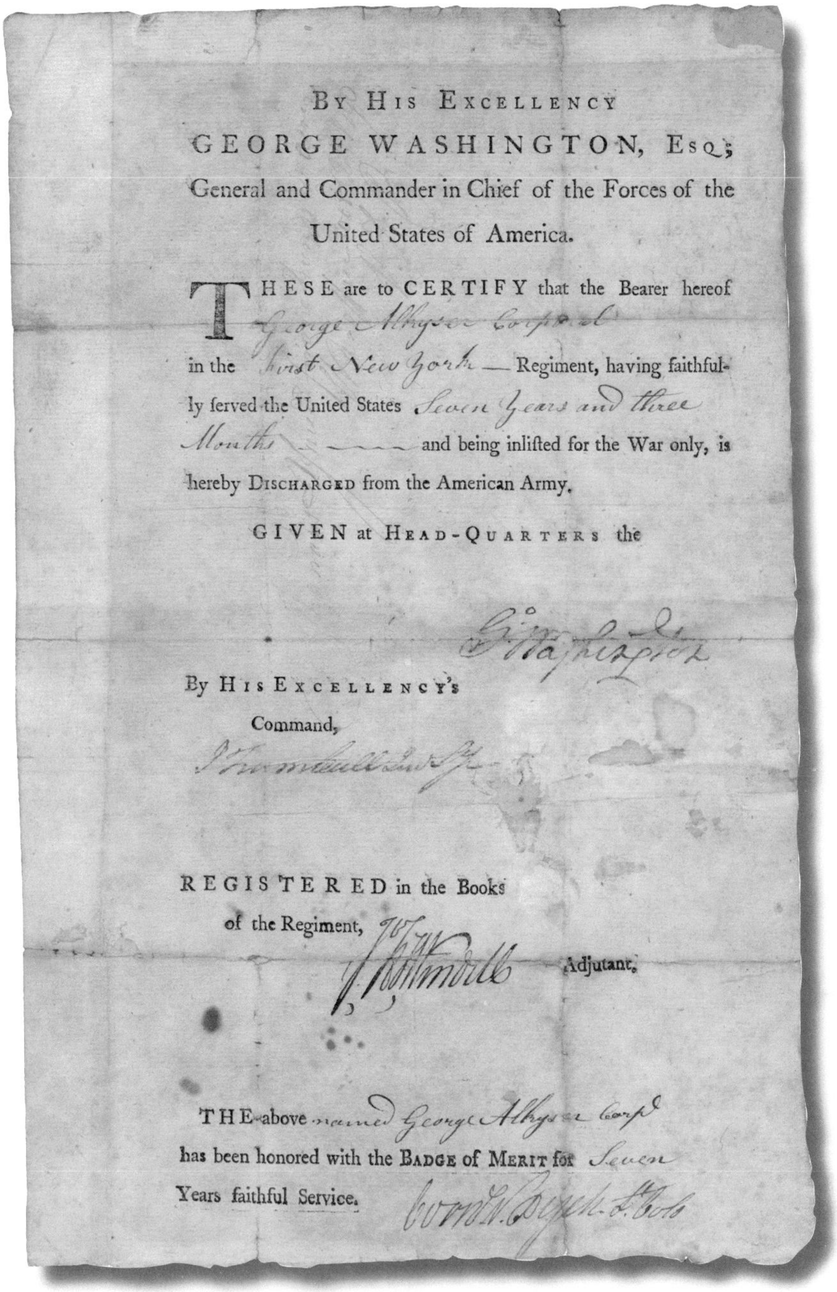

BY HIS EXCELLENCY

GEORGE WASHINGTON, Esq;

General and Commander in Chief of the Forces of the

United States of America.

THESE are to CERTIFY that the Bearer hereof
George Allyson Corporal
in the *First New York* ———— Regiment, having faithfully served the United States *Seven Years and three*
Months ———————— and being inlisted for the War only, is
hereby DISCHARGED from the American Army.

GIVEN at HEAD-QUARTERS the

G. Washington

By HIS EXCELLENCY's
Command,

Trumbull Secy Jr

REGISTERED in the Books
of the Regiment, *J. Rothmore* Adjutant.

THE above *named George Allyson Corpl*
has been honored with the BADGE of MERIT for *Seven*
Years faithful Service. *Cornelis Byek Lt. Colo*

25207 **George Washington Document Signed** *"G. Washington."* Two pages, 8.25" x
13.75", Headquarters of the Forces of the United States of America, nd. It is a discharge for
Corporal George Allyson of the First New York Regiment after seven years and three months
of service in the Army. The document also states that Allyson will receive the Badge of Merit
for his service. The document is signed by Washington, Trumbell, and Byek. From the Henry
E. Luhrs Collection. Accompanied by LOA from PSA/DNA.
Estimate: $7,000-$9,000

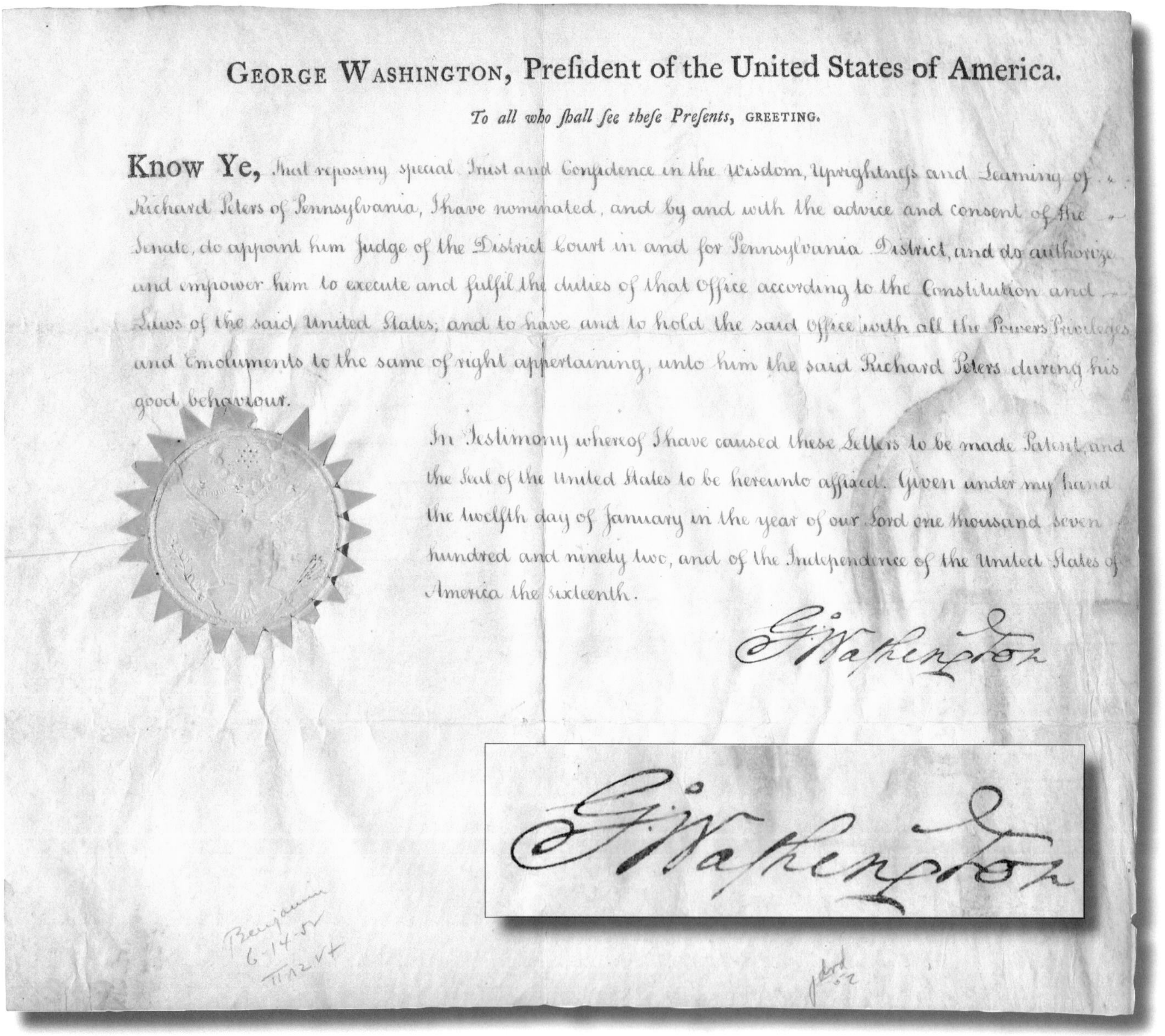

GEORGE WASHINGTON, President of the United States of America.

To all who shall see these Presents, GREETING.

Know Ye, *that reposing special Trust and Confidence in the Wisdom, Uprightness and Learning of Richard Peters of Pennsylvania, I have nominated, and by and with the advice and consent of the Senate, do appoint him Judge of the District Court in and for Pennsylvania District, and do authorize and empower him to execute and fulfil the duties of that Office according to the Constitution and Laws of the said United States; and to have and to hold the said Office with all the Powers Privileges and Emoluments to the same of right appertaining, unto him the said Richard Peters during his good behaviour.*

In Testimony whereof I have caused these Letters to be made Patent, and the Seal of the United States to be hereunto affixed. Given under my hand the twelfth day of January in the year of our Lord one thousand seven hundred and ninety two, and of the Independence of the United States of America the sixteenth.

G Washington

25208   George Washington Document Signed, as president, partially printed and accomplished in manuscript, "*G. Washington.*" One page, 13.75" x 12.75", no place, January 12, 1792. Being the appointment of Richard Peters a Judge of the District Court and for Pennsylvania. The signature of President Washington is bold and dark; wax seal intact. Docketed on verso by James Wilson, signer of the Declaration of Independence and Supreme Court Justice, attesting that Peters took the oath to serve: Wilson is scarce in any form.

The document is in Good condition; usual folds are present; the right edge is badly water damaged but the text is still very legible and the signature is unaffected. From the Henry E. Luhrs Collection. Accompanied by LOA from PSA/DNA.
Estimate: $10,000-$15,000

United States September 30th 1789

Sir,

I have the pleasure to inform you that you are appointed Marshal of the District of Virginia and your Commission is enclosed accompanied with such Laws as have passed relative to the Judicial Department of the United States. —

The high importance of the Judicial System in our National Government, made it an indispensable duty to select such Characters to fill the several offices in it as would discharge their trusts with honor to themselves and advantage to their Country. —

I am, Sir,

Your Most Obedient Servant

Go: Washington

Edward Carrington Esquire. —

25209   **George Washington appoints the first U.S. Marshal for Virginia.**

George Washington (1732-1799) President and Commander-in-Chief of the Continental Army, Letter Signed, *Go: Washington"* as President, one page, 8" x 13", [New York], September 30, 1789. In the first months of his administration, Washington informs Edward Carrington about his appointment as United States Marshal. He writes in full: "*Sir, I have the pleasure to inform you that you are appointed Marshal of the District of Virginia and your commission is enclosed [no longer present], accompanied with such Laws as have passed relative to the Judicial Department of the United States. — The high importance of the Judicial System in our National government, made it an indispensable duty to select such characters to fill the several offices in it as would discharge their trusts with honor to themselves and advantage to their country. — I am Sir, Your Most Obedient Servant Go: Washington."* Washington commissioned thirteen men to serve as United States Marshals on September 26, 1789 including such luminaries as Henry Dearborn, Isaac Huger, Clement Biddle, and Robert Forsyth. Edward Carrington (1743-1810) was a friend and confidant of Washington. During the Revolution he served in the artillery and then as a quartermaster. He served as Marshal for the District of Virginia for two years before Washington appointed him Commissioner for distilled spirits in Virginia. John Adams appointed Carrington to command the provisional army raised during the quasi-war with France. Congress established the U.S. Marshal service as a means of enforcing federal laws in the states. To this end, Washington appointed natives of each district who enjoyed the trust of the local population. Light folds some of which are repaired with archival tape on verso, light toning with a few very minor marginal chips, otherwise quite bright and clean and in fine condition. Beautifully housed in a green leather slip case with gilt titling. Early appointments of this magnitude from the first days of the Washington presidency are highly prized — this is one of the best to remain in private hands. From the Henry E. Luhrs Collection. Accompanied by LOA from PSA/DNA.

Estimate: $15,000-$20,000

25210   George Washington Document Signed *"G. Washington."* One page, 19.5" x 13.5", Mount Vernon, Virginia, October 31, 1785. For strict accuracy we must note that Washington's signature has been enhanced on this document. This document announces William Butler as a member of the Society of the Cincinnati. The Society of the Cincinnati is a patriotic organization with strict entrance rules; only officers from the Continental or French armies who had served three years, or were officed at the time of the war's end, were allowed entrance. After that, membership was passed down to the eldest son. The Society is named after the Roman farmer Lucius Quintus Cincinnatus, who took complete control of Rome during a polemic emergency, and once the war was over he returned control to the Senate and went back to his farm. The motto of the Society reflects this tradition, "He gave up everything to serve the Republic." This gorgeous document is signed by George Washington who served as the society's first president and Henry Knox, Secretary of the society and United States Secretary of War.

The document is in Fine condition; the vignettes look as if they were new, the entire document has been linen backed some time ago and is well preserved; some fraying of the linen is present. From the Henry E. Luhrs Collection. Accompanied by LOA from PSA/DNA.
Estimate: $10,000-$12,000

This Man Can Make **You** Great

25211 **George Washington and Adopted Son George Washington Parke Custis- Signatures.** A choice signature *"Go. Washington"*, closely clipped from the upper right corner of the title page of a book from his library, 3" x .75". Also included is a signature of his adopted son (and also step-grandson) *"George W P Custis of Arlington"* on a 5" x 2.25" lined sheet, laid down to a larger sheet along with his obituary. Rounding out this historical lot is a George Washington CDV, published by the New York Photographic Company, and a vintage booklet about Washington, *This Man Can Make You Great.* All in Fine condition. From the Henry E. Luhrs Collection. Accompanied by LOA from PSA/DNA.
Estimate: $4,000-$5,000

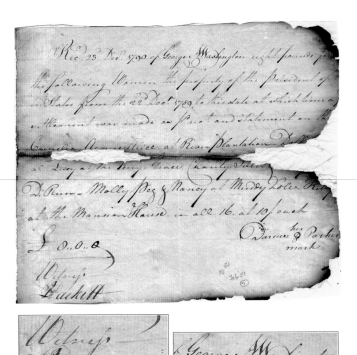

25212 **A midwife receives payment for attending to George Washington's slaves**

(George Washington) A wonderful manuscript Document Signed with the mark of midwife Dorcas Parker, *"P"* one page, 8" x 6.25", no place given, December 23, 1790. Parker, the wife of Washington's neighbor Lawson Parker, helped deliver children for slaves on Mount Vernon — as well as Washington's surrounding plantations. The document reads in most part: *"Recd. 23d Decr 1790 of George Washington eight pounds for the following Women the property of the President of the United States from the 22d Decr. 1789 to this date at which time a final settlement was made as p[e]r rec[eip]t. and statement on the Cornelia Agnus Alice at River plantation- Dollars [word missing] Lucy at the Torry Grace, Charity, Tillie & D. Run- Molly, Peg & Nancy at Muddy hole - Kitty[?] at the Mansion House - in all 16. at 10 S[hillings] each..."* At the time of his death in 1799, there were 316 slaves living at Washington's Mount Vernon estate. Dorcas Parker appears several times in Washington's ledgers detailing her services as a midwife. (Washington's vast land holdings required a small army of people to help sustain them and were not limited to slaves.) Washington's papers reveal that he hired several different people to serve as midwives, both white and free black. Often they were the wives of men in his employment. Significant losses from exposure to fire resulting in the loss of a few words of text, entire document backed with archival tissue for stability, else still legible, paper bright and in overall Good condition. From the Henry E. Luhrs Collection. Accompanied by LOA from PSA/DNA.
Estimate: $1,000-$1,500

25213   George Washington's Cabinet and Advisors- Autograph Collection consisting of 18 or more signed items including:

Samuel Osgood (Postmaster General 1789-1791): DS (1801); DS (1803).

Timothy Pickering (Postmaster General 1791-1795, Secretary of State 1795-1797, Secretary of War 1795-1796): ALS 2pp (1785); two clipped signatures (as Secretary of State).

Joseph Habersham (Postmaster General 1795-1797): ALS 2pp (1805); closing from ALS (1793).

Oliver Wolcott Jr. (Secretary of the Treasury 1795-1797): ALS 2pp (1824); ALS (1802); LS (1799); ALS (1803); ANS- third person (1817).

Henry Knox (Secretary of War 1789-1794): clipped signature laid down to engraving (nd).

James McHenry (Secretary of War 1796-1797): two clipped signatures as Secy of War.

Charles Lee (Attorney General 1795-1797): ANS (1784).

Also included are: George Taylor Jr (ALS 1795); Robert H Harrison (clipped signature 1776); Amos Kendall (clipped signature). Condition varies; generally very good. From the Henry E. Luhrs Collection. Accompanied by LOA from PSA/DNA.
Estimate: $2,000-$3,000

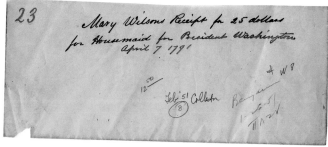

25214   (George Washington) A collection of three documents by aides of George Washington. Includes **Tobias Lear (1762-1816) secretary to Washington, Letter Signed,** "*Toboas Lear*" one page 7.75" x 7.5", Department of War, [Washington], September 14, 1815, noting the adjustments of "*The Accounts of Capn. Samuel w. butler late Pay Mater 3rd. Regt. Infy...*" Small loss at right margin, else very good; **Richard Varick (1753-1831) Aide-de-Camp to Washington, partly printed Document Signed** "*,Rich. Varick Mayr*" as Mayor of New York, one page, 5" x 7", New York, September 5, 1799 noting the posting of bail for a man "*...at the suit of Alexander McDougall of a Plea of Trespass...*". Chips at top margin, light toning, else very good; **Benjamin Walker (1753-1818) Aide-de-Camp to Washington, manuscript Document Signed twice,** "*Ben Walker*" one page, 6.5" x 8.25", no place given, November 27, 1789 attesting to the accuracy of a receipt. Remnants of a formerly affixed document at top right, else very good. Together, three pieces. A fine group. From the Henry E. Luhrs Collection. Accompanied by LOA from PSA/DNA.
Estimate: $500-$700

25215   (George Washington's Presidential Household) Manuscript Document Signed by Mary Wilson who signs with her mark, "*x*", one page, 7.5" x 3", no place given, April 7, 1791, a receipt from "*...Mr. [Tobias] Lear the sum of twenty five dollars for five months wages as Housemaid in the family of the President of the United States*" Little is known about Mary Wilson except that she worked as a washerwoman until March 1791 when she assumed the duties of housemaid. She married in the summer of 1792 and was listed as "Mary Loeffler" when she received her final wages on November 10, 1792. Tobias Lear (1762-1816) was Washington's personal secretary from 1791 to 1793. Chipped at bottom and right margins with loss of one word of text, slightly browned at edges, otherwise very good condition. A fun item with great association to our first president. From the Henry E. Luhrs Collection. Accompanied by LOA from PSA/DNA
Estimate: $600-$800

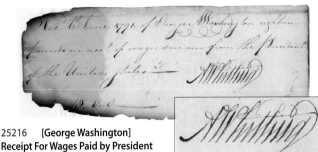

25216 [George Washington] Receipt For Wages Paid by President Washington to His Mount Vernon Estate Manager.
Anthony Whitting Document Signed ("A. Whitting"), 1 page, 7.5" by 3", no place, June 6, 1791. Fragile, and partially backed; discolored and browned at edges, the text is discernible and the signature bold - good, all in all. In full: "*Rec'd 6th June 1791 of George Washington eighteen pounds on acct. of wages due me from the President of the United States.*" Mount Vernon was badly run down when Washington inherited it, and it was the mission of his life to build it into the finest plantation in Virginia. Whiting was with him a long time; there are records of Washington complaining about him early on. But at its peak, Mount Vernon comprised more than 8,000 acres, contained five farms, and supported a few hundred people. It was always, after the cause of liberty and America, what Washington loved best. From the Henry E. Luhrs Collection.
Estimate: $600-$900

25218 [Judaica] (Martha Washington) Solomon Levy, New York merchant, Autograph Document Signed
"*Solomon Levy*" one page, 8" x 2.5", no place given [New York], June 17, 1790, a receipt for cotton purchased by First Lady Martha Washington. The document reads in full: "*Recd. from Lady Washington Three Pounds in full for 20yds Cotton June 17, 1790 Solomon Levy*" Docketed on verso in an unknown hand. Browned at irregular margins, else very good condition. A fun association piece combining early Judaica with the First Family! From the Henry E. Luhrs Collection. Accompanied by LOA from PSA/DNA.
Estimate: $400-$600

25217 George Washington Cabinet, Associates, and Descendants Collection.
This lot consists of 16 items, all of which come from people associated with Washington either by position or bloodlines. The bulk of the lot is autograph letters signed, mixed with several documents signed and signatures. That the "Father of Our Country" commanded respect and adulation is inarguable, but as with any great leader, his closest confidants and associates contributed to his success. Some of the signatures featured here include: ; William Smith, Representative from Maryland and first Auditor of the United States Treasury; a customs report signed by William S. Smith, one of Washington's aides-de-camp; autograph letter signed by Fisher Ames, congressman from Massachusetts and a great orator; signature of Charles Lee, Washington's second Attorney General; a signature of William Bradford Jr, Washington's first Attorney General; eight autographed letters signed by J.W. Washington, purported to be a distant relative of Washington; an autographed letter signed by Joseph de Jaudenes, Commissary General and Envoy from the King of Spain; an autographed letter signed by Lawrence Washington in 1834, another purported descendant of Washington; a document listing several items that were sent to the colonies for use by the Washington family; and a document discussing the bills for millinery for the Washington family.

The documents in this lot are in fine condition on average; the documents listing bills for the Washington family are incomplete, having been cut from larger documents; the signatures are also clipped. From the Henry E. Luhrs Collection. Accompanied by LOA from PSA/DNA.
Estimate: $600-$800

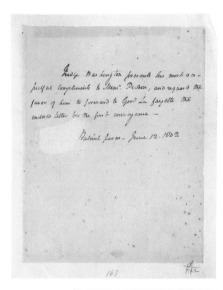

25219 Bushrod Washington Signature and Autograph Letter Signed.
Bushrod Washington was the nephew of George Washington and inherited Mount Vernon from Washington. Later, he would serve as a Supreme Court Justice. The letter presented here is one page, 7.25" x 9", Walnut Farm, Virginia, June 12, 1802. It reads, "*Judge Washington presents his most respectful compliments to Mons. Pichon, and requests the favor of him to forward to Ge. Lafayette the enclosed letter by the first conveyance.*" He signs the letter in the third person. The signature measures 3.25" x 1.5", and reads "*Respectfully yours Bush. Washington.*"

Both items are in fine condition; the letter has the usual folds and has been tipped into another sheet of paper; the letter has small areas of redox spots on the lower right edge; the signature has been clipped from a larger document and also has several visible folds. From the Henry E. Luhrs Collection. Accompanied by LOA from PSA/DNA.
Estimate: $700-$900

25220   Woodrow Wilson Signed Photograph. A 5" x 6.75" B&W photo with a Harris & Ewing blindstamp on a 7.5" x 10.75" Harris & Ewing mount which is signed *"With the Compliments of Woodrow Wilson 1922"*. Generally fine condition with mounting traces at the top and just a bit of silvering on the photo. An attractive item for display. From the Henry E. Luhrs Collection. Accompanied by LOA from PSA/DNA.
Estimate: $500-$700

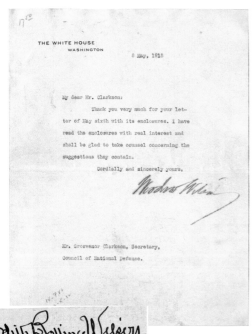

25221   Woodrow Wilson Typed Letter Signed as President along with a Signature of Edith Bolling Wilson on a card. The letter: One page, 7" x 8.75", White House stationery, Washington, May 8, 1918, to Grosvenor Clarson, secretary, Council of National Defense. In part,: "...I have read the enclosures with real interest and shall be glad to take counsel concerning the suggestions they contain..."Very good condition with general soiling and one fold.

The aforementioned signature (3.25" x 2" card) of Edith Bolling Wilson is bold and dark and in very fine condition. Also included is a 1917 Inaugural invitation with the original full-page engravings of President Wilson and Vice President Thomas R. Marshall in fine condition. From the Henry E. Luhrs Collection. Accompanied by LOA from PSA/DNA.
Estimate: $400-$600

25222   Woodrow and Edith Wilson Signature Lot. This lot features one Woodrow Wilson typed letter signed, *"Woodrow Wilson,"* and one small signature card signed by Mrs. Wilson, *"Edith Bolling Wilson."* The typed letter measures 7" x 8.8", and is dated November 15, 1918, from Washington D.C. The content discusses a debt with a George Howe, and Wilson's willingness to "forget" it. A delightful, kind letter. The signature card measures 5" x 3", and is written in crisp, dark ink. The letter is in Good condition; the blue ink of the type is beginning to bleed a bit and fade. The signature card is in Fine condition, with no visible flaws. A charming lot! From the Henry E. Luhrs Collection. Accompanied by LOA from PSA/DNA.
Estimate: $400-$500

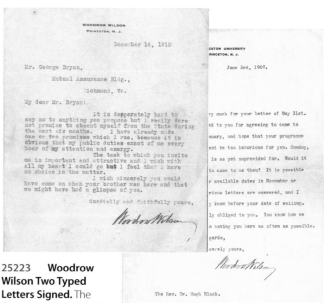

25223   Woodrow Wilson Two Typed Letters Signed. The first: one page, 6" x 8.25", Princeton University letterhead, Princeton, New Jersey, June 3, 1907, to the Rev. Dr. Hugh Black. Wilson is writing to thank Black, a Scottish-American theologian and author, for agreeing to come for a program in January. Fine condition.

The second letter: one page, 6" x 7", personal letterhead, Princeton, New Jersey, December 16, 1910, to George Bryan. In part: "It is desperately hard to say no to anything you propose but I really dare not promise to absent myself from the State during the next six months. I have already made one or two promises which I rue, because it is obvious that my public duties exact of me every hour of my attention and energy..." This letter was written in the period between Wilson's election and inauguration as governor of New Jersey. Very good condition with mailing folds and general soiling.

Also in this lot is a Signature of Edith Bolling Wilson on a small card 4" x 2.5". Very fine condition. From the Henry E. Luhrs Collection. Accompanied by LOA from PSA/DNA.
Estimate: $500-$600

25224   Woodrow Wilson (1856-1924), President, Typed Letter Signed as Governor of New Jersey, *"Woodrow Wilson"*, one page, 8" x 9.75", Trenton, October 15, 1912 to George S. Johns of St. Louis. Written during his first run for President, Wilson pens: *"I want to thank you sincerely for the two very interesting letters that arrived at Trenton in my absence. What you say with reference to the necessity for more publicity is very timely,*

and I will take the matter up at once with New York headquarters. It is fine to have the support of such loyal friends as yourself." Wilson was in a tight race with both William H. Taft (the Republican) and a rebellious third-party candidate in Theodore Roosevelt (Progressive) running against him. Interestingly, the day before Wilson wrote this letter, Roosevelt was the subject of a failed assassination attempt in Milwaukee while delivering a speech. Showing his usual fortitude, the Bull Moose refused medical treatment and gave his scheduled address with a bullet lodged in his rib. However Roosevelt cancelled the balance of his speaking tour. In a gesture of appropriate concern, both Taft and Wilson suspended their campaign activities until T.R. recovered. Despite these complications, Wilson won the election of 1912, though not with a majority of the popular vote. Light folds, one only slightly affecting end of signature, else fine condition. From the Henry E. Luhrs Collection. Accompanied by LOA from PSA/DNA.

Estimate: $500-$700

25225   Woodrow Wilson Letter Re:His 1909 Lincoln Speech Typed Letter Signed, *as president of Princeton University,* 1 page, 6"by 8", on the letterhead of "The President's Room", Princeton, New Jersey, February 26, 1909. To Albert F. Griffith. Wilson, it is worth recalling here, typed almost all his own letters. In excellent condition, albeit bearing a couple of soft pencil notes at a corner and margin. At the centennial celebration of Lincoln's birth in Chicago in 1909, Woodrow Wilson, with a gubernatorial run just a glint in his eye, delivered a memorable address on Abraham Lincoln. That speech, eventually published as "Abraham Lincoln: A Man of the People," is the subject of this letter. *"I very much appreciate your kind letter of February 23rd and regret to say that my address on Lincoln, delivered at Chicago on February 12th, has yet to be printed. It was stenographically reported and is, I think to be published with the other addresses delivered in connection with the celebration... If it is your kind wish that I should autograph your copy, I will do so with pleasure."* From the Henry E. Luhrs Collection. Accompanied by LOA from PSA/DNA.

Estimate: $300-$600

25226   Woodrow Wilson (1856-1924), President, Typed Letter Signed *"Woodrow Wilson"* as President, one page on White House letterhead, 7" x 9", Shadow Lawn, October 16, 1916 to journalist Cyrus Townsend Brady (1861-1920) thanking him for the enclosure of his letter of support published in *The New York Times.* Wilson writes: *"My dear Mr. Brady: I know you are generous and do not want me to take the time to answer your letters, but you do such fine things and do them in such a big-hearted way that I must drop you a line to thank you for your letter of October eleventh and its enclosures. You certainly are a fine friend."* Offered together with a retained and signed copy of Brady's original letter to Wilson, dated Yonkers, New York, October 11, 1916. The *Times* article was published on October 16, and was headlined "If the President is Defeated". Brady wrote in a fiery polemic that a defeat of Wilson by Charles Evans Hughes would in short "...give unbounded joy to every traitorous and disloyal hyphenate in the country..." Wilson narrowly won a second term in 1916 by stressing the fact that he had kept the nation out of war, and had managed to pressure the Germans to suspend unrestricted submarine warfare. This would not last of course, and after further attacks on American ships by German U-boats, Wilson asked Congress to declare war against Germany on April 2, 1917. Letter is overall quite clean with only minor soiling, overall fine condition. From the Henry E. Luhrs Collection. Accompanied by LOA from PSA/DNA.

Estimate: $500-$700

25227   Woodrow Wilson Letter, as President, Referring to His Impaired Health! Typed Letter Signed, *as president,* 1 page, 7" by 9", The White House, Washington, September 18, 1920. To John A. Stewart, Chairman of the Board of Governors of the Sulgrave Institute of America. In fine condition, albeit bearing a pencil checkmark, apparently a notation of the recipient. Here Wilson declines to attend a celebration of the 300th anniversary of the landing of the Pilgrim fathers and the beginnings and development- from Magna Charta and the Bill of Rights down- of the free institutions of the English speaking nations, to be held in February 1921. Why he declines, however, is the reason to bid here: Wilson makes an uncommon reference to the poor state of his health. In full: *"Thank you for your letter of the sixteenth. I certainly hope that all your plans will be matured. I shall follow the progress of the celebration with the greatest interest, and regret only that the condition of my health prevents my taking a personal part on so notable an occasion. I should be happy, if it were possible, to attempt to put into words the unique significance of the things we are commemorating."*

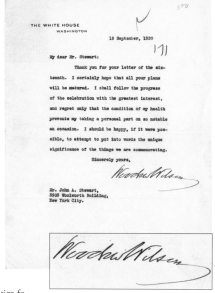

On October 2, 1919, President Wilson suffered a serious stroke that almost totally incapacitated him; he could barely move his own body. For the rest of his term in office, the extent of his impairment was kept from the public, with the First Lady acting, for months, as a kind of regent. Although Wilson slowly regained strength, he never fully recovered. His stroke, and the terrible way in which it was handled, caused the worst crisis of Presidential disability in American history - and led eventually to the 25th Amendment to the Constitution. From the Henry E. Luhrs Collection. Accompanied by LOA from PSA/DNA.
Estimate: $700-$900

25228   Woodrow Wilson Presidential Appointment - of a Notary Public! Document Signed, *as president,* partially-printed and accomplished in manuscript, 1 oblong page, 18.5" by 14.5", Washington, D.C. May 1, 1916; co-signed by Attorney-General Thomas Watt Gregory and bearing the bright orange seal of the Department of Justice. Being the appointment of Albert Harper as a Notary Public for the District of Columbia. Some age-toning and a noticeable vertical center crease, with a nascent tear at its top; otherwise, good. The District of Columbia, like the Vatican, is a City unto itself: and like the Vatican, it's God - the Federal Government - moves in mysterious ways. Hence the president, and his attorney-general, stop everything to appoint a notary. From the Henry E. Luhrs Collection. Accompanied by LOA from PSA/DNA.
Estimate: $300-$500

25229   Woodrow Wilson Typed Letter Signed Dating from Just After He Left The White House. Dated March 22nd, 1921 on his 6.75" x 8.75" personal stationery bearing the address of his Washington home. Very fine, with minor pencil notations. Wilson thanks an acquaintance for bringing the invalid former President a meal of "delicious shad." Surprising strong signature by the stroke-victim Wilson. Provenance: King Hostick, 1956. From the Henry E. Luhrs Collection. Accompanied by LOA from PSA/DNA.
Estimate: $300-$400

25230 Woodrow Wilson Administration Autograph Collection.

Offered here is an amazing collection of more than 60 autographed items from key figures in the Wilson administration between 1913 and 1921. A quick look-through shows only two of the 19 different cabinet members are missing. Included are Vice President Thomas R. Marshall and Secretary of State William Jennings Bryan with several others represented by multiple autographs. Also in this lot are senators, congressmen, ambassadors, and various other government officials. There are numerous references to World War I here for the historian. Generally fine condition. A great grouping. From the Henry E. Luhrs Collection. Accompanied by LOA from PSA/DNA.

Estimate: $800-$1,200

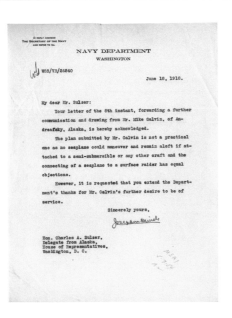

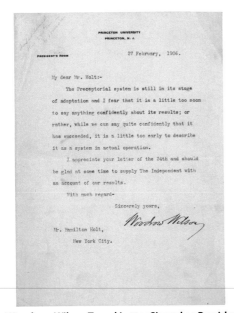

25231 Woodrow Wilson Typed Letter Signed as President of Princeton University

Dated 27 February, 1906, on his official stationery. 6.0" x 8.25", fine to very fine condition with minor light pencil notations. Wilson writes one Hamilton Holt regarding the newly adopted Preceptorial System at the University. From the Henry E. Luhrs Collection. Accompanied by LOA from PSA/DNA.

Estimate: $300-$400

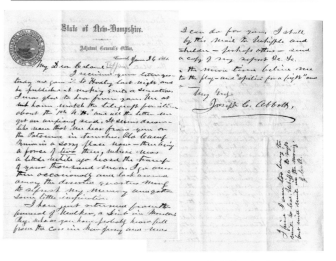

25232 Joseph Carter Abbott, (1825-1881), Officer in the 7th New Hampshire Regiment who led his troops in the capture of Fort Fisher, war date Autograph Letter Signed,

"*Joseph c. Abbott*" and "*J.C.A.*" four pages, Concord, New Hampshire, June 26, 1861, reporting on preparations for recruiting, and the funeral of "*...Walker, a Lieut. in Mouton's Reg. who as you have probably heard fell from the cars in new jersey and was killed. It was has been a melancholy day. The Home Guards, the Horse Guards, the Knight Templars of Concord and Boston, the Governor & Council and the legislature all turned out. The body was laid in State in the rotunda of the State House, and there was a great display. It was indeed splendid... there was a rumor flying about town that your Reg. had attacked the battery opposite you. A man came in and told me of it. I ... said that twenty five of your men were killed, but, said he, 'they took the battery' as if cared nothing at all about the killed. The Governor was a little long-faced about the killed, but said he thought all along that the boys would show pluck...*" Very good condition. From the Henry E. Luhrs Collection. Accompanied by LOA from PSA/DNA.

Estimate: $400-$600

25233 Fisher Ames Requests His Sons Be Taken Out of School to be Taught at Home

Third Person ALS: "*Mr Ames*", 1p, 4.75" x 3.75". No place, June 3, 1805. In full: "*Mr Ames thinks it expedient to remove his son Worthington from Mr Jenks's care for some time Nat's lame knee obliges him to get his tuition at home, and both the boys can be taught by the same preceptor. Mr Ames owes it to Mr Jenks to express his most grateful acknowledgements for his able and faithful attentions to his children.*" Addressed by Ames on verso to: "*Revd Mr Jenks*". Fisher Ames and Frances Worthington Ames

had seven children, John Worthington Ames and Nathaniel Ames were the oldest. Worthington was 11 and Nat was 9 when this letter was written. Ames represented Massachusetts in the House of Representatives in the first four Congresses, 1789-1797 and was only 50 when he died in 1808. He had been chosen President of Harvard in 1804 but declined because of ill health. Lightly browned at left and at folds, else in very fine condition. From the Henry E. Luhrs Collection. Accompanied by LOA from PSA/DNA.

Estimate: $300-$400

25234   Rare 1764 John Armstrong Military Letter ALS: "*John Armstrong,*" 1p, 6" x 7.25". [Pennsylvania], September 1, 1764. With integral leaf addressed by Armstrong "*To/Ensigne Pecke/to be forwarded/by Mr. Harris*" In full: "*I expected to have seen you at Mr. Harris's on my return from Lancaster—and shou'd be glad to know with all convenient speed how many Men you have got, where they are, and whether you have got Arms & Ammunition for them as these Articles are left with Jon. Harris for the Use of the Soldiers. I shou'd be glad to see you at Carlisle where you shall receive farther orders, and know where you will Draw Provisions wch. must be fixed wth. Mr. Callander. I am Sir your Very humbl. Servt.*" In 1763, Pennsylvania Governor John Penn had named John Armstrong as commander of frontier defenses. Armstrong headed north in October, 1763, with a force of 600 volunteers to attack an Indian village located near Big Island (near present-day Lock Haven) on the west branch of the Susquehanna River. He destroyed Indian villages and crops and was back in Carlisle by November. By July 1764, there was general peace along the frontiers. Armstrong continued to worry over what he called the "expos'd state of the Western Frontier" and called upon the government for more supplies to outfit garrison troops. During the American Revolution, John Armstrong became the first Brigadier General commissioned (March 1, 1776) by the Continental Congress. Pencil markings in blank margins. Affixed to narrow 0.5" x 7.25" strip of mounting paper on verso at blank lower edge of integral address leaf. Overall, in Fine condition. From the Henry E. Luhrs Collection. Accompanied by LOA from PSA/DNA.
Estimate: $500-$800

25235   Attempting to prevent an armed march on the Wyoming Valley

John Armstrong (1725-1795), American General in the Revolution, an important Autograph Letter Signed "*John Armstrong*" as "*Chairman of the Committee*", one page, 6.25" x 7.5", Carlisle, [Pennsylvania], November 5, 1775 to the Committee of Correspondence for Northumberland County. In the early days of the American Revolution, Armstrong attempts to quell a brewing local civil war. Overlapping colonial land grants to Pennsylvania and Connecticut in the 17th century set the stage for conflict in the Wyoming Valley of Pennsylvania when a company of Connecticut colonists attempted to settle there in 1762. To the great chagrin of Pennsylvania, the settlers claimed the region as a part of Connecticut. Open warfare erupted in 1769 and continued sporadically until 1784. In this letter, Armstrong warns the Northumberland Committee about a planned march to destroy the Wyoming Valley settlement: "*Hav[in]g rece[ive]'d information that a Cons[idera]ble. No. of inhabitants of y[ou]r Co[unty] are determined shortly to go up in hostile manner ag[ains]t. the people of Connec[ticu]t. settled at Wioming [sic] with intent to dispossess them on this alarming news we have tho[ugh]t. proper to write you our opinion; which is that such a step at this time, will be attended with very bad Consequences. Common humanity forbid at this inclem[en]t. season — expose them to g[rea]t . suffering, both hunger & cold — perhaps to the loss of life —— tend to inflame the dispute — & a disunion — it will probably embark some of the other Colonies in the dispute — and shew [sic] disrespect to advice of Congress — this dispute render our Enemies more obstinate & make them rejoice — Acting in the defensive will secure your Character in this & other Provinces — For this reason offer their opinion & make it our express request that you will forbear hostilities at least for the present until time further delib[erate] & advise.*" Armstrong's remonstrance was not sufficient to prevent the Northumberland men from marching. On Christmas Day, 1775, Connecticut settlers repulsed their attackers at Rampart Rocks near Harvey's Creek, ending open conflict for the duration of the Revolutionary War. Although the Revolution quelled the Wyoming Valley war, it did not spare its residents from tragedy. On July 3, 1778, a party of Iroquois and Loyalists raided the valley, killing 300 inhabitants. In 1782 Connecticut and Pennsylvania reached an accord agreeing that Pennsylvania had jurisdiction over the area while protecting the property claims of the Connecticut settlers. Open conflict erupted once again in 1783 concluding with another victory by the Connecticut men in 1784. A final settlement was reached two years later, along much the same lines as the 1782 agreement. Some clean fold separations, light toning, else Very Good. Tremendously rare and important historic content. From the Henry E. Luhrs Collection. Accompanied by LOA from PSA/DNA.
Estimate: $2,000-$3,000

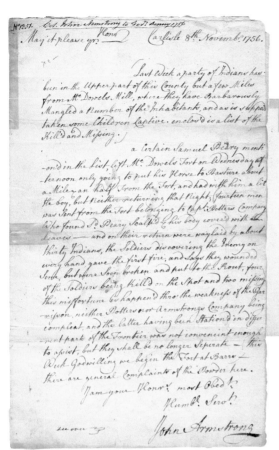

25236   Reporting on a deadly Indian raid in Pennsylvania in 1756 John Armstrong (1725-1795) American General in the Revolutionary War, fine content Autograph Letter Signed *"John Armstrong"*, two pages with integral address leaf, 7.5" x 12", Carlisle, [Pennsylvania], November 8, 1756 to Pennsylvania Governor William Denny reporting of an Indian attack on Fort McDowell (near present-day Mercersburg, Pennsylvania). He writes in part: *"Last Week a party of Indians has been in the Upper part of this County but a few Miles from McDowels Mill, where they have Barbarously Mangled a Number of the Inhabitants, and as is supposed taken some Children Captive. enclose'd is a list of the Kill'd and Missing. A Certain Samuel Peary mention'd in the list, left McDowels Fort on Wednesday afternoon only going to put his Horse to Pasture about a Mile & an [sic] half From the Fort, and had with him a little boy, but Neither returning that Night; fourteen men was Sent from the Fort belonging to Capt. Potters Company who found Sd. Peary Scalp'd & his body covered with Leaves — and on their returned were waylaid by about thirty Indians, the Soldiers discovering the enemy on every hand, gave the first fire, and Says they wounded Some, but were Soon broken and put to the rout, four of the soldiers being Kill'd on the Sport and two missing. this misfortune is happen'd thro the weakness of the garrison, neither Potters nor Armstrong's company being compleat [sic], and the latter been Station'd in different parts of the Frontier was not convenient enough to assist, but they shall be no longer Separate... there are general Complaints s of the Powder here..."* On the inside of the letter, a 4.5" x 10" manuscript has been attached listing the names of those killed or missing. Those killed included three soldiers and seven civilians. The missing included two soldiers as well as *"...Four children belonging to John Archer, Samuel Neely a boy [and] James McCoid a child"* Fort McDowell was constructed in 1755, one of numerous forts built along the Appalachian frontier to protect from raids by Indians allied with the French. The fort consisted of a rectangular stockade with four blockhouses that surrounded a gristmill. The fort was manned by about 40 militia until the competition of Fort Loudon several miles to the north. Fort Loudon would become an important post on the Forbes Road leading to Fort Pitt. Weak folds repaired with archival tape, else very good condition. Quite significant content. One has to wonder if the kidnapped children — a common practice by several tribes — were ever heard from again. From the Henry E. Luhrs Collection. Accompanied by LOA from PSA/DNA.

Estimate: $1,500-$2,000

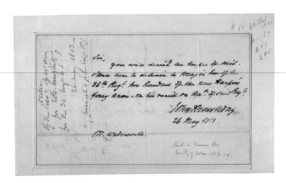

25237   War of 1812 Secretary of War John Armstrong Orders 200 Harper's Ferry Muskets On verso of a request for *"proper musket*." Armstrong writes on May 26, 1813: *"Sir : You will direct the keeper of military stores here to deliver to Major Lee of the 36th reg't. Two hundred of the New Harper's Ferry Arms on his receit on account of said reg't."* 7.75" x 4.5, fine condition with one old tape repair on verso. An appealing subject. From the Henry E. Luhrs Collection. Accompanied by LOA from PSA/DNA.

Estimate: $150-$250

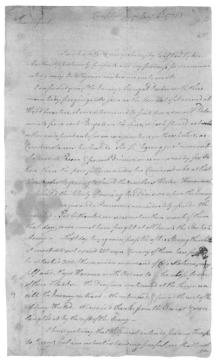

25238   An Early Letter From Valley Forge Francis Barber (1751-1783) Autograph Letter Signed *"F. Barber"*, two pages, 8" x 13", *"Camp Valley Forge"*, January 6, 1778 to Colonel Jonathan Dayton. Barber served as a Colonel in the Continental Army, was wounded at Germantown and Monmouth; he led a battalion in the final assault on Yorktown. Barber was tragically killed by a falling tree at the close of the war. An excellent letter describing a brief foray out of camp. He writes in part: *"...I informed you of the enemy's being at Derber [Darby?]with their main body foraging. As soon as the Account of it arrived at Head Quarters, it was determined to send down small Detachments from each Brigade in the Line, which should act either independent of or in conjunction with each other, as Circumstances presented. Sir L having just come out of a warm Room & from a Brimer[?], was more ready for action than the poor fellows under his command who at that time were beginning to build themselves Huts. He earnestly solicited the Liberty of moving his Division upon the Enemy and this was granted. Orders were immediately issued. We started - God be thanked, we were not within march of them that day, or we must have fought at all Events the British Amy. Next day being more sensible of his Strength, which at most did not exceed 500 men & many of them Bare foot - he detached 300 of them under command of Colo[nel] Malionee, my self and Major Harmer with orders to be close to one of their Flanks. The Division continued at the Lines until the Enemy retired. We returned, & found the rest of the Army rested. We received Thanks for the General & were laughed at by the rest of the Army. I heard yesterday that the General intends sending Troops to Jersey; but am notwithstanding fearful, we shall not go & press & use these. If Jersey Troops are sent, a Jersey General should command them. but a J[ersey]. General will scarcely be trusted. they also object to us - that were we in jersey we should be constantly running home & no service done. This may be depended on, that unless the Preference be given to us, we shall marked a d—l of a Noise — No News today —- We go on finely with our Huts, several are already completed, a few days will compleat [sic] the rest. When they are finished we shall be more easy about the matter..."*

It was an auspicious beginning to what would become one of most tragic winters for the Continental Army. While the weather remained relatively mild for that time of year, with the spring rains, disaster struck. The huts were often built into the ground (to save time of wood cutting) and soon became flooded. The fleas and rats soon followed to create a disease-ridden town of 12,000 starving, hungry soldiers. Nearly 2,000 men died that winter. On the positive side, the winter at Valley Forge was the scene of a transformation: from undisciplined, green troops, to a tightly skilled, effective fighting army. Silked, usual folds and a few minor marginal tears, a few soiled spots obscure several words including part of the signature, else very good condition. A fine content letter illustrating the somewhat lighter side of camp life. From the Henry E. Luhrs Collection. Accompanied by LOA from PSA/DNA.
Estimate: $1,500-$2,500

25239   Nicholas Biddle Autograph Letter Regarding a Land Purchase Autograph Letter Signed, 2 pages, recto and verso, Philadelphia, May 8, 1817. To Vincent Le Ray de Chaumont. In fine condition. Here Biddle, who would soon enough become president of the Bank of the United States, discusses the purchase of some land near Tioga. *"I had this morning the pleasure of receiving... the outline of your negotiation & your plans with regard to the land, in all which - if in other respects the purchase is a desirable one - I do not perceive any difficulties..."* He continues that he wishes to visit the land himself - but has missed the stagecoach, thought to travel by private carriage, decided against it, will wait until the next stage, etceteras - and shall soon be on the road to Tioga. From the Henry E. Luhrs Collection. Accompanied by LOA from PSA/DNA.
Estimate: $300-$400

25240   Financier Nicholas Biddle Autograph Letter Signed *"N. B.".* Two pages, 8" x 9.75", Andalusia, October 22, 1822, to James Worth. In regard to local politics, in part, *"...We proceeded very harmoniously by adopting a constitution & naming officers for the coming year. These consist of a President, the Vice President- in each county & four directors also in each county. Mr Jonathan Roberts was elected President..."* Andalusia is located in Bucks County just north of Philadelphia and has been, for 200 years, the home of the Biddles, one of Philadelphia's legendary families. Nicholas Biddle was the president of the Bank of the United States from 1822 until 1839, and was one of the most important financial experts of his day. Fine condition; folds, a tiny nick at the top right mentioned only for accuracy; old linen hinge at left edge. From the Henry E. Luhrs Collection. Accompanied by LOA from PSA/DNA.
Estimate: $400-$500

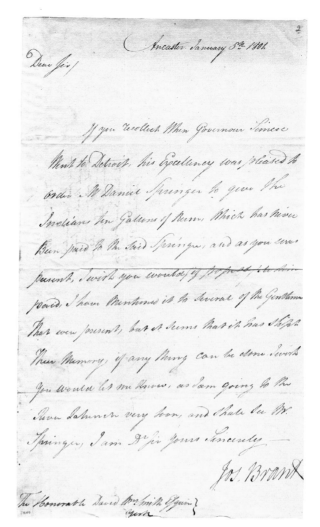

25241   Continental Congress President Elias Boudinot Document Signed. Two pages, 6.5" x 8.25", [New Jersey], July 25, 1808. A legal financial document regarding a loan office certificate, signed at close. Boudinot was President of the Continental Congress for the November 1782 to November 1783 term. Since this was the period that the Treaty of Paris, in which Britain recognized American independence, was concluded, many misguided "historians" claim that he (or his predecessor John Hanson) was actually the first U.S. President. That notwithstanding, Boudinot served his country well: he was elected to the first three Congresses representing his beloved home state of New Jersey. Afterwards, George Washington appointed him Director of the United States Mint, a position he held until his retirement in 1805 and under whom the first U.S. coins were minted. He also served (for nearly 50 years) as a trustee of the College of New Jersey (Princeton), and later in life, he co-founded the American Bible Society. Fine condition; one small paper mend, hinged to larger sheet. From the Henry E. Luhrs Collection. Accompanied by LOA from PSA/DNA.
Estimate: $400-$600

25242   A rare letter from Mohawk leader Joseph Brandt

Joseph Brandt (c. 1742-1807) Mohawk chief and British officer in the American Revolutionary War, rare Letter Signed "*Jos. Brant*", one page, 7.25" x 12", "*Ancaster*" [Ontario], January 5, 1801 to David William Smith in York, Ontario concerning a large cache of rum. He writes: "*If you recollect when Governour Simcoe Went to Detroit his Excellency was pleased to order Mr. Daniel Springer to give the Indians ten Gallons of rum which has since been paid to the said Springer, and as you was present, I wish you would (if possible) see him paid, I have Mentioned it to Several of the Gentlemen That were present, but it seems that if has slipt [sic] Their Memory, if any thing can e done I wish you would let me Know, as I am going to the River Johnson very son, and shall see Mr. Springer...*" During the Revolutionary War , Brandt led warriors of four Iroquois nations allied with Great Britain and was appointed captain in the British Army. He was made infamous for the Wyoming Valley "massacre," a Loyalist and Indian raid on a Pennsylvania settlement that resulted in the deaths of hundreds. As later determined by historians, Brandt was not even present. Indeed, though, he was known as "Monster Brandt" by the Americans. But in actuality, he was a voice of moderation and restraint during the struggle. Following the war, he migrated with his followers to the Grand River region of Ontario which was granted to them in thanks for their loyal service. For the remainder of his life he attempted to form a pan-Indian alliance to resist further encroachment on western lands by the United States. His efforts were unsuccessful, but the struggle would be continued by Shawnee leader Tecumseh. Usual folds, else very fine condition. A very difficult example to obtain; this is perhaps the finest to come to market in decades. From the Henry E. Luhrs Collection. Accompanied by LOA from PSA/DNA.
Estimate: $3,000-$4,000

25243 Cadwallader D. Colden Autograph Letter

Signed "*Cadwallader D. Colden.*" A document signed by Colden, four pages, 8" x 9.7" Harlem Near New York, October 28, 1822. It reads in part, "*The question is then, did the state of New York do an injurious act towards, Rhode Island or towards any of her sister states when she made exclusive grant to Fulton under which we claim? It seems to me that this question will be best answered by supposing that when Fulton applied to the state of New York, he had addressed himself to the state of Rhode Iland. (sic) Had by anticipation, represented all the advantages of steam navigation as they are now enjoyed; had represented that he could not make the experiments and expend the money necessary to make effectual experiments without he could be assured of an exclusive right to the use of his inventions for a limited time, without such exclusive right he would reap no advantage tho (sic) he should be ever so successful in the execution of his plans.*"

The letter is no doubt making reference to Robert Fulton and his steamboat plans. Fulton had died in 1815 and his intellectual property is what is being discussed in this letter between Colden and Caddington Billings. After the steamboat was introduced there were years of rivalry and disputes as to the originality of the idea and the actual father of the design. Regardless of Fulton's place in the pantheon of inventors who lay claim to the steamboat's inception, Fulton deserves credit for giving the steamboat the precedence as a passenger carrying conveyance as well as for transportation of freight. All attempts at this before Fulton proved fruitless and inefficient. Colden, the son of the colonial leader of the same name, himself was a statesman and politician who devoted much of his later life to the completion and technology of the Morris Canal in New Jersey. His connection to waterways and freight conveyances are what ties him so closely to Fulton and his inventions. Colden even wrote a biography of Robert Fulton's life and inventions. The content of this letter is fascinating and it would be extremely desirable for any inventor or transportation enthusiast!

The letter is in Fine condition with no major flaws whatsoever. The paper is browning slightly due to age, but the ink is crisp and dark. The letter comes with a complete typed transcription of the text! From the Henry E. Luhrs Collection. Accompanied by LOA from PSA/DNA.

Estimate: $1,000-$1,500

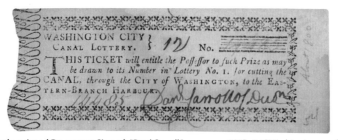

25244 Daniel Carroll (1730-1796) Partly-printed Document Signed,

"*Danl Carroll*", one page, 4.25" x 1.5", Washington, no date given. Carroll was a member of the prominent Maryland political family which included Signer of the Declaration of Independence, Charles Carroll of Carrolton and John Carroll, the first Catholic Bishop in the United States. Daniel Carroll was a member of the Constitutional Convention of 1787 and served in the First Congress of the United States. He was later appointed one of three commissioners to survey the District of Columbia and served as one of the City's Chief Administrators. A ticket for the Washington City Canal Lottery, bearing the number 14485. The ticket bears the notice: "*THIS TICKET will entitle the Possessor to such Prize as may be drawn to its Number in Lottery No. 1. for cutting the CANAL, through the CITY of WASHINGTON, to the EASTERN-BRANCH HARBOUR.*" For many years, much of Washington was a swamp, crisscrossed with canals. Indeed at this time, much of the Washington Mall was under water. This particular canal, completed before 1820 ran from just west of the Capitol (adjacent to Pennsylvania Avenue) to the Eastern Branch of the Potomac. Light toning from dampstain, else fine. From the Henry E. Luhrs Collection. Accompanied by LOA from PSA/DNA.

Estimate: $600-$800

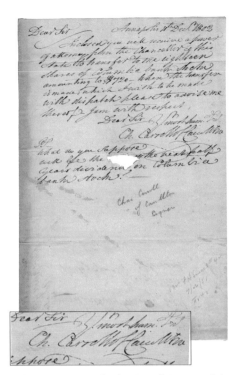

25248   Samuel Osgood (1747-1813) First Postmaster General under the Constitution, Autograph Endorsement Signed "*S Osgood N[aval] Off[ice]*" on the docket of a two page manuscript Document, 7.75" x 12.5", [New York], April 27 - May 8, 1803 a "*Return of Merchandise unladen under my inspection from on board the schooner Lion Clark Master from St Croix*" Osgood endorses the verso as Chief Naval Officer for the Port of New York, a post he held after retiring from the New York State Assembly. Light toning and soiling, usual folds, else very good. A scarce example — perfect for the philatelic collector.   From the Henry E. Luhrs Collection. Accompanied by LOA from PSA/DNA.
Estimate: $300-$500

25246   Declaration Signer Charles Carroll Autograph Letter Signed "*Ch. Carroll of Carrollton.*" Two pages with integral address leaf, 8" x 11.75", Annapolis, December 11, 1802. The content of the letter relates to Carroll's purchase of $720 of Columbia Bank stock. Charles Carroll was the only Catholic signer of the Declaration of Independence as well as the longest surviving.

The letter is in very good condition; usual folds are present; staining present on lower edge which extends into the body; circular tear in the center of the letter from the breaking of the wax seal.
From the Henry E. Luhrs Collection. Accompanied by LOA from PSA/DNA.

Estimate: $400-$500

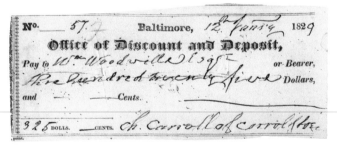

25247   Declaration Signer Charles Carroll of Carrollton Checks Signed "*Ch. Carroll of Carrollton*". Two items are included. The first: a partly printed check made out and signed by Carroll, 6.25" x 2.5", Baltimore, January 12, 1829. On the Office of Discount and Deposit to William Woodville, Esq. for $325.00. The second: a similar check, in another's handwriting and signed by Carroll, June 3, 1830, for $291.20. Carroll signed the Declaration of Independence, was a member of the Continental Congress, and a U.S. senator as a representative of Maryland. Interestingly, he was the only Catholic signer and the last-surviving signer, dying on November 14, 1832. Checks are in fine condition with expected cut cancellations not affecting the signatures. The second is mounted by the left edge to a larger sheet.   From the Henry E. Luhrs Collection. Accompanied by LOA from PSA/DNA.
Estimate: $400-$500

25249   Samuel Chase (1743-1811) Signer of the Declaration of Independence, scarce manuscript Document Signed, "*Samuel Chase*", three pages, 9" x 14", Baltimore, June 2, 1787, a lengthy document discussing a complex estate in which several of the heirs are disputing the interpretation of the will due to unclear language. The document reads in very small part: "*The World Legacy has been held to extend to a devise of Land, but such construction was given to comply with the Intention of the Testator; and because if the World Legacy was confined to pecuniary Legacies, the Divise [sic] over Could not take Effect, being after a dying without issue; and the law will not allow a pecuniary legacy to be limited after a dying without issue generally...*" Chase had a varied and eventful career. During his tenure with the Continental Congress he was sent with Benjamin Franklin and others in a delegation to Canada in an unsuccessful attempt to convince Quebec to join the American Revolution. After the war, he served as a judge in Maryland and was appointed to the Supreme Court in 1796 where he gained the dubious distinction of being the first and only Supreme Court justice to be impeached (though he was acquitted by the Senate). Moderate scattered foxing and toning, partial separation at folds, otherwise very good. A worthy example with interesting content. From the Henry E. Luhrs Collection. Accompanied by LOA from PSA/DNA.
Estimate: $1,000-$1,500

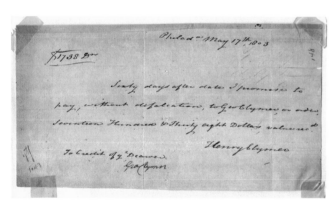

25250   Declaration Signer Samuel Chase Document Signed
"Samuel Chase." Three pages, 7.75" x 7.6", Baltimore, Maryland August 14, 1793. This document is an oath of citizenship based upon Maryland's "An Act for Naturalization." Naturalization was a large issue in colonial America, before and after the Revolution. Samuel Chase signed this document as the Chief Judge in the state of Maryland.

The document is in very fine condition; edges slightly worn with small tears. From the Henry E. Luhrs Collection. Accompanied by LOA from PSA/DNA.
Estimate: $1,500-$2,000

25251   George Clymer Makes a Loan Document Signed, 1 page, 7.5" by 4", Philadelphia, May 17, 1803. In fine condition, albeit held at corners to a slightly larger sheet with archival tape. Being the agreement whereby the Revolutionary patriot and Signer of both the Declaration of Independence and the Constitution loans a relative $1738 for sixty days. Promising to pay is Henry Clymer. From the Henry E. Luhrs Collection. Accompanied by LOA from PSA/DNA.
Estimate: $300-$400

25252   George Clymer Bends Over Backwards To Be Fair To a Debtor.
Autograph Letter Signed, 2 page, recto and verso, with integral address leaf, Philadelphia, January 6, 1796. To John Shippen Esq. In Philadelphia. A nascent tear at margin, else fine. Clymer was a wealthy merchant, a well-known politician, a Signer of the Declaration of Independence, and just as famously, a great philanthropist. It seems unlikely, in this last connection, that the point of letter

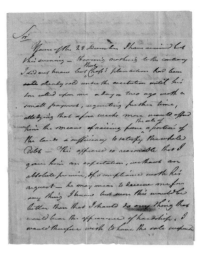

offered here was to increase the well-being of humankind by charitable aid, but it is certainly an appealing example of the man's scrupulous fairness. In part: " *...Hearing nothing to the contrary I did not know that Cross's plantation had been already sold under the execution until his son called upon me a day or two ago with a small payment, requesting further time, alleging that a few weeks more would afford him the means of raising, from the sale of a portion of the land a sufficiency to satisfy the whole debt. This appeared so reasonable that I gave him an expectation, without an absolute promise, of a compliance with his request. He may be mean to deceive me for any thing I know but even this would be better than I had to do any thing that would bear the appearance of hardship. I would therefore wish to have the sale suspended for a month or ten weeks. By that time we shall know whether the expectation he has raised is to be valued... If not, after waiting so many years, I think no one can accuse me of too great haste in ordering the sale...*" From the Henry E. Luhrs Collection. Accompanied by LOA from PSA/DNA.
Estimate: $400-$600

25253   Declaration Signer George Clymer Autograph Letter
Signed *"G. Clymer."* One page with integral address leaf, 4.75" x 8", np, nd. This letter was written to A. McCall Esquire, the content discusses land prices and taxes, it reads in part, *"Mr. Kane tells me that in consequence of a confirmation lately taken place of titles on Military grants that lands there have considerably risen in value - some up to 5 dollars!"* Clymer was a Declaration of Independence Signer representing Pennsylvania.

The letter is in fine condition; usual folds are present; edges are worn and torn slightly; residue and small hole present from wax seal removal. Also included with this ALS is a handsome engraving of Clymer, perfect for a display piece! From the Henry E. Luhrs Collection. Accompanied by LOA from PSA/DNA.
Estimate: $400-$600

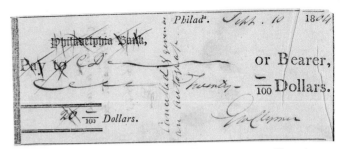

25255 **Declaration Signer George Clymer Document Signed**
"Geo. Clymer." One page, 5.2" x 2", Philadelphia Bank Check, Philadelphia, September 10, 1804. This lot features a cancelled check signed by George Clymer written for $20. George Clymer was a signer of the Declaration of Independence representing Pennsylvania. The document is in fine condition; document has been laid down on another piece of paper; cancellation marks present over some of text; staining present near the center of the document. From the Henry E. Luhrs Collection. Accompanied by LOA from PSA/DNA.
Estimate: $400-$500

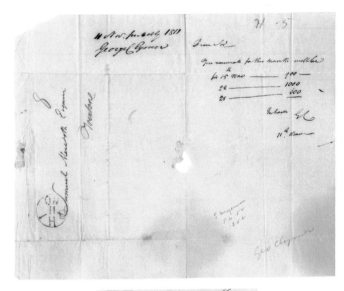

25256 **Declaration Signer George Clymer Autograph Letter Signed and Autograph Document Signed.** George Clymer was a signer of the Declaration of Independence representing Pennsylvania; he was also the first president of the Philadelphia Bank and the Philadelphia Academy of Fine Arts. The first document featured in this lot is an ALS signed, *"G.C."* One page, 8" x 10", np, August 29. The content of the letter is routine, stating Clymer's need for another copy of a note sent to him.

The second item is an autograph document signed, *"G.C."* One page, 7.75" x 9.75", np, November 11. The document is written out for a Mr. Samuel Meredith, and lists various renewals on his account.

The documents are both in very good condition; both have circular tears from the breaking of the wax seal; edges are worn and torn slightly; usual folds are present. From the Henry E. Luhrs Collection. Accompanied by LOA from PSA/DNA.
Estimate: $500-$700

25254 **Declaration Signer George Clymer Autograph Document.**
Two pages, 8.5" x 10.1", np, nd. Under Clymer's own hand, we have here a financial statement showing his exact worth; a list of all lands owned, houses, etc. According to this document, Clymer was worth around $137,000. This is an interesting document for collectors since it discloses property and possession of the signer. It reads in part, *"A house on Eight Street ———- The building cost more than 12,000 & it has been rated at 10,000 I set it at 8300 but have yet to pay on it about 1200 pounds ——- 3,300 5,000"*

The document is in very fine condition; usual folds are present; edges slightly worn. From the Henry E. Luhrs Collection. Accompanied by LOA from PSA/DNA.
Estimate: $1,000-$1,500

View color images of virtually every lot and place bids at HeritageAuctions.com/Americana

Session One, Auction #626 • Monday, February 20, 2006 • 5:00 p.m.

103

25257   Declaration Signed George Clymer Document Signed *"Geo. Clymer."*
One page, 5.1" x 2", Philadelphia Bank Check, Philadelphia, February 11, 1808.
This lot features a cancelled check signed by George Clymer written for $30.
George Clymer filled in the check and signed it. Clymer was a representative from
Pennsylvania at the signing of the Declaration of Independence. The document is
in fine condition; minor tear on the left edge; edges slightly worn. From the Henry
E. Luhrs Collection. Accompanied by LOA from PSA/DNA.
Estimate: $400-$500

25258   Constitution Signer Jonathan Dayton Autograph Letter Signed

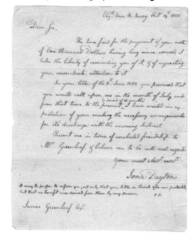

"Jona: Dayton". One page, 8" x
9.75", Elizabethtown, New Jersey,
October 14, 1801, to James
Greenleaf. In part, *"The time fixed
for the payment of your note of
One thousand Dollars having
long since arrived, I take the
liberty or reminding you of it, &
of requesting your immediate
attention to it..."* James Greenleaf
was a land speculator who, in
the 1790s, controlled as many as
one-third of the buildings for sale
in Washington, D.C. The supply
outstripped the demand and he
went bankrupt. Dayton signed
the Constitution as a representative of New Jersey and was a
member of the Continental Congress 1787-1788. A land speculator himself, he
got involved in the Aaron Burr scheme to set up an empire in the western United
States, and was arrested for treason in 1807, ending his political career. The city of
Dayton, Ohio is named after him, as he owned 250,000 acres of the state's land at
one time. Fine condition, very clear and legible writing, also signed with his initials
in the postscript. From the Henry E. Luhrs Collection. Accompanied by LOA from
PSA/DNA.
Estimate: $400-$500

**25259   Robert Dinwiddie
(1721-1770), Lieutenant
Governor of Virginia who appointed George Washington as
a Lieutenant Colonel in 1754 to
command an expedition against
the French. Letter Signed,** *"Robt.
Dinwiddie"* one page, 8" x 12.5",
London, May 20, 1769 to Andrew
Elliot concerning financial matters.
*"It is a Year ago since I received
your Letter in regard to the Debut
due me by Sir John Sinclair... In the
Meantime it is very hard upon me
to be out of the Money, lent out
of my Pocket, so long and indeed
my chief Dependence is upon your
Favour in Interfering in the Affair,
and hope you excuse the Trouble
I give you therein..."* Usual folds,
a few minor spots, a few marginal chips, else very good to fine
condition. A difficult example to
obtain; this a fine specimen. From
the Henry E. Luhrs Collection. Accompanied by LOA from PSA/DNA.
Estimate: $700-$900

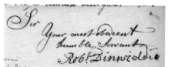

**25260   William J. Duane
1811 Autograph Letter
Signed** from an early
American journalist and author with incredible content.
Four pages, 7.75" x 9.75",
Philadelphia, March 4, 1811.
Duane was the publisher
of the Philadelphia *Aurora,*
the leading organ of the
Democratic Party. His friend
Thomas Jefferson went so
far as to attribute his election
as President to the support
of Duane's paper. This present letter comments on
various political situations
in Washington and the dis-
solution of the Bank of the
United States, in part: *"...Mr.
Madison's house is a scene of
odious intrigue. Washington is
a scene of dissipation and ex-
travagance which those which
also have seen the courts of
Europe say they do not equal...*

*Mr. Madison is like a man with his head in a noose, and these parties holding each
of them an end of the rope — he must select or perish between them...How Mr.
Hamilton fares, I know not; before he was a member of the Executive I had been
for years in constant correspondence with him. I believe him a very upright man
and that he has been sickened to the soul to see what he has seen..."* Fine condition;
hinged below a small vintage portrait. Originally purchased from Walter Benjamin
Autographs.

Also included in this lot is a Document Signed by Secretary of War John Armstrong
Jr. One page, partly printed, 8" x 9.75", Washington, March 18, 1814, commissioning John E. Calhoun as captain in the Third Regiment of Riflemen with an
officer's endorsement on the verso. Armstrong was a delegate to the Continental
Congress as well as a senator from New York. He fought in the Revolutionary War
and again in the War of 1812 before Madison named him Secretary of War. He was
forced to resign in September of 1814 when the he was blamed for the British
burning of Washington. Also fine condition. From the Henry E. Luhrs Collection.
Accompanied by LOA from PSA/DNA.
Estimate: $400-$600

**25261   Joseph Dudley
(1647-1720) Colonial
Governor of Massachusetts,
Endorsement Signed** *"J
Dudley"* on a 5.25" x 1.5"
slip removed from a larger
document, Boston, August
29, 1707. Mounted to a sheet
bearing his likeness, closely
cut, else fine condition. A
fine, representational specimen. From the Henry E. Luhrs
Collection. Accompanied by
LOA from PSA/DNA.
Estimate: $300-$500

25262   Speculation leading to the first financial panic in New York

William Duer, (1747 - 1799) Signer of the Articles of Confederation, Autograph Letter Signed, *"Wm. Duer"*, two pages, 10" x 8.75", Philadelphia, October 31, 1791. Headed *"Confidential."* Duer writes on land and financial speculation that would result in his personal ruin the following year which, in turn, resulted in the first financial panic in New York. He writes in part: *"It is probably you may see before this Reaches you, a Printed Set of Regulations which are this Evening to be taken up by the Stockholders... It is in my Judgment crude and Undigested... I have seen the Committee; and instead of their first observation about Branches; I have got them to agree to a Recommendation of their being without delay Established... I have satisfied myself that after the second Specie Payment in January, Branches will be established — will it not be therefore advisable for me to Cut quick out of the New York Stock; and still to lend my Force to the National Bank. before they raise — the account of the Branches will produce and a Rational Grounds — a considerable Raise — On this Presumption I hold as the 100, I bought of Lewis.— and if your Judgment corresponds as to mine, I wish you still to purchase about 150 Scrips... Scrip was here at the Noon Sales 155.— and there appears a movement with the Pennsylvanians to purchase— I have traced the Eastern Purchases: and find they are determine to hold in the Bank, as larger Interest than they have— after all you must Judge whether they can be bought Lower by Waiting-"* After mature Reflection, I think not, and therefore give you this opinion." "The panic in New York resulted in the loss of nearly $3,000,000 and ruined the fortunes of many investors. A excellent financial letter worthy of further research. Light creases, small hole at trimmed address leaf, else fine. From the Henry E. Luhrs Collection. Accompanied by LOA from PSA/DNA.

Estimate: $1,000-$1,500

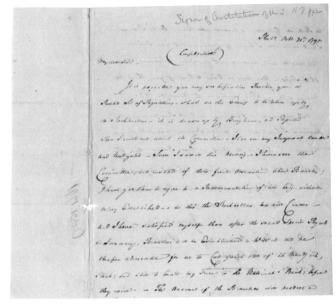

25263   Declaration Signer William Ellery Autograph Manuscript Signed in the third person. Three pages, 6.25" x 7.5", np, nd. A really interesting document that starts out: *"Extracted by William Ellery from a letter written by Alexander Garden of Charlestown, South Carolina March 1764, to Mr. William West of Philadelphia who labored under a vitiated state of blood and relaxation of solids..."* The entire item is about various natural medicines and their uses, recommending various agents and treatments for particular ailments. Ellery was an attorney by trade and training; it's interesting to discover his apparent interest in the medical field. Fine condition and, almost certainly, unique. From the Henry E. Luhrs Collection. Accompanied by LOA from PSA/DNA.

Estimate: $600-$800

25264   Declaration Signer William Ellery Endorsement Signed *"William Ellery."* Two pages (clipped from a larger document), 6.8" x 3.25", Rhode Island, July 30, 1784 (date endorsed). This document states that the General Assembly of Rhode Island owed two pounds and eight shillings to be paid to William Ellery out of the General Treasury. Ellery endorses the back and states that he received the sum in full.

The document is in fine condition; clipped from a larger document and placed in a border; usual folds are present; slight soiling has occurred along fold lines and edges. From the Henry E. Luhrs Collection. Accompanied by LOA from PSA/DNA.

Estimate: $400-$500

25265 Declaration Signer William Ellery Autograph Letter Signed *"William Ellery"*. One page, [Newport], August 13, 1794, to District Attorney Ray Greene. A letter from Ellery as customs collector of Newport, a job he held from 1790 until his death in 1820, in part: *"...Two cases have occurred which require you should be at Newport. — You will therefore I hope be here as soon as your business will admit..."* Ellery signed the Declaration of Independence as a representative of Rhode Island. He also was a member of the Continental Congress 1776-1785. This letter is written on strong laid paper and is in generally fine condition. There is a hole near his signature from the original wax seal, the integral address leaf is present and also in Ellery's hand. From the Henry E. Luhrs Collection. Accompanied by LOA from PSA/DNA.

Estimate: $500-$700

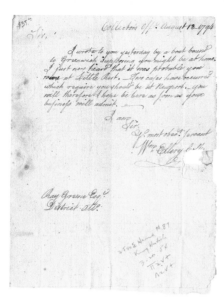

25266 Declaration Signer William Ellery Autograph Letter Signed *"Wm. Ellery Collr."* One page, 6.75" x 8", Collector's Office , Port of Newport, Rhode Island, December 4, 1810. The content of this letter regards exchange rates of foreign currency. It reads in part, *"Not receiving from you or from the Collr. of Providence, the information I wanted relative to the rate at which the money of Denmark, Sweden, and Norway should be estimated, I wrote to the Collr. of Boston and Charlestown, and now give you a copy of his letter. The Big dollar of Denmark, Sweden and Norway is a silver currency and always estimated at 100 cents. The Banco dollar is fixed for the current Dollar by the Bank & those for Denmark & Sweden are here taken at 75 cents"* William Ellery was a Declaration of Independence signer representing Rhode Island, he wrote this letter as customs collector of Rhode Island. This letter is a great look at how money was exchanged and traded at the turn of the 19th century. The letter is in very fine condition; usual folds are present; the edges are slightly rounded and worn. From the Henry E. Luhrs Collection. Accompanied by LOA from PSA/DNA.

Estimate: $600-$800

25267 William Ellery questions a bill for a Pillory for Providence Rhode Island

William Ellery (1727-1820) Signer of the Declaration of Independence, Rhode Island Representative, Autograph Endorsement Signed, *"William Ellery Cl[er]k"* on the verso of a manuscript Document, one page, 7.25" x 4.25", no place given [Providence, Rhode Island], April 8, 1769, a bill for *"... Building a Pillere [sic] for the County of Providence and finding materials of every Kind etc... £4.10.0..."* Because of the vagueness of the invoice and the large sum, Ellery notes that the lower house of the legislature *"Resolved that Benjamin Man be appointed to examin[e] into the Reasonableness of the within Charge"*. Light soiling along folds, tipped to a larger sheet, else very good. A Fine specimen. From the Henry E. Luhrs Collection. Accompanied by LOA from PSA/DNA.

Estimate: $600-$800

25268 John Ericsson (1803-1889), engineer, designer of the ironclad *Monitor,* **Autograph Letter Signed,** *"J. Ericsson"* one page, 5" x 8", no place given, February 28, 1859 asking his correspondent to *"Please take charge of the inclosed [sic] reply to Mr. Pisents [sic] letter - I cannot get up a letter or more safe drawing and description of my invention and I full well assumed that if Mr Pisant will only obtain a patent for which I consider we are proof against all interference in Cuba."* Tipped at top margin to a folder, else fine. A nice example from a man who changed military history. From the Henry E. Luhrs Collection. Accompanied by LOA from PSA/DNA.

Estimate: $500-$700

25269   John Ericsson (1803-1889), engineer, designer of the ironclad *Monitor,* **good engineering content Autograph Letter Signed,** *"J. Ericsson"* one page, 8" x 10", no place given, June 16, 1859 discussing designs for a ship.

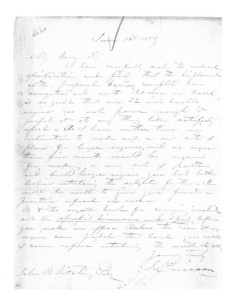

He writes: *"I have carefully read the enclosed specifications and find that the displacement of the purposed boat, compete for navigation and with 130 men on board, it so great that our 32 inch double engine has not power enough to propel it at any thing like satisfactory speed. As I have neither time nor inclination to make out a new set of plans for larger engines, and as more than five months would be required for making a new set of patterns and build larger engines you have better decline entertaining the subject further. It will be well to give your friends a positive refusal at once. As to the small boat for carrying invalids, ask for specific dimensions and specs before you make an offer. Unless the Kay engine can propel this boat, you will of course refuse entertaining the matter at all."* By this point, Ericsson was already an established naval engineer with an important resume including the invention of the screw propeller. He had also presented drawings of iron-clad battle ships with dome shaped gun towers to emperor Napoleon III of France in 1854. At the outset of the Civil War, the Confederacy began outfitting an ironclad from the hull of the burned out ship *Merrimack.* In August 1861, Congress recommended the construction of armored ships, and Ericsson presented drawings of what would become the U.S.S. *Monitor.* Though in 1862 it battled the *Merrimack* to a stalemate, it managed to save the wooden Union fleet from destruction and prove the utility of such construction. Light toning at margins, else near fine. From the Henry E. Luhrs Collection. Accompanied by LOA from PSA/DNA.

Estimate: $800-$1,200

25270   Declaration Signer William Floyd Document Signed *"Wm. Floyd".* One page, 8.25" x 8.5", manuscript, New York, April 3, 1784, certifying that *"...the state of New York is indebted unto James Post and Zebulon Jessup in the sum of Three Hundred and Two pounds..."* The document is in the autograph of Isaac Roosevelt, the great-great-grandfather of Franklin D. Roosevelt, and signed by Floyd, both acting as commissioners appointed *"...for the procuring of money on loan and Clothing for the use of this state..."* Jessup and Post sign the verso. William Floyd was a member of the Continental Congress, a signer of the Declaration of Independence, and a U.S. congressman, all as a representative from New York. Document is lightly and evenly toned, signatures bold and clear, a bit weak at the folds, else very good. From the Henry E. Luhrs Collection. Accompanied by LOA from PSA/DNA

Estimate: $800-$1,200

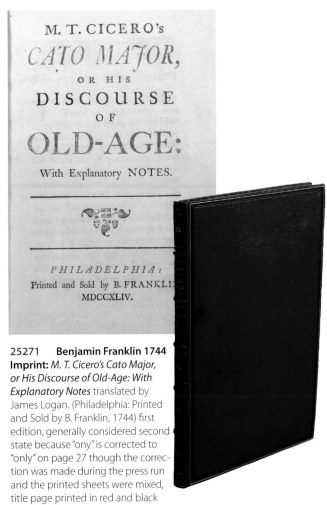

25271   Benjamin Franklin 1744 Imprint: *M. T. Cicero's Cato Major, or His Discourse of Old-Age: With Explanatory Notes* translated by James Logan. (Philadelphia: Printed and Sold by B. Franklin, 1744) first edition, generally considered second state because "ony" is corrected to "only" on page 27 though the correction was made during the press run and the printed sheets were mixed, title page printed in red and black with printer's device, viii, 159 pages, bound in full red levant morocco by Riviere & Son with gilt border and titles on the banded spine, all edges gilt, the larger and rarer issue on fine Genoese paper, 5.75" x 8.25".

This book is recognized as one of finest examples of the printer's art in Colonial times and was also the first classic work translated and printed in North America. It was Franklin's personal favorite of all that came from his press. He states in his "Printer to the Reader", in part: "I have, *Gentle Reader,* as thou seest, printed this Piece of *Cicero's* in a large and fair Character, that those who begin to think on the Subject of OLD AGE, (which seldom happens till their Sight is somewhat impair'd by its Approaches) may not, in Reading, by the *Pain* small letters give the Eyes, feel the *Pleasure* of the Mind in the least allayed...I shall add to these few Lines my hearty Wish, that this first Translation of a *Classic* in this Western World, may be followed with many others, performed with equal Judgment and Success; and be a happy Omen, that *Philadelphia* shall become the Seat of the *American* Muses." This handsome volume contains three bookplates, "Olin Lane Merriam", "Ex Museo C.A. and V. Baldwin", and "William Jephson Serjeant at Law". A fine, tight copy of an important work. Worthy of the finest library or collection. From the Henry E. Luhrs Collection.

Estimate: $6,000-$8,000

25272 **[Benjamin Franklin] His 1740 Pamphlet "A Collection of Charters and Other Public Acts"** *A Collection of Charters and Other Public Acts Relating to the Province of Pennsylvania* (Philadelphia: Franklin, 1740). Campbell 142; Evans 4583; Miller 203. Lacking the title leaf [a photostat of it is present], 46 pages, small folio, string bound but ragged at edges with pages beginning to separate at right margin. The contents are organized, for convenience and cheer, as follows. I: The Royal Charter of William Penn, Esquire - II: The First Frame of Government,

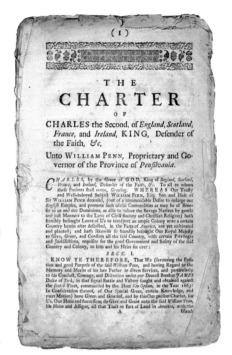

granted in England, in 1628 - III: The Laws agreed upon in England - IV: Certain Conditions or Concessions - V: The Act of Settlement, made at Chester, 1682 - VI: The Second Frame of Government, Granted in 1683 - VII: The Charter of the City of Philadelphia Granted October 25, 1701 - VIII: The New Charter of Privileges to the Province, Granted October 28, 1701. A rare and desirable item! From the Henry E. Luhrs Collection.

Estimate: $300-$500

25273 **Albert Gallatin, (1761-1849) Secretary of the Treasury under Thomas Jefferson and James Madison, Autograph Letter Signed,** *"Albert Gallatin"* as Secretary of the Treasury, two pages, 7.75" x 9.75", [Washington], April 23, 1805 to Thomas Rodney *"...and the other commissioners, &c Washington Mississippi Territory"* concerning elements of the reorganization of the Mississippi Territory following the Louisiana Purchase. Gallatin instructs the commissioners: *"It being provided by the 5th Section of the Act of March 27, 1804, that each of the Commissioners appointed to adjust the claims to lands in the Mississippi Territory west of Pearl River, shall be allowed six dollars for every day he shall attend on the Board after the last day of November 1804: it will be necessary.... [to] ascertain the number of days which each commissioner shall have this attended, and transmit the result... to this Office..."* The Pearl River became part of the western boundary of the Mississippi Territory when Jefferson acquired the Louisiana Territory in 1803. Extremely light creases, a few stray pencil marks, else Very Fine. From the Henry E. Luhrs Collection. Accompanied by LOA from PSA/DNA.

Estimate: $700-$900

25274 **Declaration Signer Elbridge Gerry Document Signed** *"E. Gerry"* with a large paraph beneath his name, as governor of Massachusetts. One page, 15" x 9.25", partly printed, Massachusetts, April 27, 1811. An officer's commission for Ezra Dodge *"...to be Lieutenant of a Company in the Third Regiment of Infantry in the First Brigade, and Second Division of the Militia of this Commonwealth..."* Also signed by the state secretary on the front and Lt. Col. Jona H. Lovett on the verso. Gerry signed the Declaration of Independence as well as the Articles of Confederation. He was also our nation's fifth vice-president, serving under James Madison, dying while in office in 1814. This handsome document is in very good condition with a bit of tattering around the edges, the paper seal is present and intact, and the signature is very fine and large. A fine, displayable document from the politician after whom gerrymandering was named. From the Henry E. Luhrs Collection. Accompanied by LOA from PSA/DNA

Estimate: $500-$700

25275 **Declaration Signer Elbridge Gerry Autograph Letter Signed** in the third person twice as, *"Mr. Gerry."* Two pages with integral address leaf, 7.25" x 9.25", Cambridge, October 25, 1798. This two-page document was written to Governor Increase Sumner of Massachusetts. The document contains a listing of books Gerry had brought back from his trip to Paris. Gerry was in France serving on the delegation over the XYZ affair, a large diplomatic scandal. The document is in fine condition; the usual folds are present; wax seal still intact; circular tear on address leaf from the wax seal being opened. From the Henry E. Luhrs Collection. Accompanied by LOA from PSA/DNA

Estimate: $700-$900

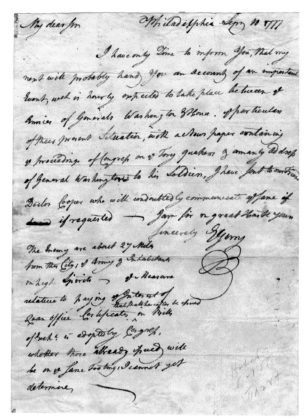

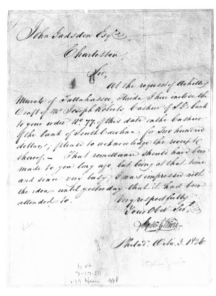

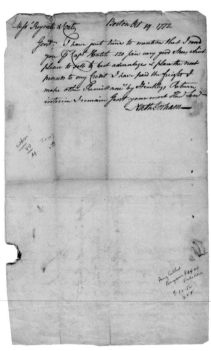

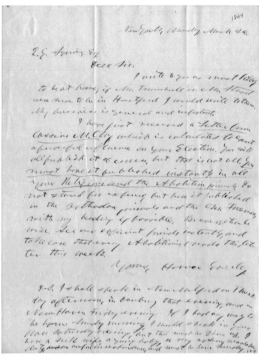

25279   Horace Greeley Autograph Letter on the Abolitionist Cassius Clay's Work. Autograph Letter Signed (twice: in full and with initials), 1 page, 7.5" by 10", Monday, March 26, no year [1844]; with integral address leaf, addressed in autograph and bearing the initialed message, "In haste - H.G." To Ephraim George Squier, the editor of the Whig Daily Journal in Hartford, Connecticut. The letter is fine, albeit there is some paper loss, not effecting text, on address leaf. With typed transcription. A quintessential example of the editor and politician who was mid-19th century America's most fiery, and dominant, agitator. In part: *"I write to you as most likely to be at home; if Mr. Trumbell or Mr. Stuart were sure to be Hartford I would write to them. My business is general and important. I have just received a Letter from Cassius M. Clay* [the American abolitionist and political campaigner] *which is calculated to excite a powerful influence on your Election* [Henry Clay's presidential bid of 1844]. *"You must have it published instantly in all your Religious and the Abolition journals. Do not stand for expense but have it published in the Orthodox journals and the Chr.* [Christian] *Freemen, with my heading if possible. Be energetic - be wise. See our efficient friends instantly, and take care that every Abolitionist reads this letter this week."* He rattles off where he is speaking in the next few days and says he'd speak in Hartford, too, *"but that must be given up. I have a sick wife, a young baby, a very arduous newspaper duty, an awful correspondence, and must be here Sunday."* From the Henry E. Luhrs Collection. Accompanied by LOA from PSA/DNA.
Estimate: $400-$600

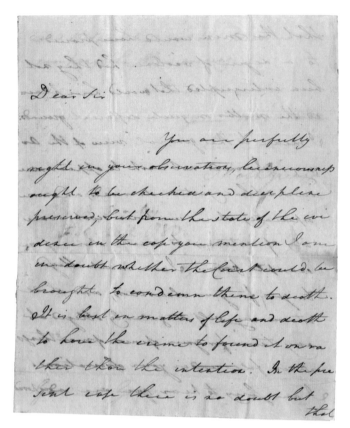

25280   Nathanael Greene Great Autograph Letter on Military Justice in the Continental Army! Autographed Letter Signed, *as Major General*, 3 pages, recto and verso, 7.5" by 9", Head Quarters, February 20, 1783. To **General Mordecai Gist**. In very fine condition, with some minor traces of mounting on margin on 4th integral leaf where, too, it is noted, there is a small hole, not affecting the text, where a wax seal was removed. Nathanael Greene emerged from the Revolution with a reputation as the outstanding patriot general of his age: this letter reveals why. *"You are perfectly right in your observations, licentiousness ought to be checked and discipline preserved; but from the state of the evidence in the case you mention I am in doubt whether the Court could be brought to condemn them to death. It is best in matters of life and death to have the crime to found it on, rather than the intention. In the present case there is no doubt but that the men would have proceeded to a degree of violence had they not been interrupted that would have placed the matter on quite different grounds: I mean to the general view of the Army. I would not want to appear more severe than justice demands; and more especially where we have such a variety of instances to make choice of an example from. I am much obliged to you for your observations; and shall esteem myself singularly obliged at any time for your opinion of men [&] things which fall under your observation..."* From the Henry E. Luhrs Collection. Accompanied by LOA from PSA/DNA.
Estimate: $3,500-$5,000

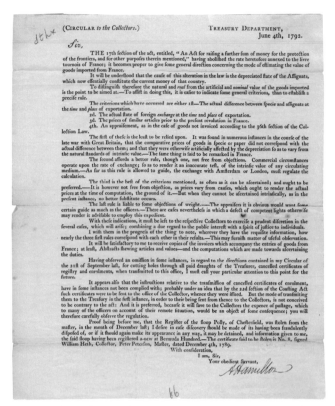

(CIRCULAR *to the Collectors*.)   TREASURY DEPARTMENT,
                                                 June 4th, 1792.

Sir,

THE 17th section of the act, entitled, "An Act for raising a further sum of money for the protection of the frontiers, and for other purposes therein mentioned," having abolished the rate heretofore annexed to the livre tournois of France; it becomes proper to give some general direction concerning the mode of estimating the value of goods imported from France.

It will be understood that the cause of this alteration in the law is the depreciated state of the Assignats, which now essentially constitute the current money of that country.

To distinguish therefore the natural and *real* from the artificial and *nominal* value of the goods imported is the point to be aimed at.—To assist in doing this, it is easier to indicate some general criterions, than to establish a precise rule.

The criterions which have occurred are either 1st.—The actual difference between specie and assignats at the *time* and *place* of exportation.

2d. The actual state of foreign *exchange* at the *time* and *place* of exportation.

3d. The prices of similar articles prior to the present revolution in France.

4th. An appraisement, as in the case of goods not invoiced according to the 36th section of the Collection Law.

The first of these is the least to be relied upon. It was found in numerous instances in the course of the late war with Great Britain, that the comparative prices of goods in specie or paper did not correspond with the actual difference between them; and that they were otherwise artificially affected by the depreciation so as to vary from the natural standards of intrinsic value.—The same thing is said to be remarked in France.

The second affords a better rule, though one, not free from objections. Commercial circumstances operate upon the rate of exchange; so as to render it an inaccurate test, of the intrinsic value of any circulating medium.—As far as this rule is allowed to guide, the exchange with Amsterdam or London, must regulate the calculation.

The third is the best of the criterions mentioned, as often as it can be ascertained; and ought to be preferred.—It is however not free from objection, as prices vary from causes, which ought to render the actual prices at the time of computation, the ground of it.—But when they cannot be ascertained intrinsically, as in the present instance, no better substitute occurs.

The last rule is liable to some objections of weight.—The appraisers it is obvious would want some certain guide as much as the officers.—There are cases neverthelefs in which a defect of competent lights otherwise may render it advisable to employ this expedient.

With these indications, it must be left to the respective Collectors to exercise a prudent discretion in the several cases, which will arise; combining a due regard to the public interest with a spirit of justice to individuals.

I with them in the progress of the thing to note, wherever they have the requisite information, how nearly the three first rules correspond with each other in their results.—This may furnish matter of useful observation.

It will be satisfactory to me to receive copies of the invoices which accompany the entries of goods from France; at least, Abstracts shewing articles and values—and the computations which are made towards ascertaining the duties.

Having observed an omission in some instances, in regard to the directions contained in my Circular of the 21st of September last, for cutting holes through all paid draughts of the Treasurer, cancelled certificates of registry and enrolments, when transmitted to this office, I must call your particular attention to this point for the future.

It appears also that the instructions relative to the transmission of cancelled certificates of enrolment, have in some instances not been complied with; probably under an idea that by the 22d section of the Coasting Act such certificates were to be sent to the office of the Collector, whence they were issued. But the mode of transmitting them to the Treasury in the first instance, in order to their being sent from thence to the Collectors, is not conceived to be contrary to the act: And it is preferred, because it will save to the Collectors the expence of postage, which to many of the officers on account of their remote situation, would be an object of some consequence; you will therefore carefully observe the regulation.

Proof being before me, that the Register of the sloop Polly, of Chesterfield, was stolen from the master, in the month of December last; I desire in case discovery should be made of its having been fraudulently disposed of, or if it should again make its appearance in any way, it may be detained, and information given to me, the said sloop having been registered a-new at Bermuda Hundred.—The certificate said to be stolen is No. 8, signed William Heth, Collector, Peter Peterson, Master, dated December 4th, 1789.

With consideration,
I am, Sir,
Your obedient Servant,
A Hamilton

25281   **Alexander Hamilton, (1755-1804) principal author of the Federalist Papers, and Secretary of the Treasury in the administration of George Washington, Letter Signed,** "*Alexander Hamilton*" one page, 7.75" x 9.25", [Philadelphia], June 4, 1792, a printed circular directed to federal customs collectors explaining that "*....having abolished the rate heretofore annexed to the ivre tournois of France; it becomes proper to give some general direction concerning the mode of estimating the value of goods imported from France. It will be understood that the cause of this alteration in the law is the depreciated state of the Assignats, which now essentially constitute the current money of that country...*" He continues the explanation setting forth a set of *ad hoc* rules to determine value of the new currency of France instituted during the French Revolution which proved to be as inflationary as Continental currency during the American Revolution. Thus in an effort to determine actual value of imported goods, Hamilton advised the collectors to primarily rely on the value of "*...similar articles prior to the present revolution in France...*" A few slight fold tears, hinged mounted to a folder, else fine. Overall a lovely document and quite desirable specimen with financial content. From the Henry E. Luhrs Collection. Accompanied by LOA from PSA/DNA.
Estimate: $3,000-$5,000

25282   **Alexander Hamilton Free Frank Signed** "*Free A. Hamilton*" inset into a paper address panel to John Nicholson, Esq., 4.75" x 2.75", np, nd. Hamilton was our nation's first (and possibly most important) Secretary of the Treasury, establishing the First Bank of the United States, public credit, and much of the basic infrastructure of our financial systems. This piece is in very good condition with general light soiling. From the Henry E. Luhrs Collection. Accompanied by LOA from PSA/DNA
Estimate: $1,000-$1,500

25283 Alexander Hamilton Letter Signed "*A. Hamilton*", one page, 8" x 12", "*War Department*", September 12, 1794 to Samuel Hodgson concerning outfitting troops en-route to western Pennsylvania to suppress the Whiskey Rebellion. Hamilton writes: "*I request that some person in character of chief Armourer who may also have charge of the Artificers be provided to accompany to Militia Army. Let him also engage such wheelwrights and other mechanics as may not certainly be found among the troops, and let every correspondent arrangement be made. One half the Intrenching [sic] tools intended for the expedition are to be forwarded without delay to Williamsport. The other half is destined for Carlisle.*" The Whiskey Rebellion arose from the 1791 tax issued on distilled spirits, a measure supported by Hamilton in his role as Secretary of the Treasury to pay down the enormous debt incurred by the United States during the American Revolution. The tax levied a six-cent per-gallon tax on large volume distillers, while smaller operations were forced to pay nine-cents per-gallon. Most of the distillery operations in the Appalachian west were of the smaller variety and were thus adversely impacted by the tax. Over the next several years, a nascent rebellion grew initially in the form of non-payment of the tax then escalated into harassment directed at tax collectors in western regions stretching form Georgia to Pennsylvania. After the tarring and feathering of a tax collector near Pittsburgh in the summer of 1794 (resulting in his death) and other mob actions, President Washington, remembering well the threat of Shay's Rebellion nearly ten years earlier, invoked the Militia Act of 1792. He summoned the militias of Virginia, Maryland and Pennsylvania to march to Pittsburgh. A force of 13,000, under the command of Washington, Hamilton and Henry Lee, marched into western Pennsylvania in September. In the wake of this massive show of force, the rebels quickly disappeared into the woods and the rebellion was easily suppressed. They managed to capture twenty barefoot men who were paraded down Market Street in Philadelphia. Two of them were charged with treason and sentenced to the gallows but Washington pardoned them on the grounds that one was a "simpleton" and the other "insane." The suppression of the rebellion had the unanticipated consequence of forcing many small whiskey producers further west into Kentucky and Tennessee, far out of reach of federal authority. Interestingly, in these regions distillers found excellent corn-growing country and discovered smooth, limestone-filtered water — both proving quite suitable for the blending of the finest whiskey. The tax itself, largely uncollectible outside of western Pennsylvania, was repealed in 1802. Hamilton, while still Secretary of the Treasury, also assumed the supervisory post over the army as Inspector General. In that role, under Washington, he addressed a variety of logistical issues that made deploying the large military force possible through what was still a relatively untamed frontier. Light horizontal creases, a very light dampstain just hits the bottom of Hamilton's dark bold signature, otherwise fine condition. From the Henry E. Luhrs Collection. Accompanied by LOA from PSA/DNA

Estimate: $7,000-$9,000

25284 (Alexander Hamilton) Gouverneur Morris (1752 - 1816), Signer and part author of the United States Constitution, **Partly Printed Document Signed** "*Gov Morris*" and also signed by **Rufus King** (1755 - 1827), "*R King*", **Oliver Wolcott, Jr.** (1760 - 1833), "*Oliv. Wolcott*" and others as Trustees of the Estate of Alexander Hamilton, one page, 7" x 6", New York, November 29, 1804. A wonderful piece of Hamiltoniana signed by some of his closest political allies. A "*Certificate*" issued to "*Dewitt Clinton for a Share in the Trust intended in a certain Writing of this date, relative to the estate of Alexander Hamilton, deceased; and this Certificate to be assignable, and to be receivable on Sales of the Estate by the Trustees, as a payment of Two Hundred Dollars: the Dividends, however, if any, which may have been paid on the Share, being first deducted.*" Alexander Hamilton was killed in a duel a few months earlier, July 11, 1804, on the heights of Weehawken, New Jersey by political adversary Aaron Burr. Their rivalry had festered for many years — Hamilton, a high Federalist, and Burr, a staunch Democratic-Republican, faced one another in a duel sparked by Hamilton's effort to deny Burr the Vice Presidency and the governorship of New York. The day before the fateful duel, Hamilton composed his last will and testament. He did not name Clinton or anyone else; his only named heir was his wife, Elizabeth Schuyler. Thus the payment to Clinton was likely resulting from a debt. A fine association piece. Very Fine condition. From the Henry E. Luhrs Collection.

Accompanied by LOA from PSA/DNA.

Estimate: $1,000-$1,200

25285   Settling the 1790 Pennsylvania Constitution.

Edward Hand (1744-1802) American General during the Revolution, Autograph Letter Signed, "*Edw:d Hand,* two pages, 6.5" x 8", Philadelphia, February 4, 1790 *...Some time ago I forwarded you the plan of the Legislative Branch, & now send those for the Executive & Judicial, as agreed on by the Committee of the whole[.] the bill of rights is gone through, one Section, (on the liberty of the press) excepted, expect the Committee of the whole will report tomorrow, and as the business has already been so amply discussed hope it will pass easily thro the Convention unless our absentees give an opening to the overhill gentleman [sic], and some of them are well dispose[d] to profit by such an advantage...*" The "overhill" gentlemen to which Hand refers were likely delegates from the western counties of Pennsylvania who had benefited from the radical democratic state Constitution of 1776. That first constitution provided for a unicameral legislature, frequent elections and a weak executive. In many respects the debate over the Pennsylvania Constitution mirrored the debate over the Federal Constitution. The revised Pennsylvania Constitution was passed just two days following this letter, on February 6, 1790. Small loss at top right corner of blank leaf, with integral address leaf, mounting strip along verso of left margin, else Fine. An amazing piece of history. From the Henry E. Luhrs Collection. Accompanied by LOA from PSA/DNA.
Estimate: $1,500-$2,000

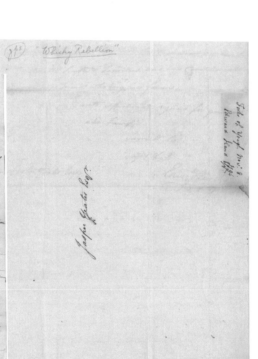

25286   General Edward Hand writes en route to suppress the Whiskey Rebellion

Edward Hand (1744-1802) American General during the Revolution, Autograph Letter Signed, "*Edwd Hand*", one page 7.5" x 9", "*Camp Forks of Youghisgeni*", November 8, 1794 to Jasper Yates. "*...the description of bad roads & deluges of rain in the mountains which would be neither new or Amusing to you — indeed even now I can only tell you that the Right column lies near buds Ferry on the N E of Youhiogeni [?] — and will I suppose soon move towards Pittsburgh — the left Column lies between Buds & Parkinson's Ferrys - the light or advanced Corps from both Columns have yesterday or will to day Cross the Monongahela into Washington County - The Judicial Gentlemen are constantly laboring and will I hope in the end bring forth something - a few days must develop the plans of government - & I hope they will be successful - Mr Smith, Fr Judge advocate Duncan & Myself are perfectly well indeed the whole Army are uncommonly healthy...*" The Whiskey Rebellion arose with the 1791 tax issued on distilled spirits, a measure supported by Hamilton in his role as Secretary of the Treasury to pay down the enormous debt incurred by the United States during the American Revolution. The tax levied a six-cent per-gallon tax on large volume distillers, while smaller operations were forced to pay nine-cents per-gallon. Most of the distillery operations in the Appalachian West were of the smaller variety and were thus adversely impacted by the tax. Over the next several years, a nascent rebellion grew initially in the form of non-payment of the tax then escalated into harassment directed at tax collectors in regions stretching form Georgia to Pennsylvania. After the tarring and feathering of a tax collector near Pittsburgh in the summer of 1794 (resulting in his death) and other mob actions, President Washington, remembering well the threat of Shay's Rebellion nearly ten years earlier, invoked the Militia Act of 1792. He summoned the militias of Virginia, Maryland and Pennsylvania to march to Pittsburgh. A force of 13,000, under the command of Washington, Hamilton and Henry Lee, marched into western Pennsylvania in September. In the wake of this massive show of force, the rebels quickly disappeared into the woods and the rebellion was easily suppressed. They managed to capture twenty barefoot men who were paraded down Market Street in Philadelphia. Two of them were charged with treason and sentenced to the gallows but Washington pardoned them on the grounds that one was a "simpleton" and the other "insane." The suppression of the rebellion had the unanticipated consequence of forcing many small whiskey producers further west into Kentucky and Tennessee, far out of reach of federal authority. Interestingly, in these regions distillers found excellent corn-growing country and discovered smooth, limestone-filtered water — both proving quite suitable for the blending of the finest whiskey. The tax itself, largely uncollectible outside of western Pennsylvania, was repealed in 1802. Fine condition. From the Henry E. Luhrs Collection. Accompanied by LOA from PSA/DNA.
Estimate: $1,500-$2,000

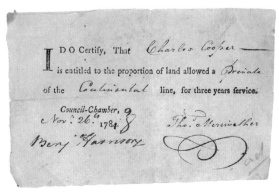

25287   Declaration Signer Benjamin Harrison V Document Signed
"Benj. Harrison". One page, 5.75" x 3.5", partly printed, [Philadelphia], November 26, 1784, certifying that a Charles Cooper *"...is entitled to the proportion of land allowed a Private of the Continental line, for three years service..."* Countersigned by Thomas Meriwether. Harrison signed the Declaration of Independence as a representative of Virginia and, of course, was the father and great-grandfather of two U.S. Presidents. Fine condition. From the Henry E. Luhrs Collection. Accompanied by LOA from PSA/DNA.
Estimate: $300-$400

25288   (American Revolution) Udney Hay, American officer in the Revolutionary War, curious Autograph Letter Signed *"Udney Hay"* two pages with integral address leaf, 7.5" x 11.5", Fish Kill, [New York] July 31, 1779 to John Fisher referring to an act of Congress of July 9, 1779 regulating the Quartermaster's Department which led to much consternation among the officers, bringing many to the point of resignation. The letter reads in part: *"In a letter form General Greene QM Genl. red. yesterday, I am officially inform'd that his Excellency the Governor, was determin'd not to exercise the Power, he was vest-ed with, but uncertain whether this was wrote to General Green[e] confidentially, or with liberty to make it public, to such part of the Department as thought themselves injured by the Resolve of the 9th Instant. I waited on his Excellency myself, and have the pleasure to acquaint you that he is not only determined not to exercise any part of the powers vested in him, by the above Resolve, but has given me liberty to inform you officially that such is determination..."* He goes on to request that *"...at least untill [sic] there is an attempt to put the Resolve of 9th Inst. into execution or Congress may again be pleased to make a new Resolve which our inclination to preserve the Characters unsullied may prevent us from submitting to..."* It appears that the Congressional resolve was designed to allow state governors to investigate the affairs of quartermasters in their respective states which diluted the power of the quartermaster general. Greene would eventually leave the post of Quartermaster to accept a much desired field command. He would distinguish himself in the southern campaign of 1781. Light soiling, small hole from seal tear not affecting text, address leaf trimmed, else fine. From the Henry E. Luhrs Collection. Accompanied by LOA from PSA/DNA.
Estimate: $600-$800

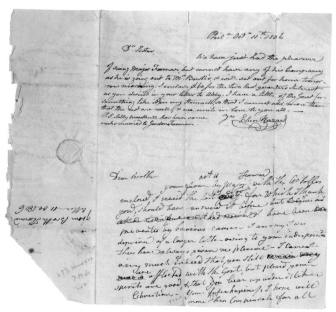

25289   Ebenezer Hazard Three Autograph Letters Signed *"Eben Hazard"* (with added paraphs) to his sister, Elizabeth Breese. The first letter: one page to his sister plus one page reply on same lettersheet, 7.75" x 9.75", Philadelphia, October 11, 1806. In part, *"...I Have a little of the Gout (or something like it) in my stomach, so that I cannot add more than that the rest are well..."* The second letter: 2.5 pages, 8" x 9.5", Philadelphia, June 8, 1807. Third letter: one page, 8" x 9.5", Philadelphia, March 26, 1813. Hazard was the first postmaster of New York City and later, the Postmaster General under the Continental government. Under his guidance, the mail was first carried in stagecoaches, an improvement over the horse and rider system. Letters are generally in good to very good condition. From the Henry E. Luhrs Collection. Accompanied by LOA from PSA/DNA.
Estimate: $400-$500

25290   Signer Joseph Hewes accounts for his slaves and other property.

Joseph Hewes (1730 - 1779) Signer of the Declaration of Independence and the first Secretary of the Navy, fine content manuscript Document Signed "*Joseph Hewes*" one page, 8" x 13", no place given, October 16, 1777 being "*A Schedule of the Taxable property of Joseph Hewes exclusive of what he has in Company with Rob. Smith delivered the 16th Octo. 1777 to Joseph Blount Esqr...*" The account lists all his land holdings including "*120 Acres of Land or there abouts, adjoining the Town of Edenton...*" which also contained a "*House & Kitchen*" together with 50 acres and a house "*...adjoining the land known by the name of McGraths...*". In addition he held 225 acres of land in Tyrrel County and 100 acres in Dauphin County as well as urban property in Edenton including "*...Stores, Kitchen, Stable & Hatters ship... Ware House Wharf etc...*" The tax schedule also includes the names of Hewes' ten slaves including "*Frank, Gun, Cuff, Will, James, Tounside, Yarmsuth, Sam, Hardy [and] Tene*" Hewes adds his name just below the names of his slaves. Hewes, born in Connecticut to Quaker parents, studied at Princeton and became a very successful merchant. Around 1760 he moved to North Carolina where he established himself in politics. In the years leading up to the Revolution, Hewes was a strong advocate for American rights and an early voice for independence. His support of war caused him to break with the Society of Friends. Light uneven toning, usual folds, else Fine condition with a dark, bold signature. Another important piece of Black Americana tying a Founding Father to slavery. From the Henry E. Luhrs Collection. Accompanied by LOA from PSA/DNA.

Estimate: $8,000-$12,000

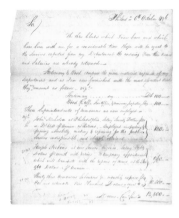

25292   Samuel Hodgdon, Washington's Superintendent of Military Stores, Details the Operation of His Department. Letter Signed, as Superintendent of Military Stores, 3 pages, recto and verso, 8" by 9.25", Philadelphia, October 6, 1796. Some wear and age-toning, with a couple folds showing some separation, but boldly signed: good, overall. This rare and interesting report, mostly likely to the Board of War, specifically concerns the personnel, functions, and salaries of the new Department. Hodgdon had a long career, in the Revolution and during the earliest days of the new nation, as a Quartermaster of the Army. He enjoyed the confidence of Washington and served at his request, as Quartermaster General and later, Superintendent of Military Stores. He retired, finally, in 1800, and went on to a successful business career, which culminated in his selection to the presidency of a trust and insurance firm, the Pennsylvania Company, in 1813. From the Henry E. Luhrs Collection. Accompanied by LOA from PSA/DNA.

Estimate: $150-$250

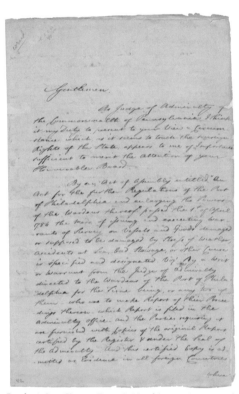

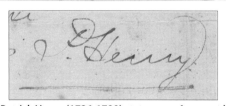

25291   Patrick Henry (1736-1799) statesman, Autograph Letter Signed "*P. Henry*" one page, 6.5" x 8" with integral address leaf in his hand, Richmond, [Virginia], November 14, 1786, to his son-in-law Spencer Roane, by Fanny, a slave girl. As he prepared to depart Richmond after declining his reelection as Governor of Virginia in favor of resuming his law practice in Pleasant Grove, he writes of "*The unexpected appearance of your Waggon [sic] & Fannys setting off prevents her being clad as we could wish — Indeed she followed the Waggon without our knowing it, being according to custom, with a Throng about us. Supposing Fanny may be usefull [sic] - to you she is now sent- with love to our dear Annie... P.S. My Wife is so busy packing up &c &c prevents her writing*" "*Annie*" was Anne Henry Roane Henry (1767-1799), his daughter. A fine, warm example. Some soiling and a tear to lower right corner affecting no text, else Fine. From the Henry E. Luhrs Collection. Accompanied by LOA from PSA/DNA.

Estimate: $4,000-$5,000

25293   Declaration Signer Francis Hopkinson Autograph Letter Signed "*Fra. Hopkinson*". Three pages plus docketing information, 8" x 13", Philadelphia, August 21, 1788, to the President and Supreme Executive Council of Pennsylvania. An interesting letter written while a Judge of the Admiralty and regarding a warrant of survey on the brig *Adventure* directed to the Board of Wardens by a British Counsul. He writes "*...as I know of no Convention between the United States of America and the Court of London investing the British Consul with this Power, I thought it necessary to submit the matter to the Consideration of your Honourable Board...*" Hopkinson signed the Declaration of Independence as a representative of New Jersey. Very good condition, weakness at folds, and edge roughness archivally repaired. Originally purchased from Walter R. Benjamin Autographs. From the Henry E. Luhrs Collection. Accompanied by LOA from PSA/DNA.

Estimate: $800-$1,200

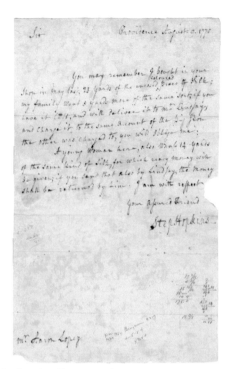

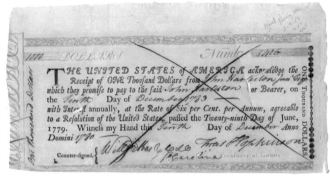

25296 **Declaration Signer Francis Hopkinson Document Signed** *"Fras. Hopkinson."* One page, 10" x 5", np, December 10, 1780. A Revolutionary War Bond for $1000, signed by the Treasurer of Loans Hopkinson and countersigned by Will Gibbes of South Carolina. Francis Hopkinson signed the Declaration of Independence representing New Jersey. The document is in fine condition; canceled with an "x" pen; very fragile paper, almost brittle; signatures are bold and crisp. From the Henry E. Luhrs Collection. Accompanied by LOA from PSA/DNA.
Estimate: $600-$800

25294 **Declaration Signer Stephen Hopkins Scarce Autograph Letter Signed** *"Step. Hopkins".* One page with integral address leaf, 7.5" x 12.5", Providence, August 9, 1770, to Aaron Lopez, merchant. Hopkins is ordering more yards of a silk previously secured from Lopez who was one of the most successful and respected Jewish merchants of the period. Hopkins signed the Declaration of Independence as a representative from Rhode Island. He was also a member of the Continental Congress 1774-1776. About very good condition; folds, general light foxing, a piece torn from right edge where opened (no text affected), wax seal still intact, old hinges present on verso. Purchased from Walter R. Benjamin Autographs with original folder present. From the Henry E. Luhrs Collection. Accompanied by LOA from PSA/DNA.
Estimate: $1,000-$1,500

25297 **Declaration Signer Samuel Huntington Autograph Document Signed** in the third person. One page, 8" x 4", Norwich, September 21, 1787. The lower portion of a partly printed document where Huntington is granted a tract of land in the state of Connecticut (of which he was governor) *"...forty six acres & one hundred & four rods of land Situated in Norwich aforesaid near Hough plain...".* Huntington was a fierce supporter of the Revolutionary cause, serving as a member of the Continental Congress and later as the first President of the United States in Congress Assembled. His writing on this lightly toned document is dark and legible; the folds are a bit weak with one old repair on the verso not affecting the docketing information, else very good. From the Henry E. Luhrs Collection. Accompanied by LOA from PSA/DNA.
Estimate: $400-$600

25295 **Declaration Signer Francis Hopkinson Document Signed** *"F. Hopkinson."* 8" x 4.25", Pennsylvania, September 20, 1779. A signed draft upon the Commissioners of the U.S. at Paris, in favor of Elbridge Gerry, signer from Massachusetts, for $12 for interest due on money borrowed by the United States. Signed by Hopkinson as Treasurer of Loans and endorsed by Gerry on the verso. A nice association of two signers.

The document is in very good condition; borders have been trimmed; edges wrinkled and folded; slight tears on upper and left edges. From the Henry E. Luhrs Collection. Accompanied by LOA from PSA/DNA.
Estimate: $1,000-$1,500

25298   Declaration Signer Samuel Huntington Document Signed "*Sam. Huntington President*". One page, 10.75" x 6.75", vellum, partly printed, The United States of America in Congress Assembled document signed by Huntington as president, Philadelphia, January 7, 1780. A commission appointing Joseph Swearingen "...Captain Lieutenant in the Eighth Virginia Regiment in the Army of the United States..." Huntington signed the Declaration of Independence as a representative of Connecticut, a state he would later govern; here he signs as President of the Continental Congress. This beautiful document is in fine condition; folds as expected, the seal is complete and intact. Originally from the collection of Oliver R. Barrett. From the Henry E. Luhrs Collection. Accompanied by LOA from PSA/DNA.
Estimate: $1,000-$1,500

25299   Samuel Huntington (1732-1796) Signer of the Declaration of Independence, Autograph Letter Signed, "*S. Huntington*" as Governor of Connecticut, four pages, 8 x 12.75", no place given, October 11, 1792. A lengthy address to the "*Gentlemen of the Council; Mr. Speaker, & Gentlemen of the House of Representatives*" discussing a wide range of issues before the legislature. He writes in small part: "*It is Expected your Committee appointed to Inspect the Grand list for a number of years past will make their Report at this Time... and Assist your endeavours to make such alterations in the mode of Taxation as may appear more Equitable & Just if such can be devised - A revision and alteration of our Militia laws for conformity to the Act of Congress as near as may be, will not Escape your attention. the Improving and repairing the more Important public roads is an object worthy the notice of the Legislature.... The applications for particular Acts of Insolvency seem to be encrasing [sic], & as Congress have made no provision in such cases, is it not Expedient that the legislature of this State, should make some regulation relative to the Subject, in particular to prevent a preference of debts in favour of the first attaching Creditors of a bankrupt Estate. there exists also another difficulty respecting those particular Acts of Insolvency: they appear, prima facie, to be expost [sic] facto laws, and in that view may perhaps be called in question as being repugnant to the Constitution of the Nation & void; to the great disadvantage of honest Debtors who may have religiously conformed to such Acts. You will remember that no provision hath been made by Government for the encouragement and Support of Schools the present year. Perhaps it may be thought by some, that this Subject hath been too frequently reiterated from the Chair; But let me observe that it arises from the Impression of a firm belief that it is Impossible for a free people to preserve their liberties & privileges... unless useful knowledge is generally diffused among them, & the principles of Virtue & religion included so as to obtain a governing Influence upon the Visible conduct & deportment of the Inhabitants; and were these favours properly upon every rising generation, I am fully persuaded that all Arbitrary & Despotic government would vanish away...*" Wonderful insight into the issues facing the state in the early days of the Republic, particularly on the subject of bankruptcy — a significant concern for many years. Samuel Huntington was a self-taught attorney who held a number of official posts in Connecticut and became active with the Sons of Liberty in 1774. He served in the Continental Congress from 1776 to 1784 and twice served as its president. In 1786 he was elected Governor of Connecticut and remained in that office until his death. Light folds, else fine condition. From the Henry E. Luhrs Collection. Accompanied by LOA from PSA/DNA.
Estimate: $1,000-$1,500

25300   Thomas Hutchinson (1711-1780) Last civilian Colonial Governor of Massachusetts, manuscript Document Signed

"*T Hutchinson*" as Judge of Probate one page, 6.25" x 7.25", Boston, November 2, 1764 certifying that "*... the Account of Jonathan Snelling Administrator Dr. Bonis now Complete annexed of the Estate of his late father Jonathan Snelling late of Boston Mariner deceased and a List of Debts remained due, it appears that the Debts will exceed the personal Estate...*" Hutchinson, in reality a political moderate, was made the scapegoat by Massachusetts radicals for British tax policies. In 1765 a mob, mistakenly informed that Hutchinson supported the Stamp Act, and ransacked his home. Though Hutchinson opposed many of the British measures to tax the colonies, he was also opposed to mob rule which placed him in a precarious position. His involvement in the importation of tea in 1773 — despite fierce opposition — made him a political liability and he was replaced by General Thomas Gage in 1774. Neatly laid in to a larger sheet, light foxing and toning along folds, else Very Good. From the Henry E. Luhrs Collection. Accompanied by LOA from PSA/DNA.

Estimate: $400-$500

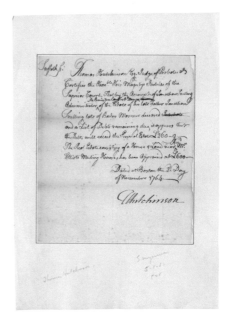

25301   A Federalist criticizes Jay's Treaty

Jared Ingersoll (1749-1822) Signer of the Constitution, Autograph Letter Signed, "*J. Ingersoll*" three pages with integral address leaf in his hand, Philadelphia, November 9, 1795 to Samuel Bayard (1767-1840), agent of the United States in London charged with prosecuting American claims in British Admiralty Courts. A fine content letter criticizing Jay's Treaty with Great Britain and the growing rift in America between supporters of the French Revolution and those advocating stronger ties with Britain. He writes in part: "*...Mistress of the Ocean, Great Britain appears to me, to disregard all considerations of Justice or the Rights of Neutral Nations, much of her conduct is in conformity with such sentiments & and admits an easy solution, but why she should at the same moment court us to a degrading Treaty, and insult us while its ratification was in Uncertainty, I do not understand. What is there at the Court of Great Britain to dazzle the eyes and turns the head of an American? have you experienced its fascinating Charms? as my three years residence was in the sequestered Chambers of the temple, I am at a loss to know why it is that the U.S. diminish so much in the eye of an American resident at [the Court of] St. James. When I say so much I mean as one would suppose from the perusal of Mr. jay's Treaty. While I thus express myself with respect to the English Court do not consider me a Partizan [sic] of France, I see with infinite regret a French & and English Interest rising up among us, and threatening to include all under those two Factions and to leave note to support an American Independent Character, that will regard French & English only as they may be rendered subservient to this national Concern- At last favor me you're your opinion as to the probable and expectable conduct of the English Court as the subject of the Spoliations on our trade, do they attempt to justify the measure? will they compensate us for our losses, is Delay their object. The revocation of the provision order as I is called, I take for granted, I only because, it is thought by Mr. Pitt, that they have less need of our Flour, now than previously to their harvest , or that they can at present hold over Accounts with us, if we threaten Sequestration, at any rate that they do not recall upon any Acknowledgement that the Order was not founded on the Law of Nations...*" Ingersoll studied law in London at the Middle Temple in the late 1760s where he made the acquaintance with Benjamin Franklin. In late 1794, John Jay had negotiated a commercial treaty with Great Britain (commonly known as Jay's Treaty) in which the British agreed to abandon their forts in the Northwest Territory in exchange for the settlement of pre-Revolutionary War debts owed to British citizens. Many regarded the treaty as a sell-out as the agreement did not address the problem of British impressments of American ship crews and those opposed to Britain's war with revolutionary France. Ingersoll accurately predicts the rift between opponents and supporters of the French Revolution in America that preoccupied political discourse for the balance of the decade. Small hole from seal tear, light creases, else fine. Incredible insight, important history... a great letter. From the Henry E. Luhrs Collection. Accompanied by LOA from PSA/DNA.

Estimate: $1,500-$1,800

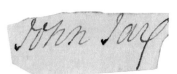

25302   Continental Congress President John Jay Signature, a small clip 1.75" x .625" laid down to a 5" x 3" card. If anyone can be called a "founding father" of the United States, Jay certainly qualifies. He served in the First and Second Continental Congress and served as president of that body from 1778 to 1779. He was then instrumental in the peace process after the Revolutionary War, helping to fashion American foreign policy in Europe. He co-wrote the *Federalist Papers* with Alexander Hamilton and James Madison. He was the first, as well as the youngest, Chief Justice of the United States, serving from 1789 to 1794. He later was elected governor of New York. From the Henry E. Luhrs Collection. Accompanied by LOA from PSA/DNA.
Estimate: $400-$500

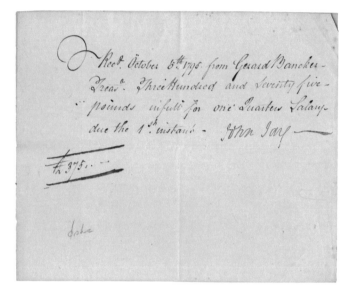

25303   Continental Congress President John Jay Document Signed. One page, 8" x 12.75", np, October 6, 1795. In full "Recd October 6th 1795 from Gerard Bancker- Treasr. Three Hundred and Seventy Five pounds in full for one Quarters Salary due the 1st instant." Signed at the close. Bancker was the treasurer of the state of New York and this was most certainly a receipt for Jay's pay as governor of New York. Fine or better condition; fresh and bright but with one paper clip impression at right, away from signature. From the Henry E. Luhrs Collection. Accompanied by LOA from PSA/DNA.
Estimate: $800-$1,200

25304   Henry Laurens (1724-1792) diplomat and President of the Continental Congress, Autograph Letter Signed, "*Henry Laurens President of Congress*", one page, 8.25" x 13.25", York, Pennsylvania, June 9, 1778 to the Vice President of Pennsylvania, informing him of the enclosure of several acts of Congress including: "*...27th May. for an Establishment of the American Army... 4 June for appointing Commissioners for holding a treaty with the Delaware Shawnese [sic] & other Indians at Fort Pitt the 23d July next... 8 June for raising a Company of foot in the county of Northumberland &c... for laying a general Embargo on certain articles of provisions...*" In the end, the Shawnee did not negotiate with the commissioners, seeing the Americans as a threat to their territory. But certain elements of the Delaware went ahead and signed the treaty of Fort Pitt in September 1778. The treaty allowed the construction of Fort Delaware on the Ohio. The act of May 27 concerning the establishment of the army was a complete reorganization of the force with a standardization in pay and personnel. It was an integral part of creating a more disciplined, professional army capable of defeating the British. Light toning at left margin, usual folds, else fine. As noted, Laurens is tough; an ALS with content of this magnitude is prohibitive. From the Henry E. Luhrs Collection. Accompanied by LOA from PSA/DNA.
Estimate: $5,000-$7,000

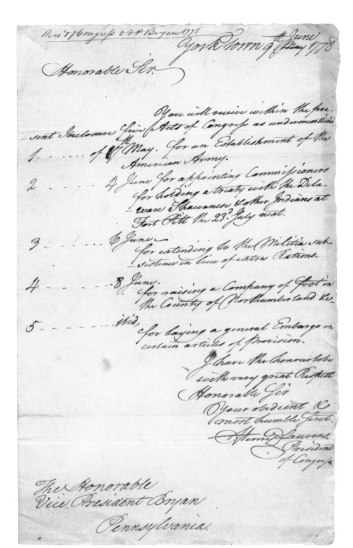

25305 Henry Laurens (1724-1792) diplomat and President of the Continental Congress, Autograph Letter Signed, "*Henry Laurens President of Congress*", one page, 8.25" x 13.25", York, Pennsylvania, January 1, 1778 to Thomas Wharton, President of Pennsylvania, informing him that he "...*had the honor of making to the State of Pennsylvania was directed to the Honorable Mr. Speaker of Assembly, having been advised to so by the Delegates in Congress... Permit me this at present the liberty o sending to your hands an Act of Congress of 31st Decem[ber] for promoting a speedy reformation in the Army discipline & economy which you will pleased to lay before the proper power...*" On December 31, 1777, Congress resolved "That as it is expedient to promote a speedy reformation in the army, as well for the purpose of discipline as economy; and the number of officers being already out of all proportion to that of the privates, to avoid further embarrassments in this respect, it be recommended to the governments of the several states, to suspend filling up any vacancies in their respective regiments, until they shall hear further from Congress on the subject." Congress convened in York, Pennsylvania for much of early 1778 as the British were occupying Philadelphia. Light creases, loss from seal tear neatly repaired, else fine. Laurens is tough; an ALS with such fine content is quite desirable. From the Henry E. Luhrs Collection. Accompanied by LOA from PSA/DNA.

Estimate: $3,000-$4,000

25306 Arthur Lee (1740-1792) and Samuel Osgood (1747-1813), Letter Signed, "*Arthur Lee*" "*Samuel Osgood*", one page with integral address leaf, 7.5" x 9.25", [Philadelphia], September 5, 1788 to Jonathan Dayton concerning the Symmes purchase of land in present-day southwest Ohio. John Cleves Symmes, a New Jersey judge who had contributed much of his wealth to support the Continental Army, requested a contract to promote and settle the region. Symmes formed a syndicate, the Ohio Company, to purchase land between the Great and Little Miami Rivers north of the Ohio River. Symmes, in his eagerness, began settlement of the country before Congress could even act to grant him the territory, causing no little consternation among the delegates. Jonathan Dayton (1760-1824), a former general from New Jersey (and at the time of this letter a delegate to Congress), was one of the shareholders in the company. Here, congressional delegates Lee and Osgood note some irregularities in Symmes' deeds. They inform Dayton that "*On looking over Mr. Symmes Deeds, which you left at this office, they do not appear in some of the Clauses to Correspond with the Acts of Congress; we have therefore thought it advisable to refer them to the Examination of Council; which will necessarily prevent the Completion of this Business till the Early Part of next Week...*" Congress finally agreed to a contract for one million acres on October 15, 1788. The subsequent survey, which was highly flawed, and continued Indian warfare prevented much settlement until after 1795. The cities of Cincinnati and Dayton were part of this purchase. Arthur Lee was one of the American agents sent to Paris to seek an alliance with France during the American Revolution and later served in the Continental Congress. Samuel Osgood also served in the Continental Congress and became the first Postmaster General under the Constitution of 1787. Light creases, a few toned spots, else fine. Another example of significant, early history that documents how the country was settled. From the Henry E. Luhrs Collection. Accompanied by LOA from PSA/DNA.

Estimate: $1,000-$1,500

25307 General Charles Lee on Adams' captured correspondence, riotous riflemen, and the Hessians

Charles Lee (1732-1782), Major General in the American Revolution and traitor, Autograph Letter Signed, "*Charles Lee*", three pages, 7.75" x 12.5", "*Camp on Winter Hill*" [near Cambridge], October 10, 1775 to Benjamin Rush (1746-1813) Signer of the Declaration of Independence. A rich, detailed (and ever colorful!) letter written in the early months of the war to his friend in Philadelphia. Lee comments on the recently captured and published letter by John Adams criticizing rival John Dickinson (as well as a veiled insult directed at Lee), on news that Great Britain would contract German troops to fight in America, and then laments the presence of wild and undisciplined Virginia riflemen whom he labels "*...soft, dirty mutinous and disaffected...*". In an interesting combination of colorful discourse and straightforward complaints, he writes: "*General Washington[']s letter I think, a very good one, but Gage certainly deserv'd a still stronger one such as it was before it was soften'd - that Gentleman has now run his race of glory. I am afraid your intended Philippic will not pass I call'd him damn him, let us leave him alone to the hell of his own conscience and the infamy which must [certainly?] attend him! You see I have not left off swearing, but am in hopes that your reproofs and time will bring about reformation. I am sorry that we have reason to apprehend bad consequences from the publication of Adams's [sic] letter - Surely Dickinson can not be so ill arm'd in zeal for liberty as to suffer private pique to slacken him in the public cause - if it has this effect, H must forfeit all title to the reputation of a truly virtuous citizen. What in the Devil's name possesses the Congress in not giving orders to seize that scoundrel Tryon [?]. Scoundrel is not too harsh an epithet for the man, who will accept of any office under the present hellish Administration, as They can only hold their office by a scoundrel Tenure any delicacy of this kind at present is not only ridiculous but must be pernicious - it confirms me in an opinion that I have long held - viz that in public contests Rogues, with inferior capacities, are an overmatch for the honest. With suspicion the latter are always hesitating lest they shou'd not act consonantly to the rule of rectitude - whereas the former finds no stumbling blocks - cato's aprts were perhaps equal to Caesars, but Cato would never have forc'd the doors of the Temple of Ops where the public Soul has lodg'd. Brutus (cou'd He have relax'd at certain junctures from his inflexible divine notions of honor and virtue), would have baffled and crush'd that reprobate Antony - indeed a thousand instances might be produc'd from ancient History in support of my Hypothesis — I suppose the Tories are in high Spirits with the news of the Hanoverians Hessian Ships of war and for my own part I maintain the same opinion the more They send, the better - the sooner they will be exhausted, and I am sure if we continue firm they cannot subdue us & then Congress must give better pay to their officers; for the present miserable pittance will not tempt men of a fortune to the low wretches who live like the Common soldiers and with the Common soldiers, but men who chuse [sic] to preserve the decent distance of Officers, must have a decent subsistence and without this difference no authority or respect can be expected. I was of opinion, that some Battalions from the Southward cou'd be necessary, but I have alter'd my opinion I am now persuaded you have not to the Southward so good materials for common Soldiers - Your [Pennsylvania] Riflemen have a good deal opened our eyes upon this subject tho[ugh] to do justice*

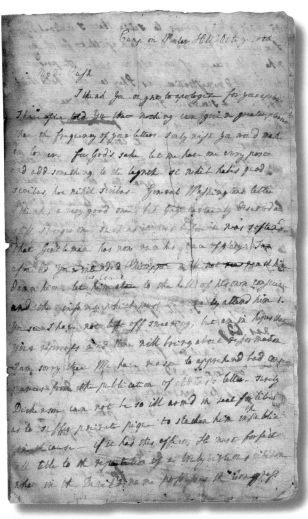

to their Officers, they are more acceptionable [sic]. Their Privates are in general degraded yet soft, dirty mutinous and disaffected, We grow very impatient for Powder..." Before Lee closed the letter he began another thought but crossed out the text which reads: "*You ought my Friend to be a little more upon your guard in declaring your Republican sentiments to the Southern People - Virginia and Carolinas are not yet prepared for such doctrine...*" A revealing letter on several levels illustrating the social distance between officers and soldiers (or a severe lack thereof) and conflicting political battles within the revolutionary movement. John Adams' confrontations with John Dickinson over the latter's propensity toward reconciliation boiled over in early months of open hostilities. In a letter to James Warren that was captured and famously published by the British, he characterized Dickinson as a "A certain great Fortune and piddling Genius whose Fame has been trumpeted so loudly, has given a silly Cast to our whole Doings. We are between Hawk and Buzzard. We ought to have had in our Hands a Month ago, the whole Legislative, Executive and Judicial of the whole Continent, and have compleatly [sic] moddelled [sic] a Constitution, to have raised a Naval Power and opened all our Ports wide, to have arrested every Friend to Government on the Continent and held them as Hostages for the poor Victims in Boston—And then opened the Door as wide as possible for Peace and Reconcilliation [sic]: After this they might have petitioned and negotiated and addressed, etc. if they would. Is all this extravagant? Is it wild? Is it not the soundest Policy?" Ironically in the same letter Adams says of Charles Lee "You observe in your Letter the Oddity of a great Man. He is a queer Creature. But you must love his Dogs if you love him, and forgive a Thousand Whims for the Sake of the Soldier and the Scholar." Lee very tactfully responded to Adams five days prior to his comments to Rush. These intramural rivalries were not limited to Congress: the elite Virginia riflemen that arrived in August under the leadership of Daniel Morgan, though fearsome to the British for their ability to pick off sentries from long distances, were a vastly undisciplined lot. Unwilling to submit to military discipline, the riflemen did not adapt well to the tedious boredom of camp life and were prone to fights amongst themselves and others. In one instance, a group of mutinous riflemen attempted to free one of their own from a military jail in Cambridge, and were faced down by 500 troops with Washington, Lee and Greene at their head.

Charles Lee was one of Washington's most experienced officers, a former member of the British Army who claimed to hold a general's commission from the King of Poland. Lee was also one of Washington's most arrogant and troublesome generals. Most famously, at the Battle of Monmouth in 1778, Lee directly disobeyed Washington's orders to advance against the British that turned what could have been a decisive victory into a stalemate. After the war, it was discovered that Lee was a traitor, offering a plan to the British high command on how to defeat Washington- while he was a prisoner of war in 1776-77. A spectacular letter written by one of the Continental Army's most colorful generals. Silked, moderate toning and soiling, otherwise very good condition. From the Henry E. Luhrs Collection. Accompanied by LOA from PSA/DNA.
Estimate: $4,000-$6,000

25309   Charles Lee
(1732-1782) Letter Signed

"Charles Lee Major General", three pages, 7.5" x 12.5", "Camp" [near Peekskill], November 22, 1776, with additional 19 line autograph postscript in Lee's hand to Brigadier General John Nixon. Charles Lee, perhaps Washington's most eneral John Nixon for a foraging expedition to the home and manor of Loyalist Frederick Phillips III.

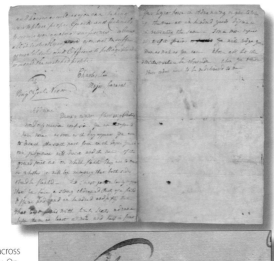

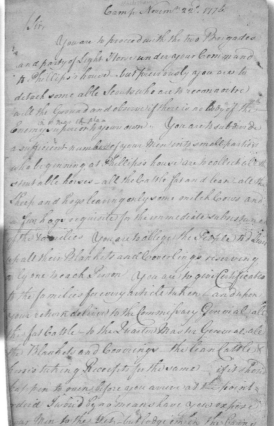

Following the Battle of White Plains on October 28, 1776, Washington split up his troops leaving Lee with a large contingent of the Continental Army near Peekskill. Washington moved the balance of the army across the Hudson River into New Jersey. On November 10th Washington received intelligence that the British were preparing to move into New Jersey, and requested that Lee and his army cross the Hudson to join forces. Lee hesitated for an entire month, answering Washington's repeated requests to move with various explanations including a wish not to expose the lush and agriculturally productive county of Westchester to the British for supplies. On November 12th, Lee communicated intelligence to Washington that the main body of Howe's army had retreated to the south, he still distrusted the ability of his scouts and feared a later attack since much of the British force still remained north of Manhattan Island and could easily turn against him. In this letter he gives highly detailed instructions to John Nixon: "Sir, You are to proceed with the two Brigades and party of Light Horse under your Command to Phillips's house - but previously you are to detach some able Scouts who are to reconnoiter will the Ground and observe if there is no body of the Enemy in or near the place superior to your own. You are to subdivide a sufficient number of your Men into small parties who beginning at Phillips's house ware to collect all the stout able horses-all the Cattle fat and lean-all the Sheep and hogs leaving only some milch Cows and a few hogs requisite for the immediate subsistence of the Families[.] You are to oblige the People to deliver up all their Blankets and Coverlings reserving only one to each Person[.] You are to give Certificates to the families for every article taken-and upon your return deliver to the Commissary General all the fat Cattle - to the Quarter Master General all the Blankets and Coverings - the lean Cattle & horses taking Receipts for the same - if it should happen to rain before you arrive at the point order'd I woul'd by no means have you expose your Men to the Wet - but loge 'em in the barns and houses as well as you can taking care to place proper Guards and Centinels [sic] to secure you against surprises - above all it is strictly inform'd you, to suffer your Soldiers and Officers to pillage[,] plunder or insult the wretched people" After signing the letter, Lee adds further instructions: "During night - flanking parties would only occasion confusion - You are therefore to have none as soon as the day appears your are to detach the sixth part of each Corps... I must particularly request that you have a strong Advanced Part of a field officer and an hundred and fifty Men — that Capt Lee is with sixty Scouts advanced before them at least as much and half in front. Your light horse in Advancing ought to bring up the rear at an hundred yards distance in retreating the same — I once more repeat that if it rains You will lodge your men as well as you can - above all let the strictest silence be observed..."

The letter clearly illustrates Lee's complete distrust of abilities of his subordinate officers and men. The level of micromanagement here betrays his attitude toward Nixon, whom he regarded as an inferior. At the same time, Lee, who possessed one of the most distinguished military rÈsumÈs in the Continental Army, thought himself vast superior than relatively inexperienced Washington. Lee actually staged a letter-writing campaign strongly criticizing Washington's command decisions, blaming him for the seemingly endless stream of defeats in 1776. Some have speculated that Lee's delay in joining Washington in New Jersey was a deliberate plot to see Washington defeated by Howe, demonstrating Washington's ineptitude, and creating an opening for Lee to command the army. This lack of confidence in the abilities of the officers and troops under his command (as well as his superiors) would continue to the end of his military career. This letter, however casts some doubt on any 'plot' to discredit Washington by letting him be defeated. It is obvious that besides being mistrustful of Nixon's judgment and abilities, he still viewed the British a threat to his position and was thus unwilling to abandon his post. Two years later, at Monmouth Court House, it was Lee's hesitation with his advance guard and subsequent retreat before a weaker British force that turned what could have been a decisive victory for the Americans into a stalemate. Lee survived a court-martial but continued to criticize Washington and was dismissed from the service in 1780.

Within two weeks of his crossing the Hudson River (on our about December 1, 1776), Lee would himself be surprised and captured by the British. On the night of December 12, he decided to spend the night away from his army at White's Tavern in Basking Ridge, New Jersey to enjoy food, drink, and the hospitality of one of the tavern's resident women. A British patrol under the command of Benastre Tarleton, arrived at the tavern the following morning on a tip from a Tory sympathizer. After a brief skirmish Lee surrendered. He remained in captivity in New York until he was exchanged in the spring of 1778. While in captivity, Lee actually presented a plan to the British command on how to defeat the American army. Fortunately for the Americans, the British ignored his plan. The treason was only exposed after his death in 1780.

Frederick Phillips's open declaration of loyalty to the crown earned him an arrest warrant from George Washington — Phillips appears to have already been in New York by late November. His signature appears with over 500 other loyalists in New York City on a petition addressed to William Howe on November 28, 1776 reaffirming his loyalty to King George III. He soon fled to British occupied New York with his family. Before the close of the War, he would flee to England with his family and remained there until his death in 1786. The State of New York confiscated his vast manor and sold it at public auction. The mansion, up on the Hudson near Tarrytown, is now a state historical site open to the public.

This fine content letter bears the usual folds, light soiling and a few minor archival repairs, overall fine condition. From the Henry E. Luhrs Collection. Accompanied by LOA from PSA/DNA.
Estimate: $7,000-$9,000

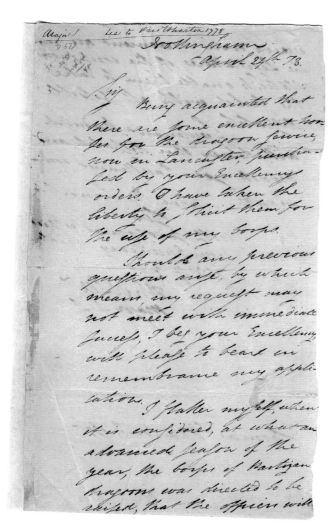

25310 Henry "Light Horse Harry" Lee (1756-1818) American general in the Revolutionary War, Autograph Letter Signed, "*Henry Lee Major L[ight]. D[ragoons]*", two pages, 8" x 12.25", Nothingham, April 24, 1778, to Thomas Wharton, President of Pennsylvania, discussing the procurement of horses for his dragoons. Soon after receiving his commission as Major taking command of an irregular regiment of dragoons, he writes in part: "*Being acquainted that there are some excellent horses for the dragoon Service, now in Lancaster, purchased by your Excellency's orders. I have taken the liberty to solicit them for the use for my Corps. Should any previous questions arise, by which means, my request may not meet with immediate success, I beg your Excellency, will please to bear in remembrance my application. I flatter myself, when it is considered, at what an advanced season of the year, the Corps of Partizan Dragoon was directed to be raised, that the officers will receive every convenient aid from the Legislatures of the contiguous states, to enable them to take the field with all possible dispatch.* " Lee's dragoons would serve with great distinction through the balance of the war including a spectacular surprise attack on the British outpost at Paulus Hook in August, 1779 for which he received a gold medal — an award given to no other officer below the rank of general during the entire conflict. Lee's dragoons would later join Nathaniel Greene in the Carolinas and prove invaluable at Guilford Court House, Eutaw Springs, and Camden. Reinforced along left margin, margins slightly irregular, one tiny pin hole, else near fine condition. Extremely scarce in war-date form; this is an excellent example. From the Henry E. Luhrs Collection. Accompanied by LOA from PSA/DNA.
Estimate: $4,000-$5,000

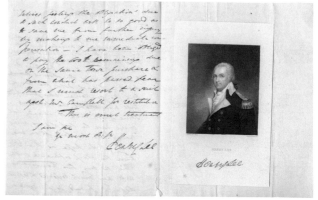

25311 Henry "Light-Horse Harry" Autograph Letter Protesting **"Cruel Treatment."** Autograph Letter Signed, 2 pages, recto and verso, Norfolk, May 22, 1807. To a Judge. In fine condition. With a steel engraving of Lee in uniform. Certainly Lee was a brilliant and dashing soldier - he won one of only eight medals voted by Congress during the Revolutionary war. But off the battlefield he lived far beyond his means and hadn't the slightest head for business: his ineptitude as a planter, and disastrous speculations in real estate, would eventually land him in debtor's prison. Here we see the gallant fighter — and father of a newborn son, Robert E. Lee — try to save himself from going under. "*I have been here for some days with the expectation of ascertaining & closing the difficulties which I experience in consequence of the incomplete title sent me... to 4000 acres of the dismal swamp land. I had sold the land but the gentleman who purchased it will not accept the deed as some of the land is already lost & 4000 acres never can be laid off in one body. I do hope as friendship had the chief influence with me in my two transactions with my much respected & beloved departed friend, so his representatives... will be so good to save me... by making to me immediate compensation... This is cruel treatment.*" From the Henry E. Luhrs Collection. Accompanied by LOA from PSA/DNA.
Estimate: $500-$700

25312 Signed by three Signers of the Declaration of Independence, Members of the Secret Committee

Richard Henry Lee (1732-1794), Signer of the Declaration of Independence, Autograph Letter Signed, "*Richard Henry Lee*" also signed by fellow Signers Francis Lewis, "*Fra: Lewis*" and William Whipple "*Wm. Whipple*" all as members of the Secret Committee, three pages, 8.5" x 13.25", Baltimore, February 6, 1777 to an unknown recipient, possibly Robert Morris. An excellent content letter describing efforts to finance the on-going Revolutionary War through trade with France and her Caribbean colonies. "...*We have received your favor of the 31st Jan[uar]y. and have laid your reasons before Congress for not complying very quickly with the desire of Congress touching the amount of our exports & imports on their account... We find ourselves here under such inseparable difficulties in the right conduct of business whilst we remain without the books or a Clerk, that we must entreat you to loose [sic] no time in getting both here as soon as your necessary attention to other things will permit... since we came here, we have purchased a Ship and a Brig, both Prize Vessels, one of them carries about 600 h[ogs]h[ea]ds Tob[acc]o. and the other between three & four hundred, which we propose to load with Tobo. so soon as the Enemies ships in the Bay will permit us to move... We have agreed with Mr. Fitzsimmons for two thirds of his Brig, and we shall put on board about 80 hhds of Fish purchased here from a Prise [sic] on pretty reasonable terms... This Cargo, will follow your advice, and go to Mr. Curson, St Eustatia. Not that we mention Mr. Curson, we must inform you that we found a Brig here that was chartered by Messrs. Lewis Livingston & Alsop about 12 months ago and loaded at N. Yorke with 710 barrels of flour to be delivered to Mr. Curson. The Captain (on various pretences) went to... Hispanola & delivered the four to a Monsr. Croix who has acknowledged the receipt to Mr. Curson but the often promising remittance to him as not [been] made... The Capt. without any authority that we know, pretends he sold the Vessel likewise to Monsr. Croix — The captt. & Vessel has since been in Monsr. Croix's employment to Old France, return to Hispaniola, and from thence came here in some business - Here we found him, his Vessel navigated with French men & with a French Captain, himself super Cargo - The Brig loaded with Flour from the sale of her Cargo here, and depts. due to the amount of £2500 over & above her Cargo on board. All this transaction shews [sic] a wicked system of fraud between the Captain and Monsr. Corix - We laid the matter before Congress & the desired the Secret Committee to do therein what was just & for the public good - We have stopt the Vessel, & the Super Cargo is fled - The French Captain is clamorous & demands his Vessel! What is your opinion of the best to be done in this matter?...*" Interestingly, a postscript notes that "*We think the*

Inclosed Letter from Mr. B. Deane should be communicated to the Clother Genl. & he to issue his orders accordingly..."

The Secret Committee was the first intelligence directorate for the United States. They dealt with a variety of issues and addressed all foreign affairs including arranging for trade to obtain military stores. They often used intermediaries to mask the fact that Congress was the purchaser of these supplies. One of those intermediaries was Samuel Curson at St. Eustatia who was a significant supplier of powder to the United States. This was a risky venture at best. In 1781, when the British captured St. Eustatia from the Dutch, Curson and his partner were arrested. Benjamin Franklin wrote from Paris, "...Mr. Samuel Curson and his Partner Mr. Isaac Governeur junr. after St. Eustatius was taken were put on board the Vengeance Man of War, Comdore. Hotham, to be sent to England stripped of every Thing but their wearing apparel, their Books, Papers & Slaves having been taken from them and Mrs. Governeur with a young Infant turned out of Doors. Special Severity, it is supposed, has been shewn to them in Consequence of their acting as Agents to Congress." Letters regarding foreign trade to finance military operations in the Revolutionary War are significant — one signed by three Founding Fathers has tremendous verve attached. An incredible piece of history. Light dampstain at top left, usual folds, else very good. From the Henry E. Luhrs Collection. Accompanied by LOA from PSA/DNA.

Estimate: $8,000-$12,000

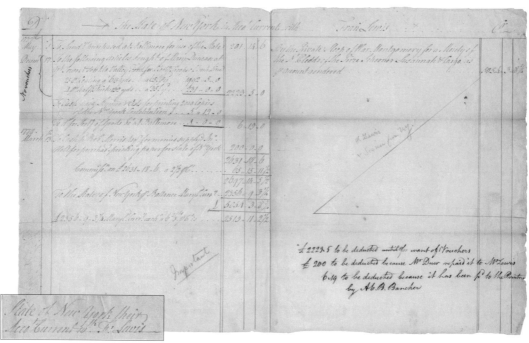

25313 **Declaration Signer Francis Lewis Autograph Document Signed** twice "*Frans Lewis*" on front and "*F Lewis*" on verso. One page, 15.5" x 9.5", New York, March 13, 1778. A handwritten itemized account submitted to the state of New York for sums due him. Entries include: items purchased at Baltimore; supplies for the army purchased at Yorktown and Valley Ford [sic Forge?]; $200 cash for paper used by the state paid by another Declaration signer Robert Morris. Lewis was also a delegate to the Continental Congress in 1775 and signed the Declaration of Independence as a representative of New York. His Long Island property was destroyed by the British during the Revolutionary War. There is a boulevard named after him in Queens, New York, as well as a high school. This war-dated letter signed by one Declaration signer (twice) and mentioning another is very important and desirable. Fine condition. From the Henry E. Luhrs Collection. Accompanied by LOA from PSA/DNA.
Estimate: $2,000-$3,000

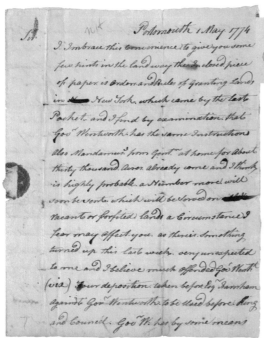

25314 **(New York - New Hampshire Land Dispute) Stephen S. J. Little Autograph Letter Signed,** three pages, 6" x 7.5", Portsmouth, May 1, 1774 to Captain Moses Little in Falmouth concerning the on-going territorial dispute between New York and New Hampshire over the region now known as Vermont. Little writes to give Moses Little "*...some few hints in the land way the Inclosed piece of paper is Orders and Rules of granting Land in New York which came by the Last Packet and I find by examination that Gov Wentworth has the same Instruction, also Mandamus from Gent.n at home for about thirty thousand acres already come and I think is highly probable a Number more will soon be sent which will be served on Vacant or forfeited land, a Circumstance I fear may affect you as there's Something turned up this last week very unexpected to me and I believe much offended Gov. [John] Went[wort]h. (vis) Four deposition[s] taken before Esq Farrham against Gov. Wentworth to be used before King and Councel [sic]... as soon as you are acquainted with the length of your charter and progress in Settlement but if forfeited you may rely on. the Gov. will clap on some of those Mandamus, which he has sent to him to fix on the spot he chuses [sic]. I Imagine some of our court party Secretly think that Col. Bagley was knoing [sic] to your sending a Deposition, and I am Inform'd (Under the Rose) [confidentially] that the Govn. a little mistrust his integrity in the affair...*" Between 1749 and 1764, New Hampshire Governor Benning Wentworth (the father of Governor John Wentworth who is mentioned above) granted an enormous quantity of land west of the Connecticut River (including 131 towns) in an area also claimed by the Province of New York. After repeated warnings by New York to Wentworth not to claim further lands in the region, the province petitioned London to adjudicate the dispute. A royal order of July 26, 1764 affirmed that "*...the western bank of the Connecticut, from where it enters the prov-*
ince of Massachusetts Bay as far north as the 45th degree of northern latitude, to be the boundary line between the said two provinces...*" New York took the decision to mean that all of Wentworth's land grants were now invalid and divided the territory into four counties and required that grantees surrender their charters with the option of repurchasing the land at much higher prices. New York's actions soon drove many in the region into open rebellion under the leadership of Ethan Allen and his Green Mountain Boys, leading to the establishment of the Vermont Republic. Vermont joined the Union as a state in 1791. *Provenance*: Heise, October 2, 1950, List 241, No., 25. Weak at some folds with minor pin holes, small loss from wax seal tear, else fine condition. From the Henry E. Luhrs Collection. Accompanied by LOA from PSA/DNA.
Estimate: $800-$1,000

25315   [New York] Philip Livingston, the Patroon, Sells Acres of Albany! Autograph Document Signed (three times: twice in the text and at bottom), 1 full page, 8" by 12.5", Albany, July 5, 1732. Co-signed by his father-in-law **Pieter Van Brugh,** Mayor of Albany, New York Commissioner of Indian Affairs, a Member of the General Assembly and a Captain at Fort Orange. A handsome document, with rudimental repairs on verso, generally very good; with red wax seals intact. With typed transcription. Here Livingston of Livingston Manor sells off part of the County he owns: gone are 83 acres, for six hundred pounds, to Jacob Borst and Adam Szee. A rare document from colonial New York.   From the Henry E. Luhrs Collection. Accompanied by LOA from PSA/DNA.

Estimate: $200-$300

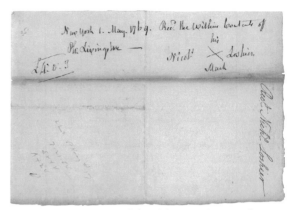

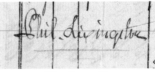

25317   Declaration Signer Philip Livingston Autograph Endorsement Signed One page, 7.5" x 5.25", signed on the back of a bill for various building materials *"New York 1 May. 1769. Rec'd the Within Contents of Ph: Livingston— Nichols (his mark) Loshier".* Livingston was a New York City merchant, a delegate to the Continental Congress 1775-1778 and signer of the Declaration of Independence as a representative from New York. Fine with lightly toned fold, a couple of minor old paper repairs, Livingston endorsement bold and clean. From the Henry E. Luhrs Collection. Accompanied by LOA from PSA/DNA.

Estimate: $300-$500

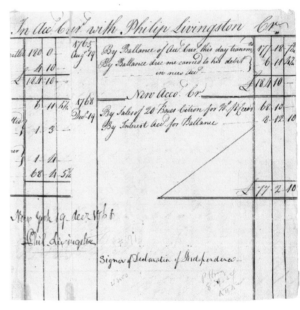

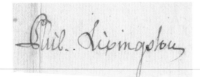

25316   Declaration Signer Philip Livingston Letter Signed *"Sir Your Most Hum Servant Phil. Livingston".* One page, 7.25" x 7.25", New York, January 9, 1764, to Richard Derby. Regarding business, it reads in part "...I am sorry to tell you that only Six Pipes of your Wine are yet sold and when I shall be able to sell the Remainder unless at Publick Sale, I know not that article is very Plenty and a large Quantity Expected and Cash very Scarce..." Livingston signed the Declaration as a representative from New York and was a member of the Continental Congress from 1775-1778. Fine condition; original light folds. Also included is a typewritten history of the Livingston family.   From the Henry E. Luhrs Collection. Accompanied by LOA from PSA/DNA.

Estimate: $400-$600

25318   Philip Livingston "The Signer" Document Signed *"Phil. Livingston."* Two pages, 7.8" x 7.6"; New York, December 19, 1768. A large detailed bill made out to Philip Livingston, amounting to 77 pounds, 2 shillings, and 10 pence. Livingston signs the bill in the lower left corner. The Verso shows credits to Philip's account. Livingston was a merchant and statesman from New York; he served on the Continental Congress and signed the Declaration of Independence. This document is an interesting look at colonial bookkeeping.

The document is very fine condition; usual folds are present; some separation occurring along fold lines; mounting traces on the lower edge of verso. Included with the document is an engraving of Livingston; slightly water-damaged but still nice for display! From the Henry E. Luhrs Collection. Accompanied by LOA from PSA/DNA.

Estimate: $300-$500

25319   Robert Livingston (1746-1813) judge, drafter of the Declaration of Independence, fine content Autograph Letter Signed, "*R Livingston*", three pages, 7.75" x 9.5", Philadelphia, Feb. 15, 1780 likely to Governor George Clinton of New York relating news of John Jay's arduous voyage to Spain to assume his post as American minister to that court. Livingston writes in part. "*We are all very happy the day before yesterday at rec[eivin]g a letter from Mr [John] Jay, but on opening we found it dated at Martinique - where he was driven after loosing all his Masts, & Bowsprit, on the Banks of Newfoundland - He got in to Martinique the 19th Decr and left it in a french frigate the 26[th] all well on board on the day of their arrival the English fleet from St Lucy engaged a fleet of merchantmen under convoy of a frigate & notwithstanding a gallant attempt of Monr. La Motte Piquet with 3 ships to relieve them took 12 of them - The English have a decided superiority at sea in the west Indias, owing to the storm that divided the French fleet - The Minister tells me that he has acc[ount]s from Europe so late as Nov[embe]r the combined fleet was then preparing for sea under Mr. Chaffunt, Count D'Olivers being removed from the command - great preparations were making on both sides to carry on the war with spirit the ensuing summer, & very little prospect of a peace.*" Despite the seeming danger, Jay arrived safely with his wife in Cadiz on January 22, 1780 — about a month after he left Martinique. While serving as Minister to Spain, he was also appointed by Congress to join the peace commission with Benjamin Franklin and John Adams in Paris. There, he would play a pivotal role in the negotiations to end the war with Great Britain. Light creases, margins just a tad rough, else Fine condition. A fine specimen. From the Henry E. Luhrs Collection. Accompanied by LOA from PSA/DNA.
Estimate: $700-$900

25320   Livingston Family, Patroons of New York, Autograph Archive. A landholder in New Netherland who, under Dutch colonial rule, was granted proprietary and manorial rights to a large tract of land in exchange for bringing 50 new settlers to the colony was called a patroon. It was essentially a feudal form of government and a Scotsman named Robert Livingston was one of these early patroons. He was awarded a tract of 160,000 acres of land that formed Livingston Manor in what is now Columbia and Dutchess counties in New York. He was the first lord of the manor and was very active in politics, acting as Secretary for Indian Affairs and as a representative in the New York provincial assembly. His descendents and family members figure very heavily in the development and success of the state of New York and the United States as a whole. Just a few of the illustrious Livingstons that are represented by autograph material in this lot are as follows:

Brockholst Livingston- Supreme Court Justice, Revolutionary War officer.

Edward L. Livingston- Secretary of State under Van Buren, Mayor of New York City.

James Livingston- Revolutionary War officer, helped expose Benedict Arnold as a traitor.

Robert Livingston Jr.- Mayor of New York CIty.

Robert R. Livingston "The Chancellor"- a delegate to the New York state constitutional convention and a member of the committee that drafted the Declaration of Independence. Administered the oath of office to George Washington at his first inauguration.

Walter Livingston- Continental Congress delegate.

William Livingston- The first governor of New Jersey, succeeded William Franklin who was the last Royal governor, also a Continental Congress delegate.

This is just a tiny sampling of the members of this important family that the winning bidder will find. It seems likely that this is the largest holding of Livingston autograph material to be offered to the public in more than 50 years. These documents and letters are in generally very good to fine condition. Extensive background and biographical material will be included with the lot. From the Henry E. Luhrs Collection. Accompanied by LOA from PSA/DNA.
Estimate: $2,000-$3,000

25321 **Robert R. Livingston (1746-1813) Judge, Drafter of the Declaration of Independence, Autograph Endorsement Signed,** "*R R Livingston*", one page, 7" x 9.5", Philadelphia, March 3, 1783 written at the bottom of a manuscript petition in another hand in which Jane Cuyler requests: "*...That your Petitioner was formerly an Inhabitant of New York from whence she went to Charles Town On the enemies [sic] taking Possession of that place your Petitioner was obliged to leave it with a Family of four children & she has suffer'd [sic] numberless inconveniences since - Your Petitioner has some Property in New York where she wishes to go, & for which purpose she begs your Permission - If you shoul'd [sic] be pleas'd [sic] to indulge her with a Pass the favor will be held in grateful remembrance...*" Livingston subsequently certifies *...that Mrs. Cuyler was a long time an inhabitant of New York and that her late husband's family possessed a considerable property there...*" At the time, New York was still occupied by British Forces who captured the city in 1776. They did not leave New York until November 25, 1783 when news of the final peace treaty arrived in America. Jane Cuyler may have been a member of the prominent Dutch New York family Corlear, and this is merely a misspelling. Extremely light creases, very light foxing, else Fine. A great, early document. From the Henry E. Luhrs Collection. Accompanied by LOA from PSA/DNA.
Estimate: $700-$900

25322 **Robert Livingston Autograph Letter Signed** "*Robt R. Livingston.*" This 9" x 7.3", two pages handwritten with integral address leaf, dated April 8, 1792 from Clarmont (Ohio). Robert Livingston, known as the "Chancellor", represented New York at the Constitutional Convention and sat on the committee that drafted the Declaration of Independence, although he was called home before he could sign it. This letter is sent to a Reverend Vanderkemp thanking him for his offer to send him a "scarificator." He offers the reverend six black sheep in exchange for this instrument. A wonderful, cordial letter with interesting early farming and trade content. The letter is in Good condition; slight staining on the first page and the address leaf; large tear on the left edge of the address leaf. Wax seal still present, and signature is bold and dark. From the Henry E. Luhrs Collection. Accompanied by LOA from PSA/DNA.
Estimate: $400-$600

25323 **William Livingston Document Signed** "*Wil: Livingston Presd.*" 7.8" x 4.3", one page handwritten document, dated May 20, 1785, in Trenton New Jersey. The document is of a legal nature, and states that Bowen Reid is entitled to four pounds and four shillings for his six days of attendance at a Court of Errors. William Livingston was the first governor of New Jersey and brother of Philip Livingston, the signer of the Declaration of Independence. The document is in Good condition; the writing is slightly faded from age; pencil notations on front and verso. From the Henry E. Luhrs Collection. Accompanied by LOA from PSA/DNA.
Estimate: $300-$500

25324 **William Livingston Document Signed** "*Wil: Livingston.*" 6.7" x 2.3", one page handwritten document, dated April 3, 1777. William Livingston was the brother of Philip Livingston who signed the Declaration of Independence. William was the first governor of New Jersey and a very important member of the new government. The document is signed with the notation of "*Gov. of N. Jersey.*" Fabulous signature lot! The document is in good condition; small hole in the upper left corner; adhesive on the verso; pencil notations on the front of the document. From the Henry E. Luhrs Collection. Accompanied by LOA from PSA/DNA.
Estimate: $300-$500

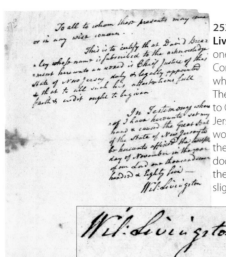

25325   Early American Document Signed by William Livingston. This 7" x 8.5" document is signed by William Livingston, one of the representatives from New Jersey at the Constitutional Convention. He was a well-known lawyer and renaissance man whose home was the center of social activity in early colonial times. The document is of a legal nature, and appoints a David Brearley to Chief Justice of New Jersey. Livingston was the governor of New Jersey from 1776 till his death in 1790. The document featured is a wonderful example of early American politics, being carried out by the very men who were responsible for our right to self-govern. The document is in good condition; the left edge has some staining near the centerfold; there are several areas of foxing in upper right corner; slight soiling present over the entire letter, but writing and signature are bold and crisp. From the Henry E. Luhrs Collection. Accompanied by LOA from PSA/DNA.

Estimate: $400-$600

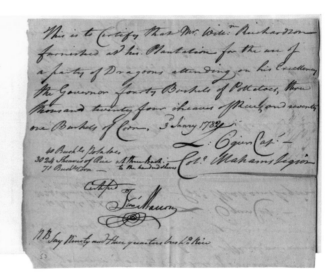

25326   Francis Marion, "The Swamp Fox": A Rare War-Date Document Signed. Document Signed, 1 oblong page, 7.5" by 6.5", no place [South Carolina], January, 1782. In Fine condition; tipped to a larger sheet. With a handsome steel engraving of the General. Here the brilliant partisan, still campaigning against the British despite Cornwallis' surrender — the fighting wouldn't cease in South Carolina until the British evacuated Charlestown in December 1782 — certifies a receipt for provisions for his Dragoons. In part: "*This is to certify that Mr. William Richardson furnished at his plantation for the use of a party of Dragoons... forty bushels of potatoes, three thousand twenty-four sheaves of rice, and seventy one bushels of corn.*" A rare and desirable autograph. From the Henry E. Luhrs Collection. Accompanied by LOA from PSA/DNA.

Estimate: $3,500-$5,000

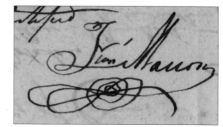

25327　Cyrus McCormick Autograph Letter Signed

"C.H. McCormick." One page, 8.25" x 10.5", Chicago, Illinois, December 23, 1832. To Jno. R. Walker in regard to a warranty on his reaper. Here is an exceptionally early reference to the invention that made McCormick's fortune, and revolutionized American agricultural production: the reaper, invented just twelve months before. In part, *"I regret your entire report of mess at mowingIt is my custom to make you my warranties & if your machine will not mow of which you can satisfy the Agent for he can show you what is wrong he will refund amt. to you to make it right."* The letter is in fine condition; usual folds are present; some light staining present on verso. From the Henry E. Luhrs Collection. Accompanied by LOA from PSA/DNA.

Estimate: $600-$800

25328　Lachlan McIntosh (1727-1806)

American General in the Revolution who killed Signer of the Declaration of Independence Button Gwinnett, Autograph Letter Signed, *"Lacn. McIntosh"* one page, 7.75" x 11.5", Haddon's Point, December 18, 1780 to Colonel Ball during his imprisonment by the British. He writes to Colonel Ball: *"I take Liberty of troubling you with the two inclosed Letters, and as you have been kind enough to promise you would deliver each of them yourself request you will keep them in this paper, untill [sic] you have done it for fear you may forget. In am*

assured your best rout[e] is over the Chawsaw & if so, Hillsburrough, will not be much out of your way - besides the Satisfaction you will give to Mrs. McIntosh, which I am sure now cou'd with more to do you upon your Indulgence, & wish you a happy Signet of your friends & family." " Below his signature, and eight days later, McIntosh adds a lengthy postscript, a *"Memorandum to Colo. Ball the 26th Decr [sic]. 1780"* with *"As I expect you will call at Hillsborrough - you will please to inform Mrs. McIntosh of my Situation here — and if you find her in any Danger where she is, from the Enemy, advise her the best place to go or Safety.- :You will please to Deliver the Letter from the Virginia Officers to Governor [Thomas] Jefferson - & inform my Son of it, that he may do anything necessary in Consequence thereof, and shall expect your own influence or support of it. — In case of our General Exchange which I expect you will plead hard for - I hope you will not allow an old Tesson[?] to walk out of it.-"* McIntosh was captured by the British at Charleston, South Carolina on May 12, 1780 after American forces surrendered the town after a forty-day struggle. He was not exchanged until February 9, 1782. That experience compromised his health for the rest of his life. A scarce example in fine condition. From the Henry E. Luhrs Collection. Accompanied by LOA from PSA/DNA.

Estimate: $1,500-$2,000

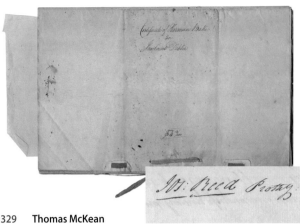

25329　Thomas McKean

(1735-1817) Partly-printed Document Signed *"Thos McKean"* as Governor of Pennsylvania, one page, 15" x 13" with an additional thirty-four attached pages of manuscript documents, Philadelphia, July 25, 1806. McKean, Signer of the Declaration of Independence, commissions Joseph B. McKean, Joseph Reed, and Charles Erdmann to administer the bankruptcy of merchant Herman Bake. In the attached documents, Bake petitions the state for protection under the newly enacted bankruptcy laws. Bake provides a *"...list of his Creditors... and the nature of their debts... [and] prays the benefit of an act of Assembly of Pennsylvania entitled an act providing that the person of a debtor shall not be liable to imprisonment for debt after delivering up his estate real and personal for the benefit of his creditors..."* The debts are categorized as *"Debtors and Creditors"* and *"Doubtful Debtors"*, the latter noting interest for several cargoes lost to French privateers. Other attached documents include a copy of Bake's father's will, dated Amsterdam, 1783 with translations from the original Dutch to English. Bankruptcy legislation was only in its infancy, and at this time only available for merchants and other business owners, not the common working person. Only a few years previous, the passage of a federal bankruptcy act allowed Robert Morris to leave debtor's prison after his speculations in western lands caused his financial empire to collapse. Usual folds, paper seals intact, a few toned spots, otherwise fine condition. From the Henry E. Luhrs Collection. Accompanied by LOA from PSA/DNA.

Estimate: $400-$600

25330　Declaration Signer Thomas McKean Document Signed as Pennsylvania Governor

"Tho M:Kean". One page, partly printed, 15.5" x 13", Lancaster, August 2, 1800. A document commissioning Samuel Heth as a *"...Captain of the fourth Company in the fourteenth Regiment of the Militia of the Commonwealth of Pennsylvania..."* Thomas McKean signed the Declaration of Independence as a representative of Delaware. His signature on this present document is at the far left, underneath the seal which is still present and intact. A very handsome document for display; very good condition with folds and scattered foxing, right edge tattered. From the Henry E. Luhrs Collection. Accompanied by LOA from PSA/DNA.

Estimate: $400-$600

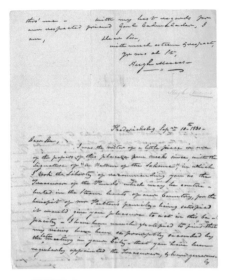

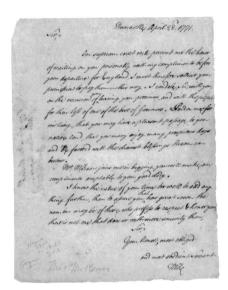

25331 Thomas McKean (1735-1817) Signer of the Declaration of Independence, Autograph Letter Signed *"M.K"*, one page, 6.5" x 8.25", New Castle, [Delaware], April 22, 1771 to Pennsylvania Lieutenant Governor John Penn (1729-1795) who was departing for England. McKean writes: *"Our supream [sic] court will prevent me the hour of waiting on you personally with my compliments before your departure for England, I must therefore solicit your permission to pay them in this way. I condole, Sir, with you, on the occasion of your leaving your provinces, and with the peoples for their loss of one of the best of Governors..."* Penn returned in 1773 as a full governor. When Pennsylvania created a new government one month after independence, Penn offered no resistance. Light toning, irregular margins, else very good. From the Henry E. Luhrs Collection. Accompanied by LOA from PSA/DNA.
Estimate: $800-$1,000

25332 Declaration Signers McKean, Morris, Ross along with the first public reader, John Nixon. This lot contains four items related to the Declaration of Independence:

Thomas McKean, signed as representative from Delaware. Signature *"Tho M:Kean"* on 2.5" x 1" sheet. Fine- bold and dark signature.

Robert Morris, signed as representative from Pennsylvania. Signature *"Robr Morris"* on 3" x 1" sheet. Good- bold and dark signature with small tear affecting first "R".

George Ross, signed as representative from Pennsylvania. Signature *"George Ross"* on 2" x 2" piece removed from larger document.

John Nixon, the first person to read the Declaration in public, which he did from the steps of the State House on July 8, 1776 in Philadelphia. Signature on verso of 7.25" x 6" 1785 document. Fine. From the Henry E. Luhrs Collection. Accompanied by LOA from PSA/DNA.
Estimate: $600-$800

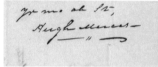

25333 (Early Steamboats) Hugh T. Mercer, Two Autograph Letters Signed *"Hugh Mercer"*, each two pages, 8" x 10", Fredericksburg, Virginia, August 21, 1830 and September 10, 1830 to Nicholas Biddle, President of the Bank of the United States, discussing the newly-opened ferry service between Fredericksburg and Baltimore. Hugh T. Mercer, the son of Revolutionary War surgeon Hugh Mercer and father of Confederate General Hugh Weedon Mercer, writes to Biddle on August 21: *"Thinking it quite probable that the Stock of our New Steamer, plying between this & Balt[im]o[re] will be good Stock, will you be so good as to inform me... whether you can procure for me... a few Shares..."* On September 10, he writes again to Biddle: *"I was the writer of a little piece in one of the papers of this place a few weeks since, with the Signature of 'a Patron of the Scheme,' in which I took the Liberty of recommending you as the Treasurer of the Funds which may be contributed in the Steam boats of our Country, or the benefit of Mr Fulton' family... at the request of Capt Noah Fairbanks of the Steamer 'Rappahannock,' plying weekly between this Town & Baltimore, I forward you a Check for twenty two Dollars & fifty five Cents, that being the amount contributed to his Box, during the short period the Boat has been in motion. The Stockholders of this very fine Boat, will always feel pleasure in reflecting that it was with some of them, this beneficent Scheme originated, & that the first impulse was given to it on board the 'Rappahannock' when she commenced her route the first of the past summer..."* With integral address panels. Extremely light toning, usual folds, small loss from seal tear, first page of one letter neatly trimmed, else fine condition. Early documents of this nature detailing the formative years of travel and commerce are quite significant. From the Henry E. Luhrs Collection. Accompanied by LOA from PSA/DNA.
Estimate: $800-$1,200

25334 **Outstanding Content and Rare Arthur Middleton Letter Describing the Early Days of the Revolution Arthur Middleton (1742-1787) Autograph Letter Signed with his pseudonym** "Andrew Marvell", four pages, 7.5" x 12.5", Charleston, South Carolina, August 12, 1775 to an unknown recipient with a few marginal explanatory notes in another hand. A rare and exceptional content letter written in the early months of the American Revolution by a Signer of the Declaration of Independence — only a year before he would sign that document. A flippant but informative letter detailing the chaos that reigned in the early days of the rebellion, Middleton, then a member of the South Carolina Provincial Congress and the Committee of Safety, describes with glee and wit the tarring and feathering of political opponents, seizures of loyalist estates, as well as measures to prepare for colonial defense and moving against prominent Loyalist Thomas Fletcher. He also notes a rumor of an overwhelming victory by Washington over the British in Boston. He writes in full: "Dr. Sir - Since I wrote the damn'd Stuff contained in the enclosed Letter, more for my own amusement during a long sitting at the Council Table in debate about nothing, than for your profit or entertainment upon receipt of it, your second Set of Letters came to hand, with one for myself dated 9th inst. for which I am obliged to you. It gives us particular pleasure to find

you gave had so much success in your Labours - what would I not have given to have been a spectator at the Dutch crying bout with an Hogarth's pencil in hand? One of you certainly must have been vastly moving, whether Tennent or yourself we are much at a loss to know, for I find you have united the orators under the word We & then confounded religion & politicks. The plan of you operations is much approved of. I like sometimes to see a man turn'd inside out; but as to Tacitus [alluding to Colonel T. Guillard] I may with such alteration of the Poet say 'ego illum intus etq in cute novi.' The Affidavit proves Capt. K[irkland] a rebellious Seditious Son of a B— & the Letter shows Capt. P. not to be one of the best sort of Folk - for God's sake as you come down seep the chimney of the State, or we may shortly have a Bonfire - as you say it shall be done, I trust it will - The general form milate are to sit Tomorrow morning upon the trial of the Two Lawyers: we have the papers in hand, & without doubt they are to be convicted; but what the devil shall we do with them? what Boot will fit Dunn, or what shall be Done to Boote? I wish they were at the provincial Camp. I suppose we shall Dine late for the business is to be concluded at one sitting- A Mr: Walker gunner of Fort Johnson had a new suit of Cloaths yesterday without the assistance of a single Taylor [sic. an allusion to tarring & feathering] - his Crime nothing less than damning us all - during his circumcartation he was stopped at the doors of the principal non-associators & was made to drink damnation to them also not excepting our friend Sr. Wm. on the Bay. A Committee is appointed & will sit on Tuesday to receive the answers of the non-subscribers whether they will swallow the oath or not - Dr. M[illiagan]'s answer to the messenger who summon'd him was 'that he should not take the oath & he did not know whether he should obey the summons;' this answer preceded the Show of yesterday; whether that will alter hi tune or not I cannot say — Nothing has yet been concluded upon but the tender of the oath to those people - I have twice pushed hard for the resolution for attaching Estates in case of desertion, but have not been lucky enough to get a Second: the matter however is not rejected, only postponed. Rawlinus postponator declares the resolution not proper to proceed from the Committee of So[uth]. Caro[lin]a. & so arbitrary that none but the Divan of Constantinople could think of promulgating such a Law. I still however do not despair & shall make another trial or two, for I believe at last the State Motto must be 'urgendo vincimus.' the proposal of having waggoners examined by the Guards before they enter the Town Gates will be taken up the first time we have leisure for considering it, & I doubt not will be adopted. I have mentioned your request respecting the vacancies in the regulars, & the blank omissions are all forwarded to Thomson by this conveyance. I also this day once more urged the necessity of entrusting you with blank commissions for Volunteer Companies on the back of [Colonel Thomas] Fletchall, & with some difficulty carried my point, so that the President will enclose you 6 setts; it is expected however that you will have the resolution of congress strictly complied with before delivery of the commissions: I mean as to the associating of 50 Men & the election of Officers; & that you will bring down with you copies of such associations & Lists. the Continental Congress strongly recommend the dividing the Militia of each Colony into Regim[en]ts or Battalions - If we should carry that point also in council it will be a means of diminishing the influence of Fletchall & every Scoundrel like him in the colony - If I mistake not Col. Laurens mentions these matters to you by order, & will also intimate that if any complaints are lodged against Fletchall he will be deprived of his commission. It is said he abuses much the authority vested in him as a Justice of the Peace, by issuing process contrary to the express laws of the Congress. If you should find that to be the case, I think

you might, I have no doubt you will, draw a very weighty argument for rendering him despicable, from his arouse of power especially in your discourses among the poorer sort: but why need I mention what must occur to you? I know not what Stuart has said to you - but his letter to us is evasive in the last degree. Muckenfoos tells me upon delivery of the express packet he turned as pale as his shirt tail — behold the 'mens conscia.' We have notice that one or two of our Vessels are upon the coast with the needful, but no particulars. We have a flying report that Washington has entirely defeated the King's Troops, but I do not credit it; I fear it is too good to be true. It grows too dark to see what I write, & I grow so stupid that you must excuse my breaking off abruptly & telling you that I am your's Sincerely Andrew Marvell."

Middleton had used the same pseudonym "Andrew Marvell" in several political pamphlets, taking his name from the English poet, political pamphleteer and satirist, Sir Andrew Marvell (1621-1678). This is a fine letter illustrating several personal dimensions of an historically elusive figure. Like many in the colonial elite, Middleton was educated in England, attending Hackney and later St John's College, and then Cambridge — where he obviously applied himself in Latin, poetry, and history among other subjects. He later spent time touring Europe and upon his return to South Carolina in 1773, be From the Henry E. Luhrs Collection.came a prominent Whig leader. He was known for his ruthlessness toward his opponents and was a strong advocate of confiscating Loyalist property and other measures meant to intimidate the opposition. Ironically the draconian measures he advocated also speak to his (albeit dark and cruel) sense of humor. His witty allusion to a tarring and feathering is but one example here.

The following year, Middleton was elected to the Continental Congress in place of his ailing father, Henry Middleton, and was present for the vote on Independence. In 1780 he was arrested by the British after they captured Charleston, and was exchanged in 1781. He served in Congress again between 1781 and 1783 and then retired from public life. Overall this is a wonderfully rich letter, giving the reader a vivid impression of the chaotic early days of the rebellion. Provenance: Goodspeed's Book Shop, 1959. Archival tape repairs at left margin, light folds, else very fine condition with rich, dark ink. From the Henry E. Luhrs Collection. Accompanied by LOA from PSA/DNA.
Estimate: $18,000-$25,000

25335 Arthur Middleton discusses the admission of Vermont into the Union

Arthur Middleton (1742-1787) Signer of the Declaration of Independence, rare Autograph Letter Signed "A.M." one page, 8" x 11", Philadelphia, January 26, 1782 on a variety of subjects, and in particular, his doubts on the admission of Vermont into the United States. He writes:

"I hear you left Stanton yesterday & proceeded on you Journey Southward — I hear you will have had many a disagreeable hour before you receive this — I find the regulation last made with regard to Promotions goes farther than I imagin'd when I mentioned it to you — It dissolves the classing of States by districts, which was injurious to some of those who were linked together like the living and the dead in the Past — The Two parts were combined that the one might carry through the other, tho' the whole [illeg.] was intended merely to clear the way for a favourite promotion; it has not been since pushed but we expect it daily — V[ermont] is still sub judice several attempts have been made to carry the point of admission to the Union - but a few are obdurate; she will probably at least be kept out for a Time if not for ever & punish'd in the law for her Iniquities — I enclose all the Newspapers which you neglected to send for — if upon your arrival you should find any ground, or any thing else to which I have a Claim, that can be of service to you, I hope beg you will make the same use of it as it were your own — remember me to Sally & Harriet & the little ones..."

The issue of Vermont was a complex problem facing Congress. The region had been in dispute between New York and New Hampshire who had both claimed it as their own. Conflicting land grants by both colonies nearly led to a civil war. In 1777 representatives of the New Hampshire settlers convened in Westminster and declared independence of the Vermont Republic and soon passed a liberal constitution allowing for universal manhood suffrage, abolition of slavery, and support of public schools. It's admission to the United States as a state was blocked throughout the confederation period by New York and New Hampshire — Vermont continued operating as a sovereign entity until 1791. Its admission to the union was finally allowed as a regional counterbalance to the admission of Kentucky that joined the Union soon afterwards. A great document from the formative period in the early days of the Republic. Professionally silked and laid down to a larger sheet with left edge repairs, the text is largely unaffected. Excellent appearance. From the Henry E. Luhrs Collection. Accompanied by LOA from PSA/DNA.

Estimate: $7,000-$10,000

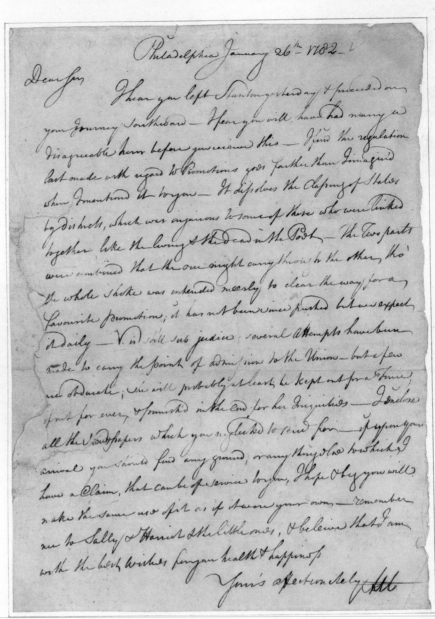

and on October 19th, after burning the Kremlin, he ordered a retreat. While his army had dwindled, the Russian forces had increased. Peace with Sweden had released a Russian army in Finland and peace with Turkey had released the army of the Danube. In July, 1812, Napoleon's Grand Army had more than 250,000 men. It had suffered no decisive defeat, yet it amounted now only to 12,000. In the retreat from Moscow alone, about 90,000 had been lost. By December, in the unbearable Russian winter, Napoleon's Grand Army ceased to exist. Kubusoff pursued Napoleon through Poland and into Prussia, where he was replaced in April, 1813, when he became ill. An exhausted Kutusoff died peacefully later that month. An important foreign affairs letter about Napoleon in Russia written by an American statesman who had served as Minister to France. Show-through, but Morris has penned his letter on each side in the spaces between the lines so that words are not behind each other. Very fine condition. From the Henry E. Luhrs Collection. Accompanied by LOA from PSA/DNA.

Estimate: $800-$1,500

25337   (Robert Morris) (1734-1806) Financier of the American Revolution, printed broadside, 8.5" x 13.25", Philadelphia, March 8, 1792. Entitled *"Plan of Association of the Pennsylvania Population Company."* The Pennsylvania Population Company was established by Robert Morris' associate John Nicholson, a shady businessman who eventually found himself in debtor's prison (together with Morris!) due to reckless investments in western land. Their company was set up primarily to aid Dutch investors interested in purchasing property in western Pennsylvania. The document reads in small part: "Whereas the forming settlements on the Western Boundary of Pennsylvania will establish a barrier to the frontiers and enable the settlement of the other lands to be made in safety, and will promote and expedite the population of the same, and therefore promises of the same, and therefore promises great public utility; and whereas it is expected such settlements may be formed by an association so as to reward the undertakers of so useful a work..." Included on the broadside is the text of an act by the Pennsylvania House of Representatives specifically written to allow non-resident aliens the right to hold property in that state. A similar concern, The Holland Company, was established to act as a trustee for a group of Dutch investors to purchase property in western New York — up to then not allowed to own property in that state. Over the course of the 1790s, speculation in these lands would run wild. The only problem? Speculation far outstripped the actual purchase of lands by settlers — arriving much slower than anticipated. Morris and Nicholson could not hold on long enough for the property to be fully valued. The Dutch investors, however, had better resources and managed to see an eventual return on their purchase. They held their lands through the 1840s when the area had been thickly settled. A fascinating and scarce document. Light scattered foxing and creases, else very good condition. From the Henry E. Luhrs Collection. Accompanied by LOA from PSA/DNA.

Estimate: $500-$700

25336   Gouverneur Morris Writes About Napoleon in Russia. ALS: *"Gouv Morris",* 2p, 8" x 9.5" (front and verso). Morrisania, 1813 August 11. Integral leaf addressed to: *"Robert G. Harper Esqr./Baltimore".* Excellent "NEW-YORK/12 AUG" postmark. Docketed by Harper. In full: *"Accept my thanks for your kind Letter and the Pamphlet enclosed. I had already twice perused and with increased Pleasure your Speech at the Festival. Your Views both Military and political appear to me perfectly correct. As to the latter the most incredulous must soon believe. Unfortunately Kutusow is no more and Bonaparte remains again unrivalled. The old Marshal's Campaign appears to me not only a Chef d'oeuvre but unique -From the time when the Russian force was collected, from the extensive Posts which the uncertainty of Bonaparte's Attack rendered necessary the French Emperor was no longer master of a single movement. He could not take the Road to Petersburgh because he would have left his Flank and Rear opposed to the grand Army of Russia - In retreating from Moscow he would I believe have taken the Road to Cracow, in order to pass his winter in Prague, if he could. This at least is the Course I had marked out for him long before we heard of his Movements and indeed immediately on receiving the news of the burning of Moscow fixed on the 20th of October for his Departure, I conceive that it was for this Purpose he fought the Battle in which he was defeated. In Possession of Prague and leaving Garrisons where he did leave them he would have secured the Cooperation of all his Vassals including Austria for the present Campaign. After we had received information of the Ruin of his Army I looked forward to every thing good if Kutusow should live, but feared much that the slender Thread of his Existence would break or be broken. The last Affairs prove that he has not left his Mantle to his Successor. Adieu believe me always truly yours."* Gouverneur Morris, a Signer of the Articles of Confederation, served in the Continental Congress (1777-1778) and the U.S. Senate (1800-1803). From 1792-1794, he was U.S. Minister Plenipotentiary to France. Robert G. Harper, Congressman from South Carolina (1795-1801), moved to Baltimore, was Major General in the War of 1812, and later represented Maryland in the U.S. Senate (1816). He was an unsuccessful Federalist candidate for Vice President in 1816. In this letter, Morris refers to Napoleon as Bonaparte, his given name, which he dropped after he became Emperor Napoleon I in 1804. In 1812, Czar Alexander had named 67-year-old General Mikhail Kubusoff (or Kubusov) as commander in chief of all his armies. Kubusoff had previously been remembered as losing the Battle of Austerlitz in 1805 to Napoleon. On September 7, 1812, near the village of Borodino, more than 100,000 men with about 600 pieces of artillery were engaged on each side. It ended in a victory for Napoleon, but he lost about 30,000 men, including two Generals; the Russians lost nearly 50,000 men. On September 14, 1812, Napoleon entered Moscow. The campaign ended in disaster for him

25338   Frederick A. Muhlenberg, (1750-1801) first speaker of the House of Representatives, partly-printed Document Signed, *"Fredk. A. Muhlenberg, Speaker"* one page, 7" x 6.5", Philadelphia, November 27, 1782, a pay warrant ordering £26 to William Montgomery *"...it being for 28 Days attendance in Assembly and mileage..."* Countersigned by **John Nicholson.** Expertly mounted to another sheet which has been hinged to a lager sheet bearing an engraving of Muhlenberg. Light toning at folds, else very good. A fine example. From the Henry E. Luhrs Collection. Accompanied by LOA from PSA/DNA.

Estimate: $300-$400

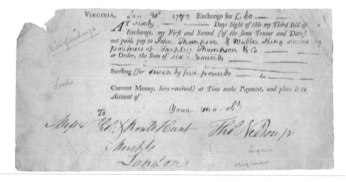

25339   **Declaration Signer Thomas Nelson Document Signed** *"Thos. Nelson Jr."* One page, 8.25" x 4", Virginia, January 30, 1773. A bill of exchange between Mess. Thos. and Rowld Hunt, Merchants in London for sixty pounds. Thomas Nelson was a signer of the Declaration of Independence as a representative from Virginia. The document is in very good condition; tears on upper left corner and lower edge near the center; soiling present on edges; bug holes on upper right corner. From the Henry E. Luhrs Collection. Accompanied by LOA from PSA/DNA.

Estimate: $1,500-$2,000

25340   **Declaration Signer Thomas Nelson, Jr. (1739-1789) Letter Clerically Signed Twice,** *"Thos. Nelson Jur."* and *"T. N.",* two pages, 7.75" x 12.5", York, Virginia, September 9, 1785 to Samuel Martin discussing trans-Atlantic shipping and the sorry state of the economy. He first informs Martin that *"The Brig Assistance being at length loaded... will proceed with all Expedition to London. I feel myself extremely hurt at this unfortunate Adventure; but I must content myself with the reflection of having done the best I cou'd with her..."* Nelson goes on to describe the general state of economic affairs only two years after the close of the American Revolutionary War: *"Our Country is so glutted with Goods that is impossible to sell any Quantity for ready Money, so that we are obliged to give Credit, which makes our Trade so precarious that the Profits are hardly adequate to the Risk the Merchant runs. Before I had heard any thing of Mr. Blackburns House, I had connected myself with the House of Wallace Johnson & Miser of London, to whom I have this Year consign'd the principle Part of my own Crop. From some late Acc[oun]ts from London I almost wish I had sold my Tobacco in the Country where the Price was very high. Very few of our Planters ship their Crops at this Time, chusing [sic] rather to sell to the merchants than to risk them across the Water, so that it wou'd be impossible to load a Vessel of any Burthen on Consignment, and to Load on Purchase at the extravagant Prices now demanded is much too hazardous to be attempted by an Individual, unless he had a very large Capitol to support him in any Loss he might sustain..."* An excellent description of the economic slump that hit the infant United States at the conclusion of the peace treaty of 1783. The letter is signed clerically but still of value and historical interest. Clean separation at center horizontal fold, a few minor chips to margins repaired with archival tape, else very good. Another important letter with revelatory content. From the Henry E. Luhrs Collection. Accompanied by LOA from PSA/DNA.

Estimate: $1,000-$2,000

25341   Declaration Signer William Paca Endorsement Signed

"Wm. Paca, February '77." One page, 7.25" x 4.25", np, February 1777. William Paca was a signer of the Declaration of Independence as a representative from Maryland. He held numerous public offices including Governor of Maryland. The endorsement is in very good condition; endorsement has been clipped from a larger document; staining and rubbing present over parts of text; mounting traces on verso. From the Henry E. Luhrs Collection. Accompanied by LOA from PSA/DNA.

Estimate: $500-$700

25342   Declaration Signer Robert Treat Paine Signed Book:
Address and Recommendations to the States by The United States in Congress Assembled. (Boston: Honorable House of Representatives of the Commonwealth of Massachusetts, 1783), first Boston printing- same year as first printing in Philadelphia, 62 pages, paper wraps, stitched, 12mo (7.75" x 5.25"), signed by Paine on the upper right of the front wrap. This important report deals with raising revenue and other issues facing the new nation. Also bound in are various papers relating to Benjamin Franklin, John Adams, and George Washington, as well as other congressional resolutions. Paine was a signer of the Declaration of Independence and a member of the Continental Congress from 1774-1778 as a representative of Massachusetts. Good condition, printed on the rough handmade paper of the day, edges rough, small paper loss on front wrap. A very rare early American imprint. From the Henry E. Luhrs Collection. Accompanied by LOA from PSA/DNA.

Estimate: $2,000-$3,000

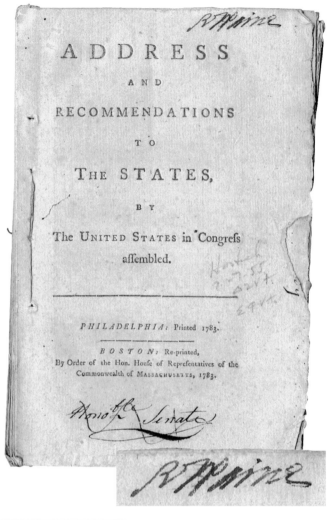

25343   On the Mason and Dixon Line Survey

John Penn (1729-1795), Lieutenant Governor of Pennsylvania & grandson of William Penn, Autograph Letter Signed, *"John Penn"*, four pages, 7" x 9", Black Point, June 17, 1767 to an unknown recipient discussing preparations for the final year of the Mason and Dixon survey and the Maryland-Pennsylvania boundary line.

"I am much obliged to your father for the trouble he took in consequence of my letter, and also to Col. Burd for his readiness in offering his Services upon this occasion. I am amazed to find both by your letter & Col. Burd's that so many Indians are expected to accompany the Surveyors in running the line. I had no idea of more than five or six deputies coming down, from what Sr. William Johnson wrote me, nor do I think he himself expected any more would come. I think the best manner of proceeding will be to call the Commissioners together with Mr. [George] Croghan to consult upon a proper method of sending these Indians home again. Six or eight would surely be enough to attend upon the Surveyors. The maintaining of so large a body would not only be very expensive, but other inconveniences would unavoidably arise whenever they had any Communication with the white People. They should at all events be sent back; and if a present upon the occasion should be thought necessary by the Commissioners it must be sent. I need not recommend frugality upon the occasion. I suppose the gentlemen will naturally think of that. I am afraid our Masters at home will be surprised as it is when the accounts of this business are transmitted to them through I believe everything relating to it, has been managed with as much regard to their interest as possible..."

Charles Mason and Jeremiah Dixon began their survey to define the boundaries between Pennsylvania, Maryland and Delaware in 1763. Their most enduring line was, of course, the long border between Pennsylvania and Maryland which would bear their name. They finished defining that line in October 1767 but halted when they reached a path used by the Iroquois... their Delaware guides refused to push any further westward fearing reprisals from that confederation of tribes. The survey ended 233 miles from the coast and was not completed until after the American Revolution. George Crohghan (1720-1782) was an experienced Indian agent and fur trader and a major player in western land speculation after the close of the Revolution. Sir William Johnson (1715 - 1774) was in charge of Indian affairs for the northern colonies. *Provenance* Walter Benjamin, 1955. Usual folds, reinforced along left margin, a few contemporary ink smudges, else fine. From the Henry E. Luhrs Collection. Accompanied by LOA from PSA/DNA.

Estimate: $1,000-$1,500

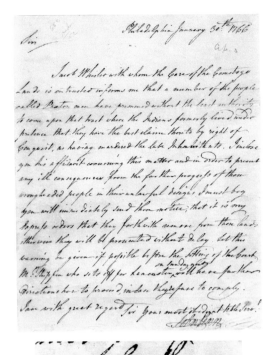

25344   Thomas Penn Signature Collection. This lot features four items signed by Thomas Penn, the two letters in this lot discuss some of his holdings in the state of Pennsylvania. The first item is a Thomas Penn signature on a 3.25" x 1.6" clipping of parchment paper that has been mounted onto rag paper of sturdy stock. He signs himself, "*Tho Penn.*"

The second item is an autograph note signed, "*Tho Penn.*" It is a small clipping of handmade paper that measures 3.75" x 2.75" and reads, "*Reced. 18th of March 1735-6 of James Stech fourty two pounds ten shillings on the Accompt of my Brother John Penn.*"

The third item is a handsome autograph letter signed, "*Tho Penn.*" Two pages with integral address leaf, 7.5" x 8.75", London, October 9th, 1762. Written to Edward Penington, Surveyor of Pennsylvania about the disposing of certain lands owned by his nephew Springet Penn and others, all descendants of his eldest brother William. It reads in part, "*My nephew has told me he has sent you a power to sell pensbury. I have desired I may have the house and a piece of land of three quarters of a Mile on the River with the house in the middle to run a mile back, to which he has consented and I desire when you lay out four thousand acres, which he is to have, in farms, that you will lay out this as I have directed for which I shal* [sic] *pay in the manner any other persons do*" Pennsbury was the famous estate built by William Penn himself some miles up the Delaware River from Philadelphia.

The fourth and final item is an autograph letter signed, "*Tho Penn.*" One page, 7" x 8.75", London, August 10, 1763. Written to Joseph Shippen, Secretary of Pennsylvania. This letter discusses the running of the Mason-Dixon Line. It reads in part, "*As Mr. Richard Peters has resigned the offices he held under us, in order to apply his time principally to the duties of his function as a Minister, we cannot any longer desire him to receive and disburse the money necessary for the Service of the Commissioners and Surveyors, appointed for running the Lines between Maryland and Pennsylvania*" The Mason-Dixon line was originally a boundary between Maryland and Pennsylvania, and it was surveyed between 1763 and 1767.

The items in this lot are in fine condition on average; the letters have the usual folds present; slight soiling present along the fold lines on both letters; the signature and note are both clipped. From the Henry E. Luhrs Collection. Accompanied by LOA from PSA/DNA.
Estimate: $600-$800

25345   Pennsylvania Governor John Penn orders the Paxton Boys off Indian land

John Penn (1729-1795) Grandson of William Penn and Governor of Pennsylvania, fine content Autograph Letter Signed "*John Penn*" one page, 7.25" x 9", Philadelphia, January 30, 1766. An important letter dealing with the continuing problem of the "Paxton Boys", a group of Scots-Irish settlers in central Pennsylvania who were responsible for the murders of over twenty Conestoga Indians in 1763 and 1764. Penn forcefully writes: "*Jacob Whisler with whom the Care of the Consestgo Lands is entrusted informs me that a number of the people called Paxton men have presumed without the least authority to come upon that tract where the Indians formerly lived under pretence that they have the best claim there to by right of Conquest, as having murdered the late Inhabitants. I enclose you his affidavit concerning this matter and in order to prevent any ill consequences form the further progress of those wrongheaded people in their unlawful designs, I must beg you will immediately send them notice, that it is my Express orders that they forthwith remove from those lands otherwise they will be prosecuted without delay. Let this warning be given if possible before the setting of the Court. Mr. Shippen who sets off for Lancaster on Sunday next will have further Directions how to proceed, in case they refuse to comply.*" The Paxton Boys, unhappy that the Quaker-dominated government wasn't doing more to guard the frontier in the wake of Pontiac's rebellion, decided to take matters into their own hands: they attacked a village of the local, friendly (many Christian converts) Consetoga (or Susquehannock) Indians, killing six. Governor Penn subsequently placed the survivors in protective custody in the Lancaster workhouse. On December 27, 1763, the Paxton men broke into the workhouse where they brutally killed all fourteen inside. The Governor issued bounties for their arrest. The Paxton men, outraged that the government in Pennsylvania would do more to protect Indians than White settlers, marched on Philadelphia in January 1764 seeking to kill more Indians. It was the presence of regular British troops and militia that prevented them from doing much damage. Benjamin Franklin negotiated a settlement that averted the immediate crisis. However, as this letter clearly demonstrates, the Paxton men continued to be a threat to the peace in Western Pennsylvania. *Provenance*: Walter Benjamin, 1955. Extremely light toning, a few minor marginal chips else fine condition. Interesting and quite rare history in this missive. From the Henry E. Luhrs Collection. Accompanied by LOA from PSA/DNA.
Estimate: $6,000-$8,000

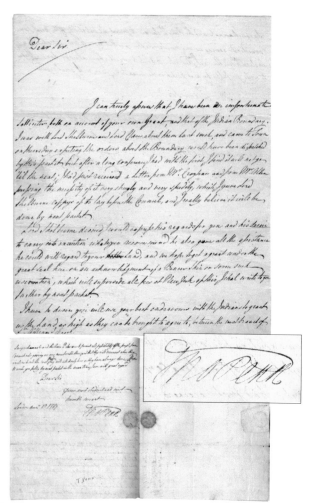

25346   John Penn ("The American") Document Signed and Autograph Letter Signed. John Penn was the son of William and Hannah Callowhill Penn, and their only child born in North America and therefore was called "The American." His parents had arrived in the colony the December preceding his birth January 31, 1699, after a hazardous voyage across the Atlantic The DS is signed, "*John Penn.*" One page, 10" x 8", Philadelphia, Pennsylvania, August 6, 1773. Addressed to John Lukens to survey 300 acres of land granted to Mordecai Holt. The ALS is signed, "*J. Penn.*" Two pages, 7.25" x 8.75", Spring Gardens, Pennsylvania, Friday, n.d. Addressed to Philip A. Hanrott, he speaks about a letter written by William Penn (his grandfather) and wants the recipient to read the book sent to him about it. The postscript in the letter reads, "*You know my sister feared the impression on the Americans might be less favorable for my grandfather's statement.*"

The DS is in fine condition; usual folds are present; one piece is completely separated from the other; edges slightly worn. The ALS is in very fine condition; usual folds are present; edges and corners worn. From the Henry E. Luhrs Collection. Accompanied by LOA from PSA/DNA.
Estimate: $300-$400

25347   Pennsylvania Proprietors John and Thomas Penn Document Signed. One page, manuscript on vellum, 29.5" x 13", Philadelphia, August 5, 1735. A legal document about a tract of land in Philadelphia 30 feet by 250 feet in size with detailed description of location. Signed on the lower folded-over border by two of the three "Proprietors" of Pennsylvania at this time under the Crown of England, "*John Penn*" and "*Tho Penn*". Fine condition; folds as expected, docketing information and intact paper seal on verso, dangling ribbon present on front but seal crumbling. From the Henry E. Luhrs Collection. Accompanied by LOA from PSA/DNA.
Estimate: $400-$600

25348   On Determining the Proclamation Line of 1763

Thomas Penn, (1702 - 1775), son of William Penn and Proprietor of Pennsylvania, Letter Signed "*Tho Penn*", two pages with integral address leaf, 7.25" x 9", London, December 12, 1767 to Sir William Johnson. Thomas Penn, the son of the founder of Pennsylvania, acted as one of the proprietors of the colony. Here he writes to Johnson, the Superintendent of Indian Affairs for the Northern District of British North America, concerning negotiations with the Iroquois over the location of the Proclamation line of 1763. The boundary was designed to separate Europeans from the Indians following the British conquest of French Canada at the close of the Seven Years War. This was an attempt to preserve both the peace and, more importantly, the lucrative fur trade. Penn advises Johnson on developments and advice from London: "*I can truly assure that I have been an imfortunate [sic] solicitor, both on account of your own Grant, and that of the Indian Boundary. I was with Lord Shelburne and Lord Clare about them last week, and came... on Thursday expecting the orders about the Boundary would have been dispatched by this packet... I had just received a letter from W[illia]m Croghan and from W[illiam] Allen pressing the necessity of it very strongly and very speedily, which I gave Lord Shelburne coppys [sic] of to lay before the Council, and I really believe it will be done by next packet. Lord Shelburne desired I would express his regards for you and his desire to carry in to execution what you recommend he also gave all the assistance he could with regard to your land, and we hope to get a grant under the great Seal here on acknowledgment of a Beaver Skin or some such reservation, which will supersede all fees at New York of this I shall write to you by farther by next packet... I have to desire you will use your best endeavours with the Indians to grant us the land as high as they can be bought to agree to, between the west branch of the Sasquehannah [sic] and the River Delaware to prevent all possibility of the people from Connecticut giving us any more trouble there, and that they will covenant when they incline to sell the rest that they will sell it only to us as they have always done...*" The situation in Pennsylvania was complex: not only did the colony have the question of a western limit of European settlement, they had a small-scale civil war brewing over a settlement in the Wyoming Valley by Connecticut. The effort to limit European settlement beyond the Appalachians became one of the significant issues that propelled the colonies toward complete separation from the British Empire in 1776. An important letter. Light toning from wax seal, else quite clean and bright and in very fine condition From the Henry E. Luhrs Collection. Accompanied by LOA from PSA/DNA.
Estimate: $2,000-$3,000

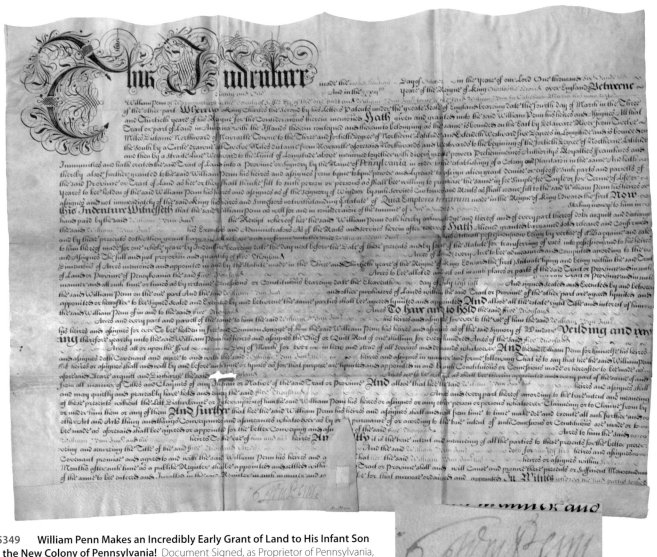

25349   William Penn Makes an Incredibly Early Grant of Land to His Infant Son in the New Colony of Pennsylvania! Document Signed, as Proprietor of Pennsylvania, accomplished in a highly ornate Old English hand, 1 page, on vellum, 50" by 20", Worminghurst, Sussex [England], October 22, 1681; with wax seal intact. Some separation and a few holes at folds, otherwise quite good, with an especially fine signature. With typed transcription.

By this document Penn, who received his charter from Charles II for the colony of Pennsylvania in March, 1681, "leases and releases" to his infant son, William Penn, Jr., for 100 pounds, 5,000 acres of Pennsylvania. In part: " *THIS INDENDURE made the two and twentieth day of October in the Year of our Lord One thousand six hundred Eighty One And in the XXXIII Yeare of the Reigne of King Charles the Second over England BETWEENE William Penn of Worminghurst in the country of Sussex of the one part and William Penn Junr Sonne of the said William Penn by Gulielma Maria the now Wife of the other part WHEREAS King Charles the Second by his Letters under the greate Seale of England bearring date the fourth day of March in the Three and Thirtieth yeare of his Reigne for the Considerations therein mentioned HATH given the said William Penn his heires and Assignes All that Tract of part of Land in America with the islands therein conteyned and thereunto belonging as the same is bounded on the East by Delaware River from Twelve Miles Distance Northward of Newcastle Town to the Three and fortieth Degree of Northerne Latitude and Extendeth Westward five degrees in Longitude and is bounded on the South by a Circle drawn att Ten Miles distance from Newcastle aforesaid Northwards and Westwards to the beginning of the fortieth Degree of Northerne Latitude and then by a straite line Westward to the Limit of Longitude above menconed... In order to the establishing of a Colony and Plantation in the same... THIS INDENTURE WITNESSETH that the said William Penn as well for and in consideration of the summe of One hundred pounds Sterling moneyes to him in hand paid by the same William Penn Junr... Doth Covenant and agree to and with the said William Penn Junr. ... that hee the said William Penn.. shall and will... Cleare acquitt and Discharge...Five Thousand Acres ... from all manner of Titles and Claymes of any Indian Native of the said Tract or Province... that hee the said William Penn Junr.... may quietly and peaceable have and hold the said Five Thousand Acres..."*

William Penn, Jr., was born at Worminghurst, his mother's estate in Sussex, on March 14, 1681 - ten days after the grant of Pennsylvania to his father. Appleton's says Junior came to the colony in 1704. Mercifully, he did not remain. While there, he quit with the Quakers; lived lavishly; had bar fights; exceeded his father's limit on expenses, kept a kennel of hounds, and engaged in affairs, it was said, with unmarried woman. He returned to England, unlamented, and sometime between his repatriation and his death in France in 1720, sold the manor at Williamstadt which had, as this early document establishes, been laid out for him at the founding of the colony. From the Henry E. Luhrs Collection. Accompanied by LOA from PSA/DNA.

Estimate: $3,500-$4,500

25350   William Penn's father reports on his voyage after the capture of Jamaica.

William Penn, Sr. (1621-1670), Admiral and father of the founder of Pennsylvania, William Penn. A scarce Autograph Letter Signed, *"Wm Penn"*, two pages, 8.25" x 11.5", *"Swiftsure in Stoaksbay"*, August 31, [1655]. Admiral William Penn, the father of the founder by the same name, was a ship's captain by age twenty and by age thirty-one rose to become Vice-Admiral of England. He served with distinction in the war with the Dutch. James II (as Duke of York) appointed him commander of the navy in 1664. Following the successful capture of Jamaica from Spain in May, 1655, Penn relates his eventful return voyage to England noting the explosion of a powder magazine on one of his ships and an engagement with a French warship. (Please note that we have not corrected the seventeenth century spellings): *"My last was from Jamaica by the Cardiff wherein was a List of the Shipps appointed to continue in those parts, and of those that then were ordered to come for England. I with ye Shipps mentioned in the margen came from hense Uppon ye 25th of June, keeping whole and Entire together, till ye 13th of J[u]ly — at w[hi]ch Tyme the Divine providence made a Sad Breach by fire aboard the Parragon (w[hi]ch it being a day sett a part— throughout ye fleet to seek the Lord) Begun in Sermon time, forenoone in the Steward Roome as tis thought, and soone proved to[o] strong for all Endeavo[r]s used against it in two houres time (the masts & upper work being first consumed, and all her Cannon fired) the Store of Powder taking fire, a horrid black & hideous Cloud of Smoak were heard & Seene w[hi]ch took her from our sight, leaving us only a Sad Remembrance. About 100 persons in shuning the fire, received their death in ye water and w[i]th them (as far as we see yet) is sunk all hope of knowledge by what meanes it kindled, & who were the unhappy Instruments. About the same time & place vist 10 Fgs of[f] ye coast Cuba neer Habanna, we lost sight of the Tulip, Heartsease & Gilliflower w[hi]ch we have not mett sinse. The rest kept together till neere the Lands End. I chase a French Vessell 200 tuns, 10 guns come from Greenland and took her on Wednesday last loosing sight of the fleet whom this day we mett againe. I humbly desire ye will be pleased to dispeed away Orders to mee, how to dispose of them for as much as I have wish to, & suddenly Expect Directions from Highnesse to Attend him at London, where I shall omit to be further tedious at present..."* Penn lists the ships that returned with him to England in the left margin. An amazing account and a startling contrast to his pacifist son who joined the Society of Friends (Quakers) in the 1660s. (This proved to be a great embarrassment to the Admiral who was considered a hero in England.) Reinforced along left margin and tipped to a larger sheet, marginal tears repaired, else Fine. A significant account and a prohibitively scarce specimen. From the Henry E. Luhrs Collection. Accompanied by LOA from PSA/DNA.
Estimate: $4,000-$6,000

25351   Two Indentures signed by Richard and William Penn. This lot features two indentures, dated 1808 and 1809 for land in Philadelphia. William and Richard Penn, relatives of the founding father Penns, signed them both, along with their lawyers and a notary. All seals are still present and intact. They measure 24" x 16" and 23" x 15". A wonderful example of early real estate deals and legal procedures. Wonderful calligraphy and seal work as well! Both indentures are in Fine condition; slight soiling present on both documents; usual folds are present; ink and signatures are still bold and dark! From the Henry E. Luhrs Collection. Accompanied by LOA from PSA/DNA.
Estimate: $400-$600

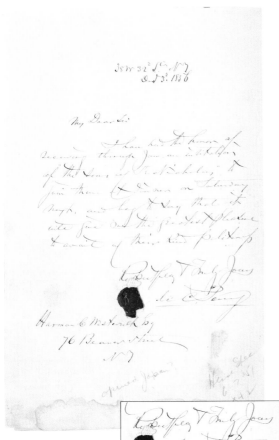

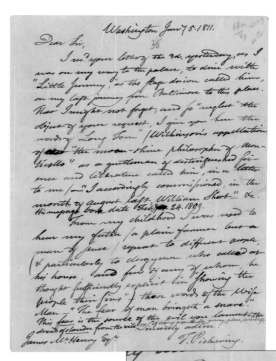

25352   Matthew C. Perry (1794-1858) American naval officer who forced Japan to open trade with the West, scarce Autograph Letter Signed, "*M. C. Perry*" one page, 5.25" x 8.25", New York, December 3, 1836 thanking his correspondent for "*...an invitation of 'The sons of St Nicholas' to join them at dinner on Saturday next and beg to say that it will give me the greatest pleasure to avail of their kind politeness...*" Some mounting remnants on bottom of letter with light soiling, part of original wax seal still affixed next to signature, else Very Good to Fine condition. Letters completely in the Admiral's hand are tough — this is a fine example. From the Henry E. Luhrs Collection. Accompanied by LOA from PSA/DNA.

Estimate: $900-$1,200

25353   Describing Jefferson as the "Moonshine philosopher of Monticello" Timothy Pickering (1745-1829) Autograph Letter signed "*T. Pickering*", one page, 7.75" x 9.75", Washington, January 5, 1811 to James McHenry with integral address leaf addressed in his hand bearing his franking signature "*Free T. Pickering*". Pickering, a high Federalist who served in the cabinets of Washington and Adams, writes to his colleague, James McHenry, who had served as John Adams' Secretary of War, lampooning their arch-rival, Thomas Jefferson: "*That I might not forget, and so 'neglect' the object of your request, I give here the words of 'Long Tom' (Wilkinson's appellation of - 'the moonshine philosopher of Monticello' as a gentleman of distinguished service and literature called him, in a letter to me) - I accordingly commissioned, in the month of August last, William Short' - etc His message book date Feb 24, 1809. From my childhood I was used to hear my father (a plain farmer but a man of sense) repeat to different people, (& particularly to clergymen who called at his house, and a few if any of whom, he thought sufficiently explicit in 'showing thes[e] people their sins') - these words of the wise man - 'the fear of man bringeth a snare'. This fear is the source of the evil you lament; the dread of slander from the vile; or of loving popularity, power, place or interest.'*"

By this date, the Federalists had been out of power for eleven years and the bitterness toward the Democratic-Republicans grew more virulent. Jefferson's trade embargos against France and Great Britain did little to endear him to New England, the center of Federalist political power. After the War of 1812 broke out against Britain, Pickering and other Federalists convened the Hartford convention which publicly proposed several constitutional amendments, but secretly discussed the possible secession of New England from the United States. Rumors of this treasonous behavior spelled the demise of the Federalist party. *Provenance*: Walter R. Benjamin, *The Collector*, December, 1951, No. 714. Very light creasing at usual folds, else very fine condition with rich ink contrast and bright, clean paper. From the Henry E. Luhrs Collection. Accompanied by LOA from PSA/DNA.

Estimate: $1,000-$1,500

25354   Autographs:Statesmen Timothy Pickering: Great Letter Protesting British Harassment of American Shipping! Autograph Letter Signed, as John Adams' Secretary of State, 4 pages, recto and verso , 8" by 10", Department of State, Philadelphia, May 8, 1799. To Rufus King, the American Ambassador to Great Britain. In fine condition. Ex-Saxon B. Gavitt.

The whole point of the Jay Treaty was to ease restrictions on American trade with the British West Indies, more or less - the less having in part to do with Article 18, which stated that any goods which served "*the purposes of war by Land or Sea*" would be, by the British, deemed contraband and seized. But what was happening, Pickering complains in this gloriously furious letter, was that now the Royal Navy was claiming that anything going from the West Indies to New Orleans, which belonged to Spain, could be military use to their allies the French. Hence household goods like nails, burlap, and leather became, as the British choose to read the law, "*just objects of confiscation...attempted to be carried to an Enemy.*" This was maddening, but Pickering, however, liked the British, and hated the French: so would Minister Plenipotentiary King, he implored, please straighten this out! "*I have again to represent to you how much the American trade is harassed by British cruisers, by what I conceive to be a perverse construction of the 18th article of the commercial treaty, relating to articles contraband. The ship General Washington, of this port, is taken by the British Armed vessels the Lynx & Pheasant, and carried into Bermuda. The pretences for the capture, as it is understood, are that she had on board some bales of Ticklenburgs [a heavy, coarse cotton fabric, used for grain sacks, upholstery, and draperies] & Oznaburgs [a coarse, mixed linen fabric], and...casks of...nails. The ship was destined for New Orleans, which is the depot of the cotton raised in our Mississippi territory, and of the skins & furs collected in traffic with the Indians. The cotton & indigo raised & the skins collected in Louisiana also find there a market. The trade between us and New Orleans is very much increased, and is daily becoming more and more important to us. Oznaburgs & Ticklenburgs are essentially for the summer clothing of the slaves & laborers, & for bags for the cotton. The nails are necessary for house building. The 18th article of the treaty declares 'sails' to be contraband: but those coarse linen are neither 'sails' nor sail-cloth. And altho' in extreme necessity, when the proper cloth is not to be obtained, some of the lightest and most trifling sails might be made of ticklen-*

burg, yet that is not, every one knows, the use for which it is imported & to which it is generally applied: and a reasonable construction of the words 'whatever may serve directly to the equipment of vessels' must exclude all three of the articles in question. It cannot be contingent & possible application of articles... but their direct and principal use and destination for that object which must determine them to be contraband."

"*...leather as I am informed has been pronounced contraband - because used in fixing the boxes of ships-pumps, and perhaps one pound in a thousand or two may be so used.*"

"*It really is important to come to an understanding with the British Government on this subject, as well for political as commercial considerations: and I hope... that you will find an early opportunity to converse with Lord Grenville [British Secretary of State, Foreign Office] upon it: and that orders will be issued to put a stop to the mischief.*"

"*I must not omit to mention another refinement in some of the Colonial Vice-Admiralty courts... a distinction made between flat and square bars of 'unwrought iron', declaring the latter contraband because they may easily be converted into ships bolts! I will only observe...that square bars of iron are wanted for common domestic uses, by every farmer in the country: I speak from my own knowledge...*"

Despite the Royal Navy's harassment, things did improve: American trade had tripled with British ports by 1800. Which of course caused the French to retaliate by seizing American ships, which caused the Quasi-War, which caused the Convention of 1800, which abrogated the Franco-American Alliance - and which still didn't stop the Americans from finally fighting the British, again, in the War of 1812. From the Henry E. Luhrs Collection. Accompanied by LOA from PSA/DNA.

Estimate: $3,500-$4,500

25355 **Charles Pinckney, (1757 - 1824), Signer of the Constitution, and Governor of South Carolina, manuscript Document Signed** *"Charles Pinckney"* as Governor and witness, two pages, 12" x 18.25", Charleston, South Carolina, June 2, 1788, a deed for 100 acres of land in Christ Church Parish, Georgia *"...Between Frances Pinckney and Rebecca Mott residuary Devisees and Leagatees of Miles Brewton esquire deceased... and William Clay Snipes of Charleston..."* Light dampstain, partial fold separation, else very good condition.From the Henry E. Luhrs Collection. Accompanied by LOA from PSA/DNA.
Estimate: $500-$700

25356 **Charles Pinckney 1753 Salary Receipt** ADS: *"Chas Pinckney,"* 1p, 7.5" x 5". [Province of South Carolina], April 2, 1753. In full: *"Receivd April 2d 1753 from George Saxby Esqr Receiver Goods the Sum of forty pounds Sterling being two hundred & Eighty Curr.t money being one Years Salary due to George Morley Esq Provost Marshall of the province of South Carolina 25th March last first deducting the Sum of one pound four shillg one penny for the Eleven days Difference in the Style Owed as Atty to Mr Morley."* The Gregorian calendar was proclaimed by Pope Gregory XIII and took effect in most Catholic countries in 1582, in which October 4, 1582 of the Julian calendar was followed by October 15th, 11 days later, in the new calendar. The Gregorian calendar was adopted by Great Britain and her colonies in September 1752, hence the 11 days mentioned in this receipt. Charles Pinckney was a noted South Carolina politician and the father of Charles Cotesworth Pinckney, a signer of the U.S. Constitution. He was long prominent in colonial affairs, serving as Attorney General of the Province of South Carolina in 1733, Speaker of the Assembly in 1736, 1738 and 1740, Chief Justice of the province in 1752ñ1753, and agent for South Carolina in England from 1753 until his death in 1758. Lightly browned. Inlaid. In fine condition. From the Henry E. Luhrs Collection. Accompanied by LOA from PSA/DNA.
Estimate: $300-$600

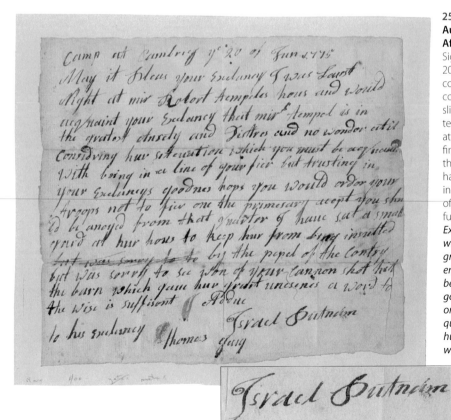

25357 **Israel Putnam Excessively Rare Autograph Letter to General Gage, Three Days After the Battle of Bunker Hill!** Autographed Letter Signed, 1 page, 7.5" by 6.5", Camp at Cambridge, June 20, 1775. To **General Thomas Gage,** under whose command Putnam had just fought at Bunker Hill. The condition of this letter, which has been affixed to a slightly larger sheet, is such that while it is boldly written in dark ink, and quite striking, it is also separated at the folds: restoration, however, will make it a very fine piece. A better letter than this, written just after the first battle of the American Revolution, will be hard to find. A Mrs. Temple's house, Putnam reports, is in the line of fire; a cannon shot hit her barn: he thus offers Gage, most respectfully, "a word to the wise." In full, and with his original spelling: *"May it Pleas your Exilancy I was Laust Night at mr Tempels hous and would acquaint your Exilancy that mrs Tempel is in the gratest anxiety and distres and no wonder at it considering her siteuation which you must be aquainted with being in a line of your fier but trusting in Your Exlancys goodnes hope you would ordor your troops not to fier on the primesary acept you shuld be anoyed from that quartor I have sat a small gard at hur hous to keep hur from bing insulted by the pepel of the contry but was sorry to see won of your cannon shot hit the barn which gave hur grait unesenes a word to the wise is suffisont. Addue..."* So started the American Revolution. From the Henry E. Luhrs Collection. Accompanied by LOA from PSA/DNA.
Estimate: $3,000-$4,000

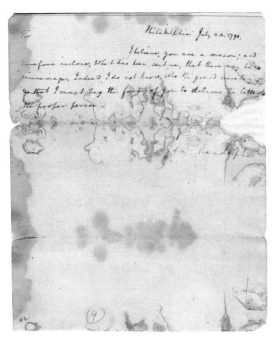

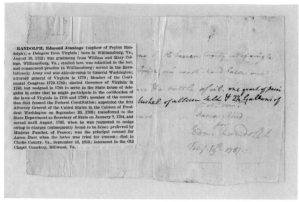

25358   Edmund Randolph Group Lot (3 ALS and 2 Signatures)
This lot features five items which have been signed or written by
Edmund Randolph. Randolph was the first Attorney General of the
United States. He also served as Aaron Burr's defense counsel during
his treason trial in 1807. This lot contains letters regarding Masonic matters, included in the lot are three autograph letters signed by Randolph,
one of which reads in part, "*Sir, I believe, you are a mason; and therefore
inclose (sic), what has been sent me, that there may be no miscarriage.
Indeed I do not known who the grand secretary is, so that I must beg the
favor of you to deliver the letter to the proper person-*"

The three letters measure 7.5" x 9", 5.3" x 8", and 5.3" x 8". The signatures
appear on pieces of paper which measure, 4.3" x 1.5", and 7.5" x 3.6". Four
documents are in very good condition, with slight signs of aging. The
two letters and two signatures show the normal darkening and erosion
that occurs with iron-gall ink. The paper is still sturdy and the writing is
dark and crisp. The letter which contains the Masonic content is in good
condition; the paper has begun separating from the lining it was dried
on and staining has begun to set in, making the writing very light and
hard to read. The signature, however, is still quite visible and clear. An
interesting lot from one of the country's early statesmen. From the Henry
E. Luhrs Collection. Accompanied by LOA from PSA/DNA.
Estimate: $1,300-$1,500

**25359   Edmund Randolph Signature and an incomplete
Autograph Document Signed.** The signature in this lot measures 4"
x 1" and appears as, "*Edm: Randolph.*" Randolph signs the ADS as "*Edm:
Randolph.*" The ADS is 1 page, 7.5" x 4.5", np, February 19, 1787. In part,
"*Gent: Be pleased to send by bearer twenty wt. of single sugar, six lbs.
of brown, one wash hand basin, one bottle of mustard & a bottle of oil,
one quart of painters oil, and 1/2 bushel of alum salt & 2 1/2 gallons of
molasses*" Randolph, a delegate from Virginia, served in the Revolutionary
Army and was aide-de-camp to General Washington; attorney general
of Virginia in 1776; Member of the Continental Congress 1779-1782; first
attorney general of the United States in Washington's Cabinet. Randolph
also served as defense lawyer for Aaron Burr during his treason trial.

The document and signature are in Fine condition. Both have been
clipped from larger documents. The ADS is creased at folds and has uneven edges: a small printed biography of Randolph has been affixed to
the page as well.   From the Henry E. Luhrs Collection. Accompanied by
LOA from PSA/DNA.
Estimate: $350-$550

**25360   Declaration
Signer Caesar Rodney
Scarce Autograph
Letter Signed** to his
brother Thomas Rodney.
One page with integral
address leaf, 7.5" x 12.25",
Dover, June 7, 1773.
Interesting personal
content, in part, "*...When
you was down you gave
me some intimation
concerning an intention
of marriage w Sally or
Rather an application to
her on that head— the
substance of what you
told me concerning it is
in most peoples mouths
now...*" Caesar Rodney
signed the Declaration
of Independence as
a representative of
Delaware. Good condi-
tion, rough at right
edge with repairs, not
affecting bold signature. Scarce in this form. From the Henry E. Luhrs
Collection. Accompanied by LOA from PSA/DNA.
Estimate: $600-$800

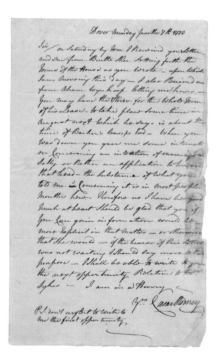

November the 27th 1775

Sir

After a very cold disagreeable ride, I am in town, and have had since I came a smart fit of the asthma; Soon after I parted with you, the evening before I left home, I began to be Strongly impressed with the thoughts of taking lodgings as soon as I should arrive in Town, And these thoughts being accompanied with many weighty reasons, (Which I will Communicate to you, when I can do it by means of my tongue, instead of my Pen & thereby save the trouble of writing so much) I went to lodgings the night I got to town, with a certain Widow Duver opposite John Cadwalladers in Second Street; This place was recommended to me by a friend of mine (one Mr. Milligan) and from what I have yet Seen She is a very genteel, well behaved kind Body, her house is fully and genteely furnished, She has no lodger but me. I have a good lodging Room and Parlour to my self — her own family consists of three Children to wit, two Girls and one boy and one servant Girl — She keeps a good Table and is very obliging, therefore you may Suppose I am so far very happy — I am to pay her 30/ a Week for my self, and 10/ a Week for my Servant, and am to find my own Wine, Spirits and fire-wood, I have already laid in my Wine, Spirits and one Cord of Wood — And pray Remember the three Cord we were planning to be brought up in the New Schooner, and remember

25361 **Caesar Rodney (1728 - 1784), Signer of the Declaration of Independence, Autograph Letter Signed**, *"Caesar Rodney"*, three pages with integral address leaf, 8.25" x 13.25", [Philadelphia], November 27 and November 29, 1775 to his brother Thomas Rodney detailing early intelligence on the fall of Montreal to Montgomery and arrival of British reinforcements in Boston.

Rodney, attending the Continental Congress then in Philadelphia, reports on his safe arrival *"After a very cold disagreeable ride, I am in town; and have had since I came a smart fit of the asthma..."* After requesting more firewood and warning his brother about a major water hazard along the Delaware River, he notes that *"Missrs. [Bushrod] Washington, Missrs. [Horatio] Gates, Collo. Custis & his Lady and one Mr. Lewis all of Virginia set out from here this morning for the Camp at Cambridge accompanied by all the military officers, the three Companies of light-infantry and the Company of light-horse - As they come up General McKinly with forty or fifty of his Battalion attended them to Schuylkill-ferry- We have certain intelligence that there are 2500 or at least 2000 troops landed at Boston from Ireland and it is thought by many, that with this reinforcement they will make a push to get out, by attacking our lines - If they should attempt it, I hope our brave American Boys who have been hitherto fortunate will give us a good amount of them -"* Rodney continues the letter two days later to report: *"You will find in this day[']s paper an account of the surrender of Montreal to General Montgomery on the thirteenth instant; The Congress has as yet received no Express, but expect one every hour as the account is generally believed; Mr Livingston being a man of Carrector [sic], Brother to a member of the Congress and brother-in-law to General Montgomery..."* He adds a postscript: *"Remember to bring up one of Caesar's frocks that I may have his Uniform made, and as you come by Land I desire you would inform yourself what State our Money printing is in, I shall want to know-"*

Richard Montgomery captured Montreal on November 12, 1775. An express rider from General Philip Schuyler reached Philadelphia on November 29 with official news from Montgomery the same day. Montgomery's express reached George Washington in Cambridge on November 28. Montgomery would soon march east to join Benedict Arnold in an attempt to capture Quebec. It was during that campaign that Rodney was killed in action, December 31, 1775. Rodney is probably best remembered for his all-night ride from Delaware to Philadelphia in order to break the deadlock in the Delaware delegation over independence. He arrived just in time to break the tie and cast Delaware's vote in favor of independence on July 2, 1776. Reinforced along left margin, a few very minor marginal tears, small loss (repaired) from wax seal tear, else very good condition. War-date Caesar Rodney letters with content are quite scarce — this is a fine example. From the Henry E. Luhrs Collection. Accompanied by LOA from PSA/DNA.

Estimate: $6,000-$8,000

25362 **Declaration Signer Caesar Rodney Signature** clipped from close of document, 3.75" x 4", February 2, 1767. Rodney was not only a signer of the Declaration of Independence as a representative of Delaware but also a member of the Continental Congress from 1774-1776 and 1778, as well as the President of Delaware during the American Revolution. Good condition, early tape mend affects signature only slightly. From the Henry E. Luhrs Collection. Accompanied by LOA from PSA/DNA.

Estimate: $300-$700

25363 **Declaration Signer George Ross Autograph Document Signed** *"G: Ross"*. Two pages, 7.5" x 12", Lancaster County, Pennsylvania, February 7, 1753. A legal document regarding a Joseph Jervis who died intestate, written early in his law career at age 22. Ross signed the Declaration of Independence as a representative of Pennsylvania and was also a member of the Continental Congress 1774-1777. Very good condition with old repairs at weak folds. From the Henry E. Luhrs Collection. Accompanied by LOA from PSA/DNA.

Estimate: $700-$900

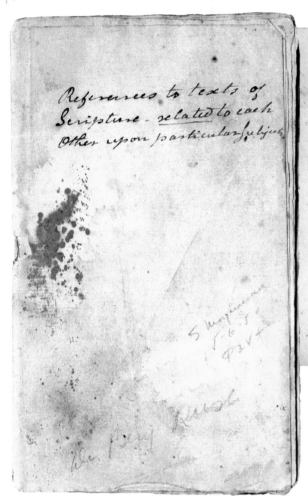

25364 **Declaration Signer Dr. Benjamin Rush Autograph Manuscript** titled *References to texts of Scripture related to each other upon particular Subjects.* This handwritten booklet of approximately 32 pages is 4" x 6.5" in size and includes Rush's writings on topics such as "Universal Salvation," "Kindness to Strangers," "The Sabbath," "Revealed Arts & Human Knowledge," "Efficacy of Prayer," and, interestingly "God's Particular Moral Government." All have various scriptural references along with his comments. In addition to being a signer of the Declaration of Independence, Rush attended the Continental Congress, and was a physician, writer, educator, and humanitarian. He founded the private Dickinson College, a liberal arts institute, in Carlisle, Pennsylvania and was the best-known physician in America at the time of his death. Very good condition; light foxing and dampstaining with one small tear at the spine in the paper wrap, yet complete and boldly penned. Also included is a 1948 Typed Letter Signed by legendary autograph dealer Mary Benjamin attributing the booklet to Benjamin Rush as well as a typewritten transcript. From the Henry E. Luhrs Collection. Accompanied by LOA from PSA/DNA.

Estimate: $4,000-$6,000

25365 **Declaration Signer Dr. Benjamin Rush Autograph Document** signed "*Dr. B Rush*" in the third person, signed at close by Hester R. McClean. One page, 6.5" x 4.25", np, May 4, 1801, receipt for payment of 20 dollars boarding costs. Rush signed the Declaration of Independence as a representative from Pennsylvania. Fine condition. From the Henry E. Luhrs Collection. Accompanied by LOA from PSA/DNA.

Estimate: $800-$1,200

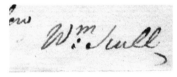

25367 John Schuurman
(?-?) Barrack Master of New Brunswick, New Jersey in 1776, **Autograph Letter Signed,** *"John Schuurman"*, one page, 8.5" x 12.75", New Brunswick, New Jersey, April 12, 1776 *"To the Honourable the Committee of Safety for the Provence [sic] of New Jersey"* informing them of his appointment and *"...in Obedience to said Appointment I have taken the Care & burden upon me until now. but finding it from the business incombant [sic] on me... So Inconvenient to Serve as Barrack masters that I Can not attend it Properly Without Incurring Either the one or the other. Perticular [sic] in the bad Situation the Barracks is in* which Causes double the trouble it Would do if it was in Order. I therefore Gentlemen pray that you will Except [sic] of my Resignation...".* Schuurman also held the position of baggage master for New Jersey. Irregular margins, light toning and folds, else near fine. A fun piece from early in the war and just before Independence. From the Henry E. Luhrs Collection. Accompanied by LOA from PSA/DNA.

Estimate: $300-$500

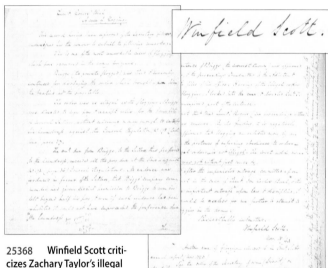

25366 (Nicholas Biddle) William Scull, Philadelphia mapmaker,
Autograph Manuscript Signed, *"Wm Scull"* one page, 7.25" x 12.25", no place, no date. A poem entitled *"Verses to the Memory of my beloved cousin Capt. Nic[ola]s Biddle of the Randolph frigate of 36 guns blown up in an Engagement with the Yarmouth British man of War of 64 guns."* The poem reads in part: *"What dread Explosion rends the distant Skies | What sulphirous [sic] flames in Spiral Volumes rise | The Randolph Swims No More, Modest and brave | The Virtious Biddle finds an early grave | ... Such was thy wish, Mysterious heaven deny'd | Deserved success to Crown thy Noble pride | Oer power'd by double force, the Trembling Main | Beheld thy Ship the Unequal fight Sustain | Amaz'd behl'd the British bands retire ... Confess'd thy Naval Skill and thundering Power | ... all haste to bind the Youthfull [sic] Wariors [sic] brow | With Wreaths Whose Verdure Shall forever glow"* Nicholas Biddle (1750-1778) was one of the first five captains of the Continental Navy. He spent much of 1775 off the coast of Newfoundland capturing British merchant ships. In June, 1776 Congress gave him command of the 32-gun Frigate *Randolph,* built in Philadelphia and launched in early 1777. On March 7, 1777 the *Randolph* encountered the 64-gun Ship HMS *Yarmouth.* Instead of fleeing in the face of a superior foe, Biddle chose to fight. After a twenty minute engagement, the *Randolph* exploded killing all but four of the 310 men aboard. This proved to be a serious blow to the fledgling Continental Navy. William Scull was a third-generation mapmaker, who during the American Revolution served in the Geographical department of the Continental Army. Slight partial fold separations, a few minor soiled spots, else fine condition. A touching, evocative tribute to one of this country's first fallen heroes. From the Henry E. Luhrs Collection. Accompanied by LOA from PSA/DNA.

Estimate: $1,000-$1,500

25368 Winfield Scott criticizes Zachary Taylor's illegal order to flog a private

Winfield Scott (1786-1866) U.S. Army General from the War of 1812 to the Civil War, lengthy **Autograph Endorsement Signed** *"W.S."* and *"Genl. Scott"* twice in text, in red ink in the margin and docket of a manuscript document bearing Scott's secretarial signature, two pages, 8" x 10", no place given, November 18, 1843. The body of the document discusses *"...one of the most remarkable cases of flogging which has occurred in the army for years. Briggs (the private flogged) was tried & severely sentenced for disobeying the order...Briggs was directed to sign pay & receipt rolls for the benefit of several Sutlers, without retaining money enough to satisfy his laundress, against the General Regulation No. 198..."* Scott notes that the flogging was *"...approved by Genl. Taylor... hearing of the illegal order & the illegal flogging, I looked into the case, & directed Genl. T. to remit the unexpired part of the sentence..."* He also condemns the court martial for the sentence and setting a bad precedent. Scott concedes, however, that *"...after the unpunished outrage committed upon me, by the court in the case of Lieut. Don Carlos Buel, & the infinitely more important outrage upon law & discipline, I suppose it would be useless for me further to attempt to suppress flogging in the army..."* In the margin of the second page and on the docket on the verso, Scott adds in own hand notes on the flogging case. A fascinating document considering the bitter rivalry that emerged during the Mexican War. Light creases, else Very Fine condition. From the Henry E. Luhrs Collection. Accompanied by LOA from PSA/DNA.

Estimate: $1,000-$1,200

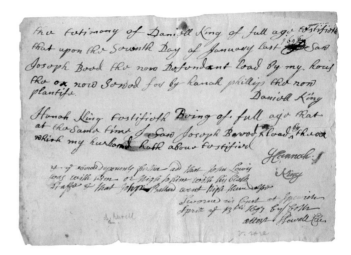

25369 William Seward Writes About Expanding Telegraph Service to the Pacific Autograph Letter Signed,

as senator, 1 page, 8" by 10", Washington, December 9, 1857. To Ezra Cornell, a founder of the Western Union Telegraph Company, for whom Cornell University is named. Traces of mounting at corners, else fine. With typed transcription. Seward wanted to expand the railroads and the telegraph all the way to the Pacific, in large part because he wanted to expand his influence from the East coast all across the country to the West: that's what it took to be President. Assumedly he was happy, then, to tell a powerful New Yorker he was listening to him carefully. In full: *"I have received and I will bestow due consideration on your suggestions concerning the proposed extension of Telegraph Communications to the Pacific."* From the Henry E. Luhrs Collection. Accompanied by LOA from PSA/DNA.

Estimate: $300-$500

25370 William H. Seward Writes About His Son Wanting to Start a New Job — Early! Autograph Letter Signed

1 page, 7.5" by 10", Auburn, March 31, 1857. To Professor Alexander Dallas Bache, superintendent of the U.S. Coast Survey. In fine condition, albeit with faint pencil notes, quite erasable, in lower right corner. Seward's eldest son, the soldier Augustus Henry Seward, having served in the Mexican American War and in Indian Territory, was apparently eager to move on - ultimately, to Utah, as part of the U.S. Coast Survey. His father makes the point for him with this intercessory letter: *" My son Lieutenant A.H. Seward desires me to say to you that although he has a furlough until the first of July next, he would prefer to go on duty at as early a day as he can be useful. Will you please inform me whether the order detailing him for the Coast Survey has been made and whether you have occasion for his services."* The Coast Survey provided the nation's earliest nautical charts, hydrographic surveys, topographic surveys, geodetic surveys, city plans and, later, Civil War battle maps. From the Henry E. Luhrs Collection. Accompanied by LOA from PSA/DNA.

Estimate: $200-$300

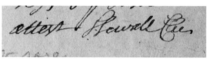

25371 Samuel Sewall (1652-1730), Salem Witch Trial Judge, Autograph Endorsement Signed

"S. Sewall Cler", one page, 7.5" x 5.5", Ipswich, April 13, 1697. A scarce legal document in which Sewall, in the role of clerk of the court, certifies the *"...testimony of Daniel King... that upon the Seventh Day of January Last 1696 Saw Joseph Bond thee now Defendant load by my house three ox..."* Sewall was one of the magistrates called in to judge the accused witches of Salem. He was most remarkable, however, for being the only former Salem judge to issue a public apology for his actions in 1692. Sewall went so far as to call for a public day of prayer, fasting and reparations. He also opened his home to one of the initial "afflicted" children, Betty Paris, daughter of Salem Village Reverend Samuel Paris. Interestingly Betty Paris'"afflictions" rapidly subsided once in the Sewall household. Besides some very light soiling at margins, the document is quite bright and clean and in very fine condition. A wonderful document from a participant in the hysteria forever recalled as a tragic period in our earliest history. From the Henry E. Luhrs Collection. Accompanied by LOA from PSA/DNA.

Estimate: $750-$1,000

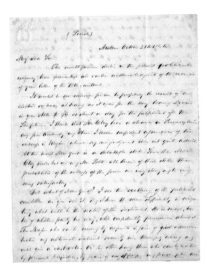

25372   Seward predicts a victory by Clay in 1844

William Seward (1801-1872), Statesman, Secretary of State in the Lincoln and Johnson Administrations, fine political content Autograph Letter Signed "*William H. Seward.*" Three pages with integral address leaf, 8" x 10, Auburn, [New York], October 28, 1844 to E. A. Stansbury, marked "*(Private).*" A rich and detailed political letter in which Seward muses on the outcome of the 1844 presidential election between Henry Clay and James K. Polk. He writes in small part: "*...those who can be excited by personal prejudice, by fears of an oppressive and persecutive aristocracy are roused and heated more than in 1840.... there is the Liberty party, which during the past three years have been suffered by our fault to withdraw from us more than any majority the Whig Party ever had... the possible civil and religious intolerance in the cities of Philadelphia and New York fostered by too many Whigs has driven nearly all the emigrant citizens from us.*" Seward believed the that "*The Loco Focos [Democrats in this context] gain in my judgment from the naturalized citizens as much as they lose to the Whigs and lose to the Liberty Party, though not considerably The result of my best observation is that two chief parties will be nearly equal throughout the states except New York City and the City decides the Election. I believe it will be Whig.*" He continues discussing the acquisition of Texas, with apparent pessimism, and is confident that the cause of Emancipation will be benefited by the Whig's appeals to the pure and patriotic mass of the Liberty Party: "*The mistake if it was of Mr. Clay has been more than counterbalanced by the absurd blunder of Mr. Birney and I feel quite confident that the cause of Emancipation practical will be benefited by the success of our appeals to the pure and patriotic mass of the Liberty party not to reason it by factions adhere to the shadows set before them by the papers.*" In the end, the Liberty Party garnered 62,000 popular votes, and probably threw the election to the Democrats and James K. Polk — he had campaigned on a pro-Texas annexation platform. The Liberty Party was absorbed into the Free Soil Party that eventually merged into the Republican Party, in 1854, when the Whig Party collapsed. Small marginal loss affecting a few words of text, otherwise very bright and mostly clean, fine condition. Early content from Seward is difficult; this is a wonderful example. From the Henry E. Luhrs Collection. Accompanied by LOA from PSA/DNA.
Estimate: $600-$800

25373   Declaration Signer Roger Sherman Autograph Document Signed "*Sherman*" as attorney for the plaintiff. Two pages, 8.25" x 5", Litchfield, 1757. Sherman was the only person to have signed all four major American federal documents: the Continental Association of 1774, the Declaration of Independence (representing Connecticut), the Articles of Confederation, and the United States Constitution. Thomas Jefferson once said that Sherman was, "*...a man who never said a foolish thing in his life.*" Very good condition; contemporary ink smears on verso. From the Henry E. Luhrs Collection. Accompanied by LOA from PSA/DNA.
Estimate: $700-$900

25374   Declaration Signer Roger Sherman Signed Book: *An Enquiry Concerning the Design and Importance of Christian Baptism and Discipline* by Nathan Williams, Pastor of the Church of Christ in Tolland (Hartford: Hudson and Goodwin, 1788), likely first edition, 86 pages, removed from bound volume, no wraps, 12mo (5.25" x 7.75"), Sherman's copy- signed by him "*Roger Sherman's*" on the title page at the upper right. A devout Congregationalist, Sherman once said to Congress in 1789 "It

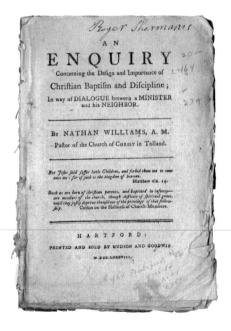

appears to me best that this article [the First Amendment] should be omitted entirely: Congress has no power to make any religious establishments, it is therefore unnecessary." Good condition, edges rough, tear on front (title) page. From the Henry E. Luhrs Collection. Accompanied by LOA from PSA/DNA.
Estimate: $800-$1,200

25375 Declaration Signer James Smith Autograph Document Signed *"Jas Smith"*. One page, 7.25" x 12.25", York County, September 8, 1782. A legal document signed by Smith as Attorney. Smith signed the Declaration of Independence as a representative from Pennsylvania. Very good condition, evenly toned, some weakness at folds, boldly written. From the Henry E. Luhrs Collection. Accompanied by LOA from PSA/DNA.

Estimate: $600-$800

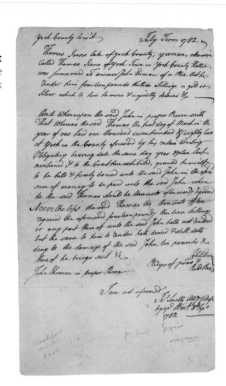

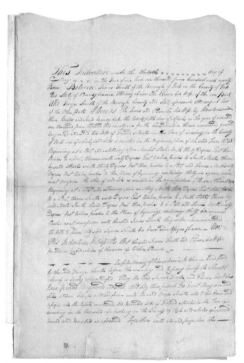

25377 Declaration Signer James Smith Document Signed Twice *"Ja: Smith"*. Two pages with docketing on verso of integral leaf, 11" x 16.5", York County, May 30, 1799. A long manuscript indenture involving Smith in a sale of land in Lewisburg to George Smith. James Smith has signed twice at the completion of the document. Smith signed the Declaration of Independence as a representative from Pennsylvania. This large document is in very good condition and has been linen-backed by a conservator to repair splitting at the folds. From the Henry E. Luhrs Collection. Accompanied by LOA from PSA/DNA.

Estimate: $300-$500

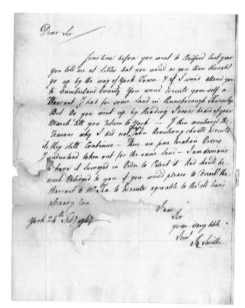

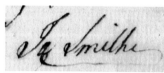

25376 Declaration Signer James Smith Autograph Letter Signed *"Ja. Smith"*. One page with integral address leaf, 7.25" x 9", York, Pennsylvania, February 24, 1767, to Surveyor General John Luken of Philadelphia. Regarding some land in Pennsborough Township, in part, *"...I am desirous to have it Surveyed in order to Patent it and should be much obliged..."* Smith signed the Declaration of Independence as a representative from Pennsylvania and was also a member of the Continental Congress 1776-1778. An attorney, he set up his first practice in Shippensburg, Pennsylvania, home of Henry Luhrs and the Lincoln Library. Very good condition, damp staining at lower left not affecting signature. From the Henry E. Luhrs Collection. Accompanied by LOA from PSA/DNA.

Estimate: $400-$600

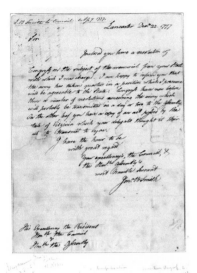

25378 Jonathan B. Smith (1742-1812) Signer of the Articles of Confederation, Autograph Letter Signed, "*Jona. B. Smith*" one page with integral address leaf addressed in his hand and an attached two page Autograph Document, 7.25" x 9.75", Lancaster, [Pennsylvania], December 22, 1777 to Thomas Wharton, President of Pennsylvania. Writing from Lancaster where Congress had fled following the British capture of Philadelphia, Smith happily reports that "*...the army has taken quarters in a position which I presume will be agreeable to the State. Congress have now before them a number of resolutions concerning the army which will probably be transmitted in a day or two to the Assembly. On the other leaf you have a copy of an act passed by the State of Virginia which your delegates thought it their [interest] to transmit to you...*" True to his word, he has transcribed the legislation from Virginia authorizing the procurement of clothing. The army's position to which Smith refers was of course Valley Forge, Pennsylvania where Washington and his army remained in great misery until the British evacuated Philadelphia in the Spring of 1778. Light toning along folds, neatly laid in to a larger sheet, small loss from seal tear resulting in loss of one word, and other tears repaired, else very good condition. Given the resonance of "Valley Forge" to all students of American history, any document noting that encampment retains incredible verve. From the Henry E. Luhrs Collection. Accompanied by LOA from PSA/DNA.

Estimate: $600-$800

25379 Baron Von Steuben *Regulations for the Order and Discipline of the Troops of the United States* ((Worcester, Mass:Isaiah Thomas, 1788) 8vo paper covered wraps, worn with tears, some loss, heavy foxing, dampstaining, edges curled. Two fold out diagrams. From the Henry E. Luhrs Collection.

Estimate: $300-$400

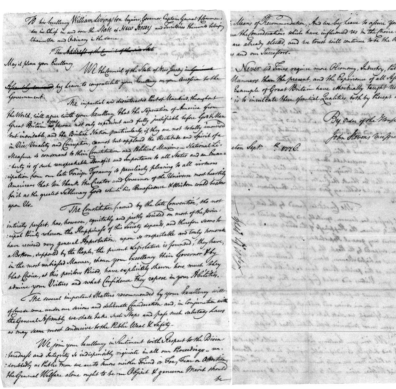

25380 **An early speech celebrating Independence**

John Stevens (1708-1792), member of the Continental Congress, Autograph Letter Signed "*John Stevens*" as Vice President the Council of New Jersey, two pages, 8.25" x 13", Princeton, September [17], 1776, a draft address to William Livingston, the newly-elected Governor of New Jersey. As the Continental Army fled the British onslaught in New York, Stevens, Vice President of the Council of New Jersey, addresses Governor Livingston:

"*We the Council of the State of New Jersey, beg leave to congratulate your Excellency on your Accession to the government. The impartial and disinterested Part of Mankind, throughout the World, will agree with your Excellency that the separation of America from Great Britain was become not only expedient and fully justifiable before God & man but inevitable, and the British Nation particularly if they are not totally immersed in Vice, Venality and Corruption, cannot but applaud the Rectitude and Spirit of a measure so consonant to their Constitution and Political Maxims - National-liberty is of such unspeakable benefit and Importance to all States and an Emancipation from our late Foreign Tyranny so peculiarly pleasing to all virtuous Americans that we thank the Creator and Governor of the Universe most heartily for it as the* greatest Sublunary Good his Beneficence & Wisdom could bestow upon Us. The Constitution framed by the late Convention, tho not intirely [sic] perfect, has, however, equitably and justly decided on most of the principal Points, whereon the Happiness of this Society depends, and therefore seems to have recieved [sic] general Approbation, upon so respectable and truly honorable a Bottom, supported by the People, the present Legislature is founded, they have, in the most unbiased Manner, chosen your Excellency their Governor & by that Choice, at their perilous Period, have explicitly shown how much they admire your Virtues and what Confidence they repose in your Abilities.... Never did Times require more Oeconomy [sic], Industry, Patriotism and sound Manners than the present, and the Experience of all Ages with the recent Example of Great Britain have effectually taught us how necessary it is to inculcate these essential Qualities both by Precept and Example...*"

Docketed "*Draught of an Address Brought in & first read Sept. 17, 1776*" An amazing and early document from the founding of the United States. The Council would soon be forced to flee Princeton as the British invaded on the heels of Washington's retreating army. In late 1776, Washington would stage a surprise attack on Trenton (December 25) completely surprising the Hessian garrison there. He followed up his success at Princeton a week later defeating British forces there and managing to give the fledgling nation some hope for victory after a disastrous campaign. Light folds and toning, else very good condition. Remarkable history. From the Henry E. Luhrs Collection. Accompanied by LOA from PSA/DNA.

Estimate: $3,000-$5,000

25381 Declaration Signer Richard Stockton Rare Autograph Document Signed. Two pages, 7.5" x 12", Middlesex County, April Term, [1766]. A legal document by Stockton as attorney for the plaintiff, signed at the end as "*Rich Stockton*" and also in the body (third person) in full. Stockton signed the Declaration of Independence as a representative of New Jersey and was also a member of the Continental Congress in 1776. While on an inspection tour for the Congress, he was captured by the British and his poor treatment at their hands hastened his death which occurred in 1781 at age 50. Near Very Good condition, split at the middle fold, easily repaired. From the Henry E. Luhrs Collection. Accompanied by LOA from PSA/DNA.
Estimate: $1,000-$1,500

25382 Declaration Signer Thomas Stone Document Signed "*T. Stone*". One page, 7.5" x 6.25", np, April 23, 1777, an itemized receipt regarding legal work. Stone was a planter and an attorney and signed the Declaration of Independence as a representative from Maryland. Good condition, staining and weakness at folds, laid down to larger sheet. From the Henry E. Luhrs Collection. Accompanied by LOA from PSA/DNA.
Estimate: $1,200-$1,500

25383 Charles Sumner, Thaddeus Stevens & Other Abolitionists Autograph Collection. An incredible grouping of items from these famous 19th century leaders in the fight against slavery and the slave trade, consisting of the following items:

Charles Sumner. 1862 ALS, 1853 ALS with free franked envelope, 1865 ALS, 1864 ALS with free franked envelope.

Thaddeus Stevens. 1859 free franked envelope, 1863 ANS, 1868 ALS, 1866 ANS, 1842 ANS.

George L. Stearns (1865 ALS); Wendell Phillips (2 Signatures); Gerrit Smith (1865 ALS); William Slade (1842 ALS); Rev. A. Booth (ALS).

Generally fine condition; excellent dealer lot. From the Henry E. Luhrs Collection. Accompanied by LOA from PSA/DNA.
Estimate: $600-$800

25384 Important Letter Group to Sculptor Horatio Greenough on his famed Semi-nude Statue of George Washington.

Charles Sumner (1811-1874), fine collection of five Autograph Letters Signed to neoclassical sculptor Horatio Greenough (1805-1852) best known for his semi-nude statue of George Washington commissioned for Congress to sit in the Capitol Rotunda. An excellent and detailed correspondence from Sumner to the noted sculptor concerning art, politics and, in a particular, Greenough's statue of George Washington — a work that caused great controversy with the heroic subject presented in the classical (semi-nude) form. Based on Phidias's statue of Zeus at Olympia, Greenough received the commission from Congress in 1833 and completed the study in 1841. Sumner, who traveled widely in Europe between 1837 and 1840, met with Greenough, his fellow Boston native, while the latter was working on his statue of Washington in Florence.

The correspondence begins with an A.L.S., four pages, 8.25" x 10.5", Berlin, January 8, 1839 with integral address leaf addressed to Horatio Greenough in Florence. Sumner discusses works in progress: "...*Columbus against the negro; that was a good exchange; will it be sufficient to make him pondering a globe? An astronomer might be so represented; Tycho Bronze is so, in the bas relief of his monument at Prague. A ship compass, a trident — can these symbols be resorted to? — I rather incline to prefer the Indian to the Virgin America. Indeed, Columbus & the Indian would be types of the two great races...*" After more discussion he notes that he

154 Session One, Auction #626 • Monday, February 20, 2006 • 5:00 PM

A 19.5% Buyer's Premium ($9 min.) Applies To All Lots

"*...should be pleased to know how you go in with yr second Govt. word...*" Usual folds, light soiling, small loss from seal tear not affecting text, else very good. Later in the year, Sumner again writes on art in an A.L.S., four pages, 8.5" x 10.25", Vienna, November 8, 1839 with integral address leaf addressed to Horatio Greenough in Florence, specifically on the Washington statue: "*...I have yr. Washington in my mind often, & the conviction has grown upon me, that you have done the great subject ample justice, & that you will produce a work that will make us all feel a pride in you as of our country. I hope you may succeed with the accessories, as you have with the figure. I would have them all pure, harmonious, & classical; by pure, I mean free from any the least thing that would tend to bring up an idea undignified or disagreeable. -& I am almost inclined to say the Indian; also the conceit of Washington passing bye [sic] the sirens [sic] Having determined upon one or more classical accessories, I would have them all of this character. This again would make against the negro & Indians. And in determining the classical, I would resort as much as possible to the actual antique, rather than to my own fancy for figures in the style of the antique...*"

Back in Boston, Sumner learns of the completion of the statue. In another A.L.S., four pages, 7.25" x 9", Boston, February 28, 1841, he accurately predicts a bad reaction from Americans: "*Let me congratulate you on the completion of yr Statue, & the distinction it has given you. From the hour, when you admitted me to see it, lighted by lamps & torches, I have not doubted for a moment the result. It will give you fame. Still I feel that it must pass through a disagreeable ordeal, one, which, as it seems unavoidable, I hope will not be annoying to you. I refer to the criticisms of people, knowing nothing of art. In Europe an artist is judged at once, in a certain sense, by his peers. With us all are critics. The rawest Buckeye will not hesitate to judge your work, & will, perhaps, complain that Washington is naked; that he has not a cocked hat & a military coat of the Continental cut; that he is not standing etc. etc. The loungers in the Rotunda, not educated in view of works of art, many, never before having seen a statue in marble, will want the necessary knowledge to enable them to appreciate yr Washington. Should you not prepare them, so far as you can? And you can do a great deal. Publish in Kickerbocker's Magazine, or such other journal... some of the papers you read me during my visit to Florence; Particularly that on the nude, for there I think you will encounter a deal of squeamish criticism...*" Small loss from seal tear, usual folds, light toning, else fine. The semi-nude statue was lampooned in the press and proved scandalous for conservative viewers. Despite the controversy, Congress voted to reimburse Greenough for his work. A copy of the act is forwarded by Sumner in another A.L.S., four pages, 7.25" x 9", Boston, September 16, 1841 with integral address leaf addressed to Horatio Greenough in Florence: "*...Above is the act, which was passed under the spur of your admirable letter to the Secretary of State... My friend Hillard... says it as good as a good statue. It touched cords of the human hart which stifled all pultry [sic], mean considerations... You will read the newspapers, & the sad revelations, as they seem at present, of Tyler's weakness & bad faith. His hand is turned by the brief hour of power to which he has come by accident...*" Clipping of the Congressional Act providing for Greenough's expenses glued to front of letter, partial fold separation, else very good.

Because of the controversy, the statue was moved in 1843 out of the Capitol Rotunda to the East Lawn on the Capitol where some joked that Washington was desperately reaching for his clothes that were on exhibit at the Patent Office several blocks north. The statue came to the Smithsonian in 1908 and now occupies a prominent spot in the National Museum of American History. Greenough died in 1852. The collection finishes with a sorrowful A.L.S. from Sumner, four pages, 4" x 6.75", Washington, December 21, 1852 to Greenough's widow: "*Sincerely & deeply I mourn with you. The death of Horatio Greenough is a loss not only to wife & children, but to friends & the worked, to Art & Literature...*" Very fine. A spectacular collection of material. From the Henry E. Luhrs Collection. Accompanied by LOA from PSA/DNA.
Estimate: $1,500-$2,000

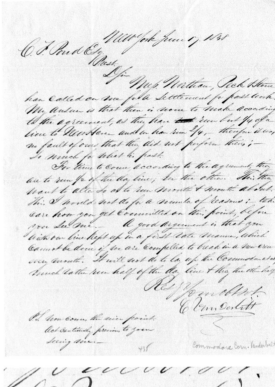

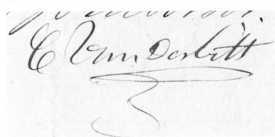

25385   "Commodore" Cornelius Vanderbilt Rare Autograph Letter - About Running His Business! Autograph Letter Signed ("C. Vanderbilt"), 1 full page, 8" by 10", New York, June 17, 1848. To C.F. Pond. In Fine condition. The Commodore's fortune, when judged in comparison to the Gross National Product of his day, was the second largest in American History - only John D. Rockefeller's was bigger. (Bill Gates, using this formula, ranks thirty-first.) Vanderbilt began with a small barge bought with borrowed money, at age sixteen - and became the leading American steamship owner. Here we see how. "*Messrs. Northam, Peck & Stone have called on me for a settlement for past work. My answer is that there is none to make according to the agreement, as they have run but a 1/4 of a line to New Haven and we have run 3/4 - therefore it was no fault of ours that they did not perform theirs; so much for what is past. For time to come... they are to run 1/2 of the day line, we the other. This they want to alter so as to run Month to Month. This I would not do for a number of reason: take care how you get committed on this point... A good argument is that you wish our line kept up in a first rate manner, which cannot be done if we are compelled to break in a new crew every month. It will not do to lay up the Commodore at all, much rather run half of the day line & they the other half... Now comes the nice point. Act cautiously previous to your seeing me*"

Later, Vanderbilt turned to railroads, and began to build his second fortune. From the Henry E. Luhrs Collection. Accompanied by LOA from PSA/DNA
Estimate: $2,500-$3,500

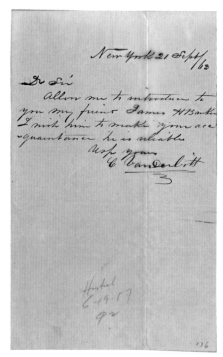

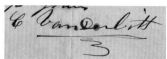

25386 **Cornelius Vanderbilt** Autograph Letter Introducing a Railroad Crony as "Reliable." Autograph Letter Signed "*C. Vanderbilt*" 1 page, 5" by 8.25", New York, September 21, 1863. Some discoloration at fold and along top margin, but not unsightly; a faint pencil notation at bottom of blank portion of letter; and tipped, by integral leaf, to a piece of cardboard: quite good, in all. Terse, as if he were paying by the word, the second wealthiest man in American history makes his point: "*Allow me to introduce my friend James H. Banker. I wish him to make your acquaintance. He is reliable.*" Vanderbilt was busy in 1863 buying up railroads — as if at almost 70, shipping hadn't made him rich enough. With his election that year as President of the New York & Harlem Railroad, the Commodore put James H. Banker on the Board. From the Henry E. Luhrs Collection. Accompanied by LOA from PSA/DNA.

Estimate: $1,000-$1,500

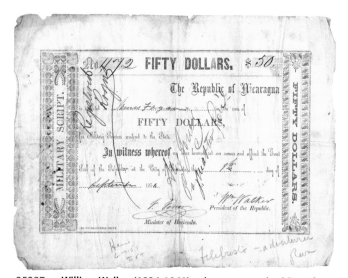

25387 **William Walker (1824-1860), adventurer, and soldier of fortune who briefly ruled Nicaragua from 1856 to 1857, rare partly-printed Document Signed** "*Wm Walker*" as President of Nicaragua, one page, 9" x 7", Granada, September 9, 1856, a promissory note issued to James Fagan for the sum of $50. Walker had a varied career and work

that included: journalist, attorney, and physician, but his most notorious occupation was as a filibusterer. Simply defined, filibusterers were Anglo-American soldiers of fortune who attempted to carve out states populated by white English speakers in Latin America. The most successful of these were, of course, the founders of Texas. Walker had attempted such a plot in Mexico in Baja California and Sonora in 1853, but met with stiff Mexican resistance. In 1855, taking advantage of a civil war raging in Nicaragua, he traveled there with a small force and allied himself with one of the factions. On September 1, he defeated the Nicaraguan national army at La Virgen, and captured the capital of Grenada a month later. Interestingly, Franklin Pierce briefly recognized the Nicaraguan government under Walker's leadership, although filibustering was contrary to federal law. Walker had the support of Cornelius Vanderbilt who wanted to construct a railroad to link the Caribbean and the Pacific. However, once in power, Walker betrayed Vanderbilt and handed the rights to build a railroad to Vanderbilt's rivals, Cornelius K. Garrison and Charles Morgan. Vanderbilt then pressured Pierce to rescinded recognition of the Walker government, and organized an opposition force led by Costa Rica to thwart Walker's attempt conquer all of Central America. In an attempt to garner Southern support, in Nicaragua, he legalized black slavery that had been outlawed in 1824. Walker was defeated in 1857, and surrendered to the U.S. Navy. He was killed in Honduras after mounting a similar expedition there in 1860. Moderate creases, light toning, else very good condition. A scarce example signed in his brief tenure as the "President of Nicaragua"... the first we've seen! From the Henry E. Luhrs Collection. Accompanied by LOA from PSA/DNA.

Estimate: $800-$1,000

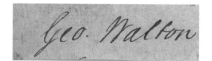

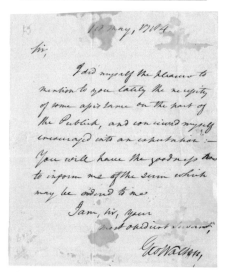

25388 **Declaration Signer George Walton Signature and Autograph Letter Signed** "*Geo Walton*". One page, 7" x 8.5", np, May 18, 1784, written as Georgia Chief Justice to Georgia Governor John Houstoun. Walton signed (the youngest to do so) the Declaration of Independence as a representative from Georgia. He was also a member of the Continental Congress 1776-1777 and 1780-1781. He had a role in the duel in which Lachlan McIntosh shot and killed Button Gwinnett. John Houstoun might himself have signed the Declaration as he was elected a delegate to the Continental Congress in 1775. However, he was in Georgia trying to put down a Loyalist uprising led by John Zubly at the time. Very good condition; folds, areas of staining not affecting signature, very minor smear on signature. Originally purchased from Walter R. Benjamin Autographs.

Also included in this lot is a Signature "*Geo. Walton Chief Justice*" removed from a document, 4.25" x 1.25", dated 1783. Fine condition. From the Henry E. Luhrs Collection. Accompanied by LOA from PSA/DNA.

Estimate: $700-$900

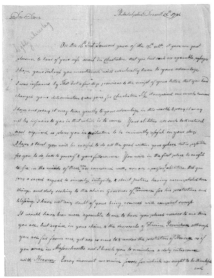

**25389	Artemas Ward Autograph Letter Blaming "the Democratic Clubs" for the Whiskey Rebellion.** Autograph Letter Signed, 2 pages, recto and verso, Philadelphia, December 15, 1794. To "Dear Dana." In fine condition, albeit an enthusiastic soul has "improved" on the clarity of two letters in pencil, as well as noted "highly interesting" in one corner, and the information that the letter came from Goodspeeds in another. With typed transcript. In this intimate letter - perhaps to his son, Henry Dana - the old Revolutionary General Ward delivers a benediction to the young man, newly removed to Charleston, ending with a warning: stay away from "the Democratic Clubs" — they caused the Whiskey Rebellion. In part: "*I hope & trust you will be careful to do all the good within your sphere that it is possible for you to do, both to yourself & your fellowmen. You will in the first place be careful to fix in the minds of those you are concerned with, you are a person of abilities, that you pay a sacred regard to sincerity, integrity, & strict Justice... daily seeking to the all-wise Governor of the universe for his protection and blessing, I have no doubt of your being crowned with complete success... Every moment we receive favors for which we ought to be thankful... I ardently pray you may through the merits of Jesus Christ be received to Zion.... God almighty bless you. (N.B) I hope you will never forsake the northern Politics & adopt the present Southern ones. Harmony is much more prevalent in Congress than last sessions. The Democratic Clubs are... reprobated, it is the general received opinion they were one cause of the late insurrection in the four Western Counties of Pennsylvania.*" From the Henry E. Luhrs Collection. Accompanied by LOA from PSA/DNA.
Estimate: $1,500-$2,500

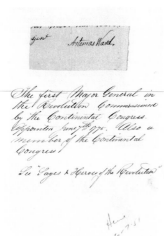

**25390	Artemas Ward (1727-1800) American Major General in the Revolutionary War, his signature** "*Artemas Ward*" on a 3" x 1.25" sheet neatly mounted onto a mid-nineteenth century 5" x 8" sheet of paper. Ward served as commander of the forces surrounding the British in Boston following Lexington and Concord in 1775. After the continental Congress appointed George Washington as Commander in Chief, Ward became a Major-General and second in command. It was Ward who gave orders to fortify Breed's Hill in June 1775 which precipitated the Battle of Bunker Hill. Fine condition. From the Henry E. Luhrs Collection. Accompanied by LOA from PSA/DNA.
Estimate: $400-$500

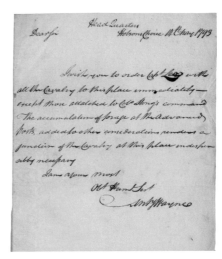

**25391	"Mad Anthony" Wayne sends for the Cavalry in Indian War!** Autographed Letter Signed, as Major General and Commander-in-Chief of the Legion Army, 1 page, 8" by 10", Head Quarters, Hobson's Choice, May 14, 1793. To his second in command, Brigadier General James Wilkinson - whose secret plots to destroy him caused Wayne no end of problems in the field. Left margin of integral leaf has been strengthened, not effecting the text; else fine. Offered here is a choice example of a scarce and desirable autograph - an urgent command given in the midst of Little Turtle's War. "*I wish to order Capt. Lear with all the Cavalry to this place immediately - except those attached to Col. Strong's command. The accumulation of forage at the advanced posts, added to other considerations renders a junction of the Cavalry to this place indispensably necessary.*" From the Henry E. Luhrs Collection. Accompanied by LOA from PSA/DNA.
Estimate: $1,200-$1,800

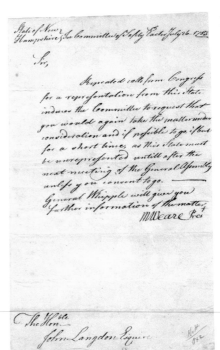

**25392	Meshech Weare Letter on New Hampshire's Representation in the Continental Congress.** Letter Signed "*M. Weare, Prest.*", as president of New Hampshire, 1 page, 7.25" by 11.5", In Committee of Safety, State of New Hampshire, Exeter, July 26, 1783. To the Hon. John Langdon. In very fine condition. Weare, as the most powerful member of New Hampshire's powerful Committee of Safety, urges Langdon to go to Congress. In full: "*Repeated calls from Congress for a representation from this State induces the Committee to request that you would again take the matter under consideration and if possible to go, if but for a short time, as this State must be unrepresented until after the next meeting of the General Assembly unless you consent to you go —- General Whipple will give you further information of the matter.*" From the Henry E. Luhrs Collection. Accompanied by LOA from PSA/DNA.
Estimate: $1,500-$2,000

25393 John Wentworth (1737-1821), last royal governor of New Hampshire, partly-printed Document Signed, "*Wentwoth*" as Governor, one page, 12.5" x 8", Portsmouth, January 20. A 1775 marriage certificate granted to "*... Francis Moore of Cambridge in the county of Middlesex Baker aged twenty seven years to Miss Bebe Preston of Boston in the county of Suffolk Aged Twenty Years...*" Why the couple came to Portsmouth New Hampshire to marry is unclear. Tape remnants along one horizontal fold, small marginal chip, otherwise on bright paper with a bold signature. From the Henry E. Luhrs Collection. Accompanied by LOA from PSA/DNA.

Estimate: $300-$500

25394 Pennsylvania President Thomas Wharton Document Signed "*Tho Wharton jun Pres*". One page, partly printed, Supreme Executive Council, 14" x 9", Philadelphia, November 6, 1777. An appointment of Stophel Whiteman "to be Adjutant of the Ninth Battalion of Militia, in the County of Lancaster." In 1777, Wharton was elected "His Excellency Thomas Wharton, junior, esquire, president of the supreme executive council of Pennsylvania, captain-general and commander-in-chief in and over the same," and served until his death a year later. Fine condition; folds, a bit of damp staining but signature is bold and clean, and the paper seal is intact and well defined. From the Henry E. Luhrs Collection. Accompanied by LOA from PSA/DNA.

Estimate: $500-$700

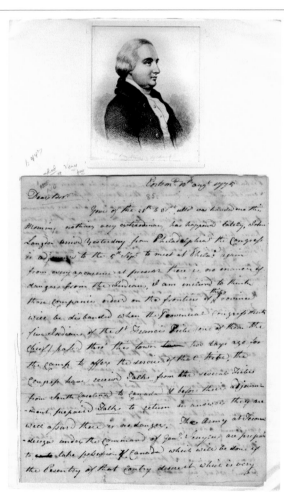

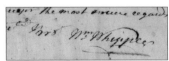

25395 William Whipple (1730-1785), Signer of the Declaration of Independence, Autograph Letter Signed "*Wm Whipple*", three pages, 7.75" x 9.5", Portsmouth, [New Hampshire], August 13, 1775. This letter is to his brother and reports on current developments including the arrival of Washington at Cambridge, the invasion of Canada, as well as Indian negotiations.

"*...John Langdon arrived yesterday from Philadelphia the Congress is adjourned to the 5th Sept. to meet at Phi[ladelphi]a. again from every apearence [sic] at present there is no man[n]er of danger from the Indians, I am inclin'd to think those companies order'd on the frontiers off this Province will be disbanded when the Provincial Congress meets five Indians of the St Francis Tribe (one of them the Chief) passed thro' this town two days ago for the Camp to offer the service of that tribe, the Congress have received Talks from the several Tribes from South Carolina to Canada & before their adjournment prepaired [sic] Talks to return in answer they are well assur'd there is no danger. The Army at Ticonderoga under the Command of Genl. Schuyler are prepared to take possession of Canada which will be done if the Pesentry [sic] of that Contry [sic] desire it which is very Probably in that case the frontiers will be much more secure then the sea Coast. The Army before Boston since the arrival of the new General [Washington] makes an appearance to the admiration of every body. Many of the cutters have been taken & Privatiers [sic] are fiti[t]ng out at Rhoad [sic] Island & all the southern Colonies for the Protection of our trade notwithstand[ing] the men of war. One thousand rifle men are arriv'd at the Camp from the Southward & two Companies more Expected dailey [sic], considerable Quantities of Powder are arriv'd & dayly [sic] arriving in the Southern Colonies, & the powder mills in York Phia. &c are fully emply'd, so that we may expect a full supply of that article very soon for any matter, for which it may be wanted, we have no certain accco[un]ts from England, how the news of the Lexington affair was received there, but no doubt that and other matters which have since happened will very much confound administration & strengthen the American party on that side the Atlantek [sic], on the whole every appearance at present is in our favor even beyond what we have reason to expect...*"

Whipple then turns to more personal matters, but notes that "*...Garrison is arriv'd from the west Indies with a load of Salt he was luckely [sic] directed in to York by a boat who shake with him on the Coast otherwise he must have fallen [sic] into the hands of the Man of war who is order'd take all vessels with salt or molasses...*"

A wonderful content-filled letter illustrating the early optimism at the start of the American Revolution. The riflemen that Whipple reports on are likely the companies under Daniel Morgan. His optimism about news from Lexington and Concord strengthening the position of America's friends in Parliament was completely unfounded. Open hostilities only strengthened the resolve of many in Parliament to bring the colonies to obedience. Ironically, it was Britain's optimism that it could easily accomplish this feat that resulted in an underestimation of the strength of the rebellion — leading to their ultimate defeat. Silked to repair fold separations, second page mounted to a larger sheet bearing an engraved portrait of Whipple, a few minor marginal chips, light toning, else very good. An important missive. From the Henry E. Luhrs Collection. Accompanied by LOA from PSA/DNA.

Estimate: $8,000-$10,000

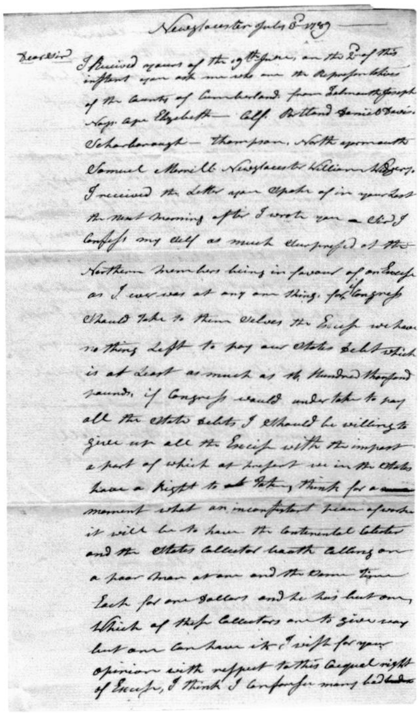

25396 William Widgery 1789 Letter to Congressman Thatcher Complaining About Congress Planning To Take The "Excess" (today, Surplus) Instead Of Letting The States Use It To Pay Their Own Debts. ALS: "*William Widgery*," 2p, 7.5" x 12". Newglocester, July 3, 1789. Integral leaf addressed by Widgery to: "*Hon. George Thatcher Esq./Representative from Massachusetts/in Congress New York.*" "*Portland July 7*" in upper left and "*Free*" in upper right. In part: "*I confess my self as much surprised at the Northern members being in favor of an Excess as I ever was at any one thing for if Congress should take to them selves the Excess we have nothing left to pay our States debt which is at least as much as 16 Hundred thousand pounds. If Congress would under take to pay all the state debts I should be willing to give up all the Excess with the import a part of which at present we in the states have a right to take, think for a moment what an inconsistent piece of work it will be to have the Continental Collector and the States Collector both calling on a poor man at one and the same time. Each for one dollar and he has but one. Which of these Collectors are to give way but one can have it...I think you would do well to give Congress the Exclusive right of Excess and Congress take upon them the payment of the States debts....*" The First Congress had convened on March 4, 1789, just four months earlier. George Thatcher represented Massachusetts in the Continental Congress (1777-1789) and in the U.S. House of Representatives (1789-1801) as a Federalist. He was District Judge in Maine (a part of Massachusetts until 1820) from 1792-1800 and Associate Judge of the Supreme Court of Massachusetts (1800-1820) and Maine (1820-1824). A lawyer in Portland, Maine, William Widgery was a member of the Massachusetts House of Representatives (1787-1793, 1795-1797) and a member of the U.S. House of Representatives representing Massachusetts (1811-1813). Slight wear at folds, hole at blank left edge as a result of opening the letter at the wax seal. Overall, in fine condition. From the Henry E. Luhrs Collection. Accompanied by LOA from PSA/DNA.
Estimate: $1,000-$2,000

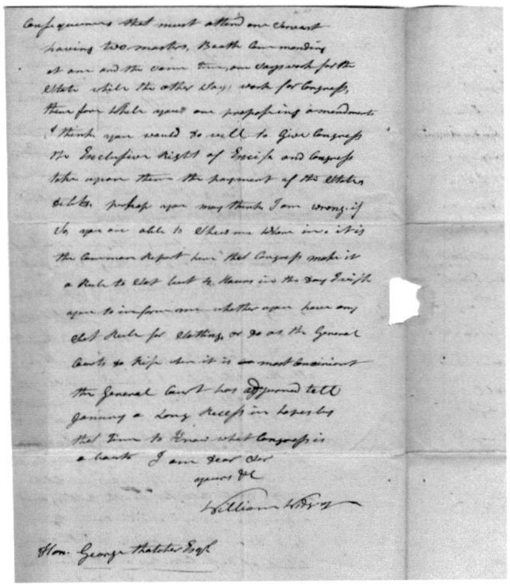

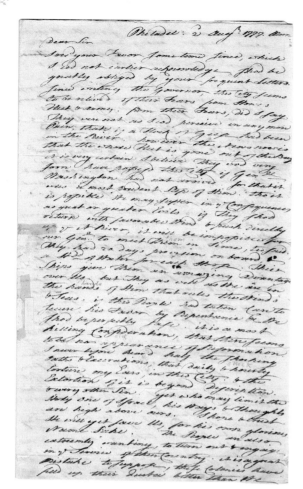

25397   On the loss of Ticonderoga, promoting Gates to command in the north, and the possible fall of Philadelphia to the British

William Williams (1731-1811), Signer of the Declaration of Independence, extremely fine content Autograph Letter Signed, *"Wm. Williams"*, three pages with integral address leaf in his hand, 7.75" x 12.75", Philadelphia, August 2, 1777 to General Jabez Huntington (1719-1786) discussing a range of war news including the fall of Ticonderoga, a congressional inquiry into the abandonment of the post, and the anticipated appointment of Horatio Gates to command the Northern Department. Williams begins by discussing a more local (and equally troubling) situation: the threat of a British capture of Philadelphia.

"...this City seems to be relieved of their Fears from Howes Fleet & Army. from their Fears, did I say... however the News now is that the whole Fleet is gone out of the Bay it is very certain I believe. They co[ul]d very soon have possessed this City if Genl. Washington had not arrived... Tho it is

possible we may suffer in ye consequences as great or greater Evils if They sho[ul]d return with favorable Wind & push directly up ye N[orth]. river, it will be impossible for our Genl. to meet Them in Time, tis said. They [the British] had a days provision on board, & a H[ogs hea]d of Water for each Horse. Their Ships give them an amazing advantage over us but they as well as we are in the hands of Him that rules the Winds & Seas. if this People had taken Care to secure his Favor by Repentance & we sho[ul]d be perfectly safe. it is a most killing consideration, that there seems to be no appearance of Reformation. I never before heard half the shocking Oaths & Execrations, that daily & hourly torture my Ears, in this City & the Extortion of it is beyond description & every other Sin..."* Williams continues in this vein before discussing the developing Saratoga campaign: *"We have at length obtained Resolves of Congress. That an Enquiry shall be made into the Reason of giving up Ty. [Fort Ticonderoga] & all ye Gen[era]l. Officers concerned, that Schuyler, St. Clair & ye rest of ye Genl. Officers repair to Head Quarters, & that Genl. Washington be directed to send a Gen. to take ye Comm[and] — in the room of Schuyler & that a Com[it]te[e] of ye House consider & point out the mode of conducting the Tryal [sic]... have no doubt but Gates ill be ye man, intend my Power to convey to you an adequate idea of the Labor it cost N[ew]. England very especially to obtain these ten times gutted Resolves, four whole Days had been spent... a Folio wo[ul]d not contain all that was said. if the whole Cause of America, was to be gained or lost forever by ye Issue, yea more, if— but I will not say it. The warmest Friends co[ul]d not possibly exert Themselves more for its Salvation, than Duane, Duer & Sundry more did, to save Schuyler from ye least imputation. if I sho[ul]d ever see you I may say more about it. tell it not in Gath, least our enemies triumph, & Congress sink in ye opinion of ye World, to ye endangering our Cause..."* In reality, the abandonment of Fort Ticonderoga in the face of Burgoyne's army was an extremely wise move. The fort had been designed by the French to repulse advances from the south. Arthur St. Clair and his garrison would have been easily surrounded by the British if they had remained. This allowed more time for a larger army to assemble and finally defeat Burgoyne at Saratoga that autumn. This spectacular victory (which had very little to do with the conduct of Horatio Gates) was overshadowed for members of Congress who were forced to flee Philadelphia after the British victory at Brandywine in early September 1777. Congress would remove to York, Pennsylvania, and Washington and his army would spend the winter at Valley Forge, north of occupied Philadelphia.

Williams is also possibly making a veiled reference (*"I may say more about it. tell it not in Gath [probably referencing Philadelphia], least our enemies triumph, & Congress sink in ye opinion of ye World"*) to the early stages to what became known as the Conway Cabal, a movement to unseat Washington as Commander-in-Chief. More a general movement than an actual plot, it was centered in the New England delegations to Congress (including Williams) who viewed Washington as an amateur responsible for innumerable defeats and delays. The move to try St. Clair, Schuyler and others over the abandonment of Ticonderoga was part of this general movement to rid the army of Washington's allies. Horatio Gates, who coveted Washington's command, was touted by New England representatives as a better candidate to lead the army. Following the losses at Brandywine and Germantown, Williams agreed with Jonathan Trumbull that the time had come when "a much exalted character should make way for a general" and suggested if this was not done "voluntarily," Congress should "see to it." The faction promoted Horatio Gates (by November the "Hero of Saratoga") as a replacement. (Historians now seriously question Gates' contribution to that victory). The "plot" lost its momentum when a letter from General Thomas Conway to Gates criticizing Washington's conduct became public. Conway resigned his commission March 1778 in disgrace. As it stands today, the tactics Washington used, which involved more maneuvering and retreating than actual battle, forcing the British to keep an enormously expensive army in the field for eight years, was one of the main factors why the British lost. Partial fold separations repaired, repaired marginal losses affect a few words of text, else bright and clean with dark ink, very good condition.

A great Revolutionary War letter rife with content. From the Henry E. Luhrs Collection. Accompanied by LOA from PSA/DNA.
Estimate: $4,000-$6,000

A 19.5% Buyer's Premium ($9 min.) Applies To All Lots

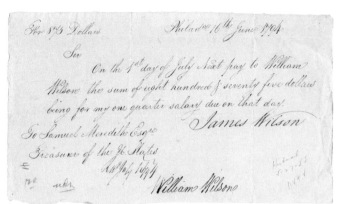

25398   Declaration Signer James Wilson Document Signed. One page, 8.25" x 4.75", Philadelphia, June 16, 1794, to Samuel Meredith, Treasurer of the United States, requesting that his $875 salary be paid to William Wilson who has also signed this document. James Wilson signed the Declaration of Independence as a representative of Pennsylvania. He was also a member of the Constitutional Convention 1775-1777, 1783, and 1785-1786, a major force in the drafting of the Constitution, and one of the first six justices appointed to the Supreme Court by George Washington. Due to some dubious land speculation that caused him to be imprisoned twice, Wilson died penniless. Fine condition; folds.   From the Henry E. Luhrs Collection. Accompanied by LOA from PSA/DNA.

Estimate: $300-$500

25400   Declaration Signer John Witherspoon Autograph Letter Signed *"Jno Witherspoon"*. One page, 7.75" x 6.75", Tusculum [Princeton, New Jersey], September 16, 1790. It begins, *"Accordg to my promise of Yesterday's letter I send the Introduction as I have drawn it up. There was very much Difficulty in determining some particulars..."* Witherspoon signed the Declaration as a representative from New Jersey and was the only clergyman to sign it. He was president of the College of New Jersey (later Princeton) during the War of Independence when the campus was nearly destroyed and Witherspoon was responsible for its rebuilding. He is one of the most elusive of all signers so don't let this opportunity pass you by. Good condition; separation at the fold repaired by professional linen backing, missing lower left corner repaired affecting no writing, staining at the fold affects the signature only slightly.   From the Henry E. Luhrs Collection. Accompanied by LOA from PSA/DNA.

Estimate: $3,000-$5,000

25399   Declaration Signer James Wilson Autograph Letter Signed. One page with integral address leaf, 6" x 8.5", Lancaster, February 3, 1779, to John Pollock of Carlisle. In part, *"Mr. Glenn informs me that upwards of two hundred cords of Pine Wood have been cut upon my Plantation for the public Works. I have received from him two hundred dollars in part payment..."* This wood was likely cut to supply the Continental Army during the Revolutionary War. Wilson signed the Declaration of Independence as a representative of Pennsylvania. Very good condition, worn and toned at folds.   From the Henry E. Luhrs Collection. Accompanied by LOA from PSA/DNA.

Estimate: $600-$800

25401   Declaration Signer Oliver Wolcott Autograph Document Signed *"O Wolcott Judge"*. One page, 8" x 8.5", np, March 22, 1786, an itemized list of expenses regarding the estate of Joshua Carter. Wolcott signed the Declaration of Independence as a representative of Connecticut though he was taken seriously ill in 1776 and was one of the last to actually sign the document. He was also a member of the Continental Congress 1776-1778 and 1780-1783. Very good condition, a light area of staining along one fold away from signature.   From the Henry E. Luhrs Collection. Accompanied by LOA from PSA/DNA.

Estimate: $400-$500

25402   Declaration Signer Oliver Wolcott Autograph Document Signed "*O Wolcott Judge*". One page, 8.25" x 11.25", np, March 22, 1786. "*An account of Debts exhibited by the Administrator on the estate of Joshua Carter late of Harwinton deceased...*" Wolcott signed the Declaration of Independence as a representative of Connecticut. Very good in appearance, separated at folds with old repairs on verso, signature unaffected. From the Henry E. Luhrs Collection. Accompanied by LOA from PSA/DNA.

Estimate: $400-$500

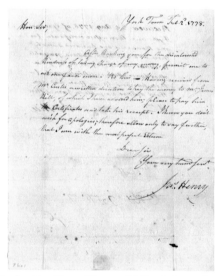

25403   Declaration Signed George Wythe Autograph Endorsement Signed in the third person on the verso of a document. Two pages, York Town, February 2, 1778. In his hand, "*Received 25 Aug. 1778, of George Wythe one loan-office certificate for three and one third dollars, payable to Isac Smith, esq; and forty six other loan office certificates, each for three hundred thirty three and one third dollars, payable to James Henry esq.*" Wythe signed the Declaration of Independence as a representative of Virginia. Thomas Jefferson once said of Wythe (his Law professor): "He was my ancient master, my earliest and best friend, and to him I am indebted for first impressions which have [been] the most salutary on the course of my life." Near fine condition; folds and mild toning. From the Henry E. Luhrs Collection. Accompanied by LOA from PSA/DNA

Estimate: $800-$1,200

25404   Declaration Signer George Wythe Autograph Endorsement. One partial page removed from document, 3" x 2.25", np, May, 1799. In full, "*May, 1799. accounts may, by consent of defendant, be refered; and, upon report, motion to dissolve the injunction, now denied, may be repeated.*" A notation on the verso reads, in full, "Autograph of Chancellor Wythe of Virginia, one of the Signers of the Declaration of Independence— Sent to me in 1829 by John Mickleson Esq of Richmond— R. Gilmor." While not a signature, Wythe material is rare enough that this would nicely serve to fill the void in most collections. Wythe signed the Declaration of Independence as a representative of Virginia from where he was a delegate to the Continental Congress in 1775-1776. Wythe was the first professor of Law in America and numbered Thomas Jefferson, Henry Clay, and James Monroe among his students. He is known as "The Father of American Jurisprudence." Very good condition.   From the Henry E. Luhrs Collection. Accompanied by LOA from PSA/DNA.

Estimate: $600-$800

25405   Mormon Leader Brigham Young Signature Signature: "*Brigham Young*" on a 3" x 1.75" card. "Died - 1878" penned along lower edge. Brigham Young succeeded Joseph Smith (1844, officially confirmed in 1847) as head of the Mormon church (Church of Jesus Christ of the Latter Day Saints) and directed and superintended the mass migration of Mormons to the Great Salt Lake Valley in Utah. He served as the first Governor of the Territory of Utah (1849-1857). Very lightly soiled, mounting remnants at corners on verso. Boldly signed. In very fine condition. From the Henry E. Luhrs Collection. Accompanied by LOA from PSA/DNA

Estimate: $400-$500

MISCELLANEOUS PRE CIVIL WAR AMERICAN HISTORY INCLUDING A COMPLETE SET OF THE SIGNERS OF THE CONSTITUTION AND ARRANGED CHRONOLOGICALLY

25406   Scarce Document Signed by Peter Zenger's Attorney, Andrew Hamilton

Andrew Hamilton (1676-1741) jurist, manuscript Document Signed, "*A: Hamilton*", one page on vellum, 29" x 12", Philadelphia, Aug. 5 1720 in which Hamilton signs as a witness to a deed between Daniel Pegg and William Chancellor for a land in the Northern Liberties. Signed on the verso by **Benjamin Chew** who attests that "*...the Name A. Hamilton Subscribed to the Execution of the within written Indentur to be the proper Hand Writing of Andrew Hamilton Esqr. late of the City of Philadelphia, deceased; And gives as a Reason for such his Belief, that he this deponent is well acquainted with the hand Writing of the Said Andrew, having often seen him Write his Name...*" Hamilton is of course best known for his vehement defense of printer John Peter Zenger (1697-1746) who was accused of sedition and libel for criticizing Governor William Crosby of New York. In a 1732 trial, Hamilton managed to convince a jury (hand-picked by the governor) to acquit Zenger. The trial was an important step in the development of freedom of the press in America. Usual folds, pin holes at margins, else Fine. From the Henry E. Luhrs Collection. Accompanied by LOA from PSA/DNA

Estimate: $900-$1,200

25408   On forming an independent government for New Hampshire

Richard Partridge (1681-1759), colonial agent and brother-in-law of Massachusetts and New Hampshire Governor, Jonathan Belcher (1682-1757), Autograph Letter Signed, "*Rd. Partridge*", three pages 6.5" x 8", London, August 28, 1739 to Belcher updating him on the progress in London to finally provide for separate governors for New Hampshire and Massachusetts: "*This day I have been w[i]th our friend Mr. T. at the Council Office to get what Information I could in thy Affairs against the Com[m]ittee tomorrow night and that Lord Presid[en]t has determined to refer back the Board of Trades Report to them about a Separate Governor for N[ew] Hamp[shi]r[e] with my Memorial for them to hear me upon it, at which I am not displeased for that We not onely [sic] gain time by it, but also that we have thus disconcerted the Measures of our Antagonists who I am apt to think will look blank upon it; And as to the appointing a day for hearing then. Hamp[shi]r[e]. Complaints that is like now to be post poned (according to my Information) till Oct[obe]r next that is— during this Vacation the Judges being gone on their Circuits, an therefore I shall defer desiring the interposition of Our Friends the Quakers in thy favour till the time draws near that there is like to be occasion And then I shall not be wanting in calling upon them. Upon further conversation at Whitehall I find my Nephew & I have been too forward in Charging Ld. P—t with being the Secret design for Separating the Governments wherefore In Justice to that Lord we must retract and Say that altho[ugh] he manifestly seems to espouse N. Hampsh[i]r[e']s Cause yet he was scarcely concern'd in any clandestine design, whatever others were... I think thou needst not be under any Apprehensions about Sh—lys superceding thee in the least or (as Capt. Coram says) of any body Else. Pray let me know at what time the Subscribers set their names to the late N. Hampsh[i]r[e]s. Address, because it is objected that it seems by the Appearance of the paper to be an old Address laid by against the present occasion...*" Belcher, like most Royal governors in the colonies, developed political enemies. A popular clamor resulted in Belcher's removal as Governor of both Massachusetts and New Hampshire in 1741. The same year, New Hampshire would be granted an independent government by George II. Belcher would soon recover his political fortunes and in 1746, George II appointed him as the Royal Governor of New Jersey. Old catalog description mounted to verso, usual folds, else fine condition. From the Henry E. Luhrs Collection. Accompanied by LOA from PSA/DNA

Estimate: $1,200-$1,500

25407   Colonial Document: Regarding Trespassing. 7.7" x 12" hand-written, one page document, dated October 2, 1693. The document is written in the specialized phrasing of the legal profession, and with antiquated language. It deals with a case of trespassing and debt between two men. A very interesting look at early colonial legal procedures and language. It the document is in Good condition; slightly soiled on the edges; writing is somewhat faded. From the Henry E. Luhrs Collection.

Estimate: $300-$400

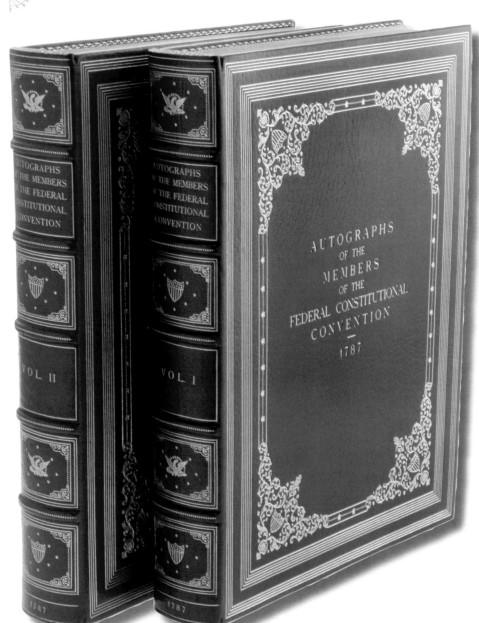

We the People...

25409   Extremely Important Bound Collection of Letters wand Documents Signed by all 55 Delegates to the Federal Constitutional Convention of 1787.

Autographs of the Members of the Federal Constitutional Convention. It became increasingly apparent after the Revolutionary War that an enduring United States of America would require the establishment of a centralized government with legally defined powers and responsibilities. To achieve this lofty goal, delegates from each of the thirteen states met in convention at Philadelphia on May 25, 1787. The attendees, although exclusively prominent white male citizens, embodied a wide range of professions, religions and sectional interests. Their combined efforts to craft a viable government over the long summer of 1787 resulted in, by September 17, the United States Constitution and earned them lasting recognition as this nation's "Founding Fathers." The drafting of the Constitution was seen as a watershed accomplishment in Western History from the outset. That the Constitution went on to survive the nation's trials of the 19th century served only to enhance its mystique and generate sober reflection upon its unique character and the great minds which conceived it. 1887 marked the Centennial of the Constitutional Convention, a commemorative event that was likely the catalyst behind the remarkable collection offered here. All 55 delegates to the convention are represented by their signatures on

manuscripts which are mostly either Autographed Letters Signed or Documents Signed. These are all neatly tipped-in on pages housed in a custom pair of large folio volumes, 11.5" x 14.75". The albums, circa 1890, each have an illuminated title page and are bound with exquisite gold tooled red morocco covers and spines protecting a combined total of 246 internal leaves on heavy stock. A facsimile of the Constitution accompanies text from Hamilton L. Carson's *Biographies of Members of the Federal Convention,* which is strategically placed throughout both volumes with engraved portraits of the delegates as a means of giving additional substance to the autographs. Carson (1852-1929) was a Philadelphia attorney who had served as Secretary of the Constitutional Centennial Commission. It is entirely possible that he assembled this collection. Red cloth slipcases incorporating sturdy board and leather-rimmed openings complete the package. The manuscripts in the collection are outlined in order of placement as follows:

 George Washington of Virginia ANS, one page, 7.0" x 3.25", Mt. Vernon, VA, January 1, 1786. A receipt in General Washington's hand for an illiterate farmer, this reads, " *Received from George Washington the sum of twenty six pounds seventeen shillings for two hundred and sixty eight and a half bushels of oats"*. Washington served as the Convention's President. His name is underscored in a fine line of red ink, else Very Fine condition;

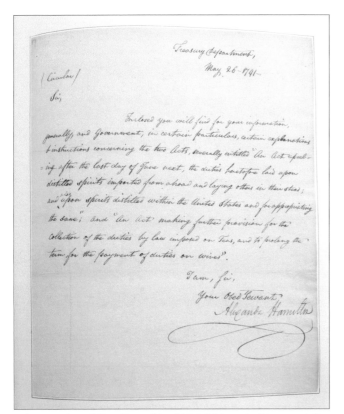

John Langdon of New Hampshire ALS, "*J W Langdon*", 3 pages, 8.0" x 10.0", Portsmouth, NH, March 2, 1803 to J. Worthington, Chillocothe, Ohio. A scarce letter to the Northwest discussing a forged deed. Stains, else Fine condition;

Nicholas Gilman of New Hampshire ALS , "*Nich. Gilman*", 2 pages, 8.0" x 10.0", Exeter, NH, May 29, 1810 to J.H. Hoac. A business letter regarding a shipment of goods. Light stains, else Fine condition;

Nathaniel Gorham of Massachusetts ALS, "*Nath Gorham*", One page, 7.0" x 9.75", Concord, MA, March 19, 1792 to Rebecca Gorham, Charlestown, MA. Gorham asks his wife to *...look on the desk and find a letter for Mr. McBond and send it on up...*". Isolated browning, else Fine condition;

Rufus King of Massachusetts ALS, 2 pages, 7.5" x 9.5", New York, February 18, 1811 to Col. Benjamin Walker, Utica, NY. King asks Walker to at least pay interest on monies owed. Very Fine condition;

William Samuel Johnson of Connecticut ALS, "*Wm Sam'l Johnson*", One page, 7.0" x 8.0", New York, April 4, 1785 to Col. Wadsworth. Treaties with Barbary pirates are discussed. Possibly a manuscript copy for Johnson's records given docketing on the verso. Very Fine condition;

Roger Sherman of Connecticut ANS, One page, 7.75" x 5.0", New Haven, CT, April 15, 1785 to John Lawrence, Treasurer. The recipient is asked to provide a Mr. Tilly with a tax credit. Sherman's constitutional legacy remains as he was behind the notion of proportional Congressional representation based upon a District's population. Very Fine condition;

Alexander Hamilton of New York ALS, . One page, 8.75" x 9.0", Treasury Department, May 26, 1791. Although in letter form, "*Circular*" appears at the top of the manuscript. It reads " *Enclosed you will find for your information, generally, and government, in certain particulars, certain explanations and instructions concerning the two Acts, severally entitled 'An Act repealing after the last day of June next, the duties heretofore laid upon distilled spirits imported from abroad and laying others in their stead; and also upon spirits distilled within the United States and for appropriating to 'same'; and 'an Act' making further provision for the collection of the duties by law imposed on Teas, and to prolong the term for the payment of duties on wines*". Large, bold signature, Very Fine condition;

William Livingston of New Jersey DS, " *Wm Livingston*", One page, 6.5" x 8.25", March 14, 1777. An affidavit attesting to the military oath of one Charles Pettett. Very Fine condition;

David Brearly of New Jersey DS, "*Dav'd Brearly*", One page with docketing, 8.0" x 12.25", Monmouth, NJ, June 22, 1774. Brearly is one of five signatories on a legal document. Browning and fading, Fine condition;

William Patterson of New Jersey ANS, "*Wm Patterson*", One page, 8.0" x 10.0", January 17, 1803 to Andrew Bayard. Payment instructions to the Bank of The United States. Fine condition;

Jonathan Dayton of New Jersey ALS, "*Jona Dayton of New Jersey*", 2 pages, 8.0" x 10.0", Washington, March 31, 1802 to Elias Boudinot. Land parcels, likely in Ohio, are discussed. Very Fine condition;

Benjamin Franklin of Pennsylvania DS, "*B Franklin Penna*", one page, 8.5" x 7.25". This undated partial legal document concerns a bankruptcy case, likely pre-Revolutionary. Franklin, born in 1706, was the oldest delegate to the convention. Very Fine condition:

Thomas Mifflin of Pennsylvania DS, " *Tho Mifflin*", one page with docketing, 9.75" x 15.0", Philadelphia, May 9, 1791. Mifflin signs this legal document as Governor of Pennsylvania. Archival repairs on folds, some stains. Very Good condition;

Robert Morris of Pennsylvania ALS, " *Rob Morris*", One page, 4.75" x 7.5", June 29, 1796 to William Tilghman. Morris inquires after a colleague's ill health. Very Fine condition;

George Clymer of Pennsylvania ALS, " *Geo Clymer*", One pa From the Henry E. Luhrs Collection.ge, 7.5" x 9.5", 1790s, to Tench Coxe, Commissioner of Revenue. It partially reads, "*...the distillers...to pay by the month according to the capacity - or to pay by the gallon on what shall be distilled...*". This letter is probably from the prelude leading to 1794's Whiskey Rebellion when farmers of Western Pennsylvania rose up over the Government's uppity decision to tax liquor. Coxe was Revenue Commissioner from 1792-1797, making this note fit in with the "Rebellion" timeline. Very Fine condition;

Thomas Fitzsimmons of Pennsylvania ALS, " *Thos Fitzsimmons*", 2 pages, 7.5" x 9.25", Philadelphia, June 19, 1798 to Mssrs. Le Roy and Bayard. A business letter regarding pricing and ships. Very Fine condition;

Jared Ingersoll of Pennsylvania ALS, " *J Ingersoll*", One page with docketing, 8.0" x 10.0", September 7, 1805. A copy, this letter begs some more time to repay a $400 debt. Very Fine;

James Wilson of Pennsylvania DS " *James Wilson*", 2 pages, 8.0" x 12.25", Philadelphia, January 27, 1794. A manuscript legal document detailing a financial arrangement between lawyer Wilson and a gentleman named

Jesse James! Light soiling, Fine condition;

Gouverneur Morris of Pennsylvania ALS, " *Gouv Morris*", 2 pages with address panel, Morrisania, February 4, 1809 to William Tilgham, Chief Justice of Pennsylvania. Morris, after an absence, sends updates regarding the legal affairs of an estate. Very Fine condition;

George Read of Delaware ALS, " *G Read*", 2 pages, 8.0" x 10.25", New Castle, DE, September 19 (1798 or before) to Malcolm Bidgeby. Read writes of legal matters. Most likely a draft letter. Light soiling, Fine condition;

Gunning Bedford, Jr. of Delaware ADS, " *Gunning Bedford, Jr.*", one page with docketing, 7.5" x 6.25", Kent County, DE, May 14, 1786. Bedford avers in this affidavit that one " *Ebenezer Griffin...did commit fornication with Hannah Spear and a female bastard child on the body of the sd Hannah...*". Some fading, else Fine condition;

John Dickinson of Delaware ADS, "*John Dickinson*", one page, 8.0" x 12.5", September 1, 1784 to Momar Porter, Philadelphia. Given the numerous lines scratched out and replaced, this letter appears to be a draft. Dickinson writes as regards a prisoner transfer from Maryland. Browning, else Fine condition;

Richard Bassett of Delaware ADS, "*Richard Bassett*", One page with verso docketing, 8.0" x 13.0", Kent County, DE, August 1, 1772. A property settlement document. Fine condition;

Jacob Broom of Delaware ALS, "*Jacob Broom*", One page, 7.0" x 6.25", Wilmington, DE, November 3, 1794 to "James". Broom's signature is perhaps the hardest to acquire. This very rare letter reads, "*I rec'd your letter of the 26th ulto. but not until yesterday and have now lsent you 7/6 more by bearer. I hope to be in N Castle some time this week when I will bring the other things written for. I hope you apply yourself closely. I have been unwell for some time. I should have been at Mrs. Hayens funeral had i been able to ride.*". Small split on lower crease archivally repaired. Fine condition;

James McHenry of Maryland ALS, "*James McHenry*", One page, 8.0" x 10.0", War Department, December 1, 1798 to Thomas Marshall. This letter, written by McHenry as Secretary of War, reads partially, "*...I directed a flag and flagpole to be procured...I also directed as many guns to be carried into the works as can be usefully employed in their defenses and such repairs made as shall be found absolutely neccessary...*".War with France was a distinct possibility when this was written. Some minor ink smears, else very Fine condition;

Daniel of St. Thomas Jenifer of Maryland ALS, "*Daniel of St Thos Jenifer*", 3 pages, 7.25" x 9.0", March 7, 1783. This letter from the "*Intendant's Office*" and is likely a true copy for files and is addressed to the "*Commrs of the Sale of Confiscated Lands*". Given the date, such lands were probably those siezed from Loyalists during the Revolution. Very Fine condition;

Daniel Carroll of Maryland ALS, "*D. Carroll*, 2 pages, 7.0" x 9.0", Baltimore, September 4, 1782. This letter to an anonymous recipient reads partially "*...I now find myself on the mending and when i good the news and when I got to town I saw the very agreeable news of the Arrival of the French Fleet in our Bay...I have not bought any Tobacco as yet..*". Fine to Very Fine condition;

John Blair of Virginia DS, "*John Blair P.*", 2 pages, 7.25" x 12.0", probably Williamsburg, circa 1760. Written in a beautiful secretarial hand, this colonial court document considers a financial dispute and names Blair as "*...president of his Majesty's Council and Commissioner in Chief of the Colony and Dominion of Virginia..*". Very Fine condition;

William Blount of North Carolina ALS, "*Wm Blount*", 2 pages, 8.0" x 10.0", "*near Nashville*",November 27, 1816 to the "*Senator & Representative of Tennessee*". A letter introducing a Dr. Larry H. Bryan. Tiny archival repair to crease split on bottom margin, else Very Fine condition. also included is a loose legal DS, "*Wm. Blount*", One page with ver-

so docketing, 8.0" x 13.0", Knoxville, TN, August 8, 1795. Blount, in his capacity as "*Governor in and over the Territory of the United States, south of the rover Ohio*", orders War Department agent David Henly to allocate funds to an infantry company. Huge, bold signature. Browning with an archival repair on one crease, else Fine condition;

Richard Dobbs Spaight of North Carolina DS, "*Rich'd Dobbs Spaight*", One page, 8.0" x 9.75", "*North Carolina in Senate*", December 29, 1785. A resolution stating that clerk's must have assembly approval before being employed by the government. Very Fine condition;

Hugh Williamson ALS, "*Hu Williamson*" and again on address panel, 3 pages, 6.5" x 8.0", Charleston, SC, July 9, 1781 to John Mease, Philadelphia. This rare wartime letter reads partially, "*...I have sent a chest of captured dry g(oods)...Whether I shall leave this (city) by water or land is yet uncertain...If you should hear of my falling into the hands of the enemy, sell the medicines immediately...*". An exceptional letter which had to have run a dicey gauntlet in order to reach its destination. Very Fine condition;

John Rutledge of South Carolina ALS, "*J. Rutledge*", One page, 8.0" x 9.75", Charleston, SC, April 8, 1800. This letter, written to an unknown recipient, imparts a bit of political advice to an aspiring candidate for office. Very Fine condition;

James Madison ALS, "*James Madison*", 2 pages, 8.0" x 10.0", May 10, 1802, Washington, D.C., to William Eaton, Consul at Tunis. Madison was serving as Thomas Jefferson's Secretary of State when the nation's tribute-driven relations with the Barbary Pirates were breaking down. This very rare lett From the Henry E. Luhrs Collection.er is important both to the history of the U.S. Navy and the history of American foreign policy. It partially reads, "*...In order to make a due impression on the Bashaw of Tripoli, the Frigates in the Mediterranean are to rendezvous before that place; and W Carthcart will attend, in order to take advantage of that impression, to meet the Bashaw in recognition for putting an end to war. This information will, the President trusts, lead you to favor the object as far as circumstances will enable you and particularly to exert yourself, if neccessary, in keeping the Bey of Tunis in proper temper towards the United States during the Crisis...*". Possibly a draft saved as a copy given

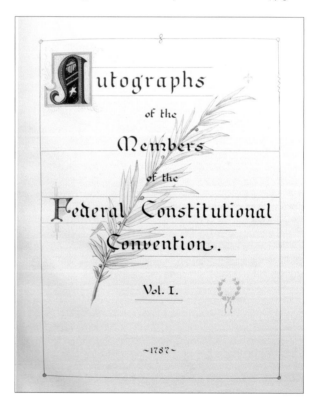

several manuscript revisions within the text. Very Fine condition;

Charles Cotesworth Pinckney of South Carolina ALS, "*Charles Cotesworth Pinckney*", One page, 7.5" x 12.0", The Hague, July 7, 1797 to John Lusac, Leyden. This personal letter tells a French friend that some American newspapers are being sent to him. Pinckney had recently served as minister to France and was in the prices of returning to the United States when he composed this letter. Very Fine condition;

Charles Pinckney of South Carolina ALS, "*Charles Pinckney*", 2 pages, 7.5" x 9.0", Madrid, November 26, 1804, to William Lee, Bordeaux. Pinckney, serving as U.S. minister to Spain inquires here as to when Monroe might be be arriving. Light stains, else Very Fine condition;

Pierce Butler of South Carolina ALS, "*P. Bultler*", One page, 7.75" x 9.75", New York, October 4-5, 1787 to unknown recipient. Travel arrangements via ship and, upon arrival, phaeton, are discussed. Very Fine condition;

William Few of Georgia ALS, "*W. Few*", One page, 8.0" x 9.5", August 31, 1804, to John Macintosh. Few records a slave purchase. The letter reads, "*Please pay unto Edward Telfair Esquire Three Hundred Dollars, it being the sum that was adjudged and awarded to be paid by you for the Negroe Woman Genny now in your possession and his receipt shall be your discharge in full for the same. from your ob'dt serv't*". Very Fine condition;

Abraham Baldwin of Georgia ALS, "*Abr Baldwin*", 3 pages, 8.0" x 9.5", Philadelphia, April 11, 1800, to Territorial Governor Thomas Worthington, Chilicothe, Ohio. Baldwin requests that his Ohio properties be examined should Worthington find himself in the neighborhood. Very Fine condition;

William Jackson of Pennsylvania ALS, "*W Jackson*", One page, 8.0" x 10.0", Philadelphia, March 16, 1802 to unknown recipient. Jackson, Secretary of the Constitutional Convention, tells of a meeting of the Society of the Cincinnati to be held in Washington. This organization was composed of former Continental officers. Very Fine condition;

Elbridge Gerry of Massachusetts ALS, "*E. Gerry*", One page, 8.0" x 9.0", Cambridge, July 31, 1811 to Jospeh Story. Here Gerry sends seven dollars to aid fire victims in Newburyport. Gerry, a perrenial politician, proposed re-drawing his state's map of voting districts. As a result of his scheming, the verb "gerrymander" was born. This letter is slightly brown on one edge, else Very Fine condition;

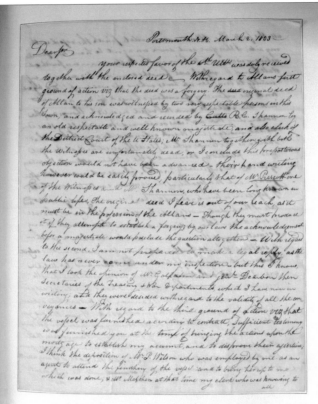

Edmund Randolph of Virginia ALS, "*Edmn: Randolph*", One page, 7.5" x 8.5", Richmond, May 10, 1788. This financial letter addresses monies owed by a client. Very Fine condition;

George Mason of Virginia ALS, "*G Mason*", 2 pages, 6.0" x 7.5", Gunston Hall, August 1, 1785 to a Mr. De Neuville in Alexandria, VA. A desirable letter in that datelined from Mason's fabulous Fairfax County estate. It partially read, "*..I hoped to have had the pleasure of seeing you here, in order to settle our Account, and to pay you the ballance [sic] due to your house for the goods formerly shipped me by the ship General Washington...but hearing that you are now in Alexandria, on your way to the northward, I have got the honour of the bearer, Mr. George Richards, to present you with a Copy of my Acct...*". Signed a second time on the address panel. Light soiling, else Very Fine condition;

Caleb Strong of Massachusetts ALS, "*Caleb Strong*", One page, 7.5" x 9.0", Boston, June 13, 1804, to Robert Parker. Strong accepts the presidency of the Agricultural Society. Very Fine condition;

Oliver Ellsworth of Connecticut DS, "*Oliver Ellsworth*", One page with verso docketing, 8.0" x 13.0", Connecticut, January 7, 1781. a partially printed copy of a deed to one Samuel Turner, Soiling, archival repairs. Very Good condition;

William C. Houston of New Jersey DS, "*William C. Houston*", One page, 9.5" x 6.5", September 9, 1777 with one page postal cover sheet, 7.0" x 3.5", addressed to Patrick Henry as Virginia's Governor, Williamsburg. This brief letter reads, "*The Hon'ble Delegates of the Commonwealth of Virginia have received your of 29 ult'o on Consequence am directed by the Hon'ble the Congress to transmit you the enclosed...*". archival repairs to creases,

Fine condition;

John Francis Mercer of Maryland ALS, "*John F. Mercer*", 2 pages, 7.5" x 9.5", Baltimore, September 19, 1784, to unknown recipient. This letter, written en route to Philadelphia discusses personal financial matters. Wax seal stain, tiny area of paper loss bordering one word. Overall Very Good condition;

Luther Martin of Maryland ALS, "*Luther Martin*", One page, 6.5" x 8.0", Baltimore, July 26, 1815, to Jonathan Merdedith. Financial matters are discussed here. Very Fine condition;

George Wythe of Virginia DS. Wythe's signature appears in full on the 1760s John Blair legal document previously listed;

James McClurg of Virginia ALS, "*James McClurg*", One page, 8.0" x 10.0", January 4, 1801, Richmond, to George Simpson, Bank of the United States. McClurg requests bank dividends be withdrawn from his account. Very Fine condition;

Alexander Martin of North Carolina DS, "*Alex. Martin*", One page, 8.0" x 13.5", July 15, 1781. Martin signs off on this fine Revolutionary War pay summary from the State of North Carolina. As a Colonel, he was due the princely balance of $12,975. Fine - Very Fine condition;

William R. Davie of North Carolina ALS, "*Wm. R. Davie*", 3 pages, 8.5" x 10.0", Paris, France, September 13, 1800, to a Mr. Peymenneau. This was penned while Davie served as a United States Envoy to France. Written during a time of painfully strained relations with France, this letter is composed in careful, caged language. It reads in small part, "*...We have agreed to commit the despatches to our government to your care, we have no doubt of your prudence and discretion...*". Very Fine condition;

William Pierce of Georgia DS, "*Wm. Pierce Jr.*". 2 pages, 9.25" x 14.2", July 5, 1784. A legal document in which Pierce, described as a merchant, signs a long list of his obligations to other parties. A few isolated stains and some fading, else F From the Henry E. Luhrs Collection.ine condition;

William Houston of Georgia ALS, "*Wm Houston*", One page, 7.0" x 9.0", Augusta, May 13, 1798, to Governor Edward Telfair in Augusta. Houston asks for monies due. Very Fine condition;

John Lansing, Jr of New York. ALS, "*John Lansing Jun.*", One page, 7.0" x 12.0", Albany, March 13, 1790, to Egbert Benson. Lansing tells Benson of other letters enclosed. The address panel carries an incredibly bold Albany handstamped cancelation. Archival repair to crease lines, else Fine condition;

Robert Yates of New York ANS, "*Robert Yates*", One page, 7.5" x 4.75", Albany, September 22, 1794, to Gerard Barker, New York Treasurer. A request that funds be deposited in his account. Fine condition.

The collection concludes with the Robert Yates ANS described above, which is followed by several blank leaves. The prospective bidder should note that there are no clipped signatures or horribly discolored partial documents included here. The overall interesting content and high state of preservation characteristic of these manuscripts reflects the fact that they were gathered with purpose at a time when some of them were less than a century old. From the Henry E. Luhrs Collection. Accompanied by LOA from PSA/DNA.

Estimate: $100,000-$150,000

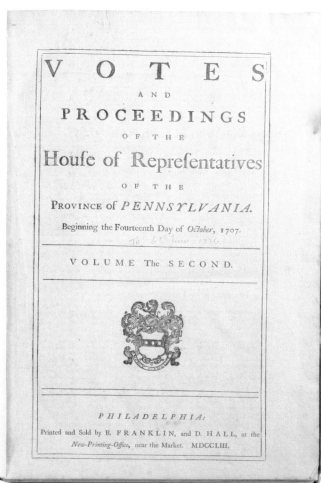

25410 *Votes and Proceedings of the House of Representatives of the Province of Pennsylvania Beginning The 14th Day of October 1707* (Philadelphia: Benjamin Franklin, 1753), Second Volume. 494 pages. Folio (9.75" x 14.75") Signed "James Wright 1754" on front end leaf. Contemporary calf with raised bands. Covers proceedings through June 6, 1726. Moderate foxing throughout. Front hinge cracked. Various abrasions and water stains on cover. From the Henry E. Luhrs Collection.
Estimate: $4,000-$6,000

25411 **Colonial & Early Americana Collection** consisting of more than 24 items, mostly manuscript legal documents dated before 1800. They offer an absolutely fascinating look at our nation's past- the names and places are, in some cases, forgotten but they live on in these wonderful pieces of history. There are dozens of signatures here — a goldmine for the researcher, historian, or dealer. Let's take a quick look at just a couple of these:

Elisha Pitkin- A one page handwritten document, 7.75" x 12.5", for a land sale, in part "*...Hartford in the County of Hartford and Colony of Connecticutt [sic] New England...this 25th Day of January AD 1775 and in the 15th Year of the Reign of our Sovereign Lord George the 3rd of Great Britain & King...*" Bears the signature of Pitkin, his son Elisha Jr., and John Pitkin as Justice of the Peace. The Pitkins were one of the earliest families in Connecticut, arriving from England in 1659.

Thomas Cadwalader- A gorgeous one page, handwritten document on vellum, 22" x 22", for a land sale in Burlington, New Jersey, in part "*This Indenture Made the Sixth day of November in the Seventh year of the Reign of King George the third And in the year of our Lord One thousand and Seven Hundred and Sixty Six...*" Cadwalader was a Physician and one of the founders of the Pennsylvania Hospital. He was one of the first to vaccinate his patients against smallpox.

The lucky winning bidder will receive many more similar to these mentioned. Great for display, would look great on your office or den wall. No doubt, a treasure trove of genealogical information could be gleaned from these great documents. Generally good to very good condition. From the Henry E. Luhrs Collection. Accompanied by LOA from PSA/DNA.
Estimate: $1,000-$2,000

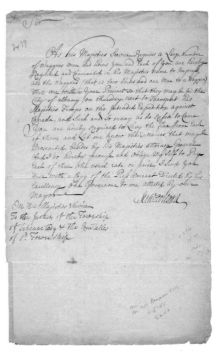

most being in the pre-Civil War period. A number of letters are included with early U.S. postage stamps such as the 3¢ Washington imperf (Scott #11). A great look back at the business and social dealings of a time long since past. These documents are unsearched as to names- a genealogical goldmine. Just a few items included:

William Walforf Astor- the legendary financier and statesman; the Waldorf Astoria was built on the site of his New York residence. Autograph Letter Signed.

August Belmont- ambassador, politician and avid sportsman; the Belmont Stakes is named after him. Signature.

John R. Bleecker- early Albany politician and New York surveyor. Autograph Document Signed.

Buffalo Corning and New York Railroad Company- large $500 bond from 1853, 35 coupons still intact.

For the New York historian, this lot would be a treasure trove of information. Generally fine condition. From the Henry E. Luhrs Collection. Accompanied by LOA from PSA/DNA.
Estimate: $750-$1,000

25412   Early American Documents Collection. This lot consists of 20 documents, dating from 1730 to 1896. The documents are of all types, from autograph letters signed, to printed patent documents. Included is the patent for the Water Wheel, several documents relating information and musings on the Whig party, and various legal documents. The documents in this collection have a wide-ranging array of subjects and material; they are waiting to be fully explored and mulled over. Collections like this offer a unique way to catch a glimpse of daily life in centuries past. Documents range from very good to very fine. Most have the usual folds; some are very soiled; the 1730 document is very yellowed from acid and age. A fascinating lot for the collector who loves to dig into collections! From the Henry E. Luhrs Collection. Accompanied by LOA from PSA/DNA.
Estimate: $400-$500

25414   (Proposed Expedition to Conquer French Canada) Henry Holland, Jr. (1704 - c.1782), prominent Albany, New York jurist and military officer, manuscript Document Signed, "*Henry: Holland*" as commissary, one page, 8" x 13", [Albany], docketed October 13, 1746 to "*...the Justices of the Township of Schenectady...*" ordering them "*...to Impress All the Waggons (that is two horses and one Man to a Waggon) That are within Your Precinct so that they bay be in the City of Albany on Thursday next to Transport his Majesties Troops on the Intended Expedition against Canada...*" The planned expedition was part of what was known in America as "King George's War" (1744-1748), one of several wars fought between Britain and France in the eighteenth century. The planned expedition did not come to fruition but was likely to have been in retaliation for the French raid on Saratoga the previous year. Usual folds, a few marginal chips and tears, else Very Good. An interesting, early document from one of the numerous aborted attempts to conquer Canada. (Maple syrup would so much cheaper if one had been successful!) The British finally succeeded in resting control of that country from the French when Quebec fell in 1759. From the Henry E. Luhrs Collection. Accompanied by LOA from PSA/DNA
Estimate: $400-$600

25413   New York Early Americana Document and Autograph Collection consisting of more than 100 separate documents, letters, and autographs. Dates range from about 1750 through the late 1870s with

25415 **(French and Indian War) Manuscript Document, two pages, 7.5" x 12", Philadelphia, September 9, 1761, with a lengthy endorsement signed by Philadelphia Mayor Benjamin Shoemaker approving a series of claims filed by Alexander McKermet.** "...*Relating to the Losses he sustain'd [sic] by the Incroachment [sic] of the French on the river Ohio in the Year of our Lord 1753 & 1754...*" The document lists the claims which are primarily listed by individuals, many of whom appear to be Indians including "...*Tassalauhervau...The Half King & his Wife...Delaware George...The Crow...The Half Kings Daughter...*" Other names include "...*Capt. Jacob... Thames Hickman... John Hickman...French Margaret's Daughter...*" McKermet was likely an English fur trader who was forced out of the upper Ohio Valley when a French expedition moved into the region to assert France's control over the area — thus touching off the Seven Years (French and Indian) War. Judging from the names on the list, McKermet lived in a mixed community of English, French and Indians. Also interesting here is the presence of a "*Half King,*" an Iroquois representative or diplomat who asserted the Confederation's authority in the Ohio Valley. The total losses amounted to £78-0-0. Mayor Shoemaker of Philadelphia signs at the bottom of the second page attesting to the accuracy of the account. Chipping to margins with the loss of a few words of text, usual folds, otherwise very good condition. From the Henry E. Luhrs Collection.

Estimate: $600-$800

25416   A French Spy's Report on America Intercepted by Britain in 1756

(French and Indian War) manuscript Letter, three pages, 8" x 12.5", [New York], January 12, 1756, a true copy of an intercepted letter addressed to the Duc de Mirepoix in Paris relating developments in North America in the early stages of the French and Indian (or Seven Years) War. This amazing piece of correspondence, from a spy for France who was based in New York, reports primarily upon recent German and "Irish" immigration into British North America and the likelihood they would fight for France. The preface notes that "*The Original [intercepted letter] I have sent under Cover to Mr. John de Neufville Merchant at Amsterdam to be forwarded from New York & the Nightingale man of War, which I heard was soon to sail the Express to London.*" The text of the intercepted letter reads: "*My Serjeants [sic] have within these three days Enlisted 600 Men my compliment is to be 15000 and if I should have Occasion I believe I could Raise 50,000 in Pensilvania [sic] Government only, for there has been Yearly vast Numbers of Germans imported from Holland, who are very Poor and wou[l]d be glad to do any thing for a living as most of them are oblig'd to sell themselves to Pay their Passage thither; These People I am Persuaded, it wou'd be a Matter of Indifference to them (if they were paid) whom they Serv'd; wether [sic] the King of France or The King of England, and I know most of them wou'd from Principle rather choose to serve my Royal [sic] Master. There has also been from time to time, Transported from England, vast Numbers of Irish to Virginia and Philadelphia, for the Peopling The*

Kings Plantation most of these are of the true Roman Cathoick [sic] Faith. There has also been continually transported form England to the above Places, what they call Convicts, for Crimes committed there, for which they are Sold in Slavery for Seven years, some of these that I have happen'd to Speak to Have Profes[e]'d the true Cathoick Religion, but their Religion is much the same with most of the Hereitcks [sic] in this Country, who (by what I can perceive) mind no other than that of getting Money; and may be hir'd to do any thing. We have an Account here that a Body of Eleven hundred Indians had appear'd at Goshen & behav'd... very insolently that all the Country thereabout were in alarm, they were said to be Delawar[e] Indians, who always had profess'd themselves friends to the English — But of late seem'd to be Wavering. Goshen is between New York and Albany up Hudsons River (call'd at New York) the North River) back of the Highlands, on the other side the River with New York at 60 miles from New York N.B. We've had the Winter hitherto very Moderate almost every day like Spring & can't hear of any Snow being fallin[g] yet to the Northward." An optimistic report based on vastly incorrect intelligence. The German and "Irish" immigrants to which the spy refers were almost entirely Protestant. The German settlers of Pennsylvania were mostly members of various Protestant sects; and the "Irish" were, in fact, mostly Scots-Irish, mostly Protestants as well. The Scots Irish settled on the Appalachian frontier and were directly threatened by Indian allies of the French. Even those who were Catholic had little reason to side with France as they did not experience a great deal of persecution in most of the American colonies, particularly in Pennsylvania. Even the spy's economic assumptions were flawed by the fact that indentured servants could just as easily escape their obligations by joining the militia to fight for Britain. Accompanied by a set of copies of another intercepted letter from the same correspondent now housed in the British Public Records Office. *Provenance,* Erik Von Scherling, Catalog 53, 1956. Light folds, a few pinholes, else Fine. Interesting, revelatory history articulating "might have been" assumptions. From the Henry E. Luhrs Collection.

Estimate: $1,500-$2,000

25417 **(French and Indian War) Printed Document,** nine pages, 7" x 11.25", (London, Printed by Thomas Baskett, 1757) an act of Parliament imposing an embargo against France prohibiting colonial exports of most food-stuffs — except to Great Britain — after war was declared against France on May 15, 1756. The legislation is entitled *"An Act to prohibit for a limited Time the Exportation, of Corn, Grain, meal, malt, Flour, Bread, Biscuit, Starch, Beef, Port, Bacon, and other victual (expect Fish and Roots and Rice, to be exported to any Part of Europe Southard of Cape Finisterre) from His Majesty's Colonies and Plantations in America, unless to Great Britain or Ireland..."* Cape Finisterre is the western-most point of land in Spain and used as a common reference point for the 43rd parallel. The real meaning behind this was to prohibit trade to the French Caribbean, dependent on American exports in the eighteenth century. Extremely light toning at margins, else Fine condition. From the Henry E. Luhrs Collection. Accompanied by LOA from PSA/DNA.

Estimate: $400-$600

during the American Revolution. Silked, minor losses, else very good; **Capt. James Patterson, Autograph Letter Signed,** one page, 8" x 12", no place given but likely Ft. Augusta, Pennsylvania, June 18, 1757, discussing recruiting efforts and military affairs: *"...the Shamokin regiment is filling fast Capt. Hambrige w[i]t[h] some others of the gentlemen officer sent - here last night about 60 men gook like w[hi]ch with the other recruits & recruiters will make a party 100 strong... I expect the favour of your Honour as I Delight to be doing something in behalf of your Honour... [and requesting that] I may be discharged from Fort and w[i]t[h] your Orders Permitted to try to find Some of these Our Enemies that's often seen five of which is said to be seen in Paxton day before yesterday; my Usage at Fort Augusta has been very good; I Suppose you have hard of the Defeat of Leuit. Halliday of the Second Battalion..."* Silked, losses affecting signature; **Charles Cruikshank, rare Autograph Document Signed,** one page, 7.5" x 6", New York, December 25, 1757, a sight draft for £164 *"...to Delancey Robinson & company..."*. Fine condition; **John Tuliken, manuscript Document Signed as Lieutenant Colonel of the 45th Regiment of Foot,** one page 6" x 5", Louisbourg, September 16, 1763 certifying the seven-year service of Private Luke Murphy. At the end of the Seven Years War, the British razed the former French stronghold. Separated at folds, silked; **Joseph Gorham, Autograph Document Signed,** one page, 7" x 5", Marblehead, April 14, 1761, concerning a debt of £15 due to *"...the Government of Nova Scotia..."*. Partial fold separation, reinforced on verso; **James Bradford, Autograph Letter Signed,** one page, 7" x 8.5", New York, Jan 4, 1755 to future Signer of the Declaration of Independence Stephen Hopkins: *"...General Shirley has order'd me to desire your honour will be pleas'd to give this Express a press Warrant..."* Fine; **Witt Browning, manuscript Document Signed,** one page, 8" x 4.5", Niagara, April 5, 1764 certifying that *"...John Steadman had four Horses employ'd five days in his majesty's Service form hence to Fort Scholsen..."* Fine; **(William Pepperrell) manuscript Document,** one page, 6" x 4", Kittery, February 12, 1750, an invoice for pitch, turpentine and tar. Pepperrell was famous for his 1745 expedition against Louisbourg. Very good. An amazing group from a difficult period to collect. Together, eight (8) pieces. From the Henry E. Luhrs Collection. Accompanied by LOA from PSA/DNA.

Estimate: $1,000-$1,500

25418 **(French and Indian War) A fine collection of eight letters and documents relative to the French and Indian (Seven Years) War.** INCLUDES: **John Armstrong (1725-1795), Autograph Letter Signed,** two pages, 8" x 13", Carlisle. [Pennsylvania], February 14, 1760 concerning the murder of two Indians: *"...Yesterday I was present when the Coroner of this County held an inquest on the dead Bodies of a Indian Man & Boy... who had been Kill'd at their Wigwam on the North Side of Canidogwinet Creek... I saw the bodies pul'd out of the water & the Mortal wounds in the heads... made either with a narrow Axe or Tamahawke [sic]; they were also both Scalp'd. The Man was a Delaware & commonly known by the name of Doctor John, — I have been told by an Old Trader he never was lik'd by his Nation, being by Some of them accounted a Wizard— he generally lived among the white people until the Indian irruptions [sic] happened... amongst the White people he always had the Character of a Sassy insolent fellow...various Conjectures arise — Some imagine the Squaw in a Drunken fit might do it... Others are of the Opinion that some of Our people... done the deed..."* Armstrong served as an officer in the Seven Years War and also served as a general under George Washington

25419 **(Pontiac's Rebellion - The Relief of Fort Pitt)** A fine collection of three manuscript Documents relative to the expedition commanded by Colonel Henry Bouquet to relieve Fort Pitt in the summer of 1763 — in the opening days of Pontiac's rebellion. The lot includes a sign-up roll for a volunteer ranger company, a payroll for the company, and a receipt signed by one of its members. At the close of the French and Indian War in 1763, the Ottawa war chief, Pontiac, based at Detroit, called for war against the English by those tribes they were formerly allied with to defeat the French. British General Jeffery Amherst ordered Colonel Henry Bouquet to mount an expedition to relieve Fort Pitt, an important western post at the site of present day Pittsburgh. The relief force defeated a body of Delaware, Mingo, Shawnee and Wyandot at Bushy Run on August 5, 1763, saving the fort. Interestingly, it was during this campaign that Bouquet advanced the idea of infecting Indian trade blankets with smallpox to act as a biological weapon against the hostile tribes. The documents offered here include a **manuscript Document Signed** by fourteen volunteers, one page, 7.25" x 9.25", Fort Cumberland, July 26, 1763, who are *"..to be lawfully enlisted [sic] in a company of Rangers under ye command of Capt. Leumel Barett for to march to fort pitt for ye space of two months..."* The second document is another **manuscript Document Signed**, *"Lemul. Barrett"*, one page, 12.5" x 7.5", Fort Bedford, August 20,. 1763, an *"Acc[oun]t of Subsistance [sic] for a Party of Volunties [sic] Commanded by Capt. Lemuel Barett"* listing the names of twelve officers and men, their dates of enlistment and discharge as well as the amounts of money owed to them. It lists Lieutenant David Bursdall who was killed on August 5, 1763 when the party was attacked by Indians near Bushy Run. On the verso several of the members have added their signed endorsements noting receipt of their pay. The third piece is a **manuscript Document Signed** by Thomas Simpson with his mark, *"x"* one page, 7.5" x 4.5", *"Fort Bedford"*, Dec. 29, 1763 in which Simpson acknowledges receipt *"...by Coll. Bouquet's Order five Pounds... on Acct of the time I have lost during the Cure of a Wound I received in the Belly at the Battle of Edge hill last August..."* A rare set of documents from one of the more tragic episodes in early American history. Overall condition is very good with some irregular margins, light soiling and the expected folds. It is almost impossible to source material from this period; this is a fine representative group. From the Henry E. Luhrs Collection. Accompanied by LOA from PSA/DNA.
Estimate: $1,500-$2,000

25420 **Early Philadelphia Merchant's Account Book of Martin Noll** 12 mo oblong. A manuscript between August. 8, 1762 to May 11, 1781 containing 144 pages of receipts, notes...written in English and German. Names of prominent early Philadelphia appear, included are R. Sewell, Michael Gratz, John Ross, John Lehman, John Priestly, Richard Chubb and more. Bound marbled boards with leather spine-some foxing and wear. From the Henry E. Luhrs Collection.
Estimate: $250-$350

25421 **(British Garrison in New York) Manuscript Document Signed** *"Da Scott Q. M."* one page, 6" x 7.5", New York, October 9, 1769. Entitled *"Return of Money in lieu of Bedding due to the Officers of the Royal Regiment of Artillery Quartered at this Place from the 3d. July 1768 to ye 3d July 1769..."*, the document lists eleven officers from major to lieutenant noting their dates of arrival and departure (most were present in New York at the time) and the funds owed, totaling £8. Docketed on verso. This seemingly innocuous bill for funds *"in lieu of Bedding"* highlights the controversy over colonial obligations to homeowners to provide shelter to regular British troops and officers under provisions of the Quartering Act. Tensions in New York would boil over into riots in January 1770 now known as the Battle of Golden Hill. A similar disturbance in Boston would result in the Boston Massacre two months later. Small tear with minor loss at top margin, very light uneven toning, else fine. From the Henry E. Luhrs Collection. Accompanied by LOA from PSA/DNA.
Estimate: $400-$600

25422 A petition to King George III for lenience toward the Colonies

An Incredible Autograph Document Signed, "*Frances Dodshon*", two pages, 7.75" 12.75", no place given but likely England, December 27, 1774, a lengthy petition to King George III to avoid conflict with the American colonies. The author writes in part: "*...Let it seem a strange thing to thee O' King that one of thy Faithful Subjects Should be impress'd [sic] with a deep inward Travail of Spirit for thy prosperity, with that of thy Amiable Consort and your royal Offspring... I have been secretly favor'd [sic] with a belief that this petition that been accepted of him who inspired it... I have Sustained... a View which I have cause to believe was given by the Holy Spirit of the Alarming tendency of the commotions that unhappily prevail in some parts of thy Dominions which if not timely & wisely suppressed will greatly I fear Involve this Nation in almost Irreparable grievances &Troubles... what Lays with the greatest weight on me is the Dreadfull [sic]Consequences that may attend should the Sword be once Drawn... O' King to thy Serious consideration... endow thee with Wisdom and Resolution to Act for thy Own and thy Subjects good and the preservation of peace and Tranquility throughout thy Extensive Dominions - And wherein thy American Subjects may be thought blame worthy, Suffer me O King to Intreat [sic] thee to Deal with them as a Tender Father & Compassionate Sovereign Chastize [sic] them not with Scorpions*

- Rebuke them not in Anger so shall thou prevent the Effusion of Blood, The ending of a potent Empire & by Lenient Measure win and Secure to thyself their Obedience Loyalty and Affection..." Unfortunately for Dodshon, matters were already spiraling out of control: the final petitions for reconciliation would be placed before Parliament in February, 1775 but they would fall on deaf ears. George III approved New England Restraining Act on March 30, 1775 and Governor Gage received orders on April 14 to enforce it and to take action to prevent a more arms from falling into the hands of the rebels. This action would result in the battles at Lexington and Concord on April 19, 1775. Usual folds with light toning, else very good condition. A remarkable document that might have changed history had it found a receptive audience. From the Henry E. Luhrs Collection. Accompanied by LOA from PSA/DNA.

Estimate: $1,200-$1,500

25423 The Quaker's response to the Non-Importation Agreements

(Society of Friends) Printed Circular Letter, two pages, 8.5" x 13", Philadelphia, September 1, 1769. (Evans #11266) An amazing piece of Quaker history, a set of statements by the Society of Friends in London and Philadelphia concerning their reaction to the non-importation agreements. The recto reprints a statement by the "*...Meeting for Sufferings, In London the 10th Day of the Third Month, 1769, To Friends in the several Provinces in North America...*" The London meeting of the Society of Friends warns their brethren in the colonies: "*In Seasons of Difficulty, we cannot be unmindful of any Part of the Body, and the present troubled State of Affairs in America, has, for some Time past, affected us with no small Degree of Concern for our Brethren there... following the very weighty Advice of our honourable Elder George Fox.. viz. 'Whatever Bustles and Troubles, Tumults and Outrages, Quarrels and Strife arise in the World, keep out of them all, concern not yourselves with them, but keep in the LORD's Power, and peaceable Truth, that is over all such Things...*" The meeting reinforces Fox's statement noting "*...we cannot but earnestly recommend it may be universally spread amongst Friends every where in North-America...*" On the verso, the broadside contains the text "*From our Meeting for Sufferings held at Philadelphia, for Pennsylvania and New-Jersey...*" reinforces the sentiments from Fox in London. They warn their brethren in "*...these and the adjacent Provinces...*

against promoting or joining in any Measures proposed for the Support of our civil Liberties, which, on mature Consideration, may appear not to be dictated by the Wisdom from above, which is pure, peaceable and gentle... Should any now so far deviate from ...[the] Practice of faithful Friends at all Times... we must declare that we cannot join with such, and that we firmly believe a steady uniform Conduct, under the Influence of that Spirit, will most effectually tend to our Relief from every Kind of Oppression... We therefore seriously exhort all carefully to guard against being drawn into Measure which may minister Occasion to any to represent us a People departing from the Principles we profess... ever bearing in Mind the deep Obligation we are, and have been under, to the King and his Royal Ancestors, for the Indulgence and Lenity granted to our Predecessors, and continued to us..." The intensifying conflict between Britain and her North American colonies caused deep divisions among Quakers, many of whom were deeply sympathetic to the cause but constrained by their beliefs. As a body, they supported reconciliation even after armed conflict erupted in 1775. Quaker attempts at neutrality in the conflict led to suspicion from both Patriots and Loyalists. Some chose to fight, including Clement Biddle who organized the "Quaker Blues". Most who chose this route were disowned by the Society of Friends. Slightly irregular margins, usual folds, light foxing, else Very Good condition. A rare and significant item. From the Henry E. Luhrs Collection.

Estimate: $4,000-$6,000

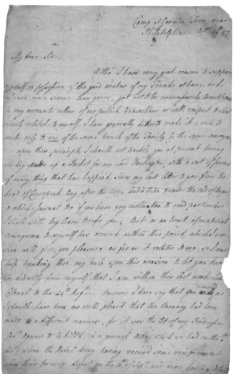

25424   A Rare Account of Battle of Germantown by a British Officer.

(Battle of Germantown) Partial Autograph Letter by an unknown British Officer, two pages, 8" x 12.5", *"Camp at German Town Near Philadelphia"*, October 14, 1777 to a relative discussing the Battle of Germantown (October 4) and the death of General James Agnew. He writes in part: *"... I should not trouble you at present having already sent up a Packet for my Lord Darlington, with a sort of Journal of everything that has happen'd since my last letter to you form the head of Chesopeak [sic] Bay after the Army landed there towards the end of August... I can't help breaking thro' my rule upon this occasion to let you know it directly form myself that I am within this last week Lieut Colonel to the 44th Regt. However I dare say that you would as I should have been as well pleas'd that the Vacancy has been made in a different manner, for it was the lot of my predecessor Genl. Agnew to be kill'd in a general action which we had on the 4th inst; when the Rebel Army having receiv'd some reinforcements since their former defeat on the 11th of Sept. and ours having detach'd thirteen Battalions upon different services three of these too [sic] Grenadier the flower of our Army, Mr. Washington to our great astonishment prevail'd upon his people to attack us; but when his whole army was beat back and oblig'd to retire by a few battalions of the British; which but for a very thick fog would have been render'd a compleat Victory and probably decisive by getting possession of all their artillery & Baggage; On this account only the pursuit could not be so rapid altho' we follo'd them above eight miles from the field of Action. Genl. Agnew poor Man! As a brave & gallant officer paid the tribute this day to Nature & his Profession, which we must all sometime or other submit to, but which none can in the ideas of a Soldier do in a more creditable way. To me it was a lucky day in every sense having not only escap'd with whole bones, but received my preferment from the Commander in Chief as a consequence of it in the most flattering manner I could have wish'd; as I am the only exception he has made at this time, having given every other preferment to the Seniors of the Line in general and not by Regimental Succession, which has brought me in before six or seven seniors actually with this army... What our next operations will be I can't tell you but should imagine that when every impediment to the Fleet; coming up to Philadelphia is effectually remov'd & that the Town is put into a posture of defense, both which ends a few days will probably effect, one more attempt will be made this Campaign to bring Mr. Washington to an Action..."* The British, however, had a much more difficult time than anticipated clearing the Delaware River — the American forts on the River were not taken for another month. However Washington was reluctant to engage his forces with the British again for the season after suffering nearly 1000 casualties. In late November he would order his army into winter quarters at Valley Forge. Provenance: Emily Driscoll, 1961. Light foxing, marginal chipping with minor losses affecting a few words, else fine. A wonderful eye-witness record of true history. From the Henry E. Luhrs Collection. Accompanied by LOA from PSA/DNA.

Estimate: $1,500-$2,000

"Live bidding and and a Virtual Simulcast of this auction will available for all bidding sessions in New York City at Shreve's Auction Gallery at the following address:

*Shreve's Galleries
145 West 57th Street
(57th St. between 6th & 7th Avenues)
18th Floor
New York, NY, 10019*

212-262-8400 (Not active until day of auction)

Heritage will broadcast the auction Live (with limited delay) from its showroom in Dallas to the off-site bidding room in New York. At the bidding room, local bidders will be able to register for bidding and bid on lots live through a Heritage phone-bidder dialed into the Dallas auction. Two projection screens will be viewable, one with the current lot and bid status, the other with a simulcasted video feed of the live auction in Dallas.

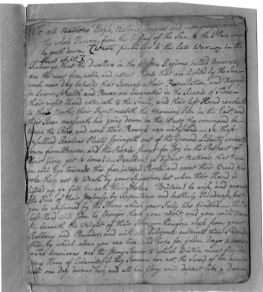

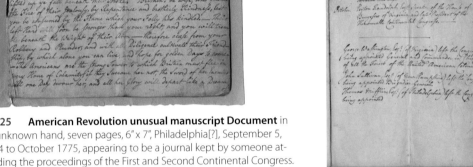

A dramatic declaration of purpose and resolve that captures the bold optimism among British colonists in North America. We have yet to find any record of this piece ever being published. The journal is written in a style suggesting it was to be read aloud to others. It was most certainly written prior to 1776 when reconciliation with Great Britain was still considered a possibility in the minds of most colonists. Thomas Paine's *Common Sense* would transform the discourse radically and swing public opinion toward outright independence.

The succeeding pages give a somewhat informal record of several key aspects of the proceedings including *"A List of the Grand American Continental Congress held at Philadelphia, in Pennsylvania, September 5, 1774."* The list notes the presence of delegates **John Sullivan, Nathaniel Folsom, Thomas Cushing, Samuel Adams, John Adams, Robert Treat Paine, Stephen Hopkins, Samuel Ward, Eliphalet Dyer, Roger Sherman, Silas Deane, Isaac Low, John Alsop, John Jay, James Duane, William Floyd, Henry Wisner, Samuel Boerum, James Kinsey, William Livingston, Stephen Crane, Richard Smith, Jospeh Galloway, John Dickinson, Charles Humphreys, Thomas Mifflin, Edward Biddle, John Morton, George Ross, Caesar Rodney Thomas McKean, George Read, Matthew Tilghman, Thomas Johnson, William Paca, Samuel Chase, Richard Henry Lee, George Washington, Patrick Henry, Richard Bland, Benjamin Harrison, Edmund Pendleton, William Hooper, Joseph Hewes, Richard Caswell, Henry Middleton, Thomas Lynch, Christopher Gadsen, John Rutledge** and **Edward Rutledge.**

As not all of the delegates listed were present on September 5, 1774, the document was certainly written at a somewhat later date. Beneath the list, the author has noted that on *"October 26, 1774 the Congress broke up, after having passed a Number of Spirited Resolves, wrote Several Letters, &c."* The author also appears to have intended to compile a similar list of the Second Continental Congress as a nearly blank page bears just two lines at top: *"A List of the Grand American Continental Congress held at Philadelphia, May 10, 1775"*

The balance of the journal includes a summary of military appointments including *"George Washington, Esq: (of Virginia) left the Congress (being appointed General and Commander in chief of all the Forces of the Unites American Colonies. John Sullivan Esq. (of New Hampshire) left the Congress being appointed Brigadier General. Thomas Mifflin, Esq. (of Philadelphia) left the Congress being appointed"* Washington was appointed to his command by Congress on June 15, 1775. The journal also includes two death notices, including Simon Boreum and Payton Randolph.

Who kept this ad-hoc journal is open to debate and we have not been able to identify the handwriting. It is quite likely that the author was transcribing his list from a newspaper or from a broadside. The heading *"A List of the Grand American Continental Congress held at Philadelphia"* closely corresponds with the title broadside editions of the 1774 Continental Association, issued on October 20, 1774. Also the order, in which the names of the delegates correspond exactly to the order on these broadsides articulate this possibility. In any event, this is an excellent relic of the early days of the American Revolution with a previously unknown patriotic speech. An amazing piece of history, rarely seen in the market. From the Henry E. Luhrs Collection.

Estimate: $5,000-$7,000

25425   **American Revolution unusual manuscript Document** in an unknown hand, seven pages, 6" x 7", Philadelphia[?], September 5, 1774 to October 1775, appearing to be a journal kept by someone attending the proceedings of the First and Second Continental Congress. Otherwise, it is possible that this manuscript was penned by someone who followed the Congress' activities closely through daily dispatches at the time. It records the names of all the members of the First Continental Congress which convened on September 5, 1774; several key events including the appointment of George Washington as Commander in Chief; concluding with the death of Peyton Randolph. Of particular interest is a two-page declaration at the front of the journal warning Great Britain that she should tread lightly in her dispute with her colonies. It reads in full:

"To all People, Nations, Tongues and Languages, under the whole Heaven, from the Rising of the Sun, to the Place here he goeth down. (wrote previous to the late War - or in the first of it) Know ye, that the Dwellers in the Western Regions, called America, are the most free, noble, and potent People that are lighted by the Sun. - each new Day beholds their Increase — their Population, and Progress in Science, Wealth and Power, are unequalled in the Records of Time — their right Hand extendeth to the South, and their left Hand reacheth to the North; their Front meetteth the Morning Sun in the East, and their Rear measureth his going down in the West; they command between the Poles, and none their Prowess can withstand. — In these unsullied Realms Plenty Springeth out of the Ground, Liberty cometh down from Heaven, and the People shout for Joy in the Prospect of their Glory yet to come! — Harken! ye distant Nations, that turn an evil eye towards this free, intrepid People; and covet their Bread provoke them not to Wrath by your Injustice, lest when their Hand is lifted up ye fall beneath their Stroke; Britain! be wise and quench the Fire of their Jealousy, by Repentance and brotherly Kindness, lest you be consumed by the Flame which your Folly has kindled. — Their left Hand will soon be stronger than your right, and you will tremble beneath the Weight of their Arm — therefore cease from your Robbery and Plunder, and which all Diligence cultivate their Friendship, by which alone you can live, and hope for golden Days to come — The Americans are the Strong Tower to which Britain must flee in every Hour of Calamity; if they Succour her not, the Sword of her Enemies will one day devour her, and all her glory will depart like a Dream and Magnificence, will no more be found, but in the dark Volume of an ancient Story. — O! Britons, rouse from your lethargic Dreams, put away your Pride of false Greatness, depart from all Iniquity, listen to the still Voice of Reason, and next to the Favour of Heaven, seek the good Will of America — She is the atlantean Prop on which you must lean for Support, or your paralytic State will crumble to Dust, never to be gathered up again. —Great George! as you would see many and good Days, and leave an unshaken Throne to your Heirs, let your Soul bless the Inhabitants of America, and your Heart and Ears ever be open to their Cry —"

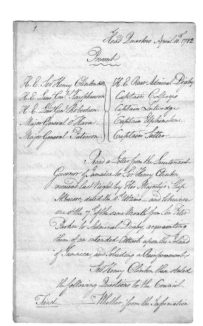

with O'Hara's analysis and decided to draw the requested reinforcements from Charleston, South Carolina. Knyphausen adds his concurrence with O'Hara's recommendations in French on the final page.

Fortunately for the British, the threat subsided only two days later when French Admiral De Grasse, who had been instrumental in the successful operations at Yorktown in 1781, was captured with his flagship off Hispaniola by British Admiral Rodney. De Grasse was assembling an invasion force for a combined French & Spanish operation against Jamaica. A revealing letter illustrating the precarious position and feelings of vulnerability by the British command, even in their New York stronghold. Before the Yorktown operation, Washington had reconnoitered New York's defenses with Rochembeau but feared a general attack could prove a disaster. *Provenance* Parke-Bernet, Carnegie Sale, Lot 6. Archival tape along left margin, very light toning, and the usual folds, else Fine. Another revelatory document. From the Henry E. Luhrs Collection. Accompanied by LOA from PSA/DNA

Estimate: $3,000-$5,000

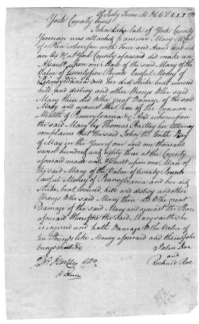

25426 **Wilhelm Baron von Knyphausen** (1716-1800) commander of German troops in America, British General Henry Clinton's second in command. In the waning days of the Revolutionary War, after the surrender of Cornwallis at Yorktown, Sir Henry Clinton and his generals consider reinforcing the island of Jamaica against a threatened invasion by France. The minutes read in part:

"Read a Letter from the Lieutenant Governor of Jamaica to Sir Henry Clinton, received last Night by His Majesty's Ship Albacore, dated the 8th Ultimo —- and likewise one of the 7th of the same month from Sir Peter Parker to Admiral Digby, acquainting them of an intended Attack upon the Island of Jamaica, and Soliciting a Reinforcement..." A lengthy discussion ensued about how to provide the requested reinforcements (2000 men) without compromising British positions in North America and from where they should be drawn. Major General O'Hara noted *"... that as the Troops at present stationed at New York & the immediate Neighboring ports are by no means equal to their defence [sic], if seriously Attacked, any diminution of those Numbers might be attended with most fatal Consequences, not only as the Season of the Year for the next Six Months is the most favorable for Military Operations in this Quarter of America, but the Rebels might in very little time collect a sufficient Body of Men for a very respectable Attack from the neighbouring Colonies, namely Pensylvania [sic], The Jerseys, & the four New England Provinces. The French Troops now actually on this Continent, would be very materially assisting in any Operations against New York, our Ports to the Southward, namely Charleston, Savannah & St. Augustine, are by no means so critically circumstanced, not only from the inclemencies of the Climate, which... renders all Military Operations impracticable, but the great difficulty likewise the Rebels would have in Collecting & supporting a large Body of Men so as to endanger the already mentioned ports, it is not probably either that the French would at this unhealthy Season of the Year risk their Troops in that part of America..."* The council agreed

25427 **Continental Congress & Founding Fathers Autograph Collection** consisting of the following signed items:

Thomas Hartley, Revolutionary War colonel and Pennsylvania congressman 1789-1800. Document Signed as attorney, York, Pennsylvania, July, 1783, very good condition with mounting traces on verso.

John Laurence, Continental Congress 1785-1787. Legal Autograph Document Signed, one page with docketing on verso, 7.75" x 12.5", New York, 1784, very good condition.

John Lowell, Continental Congress 1782. Legal Autograph Document Signed as Judge, one page, 8" x 11.5", Boston, April 20, 1790, fine condition- hinged to larger sheet, originally purchased from Walter Benjamin Autographs.

Luther Martin, attended the 1787 Constitutional Convention but refused to sign the Constitution because he was opposed to a strong central government. Autograph Letter Signed, two pages, 8.25" x 12.75", np, July 18, 1795, fine condition with mounting hinge on verso. Vintage engraving included.

Zephaniah Platt, Continental Congress 1785-1786, founder of the town of Plattsburgh, New York. Document Signed as witness, two pages, 8.25" x 13.5", Poughkeepsie, May 14, 1799, very good condition. From the Henry E. Luhrs Collection. Accompanied by LOA from PSA/DNA.

Estimate: $600-$800

176   Session One, Auction #626 • Monday, February 20, 2006 • 5:00 PM

A 19.5% Buyer's Premium ($9 min.) Applies To All Lots

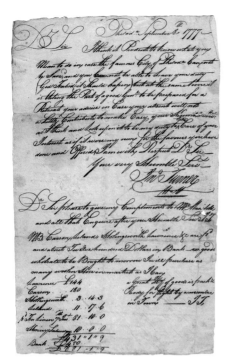

25428 (American Revolution: The Fall of Philadelphia) John Turner, Philadelphia merchant, Autograph Letter Signed, "*Jno Turner*", one page, 8" x 13", Philadelphia, September 8, 1777 to Capt. William Smith of the Philadelphia Militia at Brandywine Mills making arrangements should the British Army move on Philadelphia. An obviously worried Turner writes: "*I think it Prudent to know what you mean to do in case the famous City of Philda. Cannot be Saved, and you Cannot be able to Leave your duty (God Forbid it Should happen [sic]) but at the same time it is Acting The Part of a good Gen[t]l[eman] to be prepared for a Retreat your advice in Case your absent will not a Little Contribute to make Easy...*" He adds extra details including a note that "*...Carson, Levand, Holingsworth Lawrence &c are p[ai]d and about Twelve hundred Dollars in Bank - and goods wholesale to be Bought tomorrow I will purchase as many woolen Hose in market as I can... a Great Q[an]t[it]y of goods is pack'd Ready for flight by a number in Town - J. T.*" Turner's pessimism was not without foundation; the next day the Americans would battle the British Army under at Brandywine Creek and would be forced to withdraw toward Philadelphia on September 11. The Continental Congress would flee to Lancaster, Pennsylvania on September 19. The British Army, under command of William Howe, would triumphantly march into Philadelphia on September 26, 1777, and they occupied the city until the following Spring. Washington and the Continental Army would wait them out that winter at Valley Forge. A fantastic letter vividly illustrating the panic which reigned in the wake of the British advance on the city. Light folds a few marginal tears, light toning, else very good condition. Letters with such dramatic content seldom come on the market; an important missive. From the Henry E. Luhrs Collection. Accompanied by LOA from PSA/DNA.
Estimate: $800-$1,200

25429 Edwards Lithoprinted Facsimiles Documents of The American Revolution (J.W Edwards, Publisher Ann Arbor, Michigan) Six parts, each part in their own folder. Fine condition.

Twelve folders of various French, English, and Vatican Facsimiles of historical documents Fine condition. A collection of over one hundred facsimile of events that changed history. From the Henry E. Luhrs Collection.
Estimate: $100-$150

25430 William Loring Andrews *An Essay on The Portraiture of the American Revolutionary War* (New York: Printed by Gilliss Brothers for the author and sold by Dodd, Mead & Co., 1896) 8vo, illustrated with reproductions by the Photogravure Process of the twenty of the original engravings. Fine copy, limited edition (1 of 185). Book plate of John Page Woodbury From the Henry E. Luhrs Collection.
Estimate: $150-$200

25431 Regulations of the Quarter Master General's Department 1782 Contemporary Manuscript Document, 3p, 9.25" x 13.75". Headed: "*Regulations for the QrMaster General's Department/ By the United States in Congress assembled Octr 23rd 1782*". On July 15, 1780, the Continental Congress "*Resolved, That there be one quarter master general and one assistant quarter master general, appointed by Congress, and one deputy quarter master general for the main army, and one for each separate army, to be appointed by the quarter master general.*" On October 23, 1782, on the report of a committee consisting of members Samuel Osgood, Ralph Izard, Theodorick Bland, and James Duane, appointed by the Continental Congress to "consider and report the most just and practicable means of reducing the expenditures of the United States", the Congress repealed the 1780 resolution, replacing it with new, more detailed regulations, a contemporary copy of which is offered here. In part: "*Resolved, That there be one QrMrGenl. The present QrMrGenl to be continued in office; and hereafter, as vacancies arise, to be appointed by Congress: That the QrMrGenl with the approbation of the Commander in Chief, appoint the following Officers for the Armies of the United States, Viz. For the Main Army. One Depy QrMaster; One Waggon Master One Com[mi]s[sar]y of Forage, One Director & one Subdirector of a Compy of Artificers. For the Southern Army. One Depy QrMaster One Depy Com[missa]ry of forage One Depy Waggon Master One Director & one Subdirector of a Company of Artificers: and as many assistants as the Service may require in the Main & Southern Army, to perform the duties of QrMasters of Brigades, Store Keepers, Clerks, and Such other Duties in the QrMaster's Dept as the Service may require & also as many Waggon Conductors....Accommodations...for...Major Genl & family, one Covered four Horse Waggon & one two horse Waggon—Brigadier Genl & family one Covered four Horse Waggon....*" Individual monthly salaries and rations are also listed. At the conclusion, the resolution bears the name of Charles Thomson, Secretary of the Continental Congress. Most probably transcribed at the time for the Quarter Master General's Office. a half-inch brown ink spot on the verso of the third page (when folded) has resulted in two stains per page, one dark one on page three. Folds, else in very fine condition. Accompanied by a typed transcript. Two items. From the Henry E. Luhrs Collection.
Estimate: $800-$1,200

25432   Manuscript Directory of Philadelphia c. 1784

(Philadelphia Directory) Manuscript, five pages, 8" x 13", [Philadelphia, c. 1784]. A unique record in an unknown hand, written one year prior to the first published directories for the City of Philadelphia in 1785. The list includes many notable persons then residing in Philadelphia including "*Mr. le marquis de la Fayette, in the City Tavern*" (Lafayette was residing at the City Tavern during his five month visit to the United States in 1784); Signer of the Declaration of Independence, Francis Hopkinson; General Thomas Mifflin; Matthew Clarkson; James Varnum; Clement Biddle; Benjamin Franklin's son-in-law, Richard Bache; the noted Jewish financier, Hyam Solomon; Dutch Ambassador to the United States, Van Berkel; William Shippin; French Consul Franáois Barbé-Marbois; Spanish envoy Don Francisco Rendón, and many others. Beside each name, the author has noted their position on the street. The list itself is ordered by street, beginning with Vine and proceeding south to Race, Arch, Market, Chesnut, Quarters Alley, Walnut, Spruce and Lombard. The list continues running from east to west beginning with Water Street, Front, Second, Strawberry Alley, Third, Fourth and Fifth Streets, covering a good range of the city. Interestingly the final page lists several individuals living in other cities including Inspector General Frederick Wilhelm von Steuben, listed "*at New York*", "*Major Prévot in the country*" Before many of the listings appears an "*x*" or occasionally the notation: "*3 Cop[ies]*", "*9 Copies*" etc. We believe this document is a draft for a directory that is doubling for a subscription list to that directory. In 1785, two directories appeared in Philadelphia: these were the first two separately published directories in the entire United States. In October, 1785 *Macpherson's Directory for the City and Suburbs of Philadelphia* was published listing the residents of each street and block (houses did not bear street numbers at the time) and noting occupations as well. Three months later, Francis White printed his competing *The Philadelphia Directory* which was a bit more hurried affair and did not include many listings for those living in the suburbs. Whether this list was kept by either White or Macpherson is not certain. The printed versions of both *MacPherson's Directory for the City and Suburbs of Philadelphia* and Francis White's *The Philadelphia Directory* both sell in excess of $2,500 at auction. Some marginal folds and tears, pages bound with string, else Very Good condition. This is clearly a unique piece of history and the earliest attempt to detail the inhabitants of a major U.S. city. From the Henry E. Luhrs Collection.

Estimate: $8,000-$10,000

25433   Collection of Six Early American Manuscript Sermons totaling more than 40 pages of amazingly tiny handwritten notes for sermons delivered between 1775 and 1797. The same minister wrote the first group of four and all were delivered initially in 1775 at a (likely Protestant) church in Philadelphia. Like many pastors, the authors of these used the same sermon more than once in different years and locations, as noted at the end of the texts. Scripture references used include Psalm 1:4 ("The ungodly are not so: but are like the chaff which the wind driveth away." KJV), Isaiah 3:10 ("Say ye to the righteous, that it shall be well with him: for they shall eat the fruit of their doings." KJV), and I Chronicles 12:18 ("Then the spirit came upon Amasai, who was chief of the captains, and he said, Thine are we, David, and on thy side, thou son of Jesse: peace, peace be unto thee, and peace be to thine helpers; for thy God helpeth thee. Then David received them, and made them captains of the band." KJV). The pages are 3.5" x 6" each and all are in fine condition. All include typewritten transcripts.

The next sermon is in the hand of a different writer, 24 pages in length, 3.75" x 6.5", first preached in July 1793, and uses Matthew 10:33 as its text ("But whosoever shall deny me before men, him will I also deny before my Father which is in heaven" KJV). Based on the length, my guess is that there were a few older gentlemen in the congregation getting nudged by their wives to stay awake! Very Good condition, some soiling and a bit rough at the edges.

The last item in this lot is a sermon from still another minister, at a Baptist church this time (as noted in the text). Five pages, 4" x 7" in size, first delivered at Philadelphia on December 24, 1797. It uses Job 29:12 as its text ("Because I delivered the poor that cried, and the fatherless, and him that had none to help him." KJV). Fine condition. Typewritten transcript included.

If you're as old as this cataloguer, you may have to grab your magnifying glass to read these, but they are certainly interesting and worth the effort. This material would be fascinating to a modern-day minister or bible scholar for reading and research. The message is timeless; could these sermons be "resurrected" and preached again two centuries later? From the Henry E. Luhrs Collection.

Estimate: $2,000-$3,000

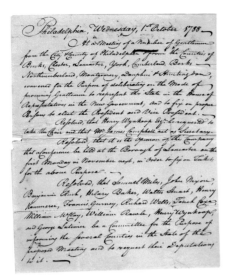

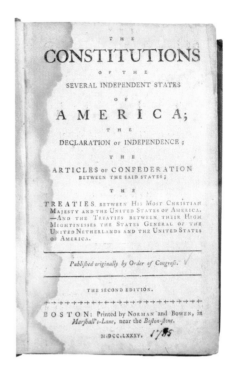

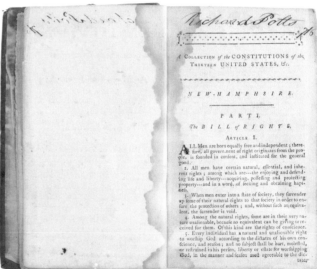

25434   Early Constitutional Manuscript- Electing the President in Pennsylvania. Two page handwritten manuscript dated Wednesday, October 1, 1788, measuring 7.5" x 9". Details the minutes of a meeting between a number of gentlemen from the counties of Pennsylvania, held in order to deliberate on producing representatives in the House of Representatives of the new government, and to fix on proper People to elect a president and vice president. Some of the names mentioned as present are; Benjamin Rush, George Latimer and John Nixon. There are 13 men listed all together. A valuable look at early governmental procedures!

The letter is in good condition with some minor issues visible. The usual folds are present, and the paper has begun to separate on some of the fold lines. No visible acid degradation or foxing. Excellent legibility. From the Henry E. Luhrs Collection. Accompanied by LOA from PSA/DNA.
Estimate: $1,000-$1,500

25435   Constitutions of the Several Independent States of America; The Declaration of Independence; The Articles of Confederation; Between and Said States, Treaties (Boston printed by Norman and Bowen 1785) Second Edition. 12mo Original full brown calf with edge wear, some weak spots along the spine. Inside hinge splitting front and rear. Some damp staining. Richard Potts copy. Signed by Richard Potts (member of the Continental Congress, United States Senator from Maryland). From the Henry E. Luhrs Collection.
Estimate: $1,500-$2,000

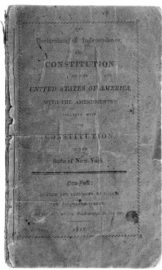

25436 *The Declaration of Independence, and Constitution of the United States of America, with the Amendments; together with the Constitution of the the State of New York.* (New York: J Low, 1812). Original printed wrappers torn and worn. Some foxing and browning throughout. From the Henry E. Luhrs Collection.
Estimate: $100-$150

25437 **Baltimore and Maryland History — Collection of Manuscript and Printed Material.** First settled in 1634 and later the seventh state to enter the union in 1788, Maryland has a long and important history. This lot contains an interesting assortment of 18th and 19th century documents and letters including a large archive of material relating to the Besore family. Approximately 25-30 items included. Generally fine condition. From the Henry E. Luhrs Collection. Accompanied by LOA from PSA/DNA.
Estimate: $400-$600

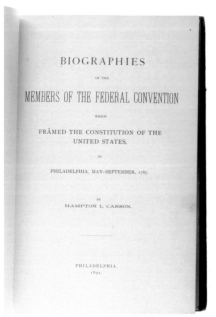

25438 **Hampton L. Carson:** *Biographies Of The Members Of The Federal Convention Which Framed the Constitution Of The United States* (Philadelphia, 1891), first edition. 4to. Original morocco. Spine splitting; rushed. Contents fine with nicely executed portrait plates. Inscribed by Carson to John F. Dillon, a prominent period attorney. Also ALS tipped in at front from Carson to Dillon. Nice Philadelphia item. From the Henry E. Luhrs Collection.
Estimate: $400-$500

25439 **(Penobscot Indians) An interesting pair of documents including a manuscript Document Signed** by six Penobscot Tribe members with their marks, one page, 7.25" x 9", Bangor, October 9, 1798, reading in part: *"received from Amasa L. Goodwin Esq. three hundred Bushels Indian corn, seventy five yards of Blue... Cloth, fifty pounds musket powder & Two hundred pounds shot... in full for the payment Due us from the Commonwealth [of] Massachudsst up to October 1898 as for agreement for Land Relinquished by us to the said Commonwealth in 1795."* Offered together with a second **Manuscript Document Signed** by seven Penobscot Indians with their marks, 7.5" x 6.5", Bangor, November 20, 1810 for similar articles *"Received of John Blake Agent for the Penobscot Tribe..."* The Penobscot relinquished their land claims in exchange for a reservation in what is present-day Washington County, Maine. Irregular margins, light creases, else very good condition. A fine Native American document. From the Henry E. Luhrs Collection. Accompanied by LOA from PSA/DNA.
Estimate: $600-$800

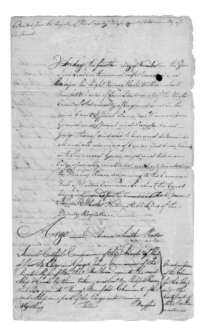

25440 **(Privateering in the Napoleonic Wars). A fascinating collection of three manuscript documents, 1803-4,** in which the owners of an American ship attempt to recover their cargo that was captured by British privateers, eleven pages total, 8" x 13", London, 1803-4. During the frequent warfare in Europe following the French Revolution between 1792 and 1812, the United States chose to remain neutral while trading in vital supplies with all belligerents. Thus American ships were also vulnerable to French and British privateers and naval vessels who captured American ships, seized cargo, and impressed sailors. Tension caused by these actions nearly drove the United States and France into open warfare in the late 1790s and ultimately led to war with Great Britain in 1812. The documents offered here deal with the cargo aboard the brig *Argo* commanded by Silvanus Smith, captured during a voyage between Cadiz and Hamburg by *"The Private Ship of War the Eliza and... the Private Ship of War Balloon..."* The first document, November 4, 1803, concerns the status of the cargo in which the judge *"...pronounce the same to belong as claimed, — and by Interlocutory decreed the same to be restored to the Claimant for he use of the Owners and Proprietors thereof with Freight to be a Charge on the Cargo - and on payment of a proportion of the Captors Expences [sic] of taking the Depositions..."* The second document, dated March 13, 1804, details the *"Particulars of Freight received of Brig Argo, Captured on her Voyage from Cadiz to Hamburgh and carried into Milford..."* The cargo is itemized and valued in mars and shillings and included Wine, Sugar, Hides, Cotton, Indigo,

Vinegar and Cochineal (for red dye), valued at 356 pounds. Also included is the "*...Bill of Expences [sic] on behalf of Mr. Henry Bromfield of London Merchant the Claimant of the ship on behalf of Nathaniel Cushing, Benj. Cushing and Silvanus Smith the Master respectively citizens of the United States of America...*" dated June 2, 1804 from the firm of Bogg & Toller for the incredible sum of pounds 115-14-6, nearly one-third of the value of the entire cargo! An amazing look into the difficulties involved in overseas commerce during the Napoleonic wars. A few minor fold separations, a few archival tape repairs, otherwise fine. Scarce records from an early chapter in our history. From the Henry E. Luhrs Collection. Accompanied by LOA from PSA/DNA.

Estimate: $750-$1,000

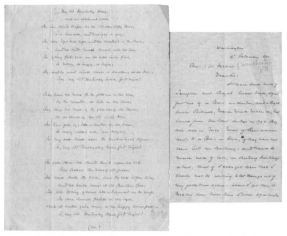

25441   Early Americana Document and Autograph Collection
consisting of approximately 50 items. Offered here is a great group of documents and letters from a wide variety of individuals and locations, most dated from the late 1700s to the mid 1800s. Just a few of the items are described below:

Albert Pike, attorney, Confederate general, Freemason. An ALS regarding Masonic ritual, handwritten lyrics to "My Old Kentucky Home" including the third verse written by Pike.

Dr. James Laurence Cabell, in charge of Confederate hospitals, professor at University of Virginia. ALS regarding university professor appointment.

Gamaliel Bradford, American privateer. ADS.

Thomas Willing, Continental Congress delegate, Bank of the United States president. DS.

This lot is full of great material such as these mentioned. Generally very good condition. From the Henry E. Luhrs Collection. Accompanied by LOA from PSA/DNA.

Estimate: $800-$1,000

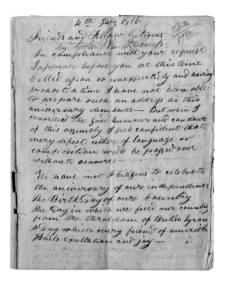

25442   (Fourth of July Oration) Manuscript, fifteen pages bound with wire, 6.25" x 7.5", Southampton, July 4, 1816. Notation on verso reads: "*4th of July Oration delivered by Wm. Jessup at Southampton in 1816*". Text for a speech given on Independence Day just about a year following the War of 1812. "*...The 4 of July 1816 is perhaps one of the most glorious ever celebrated by Republican Americans — The events and termination of the late glorious war with Great Britain — The termination of the late War with the Pirates of Africa — The extension and Diffusion of Democratic principles through out the union — The free, extensive, uninterrupted, and, prosperous commerce... are themes of exultation and joy to every true American... The American with pleasing anticipation looks forward to a time when this republic shall give laws to the world...*" Jessup then proceeds to narrate the atrocities committed by the French and the British before the War of 1812: "*... thousands of our seamen were dragged from their homes... dragged from his family and country to fight the battles of a nation which his soul abhors...* " Jessup also reminds his audience of the blessings of liberty including "*...Education, and we must consider the extension of political knowledge as one of our greatest privileges — A free and unrestricted Press is an invaluable blessing to any people —- to a republic it is indispensable — this is the Vehicle of Knowledge of our enlightened people without which how soon would they sink into insignificancy —- The first ambitious aspiring Demagogue would bind the iron brand of slavery fast upon their necks... an enlightened people can never be slaves...*" Much more fine content. Early celebratory orations recalling the Founding Fathers and their contribution to American independence are quite desirable; this is one of the finest we've encountered. Light creases, a few minor marginal chips, light soiling, else fine. From the Henry E. Luhrs Collection. Accompanied by LOA from PSA/DNA.

Estimate: $800-$1,200

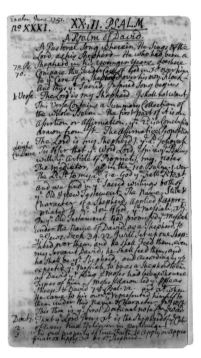

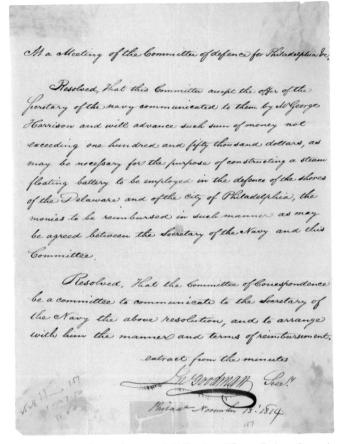

25444   Collection of Early American Religious Writings and Sermons consisting of hymns, sermons, and various letters totaling more than a dozen items. Just a few of the great pieces are described below:

C. C. Dawson, 19th century hymn writer. The words and music to "Be Ye Perfect," four verses "Be Ye Perfect" AMsS, "Rejoice Evermore" AMs/MQS.

Thomas S. Hastings, hymn writer. "Christian Submission" AMs

Ezra Ripley, long-time Concord, Massachusetts pastor, step-grandfather of Ralph Waldo Emerson. 1810 ALS.

James Freeman, Boston minister. 1811 ALS.

Ezra Griswold, Worthington, Ohio founding father. 1812 ALS to Bishop Griswold of Rhode Island.

R. H. McDaniel, hymn writer. "Since Jesus Came Into My Heart" AMsS.

Daniel Rogers, pastor of the Second Parish Church in Exeter, New Hampshire 1744-1785. Handwritten sermon on Psalm 23 dated 1751.

Generally good to very good condition. From the Henry E. Luhrs Collection.
Estimate: $500-$800

25443   War of 1812 Autograph Collection. Often called our Second War of Independence, the importance of the War of 1812 is sometimes overlooked. Though ending in a stalemate, it once and for all confirmed America's independence from Britain as well as Canada's right to exist as a British colony in North America. This amazing group of more than 100 signed items would form the basis for, or be a welcome addition to, a fine collection of this period's military and political figures. A few of the pieces included are described below:

William Bainbridge, U.S. Navy Commodore famous for his victory over HMS *Java.* ALS with vintage steel engraving.

J. Newman, Commander of Fort Pike in Louisiana. February 1, 1815 LS to British officer in the Rigolets, in part: *"Your having passed the limits prescribed for Flags of truce, this morning placed me under the disagreeable necessity of opening my batteries on your boat carrying a Flag of truce..."*

Isaac Hull, U.S. Navy Commodore, commander of the USS *Constitution* ("Old Ironsides"). LS mentioning that very ship.

James Van Cleve, ALS to historian Benson Lossing with a hand-drawn pencil sketch of the Battle of French Creek.
David Porter, U.S. Navy officer, commander of the USS *Essex.* ALS and DS (twice).

Alexander Macomb Jr., General and hero at the Battle of Plattsburg. Long ALS.

Defense of Philadelphia. Important DS dated November 18, 1814, in part: "...Resolved, That this committee accept the offer of the Secretary of the navy... and will advance such sum of money not exceeding one hundred and fifty thousand dollars, as may be necessary for the purpose of constructing a steam floating battery to be employed in the defense of the shores of the Delaware and the City of Philadelphia..."

A fabulous collection that took years to assemble. Generally very good to fine condition. From the Henry E. Luhrs Collection. Accompanied by LOA from PSA/DNA.
Estimate: $2,000-$3,000

25445 **(Thomas Paine) William Carver (? - ?)** New York author and veterinary surgeon, and associate of Thomas Paine, fine content **Autograph Letter Signed** *"William Carver"*, two pages with integral address leaf, 8.5" x 12.5", New York, July 16, 1821 to Philadelphia publishers McCarty & Davis proposing a new biography of Thomas Paine. Thomas Paine, the author of *Common Sense*, had returned to America on the invitation of Thomas Jefferson in 1800 but found little welcome due to his deistic views which he expressed in the *Age of Reason.* For the remainder of his life he moved from place to place. He spent one year (1805-1806) at the New York home of William Carver. Paine died in New York in 1809. His later radical views had alienated so many in America that only six people attended his funeral. Carver, who in 1816 had privately published *Select pieces, in prose & verse, on different subjects: containing epitaphs, and a letter to Thomas Paine, sent to him whilst on his dying bed. Also, an appeal to the Sovereign Maker of the universe, with the author's creed or belief of theological doctrines & opinions.*, pitches a new biography of Paine: *"I have been advised by a great number of citizens, to write an abridgement of the life of Thomas Paine... Cheetam's life of Paine was a scandalous work, the price two dollars, & the one published by Rickman in London, was ten and sixpence Sterling, on account of the high price of those works they met with poor sale, but it is presumed that an abridgment on duodecimo containing about 300 pages bound in boards... will meet with encouragement, the price to be one dollar... there are printers in this city that will undertake the work, Southwick was a going to do it but he died — It struck my mind that if you was to print the work, we should stand a double chance to get subscribers having two cities to collect in..."* As we have yet to discover any citations for the proposed work, we can safely assume that the publishers declined this offer. Reinforced with archival tape at edges, small loss from seal tear not affecting text, else very good. A fun piece of association history. From the Henry E. Luhrs Collection. Accompanied by LOA from PSA/DNA.

Estimate: $500-$700

25446 **Americana Document Collection** consisting of more than 50 documents, receipts, and letters with a wide range of dates (1600s to 1900s) and subjects (taxes, tobacco, oil, coffee, etc). A few of these interesting items are listed below:

Benjamin J. Russell. A wonderful series of twelve handwritten family letters dated from 1814 to 1827. The content is great — he talks not only about personal affairs but also about national happenings. Fascinating reading.

1825 Tavern Bill for Mrs. Bacon at Bush's Coffee-House, Pittsfield, Massachusetts totaling $3.24.

1771 Dated Servant Indenture. A manuscript document with multiple signatures, in part: ".. of the Town of Stoughton in the County of Suffolk in New England...place and bind out Rachel Rogers a poor child belonging to the Town and County aforesaid... after the Manner of an Apprentice to Dwell and Serve from the Day...until the 25 Day of March A.D. 1776..."

There is a particularly large group of documents in this lot that would display very well. Also, there is much material of interest to the genealogist. Consider these to be "snapshots" of life in a different day and time. Generally very good to fine condition. From the Henry E. Luhrs Collection. Accompanied by LOA from PSA/DNA.

Estimate: $700-$1,000

25447 **A manifest for a slave ship, 1833**
(Slavery) A fantastic manuscript Document Signed *"S. Bissell,* one page, 15.75" x 38", [Alexandria, Virginia], January 1833, a lengthy manifest for a schooner transporting 83 named slaves from Alexandria, Virginia to Natchez, Mississippi. The document bears the heading: *"Report and Maifest [sic] of the Cargo of Slaves on board the Schooner La Fayette of Norfolk Whereof Benj. Bissell is Master, burthen, 130/95 tons bound from the Port of Alexandria in the D.C. for the port of Natches [sic] State of Missippi [sic] via New Orleans"* Below, it lists 83 slaves, and includes: their names, height, age, complexion, the name and residence of the shipper, and consignees. The ages range from 3 months to 30 years with the average age around 20. Both men and women are represented on the list. Under *"Complexion"* they are noted as simply *"Black "* or *"Yellow"*. Shipments like this were not uncommon in the early nineteenth century as Virginia planters moved away from labor-intensive crops like tobacco to corn and wheat. While this transition was taking place, the Deep South was becoming the center of cotton production that was highly labor intensive, and fueled a ready market for slaves. The abolition of the slave importation in 1808 further increased demand. This is an amazing record of this important demographic shift which would have enormous cultural and social implications for decades to come. According to the document, the shipper of record was Franklin & Armsfield of Alexandria and the consignees were John Heyward & Company and Isaac Franklin. At the bottom, Armsfield has certified that the slaves listed *"...are legally held to service or bondage an [sic] that none of the same have been imported in the United States... subsequent to the first day of January Eighteen hundred and Eight..."* Partial separation at folds, some repair on verso, light dampstains, else good condition, and certainly worthy of professional restoration. From the Henry E. Luhrs Collection. Accompanied by LOA from PSA/DNA.

Estimate: $1,500-$2,000

25448 Cabinet Members Autograph Collection — Jackson, Van Buren, Tyler, and Harrison Presidencies consisting of the following items (generally fine condition):

John C. Spencer. Secretary of War and Treasury under Tyler. 1852 ANS.

Thomas Ewing. Secretary of Treasury under Harrison and Tyler. Secretary of Interior under Taylor and Fillmore. 1850 ALS as Interior Secretary.

Mahlon Dickerson. Secretary of Navy under Jackson and Van Buren. 1837 LS as Navy Secretary.

Edward Livingston. Secretary of State under Jackson. LS.

Amos Kendall. Postmaster General under Jackson and Van Buren. 1834 DS.

Louis McLane. Secretary of State and Treasury under Jackson. 1844 ALS.

John Forsyth. Secretary of State under Jackson and Van Buren. 1837 DS as State Secretary.

Charles A. Wickliffe. Postmaster General under Tyler. 1828 ALS. From the Henry E. Luhrs Collection. Accompanied by LOA from PSA/DNA.
Estimate: $300-$500

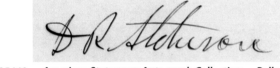

25449 American Statesmen Autograph Collection — Polk, Taylor, Fillmore, & Buchanan Presidencies. Offered in this lot are the following items (all generally fine condition unless noted):

George Bancroft. Secretary of the Navy under Polk. Two Autograph Letters Signed and one Typed Letter Signed.

Isaac Toucey. Attorney General under Polk, U.S. Senator, Secretary of the Navy under Buchanan. Autograph Letter Signed.

Reverdy Johnson. U.S. Senator, Attorney General under Taylor. Two Autograph Letters Signed.

David Rice Atchison. U.S. Senator. (Was he really president for one day?) Rare signature.

Alexander Hugh Holmes Start. Secretary of the Interior under Fillmore. Two page Autograph Letter Signed.

Horatio King. Postmaster General under Buchanan. Post Office Document Signed.

Howell Cobb. U.S. Congressman, Secretary of the Treasury under Buchanan. Autograph Letter Signed.

David R. Porter. Pennsylvania Governor. Autograph Letter Signed to President James Buchanan (Fair condition). From the Henry E. Luhrs Collection. Accompanied by LOA from PSA/DNA.
Estimate: $300-$500

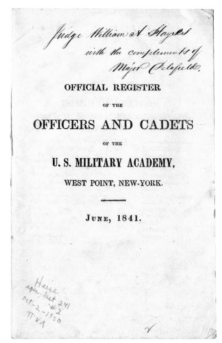

25450 [West Point] The Official Register of Class of 1841 - Signed by Richard Delafield and Joseph Hooker - and Listing Cadets Grant, Longstreet, Doubleday, Hancock, &c ... Pamphlet, entitled "Official Register of the Officers and Cadets of the U.S. Military Academy, West Point, New-York, June 1841", inscribed in ink on the front to "*Judge William A. Hayes with the compliments of Major* [Richard] **Delafield**", 23 pages, 4" by 6.5", and signed on the back cover "*J.* [Joseph] **Hooker.**" In fine condition. This fascinating version of a future Civil War "Who's Who" lists, in two sections, "Cadets arranged in Order of Merit... as Determined at the General Examination" and "Roll of Cadets Arranged According to Merit in Conduct." Some names which jump out at the modern reader are: Don Carlos Buell, John Fulton Reynolds, Alfred Sully, Abner Doubleday, Richard Brooke Garnett, James Longstreet, William S. Rosecrans, Christopher C. Auger, Ulysses S. Grant, Horatio G. Wright, Rufus Ingalls, Alfred Pleasonton, Simon B. Buckner, and Winfield S. Scott. In the "Offenses against Orders or Regulations," it is noted that Horatio Wright had the least, and Don Carlos Buell the most. A truly remarkable look at the Civil War's greatest leaders; it's like reading their report cards. From the Henry E. Luhrs Collection. Accompanied by LOA from PSA/DNA.
Estimate: $1,200-$1,800

25451 **(Mormons) An important collection of approximately sixty printed and manuscript documents from Hancock County, Illinois and in particular, Carthage and Nauvoo — where the Mormons, under the leadership of Joseph Smith, settled in 1839-1846.**

In 1838, Joseph Smith and several thousand Mormons fled Missouri by order of the Governor, and migrated to parts of Illinois and Iowa. Joseph Smith purchased swamp land from farmers and speculators on the banks of the Mississippi River, situated in between the towns of Carthage (county seat) and Quincy. By 1840, nearly 3,000 Mormons settled on this land tract, generally referred to as Commerce. Joseph Smith renamed the settlement Nauvoo ("beautiful" in Hebrew) and the Mormon migration continued en masse. The Mormons' fear of religious persecution prompted Joseph Smith to obtain a special charter for Nauvoo granting the city an independence likened to that of the State — Joseph Smith served as head of the municipal system, legal system, city government and church. As such, he issued writs of *habeas corpus* that protected Nauvoo's citizenry from law and tax enforcement agents from other states; raised a militia that was independent of the State militia; and created a fiscal shelter for the Church and it's members that held no allegiance or obligations to the larger State. By 1844, Nauvoo's population soared to 10,000. It's liberal charter, growing commercial success, and river proximity made it a safe haven for various types of criminals. This, combined with anti-Mormon sentiment, and a general disdain for the untouchable (and questionable) business and political practices of Joseph Smith, fueled anger in the neighboring towns of Quincy and Carthage. At the same time, some Nauvoo Mormons were also questioning the morality of Smith's leadership, especially after he announced his intentions to run for President of the United States. The apostate collective published a dissenting newspaper, *The Nauvoo Expositor,* but only published one issue before Joseph Smith ordered its presses destroyed on June 11, 1844. Subsequently, Joseph Smith and his brother Hyrum were arrested. Smith was murdered by a mob while he was held in jail in Carthage on June 27, 1844. His death led to a succession crisis and schisms within the Mormon movement. Brigham Young was chosen to succeed Joseph Smith, and from 1846 through 1852, he led the migration of sixteen thousand Mormons from a hostile Illinois to Utah.

Of the sixty documents, roughly one third date from the period of Mormon settlement there. A small sampling of the material reveals two documents signed by early Mormon leader **Stephen Markham (1800-1878), partly-printed Document Signed** "*Stephen Markham*", one page, 8" x 12", Nauvoo, Illinois, July 8, 1846 selling land in Nauvoo to Leonard Schusler. The collection contains a similar D.S. also signed by Markham and his first wife **Hannah Markham** and filled-out in Markham's hand, one page, 8" x 12", Nauvoo, Illinois, April 1, 1842 in which they sell a lot in Nauvoo to Mormon elder **George W. Crouse.** Crouse was excommunicated from the Church on September 15, 1844 for "unchristian conduct". Interestingly enough the collection includes **George W. Crouse and Catherine Crouse,** D.S., 12" x 16" June 26, 1843, sale to Daniel Bailey for $200 for land in Nauvoo. Markham had been in the Carthage jail with Smith and others but was allowed to leave to obtain medicine. Upon his return he was confronted by a mob and forced away at bayonet point. Also of interest is an **A. D.S. endorsed by Carthage County jailer, George W. Stigall,** Nauvoo, Illinois, June 14, 1845. Stigall was the jailer for Carthage County at the time that Joseph and Hyrum Smith were assassinated. The collection also includes numerous documents listing homes in Nauvoo that had been sold off for non-payment of tax, many of which appear to have been abandoned (or just delinquent) in the period between 1843 and 1847 when the Mormon's began their journey west to establish Deseret in modern-day Utah. A tremendous collection worthy of further research. Overall condition Very Good. An important, early Mormon archive. From the Henry E. Luhrs Collection.
Estimate: $2,000-$3,000

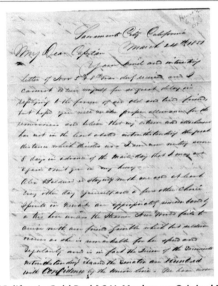

25452 **[California Gold Rush] S.H. Meeker, an Original Forty-Niner, Writes About "El Dorado."** Major S. H. Meeker. Autograph Letter Signed ("Harry"), 6 pages, recto and verso, 8" by 10.5", Sacramento City, California, March 24, 1851. To "My Dear Captain." In Fine condition. With typed transcription. Major Meeker came to California in '49, when the first reports of major gold strikes were just starting to sweep the country, and stayed until his death in '63, becoming along the way a much respected merchant. Here, just a couple years into his stay, he writes an old comrade about the wonders to behold - and reports on the booming business. In part: "*...We now have eight large class steamers plying between this place and San Francisco and the way the price of fare is knocked down occasionally is a Caution to California profits, and the rapidity with which the comforts not only but the luxuries of traveling have increased is equally surprising. Eighteen months since I paid $30 for the privilege of a deck passage from San Francisco on the old propeller McKinn - Now the fare in the saloon on first class steamers...can be had for one Dollar... The progress of civilization and refinement is equally visible in other quarters. A few months since we considered ourselves fortunate to get enough hard bread and bacon... Now an abundant supply of game and excellent vegetables are served up to us daily with all the proper appointments... We are a fast people and it is not too much to predict that some parts of this country will in less than two years equal in Splendor and luxurious living any part of the World. Both the desire for it and the gold to pay for it exist here in a great degree. The Ladies are coming too!*" Meeker continues to rhapsodize about the hunting, the climate, even the lettuce. He sends news, too, of other young men from the East who've gone West.... From the Henry E. Luhrs Collection. Accompanied by LOA from PSA/DNA
Estimate: $600-$900

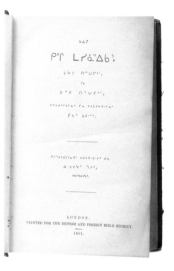

25453 *Bible (Native American)*
Cree (London: British and Foreign Bible Society 1861), 8vo (5.5" x 8.75"), full embossed brown leather spine split, edges worn. Contents fine with 855 pages in Cree syllabic. From the Henry E. Luhrs Collection.
Estimate: $800-$1,000

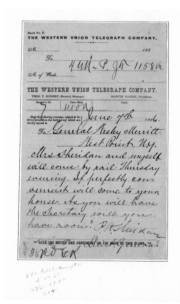

25454   Philip Sheridan Collection. This lot features three items written and signed by Philip Sheridan, the great Union Army general and architect behind the protection and development of Yellowstone National Park.

Autograph Letter Signed "*P.H. Sheridan.*" Four pages, 5" x 6.5", Chicago, April 9, 1881. The content of this letter is routine.

Autograph Letter Signed "*P.H. Sheridan.*" Two pages, 5" x 6.5", Chicago, July 18, 1882. The content of this letter is routine.

Autograph Document Signed "*P.H. Sheridan.*" One page, 5.4" x 8", Western Union Telegraph Company Letterhead, np, June 7, 1886. This telegraph was sent to a General Wesley Merritt, announcing that he and his wife would be visiting soon.

The three items in this lot are all in very fine condition; the letters have slight staining around the edges; otherwise excellent! From the Henry E. Luhrs Collection. Accompanied by LOA from PSA/DNA.
Estimate: $500-$700

25455   General Fitz John Porter Collection of Seven Autograph Letters Signed. Porter was a career army officer and Union Civil War general whose military career was unjustly ruined by a politically-motivated court martial. He distinguished himself as a defensive expert at the Seven Days Battles, being promoted to major general on July 4, 1862. Later that same year at Second Bull Run, General John Pope gave him orders which were based on incomplete information and would have been disastrous had Porter carried them out. Pope was furious and accused him of insubordination and blamed him for the defeat. He was arrested and tried by a military court hand-picked (and later promoted) by Edwin Stanton who hated Porter based mainly on his association with General McClellan. As expected, Porter was found guilty and was dismissed from the army on January 21, 1863. It took him about twenty years to get his name and reputation cleared. In 1879, a special commission reviewed the case and exonerated Porter saying that Porter's reluctance to attack likely saved Pope's army an even greater defeat. Finally, in 1886 and with the help of Chester A. Arthur, he was reinstated as a colonel backdated to 1861 (but without the back pay). Two days later, he resigned. His post-war civilian life was busy serving in New York City as Commissioner of Public Works, Police Commissioner, and Fire Commissioner as well as various positions in the railroad, construction, and other commercial industries.

This lot contains a total of eight signed letters, seven of which are completely in his own hand. Also included is an original printing of the 27 page brief and argument, *Memorial of Fitz-John Porter,* he made before Congress in 1882 asking for the court martial to be overturned. The material in this excellent lot is generally in fine condition. From the Henry E. Luhrs Collection. Accompanied by LOA from PSA/DNA.
Estimate: $400-$500

CIVIL WAR ERA AMERICANS INCLUDING THE ONLY KNOWN COPY OF MEADS FIRST REPORT OF THE BATTLE AT GETTYSBURG

25456   Confederate General Jubal Anderson Early Signature
"*J. A. Early Lynchburg, Virginia*" on a 3.75" x 1.75" sheet laid down to a heavy card. Born in Virginia, Early served in the Seminole Wars and then in the Mexican War, practicing law in the interim. At the outbreak of the Civil War, he enlisted in the army as a colonel, later rising to the rank of lieutenant general. After the war, he traveled first to Texas, then Mexico, Cuba, and Canada. He refused to take the oath of allegiance to the United States but was pardoned in 1868 by President Johnson. He is considered to be one of the most able of all rebel generals and certainly one of the scarcer autographs. Very good condition with soiling and staining. From the Henry E. Luhrs Collection. Accompanied by LOA from PSA/DNA.
Estimate: $400-$500

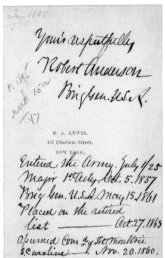

25457 Robert Anderson - Signed Photo and Signature of the commanding officer who surrendered Fort Sumter, the battle that started the Civil War. Offered here is a fine group of items. First is a CDV signed on the front *"Robert Anderson Brig Gen U.S.A."* and also on the back *"Your's [sic] respectfully Robert Anderson Brig Gen U.S.A"* above a handwritten history of his service in the Army. The second item is a clipped closing to a letter signed *"Respectfully, Your Obt Servt, Robert Anderson Maj Gen USA"* (ink smeared). Next is an ALS of transmittal from his wife, signed *"Mrs. Anderson"* in the third person, sending the CDV as requested to famous autograph collector and writer Lewis J. Cist. Also in this lot are two period engravings and a clipped contemporary article regarding the Fort Sumter battle. Except where noted, all in fine to Very Fine condition. Has original purchase invoice with handwritten note from Mary Benjamin, 1948. From the Henry E. Luhrs Collection. Accompanied by LOA from PSA/DNA.
Estimate: $1,500-$2,000

Anderson. Anderson has filled out the questionnaire with the first answer being his signature. In full (Anderson's handwritten replies in italics): *"Philadelphia, July 20, 1863. Sir, I am having prepared with great care, by an eminent author, a work embracing 'The Life and Services of the Generals of the Army,' Illustrated with fine Steel Portraits, and I would esteem it a favor if you would allow some friend or member of your staff to fill up the following blanks: Name, in full. Robert Anderson. When and where born June 14. 1805. at 'Soldier's Retreat. Jefferson Co., Ky. If graduated, when and where. July 1825. U.S. Military Academy West Point Date of your first entering the army, and present commission. July 1, 1825. Brig Genl U.S.A. List of battles in which you have participated, and any facts or particulars regarding the same. Bad Axe Black Hawk War. 1832. Jupiter Inlet Fla 1838. Vera Crux (sic), Cerro Gordo, Molino del Rey, Mexico. 1847. Fort Sumter. South Carolina 1861. If not in any battles, what other duties have you performed. [left blank] Where could I procure a satisfactory portrait of yourself. McAllister. Phila Profile by Guttekunst. To whom, or to what sources could you refer me for accurate information in regard to your life and services. Appleton's New American Cyclopedia Vol 16 Supplement, Cullum's Register of Graduates of Military Academy. Gardner's Military Dicty. As the work is in a forward state, your early attention will greatly oblige Yours truly, George W. Child."* On verso is a printed announcement for "Lossing's Pictorial History of the Great Rebellion". Slight tears in blank areas at edges of folds, else in fine condition. Accompanied by manuscript biographical information relating to Anderson, 1.5p, 5" x 8", dated November 12, 1862. This was part of the renowned Collection of Oliver R. Barrett sold at Parke-Bernet Galleries in New York on February 20, 1952; original Parke-Bernet folder is present. Three items. From the Henry E. Luhrs Collection. Accompanied by LOA from PSA/DNA.
Estimate: $800-$1,200

25459 Robert Anderson, (1805-1871), Union commander of Fort Sumter at the start of the Civil War, his Signature with closing *"Your Sincere friend Robert Anderson"* on a 3.5" x 1.5" slip removed from a letter. Mounted to a larger sheet to which has also been affixed a letter from his wife, **Eliza Bayard cinch Anderson, Autograph Letter Signed** *"E. B. Anderson"* two pages, 4" x 6", no place given, [Washington], June 18, 1896, and enclosing *"...an Autograph of Genl Anderson 'to go with the photo which your little daughter prizes so highly'. He loved children, so I send it to her..."* Offered together with an Anderson carte-de-visite photograph published by E. Anthony, New York. All three pieces in fine condition. From the Henry E. Luhrs Collection. Accompanied by LOA from PSA/DNA.
Estimate: $300-$400

25458 Fort Sumter General Robert Anderson Fills Out 1863 Questionnaire Partly Printed DS: *"Robert Anderson"*, One page, 8" x12.5". Printed letter, in questionnaire form, from George W. Childs to Robert

View color images of virtually every lot and place bids at HeritageAuctions.com/Americana

25460 **Union General William Averell: An Extraordinary Account of Bull Run!** Autograph Letter Signed, as "Bvt. Maj. USA, Late Bvt. Genl. USA", 3 pages, recto and verso, 6" by 9.5", Bath, Steuben County, New York, October 31, 1887. To Daniel S. Farrington. In fine condition, albeit an over-enthusiastic soul has penciled Averell's name at top of letter. With typed transcription. Here the distinguished Calvary commander answers the question, how did he feel in his first battle? His reply: "... *My first battle was Bull Run in 1861. My feeling on entering the battle was, as I saw the enemy hastening to their positions, that there was a great and useless Crime about to be Committed; - the second as I can remember the whizzing and hurling of my first solid shot from the enemy through the trees and tearing along the ground was of the fierce and terrible force of a cannon ball; - next I was startled, amused and horrified to see a man who had been hit on the head by a fragment of shell springing about and shedding blood like a chicken with its head just stricken off; after the wonder at the excitement amounting to a kind of delirium of some of our Chief Commanders who galloped about yelling to anyone who would listen, about what the enemy were doing and generally calling for reinforcements like frightened idiots; then the woeful lack of a capable Commander of all our forces with a headquarters was felt; and to skip to the last uncontrollable indignation and mortification at the failure of our army to win the battle... The only Consolation to be found was to know that the enemy was not much if better off than ourselves...*" From the Henry E. Luhrs Collection. Accompanied by LOA from PSA/DNA.
Estimate: $1,000-$1,500

25461 **Original Watercolor Study of Meade by Ole Peter Hansen Balling, painted in the field and signed at the time by Meade**

George G. Meade, (1815-1872), Union General, victor at Gettysburg, an original watercolor bust portrait of Meade signed *"Geo. G. Meade Maj. Gen[eral] Com[mandin]g. A[rmy of the] P[otomac].",* 9" x 11", *"H[ead] Q[uarter]rs A[rmy of the]. P[otomac]"* [likely near City Point, Virginia], October 12, 1864. This chest-up portrait was accomplished by noted Norwegian-born artist *Ole Peter Hansen Balling, (1823-1906), who also signs the portrait "H. Balling".* Balling is, perhaps, best known for his heroic oil painting, *Grant and His Generals,* which depicts Grant riding triumphantly beside twenty six of his generals, including Meade, and which was completed in 1865; it hangs at the National Portrait Gallery in Washington. In order to complete that dramatic work, Balling traveled to Union army encampments and composed from-life studies of his subjects. In the autumn of 1864, he spent five weeks in and around City Point, Virginia for the purpose of painting portraits of Grant, and his field officers. He also painted Philip Sheridan while the latter was in service in the Shenandoah Valley, as well as William Sherman and George H. Thomas, in Washington, after the war. The finished painting was published to raise funds for the Sanitary Commission, a private organization for aiding sick and wounded soldiers. After comparing this sketch of Meade for inclusion in *Grant and His Generals,* with the final work, we are confident that this was the study used. Meade adds a note at the bottom right: *"Sketched at the Hd. Qrs. A.P. Octr. 12, 1864"* Ole Peter Hansen Balling was born in Oslo, and emigrated to New York in 1856. He also painted portraits of John Brown, James Garfield, and Chester A. Arthur, all of which hang in the National Portrait Gallery. *Provenance:* the Oliver R. Barrett Lincoln Collection, Parke-Bernet Galleries, February 20, 1952, Lot 520. Feint toning along light crease, some minor age wear but the color remains quite vibrant and bears a very bold and dark signature. Fine condition.

Please Note: A similar study of General Winfield Scott Hancock by Balling also appears in this catalog. From the Henry E. Luhrs Collection. Accompanied by LOA from PSA/DNA.
Estimate: $4,000-$6,000

25462   General P. Gustave Toutant Beauregard Document Signed
"*G.T. Beauregard.*" Signed check, 8.3" x 2.5", Mutual National Bank, New Orleans, Louisiana, December 20, 1878, for the amount of $16. General Beauregard was a Confederate commander and *postbellum* he became active in the railroad industry as well as supporting voting and civil rights of freed slaves.

The check is in very fine condition; the cancellation stamp effects some of the signature but not to the point of effecting legibility. From the Henry E. Luhrs Collection. Accompanied by LOA from PSA/DNA.
Estimate: $400-$600

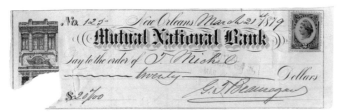

25463   General P. Gustave Toutant Beauregard Document Signed
"*G.T. Beauregard.*" Signed check, 8.5" x 2.5", Mutual National Bank, New Orleans, Louisiana, March 21, 1879, for the amount of $20. General Beauregard was a Confederate commander and one of the few high-ranking Confederates who supported the civil and voting rights of freed slaves after the war ended.

The check is in fine condition; cancellation stamp slightly touches the signature but does not affect legibility; large hole in the lower left corner. From the Henry E. Luhrs Collection. Accompanied by LOA from PSA/DNA.
Estimate: $400-$600

25464   General P. Gustave Toutant Beauregard Document Signed
"*G.T. Beauregard.*" Signed check, 8.25" x 2.5", Mutual National Bank, New Orleans, Louisiana, February 3rd, 1880, for the amount of $100. General Beauregard was a Confederate commander and *postbellum* he declined offers to command the armies of Romania and Egypt.

The check is in very fine condition; the cancellation stamp effects some of the signature but not the point of effecting the legibility. From the Henry E. Luhrs Collection. Accompanied by LOA from PSA/DNA.
Estimate: $400-$600

25465   General P. Gustave Toutant Beauregard Document Signed
"*G.T. Beauregard.*" Signed check, 8.25" x 2.5", Mutual National Bank, New Orleans, Louisiana, August 3, 1880, for the amount of $100. General

Beauregard was one of the eight full generals in the Confederate Army and after the defeat of the South he was one of the few high-ranking Confederates to support the rights of freed slaves. The check is in very fine condition; the cancellation stamp slight mars the signature though it is still completely legible; small hole under the letter "n" in bank from stamp; second stamp near the check value. From the Henry E. Luhrs Collection. Accompanied by LOA from PSA/DNA.
Estimate: $400-$600

25466   General P. Gustave Toutant Beauregard Autograph Document Signed "*G.T. Beauregard Supt.*" One page, 5.25" x 8.5", New York, April 24, 1856. The document reads in part, "*…The following is the Tonnage of shipments of marble stone Feb. 16 1856 to April 24, 1856…*" The rest is a list of ships bringing in shipments of marble, with amounts. Beauregard would go on to be a full general during the Civil War, serving the Confederacy.

The document is in fine condition; usual folds are present; mounting traces on verso as well as traces of another document; adhesive stain on center of obverse from glue on verso. From the Henry E. Luhrs Collection. Accompanied by LOA from PSA/DNA.
Estimate: $500-$700

25467   General P. Gustave Toutant Beauregard Document Signed
"*G.T. Beauregard.*" Signed check, 8.25" x 2.6", Mutual National Bank, New Orleans, Louisiana, January 6, 1880, for the amount of $17.67. General Beauregard was a Confederate General, one of the eight full generals of the Confederacy. The check is in very fine condition; cancellation stamp did not go all the way through the check but did cause two small burst tears near the signature. From the Henry E. Luhrs Collection. Accompanied by LOA from PSA/DNA.
Estimate: $400-$600

25468   Braxton Bragg: Superlative Post-War Autograph Letter on His New Life "As a Thing Contaminated." Autograph Letter Signed, 4 pages, recto and verso, 5" by 8", New Orleans, April 8, 1867; addressed to "My Dear Major." In excellent condition. A long and fascinating account of the unfortunate condition of the South during Reconstruction, and Bragg's own difficulties finding employment. In part: *"Indeed, I find what was formerly a passport to the hearts of our people - prominence in our cause - rather a drawback now. So timid have they become under the heels of the despots, especially the wealthy and large business men, that a prominent rebel is avoided as a thing contaminated... Especially is this the case with those who scorn to degrade themselves by ignoring the past, and seeking amnesty for the future in a spirit of assumed humility... Unable to resist, I shall submit as does Jefferson Davis, to the outrages and indignities heaped upon us... No human power can induce me to aid in riveting the chains which are to bind our people in the future... Not even the hope of amnesty... can alter my position."* From the Henry E. Luhrs Collection. Accompanied by LOA from PSA/DNA.
Estimate: $900-$1,200

25469   John Brown Signature. Signed: *"John Brown."* This lot features a clipped bank check signed by the famous "Old John Brown of Osawatomie," the bank seal is visible in red ink near the signature. He is best known for his failed raid on Harper's Ferry. Brown was a staunch abolitionist and his efforts, though futile at the time, helped to spark the Civil War and the ultimate freedom of slaves in America. He was tried and executed for his failed attempt. The signature is in Fine condition; the paper is slightly cut up from cancellation stamps, but the signature is untouched and very clear! From the Henry E. Luhrs Collection. Accompanied by LOA from PSA/DNA.
Estimate: $800-$1,200

25470   John Brown writes a year before Harper's Ferry: *"I felt for a number of years in earlier life; a steady strong desire to die... I am now rather anxious to live for a few years more."*

John Brown (1800-1859) radical abolitionist, fine content Autograph Letter Signed *"John Brown"* two pages, 5.25" x 8", Peterboro, New York, February 24, 1858 to Transcendentalist author Franklin Benjamin Sanborn (1831-1917) who was a member of Brown's Committee of Six (or Secret Six) and a major financial supporter of Brown's activities. A stirring letter written just two days after he had revealed his plan to Sanborn and Gerrit Smith to raid the federal arsenal at Harper's Ferry. He writes:

"Mr. Morton has taken the liberty of saying to me that you felt 1/2 inclined to make a common cause with me. I greatly rejoice at this; for I believe when you come to look at the ample filed I labour in; & the rich harvest which (not only this entire country, but) the whole world during the present & future generation may reap from its successful cultivation; you will feel that you are out of your element until you find you are in it; an entire Unit. What an inconceivable amount of good you might so effect; by your counsel, your example, your encouragement, your natural & acquired ability; for active service. And then how very little we can possibly loose? Certainly the cause is enough to live for; if not to for. I have only had this one opportunity in a life of nearly Sixty years & could I be continued ten times as long again I might not again have another equal opportunity. God has honored but comparatively a very small part of mankind with any possible chance for such mighty & soul satisfying rewards. But my dear friend if you should make up your mind to do so I trust it will be wholly from the prompting of your own spirit; after having thoroughly counted the cost. I would flatter no man into such a measure if I could do it ever so easily. I expect nothing but to 'endure hardness': but I expect to effect a mighty conquest even though it be like the last victory of Samson. I felt for a number of years in earlier life; a steady strong desire to die: but since I saw any prospect of becoming a 'reaper' in the great harvest I have not only felt quite willing to live: but have enjoyed life much; I am now rather anxious to live for a few years more."

The "Secret Six" was a group of six wealthy New England abolitionists and included Sanborn and Gerrit Smith who financially supported Brown's militant anti-slavery activities. The committee provided Brown with the funds and arms that he used in his failed attempt to raid the federal arsenal at Harper's Ferry to supply arms for a general slave insurrection. His plot failed and he was captured by U.S. Marines under the command of Lieutenant Colonel Robert E. Lee. Brown was tried and hanged for treason and fomenting a slave rebellion. John Brown remains one of the most defining figures in American history — his deeds debated as either the butchery of a madman or the zealous labors of a passionate abolitionist. Credited/blamed for being one of the dominoes that tumbled to start the War, his letters are quite scarce. Weakness at folds, starting at two, else fine- bright and clean, mounted at edge of integral leaf to larger sheet. A fine vintage engraving included. From the Henry E. Luhrs Collection. Accompanied by LOA from PSA/DNA.
Estimate: $5,000-$7,000

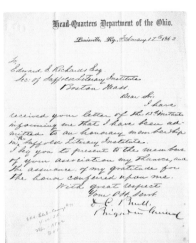

25471   Don Carlos Buell Autograph Letter Signed "*D.C. Buell, Brigadier General.*" 1 page, 7.75" x 9.75", Head-Quarters Department of the Ohio Letterhead; Louisville, Kentucky, February 17, 1862. Buell was a career soldier, he fought in three major wars; the Mexican-American War, the Seminole War, and the Civil War. He succeeded General Sherman as head of the Department of the Ohio in November of 1861, shortly before this letter was written. The content of the letter is routine; it thanks the Suffolk Literary Institute for an honorary membership that they had bestowed on him.

The letter is in very fine condition; usual folds are present; small stains present on lower right corner. From the Henry E. Luhrs Collection. Accompanied by LOA from PSA/DNA.
Estimate: $400-$600

25472   John Buford (1826-1863) Union General in the Civil War, rare war date Signature "*Jno Buford Brigadier G[eneral] Vol[unteer]s Ch[ie]f of Cav[alry]*" on a 2.25" x .5" mounted to a 3.25" x 2" card. Buford likely signed this card sometime between July 1862 and just before the Battle of Gettysburg, in July 1863. At Gettysburg, Buford's division successfully held off Henry Heth's Confederates so Major General John F. Reynolds' U.S. I Corps could deploy on the high ground west of the town. This proved to be one of the key factors in the Union victory there. Buford died of typhoid fever in December 1863. Fine condition. This is quite desirable given the scarcity of anything war-date from Buford. From the Henry E. Luhrs Collection. Accompanied by LOA from PSA/DNA.
Estimate: $1,500-$2,000

25473   [Gettysburg] John L. Burns, the Only Civilian to Fight at Gettysburg - His Autograph and Photo. Carte-de-Visite, in excellent condition, affixed to a 5" by 7" leaf on which is pasted below Burn's sig-

nature, as follows: "John L. Burns of Gettysburg." Rare.   We'll let "Liz" of the July 10, 1863 issue of the *Gettysburg Gazette* tell the tale. "*One week ago, seventy-two year old John L. Burns dropped everything to fight for his country in the battle of Gettysburg. From his house, Burns could see the armies of the Union and the Confederacy locked in battle at Gettysburg. At first he stopped what he was doing and just watched. Then he grabbed his rifle and ran to fight when the 150th Pennsylvania came to reinforce the Union forces at the end of the first day. Burns fought successfully on the second day, but he was wounded on the third, probably as he was defending the ridge against Pickett's charge. Even though wounded, he kept fighting until the battle was over. Since he was not a regular soldier, he simply went home at the battle's end and resumed his normal life.*" From the Henry E. Luhrs Collection. Accompanied by LOA from PSA/DNA.
Estimate: $800-$1,200

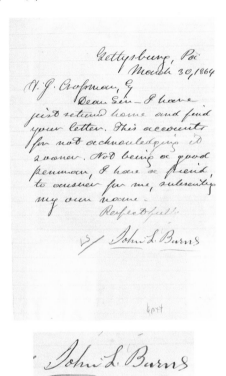

25474   John Burns, The Old Hero of Gettysburg, Letter Signed "*John L. Burns*". Also known as the "One Man Army of Gettysburg," Burns was a seventy-year-old War of 1812 and Mexican War veteran who lived at Gettysburg. When the Civil War broke out, he was one of the first to volunteer, but was rejected because of his advanced years. When the rebels invaded the Cumberland Valley and started to march toward Gettysburg, he grabbed his old musket and started shooting. When he saw the troops carrying his beloved Stars and Stripes coming in, he ran to offer his services, ending up with a Wisconsin regiment. They soon recognized his expertise with a gun and replaced his old musket with a first-rate rifle and gave him 25 rounds of cartridges. He fired 18 of his rounds, killing three rebels (by his count) and receiving three wounds himself. He was left behind on the field. When the Confederates found him there in citizen's attire, he somehow managed to talk his way into being taken home and having his wounds treated. Stories of his bravery soon spread and he became a national folk hero, with articles and poems written about him. General Doubleday even entered the account of his actions into the official report. After the war, those touring the battlefield often visited him. Upon his death in 1871, the national press carried his obituary.

This lot contains a letter signed "*John L. Burns*". One page, 5" x 8", Gettysburg, March 30, 1864, apparently in reply to an autograph request, in part: "...Not being a good penman, I have a friend to answer for me, subscribing my own name." Fine condition, lightly mounted to a folder with a group of contemporary clippings. From the Henry E. Luhrs Collection. Accompanied by LOA from PSA/DNA.
Estimate: $800-$1,200

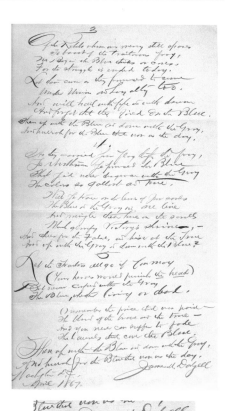

25476 Jefferson Davis Signature. Jefferson Davis Signature. Davis signs this 4.5" x 4.3" card as, "Jefferson Davis." The signature was originally on a white sheet of paper, which has been laid down on a sturdy black card stock. Attached to the card stock, aside from the signature, is a small picture of a confederate flag, and a two-line newspaper clipping stating the years of Davis' birth and death. The signature is dated, July 25th, 1853. This was likely signed shortly after he was named Secretary of War under Franklin Pierce. The signature is in very fine condition; light staining present; has been laid down, glue is visible through the paper. From the Henry E. Luhrs Collection. Accompanied by LOA from PSA/DNA.

Estimate: $500-$700

25475 Two Manuscript Fair Copies of Private Dalzell's "The Blue and the Gray"

James M. Dalzell (1838-1924), Autograph Manuscript Signed, "James M. Dalzell" with an additional two signatures in text, two pages, 8" x 13", Washington, [dated April 1867, but written much later], a fair copy of "The Blue and the Gray" which he composed in 1867 in response to the conciliatory poem by Francis Miles Finch (1827-1907). Dalzell prefaces his copy with a explanatory note: "*...In the spring of 1867 a news item went the rounds of the press, giving a touching account of how some beautiful Southern ladies had decorated alike the graves of Confederates and Union Soldiers in some cemetery in the south. The incident called forth a beautiful poem, by Stoddart. I think [he was obviously mistaken in this attribution], entitled 'The Blue and the Gray'. It has become an American classic. But the war was just over, and cooling time had not yet come, so the following poem - far inferior to the original but better expressing the sentiment of that day, went the rounds of the press in reply to the One first named...*" Dalzell's version reads in part: "*1. You may sing of the Blue and the Gray | And mingle their hue in this rhyme. | But the Blue that we use in the fray | Is covered with glory sublime. So no more let us hear of the Gray, | The symbol of treason and change. | We pierced it with bullets - away! | Or will pierce it with bullets again. | Then up with the Blue and down with the Gray, | And hurrah for the Blue that won us the day!...*" Offered together with a second fair copy, an **Autograph Manuscript Signed,** *James M. Dalzell, Private Dalzell*", two pages 8" x 13", Soldier's Home, Dayton, Ohio, May 30, 1916, entitled "*The blue and the Gray of 1867 As revised by its Author 1916*" A very different version in a much more conciliatory tone. Dalzell adds a postscript below the poem noting that at "*The great age of seventy seven, looking back over the graves of the men of both sides who fell in the war... all hate, every feeling of anger or animosity of the slightest degree, passed away forever from me...*" Dalzell was an attorney who served with the 116th Ohio during the Civil War. He later became a prominent Ohio legislator best known for patriotic speeches and articles under the name of "Private Dalzell". A fascinating pair of manuscripts illustrating how passions cool over time and heal the raw wounds of war. Two pieces, Very Fine condition. From the Henry E. Luhrs Collection. Accompanied by LOA from PSA/DNA.

Estimate: $900-$1,200

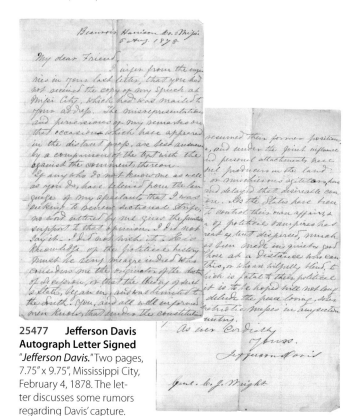

25477 Jefferson Davis Autograph Letter Signed "*Jefferson Davis.*" Two pages, 7.75" x 9.75", Mississippi City, February 4, 1878. The letter discusses some rumors regarding Davis' capture. It reads in part, "*...The facts you state in regard to captured treasure are new to me. It is probable that much of it was the property of the Richmond Banks. The item of money captured from 'Jeff. Davis' is unfounded, for the sufficient reason that I had no gold when captured, either private or public...The fact is, my dear Grafts, that I staked all my property and reputation in the defense of State rights and constitutional liberty, as I understood them...*" Interesting content since it covers both wartime propaganda and rumor as well as letting us hear Jefferson's sentiments on how his money was invested. In addition to this ALS is an ALS written and signed by Jefferson's wife Varina. The letter is in fine condition; usual folds are present; some separation has occurred on the fold lines; small stain in the upper left corner on the obverse. From the Henry E. Luhrs Collection. Accompanied by LOA from PSA/DNA

Estimate: $3,000-$5,000

25478 No Lot.

25479 **Jefferson Davis War-Date Letter About the Call-Up of Slaves to Advance War Effort!** Letter Signed, as president of the Confederate States of America, 1 page, 8" by 10", Richmond, January 30, 1863; to Governor Letcher of Virginia. In fine condition. The Confederate Army - far more than the Federal - was never reluctant to use African American labor in non-combat roles; tens of thousands of slaves were used to build fortifications, dig latrines, and haul supplies. This letter concerns their impressments - a service detested by both slave and slave owner alike, and a thorny problem for those, like Letcher, who had a constituency to please but a war to win. In full: *"I invite your attention to the enclosed communications from several members of Congress and of the Legislature, in reference to the propriety of exempting certain counties from my recent call upon you for slaves to work upon fortifications. Convinced that you can, much better than myself, decide upon the merits of the case, it is referred to you with the assurance that I will acquiesce in your judgment upon the subject, and cheerfully withdraw any call you may deem inexpedient."* On the verso is a letter in the hand of **George W. Munford**, Secretary of the Commonwealth of Virginia, replying on January 31st that Governor Letcher has *"exempted the Counties of Southampton & Sussex from the call for Slaves to work upon fortifications"* and that *"the remaining Counties will be required to meet your requisitions."* From the Henry E. Luhrs Collection. Accompanied by LOA from PSA/DNA.
Estimate: $3,000-$4,000

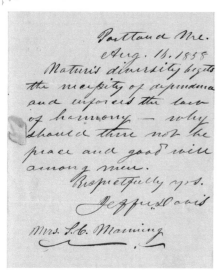

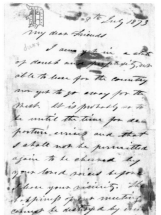

25480   Jefferson Davis Anti-Secessionist Autograph Quote With an Autograph Letter About a Jewish Officer.
1) Autograph Quotation Signed, as U.S. senator 1 page, 4.5" by 7", Portland, Maine, August 18, 1858; inscribed to Mrs. L.C. Manning. Traces of mounting on recto, not effecting text, else fine. In full: *"Nature's diversity begets the necessity of dependence and enforces the law of harmony - why should there not be peace and good will among men."* Davis' summered, and speechified, in Maine in the lead-up to the Civil War; this quote is most likely related to one of his three Portland addresses. 2) Autograph Letter Signed, as U.S. Secretary of War, 2 pages, recto and verso, 5" by 8", no place, August 23, 1855. To "Mrs. Mordecai", the wife of Major Alfred Mordecai - a southern Jew, soldier and engineer then with the Delafield Commission sent to the Crimea to study European military systems. In part: *"...Next to yourself I believe your husband's absence fell most heavily upon me, and I gave him up to the good of the service and to the gratification of his professional zeal, hoping that he would see all that was desirable and then return 'as bees fly home.' Like yourself I am not advised of the route or time of departure from among the Norseman but have some hope that the Czar will smooth the path of their return."* From the Henry E. Luhrs Collection. Accompanied by LOA from PSA/DNA.
Estimate: $2,000-$3,000

25482   Jefferson Davis Autograph Letter Signed. Two pages, 5.25" x 7.25", no place, July 8, 1873, to Mesdames Fitzgerald and Ives. A personal letter that reads, in part: "I am yet in a state of doubt and perplexity, not able to leave for the country nor yet to go away for the rest...The happiness of our meeting cannot be destroyed by even the pain of separation for the sweet memory will go with me all the weary days and long miles which are before me..." It seems likely that the ladies he is writing to are Cora Semmes Ives, the widow of his aide-de-camp Joseph C. Ives, and Cora's sister, Clara Semmes Fitzgerald.

This letter is in Poor condition with staining, tears, and cellophane tape repairs, still very interesting. Typewritten transcript included. From the Henry E. Luhrs Collection. Accompanied by LOA from PSA/DNA.
Estimate: $600-$800

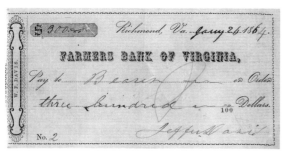

25481   Jefferson Davis Signed Check and Varina Davis Autograph Note Signed." This lot includes a signed check dated January 21, 1864, for $300 at the Farmers Bank of Virginia, it measures 6" x 3". It was only around a month after this check was signed that the first Northern prisoners arrived at the Confederate prison in Andersonville, Georgia. Accompanying the check is a 5.5" x 3.25" handwritten note from Varina Davis, she signs herself "*V. JD.*" The note has no place or date and it reads, "*Dear Sir, Please do not say to anyone that I have given you an autograph, I cannot spare another & it would inundate me with requests for them.*" A wonderful pair of signatures!

The check is in very fine condition; small tears present on the edges. The note is in very condition; usual folds are present. From the Henry E. Luhrs Collection. Accompanied by LOA from PSA/DNA.
Estimate: $2,500-$3,500

25483   Ambrose Everett Burnside Collection. This lot contains two autograph letters, signed, and one signature of Ambrose Everett Burnside. The two autograph letters are signed "*A.E. Burnside.*"

The first ALS is two pages, 4" x 6", personal letterhead, np, March 29, 1967. The content is routine, it is in response to a woman asking for a letter Burnside might have from General Sheridan.

The second ALS is two pages, 5" x 6", personal letterhead, Washington D.C., April 6, 1884. The content is routine.

The signature is a small piece of paper that has been clipped from a larger document, it measures 4.5" x 2.75". He signs it, "*A.E. Burnside R.I.*"

Burnside was a Union general during the Civil War, he fought in many key battles including the disastrous Union defeat at Fredericksburg.

The two letters are in very fine condition; the usual folds are present; they are both laid down on a larger sheet of paper. The signature is in very fine condition; slight soiling present on edges; signature has been clipped and laid down on a white card. From the Henry E. Luhrs Collection. Accompanied by LOA from PSA/DNA.
Estimate: $500-$700

25484 **Ambrose Everett Burnside Autograph Letter Signed** "*A.E. Burnside.*" One page, 4.4" x 7", Providence, Rhode Island, February 25, 1864. The content of the letter is routine, thanking the president of the Young Men's Christian Association for an honor they had bestowed on him. Burnside was a senator, politician, and Union General in the Civil War. His legacy lives on today by the popular facial hair feature named for him; "sideburns." The letter is in fine condition; usual folds are present; small stain on the lower right corner on obverse; slight soiling present on the fold lines. From the Henry E. Luhrs Collection. Accompanied by LOA from PSA/DNA.

Estimate: $400-$600

DORCHESTER IN 1630, 1776, AND 1855.

AN

ORATION

DELIVERED ON THE FOURTH OF JULY, 1855,

BY

EDWARD EVERETT.

ALSO

AN ACCOUNT OF THE PROCEEDINGS

IN DORCHESTER

AT THE CELEBRATION OF THE DAY.

BOSTON:
PRINTED AND PUBLISHED BY DAVID CLAPP.
EBENEZER CLAPP, JR.—184 WASHINGTON ST.
1855.

Maj. Ben: Perley Poore with the kind regards of his friend Marshall P. Wilder

25485 **Edward Everett Signed Book:** *Dorchester in 1630, 1776, and 1855. An Oration Delivered on the Fourth of July, 1865,* Major Benjamin Perley Poore's personal copy. (Boston: David Clapp, 1855), first edition, viii, 158 pages, half black calf over marbled boards, 8vo (6" x 9.25"), tipped into the front is an Autograph Quote Signed "*Washington was the great-*

est of good men and the best of great men. Edward Everett Cleveland, O. 13th April, 1861", also signed on a blank front page "*Maj. Ben: Perley Poore with the kind regards of his friend Marshall P. Wilder*". Book in very good condition with only minor shelf wear.

Also included in this lot is a one page Autograph Letter Signed "*Ben: Perley Poore*", one page, 5" x 8", Washington, February 12, 1886 and a period steel engraving. Both fine. From the Henry E. Luhrs Collection. Accompanied by LOA from PSA/DNA.

Estimate: $300-$400

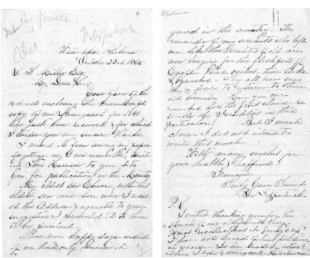

25486 **Alabama's Benjamin Fitzpatrick Writes After the War on Reconstruction and Slavery!** Autograph Letter Signed, 4 pages, recto and verso, Wetumpka, Alabama, October 23, 1866. To S.F. Miller. Some faint pencil notations on first page, else fine. Fitzpatrick was Alabama's governor, its senator, and the choice of his party to run with Stephen Douglas in 1860 - a nomination he declined. Here Fitzpatrick, who did not take a particularly active role in the Confederacy, writes shortly after the war about the "sad changes" which have come over the South. "*...It seems to me like a dream, and yet the startling reality stares in the face. Still I do not despond under the reverses that have overtaken us, and but for the dark future would set about with youthful ardor to rebuild my fortunes. There lies the rub. What is to be our fate if the Radicals obtain control of the Government as it seems they are doing! ... I have less to complain of than many others... A majority of my servants are still working with me and work very well... The remainder of my servants who left me, like the Israelites of old, are now longing for the flesh-pots of Egypt, their onions, their leeks and squashes. They all have seen me and desire to return to their old home. Have you ever remarked how the freed slaves resemble the Israelites in this particular?*" From the Henry E. Luhrs Collection. Accompanied by LOA from PSA/DNA.

Estimate: $300-$400

25487 **Confederate General Nathan Bedford Forrest Signature** "*N B Forrest*" on a lined sheet 5" x 2.5" laid down to a slightly larger page. Forrest was one of the Civil War's most successful cavalrymen and certainly an interesting character. Reputedly, he had 29 horses shot out from under him during the course of the war. His methods and tactics are still the object of study by modern military men. This piece is in very good condition with light toning and soiling. From the Henry E. Luhrs Collection. Accompanied by LOA from PSA/DNA.

Estimate: $1,000-$1,500

25488   James A. Hall Fabulous Autograph Letter Signed About Gettysburg. Fifteen pages, 8" x 10.5", Grand Army of the Republic letterhead, Damariscotta, Maine, January 23, 1886, to General Hoffman. James A. Hall was a captain in the Maine 2nd Light Artillery and participated in the Battle of Gettysburg. He was later brevetted brigadier general. This amazing letter is in response to an article Hoffman had written on Gettysburg, in part: "...*I congratulate you upon the very excellent manner, in which you so truthfully state what happened, on that memorable July 1st morning, and secondly I thank you heartily, for the justice done me and Halls battery, in placing us where we were, first ridge in rear of Willoughbys run. I had to fight John B. Batchelder for six long years, before he would put me there on his Maps and Charts he claiming I was on Middle ridge and then, only because we met on the field and I showed him, his error. Again, you are the first one to state the truth, and say, that Halls battery, was really unprotected on its right!...*" He goes on and on for pages, reminiscing about the battle and correcting various misconceptions about his participation in it. Another interesting item he mentions: "...*The fact is, (and I do not care to give it publicly now) Calef having been a gallant Soldier & Wadsworth being dead. Genl. Wadsworth ordered Calef- into my old place, and he refused point blank, to go there, for which Genl. W. wrote out charges and specifications after the battle, but they were never formally preferred...*" This letter would be a goldmine for the Civil War historian or researcher. Very good condition with some weakness at the folds, and holes in the upper left corner where originally pinned together. From the Henry E. Luhrs Collection. Accompanied by LOA from PSA/DNA.
Estimate: $400-$600

25490   Winfield Scott Hancock Letter on Civil War Artist Edwin Forbes. Letter Signed, 2 pages (1st & 4th integral leaves), 5.5" by 8.5", Governor's Island, New York, January 7, 1882. To Messrs. Estes & Lauriat. The first page is torn at bottom - but easily repaired; otherwise good. Here is an opportunity to acquire one of the Civil War's most distinguished soldiers discussing the work of the one of the War's most distinguished reportorial artists, Edwin Forbes, of the illustrated newspaper "Leslie's Weekly." "*I have carefully examined all the pictures by Mr. Forbes entitled 'Studies of the Great Army.' I, together with others, have always recognized their importance as a valuable addition to the history of the Civil War. Their reputation I think is well established - I will return them herewith.*" From the Henry E. Luhrs Collection. Accompanied by LOA from PSA/DNA.
Estimate: $250-$300

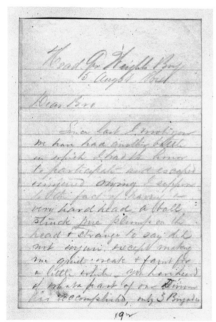

25489   Victor Jean Baptiste Girardey (1837-1864) Confederate General killed in action at Deep Bottom, Virginia, Rare War Date Autograph Letter Signed "*Victor*", four pages, 5" x 7", "*Head Quarters Wright's Brigade*", August 5, 1864 in pencil. Only eleven days before he was killed near Fussels' Mill while resisting a Federal assault on the east end of the Richmond defenses, Girardey writes to this brother, in full: "*Since last I wrote you we have had another battle in which I had the honor to participate and escaped uninjured owing I suppose to the fact of having a very hard head a ball struck me plump on the head & strange to say did not injure, except making me quite weak & faint for a little while - You have heard of what a part our Division has accomplished, only 3 Brigades retook the works held by two Yankee Corps & supported by another & slaughtered them like sheep. I never yet have seen so many Yankees dead on the same space of ground, they acknowledge a loss of 5000 men- We captured about 1200 prisoners & 18 flags, Our Division has done all the fighting for this Army at this point- since we have been here at Petersburg we have fought four (4) battles, and never had more than 3 Brigades engaged at any one time. We taken in three fine battles alone, 19 pieces of Artillery, 29 stand of Colors, about 5000 stand of small Arms & about 3700 prisoners, 300 horses, 50 wagons & 30 ambilance [sic], all this is exclusive of what we captured in the Campaign before reaching this point- this is doing very well- You have ere this heard of my promotion to Brigadier General, & at present in command of this Brigade- so you see I have at least gone up with a jump & trust I will stick- What do you think of your little Brother- no sarcasm. We also have other honors a pouring in and the Girardy boys- are come- If you can spare a little of your good old what you keep in your cellar, it would be very acceptable, & would no doubt add to comfort- very hot- & dry. My last I wrote you in relation to your forges, send them— My love to Mother & Angy kiss the Children for me. Your Affection[ate] Bro[ther] Victor Remember me to the Gals in the office- Tell Mac to Hurah*" French-born Girardey joined the Confederate Army as an aide-de-camp and soon rose to the rank of captain on the staff of General A. R. Wright. During the Petersburg operations he was transferred to the staff of General Mahone and so distinguished himself at the Battle of the Crater, four days later he was 'jumped' to the rank of brigadier general — the only Confederate officer upon whom such an honor was conferred. Neatly laid in to a larger sheet, light soiling and creases, else Fine condition. War-date missives are extremely scarce; this is one of the finest still in private hands. From the Henry E. Luhrs Collection. Accompanied by LOA from PSA/DNA.
Estimate: $1,500-$2,000

25491 Winfield Scott Hancock Sends His Photo - to the Secretary of War!

Autograph Letter Signed, 1 page, 5" by 8", Baltimore, November 25, 1865. To the famed Civil War and Lincoln photographer F. Gutekunst in Philadelphia. Fine. *"I received the Imperial Photograph yesterday: it was an excellent copy. The frame was very good and in excellent taste. I sent it to the Secretary of War today. Please send me our account at your leisure and oblige."* From the Henry E. Luhrs Collection. Accompanied by LOA from PSA/DNA.

Estimate: $300-$500

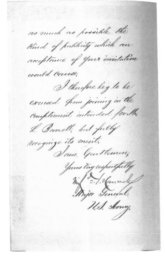

25492 General Winfield Scott Hancock Autograph Letter Signed

"Winfd. Scott Hancock Major General U.S. Army." Three pages, 4.25" x 7", New York City, May 25th, 1878. The letter was written to several men listed on the third page of the letter; the content is routine. The signature is very dark and bold. Hancock was a distinguished Union Army general. The letter is in very fine condition; light soiling has occurred; usual folds are present. From the Henry E. Luhrs Collection. Accompanied by LOA from PSA/DNA.

Estimate: $300-$500

25493 General Winfield Scott Hancock Autograph Letter Signed

"Winfd. S. Hancock." Two pages, 5" x 7.25", Governor's Island, New York, February 13, 1879. This letter was written to a Col. T.B. Parker; the content is routine. Hancock was distinguished in the Union Army, especially for his bravery at Gettysburg. He was wounded in the right leg, and continued to hold his post, and he was an inspiration for his troops. The letter is in very fine condition; usual folds are present, slight soiling has occurred. From the Henry E. Luhrs Collection. Accompanied by LOA from PSA/DNA.

Estimate: $300-$500

25494 Winfield Scott Hancock War-Date Autograph Letter About His Wound Sustained at Gettysburg.

Excellent Autograph Letter Signed (twice; in full and with initials), 2 pages, recto and verso, 5" by 8", on the letterhead of the "Headquarters Second Army Corps," Army of the Potomac, January 6, 1864. To the "Surgeon in Charge of Officers Hospital, Council "Woods', Philadelphia, Pa. In excellent condition.

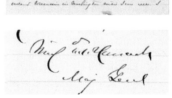

Sitting on his horse at the front of his lines during Pickett's Charge at Gettysburg, it wasn't until the final stages of the fighting that Hancock thought he'd been hit with a tenpenny nail. In fact a minie ball had passed through the pommel of his saddle and carried the bullet, and bits of foreign matter, into his right thigh. He was transported by ambulance to Westminster, then Baltimore, then Philadelphia. By October, although the wound was still open, he was able to walk with a cane and resume command of the Second Corps - a fact he reports to his surgeon here. *"My Dear Sir. I assumed command of my Corps Dec. 29th last. I have not entirely recovered; the Surgeons here, still probing my wound to the depth of six inches, but I consider myself practically well. My last Surgeon's certificate expired January 1/64."* A postscript specifically addressed to *"Surg. In Command...Philadelphia"* continues, "I write with the view of having you discharge me from your hospital, if you have not already done so. When I passed through Philadelphia, I expected to have returned for a few days, not Washington - but being ordered to remain in Washington until I am well. I failed to see you as I had intended." Hancock's wound continued to seep blood and fluid for the next year, however, forcing him from the field for weeks at a time. He finally retired from active duty during the Petersburg siege in November 1864. From the Henry E. Luhrs Collection. Accompanied by LOA from PSA/DNA.

Estimate: $900-$1,200

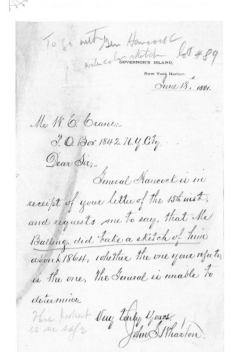

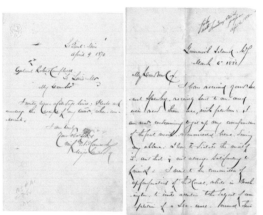

25496 General Winfield Scott Hancock- Five Autograph Letters Signed *"Winfd Scott"*. An amazing collection of five letters written and signed by this legendary Civil War general and presidential candidate of whom Ulysses S. Grant once said, "Hancock stands the most conspicuous figure of all the general officers who did not exercise a separate command. He commanded a corps longer than any other one, and his name was never mentioned as having committed in battle a blunder for which he was responsible."

Letter one: four pages, 5" x 8", Governor's Island letterhead, January 15, 1881, to Congressman S. S. Cox (of Ohio). Asking for assistance in getting a sea-wall built around the island, in part: *"Governor's Island lies in the 'jaws' of the two rivers- and the object of the Sea-Wall is sanitary...The filth from the two rivers is precipitated upon this island, now. With a Sea-wall, it would pass by instead of gathering upon the rocks..."* Fine condition with mailing folds.

Letter two: four pages, 5.5" x 8.25", Governor's Island, March 6, 1882, also to Congressman Cox. Another letter regarding the Sea-wall project. Very good condition with mailing folds and light soiling.

Letter three: one page, 5" x 8", St. Paul, April 4, 1870, to Colonel Robert Campbell. Asks for confirmation of receipt of recent letter. Very good condition with folds and some ink smearing.

Letter four: one page, 5.5" x 8.25", np, nd (9:10 a.m.), to Mr. Bader. In full: *"Will you let me look at your cards from the Aztec Dinner. I will send them right back."* Fine condition with folds, mounted by integral blank leaf to larger sheet.

Letter five: one page, 5.5" x 8.5", Governor's Island letterhead, January 31, 1882, to William A. Moore. An acknowledgement of receipt of a note. Fine condition with light folds and mounting traces on verso of blank integral leaf. From the Henry E. Luhrs Collection. Accompanied by LOA from PSA/DNA.
Estimate: $1,000-$1,200

25495 Winfield Scott Hancock, (1824-1886), Union General, an original watercolor bust portrait of Meade Signed *"Winfd. S. Hancock Major Genl. U. S. Vol[unteer]s Camp 2d. Corps."* 9" x 11", no place given [likely before Petersburg, Virginia], no date [c. October 1864]. This chest-up portrait is by the noted Norwegian-born artist *Ole Peter Hansen Balling (1823-1906)* who was in the area composing life studies his heroic oil painting, *Grant and His Generals,* which depicts Grant riding triumphantly beside twenty six of his generals, including Meade, and which was completed in 1865; it hangs at the National Portrait Gallery in Washington. In order to finish that dramatic work, Balling traveled to Union army encampments to compose life studies of his subjects. In the autumn of 1864, he spent five weeks in and around City Point, Virginia for the purpose of painting life portraits of Grant and his field officers. He also painted Philip Sheridan while the latter was in service in the Shenandoah Valley, as well as William Sherman and George H. Thomas, in Washington, after the war. The finished painting was published to raise funds for the Sanitary Commission, a private organization aiding sick and wounded soldiers. After comparing the sketch of Hancock here to his representation in *Grant and His Generals,* it appears to be quite likely that this was a study for that painting. The painting is accompanied by a letter from Hancock's assistant, John S. Wharton, A.L.S., one page, 5.25" x 8.5", Governor's Island, New York, June 18, 1881 to W. C. Crane of New York noting that *"General Hancock is in receipt of your letter.... and requests me to say that Mr Balling did take a sketch of him about 1864; whether the on your [sic] refer to, is the one, the General is unable to determine...* Ole Peter Hansen Balling was born in Oslo, and emigrated to New York in 1856. He also painted portraits of John Brown, James Garfield, and Chester A. Arthur, all of which hang in the National Portrait Gallery. *Provenance:* the Oliver R. Barrett Lincoln Collection, Parke-Bernet Galleries, February 20, 1952, Lot 489. Feint toning, pin holes at extreme corners, minor age wear, but the color remains quite vibrant and a clear, dark signature. Fine condition.

Please Note: A similar study of General George G. Meade by Balling also appears in this catalog. From the Henry E. Luhrs Collection. Accompanied by LOA from PSA/DNA.
Estimate: $3,000-$5,000

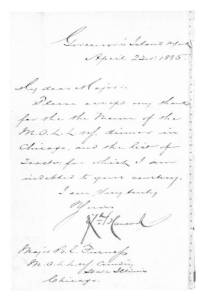

25497 General Winfield Scott Hancock-Two Autograph Letters Signed and one Letter Signed, all *"Winfd Hancock"*. The first ALS: two pages, 5" x 8", Governor's Island, New York, January 15, 1879, to D. F. Seeger, president of the Charity Association. He sends thanks and regrets for an invitation to the Flower Party of the YMCA of New York. Known to his colleagues as "Hancock the Superb," he was named after General Winfield Scott under whom he served in the Mexican War. Fine condition, light folds and minor soiling, hinged to a larger sheet.

Second ALS: two pages, 5" x 8", Governor's Island letterhead, January 20, 1880, to the same individual as above. Sending regrets for having mislaid an invitation to a party. Fine condition with light folds and soiling on the first page.

The LS: one page, 5" x 7.25", Governor's Island, New York, April 23, 1885, to Major N. E. Furness. Winfield sends thanks for a menu and list of toasts from a dinner in Chicago. Very good condition with light soiling and binding holes at the right edge. From the Henry E. Luhrs Collection. Accompanied by LOA from PSA/DNA.
Estimate: $500-$700

5" x 8", Headquarters 1st Corps., Washington, December 7, 1864, to Senator J. W. Grimes. A letter of transmittal for Orders and Circulars (not present) regarding the First Corps. Hancock was a career U.S. Army officer who served with distinction in the Civil War and later ran unsuccessfully for president. Fine condition with light folds and mounting traces to verso of integral blank leaf.

The second: five pages, 7.75" x 9.75", New York, February 10, 1873, to General J. W. Hofman of Philadelphia. In reply to a letter regarding the omission of Hofman's command in Hancock's official report of the Wilderness, in part: "...must be attributed to the neglect of those of my subordinates under whose immediate command you were, who failed to submit to me their reports of operations in that battle..." This battle took place on May 5-7, 1864, in Virginia against Robert E. Lee. Fine condition with mailing folds.

Also included is a fine, vintage engraving of Hancock, likely from the period of his presidential campaign. From the Henry E. Luhrs Collection. Accompanied by LOA from PSA/DNA.
Estimate: $400-$500

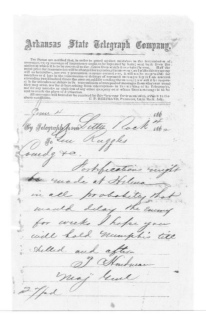

25499 Thomas C. Hindman Autograph Document Signed *"T. Hindman Maj. Genl."* Two pages, 5" x 8.25", Arkansas State Telegraph Company, Little Rock, Arkansas, June 4, 1862. Major General Hindman sent this telegraph to General Ruggles, it reads, *"Fortifications might be made at Helena in all probability that would delay the enemy for weeks I hope you will hold Memphis till shelled and after-"* Hindman was a commander in the Confederate Army and was one of the leading voices for Arkansas' succession; he was a member of the infamous "Fire Eaters" who more or less fueled the conflagration which would be the Civil War. He was assassinated in 1868.

The document is in very fine condition; slight tears and holes present on left edge. From the

Henry E. Luhrs Collection. Accompanied by LOA from PSA/DNA.
Estimate: $500-$700

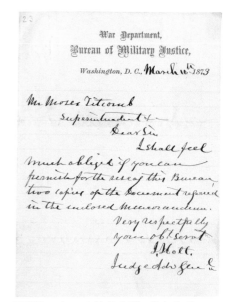

25500 Joseph Holt: A War-Date Letter of the Union Judge Advocate General. Autograph Letter Signed Signed " *J. Holt*", as Judge Advocate General, 1 page, 5" x 8", on the letterhead of the War Department, Bureau of Military Justice, Washington, March 10, 1873. To Moses Titcomb, Superintendent of the Senate Document Room. In fine condition. With typed transcription. Judge Holt could, if he wanted, hold a person in arrest without writ of habeas corpus; less terrible here, he chases a Senate document. In full: *"I shall feel much obliged if you can furnish for the use of this Bureau two copies of the Document referred in the enclosed memorandum."* From the Henry E. Luhrs Collection. Accompanied by LOA from PSA/DNA.
Estimate: $400-$500

25498 General Winfield Scott Hancock Two Letters Signed both with his stylized *"Winfd Hancock"* signature. The first: one page,

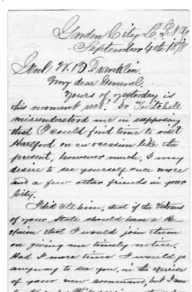

25501 Joseph Hooker criticizes using Federal troops to break the Strike of 1877

Civil War General Joseph Hooker (1814-1879) Autograph Letter Signed, "*J. Hooker Maj. Genl.*", nine pages, 5" x 8", Garden City, New York, December 20, 1877 to his former comrade-in-arms William B. Franklin (1823-1903). Hooker writes on the massive railroad strikes that crippled the nation during the summer of 1877 and the use of federal troops to break the strike.

"*You doubtless know that I was educated for a regular, or trained soldier, and until the War of the Rebellion, I had been made to believe that the strength of a Military power lay in its trained troops, and my convictions remained unchanged until the battle of Williamsburg... opened my eyes to my error. In that fight the greater part of my troops were under fire for the first time, and many of whom, I have no doubt, had never before heard the report of the discharge of a musket, and yet they went in to a battle at the earliest dawn, at one time waged with unusual violence, and stuck to it until night came, as I had never seen troops before freeze to a fight. In previously disciplining my command at Blandensburg I had remarked with how much more ease and satisfaction they were controlled, and educated than were the class of men who were recruited to fill the ranks of our regular Army. Besides they appeared to me to be more identified with our institution than the men who composed the rank and file in the regular Army, and the feeling inspired by their conduct in the first battle continued to strengthen to the end of the Rebellion, until now as it ever will be, I trust, my conviction that the strength, and perpetuity of our Nation depends upon our Militia, over any other power in the Nation, and until all our people realize this fact as I do, I fear our Militia forces will not receive the consideration from our Officials they so justly deserve. It is true strong influences were operating to the feeling of all our loyal people in the last war, as home, Country everything held dear, were involved in the issue which was not the case in the Strikers War last Summer, but under discreet intelligent Officers, I contend that the Militia are more easily influenced, and governed than corresponding numbers in an Army of trained bands... My only regret that Gov. Hartfrant was not at home in the incipient movements of the disturbers of the peace in your State, as then his prompt action would doubtless have prevented, an organization of the Mob which threatened to disturb, not only our business, but almost the existence of the Government itself... I do not now believe that it will be unwise in us to anticipate a more frequent recurrence of storms in our political World than we have yet experienced... I do not believe in the policy inaugurated by Genl. Grant in employing Soldier, and Bayonets to control, and take part in the affairs of States, and I believe it will be highly improper, and impolitic to employ the Army in any such work... We require a small standing Army to hold our Forts, and frontiers that it is all... the facilities the Rail Roads furnish us for massing troops, it is a question to my mind whether it is not better or a nation to rely on muscle, more than masonry for its defense. The latter can easily be destroyed, the former never...*"

A truly fine letter in which a former subordinate criticizes policies of his ex-commander in favor of the supremacy of states' rights. Reconstruction had come to an end in 1877 when the last federal troops left the former Confederate States. The experience left many, both in North and South, angry and bitter. The growing conflict between capital and labor in the rapidly industrializing nation would again test the limits of federal authority. *Together with* a second **Joseph Hooker Autograph Letter Signed,** *J. Hooker Maj. Genl.*", two pages, 5" x 8", Garden City, New York, September 4, 1878, again to General William B. Franklin, discussing a reunion. Very light creases, else very fine. Two fine letters between former comrades. From the Henry E. Luhrs Collection. Accompanied by LOA from PSA/DNA.
Estimate: $1,500-$2,000

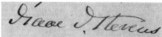

25502 Isaac I. Stevens Collection.
This lot contains seven items signed by Isaac I. Stevens. Stevens was the first governor of Washington Territory and a general in the Union Army. He was a staunch supporter of Franklin Pierce, a position which helped him gain his position as governor. Stevens was killed in action during the Civil War, charging forward with his troops at the Battle of Chantilly. The inventory of the lot is as follows:

Autograph Letter Signed "*I.I. Stevens.*" One page, 5.75" x 7.25", Washington, April 14, 1851. The content is routine.

Autograph Letter Signed "*I.I. Stevens.*" One page, 7.8" x 10", Washington, April 11, 1851. The content is routine.

Autograph Letter Signed "*I.I. Stevens.*" One page, 4.6" x 7.2", Washington, April 19, 1851. The content of this letter is routine.

Autograph Letter Signed "*I.I. Stevens.*" One page, 7.5" x 10", Washington, April 12, 1851. The content is regarding the Office Coast Survey, involving various plates of the tides of Cat Island and Boston Harbor.

Autograph Letter Signed "*I.I. Stevens.*" One page, 5" x 7.75", Washington, April 19, 1851. The content is routine.

Autograph Letter Signed "*Isaac I. Stevens.*" One page, 7.5" x 10", Boston, Massachusetts, October 11, 1852. The letter is written to Prof. James Henry, in which Stevens endorses Lt. Montgomery Hunt in his pursuit to be appointed the Inspector of the New York Light House District.

Clipped Signature, signed "*Isaac I. Stevens.*" This 2.5" x 1" slip of paper was once a part of a free franked envelope. The word "free" is still visible above Stevens' signature.

The items in this collection are in fine condition on average; the signature is slightly yellowing; otherwise excellent! From the Henry E. Luhrs Collection. Accompanied by LOA from PSA/DNA.
Estimate: $600-$800

200   Session One, Auction #626 • Monday, February 20, 2006 • 5:00 PM

A 19.5% Buyer's Premium ($9 min.) Applies To All Lots

25503   General Joseph Hooker Autograph Letter Signed and Two Signatures. First, the letter: signed *"J. Hooker Maj. Genl"*, four pages, 5" x 8", Astor House letterhead, [New York], October 4, 1873, to General H(enry) M. Cist. Concerns errors in the printed account of a speech he made at Literary Hall in Pittsburgh, in part: *"...such a botch was made of it...This is not the first time the [Army and Navy] Journal has wilfully misquoted me and no doubt designedly..."* He refers several times to Ward and Sheridan about whom he says: *"...It is only charitable to suppose that he didn't know what he was talking about..."* Fine condition with light folds and a couple of tiny minor stains. Originally purchased from Walter R. Benjamin Autographs.

One of the two Signatures is signed *"J. Hooker Maj. Genl"* on a 3.75" x 1.5" slip laid down to an album page and is in fine condition. The other is signed *"Joseph Hooker Maj Gnl"* on a lined sheet laid down to a small card 3.5" x 1.5", very good condition with light soiling.

To round out this impressive lot, a group of vintage clippings and two nice engravings of Hooker. These portraits would be excellent for matting with these signatures. From the Henry E. Luhrs Collection. Accompanied by LOA from PSA/DNA.
Estimate: $400-$500

25504   Confederate General John D. Imboden War-Date Autograph Letter Denying Depredations! Autograph Letter Signed (twice: "J.D. Imboden" and with initials"), as *Brigadier General,* 2 pages, recto and verso, 7.5" by 10", H.Q. Valley District, August 27, 1863. To Governor John Letcher of Virginia. The spine of the integral leaf has been strengthened - and the condition is fine. With a typed transcription. Here Imboden, a school teacher and lawyer before he entered the Confederate service as a gunner, defends the men under his command. He denies that soldiers with Major Gilmore - an unusually active and undisciplined man, as it happens - were guilty of plundering and burning towns. *"...The fact is this, that the whole lower valley, and all along the Blue Ridge the country is filled with deserters from the army, and these are the scoundrels who commit these outrages, and to avoid arrest claim to belong to the nearest command, and in this case Major Gilmore happening to be on duty in that part of the country, every villain who has deserted his colors, will pass himself as one of Gilmore's men, whenever questioned. The Major has informed me of his purpose to lynch some of*

these fellows, a proceeding in which I will sustain himself, as I believe it to be the only means of breaking up the rascality."   From the Henry E. Luhrs Collection. Accompanied by LOA from PSA/DNA.
Estimate: $1,000-$1,500

25505   Joseph E. Johnston Autograph Letter Signed *"J.E. Johnston."* Two pages, 5" x 8", Washington D.C., February 5, 1886. The letter is written to a C.S. Hart Esq., it explains Johnston's regret that he is unable to help Hart run for political office. Joseph E. Johnston was one of the most senior generals for the Confederacy during the Civil War, and after the war ended he served as Commissioner of Railroads under Grover Cleveland.

The letter is in very good condition; slightly soiled on the edges; usual folds are present; separation occurring on the vertical fold. From the Henry E. Luhrs Collection. Accompanied by LOA from PSA/DNA.
Estimate: $500-$700

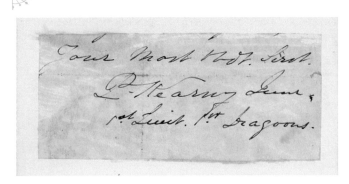

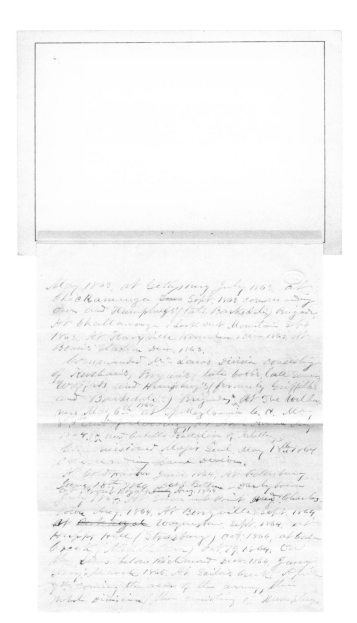

25506   General Philip Kearny Signature. Kearny signs on this 3.5"
x 1.5" piece of paper as "*P. Kearny Junior 1st Lieut. 1st Dragoons.*" He
received this rank in the year 1837. Kearny was killed at the Battle of
Chantilly in 1862. Kearny was a brave soldier who was responsible for
the use of unit insignias; he was also known to ride into battle with his
reins in his teeth bearing his pistol in his left hand. A fierce sight. The
signature is in fine condition; the glue used to lay down the signature has
soaked through and stained the obverse slightly. From the Henry E. Luhrs
Collection. Accompanied by LOA from PSA/DNA.
Estimate: $400-$500

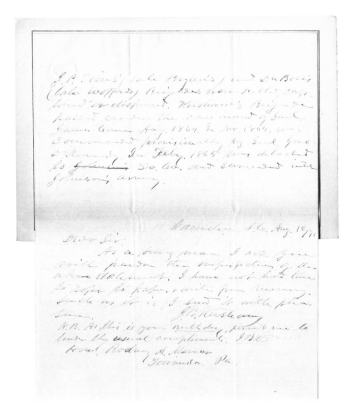

**25507   Joseph B. Kershaw (1822-1894), Confederate Major
General in the Civil War, biographical content Autograph Letter
Signed** twice "*J. B. Kershaw*" and "*Joseph Brevard Kershaw*" three pages,
7.75" x 9.75", Camden, South Carolina, August 12, 1877 to Rodney A.
Marcus summarizing his Civil War career. After apologizing for the "*imper-
fections... I have not had time to refer to paper, & write form memory...*"
he summarizes his impressive career, in part: "*While Colonel participated
in Battles of Ft. Sumter, April 1861, and Manassas and Bull Run July
18 to 21, 1861... As Brigadier engaged at Williamsburg... Savage State
and Malverne [sic] Hill... Maryland Heights (Harper's Ferry) Sept. 1862
Sharpesburg [sic] (Antietam) Sept. 1862... Stone wall at Fredericksburg...
At Chancellorsville, and Fredericksburg May 1863, at Gettysburg July
1863, at Chickamauga Sept. 1863...Chattanooga & Look Out Mountain...
Knoxville... Commanded Mr Lewis' Division consisting of Kershaw's
Bryan's... Wofford and Humphrey's... Brigades & at the Wilderness May
6th, 1864, at Spotsylvania C. H. may 8th '64... Cold Harbor... Petersburg...
Deep Bottom & Darbytown at Front Royal... On the Lines below Richmond
Decr. 1864... Sailor's [sic] Creek, April 7th covering the rear of the army...*"
More fine content. Neatly tipped to a larger sheet, usual folds, else very
fine condition. After the war, Kershaw went on to serve as an attorney
and politician. Great recollections of a distinguished military career.
Despite a long life, for some reason Kershaw remains exceptionally
scarce — and this is a fine specimen. From the Henry E. Luhrs Collection.
Accompanied by LOA from PSA/DNA.
Estimate: $2,000-$3,000

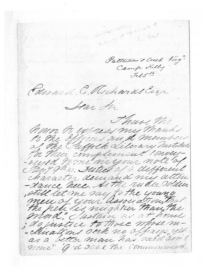

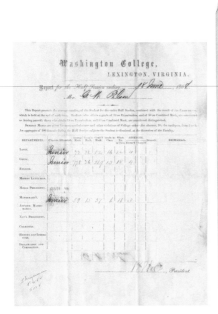

25508 **Rufus King Jr. Autograph Letter Collection.** Four letters, of varying sizes, written and signed by Rufus King. Two are on Wisconsin Active Militia Station; the other two are on personal stationery; they date between 1861 and 1863. Rufus King Jr. was an officer in the Union Army during the Civil War. He was awarded a medal of honor and brevetted Captain in June of 1862 for the bravery and courage he displayed during a seventeen hour stand off at White Oak Swamp Bridge in Virginia. His actions, and the actions of his unit, prevented the bridge from being taken by a superior Confederate force. The letters in this lot are of routine content. Rufus King served in the army until 1871; he was a brave officer and he is boldly represented by this lot. The letters in this lot are in fine condition on average; usual folds are present and slight soiling is along the fold lines. The letter dated October 1863, however, is in very good condition; several small holes as well as light staining mar the text. From the Henry E. Luhrs Collection. Accompanied by LOA from PSA/DNA.

Estimate: $400-$600

25509 **Brig. General Frederick W. Lander Autograph Letter Signed** *"Fred W. Lander."* Two pages, 7.5" x 9.8", Camp Kelly, Patterson's Creek Virginia, February 25. Lander was a brigadier general in the Union Army during the Civil War. A civil engineer by trade, he was assigned by the government to secretly investigate the southern states in order to evaluate their strength. He was given this assignment because he had successfully crossed the continent five times and lived through many hardships including Indian attacks. He was part of several key Union battles, and was responsible for a successful skirmish at Blooming Gap against a superior force of Confederate soldiers. Lander died suddenly in 1862, and his death was a huge loss for the Union Army. Lander wrote this letter to an institute in his home state of Massachusetts; it reads in part, *"As the ruder soldier still let me say to the young men of your Association, "That the pen is mightier than the sword.".. .and whether with pen or word may her young men feel what I endeavor to embody in verse- Go forth! And on her shining scroll write one enduring act of thine: God gives the birthright of the soul But our own hands must make the sign."* The letter is in very fine condition; usual folds are present; pencil notations present on first and second pages; signature is bold and dark. Accompanying this letter is a handsome engraving of General Lander. From the Henry E. Luhrs Collection. Accompanied by LOA from PSA/DNA.

Estimate: $1,500-$2,000

25510 **General Robert E. Lee Washington College Document Signed** *"R E Lee".* One page, 8" x 10.5", partly printed, Lexington, Virginia, June 18, 1868. This is basically a "report card" for a student named G. W. Pilson for the half session, signed by Lee as president of the college. Mr. Pilson took Latin (11th of 22 in class), Greek (13th of 18 in class), and Mathematics (1st of 11 in class). This venerable institution is now known as Washington and Lee University, named after George Washington who provided its first large endowment, and Robert E. Lee who served as president from just after the Civil War until his death in 1870. Very good condition with folds, light soiling, and fold over ink transference affecting the signature a bit. Also included in this lot is a period engraving of Lee and a printed 1907 centenary tribute by Theodore Roosevelt. From the Henry E. Luhrs Collection. Accompanied by LOA from PSA/DNA.

Estimate: $4,000-$6,000

25511 General Robert E. Lee Signature "*R E Lee*" clipped from a document or letter, 2" x 1", laid down to a card and then to an album page. Lee, although fighting against superior forces, managed a number of victories during the Civil War and is one of the true icons of that war. Afterwards, he urged reconciliation and spent the rest of his life as president of Washington College (now Washington and Lee University) in his beloved Virginia. Very good condition with the ink notation "#212" written in another hand just above his signature. From the Henry E. Luhrs Collection. Accompanied by LOA from PSA/DNA.
Estimate: $1,000-$1,500

25512 John Logan Signature and Mary Logan Autograph Letter Signed "*Mrs. John A. Logan.*" This lot features two items that are related to the great General John Logan. The first is a 3.6" x 2.5" card signed by the general himself. It reads, "*Yours Truly, John A. Logan, Maj. Gen.*" The second item is a letter written by Logan's wife Mary, it measures 5" x 6.1" and is handwritten on 2 pages. The date it was written was Jan. 10, 1901 from Washington, D.C. The content is patriotic and reads in part, "*I also enclose an engraving of my son which we consider very fine and I should be glad if father & son could appear together as an object lesson in patriotism and to show the tirade on the Sons of great men is outrageous and unworthy of Americans.*" John Logan is well known for founding the holiday we celebrate as Memorial Day. He was also the premiere volunteer General in the Union Army. Both items are in Fine condition; the only problem being pencil notations on the letter and card. From the Henry E. Luhrs Collection. Accompanied by LOA from PSA/DNA.
Estimate: $400-$500

25513 James Longstreet (1821-1904), Confederate General, Autograph Letter Signed, "*James Longstreet*", two pages, 8" x 10", Gainesville, Georgia, September 28, 1894 to Gettysburg Union General Daniel Sickles inquiring about publishing houses for his book *From Manassas to Appomattox: Mmemoirs of the Civil War in America.* At the suggestion of his son, Longstreet writes Sickles informing him that: "*My M[anu]s[cript] is ready and has been except the final review, but friends have advised me not to publish until business affairs are more settled. Some have written that the Publishing companies are not in condition to put out an important work. It has just occurred to me that you may be better prepared to inform me of such matters. I have thought of Longman, Green & Co of New York, and Houghton Mifflin & Co of Boston. The work may be expensive in getting maps and photographs, but it will be better, in the end, to have it complete. I have some confidence, that you will be satisfied with my Gettysburg, for I have tried to make a finish of it, and I think make it clear that it was your move that saved the field...*" An incredible letter to a former adversary. Longstreet faced Sickles on the second day of Gettysburg. Sickles had moved his III Corps forward (without orders) to a more advantageous position. Longstreet's corps slammed directly in Sickles' position. The fighting that ensued at Devil's Den, the Wheatfield, Little Round Top and the Peach Orchard virtually destroyed Sickles' corps. Sickles' leg was shattered by a cannonball and was amputated. Longstreet's men were eventually pushed back after the heroic Union defense of Little Round Top. Longstreet would publish his book two years after this letter was written; J. B. Lippincott of Philadelphia handled the work. Usual folds, light chipping at right margin, else fine condition. A fun association piece showing the accessibility of former enemies to one another in advancing years. From the Henry E. Luhrs Collection. Accompanied by LOA from PSA/DNA.
Estimate: $800-$1,200

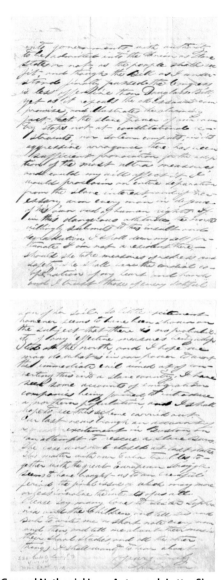

25514   James Longstreet (1821-1904) Confederate Civil War General, Autograph Letter Signed, "*J Longstreet*", one page, 5.75" x 9", Gainsville, Georgia, October 22, 1892, to Colonel D.C. Pavey of Portsmouth, New Hampshire regretting that he has "*...no photo on hand, and find it impossible to have them, friends calling oftener then it is convenient to have them... I cannot say if I can meet your wishes in regard to Gen. F. J. Porter...*" It was Fitz John Porter's reluctance to attack Longstreet's corps during the Second Bull Run campaign that resulted in Porter's court martial in 1863. Fine condition. From the Henry E. Luhrs Collection. Accompanied by LOA from PSA/DNA.

Estimate: $400-$600

25515   General Nathaniel Lyon Autograph Letter Signed "*N. Lyon.*" One page (last page of a longer letter; the rest is missing), 7.75" x 9.75", np, nd. The content of this letter reflects the staunch attitude Lyon held regarding succession, he greatly opposed Missouri's succession and even disguised himself as a farm woman in order to spy on the troops training for home defense. Lyon was the first Union General to be killed in the Civil War. The letter reads in part, "*…with authority to be admitted into the Union as Slave States or not, as the people shall see fit, and though the Bill as I understand finally passed the Congress, is less offensive than Douglass' Bill, yet as it repeals the Missouri Compromise, and illustrates the alarming fact, that the slave power of our country stops not at constitutional restraints, nor solemn compacts… If in this dangerous attitude, the north willingly submits to this insult and degradation, I shall deem myself fortunate I am not a resident there…*"

The letter is in fine condition; usual folds are present; water damage stains present on lower edge of the verso; the letter is not complete, we only have the final page of what was a longer letter. From the Henry E. Luhrs Collection. Accompanied by LOA from PSA/DNA.

Estimate: $3,000-$4,000

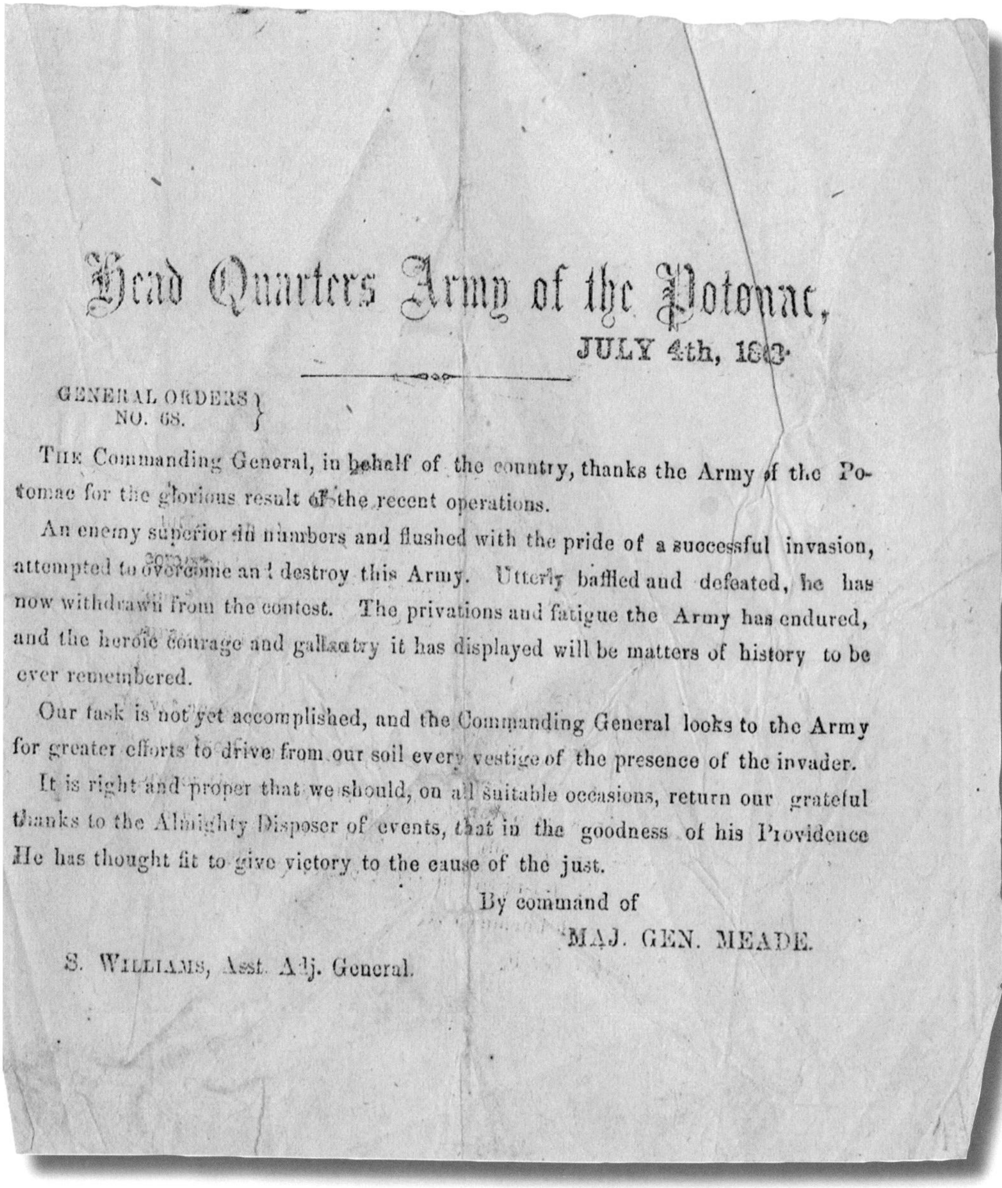

Head Quarters Army of the Potomac,

JULY 4th, 1863·

GENERAL ORDERS }
NO. 68. }

THE Commanding General, in behalf of the country, thanks the Army of the Potomac for the glorious result of the recent operations.

An enemy superior in numbers and flushed with the pride of a successful invasion, attempted to overcome and destroy this Army. Utterly baffled and defeated, he has now withdrawn from the contest. The privations and fatigue the Army has endured, and the heroic courage and gallantry it has displayed will be matters of history to be ever remembered.

Our task is not yet accomplished, and the Commanding General looks to the Army for greater efforts to drive from our soil every vestige of the presence of the invader.

It is right and proper that we should, on all suitable occasions, return our grateful thanks to the Almighty Disposer of events, that in the goodness of his Providence He has thought fit to give victory to the cause of the just.

By command of
MAJ. GEN. MEADE.

S. WILLIAMS, Asst. Adj. General.

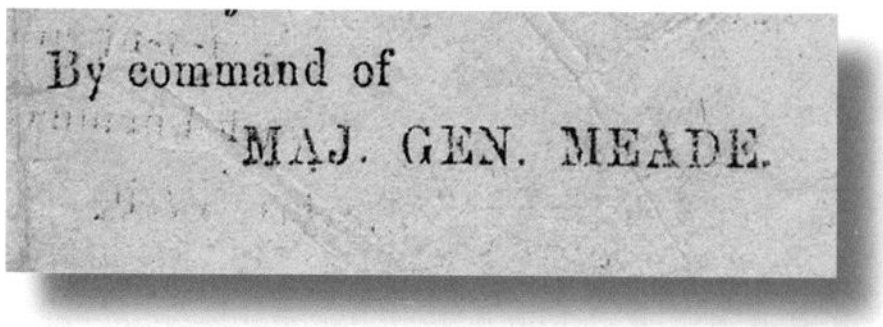

By command of
MAJ. GEN. MEADE.

25516   The only known copy of the first report of victory at Gettysburg — Meade congratulates his army, July 4, 1863 (George Meade) (1815-1872) Union Major General in the Civil War, fine content printed Document, one page, 5.5" x 61", "*Head Quarters Army of the Potomac*" [Gettysburg, Pennsylvania], July 4, 1863, a rare copy of General Order 68 congratulating Union forces on their hard-won victory at Gettysburg. The document reads: "*The Commanding General, on behalf of the country, thanks the Army of the Potomac for the glorious result of the recent operations. An enemy superior in numbers and flushed with the pride of a successful invasion, attempted to overcome and destroy this Army. Utterly baffled and defeated, he has now withdrawn from the contest. The privations and fatigue the Army has endured, and the heroic courage and gallantry it has displayed will be matters of history to be ever remembered. Our task is not yet accomplished, and the Commanding General looks to the Army for greater efforts to drive from our soil every vestige of the presence of the invader. It is right and proper that we should, an all suitable occasions, return our grateful thanks to the Almighty Disposer of events, that in the goodness of his Providence He has thought fit to give victory to the cause of the just. By command of MAJ. GEN. MEADE.*" This broadside is a "Holy Grail" of Civil War collecting as it is the only example known to remain extant. It also represents the earliest printed report on the victory at Gettysburg. A supreme rarity from the battle that changed American history, a cornerstone document.   From the Henry E. Luhrs Collection.
Estimate: $30,000-$50,000

Office Survey N. & N. W. Lakes
Detroit April 12. 1860.

Wm. Buell & Son
17. Congress Street
Boston –

Dear Sir,

Your favor of the 9th inst. is received – also the telescopes sent per express. The french glass sent, is exactly the article I have been in search of, & is in all respects adapted to my purpose. Had I have seen it when first asking for telescopes, I would have sent for a number – as it is I will retain this, and you can complete for me the one you had nearly finished when you came across this one. This will make three received from you which will answer for the present – Please when you have completed the new one now in hand & sent it – forward your account for the three to Capt. I. C. Woodruff – specifying they were received by me. I am extremely obliged to you for all the trouble you have taken in this matter – Very truly yours

Geo. G. Meade
Capt. Top. Engrs.

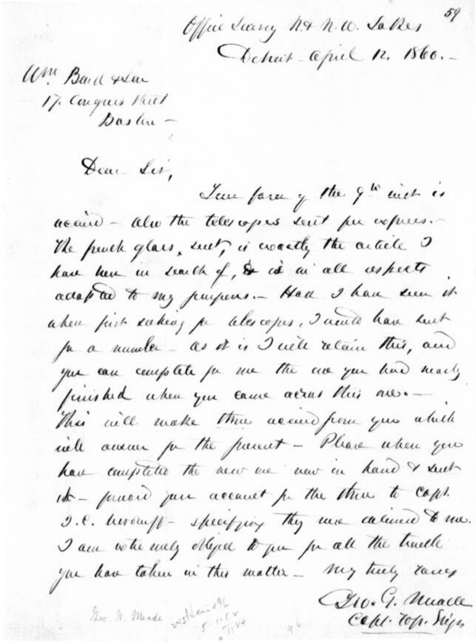

25517 General George Meade Autograph Letter Signed *"Geo. G. Meade Capt[ain]. Top[ograhpical]. S[urve]y[e]rs"* as captain, Topographical Engineers. One page, 7.5" x 9.75", Detroit, April 12, 1860, to Wm. Buell & Son. Meade, after the Mexican War, returned to his duties as a military engineer. This letter is in response to the receipt of a shipment of telescopes, in part: *"...the french glass sent, is exactly the article I have been in search of, & is in all respects adapted to my purpose...Please when you have completed the new one now in hand & sent it- forward your account for the three to Capt. I. C. Woodruff..."* In August of the following year, Meade's career would take off with a key promotion from Captain to Brigadier General in the Union Army. He would be promoted to major general for his gallant conduct at Fredericksburg. Meade would of course, make his most lasting impression leading Union forces at Gettysburg. Light soiling, else Fine. From the Henry E. Luhrs Collection. Accompanied by LOA from PSA/DNA.
Estimate: $700-$900

Head-Quarters, Army of the Potomac,
Dec. 29th 1863

My Dear Miss Harris –

I return you, your card & silk with my attempt to write my name – which you will perceive was not very successful & will not be very ornamental to your quilt. If you will favor me with some other pieces I will try again as I am desirous of evincing my sense of the compliment you have been pleased to pay me.

Most truly Yours
Geo. G. Meade
Maj Genl of Vols

Geo. G. Meade
Maj Genl of Vols

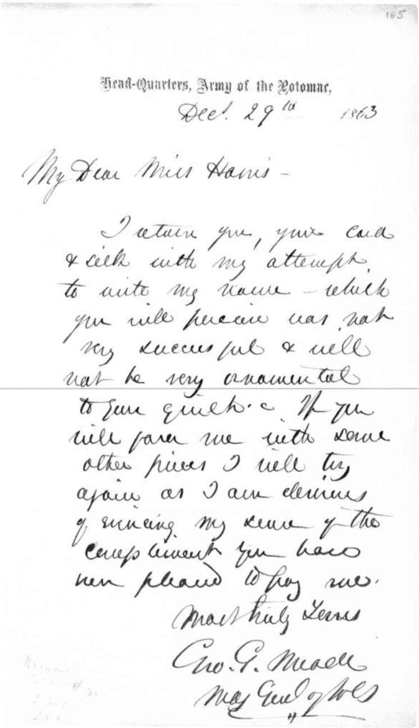

25518 George Meade Civil War Dated Autograph Letter Signed *"Geo. G. Meade Maj Genl".* One page, 5" x 8", Head-Quarters, Army of the Potomac letterhead, no place, December 29, 1863, to a Miss Harris. It reads: *"My Dear Miss Harris - I return you, your card and silk [not present] with my attempt to write my name- which you will perceive was not very successful & will not be very ornamental to your quilt. If you will favor me with some other pieces I will try again as I am desirous of evincing my sense of the compliment you have been pleased to pay me..."* During the time of the Civil War, autograph quilts were a popular pastime for the ladies left behind at the home front waiting for their sons and husbands to return from battle. Fine condition. From the Henry E. Luhrs Collection. Accompanied by LOA from PSA/DNA.
Estimate: $700-$900

1863
Philada. Sept. 24/63

Dear General –

Mr. McMillan of London, who is on a visit to this country, naturally desires to see & make the acquaintance of all distinguished men – I have therefore given him this note to you & beg you will do me the favor to grant him an interview.

Very truly Yours
Geo. G. Meade
Maj. Genl. USV

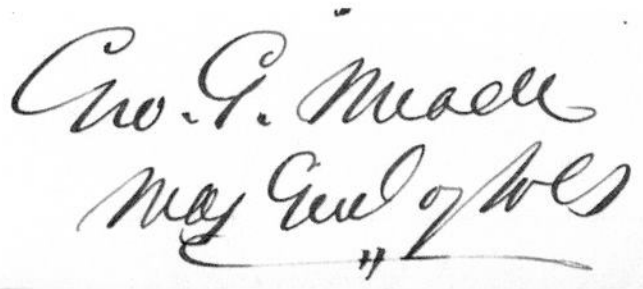

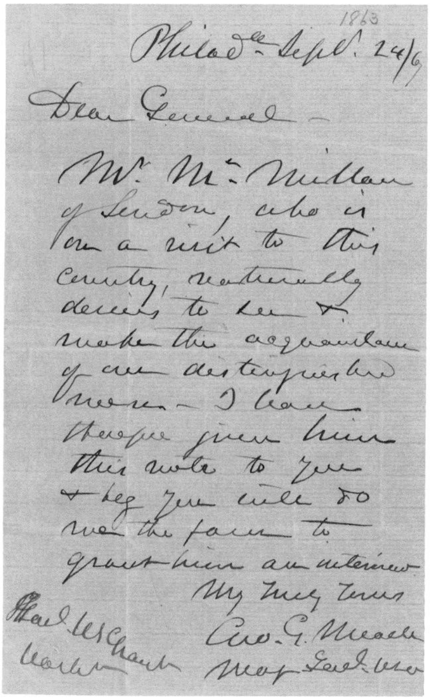

25519 George Meade War-Date Autograph Letter To Ulysses S. Grant! Autograph Letter Signed, as Major General, 1 page, 4.5" by 7", Philadelphia, September 24, 1863. To Major General Ulysses S. Grant. In fine condition. An odd wartime letter: here the patrician Meade asks "Butcher" Grant to receive an Englishman desirous of meeting distinguished men. *"Dear General - Mr. McMillan of London, who is on a visit to this country, naturally desires to see & make the acquaintance of all distinguished men - I have therefore given him this note to you & beg you will do me the favor to grant him an interview."* Grant was, at the time, engaged in the rescue of the beleaguered Union army under Rosecrans at Chattanooga. From the Henry E. Luhrs Collection. Accompanied by LOA from PSA/DNA.
Estimate: $600-$800

Geo. G. Meade
Maj. Genl. U.S.A.
Comdg. A.P.

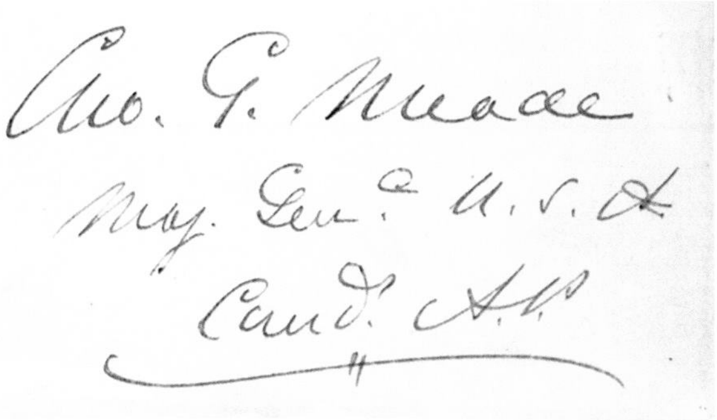

25520 George Meade Signature. 3.7" x 2.7" signature card, signed: *"Geo. G. Meade Major Gen. U.S.A."* George Meade is best known for defeating Robert E. Lee at the battle of Gettysburg. The signature is in Fine condition; no visible issues! From the Henry E. Luhrs Collection. Accompanied by LOA from PSA/DNA.
Estimate: $400-$500

Chas. G. Meade

25521   George Meade, Civil War General- Signature on 6" x 4.5" sheet,"*Geo. G. Meade Maj. Genl. U.S.A. Boston, May 13, 1871*". A career officer, Meade may be best known for defeating Robert E. Lee at the Battle of Gettysburg. Very Fine condition; just slight evidence of mounting traces on verso showing through. From the Henry E. Luhrs Collection. Accompanied by LOA from PSA/DNA.
Estimate: $400-$600

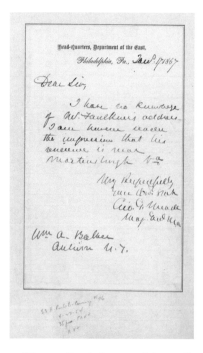

25522   General George Meade Autograph Letter Signed "*Geo. G. Meade Maj Genl*". One page, 5" x 8", Head-Quarters, Department of the East letterhead, Philadelphia, January 17, 1867. In part, "*...I have no knowledge of M. Faulkner's address- I am however under the impression that his residence is near Martinsburgh Va...*" Very Fine condition, hinged to a contemporary larger sheet. From the Henry E. Luhrs Collection. Accompanied by LOA from PSA/DNA.
Estimate: $500-$700

25523   George G. Meade, (1815-1872), Union General in the Civil War, victor of Gettysburg, Letter Signed "*George G. Meade*" one page, 7.75" x 9.75", Philadelphia, September 18, 1865 transmitting "*... a Monthly Return of the Headquarters, Military Division of the Atlantic for August 1865...*" Meade was mustered out of the volunteer service at the close of the Civil War, but remained with the regular army, and was appointed commander of the Military Division of the Atlantic. He served for some time in Atlanta during Reconstruction, but spent most of the reminder of his life in Philadelphia in a home donated by its citizens in thanks for his services to the country. Partial horizontal fold separations, else fine. From the Henry E. Luhrs Collection. Accompanied by LOA from PSA/DNA.
Estimate: $400-$450

25524   George Meade Signature. Signature card, signed: "*Geo. G. Meade Maj. Gen.*" It is dated November 23, 1864 from Headquarters of the Army of the Potomac. Meade was put in charge of this Army and held control until the end of the war. This unit was present at Lee's surrender at Appomattox. The signature is in Fine condition; there are pencil notations on the front of the card; the signature and writing are very dark and bold. Excellent! From the Henry E. Luhrs Collection. Accompanied by LOA from PSA/DNA.
Estimate: $400-$600

25525 George B. McClellan - Two Autographed Items. The first item is an Autograph Note Signed in pencil *"Geo B McClellan"*, front and back, on his personal calling card, 3.5" x 2.125", no place, no date, to a John Van Buren sending regrets about a dinner invitation. Original transmittal envelope included. The second item is an ink signature *"Sept 11 1863 Geo B McClellan Maj Gnl"* on a 4.5" x 1.5" sheet laid down to a another page to which is also attached an engraved image (likely from a *Harper's Weekly*). Both are in Very Good condition. From the Henry E. Luhrs Collection. Accompanied by LOA from PSA/DNA.

Estimate: $400-$500

25526 McClellan: *"I have made it a rule to avoid writing letters for publication..."* **George B. McClellan, (1826-1885), Union General, commanded Army of the Potomac,** fine content war-date Autograph Letter Signed *"Geo W McClellan"*, one page, 7.5" x 9.5", New York, May 20, 1863 to Charles C. Fulton., editor of the *Baltimore American"*; it denies permission to publish remarks made in a conversation between the two. Marked *"Private""I re-garded our conversation as entirely a private one, brought on in consequence of the note of introduction you brought to me from Judge [Montgomery] Blair. I have no idea of talking for the public nor that our interview should lead to any letters for publication. Your letter as a general thing expresses my views, which you have made in some cases rather stronger & wider than I intended, & in others less so. But, for reasons which I need not explain, I have made it a rule to avoid writing letters for publication, & have sought to remain as quite as possible, and I do not feel that the time has yet arrived for me to depart from my custom, and I therefore request that my conversation may not be regarded as a subject for publication."* McClellan had been sidelined by the Lincoln Administration amid accusations that he did not prosecute the war to the fullest extent as he was more concerned with his supply lines than going into battle. Viewed by many as a potential po-litical opponent of Lincoln in the 1864 election, he was continually asked for his political views. Fulton had written to McClellan to correct what he termed as the "general misapprehension prevailing as to your views on... the vigor prosecution of the war." Fulton had been led to understand that McClellan viewed any compromise with the South as "ridiculous" and that

he denied any connection with the Copperheads. Light marginal ton-ing and a minor chip, usual folds, else fine. Offered together with a cut **Signature** *"Geor B. McClellan Maj. Genl. USA"* on a 7" x 2" mounted slip of paper. Fine. Also offered together with an **A.L.S. of his son, New York Mayor, George B. McClellan,** two pages, 5" x 7.75", [New York], January 23, [19]17 declining a speaking engagement. Fine. Together, three pieces. Excellent content muzzling someone who wanted to publish the views of Lil Mac! From the Henry E. Luhrs Collection. Accompanied by LOA from PSA/DNA.

Estimate: $1,000-$1,500

25527 John S. Mosby "The Gray Ghost" Autograph Note Signed *"Jno S Mosby"*. One page, 8" x 4.5", lined paper, no place, no date. In reply to an autograph request: *"Dear Sir Your favor has been recd requesting my autograph which is subscribed. Very Respectfully Your Obt Servant..."* Mosby was a Confederate guerrilla fighter in the Civil War, known for his ability to strike fast and to elude his pursuers. Very Good condition; minor ink transfer where folded, light stains, mounting traces on verso. From the Henry E. Luhrs Collection. Accompanied by LOA from PSA/DNA.

Estimate: $700-$900

25528 Colonel John S. Mosby Autograph Letter Signed *"Jno. S. Mosby."* Three pages, 5.25" x 6.75", The Garde, Hartford, Connecticut, December 11, 1910. The content discusses his lecture tour, his cordial reception everywhere, and it reads in part, *"…Yesterday the head of Colt's Arms Factory sent his automobile for me (I have surrendered to the Automobile) & showed me over his factory. I told them that I had one bul-let still in me & four bullet holes made by Colts pistols & that I had a desire to see how they are made…"* John S. Mosby was a noted Cavalry leader in the Confederate Army, he was known as the "Grey Ghost" because of his ability to disappear and hide from Union troops along with his men. The letter is in very fine condition; usual folds are present; pencil nota-tions present on page 1,2 and 4. From the Henry E. Luhrs Collection. Accompanied by LOA from PSA/DNA.

Estimate: $800-$1,200

25529   Richard Bickerton Pernell, Viscount Lyons, (1817-1887), British Ambassador to the United States during the Civil War, Autograph Letter Signed *"Lyons"* two pages 4.5" x 7", Washington, June 20, 1861 to Second Assistant Secretary of State William Hunter, (1805-1886), asking him if *"...anything came of the enquiries concerning the two boys said to have been kidnapped by the Mater of the American Schooner 'Pebe'? Mr Seward's note to me on the subject is dated 30th April.."* Seward probably had more important affairs to attend to than to deal with a case of two kidnapped foreign nationals. Lyons' tenure as Minister to Washington was not uneventful, to say the least, as he attempted to balance British interests toward the North and South. He is, perhaps, best remembered for his masterful handling of the *Trent* affair — the capture, by the U.S. Navy, of two Confederate diplomats, aboard a British steamer bound for Europe, brought the U.S. and Britain very close to war. It was largely Lyons' tact and firmness that prevented the conflict. Mounting remnants on right margin of second page, else fine. From the Henry E. Luhrs Collection. Accompanied by LOA from PSA/DNA.
Estimate: $200-$300

25530   Benjamin Prentiss Autograph Document Signed *"Prentiss."* One-page handwritten document, measures 7.7" x 8.7", and is dated March 4, 1862. Benjamin Prentiss fought in the Mexican-American War and the Civil War, rising to the rank of General. He was captured at the Battle of Shiloh along with 2200 other Union troops. He is often credited with holding the Confederate Army at bay allowing General Grant to continue his trek into the South unfettered. The letter contains some battle content: it reads in part, *"...We had news last evening of another repulse of our forces at Manassas & the death of McLellan [sic]. The news generally credited for an hour or two was by the abolitionists well recd particularly because the death of Mc. Some even going so far as to say that if he was killed it could compensate for the loss of a battle..."*

The letter is in Good condition; it has the usual folds and some ink smearing. From the Henry E. Luhrs Collection. Accompanied by LOA from PSA/DNA.
Estimate: $2,000-$3,000

25531   Haldiman Sumner Putnam, (1835-1863), Civil War Colonel in the 7th New Hampshire Regiment, killed while leading his men on the attack of Fort Wagner, war date Autograph Letter Signed *"H. S.P."* four pages, 8" x 9.5", St. Augustine, Florida, April 26, 1863. A detailed letter describing his activities including witnessing a naval bombardment on Charleston, the burning of Jacksonville, and the use of Black troops in battle. He writes in part: *"...On arriving at Hilton Head your uncle was put in command of a brigade consisting of the three New Hampshire & 6th Conn. regmts.... we all went up to Stone inlet, lay there for one week heard the bombardment of Fort Sumter... I think... we may regret the not being in possession of Charleston, that an attack by land would only have caused us to loose more or less men, with precisely the same result..."* Describing the naval battle in the harbor, he notes *"...a magnificent spectacle... the monitors were all hit about 50 times, and but one, the Keokuk damaged. The great fight lasted about two hours. It fully demonstrated the power of the iron-clads to withstand any conceivable amount of hammering but unfortunately their offensive power is comparatively small when opposed to a casemate d fort... I came back immediately with my command of five companies after the attack had been abandoned... I am sorry you* *were not better satisfied with your place in the Grand Army... Moreover the idea that you are to be kept simply as a brigade quartermaster for any time is too ridiculous. Blood will tell my boy. And I shall not be startled to hear you a Lt. col. tomorrow- You know the sequl [sic] to the Jacksonville 'Capture'- the colored braves were there for a day or two & sent for reinforcements, the 8th Maine & 6th Conn- went down to their rescue, two darkies having been hit in the meantime - I am told the Cols. of the White regiments had orders not to assume command though we outranked Col. Higginson. They all stayed there a week or longer together and evacuated the place for the third time. After having gone brought he deep and unusual process of separating the lambs & goats & sending he former 'over the lines'. Well when they came away they concluded the town had been taken or 'captured' often enough so they promptly burnt about two thirds of it to ashes. this considering Jacksonville was at most the only place in the Department that ever manifested the least symptom of loyalty since we came here, was rather edifying. Of course the 'furniture hunters'... took good care to secure all the pianos, sofas, chairs, tables mirrors &c before burning... It is but just to say that the negroes behaved more decently than the White soldiers. the expedition was organized to secure a few hundred intelligent contrabands, to fill up the 2d S.C. Vols, they secured eighteen..."*

To this point, Putnam had yet to see combat, though he was considered one of the finest officers in the X Corps. His 7th New Hampshire, together with the famous 54th Massachusetts (Colored Troops), assaulted Fort Wagner on May 18, 1863. This futile assault, resulting in hundreds and hundreds of casualties, was made famous in the 1989 film "Glory." Light creases, else fine condition. A rich missive with real content... and tremendously rare. From the Henry E. Luhrs Collection. Accompanied by LOA from PSA/DNA.

Estimate: $800-$1,200

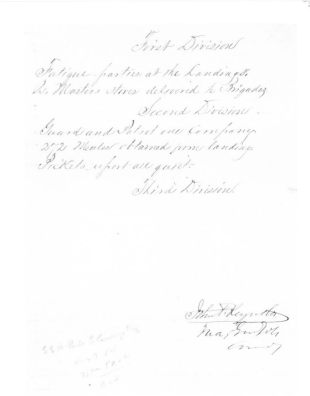

25533   General John F. Reynolds Document Signed *"John P. Reynolds Maj. General, Army."* Two pages, 7.2" x 9.8", Memoranda from Headquarters, March 15, 1863. This document has a head which reads, *"Daily Memoranda for information of the Major General Commanding."* The document was used to write down orders and various data about the officer's regiment. The verso of this document has several lines of text written about various divisions; General Reynolds signs the document in the lower right corner. Reynolds was a well-respected and capable commander; he was loved by his soldiers and peers. He was killed at Gettysburg while overseeing the fighting near McPherson's Woods. He was struck in the neck with a bullet and died almost instantly. He signed these orders only months before he was killed. The document is in very fine condition; usual folds are present; stain present on the lower right corner. From the Henry E. Luhrs Collection. Accompanied by LOA from PSA/DNA.

Estimate: $2,500-$3,500

25532   Thomas E.G. Ransom ALS *"T.E.G. Ransom, Brig. Gen. Vols."* Three pages, 7.75" x 9.75", Head Quarters, Post of Natchez, August 28th, 1863. This letter was written by Ransom concerning his fear about a fellow officer, it reads in part, *"…his men and officers can not be trusted in the country alone. They pillage and plunder and destroy beyond any men I have ever commanded and will not follow or obey my orders in this respect…the officers…seem to gave a very poor appreciation of this rights of citizens -non combatants - and very little respect for private property…"* Ransom was a Major General in the Union Army, and was highly praised by all of his superiors. Ulysses S. Grant said of him, "He has always proved himself the best man I have ever had to send on expeditions." The letter is in very fine condition; usual folds are present; signature is bold and dark. Amazing content! From the Henry E. Luhrs Collection. Accompanied by LOA from PSA/DNA.

Estimate: $400-$500

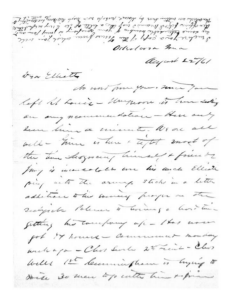

page (two pages glued together), 7.5" x 16.5", Headquarters, A.O.W.V., Clarksburg, Va., August 6, 1861. This letter was written to a Capt. Benham and it lists several orders for him to follow once he arrives at the headquarters of the Brigade of the Kanawha. It is a long and detailed list of orders.

The second ALS is signed, *"W.S. Rosecrans."* One page, 5" x 8", Washington D.C., June 20, 1888. The content of this list is interesting in that it mentions the Battle of Chickamauga, after which Rosecrans was relieved of his command. It reads in part, *"…I was so interrupted that I had not time to drop you a line or even to refer my own Mss. for the losses in killed and wounded at Chicamauga…"* [sic] The letter goes on to list the figures of those killed, wounded, and captured.

The letters are both in very fine condition; usual folds are present; the longer letter has soiling along its fold lines. From the Henry E. Luhrs Collection. Accompanied by LOA from PSA/DNA.
Estimate: $500-$700

25534   **Samuel Allen Rice: Rare War-Date Letter of the Union General Who Died of a Wounded Ankle.** Autograph Letter Signed, 2 pages, recto and verso, Oakaloosa, Iowa, August 22, 1861. To his brother, Elliott. Some nascent tearing at center folds, else very good. All the news is about Iowa readying itself for war - with the exception that *"Grim is here & tight most of the time disgracing himself."* In part: *"Palmer is having a hard time getting his company up... has now got 77... Chas Serle 2nd Lieut. - Chas Wiles 1st - Cunningham is trying to raise 30 men to go with him & raise a company from Krokus... John Lofland is getting up a rifle company to buy our men rifles - I think we will get the Minnie... We will I presume expend our patriotism shooting at a mark ... No word about your Majorship .... Have your daguerreotype taken the very first occasion..."* All this, when the War would still be over by Christmas!   From the Henry E. Luhrs Collection. Accompanied by LOA from PSA/DNA.
Estimate: $400-$600

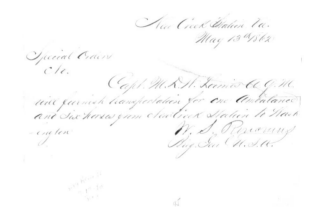

25536   **General William S. Rosecrans Autograph Note Signed** *"W.S. Rosecrans Brig. Genl. U.S.A."* One page, 7.5" x 6.25", New Creek Station, Virginia, May 13, 1862. The note is a written account of special orders, and reads *"No. Capt. M.D.W. Loomis A.Q.M. will furnish transportation for one Ambulance and six horses from New Creek Station to Washington."* William S. Rosecrans was a major Union general, although he was relieved of his command after Chickamauga. He went on to become a Congressman from California, and the U.S. Register of Treasury.

The letter is in fine condition; usual folds are present; large tear from the right edge into the center has been repaired but still visible; slight staining on verso. From the Henry E. Luhrs Collection. Accompanied by LOA from PSA/DNA.
Estimate: $400-$600

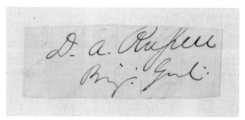

25535   **General William S. Rosecrans Pair of Autograph Letters Signed.** The first ALS is signed, *"W.S. Rosecrans Brig. Genl. U.S.A."* One

25537   **General David Alan Russell Signature.** Russell signs this 4" x 2.5" card as *"D.A. Russell Brig. Genl."* Russell was a decorated and respected General for the Union Army, he was killed at the battle of Winchester in 1864 by a cannonball.

The signature is in very fine condition; it has been laid down on the card, the signature is on a very small piece of white lined paper. From the Henry E. Luhrs Collection. Accompanied by LOA from PSA/DNA.
Estimate: $600-$800

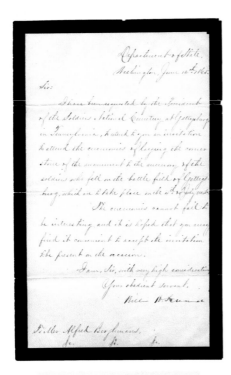

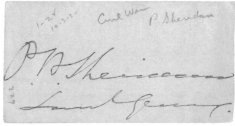

25538   William Seward: June 1865 Invitation to Laying of Corner Stone of the Soldiers' National Monument at Gettysburg. Letter Signed, as Secretary of State, 1 page, on black bordered stationery, 8" by 13", Department of State, Washington, June 12, 1865. To Alfred Berghmans. Separating at folds, else good: a particularly striking and unusual letter.   Less than eight weeks after the assassination of President Lincoln, Seward issues this formal letter of invitation to attend the laying of the corner stone of the Soldiers' National Monument at Gettysburg National Cemetery - the battlefield, of course, where Lincoln delivered his noble address. *"I have been requested by the President of the Soldiers National Cemetery at Gettysburg, in Pennsylvania, to extend you an invitation to attend the ceremonies of laying the corner stone of the monument in memory of the soldiers who fell on the battle field of Gettysburg, which is to take place on the 4th of July next. The ceremonies cannot fail to be interesting..."* From the Henry E. Luhrs Collection. Accompanied by LOA from PSA/DNA.

Estimate: $800-$1,200

25539   General Philip Sheridan Archive. Comprised of 14 Documents Signed, mostly war date, and one Signed Card from the famous General Philip Sheridan. Sheridan distinguished himself as one of the great generals of the Union Army and later as a driving force in the Indian Wars. He is also largely responsible for the preservation and protection of Yellowstone National Park. In this lot there are 14.8" x 10" receipts which are all approved and signed by Sheridan for various Army expenditures. Most of the receipts date from the Civil War. Also included is a 3.7" x 2" signature card which is signed, *"P.H. Sheridan."*

All 14 Documents are in pristine condition. The Signed Card is Good but slightly soiled.   From the Henry E. Luhrs Collection. Accompanied by LOA from PSA/DNA.

Estimate: $1,500-$2,500

25540   Edward Everett Collection. This lot contains four autograph letters signed by Edward Everett, orator, politician, reverend, and much more. He served in the U.S. House and Senate as well as being president of Harvard University, and he eventually added Secretary of State to his long resume of government positions. The first ALS is signed *"Edward Everett."* Two pages, 4.5" x 7", Boston, September 23, 1864. The letter was written to Gov. Andrew and it recommends the bearer of the letter for the post of lieutenant of the 61st regiment.

The second ALS is signed *"Edward Everett."* Two pages, 5" x 8", Boston, June 12, 1863. The letter discusses Everett's thanks for the copy of *"Notes & Comments on Shakespeare"* which was sent to him. He says he has been a long time student of "The Great Author." Everett was a well-educated man and this no doubt was of keen interest to him as a bookish person.

The third ALS is signed *"Edward Everett."* One page, 4.6" x 7.25", Summer Street, February 27, 1862. The letter was written to J.T. Fields Jr. Esq. and the content is routine.

The fourth and final ALS is signed *"Edward Everett."* Two pages, 4.5" x 7", Summer Street, September 28, 1864. The letter was written to Reverend R. Ellis and the content is routine; dealing with a dinner invitation.

The condition of the four letters is very fine on average; usual folds are present; slight soiling along fold lines. Otherwise excellent! From the Henry E. Luhrs Collection. Accompanied by LOA from PSA/DNA.
Estimate: $400-$600

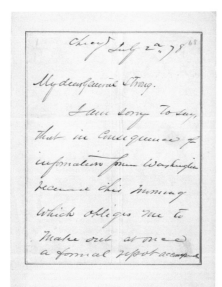

25542   Philip H. Sheridan Autograph Letter Signed *"P.H. Sheridan."* Three pages, 5" x 6.5", Chicago, July 2, 1878. The letter was written to a General Strong, and it reads in part, *"…I am sorry to say, that in consequence of information from Washington received this morning which obliges me to make out at once a formal report accompanied by statistical evidence of raids, & troubles on the Rio Grande border, that I will not*

be able to go with your party to the Opening of the Ship Canal…" Sheridan was a decorated general as well as one of the architects who secured and preserved the area known as Yellowstone National Park.

The letter is in very fine condition; usual folds are present; letter is mounted onto a larger sheet of paper. * From the Henry E. Luhrs Collection. Accompanied by LOA from PSA/DNA.
Estimate: $600-$800

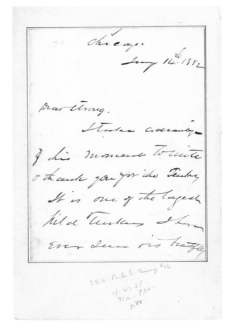

25541   Philip Henry Sheridan: Ornate Society of the Army of the Potomac Certificate Signed. Document Signed ("P.H. Sheridan"), partially-printed and accomplished in manuscript, with a decorative vignette at center and at borders, 1 page, on vellum, 15" by 12.25", , no place, no date; naming Brigadier General U.S Vols. John Mason, Third Division, Second Corps, a Member of the Society of the Army of the Potomac. Sheridan has signed as president of the Society. Worn, a little wrinkled and a tad faded, with two tiny pin holes at top center; but still handsome, and overall, good. Who better to command the honored veterans than Little Phil? He never lost a single battle. From the Henry E. Luhrs Collection. Accompanied by LOA from PSA/DNA.
Estimate: $150-$200

25543   General Philip H. Sheridan Autograph Letter Signed *"P.H. Sheridan."* Three pages, 5" x 6.5", Chicago, January 14, 1882. The letter is written to someone named Strong, the content is about various mounts which Sheridan had obtained; it reads in part, *"…I take advantage of this moment to write & thank you for the Turkey. It is one of the largest Wild Turkeys I have ever seen & is beautifully set up. The head neck & eyes are especially attractive. I have also to thank you for the Head of the Antelope you killed on the summit of the Big Horn…"*

The letter is in fine condition; usual folds are present; letter is mounted on a larger sheet of paper; soiling present on edges and along fold lines. From the Henry E. Luhrs Collection. Accompanied by LOA from PSA/DNA.
Estimate: $700-$900

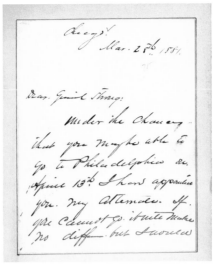

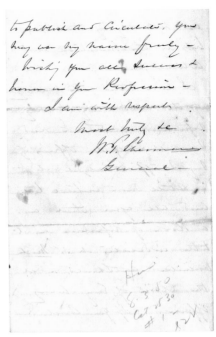

25544   Philip H. Sheridan Autograph Letter Signed To William T. Sherman Three pages, 5" x 6.5", Chicago, June 3, 1881. He signs himself *"P.H. Sheridan."* The letter reads, *"My dear general Sherman: The saddle did not belong to anyone & I am unable to say if any person ever rode on it. Tompkins the chief Q. master here found it at Leavenworth or some place down in the Dept. of Missouri. It cost nothing therefore there is nothing to pay. He gave it to me, I gave it to you, & I am glad you gave it to Ben Holliday."* Sheridan was a decorated and battle-proven general for the Union during the Civil War. This letter with the association between two legendary generals makes this piece very desirable.
The letter is in very fine condition; usual folds are present; slight soiling on edges; the letter has been mounted to a folder. Accompanying this letter is an engraving of Sheridan, perfect for display. From the Henry E. Luhrs Collection. Accompanied by LOA from PSA/DNA.
Estimate: $600-$800

25545   Philip H. Sheridan Autograph Letter Signed *"P.H. Sheridan."* Three pages, 5" x 6.4", Chicago, March 28, 1881. The letter was written to a General Strong and it reads in part, *"…I presume you will be at the meeting of the Army of the Tennessee on the 6th I have made my arrangements to be there…"* Sheridan was a decorated and accomplished Union General. His efforts lead directly to the South's surrender at Appomattox.

The letter is in very fine condition; usual folds are present; soiling present on edges; letter is mounted onto a larger sheet of paper. From the Henry E. Luhrs Collection. Accompanied by LOA from PSA/DNA.
Estimate: $500-$700

25547   William T. Sherman, (1820-1891) Civil War Union General, Autograph Letter Signed *"W. T. Sherman"*, four pages, 5" x 8", Washington, December 26, 1879 to Captain Thomas Welhelm in Benicia California thanking him for *"…the Volume of your preparation Entitled Military and naval Encyclopedia, which is most valuable to the Profession… It seems to m that you can well venture to have it Stereotyped, printed and offered for sale preferably at New York— for it cannot fail to come into demand and general use not only by the Army but by the Militia, and Citizens generally… If you conclude to publish and circulate, you may use my name freely…"* Sherman was of course famous for his "march to the sea" from Atlanta to Savannah in 1864. A few clean partial fold splits, light foxing, else very good. From the Henry E. Luhrs Collection. Accompanied by LOA from PSA/DNA.
Estimate: $400-$600

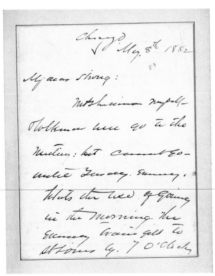

25546   Philip H. Sheridan Autograph Letter Signed *"P.H. Sheridan."* Three page, 5" x 6.5", Chicago, May 8, 1882. The content of the letter is routine; it is regarding Sheridan and his wife's upcoming visit to St. Louis.

The letter is in very fine condition; usual folds are present; transference of the ink has occurred from the second page to the third. From the Henry E. Luhrs Collection. Accompanied by LOA from PSA/DNA.
Estimate: $400-$600

25548 **William Tecumseh Sherman: A Family Letter re Life in New York** Autograph Letter Signed ("W.T. Sherman"), 1 page, 5.5" by 9", Army Building, New York, February 2, 1888. To a kinsman, Sherman Moulton. With autograph envelope. In fine condition. Not only was war hell for Sherman, but marriage too: this letter uncharacteristically finds him referring happily to his wife, newly established back in New York. "*...You can call on me always at any time —- but to increase the chances of your finding me in —- the 5th Avenue Hotel at 10 a.m., & this office at 11. Ellen [Mrs. Sherman] is now back & has Room 25 —- I am in 24 —- Lizzie [daughter] 23 —- 26 the Rushes —- Rachel [daughter] switched off a Philadelphia for Washington to return to New York about Feb. 15th —- Affectionately*" From the Henry E. Luhrs Collection. Accompanied by LOA from PSA/DNA.
Estimate: $300-$400

25549 **General William Tecumseh Sherman Autograph Letter Signed** "*W.T.*

Sherman." Three pages, 5" x 8", Headquarters Army of the United States letterhead, Washington D.C., March 27, 1874. The letter was written to General James S. Higby and it reads in part, "*...I am 'General' but have no command of the Army. I don't even see the charges against an officer nor the proceedings of his trial...I often see it in the newspapers...*" This letter is a great example of an officer's understanding of the court martial procedure.

The letter is in very fine condition; usual folds are present; slight soiling on the edges. From the Henry E. Luhrs Collection. Accompanied by LOA from PSA/DNA.
Estimate: $400-$600

25550 **General William Tecumseh Sherman Letter Signed and Signature.** This lot features two items signed by the famous Union Army general. Sherman's "scorched earth" policy ravaged some parts of the south during the Civil War. He and his men bragged that in Georgia alone they had caused $100,000,000 worth of damage. The first item in the lot is a clipped signature, it measures 3.5" x 2.1" and is signed, "*W.T. Sherman, General.*" The second item is a letter signed "*W.T. Sherman.*" Two pages, 5.5" x 9.25", New York, June 9, 1890. The content of the letter is routine. Sherman regrets that he is unable to attend the Soldiers and Sailors National Reunion at Caldwell.

The items are both in very fine condition; the letter has the usual folds present and some slight staining on the edges. The signature has pencil notations on the lower corners and some light staining. From the Henry E. Luhrs Collection. Accompanied by LOA from PSA/DNA.
Estimate: $400-$500

25551 **General William Tecumseh Sherman Letter Signed** "*W.T. Sherman, General.*" One page, 5" x 8", New York, April 19, 1890. The content of the letter is routine. General Sherman was an accomplished general for the Union during the Civil War, although he did receive some criticism for his actions, such as his "scorched earth" policy and his reported nervous breakdown. The letter is in very fine condition; usual folds are present; slight staining on the upper corners. From the Henry E. Luhrs Collection. Accompanied by LOA from PSA/DNA.
Estimate: $400-$500

25552 **Thomas L. Snead, Asst. Adj. Genl. C.S.A, War-Date Letter About Running for Confederate Congress.** Autograph Letter Signed, *as Major*, 2 pages, recto and verso, 7.75" by 10", Camp Sumter, March 27, 1864. To the Governor of Missouri, Thomas C. Reynolds in Marshall, Texas. Miniscule tears at margins of lower fold, else quite good. If war is the continuation of politics by other means, then this letter seemingly reverses the maxim: Snead says that the St. Louisans in "Parsen's & Draytin's brigades" demand that he run for office. "*I had, until the 25th of February, positively refused, on* *all occasions, to be considered as a candidate; but... I received letters from officers in Parson's & Draytin's brigades stating that it was the unanimous wish of the St. Louisans in this Division, that I would allow myself to be announced as a Candidate to represent the St. Louis Division, and... I wrote that I would, if elected, serve as the Representative from that District."* He continues that he greatly fears *"others as well as myself think that duty & honor"* require him to remain in the field, but the other likely candidates do not wish to run. Snead did run, and he won too, ending the war in Richmond. From the Henry E. Luhrs Collection. Accompanied by LOA from PSA/DNA.

Estimate: $150-$300

25553   Collection of Henry W. Slocum Letters Comprises: (1) Six ALsS: *"H W Slocum:,* three 1p, two 2p, one 3p, 5" x 8" to 5" x 8.75", 1875-1891, three undated. Concerning delivering a speech at Gettysburg, writing a book, Col. R.M. McDowell, meeting Civil war veterans, obtaining copies of the Hancock Memorial, and his inability to be present at an installation. One letter is tipped to another sheet, one has mounting remnants, and one is wrinkled. (2) Autograph Statement Signed: *"H.W. Slocum",* 1p, 5" x 8.75". Brooklyn, N.Y., June 8, 1891. In full: *"Gen Sherman was my commanding officer and my personal friend. His greatness as a soldier is acknowledged throughout the world - The last years of his life - spent in New York - endeard him to thousands for his social qualities."* General William Tecumseh Sherman had died in New York City on february 14, 1891. Glue stains and mounting remnants on verso resulting in show-through and some wrinkling on front. (3) Signature: *"Yours Truly/H. W. Slocum"* on irregularly cut 4.5" x 1.75" slip of paper affixed to a 6.25" x 9.5" sheet. "Harper's Ferry, Va./Nov. 25th 1862" has been penned in an unidentified hand at lower left of signature sheet. (4) Two different engraved bust portraits of Slocum. (5) **Daniel E. Sickles** ALS: *"D. E. Sickles",* 1p, 4.5" x 7", on his embossed monogrammed stationery. To Douglas Tyler. No place, September 13, 1853. In full: *"Please hand to bearer whatever you have for me."* Tipped to 6" x 9" page. 11 items. From the Henry E. Luhrs Collection. Accompanied by LOA from PSA/DNA.

Estimate: $300-$500

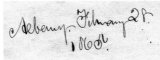

25554   Alfred B. Street Autograph Manuscript Signed *"Alfred B. Street."* A small poem titled "Our Union" written by Alfred B. Street, one page, 5" x 8", Albany, New York, February 28, 1865. It reads, *"Our Union! The lightning of battle First Kindled the flame of its shrine; The blood and the tears of our people Have made it forever divine. In battle we then defend it! Will fight till the triumph is won; Till the states form the realm of the Union As the Sky forms the realm of the sun."*

Street was the state librarian of New York and penned several poems and short stories in his lifetime. A book of his poems called, "The Burning of Schenectady and Other Poems" was published in 1842.

This lot features this charming little handwritten poem as well as a complete typed transcription. The poem itself is in Fine condition with adhesive stains on the verso. At one time it was glued into an album and the glue has stained the paper dark brown in two places. There is writing in pencil on the lower half of the page from modern cataloguing. Otherwise perfect. Onward! From the Henry E. Luhrs Collection. Accompanied by LOA from PSA/DNA.

Estimate: $800-$1,200

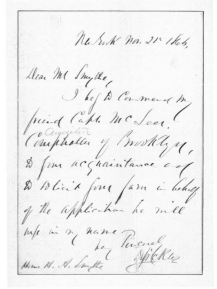

25555   Daniel E. Sickles Autograph Letter Collection. This lot features 3 letters measuring 4.5" x 7", and one letter measuring 5" x 8". The letters are all written and signed by General Daniel Sickles, a Union Army general and American politician. Sickles was a colorful man, the first ever acquitted of murder by reasons of insanity. He shot and killed the son of Francis Scott Key, Philip Key, for having a blatantly public affair with his wife. Later, he defied orders at Gettysburg, and this resulted in a severe loss of his men and a crippling wound for himself. A cannonball struck his leg which had to be amputated that same day. Sickles donated the leg to the Army Medical Museum, and he reportedly visited the limb often. The letters in this lot contain routine content about traveling to Buffalo, New York for discussions of several speeches at a Grand Army of the Republic event. This colorful general is well represented in this interesting lot. The letters in this lot are in very fine condition on average; the usual folds are present, and all are laid down on a sturdy backing sheet; signatures are bold and dark. From the Henry E. Luhrs Collection. Accompanied by LOA from PSA/DNA.

Estimate: $600-$800

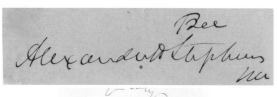

25556 **Alexander H. Stephens Collection.** This lot features three pieces signed by or relating to the Vice President of the Confederacy, Alexander H. Stephens. There are two signatures and one letter written by his nephew John A. Stephens on his behalf. Also included with these documents is a *carte de visite* of Stephens, depicting him seated in a chair wearing a dapper suit and gloves. The letter from his nephew John is regarding his uncle's inability to give a lecture that was requested. The first of the two signatures is from a free franked envelope that has been clipped down and mounted on a larger sheet of paper. The second signature reads, *"With a great deal of pleasure, yours very truly, Alexander Stephens."* He signs this card from Liberty Hall on the 21st of December 1871. Stephens was strongly opposed to abolishing slavery, and served as the first vice president of the Confederacy.

The signatures are in very fine condition; they are mounted on larger cards. The letter is in very fine condition; usual folds are present. From the Henry E. Luhrs Collection. Accompanied by LOA from PSA/DNA.
Estimate: $400-$500

25557 **An Outstanding First-hand Description of the Confederate Raid on Charleston, West Virginia, 1862.**

(Confederate Raid on Charleston, 1862) Autograph Letter Signed by Confederate officer "C. E. Thorburn - Col. & Inspcr Genl - Army Western Va.", eight pages, 8" x 9.5", Charleston, [West] Virginia, September 15, 1862 describing the Confederate raid on Charleston, the capital of present-day West Virginia. Thorburn, a member of General William W. Loring's staff, describes the foray into Union-held Western Virginia in September, 1862. He narrates (quoted in very small part here) the events in excellent detail from the outset of the mission to their brief occupation of Charleston: *"The difficulty of obtaining transportation delayed the advance of the*

Army of Western Va under Major Genl. Loring till the 6th of Sept... in Rawleigh... Our Cavy drove in the pickets capturing a few prisoners from whom we learned that the enemy would not make a stand till they had fallen back to Fayett[e] C[ourt]. H[ouse]. Raleigh C. H. was fortified & the brick houses loopholes but we entered the village without firing a shot... we had advanced to within 6 miles of Fayett C. H. when we learned from the Country people the Enemy were in strong force & well fortified.... Genl. Williams drove the enemy skirmishers from the woods & into the fortifications, slowly they taking advantage of each piece of favorable ground till he had advanced within 800 yds of the lower work when they opened on him with their artill[e]ry. Genl. Loring than [sic] ordered his artill[e]ry to take position on a slight eminence to the left about 500 yards & opened upon them From this point there was no cover for the men but our sharp Shooters picked off the gunmen & riflemen whenever they shewed [sic] theirselves [sic] finding that there were four fortifications the lower being commanded by the next higher... I went into their lines after night and found out that It could be [captured by storm]... Whilst making preparations to move to that point the Enemy evacuated his works & fled... The gallant men of our army pushed on & found the enemy in position the side of the Kanawa River Otey's Battery was moved to the front & soon discharged (with the aid of our skirmishers who occupied the hill sides) the Yankeys from their 'Stong [sic] hold') Genl Loring ordered our advance, our men answered with a cheer and the Yankees fled again after firing an immense quantity of stores. they attempted to burn their fery [sic] boats but a party of our men led by Dr Watkins of Charleston Ky / surgeon of the 22d Va. Rgt swam the river under the enemy's fire & saved them. In half an hour the ferry was established & we were advancing down both sides of the Kanawa River. Our list of prisoners was swelling every hour and our army can be more than clad & substituted from the stores saved..." Torburn continues to describe the vast quantity of captured stores and narrate the approach to Charleston: *"This brings us to the 13th At about 11 AM. Genl. Williams opened on the enemy who had now crossed to their side of he River... our Cavy drove in their rear guard till they opened on them... A running fight was kept up for some time till we came in sight of Charleston, Genl. Loring now learned that Genl. Lightburn (Yankee) had ordered the Women & Children out of town stating that if compelled to leave, that he would burn the town. He Loring ordered Col McCauslin... to push our skirmishers... rapidly up... so quickly did our men push them that they (The Yankees) fired only two store houses and a few buildings... and destroying the bridge over Elk River... the battle now became an artill[e]ry duel & the Sharp Shooters of both sides on* From the Henry E. Luhrs Collection. Accompanied by LOA from PSA/DNA.
Estimate: $100-$200

GEN LEWIS WALLACE.

25558 **Lew Wallace War-Date Autograph Letter** Autograph Letter Signed, as Major General, commanding, 1 page, 5" by 8", on the letterhead of the Head Quarters, Middle Department, 8th Army Corps, Baltimore, May 30, 1864. To Captain Smith. In fine condition. With an

engraving of the general. In full: *"Please inform me at the Eutaw House how you progress with Mr. Bernal."* From the Henry E. Luhrs Collection. Accompanied by LOA from PSA/DNA.
Estimate: $300-$400

25559   Lew Wallace: 2 Autograph Letters A twofer, for your collection of authors, Civil War generals, politicians and diplomats: this pair of autograph letters from the pen of Lew Wallace - who wrote the spectacularly successful novel "*BenHur*" - as follows: 1) Autograph Letter Signed, 1 page, 3.5" by 2.5", no place, no date; to Mrs. Townsend, very likely the wide of his fellow writer, George Alfred Townsend. Tipped to an octavo leaf, in fine condition. "*That husband of yours kept me so charmed that I came away leaving my umbrella - a brown-silk English article. Won't you be good eno' to have it looked up and returned by the bearer? Always, and truly...*" 2) Autograph Letter Signed, 1 page, 6" by 9.5", Crawfordville, Ind., June 16, 1886. To Mr. Clarence H. Bell in Boston. Fine. "*The proposal... strikes me with favor. Only I beg a little time before answering definitely. I am in negotiation which may require consultation with other parties.*" From the Henry E. Luhrs Collection. Accompanied by LOA from PSA/DNA.
Estimate: $300-$400

25560   Lew Wallace Letter Mentioning a Hero of Shiloh, Lt. Col. Julius Garesche Typed Letter Signed, 1 page, 8" by 10", Crawfordsville, Indiana, November 2, 1897. To Louis Garesche in Washington, D.C. A pencil note in lower right corner, faint imprint of folds, else fine.   Before Lew Wallace wrote one of best-selling novels of all time, *Ben-Hur - A Story of the Christ,* he was of course a Union general, who led a Division at bloody Shiloh - a battle in which Colonel Julius Garesche, riding besides General Rosecrans, was decapitated by a cannonball, bespattering Rosecrans and those around him with his blood. "Garesche's appalling death" wrote General Phil Sheridan in his memoirs, "stunned us all". This same hero was the subject of a biography written by his son, Louis, about which Wallace writes here. "Q"   From the Henry E. Luhrs Collection. Accompanied by LOA from PSA/DNA.
Estimate: $150-$250

CIVIL WAR ERA COLLECTIONS, MANUSCRIPTS, ETC.

25561   Rare 1861 Letter From Florida. Autograph Letter Signed, "*Thos Le. B*", six pages, 5.25" x 8.0", Indian River, Florida, April 1, 1861, to a friend in the North. Penned by an adventurous Northern entrepreneur less than two weeks before the bombardment of Fort Sumter, this bubbly letter from deep in rural Florida betrays the writer's near ignorance of the tumultuous events unfolding across the nation at large. It partially reads, "*...we mail as many of our letters as possible at New Smyrna... I have won the reputation of being the best cook among all the bachelors on the river...as to the political excitement, about the extent of the information we have received here is that Lincoln is President & the Southern States have Seceded. I shall be happy to see you at any time you chose to come...I intend to surprise my friends at the North by showing my handsome self when I am not expected...perhaps you would like to have a couple of Rattle snakes & two or three Aligators (sic)...I killed two of the latter to day one 6 inches long & one 4 feet in length...*". This letter comes with a memo, 3.0" x 5.0", assigning it a Luhrs Collection catalog number (37-103) and giving a synopsis of its content. There is also a 1956 dealer's receipt pricing this item at $1.50! All materials, including the 1861 letter, are in Very Fine condition. From the Henry E. Luhrs Collection. Accompanied by LOA from PSA/DNA.
Estimate: $200-$300

25562   [Union] A Civilian Reports on the Deplorable Condition of Soldiers, Sick and Well, in Baltimore. Autograph Letter Signed ("S.F.S"), 8 pages, recto and verso, 5" by 7.75", Baltimore, October 12, 1862. To "Caroline." Bound with archival tape at left margin, else quite good. This long and interesting letter touches on the everyday conditions of both Rebel and Yank, stuck in Baltimore, after Antietam. In part: "*...This morning, after overseeing the feeding of several hundred soldiers, recruits, &, besides 189 rebel prisoners from Harper's Ferry, I returned home... and went earnestly into the sleeping business... Our work, for over two months, has been very heavy, as we have received and fed... over one hundred and sixty thousand men... The character of the men, with few exceptions, is excellent... but I am saddened at the thought of what these swarming, vigorous thousands have to endure, and how few of them, comparatively, can return... At present, my chief concern is the accommodation by night of hundreds of sick and well, who are detained here from lack of transportation, yet have no shelter provided by the government. I have seen the sidewalks, platforms and woodpiles covered at night with sleeping men, some with blankets and many without... It is growing cold, and the soldiers must suffer greatly. Last night, there were hundreds, sleeping in the open depot, and those unprovided with blankets were uncomfortable indeed. I have made a formal representation to General West, and he has promised to lay the subject before the authorities...*" From the Henry E. Luhrs Collection. Accompanied by LOA from PSA/DNA.
Estimate: $150-$200

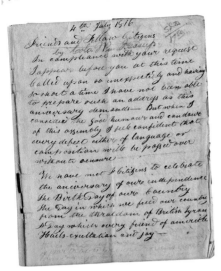

25563 (Fourth of July Oration) Manuscript, fifteen pages bound with wire, 6.25" x 7.5", Southampton, July 4, 1816. Notation on verso reads: *"4th of July Oration delivered by Wm. Jessup at Southampton in 1816"* Text for a speech given on Independence Day just about a year following the War of 1812. *"...The 4 of July 1816 is perhaps one of the most glorious ever celebrated by Republican Americans — The evens and termination of the late glorious war with Great Britain — The termination of the late War with the Pirates of Africa — The extension and Diffusion of Democratic principals through out the union — The free, extensive, uninterrupted, and, prosperous commerce... are themes of exultation an joy to every true American. The American with pleasing anticipation looks forward to a time when this republic shall give laws to the world..."* Jessup then proceeds to narrate the atrocities committed by the French and the British before the War of 1812: *"... thousands of our seamen were dragged from their homes... dragged from his family and country to fight the battles of a nation which his soul abhors..."* Jessup also reminds his audience of the blessings of liberty including *"...Education, and we must consider the extension of political knowledge as one of our greatest privileges — A free and unrestricted Press is an invaluable blessing to any people —- to a republic it is indispensable — this is the Vehicle of Knowledge of our enlightened people without which how soon would they sink into insignificancy —- The first ambitious aspiring Demagogue would bind the iron brand of slavery fast upon their necks... an enlightened people can never be slaves..."* Much more fine content. Early celebratory orations recalling the Founding Fathers and their contribution to American independence are quite desirable; this is one of the finest we've encountered. Light creases, a few minor marginal chips, light soiling, else fine. From the Henry E. Luhrs Collection.
Estimate: $800-$1,200

25564 [Union] Superb Letter About Baltimore Readying For an Invasion, Including News of "Negroes" Being Forced to Erect Breastworks. Autograph Letter Signed, in the hand of one Clara, to "Mother Hall" in Charleston, 6 pages, 5" by 8", Baltimore, June 21, 1863. In fine condition. With typed transcription. Had we but time and space enough, we would gladly run this fascinating letter in its entirety: as it is, some highlights... *"Baltimore never was so busy before... The whole place is up in arms getting ready for the Rebels... Our streets were guarded all night and our pickets extend about five miles out of the City... Last night the whole of the 'Union League' were given their arms, the 'Minute Men' were given theirs and all the known Loyal men were supplied... The Rebs here say we are marked, but they little know what is in store for them. Whole lists of names of Secesh here are being made out and are soon to go in to Genl. Schenek and ... every Secesh family is to be sent South... The police were catching all the negroes and idlers and marching them to the outskirts of the City and putting them to work on the entrenchments. They are kept at work day and night and tomorrow they talk of closing all the places of business and putting every one out to work... When the news first came that the Rebs were going to make a dash on the place, the Secesh around were very jubilant, but now they look white around the mouth.... I am going to pack up my silver and send it on... for I haven't any idea that the Rebs shall enjoy anything belonging to me... The Union people are..half crazy to get a chance at some of those sneaking Rebs around us..."* From the Henry E. Luhrs Collection.
Estimate: $250-$350

25565 [Union] Civilian Letter on Morgan's Ohio Raid. Autograph Letter Signed, in the hand of one Charlie, 5" by 7", 4 pages, recto and verso, no place [Ohio], July 12, 1863. To Charlie's girlfriend. In Fine condition. Confederate Raider John Hunt Morgan's Ohio Raid was remarkable, says Boatner, for the endurance exhibited by Morgan's command: an average of 21 hours a day in the saddle from the time he crossed the Ohio. However, the raid was pointless; he lost badly; and it marked the end of his usefulness to the Army of Tennessee. Still, as Charlie reflects, the raid upset, and terrified, Ohio for weeks. *"...I have just come from town. The excitement still continues. One meets a guard about every square. I have very nearly worn my pocket book out, showing my pass. Last night I had to show it three times on one square. There are no business houses open and all kinds of trade is suspended. We have received no mail since Friday, and none leaves the city. I hope it will not last much longer... If Morgan comes up your way I hope they will capture him. I heard he was on his way in that direction..."* From the Henry E. Luhrs Collection.
Estimate: $150-$200

25566   Libby Prison Minstrel Show A scarce printed broadside for a Christmas Show staged by Union prisoners in 1863, one page, 6" x 15.75, [Richmond], December 24, 1863. Libby Prison was created out of a tobacco warehouse in Richmond owned by the Libby and Son tobacco company. The prison was used exclusively to house Union officers until 1864 when it was converted for use to include Confederate military criminals. Overcrowding and a lack of adequate sanitation gave Libby Prison a notorious reputation — second only to the Andersonville Prison camp in Georgia. Offered here is a relic from the days before conditions had deteriorated too far, a playbill for a minstrel show in three parts: *"The Libby Prison Minstrels!"* The show included a series of songs including *"Who will care for Mother Now"* and *"Do they think of me at Home"* as well as a skit entitled *"Rival Lovers"* as well as a "Masquerade Ball" and *"The Whole to Conclude with a Grand Walk-Around."* Offered with a stereo card view of the prison by C. F. Johnston of Richmond. Backed with contemporary lined paper, a few minor marginal chips not affecting text, light creases, else near fine condition. From the Henry E. Luhrs Collection.
Estimate: $700-$900

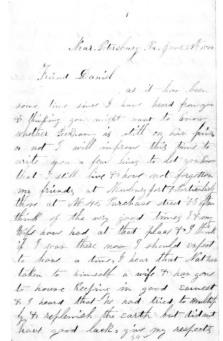

25567   Union Soldier's 1864 Superlative Account of the Carnage at Cold Harbor
Autograph Letter Signed in the hand of Private William H. Peckham of New Hampshire, a musician with the 2nd Brigade Band, 1st Division, 7 pages, 5" by 8", near Petersburg, Va., June 29, 1864; to "Friend Daniel." In Fine condition. With typed transcription. In part: *"Our Band was stationed at the 18th Corps Hospital... You have no idea of the suffering & hardships of the wounded, at the battle of Cold Harbor our corps marched 15 miles & went right into the fight so they had no Hospital fitted up & when the wounded began to come in they had to carry the men in to the woods & fit up amputating tables, as best they could.., Serious wounds were attended & then they were laid out on the ground with nothing but a rubber blanket under them & a woolen blanket over & nothing more & some of them laid 3 days in the open before they were carried into the Hospital. I tell you Daniel I don't want to see another such sight as long as I live. Some of the men had one leg off some both some with arms off some with a bullet hole in the head & in every part of the body. It was a sickening sight but one gets used to it after a few days or at least I did & could stand by & see Surgeons take off a leg or arm & not mind it much... You know more about what is going on out here than we that are right out here for there are reporters all around & they can find out by the Officers all that is going on but we cannot unless we are right there..."*
From the Henry E. Luhrs Collection.
Estimate: $300-$400

25568   Union Artillerist's Civil War Diary including details from the third day at Gettysburg

Union Artillerist's journal, an excellent manuscript, likely kept by a member of the 1st Rhode Island light artillery, approximately 175 pages, 4" x 6". A finely detailed diary which opens in the midst of the Battle of Chancellorsville and closes in the Shenandoah Valley Campaign of 1864. The diary covers the road to Gettysburg, where the diarist was present for the third day as well as the pursuit of Lee south to the Potomac. In particular the diary includes vivid descriptions of the battles leading to Petersburg including the Wilderness, Spotsylvania, and Cold Harbor. The diary, here at Gettysburg on July 3, 1863, reads in part: R *"The bal was opened by the rebels at half past 4. Our forces soon respond and the roar of artillery in unceasing for 2 hours and then it was quite till 11 o'clock when our guns open a fearful fire with artillery and is kept up till 2 P.M. this fire was the most terrific of anything of this battle and in fact the most rapid and terrific of anything I ever knew. we were ordered to the front at 1 o'clock and took up a position on the right, the firing was then severe,. the firing was brisk on the left from 5 P.M. till dark. The rebels try to break through on our right a 9 o'clock and between 12 and one....".*

His unit remained north of the Potomac for a few weeks following Gettysburg and then moved again into Virginia. Excellent content throughout. Bound in glue, original wraps missing, housed in an acid-free cover together with a slipcase with the mistaken attribution *"John Ridlon 7th Mine, Infantry"* Pages overall quite clean and bright. Comes together with a complete typed transcript. While the identity of the correspondent remains in question, there is little doubt that he was well educated and quite literate. From the Henry E. Luhrs Collection. Accompanied by LOA from PSA/DNA.
Estimate: $800-$1,000

25569 [Union] Great Letter Denouncing "Substitutions" and How Soldiers View Lincoln's Re-Election Bid!

Autograph Letter Signed, seemingly from a journalist named "Henry", 4 pages, recto and verso, 5" by 8", Before Petersburg, Va., September 19, 1864; to "Dear Mother." In fine condition. When Congress passed the Conscription Act in March 1863, it allowed draftees to pay a commutation tax to avoid service: for $300, one could hire a substitute. This practice led, not surprisingly, to charges that the system made for "a rich man's war and a poor man's fight." Here, in part, is a rousing condemnation of this Northern practice (the South disallowed it in '63) and, too, a savvy assessment of the troops' support of Lincoln." *...I am pitched into for my talk about substitutes... The whole substitute business is a work of infancy, mean, cowardly, traitorous, vile, criminal. It has prolonged the war. It has caused the death of thousands of bravest of the brave... That really good men are engaged in or approve this disgraceful business only shows that the polluting influences of the shoddy and political elements of the present Northern society have vitiated the whole... Soldiers thank me warmly for what I wrote. Soldiers' friends from the North write to me in gratitude... Politics look bad. The soldiers will vote for Lincoln because they will not vote down the war... A vast majority of the soldiers abominate Lincoln's policy, but as the single alternative tendered them is a disgraceful surrender to the foes they are fighting, they will not hesitate to vote for the only war candidate.*" From the Henry E. Luhrs Collection.

Estimate: $200-$300

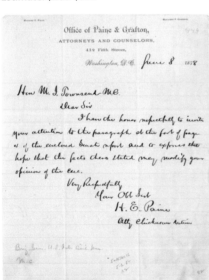

25570 Civil War Autograph Collection.

Included in this fascinating group of Civil War related items are more than 24 signed pieces from various officers and dignitaries. Just a few of the items included (with highest rank achieved): Brigadier General & Chief of Engineers John Newton (Signature); Brevet Brigadier General Albert J. Myer, Signal Officer of the Army and father of the U.S. Weather Bureau (ALS); Surgeon General Robert Murray (Signature); Justin Smith Morrill (2 ALS); Brigadier General Eleazer A. Paine (ALS as attorney for Chickasaw Nation, ALS as Congressman); Brevet Major General John G. Parke (ALS); Brevet Brigadier General Jasper Packard (AMs). Generally fine condition. From the Henry E. Luhrs Collection. Accompanied by LOA from PSA/DNA.

Estimate: $500-$700

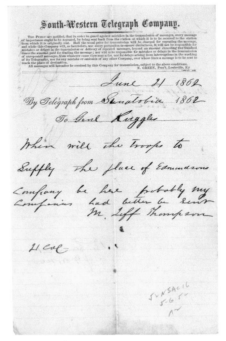

25571 Civil War Confederate Autograph Collection.

All items are in generally fine condition unless noted. Included in this lot are:

Meriwether Jeff Thompson. CSA general. Civil War dated (1862) Autograph Letter Signed (telegram form), to General Ruggles.

Joseph D. Sayers. CSA major, Texas governor. Autograph Letter Signed (very good condition).

Preston Pond. CSA colonel. Civil War dated (1862) Autograph Letter Signed.

S. F. Pennington. CSA soldier. Civil War dated (1865) Autograph Letter Signed.

Samuel W. Maurice. CSA soldier. Civil War dated (1862) Autograph Letter Signed (good condition).

Charles Marshall. CSA colonel and Robert E. Lee's *aide-de-camp.* Typed Letter Signed.

Alexander P. Stewart. CSA general. Autograph Letter Signed. From the Henry E. Luhrs Collection. Accompanied by LOA from PSA/DNA.

Estimate: $400-$600

25572 Collection of Civil War Dated Letters and Documents

consisting of at least 20 items. Most of these are war related; a few are of a personal nature. Offers great insight into the customs and happenings of a time long past and allows one to learn about the events of the war from first hand participants. The soldiers' letters are particularly interesting with one even including a hand-drawn map. The lucky bidder will not be disappointed with the quality of material included here. Very good to fine condition. From the Henry E. Luhrs Collection. Accompanied by LOA from PSA/DNA.

Estimate: $500-$800

25573   Civil War Autograph Collection. Included in this lot are about 15 Civil War-related autographs. A few of the individuals included (with highest rank achieved): Brigadier General Robert Macfeely (two bold signatures); Brigadier General R. B. Marcy (ALS as Army Inspector General); Major General Carl Schurz (four ALS, ANS); Lieutenant General Theodore Schwan (TLS); Rear Admiral Winfield Scott Schley (Signature); Major General Robert C. Schenck (Signature); Major General James Allen Hardie (ALS); Brigadier General Adolph von Steinwehr (Signature). Generally fine condition. From the Henry E. Luhrs Collection. Accompanied by LOA from PSA/DNA.
Estimate: $300-$500

25574   Civil War Autograph Collection. Included in this lot are approximately 12 Civil War-related autographs. A few of the individuals included (with highest rank achieved): Brigadier General Michael Vincent Sheridan, brother of Philip Henry Sheridan (2 LS, TLS); Brigadier General William R. Marshall (ALS); Major General J. Warren Keifer (3 TLS); Brigadier General John G. Hudson (LS); Major General Andrew A. Humphreys (LS); Major General Henry Jackson Hunt (long ALS). Generally fine condition. From the Henry E. Luhrs Collection. Accompanied by LOA from PSA/DNA.
Estimate: $300-$500

25576   Civil War Officers Signature Collection. This lot contains 11 signatures from Union Army officers. All 11 signatures are on small pieces of paper that have been laid down on larger cards. Included are: Marsena Rudolph Patrick, Army of the Potomac; William Hays, Brigadier General; John M. Schofield, Major General and Secretary of War; Rufus Ingalls, Brigadier General and Chief Quartermaster; Alpheus S. Williams "Starky"; William D. Whipple, Brigadier General; W.L. Elliot, Brigadier General; John R. Kenly, Brigadier General; E.B. Brown, Brigadier General; Gershom Mott, Brigadier General; and William S. Rosecrans, Major General.

All signatures in this lot are in fine condition on average; slight soiling on the edges of several; all have been laid down on larger pieces of paper. From the Henry E. Luhrs Collection. Accompanied by LOA from PSA/DNA.
Estimate: $400-$500

25577   Civil War Generals Signature Lot. This lot features three signatures, all on small cards. The first is a 4.1" x 2.5" card with a laid down signature of Lysander Cutler Brigadier General. He signs his name *"L. Cutler Brig. Genl."* Cutler was a Union General who fought at Gettysburg and the Second Battle of Bull Run. He was wounded at the Battle of Globe Tavern in 1864 and later died from those wounds.

The second signature is of Frank Wheaton, he signs himself, *"Frank Wheaton Brig. Genl. U.S.A."* The card measures 4.1" x 2.5". Wheaton was a Cavalry officer in the Union Army. His father-in-law was a high-ranking officer for the Confederacy.

The third signature is on a 4.1" x 2.6" card and is signed as *"A. Baird Brig. Genl. U.S. Vols."* Absalom Baird was a decorated and accomplished Union General.

The signatures are all in very fine condition; all three are on clipped pieces of paper which have been laid down on a larger sheet of paper. From the Henry E. Luhrs Collection. Accompanied by LOA from PSA/DNA.
Estimate: $200-$300

25575   Frank Bramhall *The Military Souvenir.* (New York: J.C Buttre 48 Franklin Street, 1863) Vol. 1 76 illustrations on steel engraved plates. 4to, full gilt decorated leather. aeg, hinges weak, contents fine. With an als from George B. Lincoln, Postmaster New York 1863, in reference to the book needing some corrections. From the Henry E. Luhrs Collection.
Estimate: $200-$300

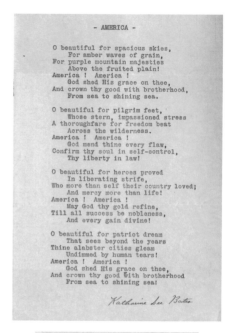

25578   John Jacob Astor III (1822-1890) Document Signed
"J.J. Astor." One page, 12" x 8.5", Canal Department, Albany, New York, November 6, 1880. This stock certificate comes from the State of New York, Canal Department in Albany and is filled out to John Jacob Astor. Astor signs the verso in bold, dark ink. Astor would only have been 16 when this stock was issued; this shows how he was involved in money and finance even at an early age. Known by most as John Jacob Astor IV, he was the Astor who served as a lieutenant colonel in the Spanish-American war and made his money in real estate, including the Waldorf-Astoria Hotel. Astor was killed along with 1500 others when the Titanic struck and iceberg and sank in 1912. Many stories circulate about Astor's heroics that night when the boat sank, including one in which he places a woman's hat on a boy to ensure that he got off the boat safely.

The document is in fine condition; the usual folds are present; the paper is brittle and separating; small hole present in the center of the value of the stock certificate. Accompanied by LOA from PSA/DNA.
Estimate: $400-$600

25579   Phineas T. Barnum Extraordinary Manuscript: *"The Noblest art, is That of Making Others Happy"* Autograph Fair Copy Signed, 1 page, on his embossed letterhead, 4.5" by 7", Marina, Bridgeport, Ct., July

19, 1889; inscribed to Mr. H.P.R. Holt of Takoma Park. In 1889, the great American impresario and self-proclaimed "Prince of Humbugs," Barnum summarized in a notebook his principles of life — which, apparently, he then wrote out for Mr. Holt."***The noblest art is that of making others happy, honesty, sobriety, industry, economy, education, good habits, perseverance, cheerfulness, love to God and good will toward men. These are the preeminent requisites for securing Health, Independence, or a Happy Life, the respect of Mankind and the special favor of our Father in Heaven."*** Barnum has added beneath his signature, at bottom, *"Born July 5, 1810, Died ——-"* A quintessential piece! From the Henry E. Luhrs Collection. Accompanied by LOA from PSA/DNA.
Estimate: $1,500-$2,000

25580   Katherine Lee Bates Rare Manuscript of "America The Beautiful" Typed Manuscript Signed, entitled "America," being all four verses of the final edition of her 1895 poem "America the Beautiful" - which, set to the tune of the hymn "Materna," is just as famous and considerably easier to sing than the official national anthem. 1 page, 5.5" by 8.5", no place, no date; rare. In excellent condition. Bates' patriotic song was a strong contender to become the country's national anthem but Congress, in its infinite wisdom, gave the nod to the "Star-Spangled Banner" in 1931. Of note, too, is that Bates never sought royalties for the poem's publication or the song's performance. From the Henry E. Luhrs Collection. Accompanied by LOA from PSA/DNA.
Estimate: $1,500-$2,000

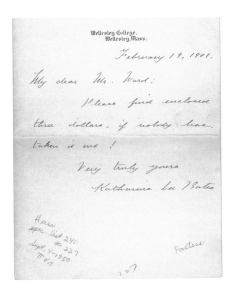

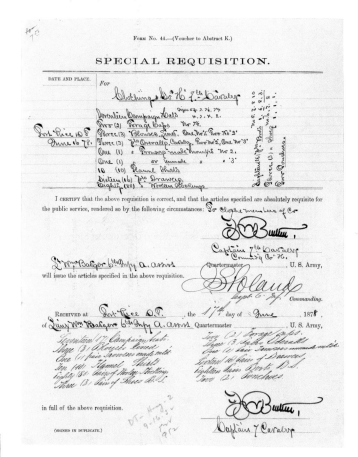

25581   Katherine Lee Bates Autograph Note Signed. One page, 4.75" x 6.5", Wellesley College letterhead, Wellesley, Massachusetts, February 14, 1901. In full: *"My dear Mr. Ward: Please find enclosed three dollars, if nobody has taken it out! Very Truly Yours Katherine Lee Bates"* Bates, of course, wrote the words to what has become the most popular American patriotic song of the current day, "America the Beautiful," a song that has taken on a whole new meaning since the September 11, 2001 attacks. She wrote the song originally in 1893 while on a trip from Wellesley to Colorado Springs, inspired by the sights she saw on the way. Fine condition, one mailing fold not affecting the signature. From the Henry E. Luhrs Collection. Accompanied by LOA from PSA/DNA.
Estimate: $300-$500

front my soul in Judgment, witness bear / To error, failure, sin: but oh, my prayer / My strife forget not! Auf Wiedersehen."* From the Henry E. Luhrs Collection. Accompanied by LOA from PSA/DNA.
Estimate: $600-$900

25583   Little Big Horn Survivor Frederick Benteen- Document Signed boldly *"F. W. Benteen"* as captain, 7th Cavalry. A "Special Requisition," one page, 8.5" x 10.75", Fort Rice, Dakota Territory, June 17, 1878. Benteen commanded a battalion consisting of Companies "D", "H", and "K" at Little Big Horn under Custer for which (along with his actions at Canyon Creek) he was brevetted brigadier general. His actions in the course of the battle have come into question as time has marched on. In 1887 he was suspended for drunk and disorderly conduct and was to be dismissed from the Army before President Cleveland intervened. Very fine condition; two original folds. From the Henry E. Luhrs Collection. Accompanied by LOA from PSA/DNA.
Estimate: $2,000-$3,000

25582   Katherine Lee Bates Autograph Poem Signed Autograph Manuscript Signed, of her poem "To The Old Year," delivered at a Wellesley College Address, 1 page, 7" by 6", Wellesley, Massachusetts, no date. Some wear and very slight discoloration at top; a tiny pencil note at bottom else fine. Best known for her patriotic lyric, "America the Beautiful," Bates was primarily a poet and an educator, serving for many years as the chair of the English department and dean of - the then new - Wellesley College. These verses, delivered at a Wellesley address, combine to represent her life's most significant work. In full: *"Auf Wiedersehen! For we shall meet before / The Throne of God. The drifting snows confuse / The foot-prints. Down the echoing wind I lose / Thy voice. So be it. We shall meet once more. / When from the grave of Time thou com'st again / To*

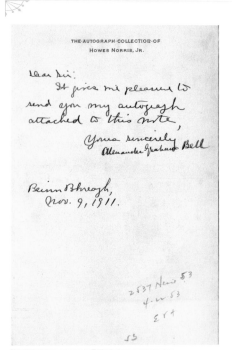

25586 **Legendary Apache Indian Chief Geronimo Bold Signature** in his interesting printline-penciled letters. On the verso of a 3.125" x 1.625" card of, and likely signed for, Richard Pearson Hobson, a Naval hero in the Spanish American War. Geronimo and his forces were the last group of independent Indian warriors who refused to acknowledge the United States government. He was captured in 1886, in Arizona, and eventually became a sort of curiosity, attending fairs and selling souvenirs and photos. Fine condition. From the Henry E. Luhrs Collection. Accompanied by LOA from PSA/DNA.
Estimate: $4,000-$5,000

25584 **Alexander Graham Bell Note Signed** "*Alexander Graham Bell.*" One page, 4.5" x 7", Howes Norris Jr. Autograph Collection Stationery, Beinn Bhreagh, Nova Scotia, November 9, 1911. This note is a response to Norris' request for Bell's autograph. Bell is widely considered to be the inventor of the telephone.

The note is in very fine condition; usual folds are present; slight staining present from smoke; mounting traces present on verso. From the Henry E. Luhrs Collection. Accompanied by LOA from PSA/DNA.
Estimate: $800-$1,200

25587 **William Jennings Bryan Autograph Collection** consisting of four items including:

Autograph Letter Signed, one page, 3.75" x 8.5", House of Representatives U.S. letterhead, Washington, January 4, 1892, to Secretary of the Interior.

Typed Letter Signed, one page, 5.5" x 8.5", personal letterhead, Miami, Florida, February 15, 1922.

Autograph Letter Signed, 1.5 pages, 5.75" x 9.25", W. J. Bryan Attorney at Law letterhead, Jacksonville, IL, May 6, 1886.

Large, bold signature on 4.5" x 2.75" sheet.
Generally fine condition, an excellent grouping from "The Great Commoner." From the Henry E. Luhrs Collection. Accompanied by LOA from PSA/DNA.
Estimate: $600-$800

25585 **William Booth: Great Autograph Manuscript About the Meaning of Life!** Autograph Manuscript Signed, 1 page, 4" by 5.5", New York, January 17, 1898. Very fine. The founder of the Salvation Army puts the ultimate question here: [in full] "*What a treasure is life? Is there any mote important question than that which asks 'How am I using it.' I ought to be able to answer the question satisfactorily to my own conscience. How is it with you, dear friend?*" From the Henry E. Luhrs Collection. Accompanied by LOA from PSA/DNA.
Estimate: $350-$450

25588 Adolphus Busch Rare Letter About Theodore Roosevelt: "I Love Him -But..." Typed Letter Signed, 2 separate pages, on the decorative letterhead of "President's Office, Anheuser-Busch Brewing Association", 8.5" by 11", St. Louis, May 20, 1913; to journalist - and later, German Spy - George Sylvester Viereck. Normal wear, and a couple pencil notations not effecting text; otherwise quite good, with an exceptionally dark and bold signature. Here the beer magnate begs off discussing Viereck's possible entry into politics, choosing instead to talk about the recent presidential election. In part: "*I believe you know my sentiments for Col. Roosevelt - I loath him - but I am not in sympathy with his actions. If he had backed President Taft for another term, he would have been the greatest and most popular man in the United States; I think he made a great mistake splitting the Republican Party, and it is a question with me whether the American people will ever forgive him...*" From the Henry E. Luhrs Collection. Accompanied by LOA from PSA/DNA.
Estimate: $1,500-$2,500

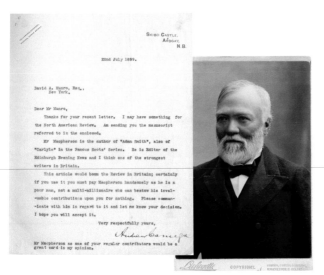

25589 Andrew Carnegie Typed Letter Signed with Cabinet Card Photo. The letter: one page, 7.75" x 10", Skibo Castle, July 22, 1899, to David A. Munro. Carnegie is sending Munro a manuscript (not present) by a Mr. Macpherson for the *North American Review,* in part: "This article would boom the Review in Britain; certainly if you use it you must pay Macpherson handsomely as he is a poor man, not a multi-millionaire who can bestow his invaluable contributions upon for nothing." Carnegie was certainly a multi-millionaire himself, making his fortune as the founder of the Carnegie Steel Company (later U.S. Steel) and then giving much of it away in his later life to fund libraries, schools, and universities. About fine condition, lightly mounted to a collector's folder, staple holes at top left.

Also included in this lot is an incredibly fine cabinet card size photo of Carnegie from approximately the same time period this letter was written- a handsome formal portrait by Lafayette of London, Dublin, Glasgow, etc. Matted and framed together, these two items would form a magnificent display. From the Henry E. Luhrs Collection. Accompanied by LOA from PSA/DNA.
Estimate: $600-$800

25590 Andrew Carnegie Typed Letter Signed *"Andrew Carnegie."* One page, 8" x 10.75", personal letterhead, New York, March 23rd, 1911. The letter is written to Joseph Choate and reads in part, *"...We are marching along the path of peace. It will trouble us to keep pace with the procession."* Carnegie was a renowned philanthropist and founder of Carnegie Steel Company, which later became U.S. Steel. The letter is in very fine condition; usual folds are present; pencil and ink notations on the obverse. From the Henry E. Luhrs Collection. Accompanied by LOA from PSA/DNA.
Estimate: $400-$500

25591 WWalter Chrysler Signature. *"W.P. Chrysler."* Signed on white paper which has been laid down on a 6" x 4" signature card. Chrysler is, of course, most noted for being a pioneer of the automotive industry. He was a part of several automobile companies then started the Chrysler Corporation in 1925. The signature is in very fine condition; laid down on a sturdy signature card. From the Henry E. Luhrs Collection. Accompanied by LOA from PSA/DNA.
Estimate: $200-$300

25592 **Dane Coolidge Autograph Archive.** This lot is comprised of some 24 autograph pieces of the prolific writer of Westerns, as follows: 1) Dane Coolidge, Autograph Letter Signed, 1 page, 8.5" by 11", Berkeley, California, August 21, 1932. To H.E. Luhrs. Coolidge encloses multiple autographs and writes that, yes, he's the husband of Mary Roberts Coolidge with whom he wrote a book, "*The Navajo Indians*", considered the "*dernier cri*" on the subject. 2) 23 Signatures - 22 of Dane Coolidge and 1 of Dane Coolide and Mary Roberts Coolidge together - on 5" by 3" slips of paper on which is printed "Autograph for H.E. Luhrs, Shippenburg, Pa." with the added proviso that the signatory is the "Author of", this information being accomplished in typescript; hence each signed slip is for a different book. From the Henry E. Luhrs Collection. Accompanied by LOA from PSA/DNA.
Estimate: $450-$550

AUTOGRAPH
for
H. E. LUHRS, Shippensburg, Pa.

Dane Coolidge

Author of   "The Wild Bunch"

Place _____ Date _____

25593 **George Custer Signature.** "*G. A. Custer.*". Q Signature on white paper which has been laid down on a 4.75" x 3.75" card; an unknown hand details his rank and regiment. Custer fought in several battles during the Civil War, and for his gallantry was appointed brigadier general of the volunteers. Custer and his entire command were slain by Sioux Indians at the battle of Little Big Horn, in Montana, June 25th, 1876. In fine condition. Accompanied by two engravings of Custer. An excellent display piece. From the Henry E. Luhrs Collection. Accompanied by LOA from PSA/DNA.
Estimate: $3,500-$4,500

25594 **Eugene V. Debs Pair of Checks Signed** "*Eugene V. Debs.*" The first check measures 6.25" x 2.75", West Town State Bank, Chicago, Illinois, September 19th, 1923. The check is made out to Eugene V. Debs for $1000, from Otto Branstetter. Debs endorses the back of the check. The second check measures 6.25" x 2.75", West Town State Bank, Chicago, Illinois, October 31st, 1923. The check is made out to Eugene V. Debs for $500, from Otto Branstetter. Debs endorses the back of the check. Debs was a prominent figure of the Socialist Party of America, and ran for president five times on the Socialist ticket; the final time he ran from prison. The checks are both in very fine condition; only the cancellation stamps mar the condition of these fine items. They do go over the signature in a few places but do not affect their legibility and crispness. From the Henry E. Luhrs Collection. Accompanied by LOA from PSA/DNA.
Estimate: $300-$400

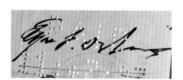

25595 Walt Disney Signed Photo. Signed Photo. Black and white, 8"x10", depicting Disney in a suit and tie. Also included with the photograph is an 10.1" x 8" glossy of the Disney cartoon, "Three Little Pigs." bearing a secretarial Walt Disney signature.

the Signed Photograph is in Very Fine condition; the ink on the paraph is slightly chipped. From the Henry E. Luhrs Collection. Accompanied by LOA from PSA/DNA.

Estimate: $2,000-$3,000

25597 Frederick Douglass writes on John Brown and slavery

Frederick Douglass (1818-1895) Escaped slave and prominent abolitionist, fine content Autograph Quotation Signed "*Frederick Douglass*", one page, 5" x 3", no place given, 1883. A remarkable statement on the legacy of "*John Brown Saw Slavery through no mist or cloud, but in a light of infinite brightness, which left no one of its ten thousand horrors concealed.*" Douglass had known John Brown through abolitionist circles but disapproved of his plan to foment a slave revolt. He thought the raid on Harper's Ferry to be a grave mistake that would inflame public opinion against the abolitionist movement. Though they had their differences, by 1883, it is obvious that Douglass had some perspective on Brown's legacy and his contribution to the end to "that peculiar institution" in America. Fine condition and ideal for display. Wonderful association for the collector of significant Black Americana. From the Henry E. Luhrs Collection. Accompanied by LOA from PSA/DNA.

Estimate: $2,000-$2,500

WALT DISNEY

January 26, 1939.

Dear Mr. Holt:

Apparently there has been some sort of misunderstanding relative to my coming down to Rollins College for the February Convocation, inasmuch as I have received letters from Edgar Grover of the Animated Magazine and Severin Bourne of New York, both of whom are under the impression that I am coming to Winter Park for the Commencement Exercises.

There has been no change in the situation here at the studio since my last letter to you, so I just cannot see my way clear to get away. However, I want you to know that I do appreciate your continued interest and regret that I am unable to accept your invitation and, therefore, must forego the privilege of receiving the honorary degree of Doctor from Rollins College.

With kindest regards.

Sincerely,

Walt Disney

Dr. Hamilton Holt,
Rollins College,
Winter Park, Fla.

WD:DV

25596 Walt Disney Typed Letter Signed "*Walt Disney.*" 7.3" x 10", one page typed letter signed by Disney in the lower right portion. It is dated January 26, 1939, and is written on his personal stationery. The letter explains that he is unable to attend an event at Rollins College, and must forego their offer to award him an honorary degree. The letter is in Good condition; the upper edge has a rust stain from a paper clip which was left on the letter as it aged; notations in pencil are present on the bottom edge. From the Henry E. Luhrs Collection. Accompanied by LOA from PSA/DNA.

Estimate: $1,000-$1,500

Sincerely,

Walt Disney

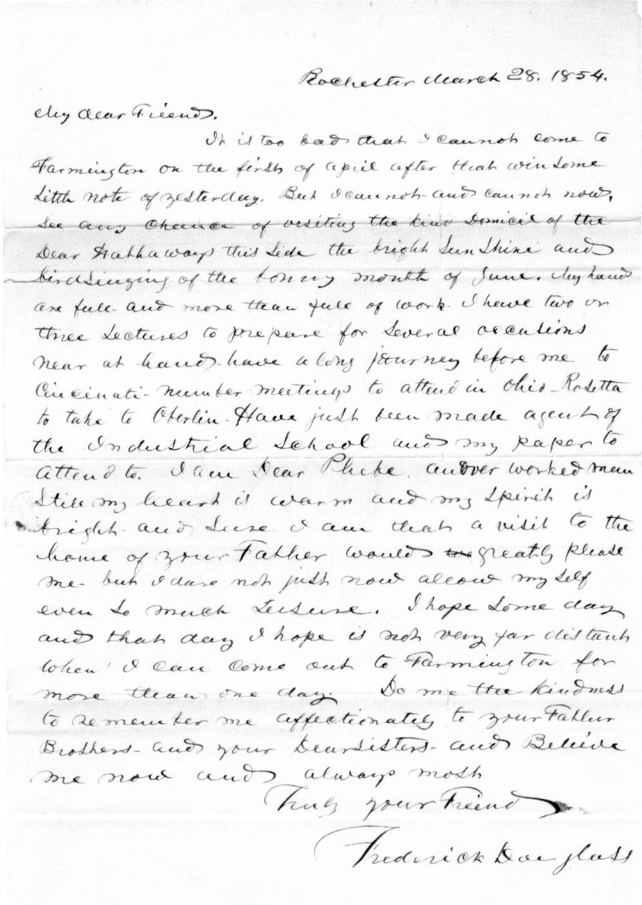

Rochester March 28. 1854.

My Dear Friend.

[handwritten letter text]

Truly your Friend

Frederick Douglass

25598   Frederick Douglass (1818-1895) Escaped slave and prominent abolitionist, fine content Autograph Letter Signed
"Frederick Douglass", one page and addressed in his hand on verso, 8" x 13", Rochester, [New York], March 28, 1854 to fellow abolitionist Phoebe Hathaway in Farmington, New York updating her on his busy lecture schedule. He writes in full: *"It is too bad that I cannot come to Farmington on the first of April after that winsome little note of yesterday. But I cannot and cannot now, see any chance of visiting the kind domicile of the Dear Hathaways this side the bright Sunshine and bird singing of the bonny month of June. My hands are full and more than full of work. I have two or three lectures to prepare for several occasions near at hand, have a long journey before me to Cincinnati, number meetings to attend in Ohio-Rosetta to take to Oberlin- Have just been made agent of the industrial School and my paper to attend to. I am Dear Phebe [sic], an over worked man[.] Still my heart is warm and my sprit is bright and sure I am that a visit to the house of your Father would greatly please me but I dare not just now allow myself even so much leisure. I hope some day and that day I hope is not very far distant when I can come out to Farmington for more than one day. Do me the kindness to remember me affectionately to your Father Brothers- and your Dear sisters- and Believe me now and always most."* Phoebe Hathaway was a Quaker abolitionist from upstate New York and likely the daughter of Joseph Hathaway, a Hicksite Quaker who accompanied Douglass in his early lecture tours in the late 1840s. By this time, Douglass could move more freely as he was no longer considered a fugitive slave — he had been formally freed by his former master. Douglass had five children including Rossetta and Charles who assisted him in the publication of his anti-slavery newspapers. As noted in this letter, Rossetta also attended meetings on his behalf. Light creases else very bright and clean and in very fine condition. A superior example with the content most coveted by collectors. From the Henry E. Luhrs Collection. Accompanied by LOA from PSA/DNA.
Estimate: $6,000-$8,000

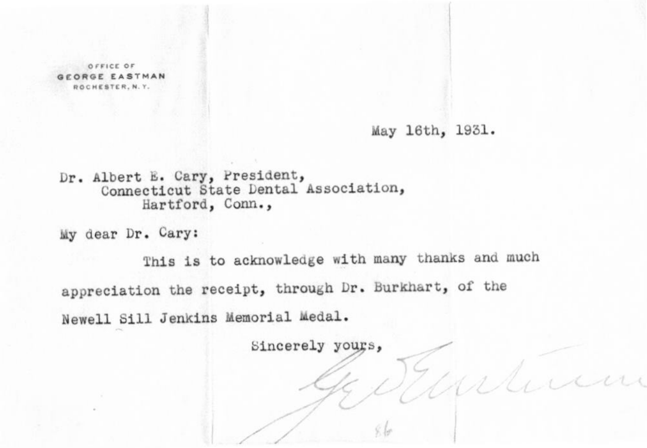

May 16th, 1931.

Dr. Albert E. Cary, President,
    Connecticut State Dental Association,
        Hartford, Conn.,

My dear Dr. Cary:

This is to acknowledge with many thanks and much appreciation the receipt, through Dr. Burkhart, of the Newell Sill Jenkins Memorial Medal.

Sincerely yours,

Geo Eastman

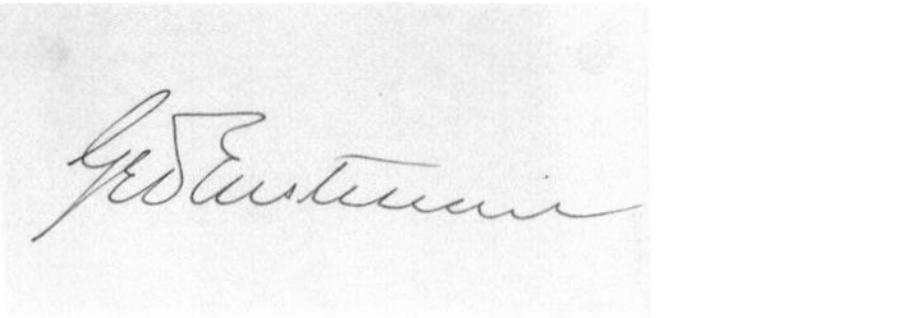

86

25599   Kodak Founder George Eastman- Typed Letter Signed and Signature both signed *"Geo Eastman"*. First, the letter: one page, 8" x 5.25", Rochester, New York, May 16, 1931, to Dr. Albert E. Cary, President Connecticut State Dental Association. A letter of acknowledgement for his receipt of the Newell Sill Jenkins Memorial Medal. George Eastman was one of a rare breed of individuals whose inventions and contributions transcend the mundane, transforming and impacting an entire society. His invention of roll film and the inexpensive camera brought photography to the common man. After earning his fortune, he retired from the day-to-day running of his company and spent the last years of his life as a philanthropist, giving away as much as $100 million, mostly to institutes of advanced learning. Very good condition with one mounting trace on the verso and a portion of the "G" clipped off at the bottom.

Also included is a Signature on a 5" x 2.5" sheet with original envelope of transmittal dated 1928. Fine condition, lightly mounted to a collector's folder. From the Henry E. Luhrs Collection. Accompanied by LOA from PSA/DNA.

Estimate: $400-$500

25600   Thomas A. Edison- A Beautiful Signature on a 5" x 3" card, signed in 1928. This is as nice as they come- a perfect *"Thos A Edison"* with his famous "umbrella" flourish in black ink on a white card. Also included in this lot is the original letter of transmittal on elaborate Thomas A. Edison Laboratory stationery as well as the envelope postmarked November 2, 1928. Signature is in pristine condition. Letter and envelope mounted to old collector's folder. From the Henry E. Luhrs Collection. Accompanied by LOA from PSA/DNA.
Estimate: $400-$600

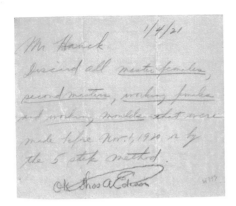

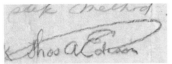

25601 **Thomas Edison Note Signed** *"OK Thos. A. Edison."* One page, 5.25" x 5", np, January 4, 1921. The note reads, *"Mr. Hancock, Discard all master females, second masters, working females and working moulds that were made before November 1, 1920 or by the 5 step method."* The letter is discussing the discarding of moulds for phonographic records, Edison was responsible for inventing the phonograph. His ideas on sound and cinema were also related to his phonographic experiments.

The note is in fine condition; usual folds are present; soiling present on verso and fold lines. From the Henry E. Luhrs Collection. Accompanied by LOA from PSA/DNA

Estimate: $1,500-$2,000

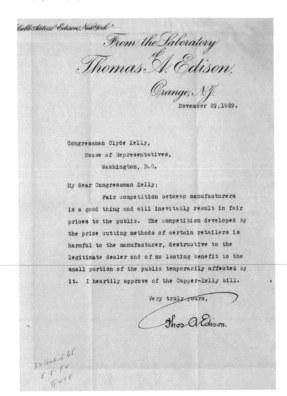

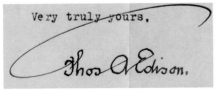

25602 **Thomas A. Edison Typed Letter Signed** *"Thos. A. Edison."* One page, 8.5" x 10.75", personal letterhead, Orange, New Jersey, November 29, 1929. The letter was written to Congressman Clyde Kelly, it

reads in part, *"…Fair competition between manufacturers is a good thing and will inevitably result in fair prices to the public. The competition developed by the price cutting methods of certain retailers is harmful to the legitimate dealer and is of no lasting benefit to the small portion of the public temporarily affected by it…"* Edison is, of course, one of the most accomplished inventors of all time, he was one of the first to combine invention with mass production. The letter is in fine condition; usual folds are present; toning is present on the obverse from framing and exposure to light. From the Henry E. Luhrs Collection. Accompanied by LOA from PSA/DNA.

Estimate: $2,000-$3,000

25603 **John Ericsson Autograph Letter Signed** *"J. Ericsson."* One page, 7.9" x 10", np, August 31, 1895. This letter discusses several of Ericsson's inventions. It reads in part, *"A letter from Sweden two days ago, brought the pleasing intelligence that, at the great agricultural fair of Ostergothland, the finest province of Sweden, a 12 inch caloric engine took the great price for its value to the farming interest- Labor has grown exceedingly costly in Sweden of late years and the Swedes look to the caloric engine…"* From an early age Ericsson was a gifted inventor and surveyor. His greatest accomplishment was the USS *Monitor* which he built for the Union Navy during the Civil War.

The letter is in very fine condition; usual folds are present; left edge is wrinkled and torn from being mounted with adhesive; mounting traces present on verso. From the Henry E. Luhrs Collection. Accompanied by LOA from PSA/DNA.

Estimate: $700-$900

inaccuracies in an article discussing the authorship of the famous song: "*Mr. Shrin has shown me the article written up in the Philadelphia Times which you sent him. It only remains for me to say that I am displeased with the person or persons who had to do with it. Mr. Shreen's article was written at my side and approved by me. No other strictly truthful account has been given out but this. I with you would do me the favor of publishing it, it is the only account that I can sanction or vouch for. You may use the photograph of the song if you desire.*" Provenance: Walter R. Benjamin, *The Collector,* December, 1949, No. 691. Slight separation at horizontal fold, minor losses at corners, else very good.

During his lifetime, Emmett's authorship of "Dixie" had been the subject of much dispute. Emmett claimed to have written the song in the spring of 1859 while performing with Bryant's Minstrels in New York. The song proved to be a favorite throughout the country and counted Abraham Lincoln among its fans. The tune also became the unofficial anthem of the Confederacy during the Civil War. Because of the song's huge success (and by the fact that it took Emmett nearly a year to secure copyright) others stepped forward to claim credit, the most prominent was William Shakespeare Hays (1837-1907), composer of such tunes as *Evangeline,* and *The Drummer Boy of Shiloh.*

Included in this lot is an excellent letter disputing Emmett's authorship of the song by former Confederate General **Edward P. Alexander (1835-1910) in an Autograph Letter Signed,** "*E. P. Alexander*" four pages, 5" x 8", South Island, South Carolina, January 8, 1908. Alexander, also alluding to an 1895 article in the *Philadelphia Times* writes to Cooper DeLeon noting that he has "*...read with great pleasure you[r] admirable & really wonderful article on the 'Belles, Beaux & Brains' of the Confederacy - but I think you're a/c[count] of the origin of Dixie is not complete, as the following narrative will show. I was married in April 60 (to Betty Mason one of the '5 Mason girls' of whom your story speaks) & in June or July of that year returned to my post at West Point. Soon after, my wife & myself went down to New York to see a play than running at Laura Kenne's called The 'Japanese Embassadors' [sic]... one of Jos[eph] Jefferson's sons told me that Jos. Jeff[erso]n was its author. It was an 'Extravaganza' & in the play some bogus 'Embasadors, ' introduced by 'Brown of Grace Church' (when the real Embassadors were not able to attend) were called upon to sing a 'Japanese Song'... George G Hull... told me about the play before taking me to hear it, & said that when the Japanese song was called for 'They played that old thing Dixie' with an accent on the 'old.' So I went that night & heard Dixie for the first time, perhaps, but I believe it was already in print in an old sort of 'circus song Book' that I had had as a boy, before I left Washington... in 1853 to go to West Point. The words given to the song then, were the same which have stuck to it ever since 'Semmon Seed & Sand Bottom'... Dixie was born from that play of the Japanese Embassadors. It was given in June or July 1860, sometime before the election*

of Lincoln in November. All the newsboys in NY were whistling it within a week. On Aug 9th 1860 I sailed for Colon [Panama], & when we arrived, then days later, Dixie was there ahead of us, & we found it had already proceeded us to San Francisco Portland & even to Washington Territory. All of our passengers made it a subject of common conversation. The stories you tell of the writing of the Wall at Mobile by Emmett, or rather for him & later occasions at Nashville & New Orleans are all far later than the appearance of 'the Japanese Embassadors' in New York & the Revival of Dixie dated from this..." Alexander continues disputing Emmett's claims noting contradictory stories and assures his correspondent that "*...I believe it was a still older 'walk around' & will be easily found by any one who will search old Theatrical & Circus records of the times...*". A fascinating pair of letters, worthy of further research. Usual folds, else very fine condition. From the Henry E. Luhrs Collection. Accompanied by LOA from PSA/DNA.
Estimate: $3,000-$4,000

25605   James Fisk Jr. "The Barnum of Wall Street" Document Signed One page, 5" x 7", ornate J F Jr letterhead, New York, August 7, 1871. A printed invitation to a ball at which the Ninth Regiment Band was to make their debut as a larger 200-member unit. Fisk has boldly signed it at the bottom. One of the "Robber Barons" of the 19th century, Fisk joined Daniel Drew and Jay Gould against Cornelius Vanderbilt in the "Erie War" in issuing fraudulent stock in the Erie Railroad Co. Their attempts to control the gold market led to the Panic of 1869. Fisk also financed theatrical shows and dated showgirls, a practice that led to his early demise. An argument over money and Broadway showgirl Josie Mansfield caused business associates Edward Stokes to shoot and kill him on January 6, 1872, just months after this document was signed. Fine condition with two mounting traces on verso, one causing a very minor paper loss at the top left corner, the original recipient's name has been erased. Seldom offered. Originally purchased from Charles Hamilton. From the Henry E. Luhrs Collection. Accompanied by LOA from PSA/DNA.
Estimate: $800-$1,200

25604   Was Daniel Emmett the Real Author of "I wish I was in Dixie"?

Daniel T. Emmett (1815-1904) Autograph Letter Signed, "Daniel D. Emmett ", one page, 5.75" x 9", Mt. Vernon, Ohio, July 6th, 1895 to R. U. Johnson Esqr. of the *Philadelphia Times.* Emmett, a pioneering mid-nineteenth century minstrel performer, is widely credited for the composition of "Dixie's Land" (or "Dixie") which became the unofficial anthem of the Confederacy during the Civil War. Emmett writes to the editor of the *Times* complaining of

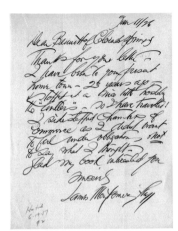

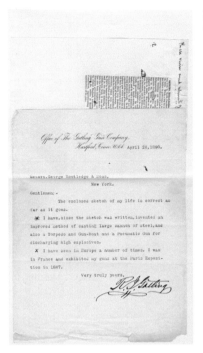

25608   Richard J. Gatling Typed Letter Signed *"R.J. Gatling."* One page, 8.5" x 11", Gatling Gun Company Letterhead, Hartford, Connecticut, April 26, 1890. Richard J. Gatling is best known for inventing the first rapid-fire gun, the gatling gun. Although this was his most widely known invention, Gatling had made a small fortune before he invented it, with inventions and devices used for agriculture. The letter in this lot discusses some corrections he made to a small newspaper article about him. The newspaper article with his corrections on it is included with this lot. The letter is in fine condition; usual folds are present; edges slightly worn. From the Henry E. Luhrs Collection. Accompanied by LOA from PSA/DNA.

Estimate: $1,000-$1,500

25606   James Montgomery Flagg Handsome Autograph Letter About Colorado Springs Autograph Letter Signed, 1 page, 8.5" by 11, no place. January 11, 1926. To *"Bennett of Colorado Springs."* In very fine condition. Best remembered as the creator of the iconic World War I *"I Want You"* recruiting poster featuring a pointing Uncle Sam (modeled on himself), Flagg was, in addition to being an artist, an author - a fact he refers to here, fleetingly, as he recalls a trip to Colorado Springs, Colorado. In full: *"Thanks for your letter. I have been to your present home town - 23 years ago - & stopped by at a nice little hostelry "The Antler" - so I have traveled! I sidestepped Chamber of Commerce as I didn't want to feel under obligation not to say what I thought - Glad my book interested you."* Flagg may have been referring to his 1925 account of a riotous road trip, *Boulevards All the Way - Maybe,* which raised, critically, riots of its own, either loved or hated. From the Henry E. Luhrs Collection. Accompanied by LOA from PSA/DNA.

Estimate: $150-$250

25607   James Montgomery Flagg: Great Letter Defining "Decency"! Typed Letter Signed, with a signature over 5 inches long; 1 page, 8.5" by 11", Biddeford Pool, Me., July 17, 1921. To reporter Mary Ethel McAuley, a nascent tear at the center fold, some wrinkles at the corners, but generally very good. With Autograph Envelope. Here the illustrator of comely *"Flagg Girls"* replies, apparently, to a question about decency. In full: *"It seems to me you might make your question easier if you named the locality - decency being indecency in different latitudes. Decency to me means a lack of ugliness. What is ugly is indecent. You know that to some people decency is something they are accustomed to. To some minds flying in the air is not decent. After they get accustomed to the fact it loses its indecency. It is the same with bathing suits. I should say that a bathing suit that was tight enough to betray an ugly sagging paunch on man or woman was indecent - tho the same tightness of garment on a beautiful body was not indecent. It isn't the suit that is indecent - it's the minds that behold it, providing the wearer is normal."* From the Henry E. Luhrs Collection. Accompanied by LOA from PSA/DNA.

Estimate: $300-$400

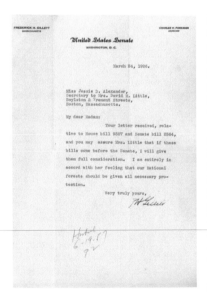

25609   Frederick H. Gillett, 3-Time Speaker of the House, Letter re Conservation. Typed Letter Signed, as senator, 1 page, on the letterhead of the United States Senate, Washington, March 24, 1926. To Miss Alexander, secretary to Mrs. David M. Little in Boston. Here the ex-Speaker, and new Senator, tends the home front. In full: *"Your letter received, relative to House bill 9387 and Senate Bill 2584, and you may assure Mrs. Little that if these bills come before the Senate, I will give them full consideration. I am entirely in accord with her feeling that our National forests should be given all necessary protection."* From the Henry E. Luhrs Collection. Accompanied by LOA from PSA/DNA.

Estimate: $400-$500

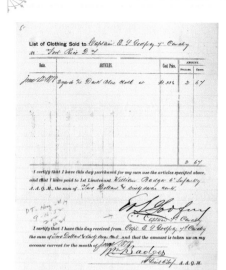

25610 Little Big Horn Survivor Edward S. Godfrey- Document Signed
boldly "*Ed. S. Godfrey*" as captain, 7th Cavalry. A "List of Clothing Sold," one page, 7.5" x 9.75", Fort Rice, Dakota Territory, June 12, 1878. Godfrey served as an enlisted man in the Ohio Infantry during the Civil War before attending West Point. He spent most of his career in the legendary 7th Cavalry. As a 1st lieutenant under Captain Benteen at Little Big Horn, he commanded Company "K" and took a prominent part in the battle, later writing about what really happened. Godfrey was awarded a Medal of Honor for his bravery at Bear Paw Mountain in 1877 and later rose to general. Fine condition; two folds. From the Henry E. Luhrs Collection. Accompanied by LOA from PSA/DNA.
Estimate: $700-$900

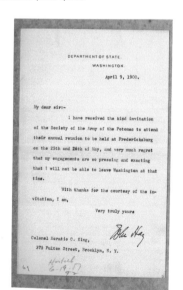

25611 John Hay Declines to Attend the 1900 Reunion of Society of the Army of the Potomac. Typed Letter Signed,
as Secretary of State, 1 page, 4.5" x 8", on the letterhead of the Department of State, Washington, April 9, 1900. To Colonel Horatio C. King. In very fine condition, with tiny pencilled dealer's note at bottom, with an blank integral leaf tipped to a slightly larger cardboard page, making for a handsome presentation. Lincoln's young personal secretary went on to great things, becoming the Ambassador to Great Britain, and serving as Secretary of State to two presidents. Perhaps not surprisingly, this letter finds him too busy to attend a Civil War reunion. " *I have received the kind invitation of the Society of the Army of the Potomac to attend their annual reunion to be held at Fredericksburg on the 25th and 26th of May, and very much regret that my engagements are so pressing and exacting that I will not be able to leave Washington at this time.*" The Society of the Army of the Potomac was founded in 1869 by General George McClellan and was, at the turn of the century, the largest Union veterans group in the country. Because its 1900 Annual Reunion was held in Fredericksburg — the first time the Society met in the South - the meeting attracted national attention. President William McKinley had time to go — but his Secretary of State, we read here, had too much work to do. From the Henry E. Luhrs Collection. Accompanied by LOA from PSA/DNA.
Estimate: $150-$250

25612 Will H. Hays: Fine Letter on How to Propagate the 1919 Republican Message.
Typed Letter Signed, *as chairman of the Republican party*, 8.5" x 11", on the letterhead of the Republican National Committee, New York City, April 21, 1919. To B. Loring Young, Speaker of the Massachusetts House. A bit of the right margin has a faint red smudge, easily trimmed or matted out; else Very Good. If you've ever wondered how Warren Harding won in a landslide in 1920, or why a man gets to be Postmaster General, this letter will help you understand. Here he suggests the propagation of the National Republican as a guide to talking points and party unity: "*... I have thought that it would be a fine thing if those who are going to make speeches would get in the habit of reading this... in order that they may get the benefit of the political matter... which quotes many speeches made in House and Senate, and gives every week a great deal of interesting political information... The paper is getting into the hands of a great many thousand political workers and of

course we all want it to be as effective as possible."* If you're wondering, though, why Hays only stayed a year as Harding's Postmaster, and then went on to rule as Hollywood's infamous "Censorship Czar" for 20-odd years, you'll need to read something racier than this pioneering political letter. From the Henry E. Luhrs Collection. Accompanied by LOA from PSA/DNA.
Estimate: $100-$200

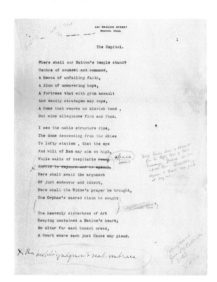

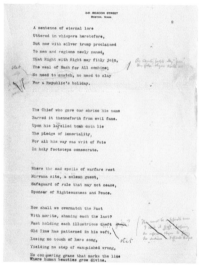

25613 Julia Ward Howe Typed Manuscript, Signed ,
being a working draft of her poem "The Capitol", bearing numerous autograph notations and containing, too, an Autograph Note Signed ("J.W. Howe") to her editor written on the verso. 3 pages, 8.5" x 11", on her personal letterhead, Boston, Massachusetts, no date. Her Note reads reads, "*I have done what I could, would wish to see proof "Stet" means must stay as it is. J.W. Howe.*" The notations made by Howe are in answer to suggestions written on the poem by Robert U. Johnson, editor of "The Century Magazine", who wrote on the last page of the manuscript, "*A beautiful poem,*" Julia Ward Howe is famous for her song, "Battle Hymn of the Republic". In very fine condition; usual folds are present; slight soiling from age. Accompanied by LOA from PSA/DNA.
Estimate: $600-$800

*entertainment one
night. I shall
hope to hear from
you later as to your
choice of a subject.
Yours sincerely,
Julia Ward Howe.*

poetess

*241 Beacon St.
Mar. 2nd 1896.
My dear Mrs Hoyt,
This is to say
that I accept the
terms offered in
your letter for a
lecture on the
evening of March
26th there will
twenty dollars and*

25614   Julia Ward Howe Autograph Letter Signed. Two pages, 3.5"
x 5.25", [Boston], March 2, 1896, to Mrs. Hoyt. Howe accepts an invitation
to lecture upon the terms of "*...twenty dollars and entertainment one
night...*" on March 26th, the subject to be decided. Howe was a prominent abolitionist, activist, and poet whose stirring "Battle Hymn of the
Republic" became a rallying song for the Union during the Civil War. She
was also the first to proclaim Mother's Day (in 1870). Very good condition with a bit of staining, not affecting the signature. From the Henry E.
Luhrs Collection. Accompanied by LOA from PSA/DNA.

Estimate: $300-$400

*Men saw the thorns on Jesus's brow,
But Angels saw the roses.
Julia Ward Howe.
Boston. March 10th 1873.*

25615   Julia Ward Howe Autograph Quotation Autograph
Quotation Signed, 1 page, 5" by 4.5", Boston, March 10, 1873. In excellent condition. "*Men saw the thorns on Jesus's brow / But Angels saw the
roses.*" From the Henry E. Luhrs Collection. Accompanied by LOA from
PSA/DNA.

Estimate: $400-$600

*aboard "Los Angeles
Limited" Eastbound
Jan. 26, 1942.
Jack Johnson
Ex Worlds Heavy
weight Champion*

POST CARD

*Sgt Fryer
DEML
Ft Totten
New York*

25616   Rare Jack Johnson Signature Signature: "*Jack Johnson*"
on verso of a color picture postcard, 5.5" x 3.5", depicting "The Famous
Streamliner '400' - Chicago and North Western Line". Above the message
is a caption beginning: "Powerful Diesels provide a smooth flow of pow-

er...." A collector has penned: "Aboard 'Los Angeles/Limited' Eastbound/
Jan. 26, 1942." above Johnson's signature and: "Ex Worlds Heavy/weight
(sic) Champion" below it. Penned on the address portion on the right,
probably by the collector: "Sgt Fryer/DEML/Ft Totten,/New York". Boxer
Jack Johnson had won the World Heavyweight Championship in a 14
round decision over Tommy Burns on December 26, 1908. On April 5,
1915, he lost his title to Jess Willard by a knockout in the 26th round. In
very fine condition. From the Henry E. Luhrs Collection. Accompanied by
LOA from PSA/DNA.

Estimate: $200-$400

**25617   Noteworthy 1918 Letter from Secretary of State Robert
Lansing Regarding the Registration of Aliens.** Dated May 17, 1918,
on Department of State Letterhead. 2pp. TLS 8.5" x 11.0". Very fine.
This is a formal communication, during wartime, to the Governor of
Massachussetts regarding a pending bill in the legislature regarding the
registration of aliens, and confirming the enclosure of a memorandum
regarding treaties with foreign governments which might affect such
legislation. This was a "hot button" issue in the paranoid atmosphere
surrounding the War, especially with regard to resident Germans
whose allegiance was in question. From the Henry E. Luhrs Collection.
Accompanied by LOA from PSA/DNA.

Estimate: $100-$200

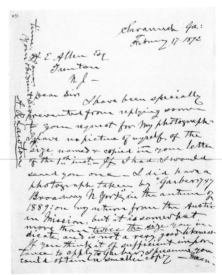

25618   Alexander Robert Lawton Autograph Letter Signed "*A.R.
Lawton.*" One page, 8" x 9.8", Savannah, Georgia, February 17, 1892. The
content discusses Lawton's regret that he is unable to send a photograph
in the size the addressee wanted. Lawton was a commander on the
Confederate side during the Civil War.

The letter is in very fine condition; usual folds are present; some of the ink
is smudged. From the Henry E. Luhrs Collection. Accompanied by LOA
from PSA/DNA.

Estimate: $400-$600

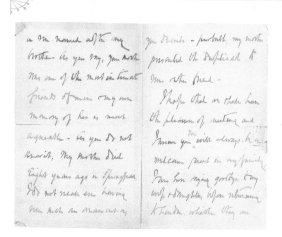

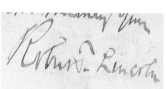

25619   Robert Todd Lincoln Collection. This lot contains five Autograph Letters Signed and three Typed Letters Signed by Robert Todd Lincoln. Robert Todd Lincoln was the eldest son of Abraham and Mary Todd Lincoln, and the only one of the four boys to reach adulthood. He served in the Civil War and held the rank of captain and later he went on to serve several government positions such as Secretary of War and U.S. Ambassador to the United Kingdom. The items in this lot are as follows: The first ALS is signed *"Robert T. Lincoln."* Two pages, 4.5" x 6.75", personal letterhead, Chicago, May 7th, 1896. The letter discusses fishing at Lake Eerie.

The second ALS is signed *"Robert T. Lincoln."* Three pages, 4.5" x 6.75", Rye Beach, New Hampshire, July 24, 1894.Excellent Political content: In part, *"… In the absence of any incident we ought to have either Harrison or McKinley. There never was a better President than Mr. Harrison & if he wants it, the Country owes him a second term…"*

The third ALS is signed, *"Robert T. Lincoln."* Four pages, 4.5" x 7", mourning stationery, Mt. Pleasant, Iowa, December 26, 1890. Mentioning the death of his mother eight years before.

The fourth ALS is signed *"Robert T. Lincoln."* Four pages, 4.25" x 6.75", July 5, 1893, Little Boar's Head, New Hampshire. About Lincoln's lack of desire to hold any public office at the end of his life.

The fifth and final ALS is signed *"Robert T. Lincoln."* Three pages, 4.5" x 6.75", Chicago, April 30, 1895. It reads in part, *"…As I have said to you, I am first for Mr. Harrison (who was defeated not worse than Cleveland) because he has demonstrated his commanding fitness for the position but whoever may be the man at the head of the ticket, it will not be myself…"*

The handwritten letters are all in very good condition overall; they have all been silked and trimmed slightly by a conservator.

The first TLS is signed *"Robert T. Lincoln."* One page, 4.8" x 7.8", Pullman Palace Car Company Stationery, Chicago, December 16, 1898. The content expresses Lincoln's sympathies at the addressee's loss of his father.

The second TLS is signed *"Robert T. Lincoln."* One page, 4.75" x 7.25", Pullman Palace Car Company stationery, Chicago, December 23, 1897. The content is routine.

The third and final TLS is signed, *"Robert T. Lincoln."* Two pages, 7" x 8.9", Manchester, Vermont, September 2, 1920. The letter discusses a letter which his mother had written in 1859 as well as his failure to pass the examinations for Harvard Law School the first time through.

The Typed Letters are in Very Good condition, albeit silked, and with some ink bleeding. From the Henry E. Luhrs Collection. Accompanied by LOA from PSA/DNA.
Estimate: $700-$900

25620   Three Significant-Content Letters Signed by Important Massachussetts Senator Henry Cabot Lodge (1850-1924) All on U.S Senate letterhead, and dating from 1898, 1909, and 1911. Each approximately 8.0" x 11.0" size, and in very fine condition with minor pencil notations. All three are written to a Prof. William Sedwick at M.I.T. The first, dated April 5, 1898, apparently refers to a letter Sedwick had sent which might have affected a bill already passed by the Senate. It presumably had to do with foreign affairs, for Lodge Concludes, *"Everyone feels with you, I am sure, that if it can possibly be obtained we want peace with honor, and I have been doing all I can to help the President in this direction, but it looks very much as if, owing to the attitude of Spain, we could not avoid a conflict."* The second declines to sign an Anti-Woman Suffrage petition as a matter of procedure, but assures Sedwick that *"I have been always openly and publicly opposed to Woman Suffrage..."* The third refers to a brief Sedwick had sent him regarding a Senate bill. From the Henry E. Luhrs Collection. Accompanied by LOA from PSA/DNA.
Estimate: $200-$300

25621   John Lowell Jr. On the Difference Between New York's & Boston's Ladies Autograph Letter Signed, 3 pages, with integral address leaf, New York, November 1, 1923. To B.A. Gould in Boston. A small piece of paper is missing from the right corner of the third page, apparently effecting a word; otherwise good.   Even great financiers think, sometimes, of other things than money: and John Lowell, Jr., one of the greatest, thought of much else. Here, on business in New York, he thinks of women - comparing and contrasting those of New York with those back in Boston. In part, and in brief:*"...I spent a pleasant evening at Mrs. Van Rensselaer's who does not forget her Boston friends... The ladies here look beautifully in the street and carry themselves with an air of gracefulness & graciousness in public unknown to our sterner climate. It is a never failing Spectacle to walk in Broadway... and the man who does not enjoy it must have his heart hardened against pleasurable sensations through the medium of the eye. The ladies here 'tis true do not converse so instructively as with us.... Could I choose I should wish to associate with those beautiful butterflies the 15 finest days of the year. Give me the cultivated minds of my own townswomen the remaining three hundred and fifty..."* From the Henry E. Luhrs Collection. Accompanied by LOA from PSA/DNA.
Estimate: $300-$400

25622 Douglas MacArthur Autograph Collection consisting of four items, two signed by MacArthur. The first is a signature on the bottom of a typewritten autograph request, 7.25" x 10.5", H. Ernest Luhrs letterhead, New York, Jul 2, 1951. The second is a signature on a 4" x 1.5" sheet laid down to card stock. The third great item in this grouping is a 5" x 4" official U.S. Army press photograph of MacArthur addressing members of Congress on April 19, 1951. This is the famous speech where he uttered the well-known phrase "Old soldiers never die, they just fade away." Vice President Alben Barkley and Speaker of the House Sam Rayburn, who are both pictured, have signed this photo. The last item is a printed announcement for Poor Richard's 47th Annual Banquet in Philadelphia in 1952 at which MacArthur was to speak. All items in Very Fine condition. From the Henry E. Luhrs Collection. Accompanied by LOA from PSA/DNA.

Estimate: $500-$600

25623 Douglas MacArthur Typed Souvenir Manuscript Signed of his famous speech before a Joint Session of Congress on April 19, 1951. The actual spoken text of the speech was neatly typed (double spaced, front only) on 14 pages of *Lincoln Library* stationery and MacArthur added his ink signature just above the title on the first page. This is the famous speech in which he says in closing, "Old soldiers never die; they just fade away. And like the old soldier of that ballad, I now close my military career and just fade away, an old soldier who tried to do his duty as God gave him the light to see that duty. Good-by." Fine condition, one barely visible spot on the front page. A most desirable item from this legendary military figure. From the Henry E. Luhrs Collection. Accompanied by LOA from PSA/DNA.

Estimate: $800-$1,200

View color images of virtually every lot and place bids at HeritageAuctions.com/Americana

25624 Douglas MacArthur Famous Quotation Signed. Typed Quotation Signed, as *General of the Army*, 1 page, 8" by 10.5", no place, no date [prior to 1951]; in Fine condition. Here the legendary and controversial American soldier offers this heartfelt, and famous, paean to fatherhood: "*By profession I am a soldier and take pride in that fact, but I am prouder - infinitely prouder - to be a father. A soldier destroys in order to build: the father only builds, never destroys. One has the potentialities of death; the other embodies creation and life. And while the hordes of death are mighty, the battalions of life are mightier still. It is my hope that my son, when I am gone, will remember me not from the battle but in the home repeating with him our simple daily prayer: "Our Father Who Art in Heaven."*" From the Henry E. Luhrs Collection. Accompanied by LOA from PSA/DNA.

Estimate: $300-$500

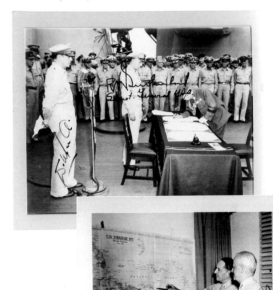

25625 General Macarthur and Others Signed Photographs. The men featured in this lot are Douglas Macarthur, Chester Nimitz, and Richard Sutherland. Two black and white photographs, measuring 5" x 4.25", picturing military scenes. The first one features the signatures of Macarthur and Nimitz, and depicts them examining a map of the Pacific Oceans and surrounding islands. The second photograph is signed by Macarthur and Sutherland and depicts the two generals watching General Yoshira Umeza sign over Japan's surrender in 1945. A nice set of photos commemorating great officers from the second World War. The photographs are both in very fine condition; typed information on the verso; pen marks present on the verso as well. From the Henry E. Luhrs Collection. Accompanied by LOA from PSA/DNA.

Estimate: $600-$800

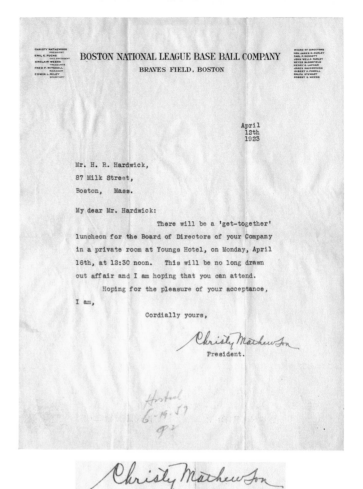

25626 **Horace Mann, the Father of Public Education, Salutes A Fellow Pioneer. Autograph Letter Signed,** 2 pages, recto and verso, 4.75" by 7.5", Yellow Springs, November 3, 1853. To Lorin Andrews of the Ohio Teachers' Association. In very fine condition, although the left margin is a just a tad ragged, and a couple of tiny soft pencil dealer's notations are tucked into the corners. With typed transcription.

That you're reading this catalogue may well be the end result of the momentous work undertaken, in the mid-19th century, by Horace Mann and the recipient of this letter, Lorin Andrews, to establish universal, nonsectarian education. That struggle forms the backdrop of this letter, as Mann expresses his appreciation of Lorin's work - he had just gotten the Ohio legislature to pass the state's first property tax to support public schools - and accepts an invitation to deliver the keynote speech at the State Teacher's Association. In part: *"...I thank your Society, most sincerely, for the invitation... and I sincerely hope the time has now come when I can establish cordial relations with a Society which I have long regarded with so much honor & respect. I should not suffer any ordinary occasion to take me away from the college [he was president of Antioch College]; but I consider this an extraordinary one... I shall gladly avail myself of this occasion to show the deep interest which I feel in the noble efforts of the Ohio Teachers of Common Schools."* From the Henry E. Luhrs Collection. Accompanied by LOA from PSA/DNA.
Estimate: $400-$500

25627 **Christy Mathewson Extremely Rare Letter on Boston Braves Letterhead!** Typed Letter Signed, as president of the Boston Braves, 1 page, 8.25" x 11", on the letterhead of the Boston National League Base Ball Company, Braves Field, Boston, April 12, 1923. To H.R. Hardwick, probably one of the ball club's 85 minority shareholders. In fine condition, with a soft pencil dealer's notation at bottom, not effecting text. A very desirable, and hard to find, autograph.

"Big Six" had all the right numbers: 78 shutouts (third all-time); 372 wins (fourth); and a lifetime 2.13 E.R.A. (fifth). Add to that four seasons when he won 30 or more games, five when he won both the E.R.A. title and strike crown, and it's no surprise that in 1936, he joined Babe Ruth, Honus Wagner, Ty Cobb and Walter Johnson as the first class of baseball Hall of Famers. In 1923 he became the president of the Boston Braves and here, five days before the start of the season, he alerts Mr. Hardwick of a Board of Directors meeting. In full: *" There will be a 'get-together' luncheon for the Board of Directors of your company in a private room at Youngs Hotel, on Monday, April 16th, at 12:30 noon. This will be no long drawn out affair and I am hoping that you can attend. Hoping for the pleasure of your acceptance, I am..."* From the Henry E. Luhrs Collection. Accompanied by LOA from PSA/DNA.
Estimate: $2,000-$3,000

25628   General Anthony C. McAuliffe Signed Photograph. Black and white photograph, 8.25" x 10", np, nd, signed as *"A.C. McAuliffe Maj. Gen. U.S. Army."* General McAuliffe commanded several successful battles during World War II, including the Battle of the Bulge. He parachuted into Normandy on D-Day and even had a chance to make his mark by giving the German commander his famous reply when asked to surrender; *"Aww Nuts!"* This handsome photo features McAuliffe in full uniform backed by an American flag.

The photograph is in very fine condition; some minor creases are visible. From the Henry E. Luhrs Collection. Accompanied by LOA from PSA/DNA.
Estimate: $500-$700

25629   General Anthony McAuliffe Signed Photograph. 8" x 9.75" black and white photograph of McAuliffe wearing his full uniform and all his decorations. He signs himself, *"A.C. McAuliffe, Lieut. Gen., US Army."* McAuliffe was a general during WWII, and was famous for his one word reply to a German surrender ultimatum. McAuliffe and his men were surrounded by Germans, and when the German commander General Heinrich von Luettwitz demanded his surrender, McAuliffe sent his famous reply, "Nuts!" The photograph is in very fine condition; writing has slightly faded. From the Henry E. Luhrs Collection. Accompanied by LOA from PSA/DNA.
Estimate: $300-$400

25630   J.P. Morgan: A Rare Letter - With Fiery Content! Typed letter Signed, 1 page, 5" by 8", on the printed letterhead of 23 Wall Street, New York, September 21, 1911. To George Sylvester Viereck, publisher of "Rundschau Zweier Welten" in New York. In fine condition. J. Pierpont Morgan was, in a word, colossal: the organizing force behind General Electric, U.S. Steel, and vast railroad empires, he served for decades as America's unofficial central banker. It didn't do, as this letter makes abundantly clear, to rile him. "<iln>" From the Henry E. Luhrs Collection. Accompanied by LOA from PSA/DNA.
Estimate: $700-$900

25631   Samuel F.B. Morse Autograph Letter Signed *"Saml. F.B. Morse."* One page, 4.9" x 7.9", No. 5 West 22nd Street, December 31, 1861. This letter was written to several men from Lecture Committee of the Mercantile Library Association. The content is routine, he accepts a dinner invitation for the 7th of January. Samuel F.B. Morse was an American inventor and artist, renowned for his invention of the Morse Code among other things. The letter is in very fine; usual folds are present; slight soiling around edges. From the Henry E. Luhrs Collection. Accompanied by LOA from PSA/DNA.
Estimate: $800-$1,200

Phil. F.B. Morse

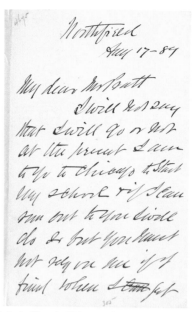

Saml. F.B. Morse.

25632   Samuel F.B. Morse Autograph Letter Signed "*Saml. F.B. Morse.*" Four pages, 5.25" x 8.2", New York, March 11, 1862. This letter is written to Samuel's sister Cornelia, it is a lengthy letter with many subjects, including war, family, and school. This letter is full of interesting sections, for example, "*…in that while so many in our beloved North & South are in deepest sorrow, our loved family circle are So exempt from trouble except in the profound Sympathy which every American heart must entertain, not entirely callous to all feelings of humanity…*" This is just one of the sections where Morse discusses the war and his feelings on the Union divided. Morse was a well-known defender of the institution of slavery, believing it to be divinely sanctioned. The letter is in very fine condition; usual folds are present; corners are slightly torn and wrinkled. Included with this letter is a handsome engraving of Morse, perfect for display. From the Henry E. Luhrs Collection. Accompanied by LOA from PSA/DNA.
Estimate: $1,500-$2,000

25633   Dwight L. Moody Writes He's on His Way to Start the Moody Bible Institute in Chicago. Autograph Letter Signed ("D. L. Moody"), 2 pages, 1st and 4th integral leaves, 5.5" by 8", Northfield, August 17, [18]89. To Mr. Pratt. Strengthened at left margin, otherwise fine. Here the Protestant evangelist sets out to spread his simple, conservative and personal Christianity; clearly, in his focus, a man on a mission. "*…I am to go to Chicago to start my school* [the Moody Bible Institute] *& if I can run out to you I will do so but you must not rely on me…*" From the Henry E. Luhrs Collection. Accompanied by LOA from PSA/DNA.
Estimate: $400-$500

25634   Robert E. Peary (1856-1920), Partial Autograph Letter (unsigned), one page, 8" x 10.5", Payer Harbor, [Ellesmere Island], August 29, 1901 to fellow Arctic explorer and anthropologist Albert Operti. While on one of his pre-Polar Arctic expeditions, Peary writes to Operti (who accompanied him to Greenland in 1897) in part; "*I was tramping [sic] along the ice foot near Hayes Pt. on my return from [Fort] Conger when suddenly a team of howling dogs appeared upon the scene dragging a sledge on which as a long-haired, shout-ing Eskimo (Karadahsu, whom you may remember). He handed me my mail bag, & my first news for two years. Your letter I read that night in a snow igloo at Cape Louis Napoleon. Don't 'bust' just yet. You have a year's extension of time for it. Besides I want to see you again…*" Mounted to a larger sheet, on the verso of which has been affixed a second **Robert E. Peary Autograph Letter Signed,** *Hastily Peary,* one page, 6" x 9.25", no place given, June 17, 1904 in pencil to Operti concerning a photograph. In part: *Can you strengthen & more clearly define the features in this photo & also complete the hood as indicated by the pencil lines, all in a way that a good photo reproduction can be made…*" Peary would begin his final expedition to the North Pole in 1908 reaching the spot deemed magnetic North at 0-degrees on April 7, 1909. Both letters bear a few marginal chips, mounted to a larger sheet, else Very Good to Fine condition. From the Henry E. Luhrs Collection. Accompanied by LOA from PSA/DNA.
Estimate: $300-$500

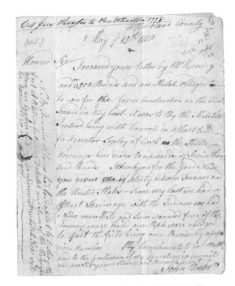

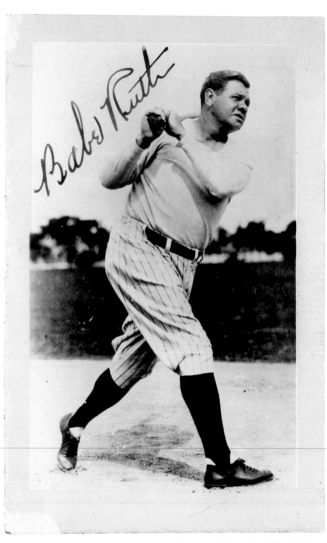

25637   Will Rogers Signature Pair. This lot contains two small signature cards signed by the legendary Humorist, Will Rogers. The first card measures 3.8" x 1.8", dated July 15th, 1930, signed, *"Will Rogers."* The second card measures 5" x 3", and is signed, *"Sincerely yours, Will Rogers."* Will Rogers is most recognized for his early career as an entertainer, and later as one of the most widely read newspaper columnists in his day. The signature cards are in very fine condition; slight soiling is present; pencil notations present on both cards. From the Henry E. Luhrs Collection. Accompanied by LOA from PSA/DNA.
Estimate: $300-$400

25635   (American Revolution) John Proctor, Pennsylvania militia officer, Autograph Letter Signed *"John Proctor"*, one page with integral address leaf, 6.25" x 8.25", Westmorland County, [Pennsylvania], May 15, 1778 to Pennsylvania President Thomas Wharton, Jr., thanking him, among other things: *"...for the good nuse [sic] you gave me of a traty [sic] between France and the United States - Sine my last we had - Ye smart Scrimage [sic] with the Indeons [sic] we had nine men kild [sic] and sum [sic] wounded four of the enemy ware [sic] kil'd and our people ware obligded [sic] to quit the field being over powered by a superior numbor [sic]..."* Proctor adds a short postscript in the left margin: *"...A numbor [sic] of torys [sic] had laid a plot to destroy the fort at Pit[t]sburg, but were detected and sum of the Principle [sic] men are tackin [sic] and in confinement..."* A fine content letter documenting the often overlooked western theatre of operations during the Revolutionary War. From the Henry E. Luhrs Collection. Accompanied by LOA from PSA/DNA.
Estimate: $700-$900

25636   Joseph Pulizer Jr. Thanks a Foxhunter-Editor for "Valuable Leads." Typed Letter Signed, 1 page, 7" by 10.5", on the letterhead of the "St. Louis Post-Dispatch", St. Louis, February 2, 1928. To Richard Ely Danielson of "The Sportsman." Tallyho! Here Pulitzer, poised to take the newspaper business he inherited into a modern media company, thanks the editor of an amateur sports-who is, more importantly, Master of the Groton Hunt - for a letter. "It contains many valuable leads," he declares, "and we all here in the office appreciate the trouble you have taken to help us out." From the Henry E. Luhrs Collection. Accompanied by LOA from PSA/DNA.
Estimate: $400-$600

25638   George Herman "Babe" Ruth Signed Photograph. Black and white photograph of the Babe in action; this photo shows Ruth swinging his bat and looking off into the stands. It measures 3.5" x 5.5" and is signed in bold, blue fountain pen as *"Babe Ruth."* Babe Ruth is considered by many to be the greatest baseball player of all time.

The photograph is in very fine condition; slight soiling present on the edges. From the Henry E. Luhrs Collection. Accompanied by LOA from PSA/DNA.
Estimate: $4,000-$5,000

25639 **"Babe" Ruth Ink Signature on Paper Sheet** 5" x 3" in size. Known also as the *Bambino* or the *Sultan of Swat,* Ruth was one of the first five inductees into the Baseball Hall of Fame in 1936. His 1921 season will likely never be equaled statistically and he is consistently voted as the top baseball player of all time. Ruth transcended being just an incredible baseball player though. He was, and still is, a national icon, a hero, and a treasure for the ages. No one will ever take his place as the fans' favorite. This is a particularly nice signature worthy of inclusion in the finest of collections. Accompanied by LOA from PSA/DNA.
Estimate: $1,200-$1,800

25641 **Samuel Francis Smith (1808-1895), composer of "America",** **Autograph Quotation Signed** *"S. f. Smith.",* one page, 4" x 2.5", no place given, January 16, 1878. A four line inspirational poem which reads: *"Live nobly, let high aims inspire thy mind; | Cast off all dross, be gracious, pure, refind; | Let works for God, for man, thy zeal employ, | And strew in all thy pathways love and joy."* Extremely light toning, else fine. From the Henry E. Luhrs Collection. Accompanied by LOA from PSA/DNA.
Estimate: $500-$700

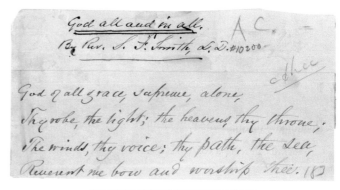

25642 **Samuel Francis Smith Autograph Quote Signed** *"Rev. S. F. Smith, D.D.".* One page, 5.25" x 2.75", np, nd. Smith is best known for the popular patriotic song "America" (aka My Country 'Tis of Thee) though he wrote dozens of other hymns and songs. Offered here are the title, signature, and first four lines of "God All and in All" (circa 1890) in Smith's hand consisting of two paper slips laid down to another sheet. Very good condition with minor ink smearing and very light staining. From the Henry E. Luhrs Collection. Accompanied by LOA from PSA/DNA.
Estimate: $300-$400

25640 **E. Kirby Smith Autograph Letter Signed** *"E. Kirby Smith."* Three pages, 5" x 8", New Orleans, Louisiana, February 24, 1893. The letter was written to Darwin C. Pavey and discusses Smith's admiration for Fitz John Porter. Porter had been the victim of an unjust court martial by rival generals when in reality he had been a model general and soldier. Smith explains this by saying in the letter, *"…his friendship for and attachment to McClelland* [sic] *was his cardinal sin and produced that cruel and unjust finding of the court, which degraded Porter as a Soldier & citizen. The whole country now recognizes his loyalty & devotion to the country and know that his merits & services as a soldier are deserving of the highest commendation…"* Smith was himself a general, although it was for the confederate side.

The letter is in very fine condition; usual folds are present. From the Henry E. Luhrs Collection. Accompanied by LOA from PSA/DNA.
Estimate: $600-$800

AMERICA.

My country! 'tis of thee,
Sweet land of liberty,
    Of thee I sing ;
Land where my fathers died!
Land of the Pilgrims' pride!
From every mountain side
    Let freedom ring!

My native country, thee—
Land of the noble free—
    Thy name I love ;
I love thy rocks and rills,
Thy woods and templed hills,
My heart with rapture thrills
    Like that above.

Let music swell the breeze,
And ring from all the trees
    Sweet freedom's song :
Let mortal tongues awake ;
Let all that breathe partake ;
Let rocks their silence break,—
    The sound prolong.

Our fathers' God! to thee,
Author of liberty,
    To thee we sing :
Long may our land be bright
With freedom's holy light ;
Protect us by thy might,
    Great God, our King!

S. F. Smith.

25643   Samuel Francis Smith Printed "America" Lyrics Signed.
Four complete stanzas of this popular patriotic song are printed on a 4.5"
x 7.5" card with a decorative border. He has signed as "*S. F. Smith.*" at the
bottom. This long-popular song was written in 1832, and is sometimes
referred to by its first line "My country! 'tis of thee." Very Fine condition, one horizontal fold as made. From the Henry E. Luhrs Collection.
Accompanied by LOA from PSA/DNA.
Estimate: $500-$700

**25645   John Wainwright Signed Photo and Autograph Letter
Signed.** This lot highlights the career of John Wainwright, an American
hero during WWII; he was responsible for defending the Philippines
late in the war. He was awarded the Medal of Honor for his efforts by
President Truman. The first item is an autograph letter signed, *"John
Wainwright, Rear Admiral, Class of 1900, U.S.N.A."* One page, 6" x 8",
Tucson, Arizona, April 11th, 1947. The content of the letter is routine. The
second item is a signed and inscribed black and white photograph. It
measures 8" x 10", and reads, *"To H. Kaulie- Sincerely J.M. Wainwright,
General USA."* The items are both in very fine condition; usual folds are
present on the letter; signature is slightly faded on the photograph. From
the Henry E. Luhrs Collection. Accompanied by LOA from PSA/DNA.
Estimate: $300-$400

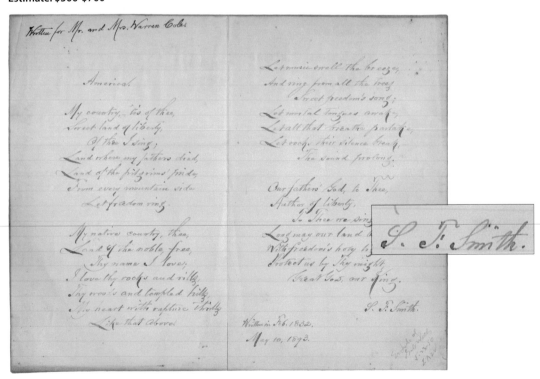

25644   Samuel Francis Smith Complete "America" Autograph Manuscript Signed, a fair copy, "*S. F. Smith*". One page, 9.75" x 7.75", np,
May 10, 1893, *"Written for Mr. and Mrs. Warren Cole."* Smith writes, by hand, all four stanzas of this beloved patriotic paean often known as
"My Country 'Tis of Thee." As noted at the bottom by Smith, he originally wrote this song in February 1832. This was the year that he became
a Baptist minister and editor of the *Baptist Missionary Magazine*. A friend asked him to translate a German poem for him. Smith liked the
music so much that he wrote new English words for it. The song became popular in his lifetime and was performed at his funeral in 1895.
Fine condition with light toning only at the very edges, presents very well. From the Henry E. Luhrs Collection. Accompanied by LOA from
PSA/DNA.
Estimate: $4,000-$6,000

25646 **Mary E. Waller Sentiment Signed.**
Autograph Sentiment Signed, 1 page, 5" by
3.25", reading *"Always Sincerely, Mary E. Waller."*
In fine condition. A handsome memento of
this popular early 20th century New England
novelist. From the Henry E. Luhrs Collection.
Accompanied by LOA from PSA/DNA
Estimate: $300-$400

25647 **Booker T. Washington Letter
Fundraising for His Tuskegee Institute** Typed
Letter Signed, accomplished in purple carbon
typescript but signed in ink, 1 page, 8" by 11",
on the letterhead of "the Tuskegee Normal
and Industrial Institute... For the Training of
Colored Young Men and Women" but headed
Fifth Avenue Bank, New York, N.Y., no date. To
James D. Perkins in New York. As founder of
the Tuskegee Institute, the African-American
leader sets out to raise money, up north, for
his groundbreaking school which in time,
would become Tuskegge University. *"I am
spending some days in the city for the purpose
of securing help for the Tuskegee Normal and
Industrial institute... We are in need, just now,
of money for current expenses and the increas-
ing of our endowment fund. I shall be glad of
any help which you can see your way clear to
give... Anything sent to the above address will
reach me."* From the Henry E. Luhrs Collection.
Accompanied by LOA from PSA/DNA.
Estimate: $300-$400

25648 **Booker T. Washington (1856-1915)
African American educator and reformer,
Letter Signed,** *"Booker T. Washington"* as
Principal of the Tuskegee Institute, one page,
6" x 9.5", Tuskegee, Alabama, October 22, 1904
to Miss Caroline E. Wing of Manchester, New
Hampshire noting the enclosure of *"...my
last annual report to he Board of Trustees...
I thought you might like to read it or at least
glance through it..."* Besides his contributions
to education, Washington was also a significant
African American leader of the late nineteenth
and early twentieth centuries advocating self-
reliance. The Tuskegee Institute was a means
to this goal. Two minor losses toward bottom
margin, usual folds, else fine. From the Henry
E. Luhrs Collection. Accompanied by LOA from
PSA/DNA.
Estimate: $300-$500

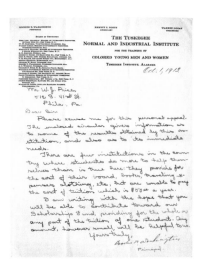

25649 **Booker T. Washington Letter
Signed** *"Booker T. Washington."* One page
handwritten document, measures 8.5" x 11",

dated October 1, 1913. This document is not
written in Booker Washington's hand but is
signed by him. The letter asks Mr. J.W. Price for
donations of cash or items to help his students
with expenses. The letter is written on Tuskegee
Normal and Industrial Institute stationery. The
letter is in Fine condition; the normal folds
are present; it is glued into a folder where it is
folded in half for storage. From the Henry E.
Luhrs Collection. Accompanied by LOA from
PSA/DNA.
Estimate: $500-$700

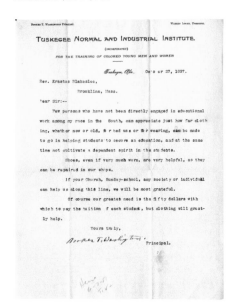

25650 **Booker T. Washington Lot of Two
Letters Signed and One Typed Letter Signed**
"Booker T. Washington." This lot consists of
three letters, all signed by Booker T. Washington
the famous educator and civil rights advocate.
None of the letters are in his own hand, but
all are signed by him. All three letters measure
8.5" x 11" and are on the Tuskegee Normal
and Industrial Institute stationery. The first
letter is a one-page typed document that is
dated October 27, 1897. The content consists
of Washington requesting clothes, bedding
items and shoes for his students. He also states
that the fifty-dollar donation for tuition is best
of all. The second letter is a two page handwritten document dated, February 12, 1901.
Booker writes Mrs. M.E. Clark thanking her for
her two-dollar donation. The third and final
letter is a one page handwritten document.
The content contains a request to Reverend
Erastus Blakeslee for money or items to help
his students with their expenses. All three
letters are in Good condition; all letters have
pencil notations on the versos; usual folds are
present; writing and printed letters are fading
slightly. A nice lot for Booker T. Washington
collectors! From the Henry E. Luhrs Collection.
Accompanied by LOA from PSA/DNA.
Estimate: $1,000-$1,500

25651 **No Lot.**

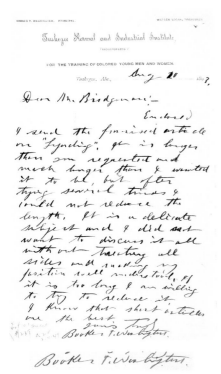

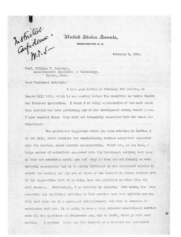

25652 Booker T. Washington on Lynching

Booker T. Washington (1856-1915) African American educator and reformer, very fine content Autograph Letter Signed "*Booker T. Washington*", one page on Tuskegee Institute letterhead, Tuskegee, Alabama, August 10, 1893 to Mr. Bridgman concerning an article on lynching slated for publication. During the height of the lynching epidemic at the turn of the twentieth century, he writes: "*Enclosed I send the finished article on 'Lynching.' It is longer then you requested and such longer than I waned it to be, but after trying several times I could not reduce the length. It is a delicate subject and I did not want to discuss it all without treating all sides and making my position well understood. If it is too long I am willing to try to reduce it. I know that short articles are the best. —- Yours truly Booker T. Washington.*" Despite Washington's advocacy of reconciliation between the races, lynching in the South continued unabated. According to the N.A.A.C.P.'s Anti-lynching Committee, 3,224 people were lynched between 1889 and 1918, of those 2,522 were black and 702 were white. The justifications for lynchings included such excuses as "using offensive language, refusal to give up land, illicit distilling" and other "offenses." Bright and clean and in extremely fine condition. Important content from one of America's towering figures in Black history. From the Henry E. Luhrs Collection. Accompanied by LOA from PSA/DNA.
Estimate: $1,500-$2,500

25653 John W. Weeks: 2 Good Content Letters, as Senator and as Secretary of War.

Here is an opportunity to obtain two letters of the Secretary of War who served two presidents, Harding and Coolidge, well and faithfully. 1) Typed Letter Signed, *as Senator,* 2 pages, 8" x 10.5", on the letterhead of the United States Senate, Washington, February 6, 1914. To William T. Sedgwick at the Massachusetts Institute of Technology; Professor Sedgwick, a biologist, was a key figure in shaping federal Public Health policy. With an initialed note in Sedgwick's hand in upper left corner "*In strictest confidence - W.T.S.*". Held by bracket, upper left, and Fine. In part: "*There are, as you know, a large number of scientists connected with the Government service; very many suitably compensated but it is pretty difficult in the Government service to select for special pay any man or class of men because it always carries with it the supposition that it is being done for political or other than reasons.*" 2) Typed Letter Signed, as secretary of war, 1 page, on the letterhead of the War Department, Washington, April 14, 1922. To the Hon. Benjamin Loring Young. Bearing the faintest imprint of a paper clip at top, else Fine. Listing the three men from Massachusetts who won the Congressional Medal of Honor in World War I. In part: "*Private George Dilboy, deceased... Private 1st Cl. Michael J. Perkins, deceased... Major Charles W. Whittlesey, deceased... The records of First Lieutenant William Bradford Turner show that he was born in the State of Massachusetts but when appointed temporarily an officer during the World War, his residence was that of New York State*". The Congressional Medal of Honor is the nation's highest military award for "uncommon valor" and given for actions that are above and beyond the call of duty in combat against an armed enemy. The names of those awarded them will always be remembered. From the Henry E. Luhrs Collection. Accompanied by LOA from PSA/DNA.
Estimate: $100-$200

25654 Roy Owen West, Coolidge's Secretary of the Interior, Rents a Cadillac!

Autograph Letter Signed, 2 pages (1st and 3rd of an integral lef), on his personal letterhead, 5.5" by 7", Chicago, April 24, 1914. To Mr. Carter. In excellent condition. Collectors of Cabinet members, certainly, and collectors of automotive history, probably, will want to bid on this letter, in which the rising Republican power broker arranges a vacation. In part: "I note that a Cadillac and driver could be furnished. I assume that the price named - $25 - is by the day... Please advise me further as to the car." He also lobbies for a quiet suite with two baths. From the Henry E. Luhrs Collection. Accompanied by LOA from PSA/DNA.
Estimate: $400-$500

25655 Orville Wright Signed Photo of First Manned Flight. On December 17, 1903 at Kitty Hawk, North Carolina, man finally conquered flight, a feat that changed the world. In that very first powered airplane flight, a bicycle repairman from Dayton, Ohio named Orville Wright stayed aloft for 12 seconds and traveled 120 feet. A photograph was taken of that quick trip and it is that image that is offered here. A 6.25" x 4.5" printed image neatly signed in black ink, in fine condition with a light crease near the top that does not detract. The original transmittal envelope is included with a March 1, 1929 Dayton, Ohio postmark. This is possibly the most desirable form of Orville Wright's autograph. From the Henry E. Luhrs Collection. Accompanied by LOA from PSA/DNA.
Estimate: $2,000-$3,000

First Man-Flight, December 17, 1903
Kitty Hawk, N. C.

25656 Sergeant York Signature and Signed Photograph. This lot features two items which highlight Sergeant Alvin York, legendary World War I hero. The first is a 5" x 3" lined note card signed, *"Sgt. Alvin C. York."* The second item is a 5.5" x 7" magazine photograph of York which he signs, *"Sgt. Alvin C. York."* York was decorated with the military's highest honor, The Medal of Honor, in 1919. The pieces in this lot are in very fine condition; signatures are bold and dark! From the Henry E. Luhrs Collection. Accompanied by LOA from PSA/DNA.
Estimate: $300-$500

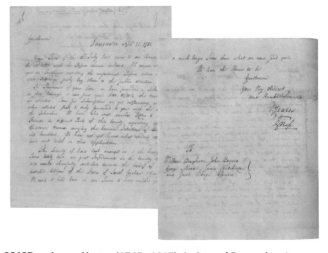

25657 Jasper Yeates (1745 - 1817), Jurist and Pennsylvania revolutionary, Autograph Letter Signed *"J: Yeates"*, two pages, 7.5" x 9.25", Lancaster, Pennsylvania, September 21, 1781 discussing support for refugees in South Carolina and Georgia. He writes in part: "*...We have also wrote circular Letters to our Friends in different Parts of this County, requesting their Assistance towards carrying the humane Intentions of congress in to Execution... The Scarcity of hard Cash amongst us & the heavy Taxes lately laid are great Impediments in the County to many who would cheerfully [sic] contribute towards the Relief to he distressed Citizens of the States of South Carolina & Georgia...*" The British ravaged the South between 1779 and 1781 and remained in possession of Charleston, South Carolina until 1782. Many of the refugees were from the captured cities of Charleston and Savannah... their plight would remedied with the British withdrawal in 1782. Light soiling, else Very good. A fine specimen. From the Henry E. Luhrs Collection. Accompanied by LOA from PSA/DNA.
Estimate: $500-$800

25658   7th Cavalry Autograph Collection consisting of six signed documents and letters. The 7th Cavalry Regiment was organized on September 21, 1866 at Fort Riley, Kansas as part of an expansion of the Regular Army following the Civil War. From 1866 through 1871, the Regiment was posted at Ft. Riley and fought in the Indian Wars. From 1871 through 1873, it participated in occupation duties during the Reconstruction period in the south before being sent north once more to the Dakota Territory. Lt. Col. George A. Custer's disaster at the Battle of the Little Bighorn on June 25-26, 1876, while a stunning defeat, demonstrated the sheer bravery of the 7th Cavalrymen: fourteen soldiers received the Congressional Medal of Honor during that battle. The Regiment was present at the Wounded Knee Massacre on December 29, 1890, the end of the Indian Wars.

This lot includes the following items related to this legendary unit: Henry J. Nowlan (1875 DS); Winfield Scott Edgerly (1876 DS also signed by William Passmore Carlin); Edwin Eckerson (1878 DS); William H. Baldwin (1879 ALS); Elmer Otis (1877 DS); Samuel D. Sturgis (1877 ALS). Generally fine condition. From the Henry E. Luhrs Collection. Accompanied by LOA from PSA/DNA.
Estimate: $500-$600

can find instruction in any study." His dream came true, as Cornell has grown to be one of the top institutes of higher learning in the world with a current enrollment of about 20,000 students. Offered here is a collection of autographed material relating to this university. Just a few of the more than 20 items in this lot are described below:

Ezra Cornell. Co-Founder. ALS, DS (check), Signature (clipped from a letter).

Andrew D. White. Co-Founder. TLS (3), AQS, LS (3).

Souvenir program. Fall Regatta of the Cornell Navy, 1873.

Jacob Gould Schurman. President of Cornell (1892-1920). TLS (4), Signature.

Other names represented here are: H. McCandless, William I. Myers, George H. Sabine, Livingston Farrand, and T. F. Crane. Items generally are in fine condition. From the Henry E. Luhrs Collection. Accompanied by LOA from PSA/DNA.
Estimate: $400-$600

25660   1860s-1870s New York Fire Insurance Policy Collection consisting of more than 25 documents, all related to the estate of John H. Dykers. These range in size from about 8" x 5" up to 14" x 17". Most all are partly printed forms, filled in by hand with various U.S. Revenue stamps attached. Many have beautifully engraved vignettes and decorative borders. A number of different insurance companies are represented. Generally fine to very fine condition. These would look great matted and framed on the wall of an Insurance Agency! From the Henry E. Luhrs Collection.
Estimate: $300-$400

25659   Cornell University Autograph and Memorabilia Collection. A research university based in Ithaca, New York, Cornell is the newest of the "Ivy League" universities. Ezra Cornell and Andrew Dickson White, who both valued egalitarianism, science, and education, founded it in 1865. Cornell said at the time "I would found an institution where any person

Fine condition. Plates are very clean. From the Henry E. Luhrs Collection.
Estimate: $300-$400

25661   (Russo-Japanese War) J. M. Hanihara, member of the Legation of Japan at Washington, Typed Letter Signed, "*J.M Hanihara*", two pages, 8"x 10", Washington, September 23, 1905 with short holograph post-script to Richard V. Oulahan of the *New York Sun,* thanking him for "*...the copies of the Daily and Sunday Sun from June 1st to September 7th, inclusive, containing full reports of the Peace Conference, held at Portsmouth, N.H., which, in compliance with the request I made to you on behalf of the Library of the Waseda University, Tokyo, Japan, my alma Mater... the papers will be bound and placed in the Library, where they will be highly prized as an invaluable record of the historic event, which you, as a special correspondent of one of the greatest papers of the age, have witnessed at a close range.*" The treaty ending the Russo-Japanese War was facilitated at a conference hosted by President Theodore Roosevelt at Portsmouth, Hampshire. Light paperclip stain, usual folds, else Fine. From the Henry E. Luhrs Collection. Accompanied by LOA from PSA/DNA.
Estimate: $200-$300

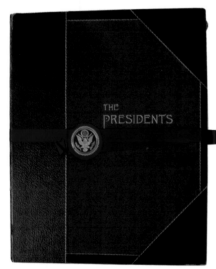

25662   *The White House Gallery of Official Portraits of the Presidents.* Published in 1901 by the Gravure Co. of America New York and Washington. No. 30 of the limited Mckinley memorial edition. 24 fine gravure portraits on deckled paper. Atlas Folio bound in three quarter leather with gilt decorations, front board detached, edges are worn through. Original ribbon with presidential seal. Contents in Very

25663   Autograph Collection Related to Presidencies of McKinley, Taft, and Theodore Roosevelt. Six autographed items: Edith K. Roosevelt, the First Lady from 1901-1909 (free franked envelope, ANS); Elihu Root, Secretary of State under Roosevelt (Signature on State Department card); John D. Long, Secretary of the Navy under McKinley and Roosevelt (ANS); William H. Moody, Secretary of the Navy and Attorney General under Roosevelt (TLS); Frederick J. Manning, Taft's son-in-law (ALS). Generally fine condition. From the Henry E. Luhrs Collection. Accompanied by LOA from PSA/DNA.
Estimate: $300-$500

25664   Literary Autograph Collection "G-H-I". A very nice lot of approximately 17 signed items that includes a number of very influential publishers, as well as authors and poets. Among the items included: Horace Greeley (ADS & ALS); Elbert Hubbard (Signed Portrait Engraving); Henry Irving (Signature); Louis A. Godey (ALS). Some important figures represented here; condition generally fine. From the Henry E. Luhrs Collection. Accompanied by LOA from PSA/DNA.
Estimate: $400-$500

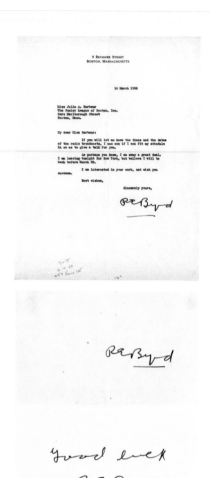

25665   Polar Explorers Group Lot. This lot features five items signed by legendary Polar explorers. The first is a 4" x 1.5" card signed: "*Frederick A. Cook.*" Cook was an Arctic explorer with a somewhat tarnished reputation. He claimed to have reached the North Pole before Peary but this was never proven. Second, we feature a 8.5" x 3.5" sheet of paper signed by James Booth Lockwood. He signs, "*J.B. Lockwood.*" Lockwood was part of the ill-fated Greely Expedition in 1881. He performed several noteworthy feats while on the expedition before perishing along with the rest of the crew. Third, we offer a typed letter signed by Richard Byrd as "*R.E. Byrd.*" It measures 8.5" x 11", dated March 16, 1938. Byrd is, of course, known for his polar expeditions and flights. Next we offer two cards with Richard Byrd's signature on them. They both measure 5" x 3" and are signed: "*R.E. Byrd.*" All five items are in Fine condition; no visible issues except for a few pencil notations on the front of the items. From the Henry E. Luhrs Collection. Accompanied by LOA from PSA/DNA.
Estimate: $300-$500

GLENN H. CURTISS
HAMMONDSPORT
NEW YORK

25666 **Pioneers of Aviation Autograph Collection.** A fine group that includes a couple of the "big" names as well as some of the other important, but less-remembered, individuals in the history of aeronautics. Included are:

Glenn H. Curtis: a large (6" long), bold signature on his personal letterhead.

Capt. Eddie Rickenbacker: a signed early Eastern Air Lines Inc. unused company envelope.

W. J. Tate: Captain Tate and his wife befriended and helped the Wright Brothers while they were at Kitty Hawk building and flying their first gliders and planes. A Typed Letter Signed and a signed (twice) privately published booklet, *Brochure of the Twenty-Fifth Anniversary Celebration of The First Successful Airplane Flight....*

Also included: Sir Charles Kingsford-Smith, Australian aviation pioneer, Signature; John Stannage, Signature; C. E. Rosendahl, Commander of the Dirigible *Los Angeles,* Signature and Signed Photo; a vintage 1927 printed photo of Charles Lindbergh; one other item. Condition generally fine or better. From the Henry E. Luhrs Collection. Accompanied by LOA from PSA/DNA.
Estimate: $400-$600

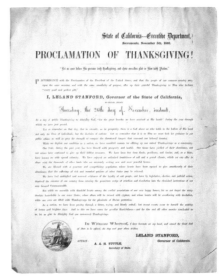

25667 **Thanksgiving Proclamation Broadsides- Massachusetts and California.** A fascinating and unique collection of these historic documents wherein the state governor annually issues "A Proclamation For a Day of Public Thanksgiving and Praise" (or similar wording). Offered here are 13 Commonwealth of Massachusetts Proclamations, ten of which are actually signed by the governor: 1892 (19" x 24"); 1907 (19" x 25"); 1908 (19" x 25"); 1910 (19" x 25", signed by Eben S. Draper); 1911 (8.5" x 11", signed by Eugene N. Foss); 1912 (8.5" x 11", signed by Eugene N. Foss); 1913 (8.5" x 11", signed by Eugene N. Foss); 1914 (10" x 14", signed by David I. Walsh); 1915 (10" x 14", signed by David I. Walsh); 1916 (10" x 14", signed by Samuel W. McCall); 1917 (10" x 14", signed by Samuel W. McCall); 1918 (8.5" x 17", signed by Samuel W. McCall); 1922 (10" x 14", signed by Channing H. Cox).

Also included is a very rare California Proclamation of Thanksgiving from 1863, in part: "In accordance with the Proclamation of the President of the United States, and that the people of our common country may, upon the same occasion, and with the same unanimity of purpose, offer up their grateful Thanksgiving to Him who bestows 'every good and perfect gift'..." The governor at the time was Leland Stanford, who would later found Stanford University.

The documents are generally in Fine condition, all have been folded. All are suitable for display. From the Henry E. Luhrs Collection.
Estimate: $1,000-$1,500

25668 World War I Autograph Collection. Included in this lot are at least 35 World War I-related autographs from both military and political leaders from around the world. Just a few of the included items: Raymond PoincarÈ, president of France 1913-1920 (Signature); General John J. Pershing (war-date TLS w/ envelope); Robert M "Fighting Bob" La Follette, Sr., one of the major opponents to the war (TLS as senator); Major General John A. Lejuene, "the greatest of all Leathernecks" (AQS, TLS); Henry Cabot Lodge (ANS, TLS); David Lloyd George (SP); Count Leopold von Berchtold, played a large part in starting World War I (ALS); Ferdinand Foch (2 Signatures); Charles Whittlesey, Commander of the "Lost Battalion" (Signature). Please note that this is just a sampling of what is included in this historical lot. Generally fine condition. From the Henry E. Luhrs Collection. Accompanied by LOA from PSA/DNA.

Estimate: $800-$1,200

25669 Polar Flight 1928 Crew Signatures. The signatures appear on an 11.5" x 8.5" sheet, with Nobile's signature in the very center, surrounded by the autographs of his entire nine man crew. Nobile's 1928 flight over the North Pole was historic, not only in its accomplishment, but also in the rescue that took place when he and his crew crashed. The rescue was a multi-national effort and Nobile and the crew of his airship were eventually rescued. Aside from Nobile, the crewmembers' signatures on the card include such names as Zappi, Lundborg, and Marian. An interesting lot; one which includes triumph and tragedy all in one. The signature sheet is in very fine condition; slight mounting traces on the verso; edges slightly worn. From the Henry E. Luhrs Collection. Accompanied by LOA from PSA/DNA.

Estimate: $300-$400

25670 Literary Autograph Collection "T". A large collection of autograph material in the fields of literature, education, publishing, and even sports! A few of the approximately 60 signed items: Gene Tunney (ALS); Martin J. Tupper (Signature laid down to Engraving); Francis Trollope (numerous ALS); Deems Taylor (Signature); Bayard Taylor (multiple ALS); Booth Tarkington (Signature); Rose Hartwick Thorpe (AMsS); Lowell Thomas (Signature, TLS, SP); Augustus Thomas (Signed Drawing w/ AQS); James Thacher (ALS); Albert Payson Terhune (ALS); Arnold J. Toynbee (Signatures); Tom Taylor (Signature, ALS); Ida M. Tarbell (SP); William Makepeace Thackery (ALS). This is an amazing collection with many high-dollar items included making it a perfect dealer lot. Generally fine condition. From the Henry E. Luhrs Collection. Accompanied by LOA from PSA/DNA.

Estimate: $1,200-$1,500

25671   Will Rogers, John Ringling, and assorted Signatures on Large Card. One page, 8.5" x 11.8", card stock sheet, np, nd. This is either a birthday card or a sign in sheet for a party, for Colonel W. Scott. It is hard to say what the function was; all we see is a small inscription reading, *"For Col. W. Scott, with best wishes from-"* The card is signed by 31 individuals from all walks of life. Most notable are: Will Rogers, famous humorist. John Ringling, the most successful of the Ringling Brothers, (he was responsible for combining Barnum and Bailey's Circus with Ringling Brothers Circus to create a huge monopoly on the circus industry). Kenesaw Mountain Landis. Landis was baseball's first commissioner, and helped to restore some respect to the league after the Black Sox scandal of 1919. George M. Cohan, is probably the most honored American entertainer; among many other things, he was called the father of the musical comedy. William H. Hays was the man responsible for the Hays Production Code which instituted early censorship in Hollywood. Dewolf Hopper, best known for his recitations of *Casey at the Bat.* Hopper would make a living reciting this poem. A wonderful group of characters on one sheet! The document is in very fine condition; all signatures appear in pencil and are very clear and free of smudges. From the Henry E. Luhrs Collection. Accompanied by LOA from PSA/DNA.
Estimate: $400-$600

25672   1949-1953 Vinson Court Signature Collection. This lot consists of three items signed by Supreme Court Justices from the Vinson Court. There are two signature cards, and one first day cover. The signature cards measure 4.25" x 3.5", one is signed and inscribed, *"To H. Ernst Luhrs with best wishes from Harold H. Burton, May 19, 1951."* The second card is signed by Justice Stanley Reed. The first day cover is the gem of this lot; it is signed by all nine justices including Chief Justice Vinson. The first day cover features a cache of the Supreme Court Building, and the stamp is the National Sesquicentennial 3 cent stamp; the cover is postmarked August 29th, 1950, 9 A.M. The justices whose names appear on the cover are: William O. Douglas, Hugo L. Black, Stanley Reed, Felix Frankfurter, Robert H. Jackson, Fred M. Vinson, Tom C. Clark, Harold H. Burton, and Sherman Minton. From the Henry E. Luhrs Collection. Accompanied by LOA from PSA/DNA.
Estimate: $400-$500

25673   Queen Anne of Great Britain Document Signed *"Anne R".* One page, 9.25" x 14", Windsor Castle, September 6, 1711, to Robert, Earl of Oxford, High Treasurer. A warrant for the payment of £1500 to "...Our Right Trusty and Right Welbeloved Cousin and Counsellour Charles Earle of Peterborough (whom Wee appointed to go to the Court of Vienna)... Which Wee are gratiously pleased to allow him for the charge of his Equipage and preparation for that Service..." Countersigned by Oxford. Very good condition; folds, some soiling and minor foxing. From the Henry E. Luhrs Collection. Accompanied by LOA from PSA/DNA.
Estimate: $750-$1,000

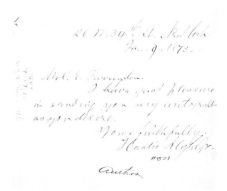

25674   Horatio Alger Jr. Rare Autograph Letters Signed. This lot consists of four items. The first two are short Autograph Letters Signed on lined paper answering two different requests for autographs. The third is a clipped 2" x 0.5" Signature laid down to a larger card. The fourth is a blank front endpaper from a book signed in the upper right *"Horatio Alger. Chelsea"*, likely written by Horatio Alger Sr. Alger was one of the most widely-read authors of the 19th century. Many of his "dime novels" were rags-to-riches stories about poor young men who achieved the American dreams of wealth and social position through hard work and determination, or sometimes, just really good luck. Often, even today, accountings of this type of success are called "Horatio Alger" stories. Generally fine condition. From the Henry E. Luhrs Collection. Accompanied by LOA from PSA/DNA.
Estimate: $500-$600

25675   Literary Autograph Collection "B" (Lot 1). The lucky bidder for this lot will receive 90 or more autographs from leaders in the field of literature, religion, education, music, history, and poetry. Included: Edward W. Bok (AQS); Louis Blanc (2 ALS); Thornton W. Burgess (ALS, ANS); Henry T. Burleigh (2 AMuQS); John Burroughs (ALS); Ellis Parker Butler (Signature, ANS); Irving Bacheller (ALS); Park Benjamin (AMs); William W. Belknap (ALS); Phillips Brooks (multiple ALS); Marc Isambard Brunel (ALS). A very desirable grouping; generally fine condition. From the Henry E. Luhrs Collection. Accompanied by LOA from PSA/DNA.
Estimate: $400-$600

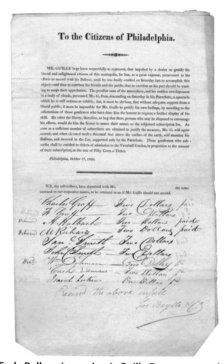

25676   Literary Autograph Collection "B" (Lot 2). Another magnificent collection of fine autographs from authors, poets, historians, clergymen, and other notables, consisting of more than 90 pieces. Included: William Cullen Bryant (Signature, ANS, AQS); Mary L. Booth (long ALS to Susan B. Anthony); Sir James M. Barrie (ALS); M. E. Braddon aka Mary Maxwell (AQS); Irving Bachellor (SP, ALS, Signature); Henry Ward Beecher (ANS); Dan Beard (Signature); Louis Bromfield (TLS, ANS). Generally fine condition. From the Henry E. Luhrs Collection. Accompanied by LOA from PSA/DNA.
Estimate: $800-$1,000

25677   Arthur James Balfour Autograph Letter Signed. Two pages, 4.75" x 7.25", House of Commons embossed stationery, London, nd. Marked "Private" this letter's recipient is not named, but is likely a newspaper or magazine editor. Body in full: *"I shall be glad to know whether you will be inclined to admit into your next number a reply to the Duke of Argyll's attack in the current number on the accuracy of the statements put forward of the present government in regard to Afghanistan- and if so what is the latest date on which such reply will have to be ready for press."*

Balfour was a British statesman, serving in many capacities throughout a long and distinguished career including as Prime Minister from 1902-1905. He is the author of the Balfour Declaration of 1917 that promised a homeland for the Jewish people. Fine condition with light folds, lightly mounted to a collector's folder. From the Henry E. Luhrs Collection. Accompanied by LOA from PSA/DNA.
Estimate: $300-$400

25678   Early Ballooning — Louis Guille Document and Charles Green ALS. The Montgolfier brothers discovered in the 1780s that when heated air was collected inside a large lightweight bag, it would cause the bag to rise. The first manned flight took place in France in 1783, and the French would bring ballooning to America about ten years later, causing only a minor stir at the time. The individual most responsible for transforming ballooning into a form of entertainment in America was another Frenchman named Louis Guille. He made exhibition flights along the east coast of the U.S. in 1819-1820. This lot contains a partly printed document, 8" x 13", Philadelphia, October 17, 1820, where Guille is asking for subscribers to "...give him the honour to request a further display of his skill...those persons who may be disposed to encourage his efforts to annex their names to the subjoined subscription list..." Nine subscribers are listed as having given fees of one to five dollars "...to be returned if Mr. Guille should not ascend." Very good condition.

Also in this great lot is an Autograph Letter Signed "*C Green*". Two pages, 3.5" x 5.5", Highgate(?), September 14, 1847. In full: "*Dear Sir. In consequence of the unfavourable state of the weather yesterday my ascent from ?? is postponed to this evening and as it is probably the last ascent of the Nassau this season you will not have an opportunity to ascend after this day. I am Sir Yours Respectfully*" Green would make 526 successful ascents between 1821 and his retirement in 1852. That and his 18-hour flight from London to Germany in 1836 made him the most famous of all British pre-20th century balloonists. Fine condition. From the Henry E. Luhrs Collection. Accompanied by LOA from PSA/DNA.
Estimate: $300-$500

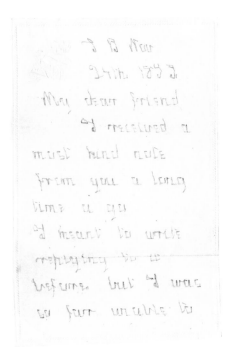

4.5" x 7", personal letterhead, np, May 24, 1866. This letter reads in part, *"…Now I am going to confide an awful secret to you- I am sure you will understand my feeling in it. The fact is, I am frightened to death by the thoughts of our dear Lord & Master suddenly inquiring into the matter- next time we meet- for he told me 'he had left it to you!' -I was really on hot coals last Sunday week- for fear he should say anything about it 0 so, I resolve to relieve my mind and enclose you 'The little bill' - Don't you understand my motive? I am sure you do."* Both of these letters are whimsical and provide a wonderful insight into the personal side of this great English poet and playwright. The letters are both in very fine condition; usual folds are present; slight mounting traces on the verso of the of the 1866 letter. From the Henry E. Luhrs Collection. Accompanied by LOA from PSA/DNA.

Estimate: $1,200-$1,600

25679   Laura Bridgman Autograph Letter Signed *"L. Bridgman."*
Three pages, 4" x 6", np, November 27th, 1893. The content is routine, but the true character of the letter is in her keen and skillful handwriting. Bridgman was the first blind, deaf, mute to learn to read and write. Included in this lot are three secretarial versions of Helen Keller's signature. Accompanying these three letters, are several items from her organization: a small card detailing the needs of the blind children in the world, a small pamphlet on Keller's work with the blind in Africa, and a small card with the Braille alphabet on it.
 The items in this lot are all in very fine condition on average; usual folds present. From the Henry E. Luhrs Collection. Accompanied by LOA from PSA/DNA.

Estimate: $300-$400

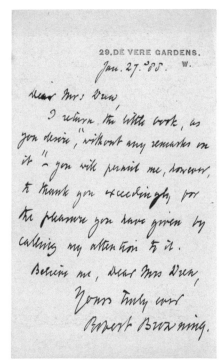

25681   Robert Browning Autograph Letter Signed *Robert Browning."* One page, 4.25" x 7", De Vere Gardens, London, January 27th, 1888. The letter was written to a Mrs. Drew; the content is routine. The signature is bold and dark, a very nice example! The letter is in very fine condition; the usual folds are present; light toning along the upper edge. From the Henry E. Luhrs Collection. Accompanied by LOA from PSA/DNA.

Estimate: $400-$600

25680   Robert Browning Pair of Autograph Letters Signed.
Letter 1: One page, 4.5" x 7", personal letterhead, np, "Black Monday", December 18 1865. Both letters in this lot were written to a Mrs. Forester, the content of this particular letter is routine. r Letter 2: Two pages,

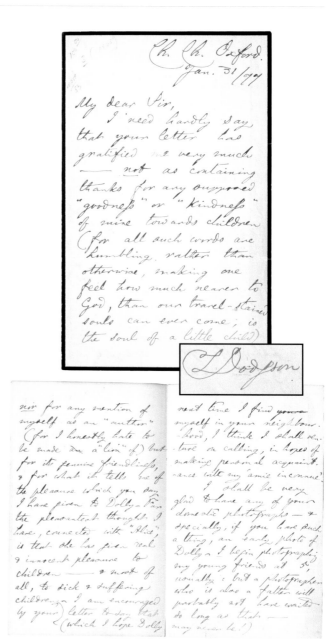

25682   Robert Burns Autograph Letter Signed *"Robt. Burns."*
Two pages, 7.5" x 8.65", Edinburgh, Scotland, nd. The letter is written to
a Mr. James Candlish in Glasgow; it reads in part, *"…At present I have
time for nothing. Dissipation and business engross every moment. I am
engaged in assisting an honest Scots enthusiast, a friend of mine, who
is an Engraver, and has taken it into head to publish a collection of all
our songs set to music…Pompey's Ghost, words and music, I beg from
you immediately, to go into this second number; the first is already published…"* The book mentioned here is James Johnson's *The Scots musical museum.* It was published in two volumes and many of Burns' contributions are present therein. Robert Burns is regarded by many as the
national poet of Scotland, and was one of the pioneers of the Romantic
Movement. His poem "Auld Lang Syne" is sung at nearly every New Year's
celebration.

Accompanying this letter are the original envelope it was delivered in
from Walter R. Benjamin Autographs, a letter from Charles Sessler Book
Sellers detailing some of the provenance, as well as a typed transcription. The letter itself is in very good condition; the usual folds are present;
some dark staining present on the front page; smudging of the ink is
evident in several places; the integral address leaf has been removed and
replaced by a new sheet of paper which was reapplied to the first page
by silking; the original text on the address leaf has been cut and laid
down onto the new sheet. The job was well done and very clean, however, it must be noted for accuracy of condition. From the Henry E. Luhrs
Collection. Accompanied by LOA from PSA/DNA.

Estimate: $1,000-$1,500

25683   Lewis Carroll Pair of Autograph Letters Signed. Letter 1:
Signed, *"Lewis Carroll."* Three pages, 4" x 6", Christ Church, March 5th,
1877. The letter is written to a child named Dolly; it reads in part, *"…Are
you gradually making up your mind to the catastrophe of a call from
me? For I really think you will see me some day soon---Please picture to
yourself a tallish man (about 6 feet 4 inches), very fat, with a long white
beard, a bald head, & a very red face--& and then, when you see me, you
will be agreeably disappointed."* Almost invariably Carroll signs himself
with his real name, Charles Dodgson, so this signature and interesting
self evaluation is very intriguing! Letter 2: Signed, *"C.L. Dodgson."* Four
pages, 4.5" x 7", Christ Church Oxford, January 31st, 1877. The letter is
written to a man whose children Carroll had befriended. It reads in part,
*"…I am encouraged by your letter to say that next time I find myself in
your neighborhood, I think I shall venture on calling, in hopes of making
personal acquaintance with my 'amie inconnue.' I shall be very glad to
have any of your domestic photographs--& specially if you have such a
thing, an early photo of Dolly. I begin photographing my young friends
at 5, usually; but a photographer who is also a father will probably not
have waited so long as that…"* This letter reveals Carroll's gentle nature
with children, his desire to write for them, and even his wish to raise the
spirits of the sick. Both letters are in very fine condition; usual folds are
present; pencil notations are present on the first page of each letter.
From the Henry E. Luhrs Collection. Accompanied by LOA from PSA/
DNA.

Estimate: $500-$700

25685 **George Washington Carver Autograph Letter Signed** *"G.W. Carver"* Two pages, 8.5" x 11", Tuskegee Normal and Industrial Institute Stationery, Tuskegee Institute, Alabama, August 15th, 1934. George Washington Carver is the African American scientist who, among many other things, researched and discovered many Industrial uses for the peanut. This letter was written to a young man named B. Robertson, and it reads in part, *"I am glad you like your new job and that it takes you out where you can commune with nature, the very thing in which you are interested and with which your soul is filled."* The letter is in very fine condition and comes complete with its original envelope; usual folds are present; writing has slightly faded; signature is still dark and legible. From the Henry E. Luhrs Collection. Accompanied by LOA from PSA/DNA.
Estimate: $400-$500

25684 **[Charles I] Collection of Regicides: The Judges Who Sent Him To The Scaffold.** This lot is comprised of four pieces, chief among them a very scarce item signed by three of the men appointed to try, in high court, the reigning monarch, Charles I. **Cornelius Holland, Denis Bond, & John Downes** Letter Signed, 1 page, 7.5" by 11", Whitehall, January 5, 1652; a small hole at center, effecting two words, else quite good. With typed transcription. This intriguing letter is seemingly about financial matters but mentions a Mr. Hutchinson who is involved with a trial: said Hutchinson has been *"furnisht sufficiently money for standing guards and hath his Convoys..."* England's Civil War, like America's, also ended in the murder of the country's lawful leader - though there the deed was done by trial and execution. Cornelius Holland and Denis Bond did not sign the King's death warrant; John Downes claimed to have done under duress.

Also with a Document Signed by one Thomas Harvey in 1707; a Document Signed by one Robert Day in 1706; and a Document Signed by one John Brookhall in 1685. From the Henry E. Luhrs Collection. Accompanied by LOA from PSA/DNA.
Estimate: $800-$1,200

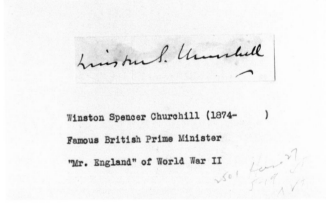

25686 **Winston Churchill Signature.** The signature is on a small white piece of paper which has been laid down on a 5" x 3" card; the following information has been typed below the signature: *"Winston Spencer Churchill (1874-) Famous British Prime Minister 'Mr. England' of World War II."* Winston signs himself as *"Winston S. Churchill."* The signature card is in fine condition; adhesive residue has seeped through the paper and has stained the signature. The signature is still dark and very legible. From the Henry E. Luhrs Collection. Accompanied by LOA from PSA/DNA.
Estimate: $700-$900

105, MOUNT STREET,
W.

Nov: 4. 1904

Dear Kuiloch Cooke,

I am very sorry to say
that I am already engaged
for dinner on the 8th, so
cannot accept your very
kind invitation.

Yours very truly

Winston Churchill.

25687   **Winston Churchill Signed Photo.** A 2.75" x 3" B&W magazine photo of Churchill on a 3.75" x 6" mount which has been signed *"Winston S. Churchill"*, possibly as Prime Minister. Fine condition save for a very minor paper clip stain at the very top affecting neither the photo nor the signature. Also included is a mailing envelope from "10 Downing Street, Whitehall" dated during World War II, August 15, 1940. From the Henry E. Luhrs Collection. Accompanied by LOA from PSA/DNA.
Estimate: $2,000-$3,000

25688   **Winston Churchill Autograph Letter Signed** *"Winston Churchill."* One page, 5" x 8", personal stationery, London, November 4, 1904. The content of the letter is routine, Churchill declines a dinner invitation. The letter is in fine condition; usual folds are present; staining present in upper right corner and down the right edge. From the Henry E. Luhrs Collection. Accompanied by LOA from PSA/DNA.
Estimate: $2,000-$3,000

Home Office,
Whitehall,
S.W.

7th April, 1910.

Dear Mr Norton,

I have to thank you very
much for your kind letter of the 1st
instant, which I received with great
pleasure.

Yours very truly,

Winston S. Churchill

25689   Winston Churchill 1910 Autograph Letter Signed "*Winston S. Churchill*" as Home Secretary. One page, 5" x 8", Home Office, Whitehall letterhead, London, April 7, 1910, to a Mr. Norton. A brief letter of acknowledgement with a handsome signature. At this time in his life, Churchill was Secretary of State for the Home Office, a senior position in Herbert Henry Asquith's Liberal Party government. Fine condition; one fold and some light soiling that could easily be cleaned. From the Henry E. Luhrs Collection. Accompanied by LOA from PSA/DNA.
Estimate: $2,000-$3,000

25690   George Cruikshank Collection. This lot contains four pieces, all of which have been drawn or written by George Cruikshank. 1. A three page letter, 4.5" x 7", Hildare Terrace, August 23rd, 1855. The letter is signed on the third page as, "*G. Cruikshank.*" The content is routine. 2. Three pages, 7.25" x 9", London, November 20th, 1835. The letter was written to a man named Barker, and contains Cruikshank's choices for illustrations in an unnamed book. He gives his ideas for titles and sketches. Wonderful content. 3. Unsigned Sketch; two pages, 4.5" x 7", np, nd. The sketch is drawn on the verso of a list of names, written in Cruikshank's hand, as well as a small map drawn, also, in his hand. The sketch is of an old woman wearing a veil, as if in mourning. The list of names appears to be soldiers, and in one corner the word "*Fallen*" has been scribbled. Perhaps, this is a list of soldiers that had fallen in the war. 4. Unsigned Sketch; one page, 4.75" x 4.25, np, nd. The sketch features several people looking out of windows, appearing rather distressed. Cruikshank is most renowned for his illustrations of Charles Dickens' famous works. The items in this collection are in very good condition on average. The larger letter and the small sketch have been laid down on sturdy backing sheets; the small ALS has several tears on the fold lines; slight areas of foxing. From the Henry E. Luhrs Collection. Accompanied by LOA from PSA/DNA.
Estimate: $300-$500

25691 Literary Autograph Collection "D-E-F". An interesting group of 18 autographed items- all of literary figures including: Alexandre Dumas, fils (ANS); Timothy Dwight IV (2 ALS); Edward Dowden (ALS); John Dos Passos (Signature). Generally fine condition. From the Henry E. Luhrs Collection. Accompanied by LOA from PSA/DNA.
Estimate: $200-$300

25692 Charles L. Dodgson Autograph Letter Signed *"C.L. Dodgson."* Two pages, 4" x 6.2", Calverton House, Sandown, September 17th, 1875. To a Mrs. Barrow. A superlative letter mentioning Dodgson's most famous works! In part, *"Would you kindly tell me whether 'Evelyn Alice' does or does not posess copies of both the books 'Alice In Wonderland' and 'Through The Looking Glass' ---Also would you tell me what days & hours the children are free of lessons…"* The letter is in very fine condition; usual folds are present; mounting traces on the verso. Accompanied by LOA from PSA/DNA.
Estimate: $300-$500

25693 Arthur Conan Doyle: An Extraordinary Manuscript on Spiritualism & an Autograph Letter! This lot is comprised of three pieces: a Typewritten Manuscript, bearing copious Autograph corrections and interpolations, an Autograph Letter Signed, and a Typed Letter Signed of Conan Doyle's widow, Jean Conan Doyle. They are, then, as follows: 1) Typed Manuscript, with numerous Autograph additions, deletions and corrections in dark ink, entitled *"The Religion of Conan Doyle"* and being in the form of an interview, 11 pages, 8.5" by 11", no place, no date. Some wear at being handled, else fine. 2) Autograph Letter Signed (*"A. Conan Doyle"*), 1 page, 4/5" by 6.75", 23 Oakley Street, Monday, no month or year; to Marillier. In very fine condition. 3) [Arthur Conan Doyle] Jean Conan Doyle, Typed Letter Signed, 1 page, 7" by 8", Windlesham, Crowborough, Sussex, August 19, 1930. To editor and writer George Sylvester Viereck. Here the least shall go first: the letter of Lady Conan Doyle to Viereck refers to the above described manuscript (*"the excellent interview which you published"*) and the recent death of her husband some weeks before. The Conan Doyle A.L.S. concerns his schedule of engagements for the week, and refers to his wife and his sister. Best and last is the manuscript...

Spiritualism became Conan Doyle's religion - and driving force - from World War I on. In this remarkable manuscript, he discusses his personal experience with spirits, Henry Ford, Oscar Wilde and Einstein; of course, such Spiritualist concepts as the soul, reincarnation, telepathy, even the (notoriously fraudulent) Cottingley Fairies come up too. In part, in brief:*I [the interviewer] Do you believe in reincarnation like Henry Ford? Doyle: I believe the soul is born and reborn many times. I am not sure that it is dons the human form after it has discarded that garment, but my thoughts incline that way… I: Do you consider Ford a great man? Doyle: He is a great personality. I: Why? Doyle: Because he is uncorrupted by his millions. No man can tell if he is incorruptible until such wealth is thrust upon him… I: Did you have any personal contact with the spiritual world? Doyle: When Geley, the French savant and spiritualist, died I was sitting with a medium in England. Suddenly I heard a whispered word, 'Geley.' I asked, in French, "When you had your accident were the moulds you carried broken?' The answer was 'Oui, Oui, ils etaient casses.' Though the medium did not know a word of French, the spirit communicated through him in that language.'…* [The interviewer asks about a posthumous book of Oscar Wilde's psychic utterances, Oscar Wilde from Purgatory by Hester Travers-Smith] *Doyle: I knew Oscar Wilde when he was living. In that book I recognize poetic and epigrammatic passages which are as characteristic of Wilde as anything that bears his imprint… I: Einstein told me modern mathematicians include in their calculations an infinite number of dimensions. Doyle: Einstein merely expressed what every Spiritualist knows…* Covered too are Conan Doyle's thoughts on fairies, marriage, death, the Buddha, Moses, Christ, Mohammed and heaven. A fascinating, heavily marked manuscript! From the Henry E. Luhrs Collection. Accompanied by LOA from PSA/DNA.
Estimate: $1,500-$2,000

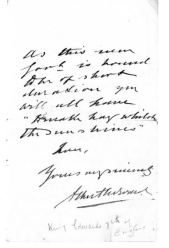

25694   King Edward VII of England Autograph Letter Signed
"Albert Edward". Three pages, 4.5" x 7", Easthampstead Park letterhead, Wokingham, June 18. 1885. An interesting letter, written as Prince of Wales (a title he held longer than anyone else 1841-1901), in part: *"Private. My dear henry, As I know Abergaruing [?] so well as he 'pulls the strings' just now. I thought I would not do better than send your letter on to him & beg him to bring your name before Salisbury...you must not lose a moment when the new admiralty comes into office- as this govt is bound to be of short duration you will all have 'To make hay whilst the sun shines'..."* The future king was right in his prediction; the Marquess of Salisbury of the Conservative Party became prime minister the month after this letter was written, but remained in office only seven months! Very Good condition; some weakness and minor separation at the folds. From the Henry E. Luhrs Collection. Accompanied by LOA from PSA/DNA.
Estimate: $400-$600

In Honor of
His Royal Highness the Prince of Wales
Mr. and Mrs. Rodman Wanamaker
request your presence at a Reception
Friday evening, November twenty-first
nineteen hundred and nineteen
at nine o'clock
Seventh Regiment Armory
New York City

R.s.v.p.

25695   King Edward VIII Signature and Wedding Memorabilia. A collection of items related to the only British monarch ever to voluntarily relinquish the throne, including:

Edward 1919 Wanamaker invitation for reception at New York City, signed *"Edward P"* in pencil as Prince of Wales.

Rev. R. A. Jardine ALS and signed photo of the minister who married the Duke and Wallis Warfield Simpson.

Marcel DuprÈ 1937-dated signature on card of the world-famous organist who played at their wedding

Major Edward Dudley Metcalfe bold signature of the Duke's best man.

Charles Mercier ALS of the Mayor of Monts, France who performed the civil ceremony at the wedding of the Duke and Wallis.

Piers Legh ALS dated 1927 from aboard the S.S. *Empress of Australia*, by Edward's equerry (personal attendant).

Other autographs, clippings, and transcripts also included. Generally Fine condition. From the Henry E. Luhrs Collection. Accompanied by LOA from PSA/DNA.
Estimate: $1,000-$1,500

25696   King Frederick II of Prussia (Frederick the Great) Letter Signed *"Friedrich"* as king. One page with integral blank leaf, in German, 7.5" x 9.25", Potsdam, November 17, 1747, to the Major v. Wolfradt. In full: "My best, Especially Dear One, on account of your petition of Sept. 27. I have decided to prolong the furlough of your son, Staff Captain Wolfradt at Emden, for one more month, but at the end of this time he has to report to his post immediately. I am your well affectionate Friedrich." Dated during the War of the Austrian Succession, this letter is in Fine condition with folds and minor soiling. From the Henry E. Luhrs Collection. Accompanied by LOA from PSA/DNA.
Estimate: $800-$1,000

Frederick William had a passion for soldiering and anything that might help his army. Here we see him at his best, encouraging native - and national - industry. "*I have seen... that your new ship is finished and launched... I congratulate you and wish that you... may build more ships, so that one does not have to have the trouble of to leave the advantage of transportation and freights to the foreigners.*" This, then, is how he laid the foundations for Prussia's power, which his son, Frederick the Great, would exploit so brilliantly. From the Henry E. Luhrs Collection. Accompanied by LOA from PSA/DNA.
Estimate: $300-$400

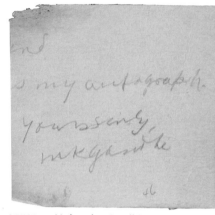

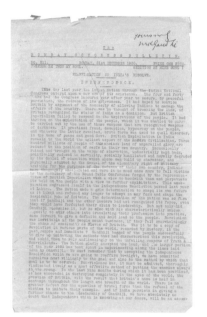

25697   King Frederick William I of Prussia Document Signed "*Friedrich Wilhelm*" as king. One page, in German, 8.25" x 13", Wusterhausen, September 22, 1725. This document begins, "His Royal Majesty in Prussia- Our all graceful sovereign have the day before yesterday considered well the new uniform rule and have condescendingly approved and confirmed same in all its points..." Impressive in appearance with royal wax seal still intact, one fold, bold signature, overall near Fine condition. Typewritten translation included. From the Henry E. Luhrs Collection. Accompanied by LOA from PSA/DNA.
Estimate: $300-$400

25700   Mohandas Gandhi Signature. 3.25" x 3", np, nd. Gandhi signs himself, "*MK Gandhi.*" Gandhi was a spiritual and political leader for India during their struggle for Independence from Britain. Gandhi rejected all forms of violence and violent protest, his philosophy of nonviolent resistance, which he named *satyagraha,* is still used by nonviolence resistance movements today. The signature is in fine condition; the signature has been clipped from a larger document; the upper and lower left corners have been lifting from the mounting and are very thin and torn; mounting traces present on verso. From the Henry E. Luhrs Collection. Accompanied by LOA from PSA/DNA.
Estimate: $400-$500

25699   Mohandas K. Gandhi, (1869-1948), leader of the Indian independence movement, his Signature "*yours truly M. K. Gandhi*" at the top of a mimeographed copy of *The Bombay Congress Bulletin,* two pages, 8" x 13", Bombay, December 31, 1930. The bulletin provides a wonderful view into the independence movement, midway through the struggle, and reads in small part: "*British Exploitation in India reveals to the world the ugliest aspect of the modern civilization. three hundred millions of people of this ancient land of unparalleled glory are reduced to the position of serfs in their own country... this exasperation expressed itself in the Independence Resolution passed last year at Lahore. The Nation made a grim determination to shape its own future as it liked and refused any longer to accept in any form and shape the despicable yoke of Britain.... Nonviolence has, it must be admitted, thoroughly vindicated itself as a most effective method of putting the enemies always in the wrong. In the last Nine months during which it has been practiced, it has succeeded in destroying completely in the eyes of the world, the prestige of Britain...*" More fine content. Small chip at top margin, usual folds, else fine condition. A nice specimen. From the Henry E. Luhrs Collection. Accompanied by LOA from PSA/DNA.
Estimate: $400-$600

25701   Giuseppe Garibaldi Document Signed. A check, 6" x 2.625", partly printed, Firenze (aka Florence), May 1841. Garibaldi was an Italian patriot credited for helping bring about the formation of a unified Italy in the 1860s. Good condition with toning and stains, laid down to a larger card. From the Henry E. Luhrs Collection. Accompanied by LOA from PSA/DNA.
Estimate: $300-$500

25698   Frederick William I, King of Prussia, encourages domestic ship-Building - so as not to have to depend on foreigners! Letter Signed, *as King,* in German, 1 page, 7.5" by 10", Potsdam, November 7, 1732. To Saturgus. Normal wear, some pencil notations, but altogether very good. With full English translation. Boorish and contemptuous of art and learning, but thrifty and practical, too,

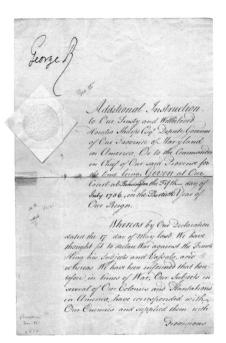

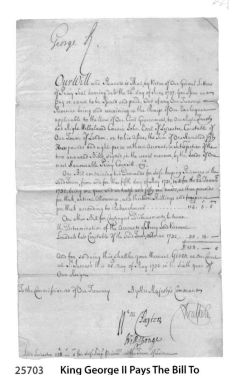

25702   George II Issues Wartime Orders to the Governor of Maryland

George II (1683-1760), King of Great Britain, Document Signed twice, "*George R*" and "*GR*", two pages, 9.5" x 13.5", Court at Kensington, July 5, 1756. In the early years of the Seven Years War (the French and Indian War), George II provides "*Additional Instruction to... Horatio Sharpe Esqr. Deputy governor of Our Province of Maryland in America...*" He notes that "*Whereas by Our Declaration dated the 17 day of May last, We have thought fit to declare War against the French King his subjects and Vassals, and whereas We have been informed that heretofore, in times of War, Our Subjects in several of Our Colonies and Plantations in America, have corresponded with Our Enemies and supplied them with Provisions and Warlike Stores, whereby Our Service has been greatly prejudiced and the safety of our Dominion endangered, It is therefore our express Will and Pleasure that you do take the most speedy and effectual Measure to hinder all Correspondence between any of Our Subjects inhabiting Our Province of Maryland... and the Subjects of the said French King, and to prevent any of the Cononys [sic] or Plantations belonging to Our Enemies... with provisions or warlike Stores of any kind.*" Preventing trade between the British colonies and French possessions in Canada and the Caribbean proved quite difficult. Explicit orders like these which only partially successful. Trade to the French Caribbean was particularly lucrative for American merchants who had been flagrantly evading British trade laws for nearly a century. Only at the close of the war in 1763 did London seriously attempt to regulate American trade; all of which met with stiff resistance and eventually open rebellion. Partial separation at center horizontal fold repaired, very light foxing, with intact paper seal, else Fine. From the Henry E. Luhrs Collection. Accompanied by LOA from PSA/DNA.
Estimate: $1,000-$1,500

25703   King George II Pays The Bill To Keep Prisoners in the Tower of London!
Document Signed, *as King,* 1 page, 9" by 14", Court of St. James, May 28, 1733; co-signed by Great Britain's first Prime Minister, **Sir Robert Walpole.** "*To the Commissioners of Our Treasury.*" Some tiny cracks at the margins of folds, else fine: a handsome document - with excessively rare content. Here George II pays to keep prisoners in the most famous prison in the world: the Tower of London. To "*our Right Well beloved Cousin John, Earl of Leicester, Constable of our Tower of London*" George directs the sum of "*One Hundred Fifty Three pounds and eight pence*" to satisfy "*One Bill... for Safe-Keeping prisoners in the said Tower, from and for the fifth day of May 1731 to & for the 24th December 1732, being one year and a half and fifty one days, at three pounds per Week... and thirteen Shillings and four pence per week...*" Connoisseurs of penal institutions will recall that the Tower of London goes back to the Norman Invasion; that it was built by William the Conqueror, although Henry II, Constable of the Tower of London got on a right footing mid-12th century, no longer a legacy but an appointed job. The more romantic among us will want to remember that the Tower is where the two little Princes were last seen oh, in the summer of 1483 — where Henry VIII decapitated some wives — where Lady Jane Grey nobly went to the block. Thomas More lost his head there, too, and the young Princess Elizabeth almost, suspected of wanting to dethrone "Bloody" Mary ("Here lands as true a subject, being prisoner," she said, "as ever landed these stairs").... George II killed no relatives there, but kept the place going: the last prisoner was a German spy, shot by a firing squad, on August 15,1941 - the 841st anniversary of the arrival of the Tower's first prisoner. From the Henry E. Luhrs Collection. Accompanied by LOA from PSA/DNA.
Estimate: $600-$900

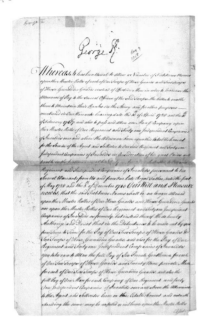

25704   King George II Orders an End to Chicanery Involving Military Payrolls. Document Signed, "*George R,*" as king, 2 pages, recto and verso, 11" by 17", Court at Kensington, August 9, 1758; co-signed by Chancellor of the Exchequer H.B. Legge and two others. Weakness at folds shows signs of unartful but sound repair; yet the signature of the monarch is exceptionally large and so this document, with some slight restoration, will be handsome indeed. In part: "*Whereas it has been usual to allow a Number of Fictitious Names upon the Muster Rolls of each of our Troops of Horse Guards and Two Troops of Horse Grenadier Guards... in order to Increase the Allowance of Pay to the several Officers of the said Troops, the better to enable them to maintain their Ranks in the Army and for other purposes... OUR WILL AND PLEASURE NOW IS, that the said Fictitious Names shall no longer be allowed...*" Instead, His Majesty orders a pay raise for his much beloved Guards. An unusual document. From the Henry E. Luhrs Collection. Accompanied by LOA from PSA/DNA.
Estimate: $500-$700

25705   King George III of England Document Signed "*George R.*" One page, 24" x 16", Court at St. James, December 18, 1789. The document reads in part, "*…Whereas we have thought it necessary for the encouragement of our Subjects trading to or residing in North America, to appoint a Consul to the States of Massachusetts Bay, Rhode Island, Connecticut and New Hampshire to take care of their Affairs and to aid and assist them in all their lawful Concerns, and endeavor to procure for them that Justice and Equity which shall be agreeable to the Peace and good Correspondence established between us and the United States…*" It was during George's reign that Britain lost many of its colonies in North America. He is believed to have suffered from the blood disease, porphyria that caused his legendary mental illness and odd behavior.

The document is in Very Fine condition; usual folds are present; docketing information present on verso. From the Henry E. Luhrs Collection. Accompanied by LOA from PSA/DNA.
Estimate: $800-$1,200

25706   King George III of the United Kingdom Document Signed "*George R.*" as king. Two pages (one leaf front and back), 8" x 12.5", November 17, 1786. This document instructs the paymaster to pay "...unto Robert Anderson the Sum of Five Shillings a day for his Half pay as Surgeon to Our Forces in the East Indies, to commence..." King George III is significant from the American point of view, as he was the last king to reign over us! Good condition with general aging and various tears in the margins, a few old repairs on verso at weak folds, Fine signature. From the Henry E. Luhrs Collection. Accompanied by LOA from PSA/DNA.
Estimate: $500-$700

25707   King George III Document Signed Appointing a Lieutenant Document signed *as King,* 1 page, vellum, 13.5" by 9.25", Court of St. James's, March 9, 1807; being the appointment of John Spinks a lieutenant in a Regiment of Foot commanded by General William Picton. Boldly signed, with the King's paper and wax seal fully intact, as is the blue revenue stamp: but foxed and discolored throughout - the condition is only good, then overall. Here the King of Ireland and England appoints John Spinks, Gentleman, to be a lieutenant and commands him to"*carefully and diligently to Discharge the Duty of Lieutenant by Exercising and Well-disciplining both the inferior Officers and Soldiers*" From the Henry E. Luhrs Collection. Accompanied by LOA from PSA/DNA.
Estimate: $200-$300

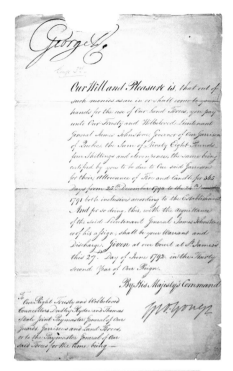

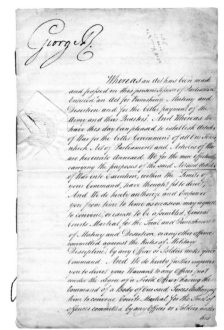

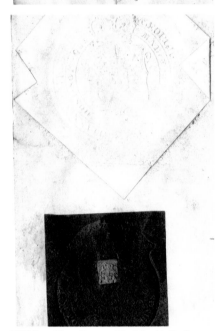

25708   King George III of the United Kingdom Document Signed *"George R."* One page handwritten document, measures 7.8" x 12.5", dated June 27, 1792, from St. James court. The content is of a legal nature. King George III sat on the throne for over sixty years, during which time he presided over the loss of Britain's vital colonies in America and still reigned during the War of 1812. His last years were marred by bouts of insanity now believed to have resulted from a blood disease or poisoning from long-term exposure to a toxic substance.

The letter is in Very Good condition with several tears; one large tear on the upper edge slightly stretches across part of the king's signature, several small tears on the right edge, light toning on the right edge, and tape on the verso, slight soiling over entire document. From the Henry E. Luhrs Collection. Accompanied by LOA from PSA/DNA.

Estimate: $500-$600

25709   King George III of the United Kingdom Document Signed *"George R."* as king countersigned by the Duke of Portland. Four pages, 9.75" x 15", Court of St. James, March 25, 1796. In part, "...we do hereby authorize and empower you from time to time as occasion may require, to convene, or cause to be assembled, General Courts Martial, for the Trial and Punishment of Mutiny and Desertion, or any other offence committed against the Rules of Military Discipline, by any Officer or Soldier under your command..." Very Good condition; minor old repairs on weak folds, seal mostly intact, very large and bold signature. Great for display. Typewritten transcript included. From the Henry E. Luhrs Collection. Accompanied by LOA from PSA/DNA.

Estimate: $600-$800

25710   King George III of the United Kingdom Document Signed *"George R."* This document was signed by George III as king, as well as Lord Liverpool. The document has both the king's seal and Lord Liverpool's dark blue one. It measures 15.5" x 11.8", and is dated March 10, 1810 from the court of St. James. The document is an officer's commission for a William Riddle Esquire. The document is in Good condition; there are severe areas of soiling, namely on the left edge; the usual folds are present as well as some burst marks near George's seal and signature. From the Henry E. Luhrs Collection. Accompanied by LOA from PSA/DNA.

Estimate: $400-$600

25711   Rodgers & Hammerstein Two Signed Pieces of Sheet Music
from *The Sound of Music* starring Mary Martin, "Climb Ev'ry Mountain" and "The Sound of Music." Both are 9" x 12", have identical cover graphics, and both are signed by the legendary composers "*Richard Rodgers*" and "*Oscar Hammerstein*" in blue ink with great contrast. One of the greatest songwriting teams of all time, Rodgers and Hammerstein had an amazing string of successful Broadway musicals in the 1940s and 1950s garnering them 34 Tony Awards and 15 Academy Awards. Condition is fine with just a bit of staining along the left border of "The Sound of Music." From the Henry E. Luhrs Collection. Accompa...

Estimate: $700-$900

25713   Paul von Hindenburg Typed Letters Signed "*von Hindenburg.*"
This lot features two letters written by noted German general and President von Hindenburg. He was the man who appointed Hitler chancellor in 1933. The first letter measures 8.3" x 11.5", and is one typed page. The signature is in bold, dark marker. It is dated October 4, 1927, and is on the president's personal stationery. The content is a "Thank You" letter written to someone who had remembered his 80th birthday. The second letter measures 8.3" x 11.7", and is one typed page. The signature is in bold, dark marker. It is dated July 29, 1933. The content is standard.

Both letters are in Good condition with little wear. The letters both have the usual folds. The second letter has a wonderful seal impressed in the lower left corner. Blue marks from a pen are present on the upper right half of the second letter. From the Henry E. Luhrs Collection. Accompanied by LOA from PSA/DNA.

Estimate: $450-$550

25712   Adolf Hitler World War II Dated Document Signed "*A Hitler*". One page, 7.25" x 9.25", typewritten, Führer headquarters, August 11, 1943. A promotion of [Walther] Lucht to lieutenant general, general of the artillery "In the name of the German People." The document has been countersigned by Hitler's adjutant, Lt. Gen. [Rudolf] Schmundt as Chief of the Army Personnel Office. Less than a year later, on July 20, 1944, Schmundt would die in the bunker at Wolfsschanze when Stauffenberg tried to assassinate Hitler with a bomb. About fine condition with one fold and some light soiling.

Also included in this lot is an original 4.75" x 6.75" B&W German printed photo taken at Reichsparteitag in 1934. These meetings were held annually as rallies for the National Socialist German Workers Party and are also referred to as the Nuremberg Rallies. Fine condition. From the Henry E. Luhrs Collection. Accompanied by LOA from PSA/DNA.

Estimate: $2,000-$3,000

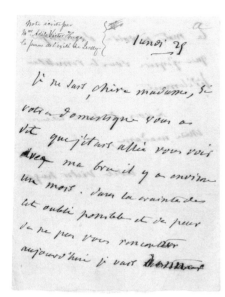

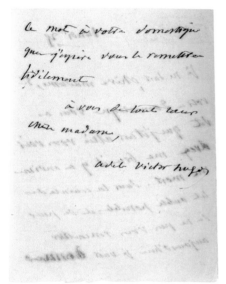

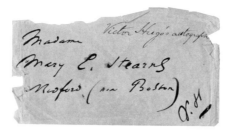

25715 Victor Hugo Autograph Envelope Addressed to a Boston Abolitionist

Autograph Envelope Signed ("V.H."), 5" by 2.5", no place or date. Boldly penned in dark ink on a blue envelope albeit ragged all on sides and containing, in the upper right corner a note in an unknown hand identifying the autograph as Hugo's. Comprised of four lines, as follows: "Madam / Mary E. Stearns / Medford (near Boston) / "V.H." Mrs. Stearns, celebrated for her glittering salon, was the wife of the wealthy Boston businessman and noted abolitionist, George Luther Stearns. From the Henry E. Luhrs Collection. Accompanied by LOA from PSA/DNA.

Estimate: $150-$250

25714 Adele Victor Hugo Autograph

Note Signed *"Adele Victor Hugo."* Two pages, 4" x 5.25", np, July, 25th. This note is written entirely in French and is untranslated. Adele Hugo was Victor's wife whom he loved passionately all his life, as is evident from many famous and popular love letters. One of which reads in part, *"When two souls, which have sought each other for, however long in the throng, have finally found each other…a union fiery and pure as themselves are…begins on earth and continues forever in heaven…This is the love which you inspire in me…your soul is made to love with purity and passion of angels; but perhaps it can only love another angel, in which case I must tremble with apprehension."* The letter is in fine condition; usual folds are present; slight brittleness has set in, pencil notations present. From the Henry E. Luhrs Collection. Accompanied by LOA from PSA/DNA.

Estimate: $400-$600

25716 Aldous Huxley Autograph Letter

Signed *"Aldous Huxley."* Two pages, 4.5" x 7", Sanary, France, September 9th, 1932. This letter was written to an unnamed woman, and it reads in part, *"I think that your idea of using the gramophone to popularize good music is cheaply excellent. Personally, I don't very much like Wagner's music & I hope that when you have given his dramas you will go on to recitals of other equally inaccessible music in the same way…why not other operas, as little accessible as Wagner's- Don Giovanni (never I fear recorded in its entirety), Verdi's magnificent Othello."* Huxley was the author of the acclaimed book *Brave New World* and many more. His works range from the scientific to the spiritual. The letter is in very fine condition; pencil notations are present on the letter. From the Henry E.

Luhrs Collection. Accompanied by LOA from PSA/DNA.

Estimate: $300-$400

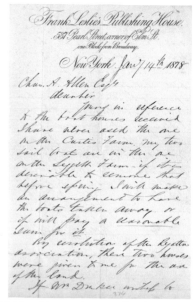

25717 Literary Autograph Collection

"J-K-L". A significant lot containing 65 or more items, each bearing the signature of an author, publisher, educator, historian, or poet. Just a few of the autographs offered here: Marie Adelaide Lowndes (3 TLS); James Russell Lowell (2 ALS); Sinclair Lewis (ALS); Dudley Leavitt (ALS); Mary Elizabeth Lease (AQS); Selma Lagerlˆf (Signature); Charles Godfrey Leland (ALS); Frank Leslie (ALS); Charles Lever (ALS); Walter Lippman (TLS); Anita Loos (Signature); Charles Battell Loomis (ALS). There are some great items here! Generally fine condition. From the Henry E. Luhrs Collection. Accompanied by LOA from PSA/DNA.

Estimate: $400-$500

25718   William James Autograph Letter Declining an Article - on Herbert Spencer Autograph Letter Signed, 1 page, 5.5" by 8.5", Chororua, New Hampshire, September 4, 1902. To Hamilton Holt. A nascent tear at a fold, and a couple pencil notations at borders, otherwise quite good. William James has been variously described as the greatest of American psychologists, the most famous American philosopher since Emerson, and a completely original thinker in and between the disciplines of physiology, psychology and philosophy. His first great work was on Herbert Spencer, in 1878, but now - his twelve-hundred page masterwork, *The Principles of Psychology* behind him and his classic *The Varieties of Religious Experience* just out - he declines to go back to where he started. "*I much regret my inability to write the article you so kindly propose, on Mr. Spencer's chapter, and remain truly yours...*" From the Henry E. Luhrs Collection. Accompanied by LOA from PSA/DNA.
Estimate: $250-$350

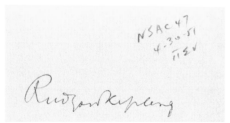

25719   Rudyard Kipling Signature Collection. Three items signed by Kipling are the focus of this lot; three signature cards, measuring 6" x 4"; 5" x 2"; and 3.8" x 2.8". The largest card has a clipped signature laid

down on the larger card and is seated next to a photograph of Kipling which is also laid down on the card. The second card is simply signed in the center. The final and the smallest card is signed and inscribed as follows, *"You have had the forethought to stamp your return envelope with a 2 ½ English stamp which makes it possible for me to return your letter promptly and, incidentally, to sign myself. Yours autographically, Rudyard Kipling."* The signatures are in very fine condition on average; the smallest card is slightly smudged. Otherwise, excellent! From the Henry E. Luhrs Collection. Accompanied by LOA from PSA/DNA.
Estimate: $500-$700

25720   Rudyard Kipling Signed Photograph *"Rudyard Kipling."* 3.5" x 5.5" postcard size photograph of Kipling as a fairly young man. He is leaning against a couch, wearing a fine suit, and smoking a cigar. Kipling is most renowned for his children story, *The Jungle Book,* and other stories which take place is his birthplace, India. The photograph is in fine condition; light soiling on picture side; two small holes in the upper left corner. From the Henry E. Luhrs Collection. Accompanied by LOA from PSA/DNA.
Estimate: $500-$600

25721   Literary Autograph Collection "A" and "C". A fine grouping of signed items from authors, historians, poets, and various notables, totaling 60 or more items. A few featured pieces: Thomas Bailey Aldrich (ALS, Signature); Joseph Auslander (TLS); Mary Raymond Shipman Andrews (ALS, Signature); Sir Edwin Arnold (AQS); Conrad Aiken (Signature); Dr. Alfred Adler (Signature); William T. Adams "Oliver Optic" (Signatures, AMsS); Charles Follen Adams (AMsS); John S. C. Abbott (3 ALS). Generally fine condition. From the Henry E. Luhrs Collection. Accompanied by LOA from PSA/DNA.
Estimate: $300-$500

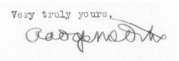

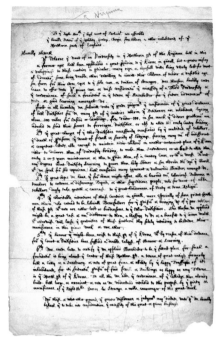

25722   Literary Autograph Collection "M-N". This amazing lot consists of approximately 150 separate autographs of a wide and varied assortment of writers, poets, educators, publishers, and religious leaders. Just a few of the items included: H. L. Mencken (TLS); Thomas Moore (Signature); E[dgar] W[ilson] Nye (ALS); Adolph S. Ochs (TLS); Ivor Novello (TLS); Edgar Lee Masters (SP); Charles Major (Signature); Archibald MacLeish (TLS *"Archibald"*); Christopher Morley (Signature); George Barr McCutcheon (ALS); William Vaughn Moody (Signature); Ferenc Molnar (Signature); George P. Morris (ALS); Lord Morpeth (ALS). There are many great items in this lot, generally fine condition. From the Henry E. Luhrs Collection. Accompanied by LOA from PSA/DNA.
Estimate: $800-$1,000

25723   Petition for University in Manchester, England. One page, 8.5" x 12.5", Manchester, England, n.d. This document likely dates to the late 16th century or early 17th century. We make this assessment based on several linguistic and religious features of the document; for instance a portion of the letter reads, *"…them wth out any degrees without University learning to pcure them holy-Orders & soe obtrude them upon ye gladly Ye great hopes we have ye from hence might issue able & learned men, laborious Pastoures & teachers to convince & discourage Papists & other sup-stitious people, who for want of able scholars, dayly take growth of exercise to ye great hindrance of Piety & true Religion…"* [sic] The term papist is a slur referring to Roman Catholics. It was coined during the English Reformation to identify anyone who believed in the papal supremacy. It was mainly a pejorative term and can be seen as such by the Act of Settlement of 1701, which says that no one who professes the "popish religion" or marries "a papist" may succeed to the throne of the United Kingdom. This term allows us to ascertain that this document was possibly written during the Reformation. Secondly, the language itself is very archaic and looks to date to about the same time. The document itself is a request to Parliament for a University in Manchester. Five long reasons are laid out by the document. However, it unlikely that the request was granted since the University of Manchester was not established until the 19th century. Regardless of the acceptance or rejection of the petition, it is an excellent document to examine legal procedure and language of the Reformation.

The document is in Fine condition; usual folds are present; the bottom edge of the document is worn and torn; soiling present on face. From the Henry E. Luhrs Collection.
Estimate: $600-$800

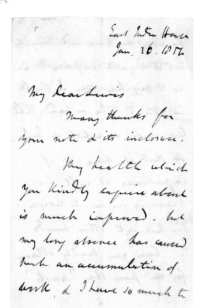

25724 John Stuart Mill Autograph Letter Signed *"J.S. Mill."* Three pages, 4.5" x 7.25", East India House, January 16, 1856; to "My Dear Lewis." In part, *"…I have so much to occupy my time and thoughts that it is quite impossible for me to say how soon I shall be able to take in hand, still less finish an article on India…Can you kindly obtain for me from the "Waste" two sets of the sheets of the article on Grote?"* John Stuart Mill is today remembered as brilliant philosopher and advocate of Utilitarianism; in his day, however, he earned his living as a senior official of the East India Company. George Grote, the philosopher, was a dear friend of Mills, and active too in the Unitarian Society. The letter is in very fine condition; the usual folds are present; the signature is bold and dark! Accompanied by LOA from PSA/DNA.
Estimate: $500-$700

25725 British Prime Ministers Autograph Collection consisting of the following items:

Arthur James Balfour. Prime Minister (1902-1905), author of the Balfour Declaration that promised a homeland for the Jewish people. Signature.

William Gladstone. Prime Minister (four times between 1868 and 1894). 2.5 page ALS, ANS, Signature. Also LS of Catherine Gladstone.

Ramsay MacDonald. Prime Minister (1924, 1929-1935). Signature, Typed Letter Signed.

Lord Palmerston. Prime Minister (1855-1858, 1859-1865). DS

David Lloyd George. Prime Minister (1916-1922), Britain's last Liberal Prime Minister. Signature.

Anthony Eden. Prime Minister (1955-1957). Signature.

Generally very good condition. From the Henry E. Luhrs Collection. Accompanied by LOA from PSA/DNA.
Estimate: $600-$800

25726 Christopher Morley: the Original Manuscript of his Great Homage, "Sherlock Holmes' Prayer." Autograph Manuscript Signed ("C.M."), "Sherlock Holmes' Prayer" and bearing the author's inscription at top, *"This first draft of S.H.'s Supplication is given to L.G. for his amusement, with much regard from his friend"*, 2 full pages, 8.5" by 13", no place, no date. The original working draft, in Fine condition. Since 1887, when *A Study in Scarlet* first appeared, there have been over 10,000 novels, short stories, parodies, burlesques, pastiches, critical studies, reviews, essays, appreciations and scholarly examinations - to say nothing of plays, television programs and films - devoted to Sherlock Holmes. Virtually all of the material is important in that it refers to the world's greatest detective. First among men to discern that anything and everything to do with Holmes must be collected, was Christopher Morley, the author, who founded in 1934 the Baker Street Irregulars. Because of Morley, and others like him, we now know that Holmes, Watson, and - ah!- Irene, are realer than ourselves. Here, then, is a very great treat: all ten stanzas of Holmes' supplication, ala Morley. It begins *"Grant me, O Spirit of Reason, matter for deduction, Intuition, and Analysis; plenty of three-pipe problems, that I may avoid the cowardice of seven percent cocaine..."* and ends with a note, by Watson, correcting Holmes' *"usual grammatical error: between when he should have said among"*, and alluding to *"IRENE."* From the Henry E. Luhrs Collection. Accompanied by LOA from PSA/DNA.
Estimate: $300-$400

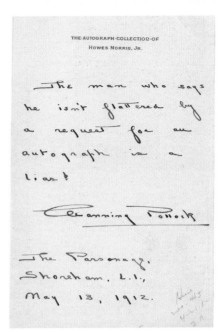

THE·AUTOGRAPH·COLLECTION·OF
HOWES NORRIS, JR.

The man who says he isn't flattered by a request for an autograph is a liar!

Channing Pollock

The Parsonage,
Shoreham, L.I.,
May 13, 1912.

25728 **Literary Autograph Collection "O-P".** An outstanding group of at least 85 different autographed items from various authors, poets, and educators. Included are: Channing Pollock (ANS); Theodore E. Perkins (AMuQS); Phoebe Palmer (AMsS *"The Shepherdess"*); Baroness Orczy (TLS); J. B. Priestley (TLS); John Poole (ANS); Dr. Mario A Pei (TLS); Henry Fairfield Osborn (AQS); Benjamin Park (ALS to Horace Greeley); Dawn Powell (Signature). This lot contains a wide range of material and the items are generally in fine condition. From the Henry E. Luhrs Collection. Accompanied by LOA from PSA/DNA.
Estimate: $800-$1,000

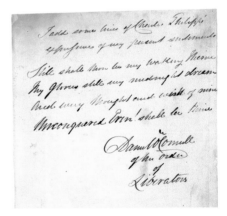

25729 **Daniel O'Connell Autograph Quotation Signed** "*Daniel O'Connell of the Order of Liberators.*" This 8" x 9.5", one page handwritten document features a small quotation from Charles Philipps written and signed by Daniel O'Connell. The quote reads, "*Still shall thou be my waking theme My glories still my midnight dream And every thought and wish of mine unconquered erin' shall be thine.*" O'Connell was a prominent politician in Ireland during the 19th century who openly opposed the discrimination against Catholics. The quotation is in Fine condition; written on very sturdy paper, the paper is slightly soiled around the edges, but signature is bold and dark! From the Henry E. Luhrs Collection. Accompanied by LOA from PSA/DNA.
Estimate: $500-$600

25727 **Eadweard Muybridge Autograph Letter Signed** *"E. Muybridge."* Two pages, 5" x 8", personal letterhead, New York, March 4, 1888. Written to Frank W. Hoyt Esq., the letter reads in part, *"…If I am not quite punctual you can be entertained very agreeably by Mr. Bradford who will tell you all about the North Pole while you examine his pictures; or, you can sit right down and endeavor to solve the problem of Animal Locomotion by means of the plates, of which you will find nearly 800 awaiting your inspection…"* Muybridge was responsible for developments in photography which eventually helped lead into the birth of the motion picture. He used multiple cameras to capture motion and he was the man who proved that when a horse runs, there is a point at which all four of the horses hooves are off the ground. The letter is in fine condition; usual folds are present; small stain in the center of the letter on the verso; signature is bold and dark. The content and signature in this letter is superb! From the Henry E. Luhrs Collection. Accompanied by LOA from PSA/DNA.
Estimate: $1,000-$1,500

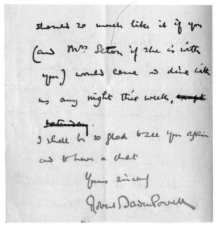

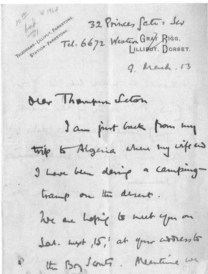

the Henry E. Luhrs Collection. Accompanied by LOA from PSA/DNA.

Estimate: $300-$400

25731   Anna Pavlova Signed Photograph *"Anna Pavlova."* Black and white printed photo of the legendary *Dying Swan* ballerina, measuring 3.25" x 5.5". The photo depicts Pavlova sitting among dozens of roses, wearing her toe shoes and fancy costume. A gorgeous photo. The printed photograph is in very fine condition; slight fading in the upper quadrants; the signature is dark and bold. From the Henry E. Luhrs Collection. Accompanied by LOA from PSA/DNA.

Estimate: $300-$500

25730   Frederick Opper Signed Sketch and Autograph Letter Signed *"F. Opper."* Two pages, 8.25" x 7", New York American and Journal Stationery, New York, September 24th, 1902. The letter mentions Opper's dismay at having to pay shipping charges on some original prints of his that were sent to him from England. The letter is in fine condition; usual folds are present; paper clip has rusted and stained the paper in the upper left corner; mounting traces present on verso. The sketch is one page, 3.5" x 5.5", np, dated May 14th, 1927. It is signed in the lower right as, *"F.B. Opper."* The sketch is of one of Opper's famous characters, named Happy Hooligan. Happy appeared in William Randolph Hearst's newspapers beginning in 1900, as the good-natured hobo who was always smiling despite his misfortunes. He was a doer of good deeds and was often a foil for his brother Gloomy Gus. The sketch is accompanied by a 4.5" x 7" photograph of Opper; both items have been laid down on a sturdy backing sheet. The sketch is in very fine condition. A wonderful set of items from one of America's favorite illustrators. From

25732   Robert Baden-Powell Autograph Letter Signed Mentions Boy Scouts. Two pages, 5.5" x 7", 32 Princes Gate, March 8, 1913, to [Ernest] Thompson Seton, the founding pioneer of the Boy Scouts of America. In part, *"...We are hoping to meet you on Sat. next, 15,: at your address to the Boy Scouts. Meantime we should so much like it if you (and Mrs. Seton if she is with you) would come to dine with us any night this week..."* Baden-Powell was a hero in the Boer War and the founder of the Scout movement. These two men first met in 1906 and shared many common ideas. About fine condition with light soiling and one minor stain on front. Originally purchased from Walter R. Benjamin Autographs. From the Henry E. Luhrs Collection. Accompanied by LOA from PSA/DNA.

Estimate: $300-$400

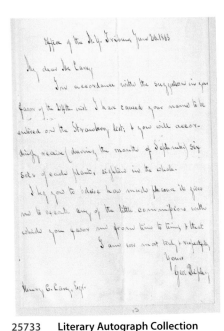

25733 Literary Autograph Collection

"Q-R". A fabulous collection of autographed material, approximately 80 items, all of famous writers, poets, and educators. Highlights include: Robert Ripley (TLS); John Clark Ridpath (TLS); Elmer Rice (Signature); Eben E Rexford (AMsS); George Ripley (ALS); Sigmund Romberg (Signature); John Rusking (Signed Pen Drawing); Whitelaw Reid (TLS); Jacob A. Riis (ALS); James Whitcomb Riley (AQS); Samuel Rogers (AQS); Henry J. Raymond (ALS); Josiah Quincy (ALS); Ellery Queen (Frederick Dannay-TLS). There are some rare items included here; generally fine condition. From the Henry E. Luhrs Collection. Accompanied by LOA from PSA/DNA.

Estimate: $600-$800

25734 Sergei Rachmaninoff Signature.

The legendary Russian-born American composer, pianist, and conductor has signed this 4" x 2.25" lined card and added the date *"April 2, 1928"*. Fine condition. From the Henry E. Luhrs Collection. Accompanied by LOA from PSA/DNA.

Estimate: $300-$400

25735 Nikolai and Anton Rubinstein Pair of Autograph Letters Signed.

This lot contains two letters, one written by Anton, and the other by Nikolai. Letter 1 (Anton): One page, 5" x 8", personal letterhead, Riga, Latvia, October 14th, 1869. The letter is written in German; the content is routine. Anton signs himself, *"Ant. Rubinstein."* Letter 2 (Nikolai): One page, 5.25" x 8.25", Moscow, October 2nd, 1898. This letter is also in German, the content discusses an upcoming concert featuring Russian musicians and composers. Nikolai signs himself, *"N. Rubinstein."* Both Rubinstein brothers were extremely gifted; Anton was a great composer, and Nikolai was a great pianist. The letters are both in very fine condition; usual folds are present on both; Nikolai's letter has several creases on the corners and dark scuff marks on the lower left edge. From the Henry E. Luhrs Collection. Accompanied by LOA from PSA/DNA.

Estimate: $800-$1,200

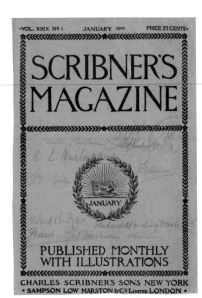

25736 Literary Autograph Collection

"S". An incredible lot of at least 110 separate autograph items from various and sundry au-thors, writers, publishers, poets, and educators from the U.S. and around the world. Included: Upton Sinclair (Signature); George R. Sims (AQS); Margaret Sidney (AQS); Frank Dempster Sherman (ALS); Philip Stanhope (ALS); Jared Sparks (ALS); Irving Stone (Signature); Charles Scribner (Signed 1901 *Scribner's Magazine* Cover); Epes Sargent (ALS); Carl Sandberg (Signature); Harriet Spofford (AMs); Goldwin Smith (ALS); Betty Smith (Signature); Cornelia Otis Skinner (SP); Margaret Sangster (ALS). A wonderful grouping for the collector or the dealer; generally fine condition. From the Henry E. Luhrs Collection. Accompanied by LOA from PSA/DNA.

Estimate: $800-$1,000

25737 Francis M. Cockrell Collection.

This lot contains eight autograph letters signed by Francis M. Cockrell. Also included are two images of Cockrell, one a photograph from a book, the other is a drawing clipped from a newspaper or pamphlet. The eight autograph letters signed date from April 1, 1881 to May 3, 1898. In all eight letters he signs himself, *"F.M. Cockrell."* Francis M. Cockrell was a Confederate military commander as well as a United States Senator from Missouri, he served in this office for five terms. The letters in this collection contain routine content and the majority of them are written on United States Senate letterhead. One letter, dated August, 1881 reads in part, *"... When I was captured at Blakely Ala. about dark on April 9, 1865 all my official papers, orders & c. were delivered to my captors and I have not the Scratch of a pen of any orders & c. issued by me in the army..."*

The letters in this collection are in fine condition on average; usual folds are present; soiling has occurred on the edges of several; signatures all look bold and crisp! From the Henry E. Luhrs Collection. Accompanied by LOA from PSA/DNA.

Estimate: $800-$1,200

25738 Clara Schumann Scarce Autograph Letter Signed *"Clara Schumann."* One page, in German, 5.5" x 8.5", Baden, Germany, June 7, 1872. To an unnamed addressee. The translation reads, *"Heartiest thanks for your parcel which gave me great pleasure, especially as the work for the organ is one I have coveted for years."* Clara Schumann was one of the leading pianists of her day, and an accomplished composer. The letter is in very good condition; usual folds are present; tears are present on the left edge; staining is light on the obverse; slight smudging. Accompanied by LOA from PSA/DNA.
Estimate: $300-$500

25739 Sir Walter Scott Writes to Southey about Coleridge ALS: *"Walter Scott",* 3p, 7.75" x 10". Edinburgh, November 28 [1825]. Addressed by Scott on verso of third page to: *"Robert Southey Esqr/Kerwich/Cumberland"* Clear "NOV 29 1825 W E" postmark. Concerning publisher John Murray's treatment of Samuel Taylor Coleridge. Thanks to Lord Byron's intervention years earlier, Murray had accepted three of Coleridge's works for publication, including "Kubla Khan". In part: *"Whatever you may complain of with respect to Murrays conduct was wholly unknown to me. Till the middle of rather the end of October I had no more idea of Lockharts being the Manager of the Quarterly Union as my being brought in the copy of the review...In respect to Mr. Coleridge nothing would give me more pain than the idea that either Lockhart or I were edging him out of a lucrative and honourable situation. The situation was offered to Lockhart by Mr Murray as open and disengaged- he put the question whether Mr. Coleridge retiring was a thing determined on & he received a positive answer in the affirmative. He had no access to Mr Coleridge personally but never doubted that a full explanation had taken place between Mr Murray & him. The first question I asked was concerning Mr Coleridges connection with the Review & I was assured it terminated with the New Years commencement...As for Joannes de Mevaires I think his conduct to you is inadvisable but I am perfectly convincved it arose out of an unintentional curiosity. Byron called him the most homourously Gods bookseller and I am sure it was not and could not be any depreciatory feeling of the great services you have rendered to the Quarterly to which we can all bear witness...."*

Minor soiling and light stains. Irregular edge at left of first page. Second sheet (third page) has been inlaid; address leaf and three line Scott postscript on verso of third page. Small triangular portion missing from blank area on second sheet when wax seal was cut to open letter. Overall, in fine condition. **Accompanied by lightly stained signature:** *"Walter Scott/Castle Grove"* **on 1.75" x 1.25 card and portrait.** Three items. From the Henry E. Luhrs Collection. Accompanied by LOA from PSA/DNA.
Estimate: $400-$600

25740 Robert Simson Autograph Letter Signed *"Rob: Simson"* (1687-1768). Three pages, 7.25" x 9.25", Glasgow, June 11, 1760. Simson comments on another mathematician, discusses Euclid, and mentions his forthcoming edition of *Data,* in part: *"the Data will be longer than what we have in the former editions...the book shall be sold at 5 or 6 shillings, tho I should be a loser by it..."* A British mathematician and professor of mathematics, Simson is known for his criticisms and commentaries on the ancient geometers, specializing in Euclid. His *Euclid's Element* was long the standard Euclid text in England. The pedal line of a triangle is sometimes called the Simson line after him. Our research shows no record of a sale of any Simson autograph material in recent years. This is a special opportunity to own a content letter from a legendary geometer. Having a paper conservator repair the fold splits and clean the light soiling would make this letter worthy of display in any fine collection or museum.

Also included is a 1776 dated engraving of Simson in excellent condition. From the Henry E. Luhrs Collection. Accompanied by LOA from PSA/DNA.
Estimate: $1,200-$2,000

oversee and guide the process of its inception. He also served as Prime Minister of South Africa; among other things he was also a military man and an intellectual. Sadly, he died before he could institute his ideas about abolishing segregation altogether in South Africa. All three documents are in Fine condition with no visible issues, except that all three items have notes written on them in pencil from previous cataloguing. From the Henry E. Luhrs Collection. Accompanied by LOA from PSA/DNA.

Estimate: $250-$350

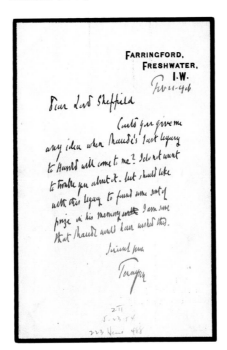

is in very fine condition, usual folds are present; signature is bold and dark. From the Henry E. Luhrs Collection.

Estimate: $300-$400

25744   Literary Autograph Collection "U-V". A fine lot containing at least 25 autographed items from various writers, educators, and journalists. A few of the featured pieces: Henry Van Dyke (AQS, ALS); John Van Druten (Signature); Carl Van Vechten (Signature); Rev. E. S. Ufford (AMuQS); Oswald Garrison Villard (Signature); Hendrik Van Loon (AMs); George Sylvester Viereck (TMsS with hand accomplished corrections by John D. Rockefeller). Generally fine condition. From the Henry E. Luhrs Collection. Accompanied by LOA from PSA/DNA.

Estimate: $200-$300

25741   Samuel Francis Smith Autograph Letter Signed *"S.F. Smith."* One page, 5.5" x 8", Newton Centre, Massachusetts, September 28th, 1894. The content of the letter describes Smith's regrets that he cannot send a current photograph, but sends, instead, an autographed poem. The poem is not included with the letter. Smith is, of course, the man who penned the famous song, "America". The letter is in very fine condition; small tears present along the vertical edges, usual folds are present; adhesive tape present on the upper edge. From the Henry E. Luhrs Collection. Accompanied by LOA from PSA/DNA.

Estimate: $600-$800

25742   General Jan Smuts Group Lot. This lot contains one typed signed letter and two signatures on 3" x 5" lined notecards. The letter is a typed one page document, measuring 8" x 10". The content is routine, and he signs it in the lower right portion of the page. Smuts is one of the men who was responsible for the establishment of the "League of Nations," he helped

25743   Alfred Lord Tennyson Autograph Letter Signed *"Tennyson."* One page, 8vo, Farringford Freshwater I.W. (Isle of Wight), February 21, 1876. The recipient of this letter is Lord Sheffield, it reads, "*...Could you give me any idea when Maude's last legacy to Harold will come to me? I do not want to trouble you about it, but should like with this legacy to find some sort of prize in his memory. I am sure that Maude would have wished this...*" Tennyson was one of the most popular English poets of his time. Most of his verse is based on classical or mythological themes. This particular letter refers to a work he wrote called *Harold* which was a tribute to King Harold II of England, he was killed at the battle of Hastings. A vintage engraving is also included in the lot. The letter

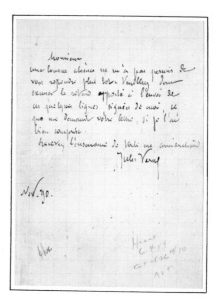

25746   Jules Verne Autograph Letter Signed *"Jules Verne."* One page, 4.25" x 5.75", np, November, 1890. Untranslated letter in French, signed in bold black ink. Verne is famous for his fantastic stories, many of which have been made into movies. The letter is in very fine condition; usual folds are present; letter has been laid down on a sturdy white backing sheet. From the Henry E. Luhrs Collection. Accompanied by LOA from PSA/DNA.

Estimate: $1,000-$1,500

25745   Jules Verne Autograph Letter Signed *"Jules Verne."* One page, 3.5" x 5.5", Amiens, France, June 17th, 1897. The letter is written in French to an unnamed woman. The translation reads, *"Very readily & respectfully I herewith address these few lines to you. The moment I set my eyes on Your American Postal (The romance (novel) which I am preparing just now has in-plot laid in the U.S. exclusively, but will not be published before two years. I only hope that- the story may please you. In the meanwhile, reserve the greetings of an old French scribbler."* Jules Verne is best known, basically, for being a pioneer of the science fiction genre. He was writing about air and underwater travel before either concept was a reality. The letter is in very fine condition; some slight staining on the edges; usual folds are present. From the Henry E. Luhrs Collection. Accompanied by LOA from PSA/DNA.

Estimate: $700-$900

25747   Literary Autograph Collection "W-X". Here is a lot with material for the most discriminating of collectors; more than 100 signed items from authors, hymn writers, educators, politicians, and poets. Just a few of the highlights: Walter Winchell (2 TLS); Kate D. Wiggins (ANS, ALS); Rabbi Stephen S. Wise (2 TLS); Owen Wister (ANS); Henry A. Wise (ALS); Horace Walpole (Signature); Charles Dudley Warner (Signature, ALS); Thornton Wilder (ALS); Henry J. Wood (TLS); Alexander Woollcott (Signature); Andrew D. White (2 TLS, ALS); Ella Wheeler Wilcox (AQS); P. G. Wodehouse (MsS). Generally fine condition. From the Henry E. Luhrs Collection. Accompanied by LOA from PSA/DNA.

Estimate: $600-$800

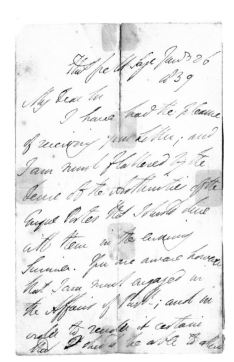

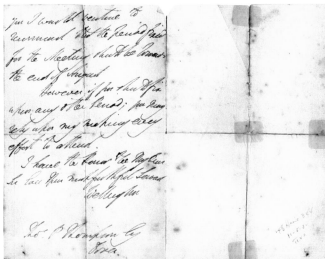

25749 **H.G. Wells Autograph Letter** Autograph Letter Signed, 1 page, 7" by 9", Little Easton Rectory, Dunmow, no date. To Bushnell Hart. A tad worn at folds, and there is a pencil note, not effecting text, in lower left corner; else quite good. Here Wells, who pioneered the genre of science fiction - as well as writing popular history and comic novels - seems to be turning down writing yet another book: "*Sears shall be suitably talked to when he comes, but I doubt it I can do that book.*" From the Henry E. Luhrs Collection. Accompanied by LOA from PSA/DNA.
Estimate: $300-$500

25748 **Arthur Wellesley, Duke of Wellington Autograph Letter Signed** "*Wellington*". Two pages, 4.75" x 7.25", Westfield, January 26, 1839, to Thomas P Thompson of Dover. A reply to a request for a dining engagement, in part, "*...You are aware however that I am much engaged in the affairs of Parl[iamen]t; and in order to render it certain that I shall be able to attend I would venture...*" Good condition; foxing and old tape repairs to folds where separating. Also included is a period engraving of Wellington. From the Henry E. Luhrs Collection. Accompanied by LOA from PSA/DNA.
Estimate: $300-$400

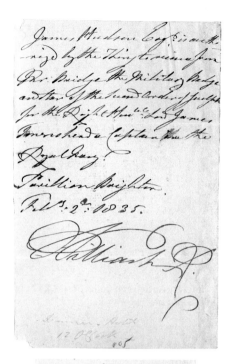

25750   **King William IV of England- Autograph Document Signed**

"William R." One page, 4.5" x 7.25", Brighton, February 2, 1835. In full: *"James Hudson Esqr. is authorized by the King to receive from Thos. Bridge the Military Badge and Star of the Second Order of Guelph for the Right Honble. Lord James Townshend a Captain in the Royal Navy. Pavillion Brighton. Feby. 2d. 1835."* Very Good condition; folds, small tears at top and bottom left, mounting traces on verso, large signature. From the Henry E. Luhrs Collection. Accompanied by LOA from PSA/DNA.

Estimate: $300-$400

25751   **John Greenleaf Whittier lot comprised of four fine pieces ,** as follows:. 1) Autograph Letter Signed, *"John G. Whittier."* 2 pages, 4.15" x 6.55", Amesbury Massachusetts, November 6, 1867. In part, *"…I never advise any one to depend on authorship for a living: anything is better than that. But it is very pleasant to be able to express one's self in rhythmical numbers & perhaps is "it's own reward" …"* 2) Autograph Letter Signed, *"John G. Whittier."* 2 pages, 4.25" x 8.5", Amesbury, Massachusetts, December 3, 1855. To the legendary writer and abolitionist Harriet Beecher Stowe. 3) Autograph Letter Signed, *"John G. Whittier."* 3 pages, 5" x 8", Amesbury, Massachusetts, June 24, 1869. The content of this letter is routine, but it does contain some of his musings on life and happiness. It reads in part, *"…Thee have not lived for thyself alone-and there are many grateful hearts to cherish the recollections of thy kindness and self sacrifice. When I think of myself life looks very and & disconsolate, but when I think of others, of dear friends whom I love, here & beyond, I am almost happy…"* r2) Card Signed, *"John G. Whittier."* The card measures 3.5" x 2", and is signed in blue ink. Whittier was a poet and transcendentalist and, like Stowe, an early proponent of abolishing slavery. His poem "Maud Muller" features the famous line, "For all sad words of tongue and pen/ The saddest are these, 'It might have been.'" The condition of these items is very fine on average. The Harriet Beecher Stowe letter has two newspaper clippings taped onto the letter as well as the address portion of the envelope. The signature card is laid down on a folder. Accompanied by LOA from PSA/DNA.

Estimate: $400-$600

25753 **Literary Autograph Collection "Y-Z".** Approximately 12 literary autographs are contained in this fine lot, includes: Stefan Zweig (Signature); Edmund Yates (ALS); Francis Brett Young (ANS); Rida Johnson Young (AMsS). Generally fine condition. From the Henry E. Luhrs Collection. Accompanied by LOA from PSA/DNA. Accompanied by LOA from PSA/DNA.
Estimate: $200-$300

End of Session One

25752 **Wilhelm II of Germany Document Signed** *"Wilhelm R"*. One page, partly printed, 8.25" x 13", New Palace, September 1, 1890. A gorgeous and decorative document, bestowing upon Robert Schnitzler, chairman of the board of the music conservatory in Cologne, the order of the Red Eagle, third class. Wilhelm was the last Emperor or Kaiser of Germany and the last King of Prussia. This document with a bold signature nearly 5.5" long is in very fine condition with light folds. Perfect for display. From the Henry E. Luhrs Collection. Accompanied by LOA from PSA/DNA
Estimate: $300-$400

RARE BOOKS FROM
THE LUHRS COLLECTION

A broad selection of rare and interesting books from this collection are

to be found in the afternoon session of our Feb. 21, 2006 catalog.

Each is identified as being from the Henry Luhrs Collection. Please do take

the opportunity to peruse these significant offerings.
